THE ECONOMIES OF AFRICA

THE ECONOMIES OF AFRICA

Edited by

P. ROBSON
Professor of Economics
University of St Andrews

and

D. A. LURY
Senior Lecturer in Economic and Social Statistics
University of Kent at Canterbury

Economics is the study of Economies
DUDLEY SEERS

London
GEORGE ALLEN AND UNWIN LTD
RUSKIN HOUSE MUSEUM STREET

FIRST PUBLISHED IN 1969

SBN 0 4330124 X

PRINTED IN GREAT BRITAIN
in 10 on 11 pt. Times type
BY UNWIN BROTHERS LIMITED
WOKING AND LONDON

PREFACE

With the coming of independence to a large part of the African continent during the last fifteen years there has arisen a growing interest and concern with its problems of economic development. In the new countries themselves this is reflected in their deliberate efforts to bring about a much greater rate of economic growth than was achieved in the past under colonial rule. A variety of paths and strategies has been adopted for this purpose but all find a common focus in economic planning procedures which in objectives are uniformly more ambitious than those practised earlier. Emphasis on growth and development has been accompanied by a steady improvement in the availability and quality of statistical data and by the publication of economic surveys and plans. Outside Africa, concern with African economic development, which of course is part of a widespread concern with the problems of less developed countries generally, finds expression in foreign aid and a proliferation of academic inquiries. From the standpoint of those seeking a broad understanding of the progress and problems of Africa since independence, official documents of both national and international agencies are useful. There are also an increasing number of academic investigations but many of these are concerned with specialized aspects of the economies they study. There is, however, a dearth of critical general studies of African economies, and those available often rest on foundations which do not facilitate inter-African comparisons.

There thus seems to be a place for a set of studies of African countries written by economists who possess an intimate knowledge of their working, making use of official and private studies (some of which they themselves have undertaken) and evaluating the policies, structures, and achievements of these economies for the student of African economic affairs. Such studies make up this book. It consists of seven descriptive and analytical studies of single African economies together with two further studies of groups of countries which, although now politically separate, have had close economic links in the past and which, in the one case at least, continue to enjoy them. The book also contains an introduction, based partly on the country studies and partly on other material, which reviews the general economic situation in relation to a number of key economic issues which have a wide relevance throughout Africa today.

Preliminary discussions among the authors took place in 1964 and the studies were written during the next two to three years. They consider developments culminating in the early and mid-sixties. By then many of the major economic problems of the post-independence era had begun to emerge clearly. In analysing economies in a continent in which change is so rapid, it is inevitable that some data will have been overtaken by events during the period in which a project of this size is in gestation. But no coherent statistical picture for a substantially later date is likely to be available by the time that this book is in the hands of the reader, nor is it probable that later information would significantly alter the main lines of analysis which will be found in this book. It may be claimed moreover that, at the time of writing, comparable economic analyses using later data are not available for most of the countries concerned.

The objectives and limitations of comparative studies in the social sciences are too well known to be elaborated here. Too often what are presented as comparative studies in economics are nothing more than loosely connected essays by a variety of authors on some general theme. They fail to provide a sample which is representative of the variety of conditions prevailing. The data employed often represent simply what was available. For a variety of reasons it is difficult to use it to illuminate, in a comparative way, such things as efforts, policies and achievements, and the ways in which varying institutions and patterns of social and political relationships influence economic policies. This book does not claim to have surmounted all these difficulties but in an attempt to avoid some of them, each of the authors was provided by the editors with an outline which specified the topics to be considered and the focus—economic development. In addition, the nature and basis of the supporting statistical data required was specified. In some cases data were available from official sources, but in others the authors had to undertake original statistical enquiries. Within the broad outline provided, the authors were given unfettered discretion to treat their material as they chose. There was no attempt to fit the material into a strait-jacket. The variety of the countries considered, the diversity of their resources and problems, would in themselves have made this undesirable. Nevertheless, in the revision of the material, the editors have sought to ensure that balance was preserved, and that key issues of widespread interest in Africa received discussion in each case. At the same time it is recognized that the specialized interests of the contributors has affected the balance of their discussions.

The individual studies were each circulated as they were completed to all contributors. There has, however, been no attempt at revision or reconciliation except by the editors. Each of the authors is solely responsible for the views expressed in his study. The introduction is the responsibility of the editors, who wish to acknowledge the benefits they derived from the comments of the authors of the country studies to whom they circulated it in draft form.

As can be seen from the biographical note on the authors, the contributors have had considerable experience of the areas with which they are concerned and in most cases have travelled widely in other parts of Africa. Most of the authors are, or have been, teachers in African universities, and one of their reasons for participating in this project was their desire to provide material for students. Several of the authors have participated in the formulation or execution of development policy in African countries. It is hoped that this experience will have brought to their assessments an insight which might otherwise have been lacking.

A word about the order in which the contributions have been placed may be called for. Of the various possible arrangements which might have been adopted, it was decided to group together the countries of West Africa and then those of Eastern Africa, with Algeria coming at the end. Within the Eastern and Western groupings the order is roughly on the basis of relative levels of development.

Unfortunately the structure and problems of African economies cannot yet be studied as profoundly as those of more developed economies. It is hoped however that this volume of comparative studies will serve as a useful handbook to students and to practising economists concerned with the continent, and that it may point the way to areas in which further study could usefully be directed. Apart from its use to students, it may be that specialists in one part of the continent will find some stimulus and enlightenment from the material presented for those parts of Africa with which they are not so familiar.

We should like to conclude with an acknowledgement on the part of the editors and contributors to the Teaching Materials Fund of the University of East Africa. A generous grant from this fund financed the initial preparation of much of the material presented in this book. We also wish to acknowledge a grant from the University of Kent at Canterbury which helped the editors after one of them moved there during the preparation of this book.

PR

DAL

CONTENTS

MAPS

ABBREVIATIONS USED FOR INSTITUTIONS IN FRANCOPHONE COUNTRIES

AOF	Afrique Occidentale Française.
BCEAO	Banque Centrale des États de l'Afrique de l'Ouest.
BIDI	Banque Ivoirienne de Développement Industriel.
CAA	Caisse Autonome d'Amortissement.
CAITA	Compagnie Agricole et Industrielle des Tabacs Africains.
CCCE	Caisse Centrale de Coopération Économique.
CCFOM	Caisse Centrale de la France d'Outre-Mer (CCCE since 1958).
CCI	Crédit de la Côte d'Ivoire.
CCP	Compagnie des Caoutchoucs du Pakidie.
CEGOS	Compagnie d'Études de Gestion et d'Organisation Scientifique.
CFA	Communauté Financière Africaine.
CFDI	Compagnie Française pour le Développement des Fibres Textiles.
CNCA	Caisse Nationale de Crédit Agricole.
FAC	Fonds d'Aide et de Coopération.
FED	Fonds Européen de Développement.
FIDES	Fonds d'Investissement et de Développement Économique et Social des territoires d'Outre-Mer.
FNI	Fonds National d'Investissement.
MTC	Manufacture de Tabac de la Côte d'Ivoire.
ORSTOM	Office de la Recherche Scientifique et Technique Outre-Mer.
SAPH	Société Africaine des Plantations d'Hévéas.
SATAMACI	Société d'Assistance Technique pour la Modernisation Agricole de la Côte d'Ivoire.
SEMA	Société d'Économie et de Mathématiques Appliquées.
SMIG	Salaire Minimum Interprofessionnel Garanti.
SODEPALM	Société pour le Développement et l'Exploitation du Palmier á Huile.
SONAFI	Société Nationale de Financement.
UDE	Union Douanière Équatoriale
UDEAC	Union Douanière et Économique de l'Afrique Centrale.

NOTES ON CONTRIBUTORS

OJE ABOYADE is Professor and Head of the Department of Economics at the University of Ibadan. He was educated at Hull University and Pembroke College, Cambridge. He has been Visiting Professor at the University of Michigan and Visiting Fellow at the Economic Growth Center, Yale University. He has written *Foundations of an African Economy: A Study of Investment and Growth in Nigeria* (1966) and several journal articles. He has edited the *Nigerian Journal of Economic and Social Studies* since 1961, and has served on many Federal and West Regional governmental bodies concerned with economic development and organization.

BRIAN VAN ARKADIE was born in 1930 in London and is currently working as Economic Adviser, Ministry of Planning and Development, Tanzania. In the past he has been on the staff of the Economic Growth Center, Yale University, Makerere University College, the Ministry of Overseas Development, UK, and the Ministry of Economic Planning, Uganda. He is the author of *Economic Accounting and Development Planning*. He has written several articles on the economic problems of East African countries, and is at present completing a book on the structure and growth of East African economies.

GEORGE DALTON was born in 1926 in Brooklyn, New York. He is Professor of Economics and Anthropology at Northwestern University and a staff member of its programme of African Studies. In 1961–62 he was Deputy Director of Northwestern University's Economic Survey of Liberia. At present he is collaborating with Irma Adelman on a statistical analysis of local community development in Africa, Asia, and Latin America. He is co-author of *Growth Without Development: An Economic Survey of Liberia* (1966). With Paul Bohannan, he edited *Markets in Africa* (1962). He has also edited a collection of articles in economic anthropology, *Tribal and Peasant Economies* (1967), and a volume of Karl Polanyi's essays, *Primitive, Archaic and Modern Economies* (1968).

DHARAM P. GHAI was born in Kenya in 1930 and is currently Deputy Director of the Institute for Development Studies, Social Science Division, University College, Nairobi. He wrote *Taxation for Development: a Case Study of Uganda*, and edited *Portrait of a Minority: Asians in East Africa*. He has written several articles on the development problems of East African countries, and has acted as consultant to the governments of Kenya, Uganda and Tanzania. He is now working on employment, wages and income distribution in Kenya.

REGINALD HERBOLD GREEN was born in 1935 at Walla Walla,

Washington, USA. He is currently Economic Adviser, Tanzania Treasury, and was formerly a faculty member of Harvard and Yale Universities, University of Ghana and Makerere University College. In research in Cameroon, Ghana, Nigeria, Sudan, East Africa, Burma, Ceylon, and Malaysia-Singapore he has concentrated on economic development strategy and policy, international economic relations and economic integration. He is at present working on economic structure, strategy, policy and development in Africa and S.E. Asia and on the financial and economic planning aspects of education for development. He is co-author with K. G. V. Krishna of *Economic Co-operation in Africa* (1967) and with A. Seidman of *Unity or Poverty? The Economics of Pan-Africanism* (1968) and has written numerous articles, especially on African development problems.

TONY KILLICK was born in Crowborough, Sussex in 1934. At present he holds the post of Economic Adviser at the Ministry of Overseas Development, London. He was formerly Tutor in Economics at Ruskin College, Oxford and before that was Lecturer in Economics at the University of Ghana. Whilst in Ghana he undertook a substantial amount of research into that country's economic structure and is at present working on a study of the problems of industrialization in the African context. Besides articles in various journals, he is joint author (with H. A. Clegg and Rex Adams) of *Trade Union Officers* (1961) and a contributor to *A Survey of Contemporary Ghana: Vol. I. The Economy of Ghana* (1966). He is married and has a daughter.

D. A. LURY read economics and statistics at the London School of Economies. He spent many years in government statistical organizations, concluding with a period as Government Statistician, Uganda. After leaving the service of the Uganda Government, he lectured at University Colleges in Sierra Leone and Nairobi, and is now Senior Lecturer in Economic and Social Statistics at the University of Kent at Canterbury. He is a Fellow of the Institute of Statisticians. Mr Lury has written *Elementary Quantitative Methods*, (1967) and several journal articles dealing with African problems.

MARVIN P. MIRACLE, born in Oklahoma in 1933, is Associate Professor of Agricultural Economics in the University of Wisconsin, and Chairman of its Comparative Tropical Economics Programme. He was formerly a staff member of the Food Research Institute at Stanford University and of San Francisco State College. He has recently published books entitled *Maize in Tropical Africa*, and *Agriculture in the Congo Basin; Tradition and Change in African Rural*

Economies. He has written numerous articles and monographs on Africa, with particular reference to marketing and agricultural development and economic change.

OLE DAVID KOHT NORBYE, born in Oslo in 1919, is senior economist at the Chr. Michelsen Institute, Bergen, Norway. Since 1965 he has been on secondment as adviser to the Ministry of Planning and Development, Kenya. From 1961 to 1965 he was head of the Chr. Michelsen Institute's development research project office in Paris. In 1959–61 he was adviser in the Planning Commission, Pakistan and earlier, during 1950–58 was with OEEC Paris, most of the period as Head of the Economic Factors Division of the European Productivity Agency. His publications include contributions in *Education, Employment and Rural Development*, published in 1967 for University College, Nairobi; *Development Prospects of Pakistan, 1960–1985*, and *Poor and Rich Countries and People* (both 1968).

O. M. OSMAN is Professor of Economics and Dean of the Faculty of Economic and Social Studies at the University of Khartoum. He studied economics at the University of Alexandria, and did postgraduate work at the Universities of Leeds and London. He has played an important rôle in the development of economic policy in Sudan, and is a member of the National Planning Economic Committee and a member of the Board of Directors of the Central Electricity & Water Corporation and of the Sudan Railways. He has published several articles on the economy of the Sudan and has a book on transport and economic growth in the Sudan in the course of publication.

PETER ROBSON studied economics at University College London. Before going to Africa in 1960 he carried out research and taught at London, Belfast and Cambridge. During his stay in Africa he has lectured, served as Economic Adviser to the Uganda Government, and has undertaken economic investigations in a number of African countries. In 1966 he was Visiting Professor of Economics at the University of Illinois. Professor Robson has edited (with Professor C. Leys) *Federation in East Africa, Opportunities and Problems* (1965). He has written numerous journal articles on problems of taxation, economic growth and integration, and a book *Economic Integration in Africa* (1968). Professor Robson was Professor of Economics at University College, Nairobi, from 1963 to 1968, and is currently Professor of Economics at the University of St Andrews.

ROBERT SZERESZEWSKI was born in Poland in 1936 and later emigrated to Israel. In 1959 he graduated from the Hebrew University of Jerusalem and received his M.Sc. two years later. From 1961 to 1964 he was a research student at the London School of Economics and was awarded a Doctorate. He then joined the staff of the Hebrew University of Jerusalem in the Department of Economics where he remained until he was killed in the battle of Jerusalem, June 1967. He was the author of *Structural Changes in the Economy of Ghana, 1891–1911* (1965), contributed to a number of learned journals, was a major contributor to *A Study of Contemporary Ghana: Vol. I. The Economy of Ghana* edited by Birmingham, Neustadt & Omaboe (1966), and was working on a study of the Israeli economy at the time of his death. He left behind a wife and two children.

ALI AHMED SULEIMAN, born in 1933 in Omdurman, is lecturer in public finance in the University of Khartoum. He is a member of the Workers' Cadre Commission which advises the Government on the wages and conditions of employment of workers in the Public sector. and was the Chairman of two wages tribunals in 1966–67. In 1966 he was appointed a member of the Transport and Distribution Committee of the Planning Organization. His publications include 'Stabilization Policies for Cotton in the Sudan', in *African Primary Producers and International Trade*, edited by I. G. Stewart and H. W. Ord (1965), and with D. J. Shaw, 'Stabilization Policies in Developing Countries, a Study case of the Gezira Scheme', in *Agricultural Economics Bulletin, UN*, December 1965. He is preparing a book on *Taxation in the Sudan*, in Arabic.

W. L. TAYLOR was born in New Zealand and educated at the University of Otago, Dunedin, New Zealand, and the London School of Economics. He has been Lecturer in Economics, University of Cape Town and was Professor of Economics and Head of the Department of Economics, University College of Rhodesia and Nyasaland until 1966. He is currently working in the Division of Educational Financing, Unesco, Paris. He has written *Francis Hutcheson and David Hume as Predecessors of Adam Smith* (1965) and contributed 'Problems of Economic Development of the Federation of Rhodesia and Nyasaland' to *Economic Development for Africa South of the Sahara*, edited by E. A. G. Robinson. He has also written numerous other articles on economic development in Africa for academic journals and for the Phoenix Group, Salisbury.

ALAN A. WALTERS, born in 1926, was appointed to the Cassel Chair of Economics at the London School of Economics in 1968 after having been Professor and Head of the Department of Econometrics and Social Statistics at Birmingham University. He has served as consultant to the Liberian Government, USAID, and United Nations Agencies. He has been Visiting Professor at

Northwestern University, Oregon, Virginia and MIT. His primary fields of research are transport economics and monetary economics. He has acted as adviser to the Ministry of Transport and is the author of numerous articles and papers in academic journals. He is the author (with G. Dalton and R. W. Clower) of *Growth Without Development, An Economic Survey of Liberia, The Economics of User Charges* (1968) and *Introduction to Econometrics* (1968).

1

INTRODUCTION

The group of countries collectively known as 'under-developed', or 'developing' or 'the third world' have several problems and attitudes in common. A natural desire for generality in the analysis of their problems, however, sometimes hinders useful discussion by too great an emphasis on their similarities and too little attention to their differences. Economists who have worked in one region soon find they have to discard several preconceptions when they begin work in another. The issues in India and Togo are not identical. Even within a region, problems and priorities vary considerably. One of the aims of the comparative studies in this book is to provide material whereby similarities and differences within Africa can be assessed.

A number of factors were considered in the choice of countries to be studied. South Africa was excluded as a special case. Countries from both the 'anglophone' and 'francophone' groups were needed. The economic structure of African countries varies from relatively primitive to relatively advanced levels and examples throughout the range were desired. Their approach to economic problems also varies, from *laissez-faire* to 'dirigiste' socialist direction. Some countries continue to have at least some 'settlers', whereas in others the expatriates, apart from a residue of former colonial administrators, are mainly transient, being diplomats, representatives of international firms or aid workers. In some areas federal issues or integration arrangements are important, or seem likely to become so. Since statistical data are essential for any useful study, the existence of a certain minimum of such data was a precondition for selection. A final requirement was that the chosen countries should be widely spread geographically.

This geographical spread is shown on Map 1. Three of the nine countries are francophone (Ivory Coast, Cameroon Federal Republic, Algeria). Federal or common market issues are important in East Africa, Central Africa, Nigeria, Ivory Coast and Cameroon, and Algeria. The Liberian economy is, except for its plantation and mining enclaves, relatively primitive, whereas that of Ghana is sufficiently developed for inter-industry analysis to be of some interest in planning. The Ivory Coast has a generally *laissez-faire* attitude towards economic policy, whereas Algeria and Ghana (for most of the period covered) were directed economies. Settlers continued to be important in East and Central Africa, and in Algeria their departure altered the whole economic structure.

Detailed statistical data are presented in the country studies. Some of it, supplemented by other data, is utilized in this Introduction. It seems desirable to preface this with some general comments on the limitations of the statistical data, in particular for comparative purposes. Since most of the country studies lean heavily on national accounts data, comment will be focused on these, but much of it applies also to other statistical data as well.

It is a common practice to employ national income data as an indicator of differences in or changes in, real income within a country. In such a context, to estimate changes in real income over time first requires that correction should be made for price changes. There are of course many difficulties involved in equating changes in national product at constant prices with changes in real income or welfare. Some of these revolve around the problem of changes in tastes and in the nature and quality of products. Other problems are that some parts of the national product like government and defence are only tenuously linked with what is usually associated with the term 'levels of living' whereas, on the other hand, many aspects of real income find no place in national product calculations.

Similar difficulties in an extreme form confront attempts to use national income data as guides to levels of real income in different countries at a particular point in time. One basic problem in using national product data as an indicator of relative real incomes on an international basis arises from the inappropriateness, for well known reasons, of exchange rates as indicators of the internal purchasing powers of the respective currencies. An indication of this problem is provided by the following figures which relate to Cameroon and

1958 GDP per capita ($)

	Cameroon	Nigeria	Ratio: Cameroon/Nigeria
Converted by official exchange rate	92	48	1·92
Converted by UN parity rate	65	58	1·12

Source: U.N. Yearbook of National Accounts, 1965, Tables 9A and 9B.

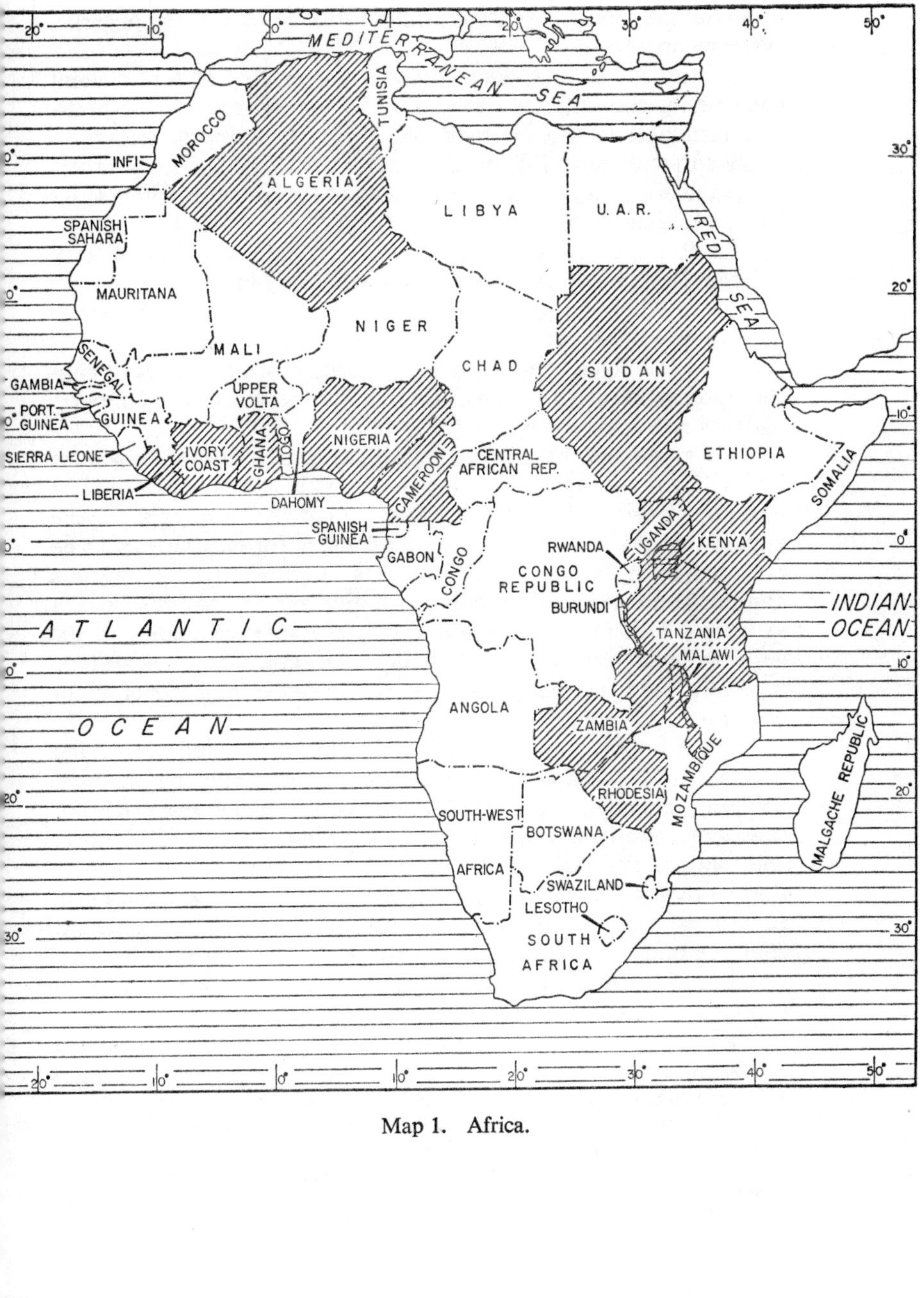
MEDITERRANEAN SEA
MOROCCO
INFI
ALGERIA
TUNISIA
LIBYA
U. A. R.
RED SEA
SPANISH SAHARA
MAURITANA
MALI
NIGER
CHAD
SUDAN
SENEGAL
GAMBIA
PORT. GUINEA
GUINEA
UPPER VOLTA
SIERRA LEONE
LIBERIA
IVORY COAST
GHANA
TOGO
DAHOMY
NIGERIA
CAMEROON
CENTRAL AFRICAN REP.
ETHIOPIA
SOMALIA
SPANISH GUINEA
GABON
CONGO
CONGO REPUBLIC
RWANDA
BURUNDI
UGANDA
KENYA
TANZANIA
MALAWI
INDIAN OCEAN
ATLANTIC OCEAN
ANGOLA
ZAMBIA
RHODESIA
MOZAMBIQUE
MALGACHE REPUBLIC
SOUTH-WEST AFRICA
BOTSWANA
SWAZILAND
LESOTHO
SOUTH AFRICA

Map 1. Africa.

Nigeria. Before the establishment of the Federal Republic of Cameroon in 1961, its western member formed part of the Nigerian currency area.

But even if 'real' product estimates are arrived at for different countries by conventional methods[1] or by less conventional methods[2] is it justifiable to use the indicated levels of *per capita* income to imply corresponding differences in welfare? Although such a procedure may not be too misleading if adopted for countries with similar backgrounds and at similar levels of development it may not be helpful if employed for comparisons between countries at very different levels of development any more than domestic real product figures would be as a guide to living standards in Britain for periods as far removed as, say, 1850 and 1950.

One of the biggest problems arises because of differences in consumption patterns. Between countries, differences in consumption patterns reflect partly differences in price structures, but also differences in tastes and 'need'. One attempt to get round the problem of international comparisons of income takes into account need. For instance, since people in hot countries do not need heating it may be argued that resources used in a cold country for heating should be excluded from its income for purposes of comparison. Using this approach and taking into account also differences in coverage and in valuation, Usher[3] reduces the ratio of *per capita* income in the UK and Thailand from 14 to 1 to about 2·5 to one. The calculation is revealing but it evidently depends on subjective judgements about need on which opinions may differ.

Another important point which must be borne in mind when using national product estimates for comparative purposes is that different countries employ different criteria for determining the extent of subsistence production which should be included in the calculations, and that practice varies in the valuations placed upon such production.[4] For instance, the treatment of traditional house building in rural areas and of beer brewing has been different in different countries and—in some cases—different at different times in the same country. The varying treatment of items such as these gives rise to substantial differences in the resulting estimates.

Another difficulty in the comparative use of national accounts data

[1] See for instance M. Gilbert and M. Kravis *An International Comparison of National Products and the Purchasing Power of Currencies*, OECD, Paris, 1954.

[2] See for instance W. Beckerman and R. Bacon, 'International Comparisons of Income Levels', *Economic Journal*, LXXXVI, 1966.

[3] See D. Usher, 'The Transport Bias in Comparisons of National Income', *Economica*, No. 118, May 1963; Appendix.

[4] See D. Lury, 'National Accounts in Africa', *Journal of Mod. Afr. Studies* 2 (1).

arises from differences in presentation which arise in part from different solutions to conceptual problems. Such differences are particularly important in Africa, where differences in the French and British systems have been carried over into the anglophone and the francophone countries. Only major differences can be mentioned here.[1] The most common aggregate in anglophone countries is Gross Domestic Product (GDP). The nearest comparable figure in the French system is Production Intérieure Brute (PIB). The main difference between the measures is that wages and salaries paid to workers in central and local government, certain other public and private non-profit making institutions and the wages of domestic servants are all excluded from PIB but are included in GDP. Also, PIB is calculated at market prices whereas although GDP may also be calculated at market prices, the factor cost basis is more commonly used in Africa. Another difference of importance is that the French system employs a commodity rather than an industrial classification. Resource availability and use are compared in terms of a commodity classification. Some of the differences between the two systems may become less important when the new UN System of National Accounts adapted for Africa is generally adopted. At present they considerably handicap comparative studies.

Finally, the purely statistical limitations of the data must be borne in mind, with particular reference to the quality of the estimates and of possible errors in compilation. These limitations apply of course to all the statistics employed in this book, not merely the national accounts data, and to national, as well as to comparative analysis. It is often impossible to get comparable figures for any considerable time period. Many entries in annual series are derived by making approximate adjustments to previous and sometimes already ancient figures rather than from the results of regular current enquiries. This should be remembered in particular in relation to estimates of subsistence production. The quality of the estimates is also particularly important in the case of traditional capital formation. Whereas in most African countries capital formation by the Central government and the modern private sector is recorded adequately, capital investment by local government and by peasant farmers in land clearing and improvement, tree crops and livestock is either poorly estimated or altogether overlooked. These deficiencies are particularly serious in view of the widespread use of average and incremental capital output ratios for planning and plan evaluation.

Despite all these limitations the statistics can be used to illuminate

[1] For a detailed discussion, See P. Ady and M. Courcier, *Systems of National Accounts in Africa*, OECD, Paris, 1960.

many aspects of structure and development: but care is needed to distinguish the cases where the light they shed is relatively clear and steady from those where it flickers and almost goes out.

THE PHYSICAL, DEMOGRAPHIC AND ECONOMIC BACKGROUND

Africa has an area of about 11·7 mn. sq. miles and forms about 22 per cent of the world's land area. Its population is estimated at about 300 mn. (about 9 per cent of the world total). Corresponding totals of areas and populations of the countries included in the studies collected here are nearly 4 mn. sq. miles and 130 mn. people. Although the areas of some African countries are large—Sudan and Libya have areas of about 1 mn. and 700,000 sq. miles and together are nearly half the size of China or the USA—their populations are usually small. The most populous country is Nigeria which has a population of some 50 mn. The average population of African countries is just over 5 mn. and is thus about 35 per cent of the average for the world as a whole. The distribution of all African countries by population size, and of those countries selected for this volume is shown in Table 1.

Table 1. *African countries by population size, 1963*

	All countries	Countries selected for study
Under 1 million	3	—
1 —	20	5
5 —	5	4
10—	4	3
15—	1	—
20—	1	—
25—30	1	—
About 50	1	1

Note: Excludes South Africa and countries shown in source as 'Non-sovereign' (except Rhodesia).

Source: *U.N. Demographic Yearbook* 1964, Table 1, New York, 1965.

Population size has an important bearing on the size of the market. From other standpoints, such as agricultural development, population density is more relevant. The population density for Africa is about 25 a square mile, but the figures for individual countries vary greatly from 2–3 a square mile in arid countries such as Libya to about 280 a square mile in Rwanda. The range of densities within each country is also wide. The overall rate of population growth is high, at about 2·4 per cent a year. Its range in the countries dealt with here is from 1 to 3·2 per cent, and the median figure is 2·5 per cent. One of the implications of such rapid rates of growth is that a high proportion of the population—from 40 to 50 per cent—is under 15.

An important consequence of the high rates of population growth is that increases in *per capita* income have been held back. Table 2 summarizes data on the annual rates of growth. There are statistical incomparabilities, but the general picture is one of relatively large rates of aggregate growth in terms of current prices. If these rates

Table 2. *Annual rates of change of GDP*
(per cent)

	Period	Population growth	Total current prices	Total constant prices	*Per capita* current prices	*Per capita* constant prices
Algeria	1954–63	2·0	4·4	−0·7	2·4	−2·7
Cameroon[b]	1951–65	2·0–2·5	6·0	3·5	3·7	1·2
Ghana	1955–64	2·5	8·0	4·7[a]	5·4	2·1[a]
Ivory Coast	1956–64	2·5	10·3	6·6	7·5	4·0
Kenya	1955–64	3·2	4·9	n.a.	1·6	n.a.
Liberia	1955–60	1·0	12·0	10·0	11·0	9·0
Malawi	1955–64	2·2	4·6	2·8	2·3	0·6
Nigeria	1950–62	2·5	6·6	2·5	4·0	0·0
Rhodesia[b]	1955–64	3·0–3·5	6·5	5·2	3·3	2·0
Sudan	1955–63	2·8	4·7	4·3	1·8	1·5
Tanzania	1960–64	1·8	8·6	4·7	6·7	2·8
Uganda	1955–64	2·5	4·2	3·5	1·7	1·0
Zambia[b]	1955–64	2·5–3·0	4·2	6·0	1·5	3·3

Notes: [a] 1955–1963.
[b] The mid range of the population growth estimates has been used for calculation of *per capita* growth.

It should perhaps be emphasized that calculations of GDP in terms of constant prices make no allowance for changes in the barter terms of trade. As noted below (page 53), these changed adversely over the period 1956–1961. For countries for which this effect was significant, the growth rate of real *per capita* product will overstate the rate of growth of 'real *per capita* consumption'. For a discussion of some of the implications of changes in the terms of trade and some suggested means of taking them into account in national income calculations the reader is referred to: C. P. Haddon-Cave, 'Real Growth of the East African Territories, 1954–60', *East African Economics Review*, Vol. 8, No. 1 (June 1961), and the subsequent discussion by Tyrrell, Lury and Massell.

Source: Contributors to this book and *U.N. Yearbook of National Accounts Statistics 1965*, New York, 1966.

of change are corrected for price changes, the rates of real growth are generally lower (Zambia is an exception) but are still sizeable. The median rate of increase is 4·5 per cent a year, which would lead to a doubling of total income in sixteen years. *Per capita* rates of real growth are much lower, the median figure being 1·8 per cent. At this rate 39 years would be required to double income. Nevertheless, the rates of growth are not negligible and they have been achieved in the face of a rapidly changing political and economic scene. During this period much energy was devoted to the struggle for independence and the subsequent search for a stable political order; the structure and character of governments has changed; with Africanization of administration, commerce and industry, large and rapid re-adjustments have been needed, which in many cases in the short run cannot have been conducive to growth.

Current development plans call for even quicker rates of growth. Table 3 sets out some indicators taken from the following chapters. The differences of rates in the first two columns may look small, but they entail on average the stepping up of existing rates of growth by more than a third. Average annual capital expenditure over the plan period is also to be higher—from about a quarter higher in Sudan, Nigeria, and Cameroon to nearly twice as high in Kenya and Uganda.

These higher rates of growth and greater capital expenditures are shown in the plans to be dependent to varying extents on foreign finance. The lowest expectation, in relative and absolute terms, is that of Sudan which budgets for a quarter of its plan finance coming from abroad. The maximum proportion budgeted for is about one half, in Kenya and Tanzania. A comparison of amounts of aid per head is one where absolute figures are not misleading, and it is worth particularizing the very high expectations under the now discarded Ghana plan: nearly £8 per head annually was required to meet the proposals there, compared to £2—£3 elsewhere.

The share of manufacturing in planned investment is high (about one fifth or more of the total) in Ivory Coast, Ghana, Tanzania, and Kenya. But investment in primary production in some of the countries is also to be high. In general the relative shares do not present a picture of countries neglecting primary production and hell-bent on industrialization. This is not to suggest that the proportions are right; but merely that widely expressed allegations of an over-emphasis on industrialization in plan patterns in Africa have been made too readily and need more detailed support.

One important feature of the development plans is the high proportion of the planned capital expenditure that is expected to be in the public sector. Although the figures in the relevant column of

Table 3. *Development Plan magnitudes*

	Period	Recent rate of growth (% p.a.)[b]	Planned rate of growth (% p.a.)	Annual capital expenditure planned (£m)	Annual capital expenditure as % of GDP[c]	Annual capital expenditure as % of gross cap. formation[c]	% of plan in public sector	% of expenditure in: Primary production	Manufacturing	Education and Health	Planned annual increase in manfg. (% p.a.)	Foreign financial requirements: £ per head p.a.	as % of total plan
Cameroon[a]	1961–6	4·8	5·5	22	13	129	43	22[f]	7[f]	13[f]	n.a.	1·8	42
Ghana	1963/4–69/70	4·7	5·5	145	25	138	57	22	20	9	29	7·9	33
Ivory Coast	1960–9	6·6	7·0	44	22	151	51	12	39	8	n.a.	n.a.	n.a.
Kenya	1965/6–69/70	2·5	6·3	65	23	198[d]	45	20	19	7	8·0	3·8	51
Nigeria	1962–8	2·5	4·0	197	17	123	41	14	n.a.[e]	13	n.a.	1·8	41
Sudan	1961/2–70/1	4·3	5·2	57	16	123	60	26[f]	16[f]	10[f]	21	1·2	27
Tanzania	1964–9	4·7	6·7	49	20	160	61	17	21	10	14·8	2·6	52
Uganda	1966–71	3·5	6·3	46	23	189	63	14	15	13	12·6	2·4	35

[a] East Cameroon only.
[b] See Table 2 except for East Cameroon, for which see Chapter 5, and Kenya, which is a 'guesstimate'. Figures are of rate of growth at constant prices.
[c] At or about beginning of plan period.
[d] But 142 per cent of previous highest figure (£45·6 m in 1957).
[e] Not available separately: trade and industry account for 13 per cent.
Assumes replacement investment distributed as expansion investment.

Sources: Contributors to the book, plan documents, *Outlines and Selected Indicators of African Development Plans* (UNECA, E/CN 14/336), and R. H. Green 'Four African Development Plans', *Journal of Mod. Afr. Studies* 3(2).

Table 3 which vary from 41 to 63 per cent look very high, they do not in most cases represent a particularly striking change from the past. Table 4 gives the two sets of percentages. Nevertheless, given the rapid prospective increase of total capital expenditure, its recurrent implications, and the tendency of Government recurrent expenditure to grow 'naturally', revenue sources are likely to come under considerable strain, despite the expectation of substantial foreign aid.

Table 4. *Government capital expenditure as proportion of total capital expenditure*
(per cent)

	Recently	Plan
Ghana	52	57
Ivory Coast	42	51
Kenya	39	45
Nigeria	42	41
Sudan	59	60
Tanzania	49	61
Uganda	66	63

Source: Plan documents, *U.N. Yearbook of National Accounts*, and contributors.

THE ROLE OF GOVERNMENT IN DEVELOPMENT

The role of Government as *the* pace-making instrument for economic change is now undisputed in all of these countries. This is so in spite of differences in governmental attitudes to economic policy which range them along a spectrum from *laissez-faire* and encouragement of expatriate private enterprises to centralized planning and rapid Africanization of all economic units (the scale polarized by Professors Coleman and Rosberg in the wider political scene into two patterns of 'pragmatic-pluralistic' and 'revolutionary centralizing').[1] All the countries are effectively one party states, although for economic analysis a better institutional description is to say that they are controlled by small elites. These elites have established interlocking key positions in the party, the political and administrative Government structures (and the distinction between the functions and powers of ministers and senior civil servants is often not so well defined or applied as it is elsewhere), the military command, and, where it exists, the indigenous business class. They can be characterized by educational qualification and tribal allegiance[2] and they control what

[1] J. S. Coleman and C. G. Rosberg (eds.) *Political Parties and National Integration in Tropical Africa*, California, 1964. The conclusions provide an excellent discussion of the political similarities and differences among African states.

[2] 'Tribalism in modern Africa does sometimes recall sex in Victorian Britain.... It may have to be brutally discussed in some circumstances. But not in mixed

established points there are for making and putting into effect decisions on all major issues confronting their countries, including those concerned with economic policy. But the power vacuums that exist, the absence of generally accepted 'rules of the game', the often rudimentary nature of the administrative structures and the dependence of their economic policies upon international trade and on expatriate enterprises and expertise prevent these elites from implementing many of their desired policies.

When they start preparing inventories of their available economic resources they are immediately made aware of supply constraints resulting from a large, traditional, slow moving agricultural sector with its accompanying poorly trained and badly educated labour force. On the demand side they confront strong and persistent claims for services, both economic and social, deriving from rising populations and from the revolution of rising expectations which they encouraged, rightly, if not always judiciously, during the struggle for independence. In their endeavour to increase resources and to allocate existing capacity more appropriately, they turn to planning as the best means for handling national economic problems.

There was some tradition to build on. In anglophone countries, attempts to co-ordinate public expenditure into medium term plans go back at least to the wartime Colonial Development and Welfare programmes, if not earlier. In francophone countries two main organizations, the Fonds d'Investissement et de Développement Économique et Social (FIDES) and the Caisse Centrale de France Outre-Mer (CCFOM) provided funds and co-ordinated their use. These early programmes were deliberately limited to public expenditures, and they are now commonly referred to pejoratively[1] as 'colonial', 'limited', or 'partial' planning. In their project by project approach and their lack of attention to real resources they were clearly defective. Nevertheless, their effectiveness in raising the level of infrastructure and in providing a base for a rapid expansion in education and in health services should not be underrated. Some, such as the Hall-Worthington plan for Uganda, were for their time remarkable in scope and vision.

The planning which has made its appearance in Africa since in-

company—that is in front of non-Africans'. Roy Lewis in *The Times*, August 25, 1967. A brief account using non-emotive terms is given in pp. 687–91 of Coleman and Rosberg *op. cit.*

[1] A. O. Hirschman's thoughtful words on 'The Semantics of Problem-Solving' are worth looking at. See 'Problem-Solving and Policy-Making; A Latin American Style?' in his *Journeys into Progress*, Doubleday, New York, 1965.

dependence is of a more inclusive character. One obvious difference between it and earlier attempts are the widespread endeavours to 'integrate', or at least to take into account, private sector activities, towards whose existence and possible growth it must be said that most African states adopt an ambiguous attitude. Most post-independence plans include data on the development of the private sector and often give specific attention to policy measures designed to influence it. So far, however, effective methods of controlling the operations of the private sector in detail without in effect taking it over have not been evolved. The most usual control mechanism has operated through development corporations, but even where these have been effective in their operations they have been unable to do more than supplement private enterprise or to intervene in limited specific fields.

Perhaps the most notable difference between the earlier approaches to planning and more recent initiatives lies in methods of formulation. Many plans are professedly formulated within a comprehensive plan framework and nearly all plans make gestures in this direction. Comprehensive planning has three main elements: it involves (i) macro-economic projections, the selection of targets and the use of aggregative frameworks to influence and guide detailed plan activities; (ii) sector co-ordination to ensure that planned investments are consistent with each other and feasible in terms of resources; (iii) a systematic selection of projects which contribute to the national objectives, not only for the public sector but also for the private sector. Morocco, Egypt, Cameroon and Tanzania are all countries in which some emphasis has been placed upon the formulation of medium and long term plans in a comprehensive framework with particular attention being given to the plan frame and internal consistency in terms of resources and financial balances.

The gap between appearance and reality in planning practices must of course be borne constantly in mind, and in many countries the actual emphasis on the aggregative aspects is not large. In Kenya, for example, work on plan frameworks, etc., has occupied only a small part of the efforts of planners. But even in the countries in which comprehensive planning has been stressed, there is little evidence that model building and aggregative plan frameworks have actually influenced plans and the link between aggregative data and specific investment choices is tenuous. Some see in this a need for extending comprehensive planning. For instance, in relation to East Africa, it has been argued by Clark that, with respect to the acceleration of economic growth 'the most important improvement immediately available is to introduce more inclusive and coherent aggregative plan frameworks'[1] Waterston, on the other hand, after a world-wide survey of planning experience, though conceding that in the long run comprehensive planning may give better results, says '. . . a reading of the record suggests that less developed countries have fared better in practice, both in the short and the long run, by first learning how to prepare and carry out integrated public investment plans than by going from *ad hoc* project preparation and execution directly into comprehensive planning. The weight of evidence and logic favours partial planning'.[2]

At bottom the debate on planning, in so far as it is concerned with formulation, concerns the role which should be played by the aggregative plan frameworks as guides to policy, as opposed to project selection, initiation and evaluation. Is it desirable to attempt to derive development activities from the aggregative analyses or is it better to build from the bottom up on the basis of individual projects or sector programmes whose feasibility and viability can be reasonably well established? Ultimately the answer turns on the contribution which each can make, at the present level of development, to the taking of effective decisions about the use of resources and institutions to promote growth.

Although different opinions are obviously current, it is fair to say that in Africa at the present time, among economists who have actually engaged in planning, there is some scepticism about the importance which should be attached to aggregative frameworks and their usefulness. In the first instance there is in many cases such a lack of dependable data about the economic magnitudes that the results of the calculations simply cannot be taken seriously. Stolper has characterized planning in Nigeria, one of the more advanced of African countries, as 'planning without facts'.[3] Apart from this, in African conditions, many of the relationships are subject to great instability. In these circumstances to place great weight on aggregative analysis as a basis for long term planning or concrete investment decisions may represent an act of faith rather than of reason. It is also clear that, the value of comprehensive planning is likely to be greater if there is a large number of projects well worked out amongst which a choice has to be made because of financial constraints. But it is becoming increasingly obvious that in some African countries (Sudan, Nigeria, Kenya) the problem is one of a lack of well-worked-out projects. Project stimulation rather than project choice becomes a major constraint. It is considerations of this kind which have led Waterston

[1] See P. G. Clark, *Development Planning in East Africa*, Nairobi, 1966.
[2] A. Waterston, *Development Planning*, London, 1966, p. 98.
[3] See W. F. Stolper, *Planning Without Facts*, Harvard University Press, 1966.

and others to argue in favour of partial planning. This is not to advocate a return to the *ad hoc* approach of colonial days but in effect is a plea to emphasize planning from the bottom up. In principle there may be no conflict, but it has been argued that in practice aggregative planning encourages a fascination with planning methodology. The other approach with its concern with projects compels planners to get involved with schemes and their implementation from the start.

Implementation itself is an area which has received overdue attention in recent years, both inside planning organizations and from outside critics, and it is sometimes alleged that it is in this area, rather than in formulation, that the major weaknesses of planning in Africa reside, if a clear distinction can usefully be drawn between the two aspects. A synoptic view on plan implementation is impossible to provide because most countries do not report regularly on plan implementation. Nevertheless it is plain that in many cases, even in the public sector, plan objectives in terms of expenditures, output or growth have fallen markedly short of intentions. Less surprisingly, private activities differ markedly in character, if not always in volume, from those expressed in the plans. These facts are indisputable. The interpretation to be placed upon them is of course another matter. It is questionable whether a valid appraisal of planning can be based on a comparison of plans and achievement. Some plan targets demonstrably embody an extreme attitude of plan fantasy, and even where this is not the case, targets may be set unattainably high for the purpose of stretching the nation and aid-donors. But apart from this, fulfilment or non-fulfilment may have little to do with the quality of the plan or the realism of its assessment of administrative capacity, but may largely reflect exogenous changes to which an appropriate response must be made.

This is not the end of the story: even where expenditure or growth targets have been realistically set and have not been upset by exogenous factors such as political upheaval, many plans have not been implemented. In some instances this has been due to a lack of well-worked-out projects of demonstrable viability and feasibility with which to clothe the sectoral allocations. Bad timing has also hindered implementation, often because of optimism about the period needed to complete contracts or obtain imports. Delays in one sector may impinge on others if vital projects get out of step. Such factors may result in less being spent than was planned. But they may just as well mean, if domestic financial resources are available, that, as in Sudan, projects are embarked upon without any prior justification, in order to keep up the level of 'development' expenditure. Either way, to the extent that this is the case, it reinforces the argument for a direction of planning effort into this area.

Aid practices are a second factor which have sometimes hindered plan implementation, for various reasons. Aid is given for projects rather than programmes and often only import costs can be financed, and imports from particular donors at that. Administrative bottlenecks prevent the release of allocated funds because documentation or justification cannot be effected in time. This of course raises questions of administrative capacity in the broadest sense which have a relevance going far beyond the relationship between aid and planning. Finally, of course, there is the extent of the political commitment to making planning work. One significant indicator of the commitment to planning is provided by the location of the planning organization in relation to the seats of power, and the status of the responsible minister.

Despite the evident difficulties encountered in the search for effective means of planning for economic development in Africa, the process has had some useful results. A necessary background for aid negotiations has been provided. It has stimulated the improvement of statistical data and its articulation within a general framework. This has provided a better basis for decision making processes. Planning methods of a fairly technical nature (sometimes leading to an appearance of precision not justified by the nature of the data used) have helped to give consistency to targets, and have helped to ensure that second round considerations such as implications for recurrent expenditure and for the balance of payments have been taken into account. In the process important lessons have been learned. In the last resort, planning has to be judged, not in terms of the sophistication of the plan, or in terms of a comparison between what was planned and what was achieved, but in terms of the difference it makes to growth, not merely in the short run but in the longer run. This is a function of the improvement in the quality and effectiveness of the decision making process in relation to resource allocation and in the use of generalized policy instruments which is brought about by planning. In the nature of the case, this contribution is virtually impossible to quantify. The record makes clear however, that planning is not a sufficient condition for accelerating economic growth.

AGRICULTURAL DEVELOPMENT

Agricultural improvement is recognized in most plans as one of the most important but yet most difficult tasks. The targets for growth in this sector are commonly more cautiously fixed than for the rest of the economy; the median annual growth rate proposed in the fourteen countries' plans is 4 per cent compared with 10·5 per cent for manufacturing, 7 per cent for basic facilities, and 9 per cent for construction.[1] But even a small percentage increase may be difficult to engender given the nature of the agricultural sector in most African countries. Admittedly, if population in agriculture is growing at 2½–3 per cent a year as it has been doing in most of these countries, a comparable increase in production should be obtainable so long as there is enough land for the newcomers to reproduce the existing traditional pattern. It is, of course, this process which lies behind much of the increase in agricultural production for export and home consumption of the post 1945 period. But there are signs that this quasi-spontaneous process is coming to an end because of growing pressure on land and the deterioration of its fertility.

Some success has been achieved in improving traditional agricultural practices, but in most countries the possibilities for expanding returns by increasing specialization, better marketing arrangements and the introduction of improved techniques and new, relatively inexpensive tools still remain to be exploited. An instance of what can be achieved by improvements in marketing and the introduction of improved techniques is shown by the considerable growth which has occurred in the fishing industry in many African countries following the introduction of outboard motors, nylon nets and cold storage facilities. All the indications so far, however, are that changes in the traditional agrarian structure can be brought about only slowly, depending as they do on the dissemination of knowledge, and changes in attitudes and practices in an uncertain environment where established techniques have demonstrated their ability to produce a living.

A further problem may arise because of special characteristics of the supply curve of agricultural products. It is often suggested that in Africa, increases in the returns to agricultural labour may elicit less effort, or may result in a reduced marketable surplus. Such phenomena have been documented elsewhere[2] and it would not be surprising if they should have occurred in Africa. Their existence would not mean that Africans are not responsive to economic

[1] See *A Survey of Economic Conditions in Africa, 1960–64*, UNECA, Table 4, p. 550.

[2] A perverse relationship between return and effort has been noted in economic development elsewhere in, for instance, S. Pollard, 'Factory Discipline in the Industrial Revolution', *Econ. Hist. Review* XVI (2), December 1963. See also, E. S. Furniss, *The Position of the Labourer in a System of Nationalism*, Boston, 1920. Other relevant references to the issues discussed in this paragraph are: R. M. Stern, 'The Price Responsiveness of Primary Producers', *Review of Econ. and Stats.* May 1962; V. Dubey, 'The Marketed Agricultural Surplus and Economic Growth in Underdeveloped Economies', *Econ. Journal* December 1963

incentives, but if these particular responses are widespread and important, public policy in agriculture would have to be designed with them in mind. In particular, one of their implications is that the securing of adequate increases in agricultural production and productivity may be dependent on the provision of more effective, and perhaps non-traditional, incentives to maintained or increased effort.

Moreover, programmes of agricultural improvement typically have a high local cost component. Aid cannot so readily be obtained for them, and domestic financial constraints may therefore particularly impede their development.

In the light of the difficulties encountered in improving traditional agriculture, it is perhaps not surprising that the 'transformation approach' to agricultural development, which relies on the introduction of large scale modern agricultural schemes using directed labour, should have been seen by many in African countries as offering a more practicable and shorter path to expansion. But although numerous attempts have been made, there are few successes to cite. On the contrary, although the Gezira scheme in the Sudan is one example which has achieved good results (it is notable that it embodies a considerable element of traditional practice), other parts of Africa are littered with the remains of transformation schemes which have proved to be unprofitable, such as the Niger scheme and the Tanganyika groundnuts scheme, to cite only conspicuous examples. Such failures moreover are not just a feature of the colonial era. The Tanzanian Government, whose 1964–69 Plan allocated a large part of its funds for agriculture to 'transformation' schemes rather than 'improvement' schemes was soon forced by economic considerations drastically to curtail the transformation element of the programme. Kenya which had specific opportunities for agricultural transformation in the course of the transfer of land from European settler to African farmer has found it desirable, in the light of the relatively poor rates of return from many of these farms, to emphasize improvement in the traditional sector, where the land consolidation programme and other improvements achieved considerable success in the pre-Plan period.

Difficulties in bringing about an adequate improvement in agriculture partly explain why the local food supply itself is beginning to emerge as a serious constraint in some countries (see the chapter on Ghana). Food imports (some of which are due to changes of taste) are growing and are making unexpected demands on foreign exchange supplies. Some comments on these imports are unnecessarily charged with moral condemnation. There is no 'divine' reason why these countries should never import food: indeed, if Sir Arthur Lewis's vision of the temperate countries as the granary rather than the workshop of the world ever materializes, they will necessarily be doing so. But this is not a consideration to influence medium term planning. Current plans will certainly be held back considerably if unintended imports of food continue: indeed their existence on a substantial scale in any country provides a prima facie reason for re-examining agricultural policy in that country's plan.

Problems of food supply lead on to a consideration of population policies. Only two African Governments—Tunisia and Kenya—have so far supported detailed family planning programmes. Admittedly a number of African countries are still under-populated; but in the face of demands to produce a rising *per capita* income, it is difficult to contemplate with equanimity the continuance of current population trends for any considerable period. There are as yet few signs that African family size will adjust spontaneously to the new mortality levels. If this does not soon occur, most African countries may be forced to promote family planning if they hope to achieve their current growth objectives.

MONEY, BANKING AND FINANCE

In view of the overwhelming importance attached to development it is not surprising that, in African countries, monetary and fiscal policies are judged primarily by their contributions to economic progress. These contributions may take three main forms: the provision of finance for capital formation; stabilization measures, which are widely felt to be beneficial to growth; and the development of institutions and arrangements which may stimulate growth through their impact on the level and utilization of capital funds. Fiscal policy has generally been the main instrument through which governments in Africa have operated hitherto. Unfortunately a comparative analysis of such policies and of fiscal performance is hindered by data problems. Conventional budgets vary in coverage; revenue and expenditure categories are not standardized; often budgets are not consolidated; the dividing line between current and development expenditure varies; finally, there are marked year to year fluctuations in revenues.

There has been a marked change from the fiscal position in the fifties when high commodity prices and a more limited development effort made it possible for a high proportion of development expenditure to be financed by budgetary savings. For instance, in Ghana, the share of capital expenditure financed by budgetary savings declined from nearly nine tenths in 1957–58 to one third in 1965. Sudan planned to make substantial contributions to development finance from the recurrent budget during the current plan period, but the contribution soon fell to zero and it is now negative. Although in Nigeria a contribution was made until 1960, it was small and only half of what was planned during the period 1955–60. There are some exceptions to this pattern. In Liberia for example, budgetary savings have been important. In Zambia too, recurrent revenue is still a major source of development finance. Both of these countries rely on mineral royalties to an important extent. It is notable that in many countries tax revenues are not significantly—if at all—higher than aid expectations expressed on a *per capita* basis (cf. Tables 3 and 5).

Table 5. *Tax performance*

Country	Year	GDP per head (£)	Tax revenue per head (£)	Tax revenue as percentage of GDP
Ivory Coast	1964	82	10·4	13
Ghana	1962–63	71	9·9	14
Algeria	1964	70	16·8	24
Liberia	1960	57	11·8	21
Cameroon	1964–65	47	5·8	12
Central Africa	1963	52	8·7	17
Kenya	1963–64	31	4·0	13
Sudan	1961–62	31	3·6	12
Nigeria	1960	27	2·6	10
Uganda	1963–64	27	3·4	13
Tanzania	1963–64	24	2·3	10

Source: Contributors; Okigbo, *Nigerian Public Finance*, Longmans, London 1965.

More often than not the tax structure has proved unable to tap increments to income on an adequate scale. The proportion of income taken in taxes has remained fairly static, despite the fact that, since total government expenditures have grown more rapidly than the gross domestic products of these economies, there has been an urgent need to increase the share of taxation in national income. Although political obstacles to the more effective exploitation of the tax systems certainly exist, a large part of the explanation for their inadequate response must be sought in the accessibility, size and rate of growth of the tax base. Table 6 sets out some of the facts about tax revenues in the countries included in this book. They are not unrepresentative of African countries as a whole.

Although there are important differences among the countries included, the general revenue pattern may be summed up as follows. About four fifths of revenue is derived from taxation; three quarters

Table 6. *Tax structure: major taxes as % of total tax revenue*

Revenue	Kenya 1963–4	Uganda 1963–4	Tan-zania 1963–4	Ghana 1962–3	Cent. Africa 1963	Came-roon 1964–5	Liberia 1960	Ivory Coast 1964	Nigeria 1960	Sudan 1960–2 (AV)	Range	Median
All taxes as % of total revenue	79·0	76·0	83·7	85·5	77·7	82·6	92·3	90·6	76·4	64·2	64·2–92·3	80·8
Income taxes as % of total tax revenue	36·4	14·6	29·5	14·8	63·2	18·2	51·3	8·6	12·6	3·7	3·7–63·2	16·5
Export taxes as % of total tax revenue	0·3	31·2	3·8	20·6	—	15·3	}	28·5	16·3	12·1	0·0–31·2	15·3
Import taxes as % of total tax revenue	37·2	35·2	43·9	47·8	} 26·3	48·1	} 48·7	} 61·4	61·2	51·7	35·2–61·2	47·8
Excise taxes as % of total tax revenue	16·3	15·0	16·5	8·7	}	4·8	}	}	6·9	22·8	4·8–22·8	15·0
Export + import taxes as % of total tax revenue	37·5	66·4	47·7	68·4	n.a.	63·4	n.a.	n.a.	77·5	63·9	37·5–77·5	63·9
Export, import and excise taxes as % of total tax revenue	53·8	81·4	64·1	77·0	26·3	68·2	48·7	89·9	84·4	86·7	26·3–89·9	72·6

Source: As for Table 5.

of tax revenue is derived from export, import and excise taxes; nearly one half of tax revenue comes from import duty; excise duties, export taxes and income taxes are of approximately equal importance and each contribute about 15 per cent of total revenue. Indirect taxes thus predominate. Income taxes are relatively unimportant but their importance is higher in those countries which possess a mining or industrial enclave producing for export. The small importance of progressive income taxes in the tax structure of these countries produces an inelastic tax system in the sense that a growth of national income tends to be accompanied by a less than proportionate increase in public revenue. Increases in the share of revenue to national income have to be effected by increases in tax rates. Since only a minute fraction of the population is subject to conventional income taxation, and effective substitutes have not yet been developed, this means increases in indirect taxation. The scope for these on articles of mass consumption when incomes are low is necessarily restricted. Many imports of capital goods come in duty free or at a low rate. Import substitution reduces revenue from import duties and in many cases local industries are unable to support excises without increased protection, which in the short run will lead to higher prices. In some cases scope for alteration of import duties may also be limited by the need to conform to a federal or common market determined revenue structure.

A striking feature of African tax systems is how little they have changed since independence. All continue to bear the stamp of their colonial predecessors. The systems of French-speaking Africa on the one hand are characterized by a multiplicity of different taxes and by a tendency for even the direct taxes to be levied on a proportional basis because of the schedular system which takes no account of total income. The progressive personal income tax is a negligible component of the tax systems of most francophone countries. Tax systems in anglophone Africa tend to be simpler; the centrally administered direct taxes tend to be steeply progressive and income from all sources, wage income, property and dividends, is aggregated for this purpose. Nevertheless, the proportion of the population outside the salariat which is subject to such progressive income taxes is in many cases small, although in some countries, particularly Nigeria and Ghana, attempts have been made with some success to widen the base.

It is easy to point to the deficiencies of existing tax systems, but difficult to see how to modernize them or to align them better with the underlying economic structures so as to make it possible to extract larger revenues without deleterious effects. Increased reliance on a progressive personal income tax on all sources of income is likely to be one important ingredient of any effective solution. Among other advantages this could diminish the disincentive to grow export crops which exists when export taxes are a major source of revenue, and in general reduce the discouragement of particular activities which arises when they are taxed more heavily merely because they are accessible. But progress towards a more efficient tax structure on such lines is so far demonstrably limited. Moreover, it must not be overlooked that in some situations business profits may be the most appropriate source of finance for the active innovator. Some economists argue that the possibility of raising adequate fiscal revenues in less developed countries depends on finding a solution to the problem of taxing land rather than its produce.[1] If this is so, improvement may be long postponed, for in many countries there are few individual land titles and even where these exist the problems of determining land productivity are immense. In Colombia, a country which is at least as advanced as most African countries, an attempt to do this, admittedly in the interests of resource allocation rather than revenue, proved a total failure.[2]

Fiscal policy may be considered not only as a source of finance but also as an instrument of stabilization. In African countries the main factors giving rise to economic instability are fluctuations in their export proceeds resulting from fluctuations in prices and output. The extent to which growth and stability are correlated in African countries may be debated, but there is undoubtedly a strong and widespread belief that this is true, and consequently there is a demand for stability measures. Such measures might operate in principle through the accumulation of budget surpluses in good times which would be held in external reserves, and their subsequent disbursement in times of depression. But when demands on development finance are so large as they currently are, it is rarely likely to be feasible deliberately to plan for surpluses. Moreover, even if favourable price trends may facilitate such policies the possibility of successful stabilization through budget operations evidently much depends on accurate forecasts of revenue, production, exports and export price.[3] But the very instability which gives rise to the problems inevitably

[1] See for example, N. Kaldor, 'Taxation for Economic Development', *Journal of Modern African Studies*, Vol. 1, No. 1 (1963), p. 16.

[2] See A. O. Hirschman, 'Land Taxes and Land Reform in Colombia', in (ed.) R. Bird and O. Oldman, *Readings on Taxation in Developing Countries*, The Johns Hopkins Press, Baltimore, 1964.

[3] A measure of built-in stabilization may be provided where, as in some African countries, export duties have been imposed on a sliding scale basis.

makes forecasting extremely difficult. Not surprisingly, budget estimates often diverge very widely from actual achievements. In Ghana during 1952–53 to 1965 the achieved budget balance differed from the planned balance by a mean of plus or minus 110 per cent. Such divergences are not uncommon in African budgets and the use of the budget as an instrument of stabilization is consequently fraught with difficulties.

In practice, such stabilization as has been attempted has been done for producers of particular major crops through the operations of marketing boards in anglophone Africa, and the *caisses de stabilization* in French-speaking Africa. Stabilization operations through marketing boards equally involve a need to forecast price trends and annual outputs (although only for particular commodities), so that in principle they confront the same problems as stabilization through the budget. The extent to which the operations of the various boards have contributed to income stabilization in different countries, and their impact on the economy in other ways has been the subject of prolonged debate. No attempt will be made to summarize this debate here, but it may be said that Marketing Boards became institutions with accepted roles not only in the marketing process itself, but also in stabilization, and in the accumulation of funds for development.[1] Their efficiency of course varied. Although it is not possible to generalize for all boards and all commodities, two things seem clear. Firstly, although boards have seldom been very effective in achieving short term stabilization of growers' incomes or crop prices, some have exercised a smoothing influence on total domestic income in the longer term. Secondly, the boards in such countries as Nigeria and Uganda have played an important role in financing economic development through the application of part of their large reserves to public development projects.

However, with widespread exhaustion of their reserves, either for development projects or to support incomes in the face of declines in commodity prices, the scope for any future stabilization or development financing measures operating through such boards is very limited, unless indeed there should occur a marked upturn of primary product prices of the kind which facilitated the initial building up of their reserves in the fifties. In any case it is questionable whether they should be allowed to resume these functions in the future, even if conditions were favourable, in part because the creation of 'earmarked' reserves places obstacles in the way of the effective use of reserves in depression, and in part because if some special form of

[1] See D. Walker, 'Maketing Boards' in (ed.) E. A. G. Robinson, *Problems of Economic Development*, London, 1965

tax on exports has to be maintained, it is on general grounds desirable that it should be an explicit rather than a concealed tax. Both the stabilization and tax functions should be clearly in the hands of Government.

It is only recently that African countries have been able to complement fiscal policy with monetary instruments. This is because, until independence, their public monetary institutions were largely engaged merely in the automatic issue of currency. A large part of the money supply consisted of the deposits of the expatriate commercial banks; it was their operations which determined the total money supply through their advances policies and which ensured that the currency issue expanded to maintain an appropriate relationship with the total money supply. Complete convertibility existed between the metropolitan currency and the colonial currency. The issuing authorities were purely passive and could not generally make advances to the colonial governments whose deficits, if any, had to be covered in other ways. Following independence the currency issuing authorities were transformed into central banks, and all of the countries covered in this book now have such institutions—except Liberia which lacks even an effective institution of the currency board type, employing instead the US dollar as currency.

Virtually all of former French tropical Africa is served by two multinational central banks, the Banque Centrale des États de l'Afrique de l'Ouest, covering West Africa, and the Banque Centrale des États de l'Afrique Équatoriale et du Cameroun, which covers Equatorial Africa. The organization and operation of these two banks is very similar. The board fixes credit supplies in each country. Bank notes are freely interchangeable within each of the two areas but are identifiable by letter or number or pictures. There is freedom of payments within the area. There is also free transferability in both directions with the French franc, facilitated by the 'operations account' system with the French Treasury which ensures unlimited over-draft facilities for the central banks. Separate accounts are kept for each member country with their central bank; individual balances of payments are computed for each member and the ownership of the pooled external reserves is attributed to each member. Each of these banks is authorized to extend short term credit to the member governments within certain limits but these facilities are of little significance since such credits can readily be obtained from the French Treasury at low rates. Medium term credits (up to five years) may also be extended to the member Governments within limits and for prescribed purposes.

The formation of the new institutions in francophone Africa is a reflection of the political situation created by independence and represents an important step towards modern central banking. Nevertheless, the basic principles governing the monetary relations between these institutions and France are virtually the same as those of their predecessors. The reserves are managed in common with those of the rest of the franc area and the currency itself is still largely managed by the Banque de France and the French Treasury. There is no formal reserve backing. The system clearly has many advantages, in particular that of the provision of unlimited support in French francs to the currency of the member countries; but they are required in return to subject their monetary and financial affairs to close control by France, a control which is reflected in the composition of the Governing Boards of the banks. As the Jeanneney Report put it, 'the member states accept a certain monetary tutelage, particularly in the matter of deficit financing.'[1]

In the English speaking countries of Africa, the growth of central banking has taken a more diverse and less fettered form. The three currency boards which served West, East and Central Africa have been broken up, and nearly every country now has its own central bank. The Sudan, which was formerly part of the Egyptian currency area, also has its own bank. Between the new countries and between them and sterling there is no automatic two-way transferability and each is subject to its own regulations. The new central banks naturally are responsible for currency issue and the management of the reserves and for converting the local currency into foreign currencies. In all cases they are authorized to create a fiduciary issue and are charged in addition with many of the usual functions of central banks including the promotion of economic development. Limitations to their powers to make fiduciary issues are often specified in their constitutions. In addition, minimum external reserves are specified. Sometimes this is in terms of a proportion of imports; sometimes it is specified in terms of a proportion of demand liabilities or, as in the case of Ghana, as a proportion of the currency issue. The older established central banks in English speaking Africa have made a start on the improvement of the banking structure and the development of local money and capital markets. Nigeria and Rhodesia are relatively well advanced in this direction, but progress elsewhere is rather limited. Wider functions have sometimes been advocated for these new central banks, including the provision of commercial banking facilities for the general public, but so far little has been attempted along these lines.

[1] See *The Jeanneney Report*, Overseas Development Institute, London, 1964, p. 38.

The limitations to employing the banking system as a source of finance for capital formation in less developed countries are well enough known to economists. Even where supply conditions are such than an expansion of demand for local factors and products could result in an increase in their supply without generating unduly inflationary price increases, expenditure financed by credit creation rapidly results in a decline in external reserves, both directly because of the often high import content of capital expenditure, and indirectly because of the high marginal propensity to import. Thus the size of the reserves is a major factor in limiting the scope for credit financed expenditure. Nevertheless, if reserves are high in relation to the size of the currency issue, demand deposits or import requirements, there may be scope for a measure of borrowing from the central banking system. This was in fact the position in several African countries in which conservative financial policies pursued prior to independence had endowed the new central banks with initial reserves which were large in relation to the criteria normally employed, as in Ghana and Nigeria. In other countries however, even though there had been no or only small fiduciary issues prior to independence, reserves were not high in relation to requirements, in part because of the large expansion of credit which had been brought about by commercial banks, and in part because capital flight or unduly high outflows of monetary assets due to an overvalued exchange rate (as in the case of the CFA franc) had reduced reserves to modest dimensions in relation to requirements.

In the countries with which this book is concerned, the financing of expenditure programmes by credit creation has been marked in Sudan, Ghana and Nigeria. In East Africa, although credit creation has provided some short term finance its importance has been small, but these central banks have existed for only a short time so nothing else is to be expected. In French-speaking tropical Africa generally, and in Ivory Coast and Cameroon, credit financed expenditure has not been important for reasons indicated above. Guinea and Mali which left the BCEAO are of course another story, and their recent financial history provides an object lesson of the dangers of financial laxity. Almost immediately after Mali signed an agreement with France in February 1967 looking forward to readmission to the West African Monetary Union, it was necessary for Mali to devalue its currency by 50 per cent to re-establish prices corresponding to those obtaining in other countries in the group.

Recourse to credit financed expenditure and the possibilities for its further use are reflected in and indicated by data relating to the foreign reserves of the countries in question. It must be borne in mind that changes in foreign reserves may be produced by factors other than credit creation. Table 7 shows the movement of foreign reserves in the past few years and the relation between these and imports for most of the countries included in this book. This ratio is included because it is widely accepted that countries ought ordinarily to maintain foreign currency reserves equal to at least four months imports. In some cases this requirement has been built into the constitutions of the central banks, as in the cases of Kenya and Tanzania. Virtually all central banks in English speaking Africa south of the Sahara have prescribed minimum reserves although these are sometimes related to their demand liabilities to the public as in Nigeria, or to the currency supply as in Ghana. In the case of two multinational central banks serving French speaking Africa, there is no formal reserve requirement.

To the extent that the rule of thumb mentioned above is a valid one, it appears that few African countries have now any margin for financing expenditure from central bank credit though this does not rule out the possibility of finance from genuine savings. Moreover, as their economies expand, and with this, their money holdings, there will be scope for some additional credit creation; indeed this will be necessary to overcome deflationary biases in the banking system. The low reserves with which the constituent members of the two francophone multinational central banks operate (indicated in the table by the figures for Cameroon and the Ivory Coast) are noteworthy. The fact that operations are possible at these levels in no way disproves the rule of thumb but reflects the ability of these countries to have recourse through the central bank to the French Treasury. It should also be noted that the movement of the reserves of the members of these groups has recently been somewhat contrary to the general picture in that they show some tendency to rise; but they are still low by reference to the usual indicators and if each country had to operate its own currency and could not rely on the French Treasury, reserves would certainly have to be built up much further.

If the scope for financing development by credit creation is limited in the African context, what can be said of the other contributions of monetary institutions and policy to development which operate through their influence on stability and through the promotion of a higher level of capital funds and their better utilization? It seems probable that one of the most important ways in which the new central banking institutions contribute to stability in Africa is through the exercise of their advisory functions to government, bearing on such matters as price policy etc., although it is clear that

Table 7. *African banking systems: foreign exchange reserves*[a]

	1959		1960		1961		1962		1963		1964		1965		1966	
	$ m	% of imports	$ m	% of imports	$ m	% of imports	$ m	% of imports	$ m	% of imports	$ m	% of imports	$ m	% of imports	$ m	% of imports
Cameroon	n.a.	n.a.	19	23·1	20	21·1	28	27·2	35	32·2	36	31·0	27	20·0	34	25·6
East Africa	136	39·9	132	35·1	136	35·9	152	39·9	166	40·9	155	36·1	143	28·4	217	35·3
Ghana[b]	433	136·9	388	106·8	191	48·6	196	58·8	122	33·4	123	36·2	132	35·2	126	42·9
Ivory Coast	n.a.	n.a.	n.a.	n.a.	n.a.	n.a.	34	21·8	41	24·1	39	16·6	60	25·4	61	23·0
Nigeria	439	87·8	434	71·8	390	62·6	338	59·4	232	39·9	245	34·5	246	31·9	227	31·6
Sudan	132	99·9	167	91·0	153	64·2	146	55·8	101	35·5	71	26·5	60	28·9	57	26·3

Notes: [a] Reserve position refers to end of year.
[b] The figures for 1964–66 are misleading since they do not include many official short term liabilities.

Source: *IMF International Financial Statistics*, June 1967.

in notable instances the proffered advice has not been accepted. Even in Africa, central bankers resign!

Perhaps not surprisingly, the contributions of African institutions of central banking to stabilization through the exercise of the traditional instruments of monetary control is, in almost all African countries, still potential rather than actual. This is not solely, or even mainly, due to the absence of local capital or money markets although this is obviously relevant. Even if such markets were more fully developed, the facts of economic dependence discussed earlier, and the almost universal dominance of the agricultural sector, would place narrow limits on the extent to which the level of economic activity could be controlled by monetary policy, or indeed by fiscal policy. The banks cannot control or influence the rate of capital formation significantly; nor can they influence the terms of trade or the weather. Nevertheless by various means of a non-orthodox nature it is possible for them to influence the supply of bank credit itself, and the adverse effects of fluctuations may, by this means, be moderated. To do this effectively however, demands the co-ordination of banking policy with the policies and operations of marketing boards, for in many African countries the price and distribution policies of these boards can be major determinants of the supply of money and credit.

The rate of growth may also be influenced by ensuring that such capital as is forthcoming is used in the most efficient way in terms of the chosen criteria. In addition it may be possible to influence the supply of capital itself by improving the system of payments and facilitating the development of institutions for bringing borrowers and lenders together. It is indeed for these purposes rather than as a means of creating the instruments for the exercise of traditional monetary policy that many African countries, through their central banking machinery, are attempting to build up local capital markets, and, less commonly, local money markets.[1] Nigeria has made considerable progress in this direction and has a stock market and building societies. Nairobi has a stock market. Salisbury possesses both a stock market and a fairly advanced money market. Nevertheless, the scope of these institutions is, even in the more advanced countries, very limited, and the market typically operates in a very imperfect manner.

Despite the changes which have occurred in the last ten years to develop effective monetary and fiscal institutions and policies in African countries, it is clear that much remains to be done. It is

[1] Arguments for specialized money markets in less developed countries are critically discussed by W. T. Newlyn in 'Money Markets in East Africa', *Journal of Modern African Studies*, Vol. 4, No. 4, 1966, pp. 471–78.

particularly urgent for African countries to expand their domestic contribution to capital finance by improving their tax performance and by gathering and using their savings more effectively, if development plans are not to be held back for want of finance. Even where finance is not a constraint, the ideology of self-reliance—as in Tanzania following the Arusha declaration of 1967—points in the same direction.

EXTERNAL TRADE

External trade is, after subsistence activities, the most important feature of the African economic scene, not merely because of its size, but also because it provides the means through which modernization enters these economies and by which the process can spread. Its potential effects have sometimes been frustrated when the main flows have operated through mining and plantation enclaves; the international depression in the 1930's also limited its benefits. But no other economic factor has exerted such a sustained pressure to monetize the economy and to open it to outside influences.

The ratio of commodity exports to gross domestic product in Africa is higher than in other continents. In 1958 the African figure excluding S. Africa was 21 per cent: in Europe it was 17 per cent, in S. America 13 per cent, in Asia (excluding Japan) 10 per cent, and in N. America 5 per cent. The ratio for under-developed countries would of course be lower if, for reasons discussed earlier, the product figures in the denominator are regarded as too low. On the other hand it can be argued that for estimating the effect of exports in the modern sector, the denominator of the ratio should be the *monetary* product. Since this is probably about two thirds of estimated total product, this adjusted ratio in Africa would be about 30 per cent. Reasons for the high ratio lie partly in the way in which Africa was brought into the international economy by colonization, and partly in its current stage of economic development; but one enduring factor is that African countries are small, and small countries tend to have a relatively more important external trade sector than large ones.[1]

The rate of growth of the volume of foreign trade in the last 50 years has been faster in Africa than elsewhere, in both total and *per capita* terms.

But the position looks less satisfactory if exports in the last 15 years are considered separately. The trade of industrial countries was

[1] E. A. G. Robinson (ed.), *Economic Consequences of the Size of Nations*, London, 1960, particularly the paper by S. Kuznets, 'Economic Growth of Small Nations'.

Table 8. *Increase in foreign trade by area, 1913–63*
(*per cent per decade: constant prices*)

	Total	*Per capita*
Developed countries	22·5	10·4
Underdeveloped countries	26·8	11·0
Africa	35·2	16·9
Asia	29·4	14·8
Latin America	23·0	−2·3

Source: S. Kuznets; 'Quantitative Aspects of the Economic Growth of Nations', *Econ. Dev. and Cultural Change*, 15 (2), January 1967, p. 16.

then growing much faster. Export growth in Africa was certainly faster than in the rest of the underdeveloped world (i.e. the world less the industrial countries and Africa), but only because of the very rapid increase of petroleum exports in the last 5 years. Over this period of 15 years, export prices of African goods fell by about 15 per cent so that the increase in the volume of exports was correspondingly greater than the increase valued at current prices shown in Table 9. The prices of Africa's imports did not alter much over this period so that the barter terms of trade moved against the continent. The adverse movement was marked in the period 1956–61, when export prices fell heavily in face of steady import prices. Since 1961, however, export prices have kept pace with import prices.

Table 9. *Percentage increases in exports* (*current prices*) *1951–66*

			Africa (ex. S. Africa)		
	World	Industrial countries	Total	Total excluding petrol	Rest of world
1951–56	22	34	13	13	3
1956–61	26	34	15	7	11
1961–66	53	57	59	28	40
1951–66	136	181	106	66	60

Source: International Financial Statistics, September 1962 and July 1967.

The most striking characteristic of African export trade is its concentration, both in the range of commodities of which it is composed and in its markets. In 1965 six commodities—petroleum, copper, cotton, coffee, cocoa and groundnuts—accounted for 52 per cent of African exports. If petroleum is excluded, the remaining five commodities formed two fifths of the remaining total. In 1965, 35 per cent of exports went to France and the UK and 34 per cent to the rest of Western Europe. The country composition of imports was not so concentrated, but 32 per cent came from France and UK and another 24 per cent from the rest of Western Europe.

The degree of export concentration is seen to be considerably higher if the African figure is disaggregated into country figures. Table 10 shows the position for the economies studied in this book. This high degree of concentration is undoubtedly a major cause of the fears of economic dependence that are widely experienced in African states.[1] African leaders resent the dependence of their countries on the fortunes of a few primary commodities and their

Table 10. *Concentration of exports*

Country	Year	Percentage due to leading three commodities	Percentage to ex-Metropolitan power
Sudan	1962–65	77: cotton, gum arabic, groundnuts	13
Ghana	1962–65	87: cocoa, timber, gold	30
Nigeria[a]	1962–65	54: cocoa, groundnut products, palm products	39
Algeria	1963	79: petroleum, wine, citrus	75
Cameroon	1963	63: cocoa, coffee, aluminium	55
Central Africa	1963	83: copper, tobacco, tea	40
Liberia	1960	82: iron ore, rubber	40[b]
Ivory Coast	1964	86: coffee, timber, cocoa	36
East Africa	1963	66: coffee, cotton, sisal	41

Note: [a] By 1966 these three products had fallen to 40 per cent, and petroleum had risen to 33 per cent.
[b] To USA.

Source: Contributors and Statistical Abstracts.

claustrophobic ties with the ex-colonial powers. Although the possibilities of economic independence that might be derived from a more diversified trading pattern are certainly greatly exaggerated, the drive to reduce this concentration finds justification in the relatively poor growth prospects of markets for primary products. As the Development Decade falters to its end, the need for the poorer countries to produce a sound international trade programme for which they can fight through the United Nations Conference on Trade and Development (UNCTAD) emerges as the key issue for the immediate future. A reduction in the very high rates of effective protection confronted by their processed primary products with the

[1] See W. A. Lewis, 'Economic Development and World Trade', in E. A. G. Robinson, *Problems of Economic Development*, London, 1965.

markets of the advanced countries should surely be an ingredient of such a programme. For instance, cocoa powder and cocoa butter are subject to an effective duty of over 100 per cent in the EEC whereas the duty on raw cocoa beans is only 5 per cent. The danger is that impatience and resentment will lead African countries to underestimate the benefits that are obtained even with present trading patterns and policies, and may thus lead to policies which will hinder development because they do not properly exploit local participation in the international division of labour.

The high degree of concentration of the exports of African countries has usually been thought to be associated with a high degree of instability in their export proceeds. Fluctuations in export proceeds in turn have been thought to give rise to damaging consequences for the economies. Recently however, the association of export concentration with export instability has been questioned. It has also been suggested that export instability in less developed countries is not significantly greater than in advanced countries. Finally, it has been argued that there is little to show that export instability is damaging to less developed economies since there is little evidence that fluctuations in export earnings are strongly associated with such domestic variables as income and investment.[1]

It is perhaps not surprising that specialization and instability of export proceeds should not be closely correlated since it is not specialization as such that gives rise to instability, so much as specialization on particular commodities which are particularly prone to severe fluctuations. However, in considering those arguments which suggest that, in any case, export instability is not significant, it must be borne in mind that the supporting studies are mostly based on data which relate only to a decade. It is arguable that this is an inadequate period on which to base firm conclusions. Particularly for tree crops (in Africa mainly coffee and cocoa), a longer time scale is required. Furthermore, during the period of the studies the effects of fluctuations will to some extent have been cushioned by automatic and planned changes in domestic disbursements. Finally, not all of the possible adverse effects of export instability will be adequately revealed by the measured magnitudes. A detailed analysis of the effects of fluctuations on resource allocation in particular countries would be needed before definitive answers could be given to the

[1] See A. I. MacBean *Export Instability and Economic Development*, Allen & Unwin, London, 1966 and the references there. The most effective discussion from an African point of view so far is O. Aboyade on 'External Trade, Capital Distortion and Planned Development', in I. G. Stewart and H. W. Ord (eds.), *African Primary Products and International Trade*, Edinburgh, 1965.

impact of instability on development. The chief value of recent discussions of export instability is that they have focused attention on areas in which further research is needed to provide the better evaluation of the domestic implications of export instability which is itself a necessary basis for evaluating the costs and benefits of possible stabilization schemes.

One very noticeable characteristic of external trade of African countries is the very low share which is represented by intra-African trade. In 1961 it was—including an estimate of unrecorded transfers —a mere 7·5 per cent of total African trade,[1] and the proportion has declined since because products like petroleum, iron ore and diamonds account for an increasing share of total African exports, but make hardly any appearance in intra-African trade. The recorded figures do not show the full extent of intra-African trade flows but it is unlikely that adjustments on this account would substantially alter the trend.

Although intra-African trade thus plays a very modest role in the economy of Africa as a whole, it is nevertheless of major significance for several countries. It is particularly important for a number of land-locked countries like Mali, Upper Volta and Niger which depend heavily on exports to neighbouring countries of such products as live animals, and fish, and is also relatively important for a few other countries, such as those of East Africa, where special institutional arrangements have encouraged it. Three prominent features of the structure of intra-African trade may usefully be mentioned. First, a high proportion of this trade has hitherto been accounted for by a small group of countries. Disregarding the trade of South Africa and the Rhodesia, Zambia and Malawi group, which accounts for over 40 per cent of both total exports and imports, about 35 per cent of remaining intra-African imports were absorbed in 1961 by four countries (Algeria, Ghana, Tanganyika and Kenya), and five countries (Kenya, Morocco, Ivory Coast, Mali and UAR) were responsible for 36 per cent of intra-African exports. Secondly the trade exhibits a marked clustering within the north west, north east, west and central areas of the continent. These are areas in which population, production, and transport facilities are highly concentrated, and which are isolated from each other by reason of the poor transport links between them. Thirdly a large share of the trade is represented by foodstuffs. About three fifths of the total value of the trade is in foodstuffs, if South Africa is excluded. If unrecorded trade were included, the share of foodstuffs would be even higher.

[1] See *Proceedings of the United Nations Conference on Trade and Development*, Vol. VII, part 2, pp. 256–78. New York, 1964.

Table 11. *Commodity structure of intra-African trade*, 1960
(excluding trade to and from South Africa)

		%
Food, beverages and tobacco		59
Crude materials		15
Fuels		3
Manufactures		22
Total	(£75 million)	100

Source: Intra-African Trade, ECA 1963.

Any discussion of external trade must include some mention of the terms of trade. There is a multiplicity of published indexes, calculated from different formulae, using different base dates, and often telling different stories. Sometimes the indices used refer to under-developed countries and sometimes to primary products which are not identical categories for most analytical purposes. The barter terms of trade of African countries have undoubtedly declined since the early 1950's—as was to be expected—but they are still better than they were in the 1930's. The last five years has been a period of marking time with both export and import prices fluctuating about a small rise. The rapid decline of export prices of the fifties has been arrested, but the arguments for expecting a relatively weakening market for Africa's traditional exports are powerful; the outlook is not bright. One estimate[1] of the expected prices in 1975 of Africa's main export commodities and of manufactured goods (1960 = 100) is summarized in the following Table. These projections imply a

Coffee, arabica	100	Cotton	93–94
Coffee, robusta	105	Vegetable fibres	93–94
Cocoa	90–91	Petroleum	85–88
Tea	93–94	Copper	94–95
Hides and skins	90–91	Aluminium	94–95
Forest products	115–117	Manufactured goods	100

decline in Africa's overall barter terms of trade of about 5 per cent. Although this may not seem a particularly disastrous fall compared with some previous fluctuations, it is a heavy burden to confront countries desperately seeking resources, and avid for foreign exchange.

[1] B. A. Balassa, *Trade Prospects for Developing Countries*, Homewood, USA, 1964.

The prospective needs for foreign exchange of African countries are dramatized by the trade gap argument. At the UNCTAD conference, estimates made by the United Nations claimed to show that, on the basis of present economic structures and policies, the achievement of an annual compound rate of increase of 5 per cent in the gross domestic products of the developing countries in Africa as a whole would imply a hypothetical current payments gap of 6 th. mn. dollars by 1970, disregarding long term capital and aid flows. If allowance is made for these flows on the basis of experience in the 1960's the gap would still be 3 th. mn. dollars. Obviously too much cannot be made of these estimates. The gap cannot materialise, but the need to maintain external equilibrium will imply a lower rate of growth, or increased foreign aid or increased exploitation of domestic resources for the promotion of capital formation. Aid prospects are not such as to encourage a belief in a dramatic improvement from this source in the next few years. And whatever contribution may be made by import substitution or increased exports, these estimates, if they are anywhere near right, underline the urgency for African countries of a new deal in international trade.

LABOUR AND EMPLOYMENT

The basic issues of economic development and the implications of alternative policies and strategies all find a human focus in problems of labour and employment. The modernization of economies is reflected in, although not necessarily paralleled by, the growth of opportunities for paid employment, particularly in industry. The wages policies employed and the institutions of collective bargaining not only influence the numbers seeking work but also the extent to which employment opportunities will be provided for any given expansion of industrial output. The literacy and skill of the population affects its employability in the modern sector. At the same time, the degree of pressure on resources in the traditional sector and the scope for bringing about significant economic expansion on the basis of that sector affect both the need to provide employment opportunities in the modern sector and the economic significance of the trend of employment opportunities in relation to the growth of population. The factors underlying the widespread demand for wage employment and in particular for improved urban employment opportunities are, of course, not purely economic, but also reflect the quality of urban and rural life and a variety of non-economic aspirations. Nevertheless the relative returns to be obtained from wage employment as opposed to self employment are certainly material although the relationships of the differential to labour flows have not yet been fully explored.[1] For all these reasons, wage employment trends cannot be evaluated in isolation. The opportunities for wage employment, the demand for wage employment, and the need for wage employment opportunities all reflect the effects of basic policy decisions and institutional arrangements upon the allocation of resources between and within the urban and rural sectors. The size and character of the sectors themselves reflect the resource base and will be influenced both by economic and non-economic objectives of economic policies.[2]

The employment situation must be viewed first against the demographic background. As a result of high birthrates the proportion of African populations aged under 15 is about 45 per cent. Comparable figures for the UK, US and USSR are 23, 31 and 37 per cent. The proportion of the aged in Africa is low: about 5 per cent are 60 or over—compared to the UK (17 per cent) and the US (13 per cent). If the 'burden of dependency' is calculated as the ratio of the number of those aged under 15 and of those 60 and over to the rest of the population, the figure is about 1 for African countries compared with 0·7 for the UK, 0·8 for the US and 0·9 for the USSR. These figures inadequately indicate the effective differences in the economic implications of population structure, mainly because African countries are confronted by a need to expand their educational systems in a manner unparalleled elsewhere. The proportions of African populations that qualify as literate range from 10 to 30 per cent. Those having secondary or higher educational qualifications form, of course, a much lower proportion of the population. For instance, even in Kenya where education compares favourably with many other African countries, only 1 per cent of adult males and 0·2 per cent of adult females had completed 9 or more years schooling, according to the 1962 Census.[3] Even if full use is made of literacy-campaigns, for example of the 'each one teach one' kind, the prospective capital and current expenditures involved are daunting in relation to resources available.

[1] But country studies are beginning to accumulate: see, e.g., W. Elkan, *Migrants and Proletarians*, Oxford, 1960, and W. J. Barber, *The Economy of British Central Africa*, Oxford, 1961.

[2] The theories of development in labour surplus economies (W. A. Lewis, 'Economic Development with Unlimited Supplies of Labour', *Manchester School*, 22, 1954, 'Unlimited Labour: further notes', *Manchester School*, 26, 1958; and Ranis and Fei *Development of the Labour Surplus Economy; Theory and Practice*, Irwin, 1964) are often referred to in this context. At the present time, however, only certain aspects of these theories are relevant in most African economies.

[3] These figures exclude the *Northern Province* for which estimates were not available. The inclusion of this Province would certainly have lowered the proportions.

The proportion of the labour force in wage employment is low—a little over 10 per cent (see Table 12). One quarter of such wage employment is in agriculture. Two fifths of non-agricultural employment is in the public sector. Since African wages in the public sector are generally higher than in private enterprise the relative importance of the public sector for total earnings is even higher.

Table 12. *Population, labour force and wage employment circa 1960*

	Pop. (millions)	Labour force: millions	Labour force: % of pop.	Wage employment: millions	Wage employment: % of labour force	Non-agricultural wage employment: millions	Non-agricultural wage employment: % of labour force	Non-agricultural wage employment: % of total wage empl.
Eastern Africa	67·6	24·7	36·5	3·8	15·4	2·5	10·1	65·8
Central Africa	32·8	13·8	42·1	2·1	15·2	1·6	11·6	76·2
West Africa	71·8	32·9	45·8	2·0	6·1	1·7	5·2	85·0
Total tropical Africa	172·2	71·4	41·5	7·9	11·1	5·8	8·1	73·4

Source: K. C. Doctor and H. Gallis, 'Size and Characteristics of Wage Employment in Africa: Some Statistical Estimates', *Inter. Lab. Rev.* 93, February 1966.

Male workers account for nearly all wage employment (usually 90 per cent or more). A comparison of male employment and the male labour force is made for a number of African countries in Table 13. The most striking feature is the wide range in the percentage of the male labour force which is employed—from less than one to nearly fifty per cent: the median figure is in the range 25–30 per cent.

The most disturbing feature of the employment situation in Africa in recent years has been that the absolute level of wage employment has changed so little, despite high capital investment and the rapid growth of the public sector. Comparable figures are difficult to obtain[1] but the changes in some of the better series are given in Table 14. The peak figure of employment in the series on which Table 14 is based occurs in the late fifties for all countries, except Ghana and Gabon.

[1] Where they are collected by an enumeration of employers, different levels of exclusion (employers with 5, 10 or 20 workers) are applied at different times and different places: the lists of employing units are deficient and their relative coverage changes over time: response varies from year to year: domestic servants and employees in African agriculture are incompletely and variously recorded: some series do not distinguish consistently between African and non-African workers.

Table 13. *Male wage employment and male labour force*

Country	Date	Male labour force (thousands)	Male wage employment thousands	Male wage employment Percentage of labour force
Africa				
Algeria	1954	2,417	1,193	49·4
Congo DR	1955–57	3,063	1,079	35·2
Dahomey	1961	497	34	6·8
Gabon	1963	120	39	32·5
Ghana	1960	1,736	499	28·7
Guinea	1955	621	37	6·0
Kenya	1960	2,005	567	28·3
Libya	1954	326	114	35·0
Malagasy	1961	1,264	153	12·1
Malawi	1961	499	131	26·3
Niger	1959–60	690	6	0·9
Nigeria	1962	9,480	854	9·0
Tanzania	1962	2,531	349	13·8
Tunisia	1956	1,027	477	46·4
UAR	1960	7,191	3,497	48·6
Uganda	1960	1,670	210	12·6
Zambia	1961	596	253	42·4

Source: As for Table 12.

One reason for the failure of numbers in employment to grow more rapidly is the dramatic decline, both relative and absolute, in the construction industry which was due mainly to the uncertainties created by the approach of independence and the slackening of economic momentum, associated with the depressed state of several export markets. Only two of the eleven countries for which figures are available show a rise in employment in construction in recent years; in seven of the remaining nine countries employment in this industry in 1962–64 was only 45 to 60 per cent of its 1954–56 level. Construction is particularly important for employment not only because it is

Table 14. *Annual percentage changes in wage employment*

Country	Period	Total	Private	Country	Period	Total
Ghana	1954–64	6·9	0·0	Gabon	1956–63	2·4
Kenya	1954–64	0·7	0·3	Malawi	1954–62	0·2
Tanganyika	1954–63	−2·6	−4·0	Rhodesia	1954–64	1·2
Uganda	1954–64	−0·6	−0·5	Zambia	1954–64	0·0

Sources: Official series taken from various Government and International statistical digests.

labour-intensive, but also because of its backward and forward linkages (e.g. into building materials and transport).

A more permanent factor which has operated to restrain the growth in employment is the rise in real wages. Reliable statistics are not plentiful, but annual rates of change calculated from such figures as are available are given in Table 15 alongside the annual percentage change in numbers taken from the previous table. The negative correlation is marked.

Table 15. *Annual percentage changes in African wage employment and real wages, circa 1954–64*

	Employment	Wages
Tanganyika	−2·6	14·1
Uganda	−0·6	8·2
Zambia	0·0	8·0
Kenya	0·7	3·4
Rhodesia	1·2	3·5
Ghana	6·9	3·0

Note: The real wage series were calculated by deflating a wage series (derived from employment and wage bill figures) by the most appropriate price index available. Wage bill figures are affected by the same sources of error as employment series (see footnote 1 on p. 60) and in addition frequently do not correct sufficiently for the conversion of housing and ration allowances to cash wages. The price indexes used for deflation usually do not include rent; since rent has in many countries risen more than other prices this omission may lead to an over-estimate in the rise of real wages.

Source: As for Table 12, and official wage and price series from Government and International statistical digests.

Events in the sisal industry in Tanzania provide a striking illustration of the changing situation for employment, wages and productivity. Increases from 1959–64 were as follows:

	Unit	1959	1964	Per cent increase
Production	million tons	202·1	222·6	10
Employment	thousands	133·2	83·0	−38
Cutters wage rate	Shs. per kipande	60[a]	175	119[a]
Cultivators wage rate	Shs. per kipande	40[a]	139	132[a]

Note: [a] Excluding rations. Percentage increase assumes value of rations in 1959 was 20 shs.

Source: C. W. Guillebaud, *An Economic Survey of the Sisal Industry in Tanganyika*, 3rd Edition, 1966.

The social desirability of higher wages is indisputable; but if wages rise at the rate experienced in at least some of the countries under discussion, and this is accompanied by an increase in the cost of labour relative to the cost of other factors, opportunities for increased employment in the modern sector, which are not in any event large, may be reduced or eliminated. Some idea of the order of magnitude of potential new employment opportunities in the modern sector is given by the following very approximate procedure. Net capital formation may be put at about 10 to 15 per cent of domestic product. If the existing average aggregate capital output ratio is about 2:1 annual net additions to capital stock will be about 7·5 per cent of total capital stock; if a capital output ratio of 3:1 is used instead, net additions would be about 5 per cent of capital stock. If new capital additions are assumed to be, on average, as labour intensive as existing installations, opportunities for wage employment would also rise at about 5–7·5 per cent a year. However, in recent years, as has been seen, real wages have risen considerably in a number of countries. If as seems likely, this has been accompanied by a rise in the cost of labour relative to other factors, employment could be expected to increase even less. Data on this crucial point are not readily available, but there are certainly indications that new investment has been less labour intensive so that it is not surprising that employment has not expanded substantially. Changes in the structure of output (particularly the decline in construction, already mentioned) have also contributed to this result.

Even if employment opportunities grow more in the future than they have in the recent past, the prospects of providing paid employment for more than a part of the increase in population would not be good. The following calculation indicates the scale of the problem, assuming perhaps optimistically that a 5 per cent increase in employment could be attained. In the initial position, 25 per cent of adult males are assumed to be in wage employment. An annual increase of 2·5 per cent a year in total adult males is assumed, and the changes over a ten year period are calculated. It can be seen that only about

Adult males

Year	Total	In wage employment	Not in wage employment	Percentage in wage employment
1	1,000,000	250,000	750,000	25
10	1,280,000	400,000	880,000	31
Increase	280,000	150,000	130,000	54

half of the increase in the adult male labour force would be able to find wage employment even with this optimistic assumption for the increase in employment opportunities. To express the problem from the other side, the increase in the number of positions would have to be nearly twice as great as is assumed if all the men in the net addition to the labour force were to be found wage employment. Family planning policies cannot affect the likely pressure on employment opportunities in the next twenty years, for the children who will enter the labour market are already born. This prospect naturally redirects attention to the question of the absorptive capacity of the agricultural sector, which is bound up with the problem of increasing its productivity, discussed earlier.

Although the numbers in wage employment have not grown, the numbers of Africans living in towns has increased very rapidly—probably by an average of about 10 per cent a year over the last 10 years. Towns in Northwestern and Western Africa have a long history and were indigenous, whereas towns in Eastern and Central Africa have been, until very recently, justly described as 'alien enclaves', and are still mainly places where the non-indigenous communities reside. Despite the expansion of the urban population the degree of urbanization in Africa is still very low. The percentage of population living in towns of 20,000 or more is less than 10 per cent, except in Northern Africa where it is just above 25 per cent.

The difference in the rates of growth of wage employment and urbanization has not yet shown itself in a comparable rise in urban unemployment. One reason for this is that the recent growth of African urban populations is partly the result of a move towards a more normal population profile; the proportion of adult males is decreasing as more woman and children arrive. Further, there seems to have been an increase in self-employment and, in some cases, in domestic service (which has always been an important but erratically estimated source of employment). Nevertheless, urban unemployment is already causing difficulties in many countries, and may become an extremely serious social and political problem if employment opportunities do not improve.

One expedient has been to return the unemployed to their rural origins but this does not touch the roots of the problem, and can hardly be maintained for any long period without stringent controls. Policies which seek to increase urban employment opportunities are likely on the other hand to add to the already high costs of urbanization, which are often overlooked when the economic balance for industrialization and modernization is struck. In Morocco and the UAR two-thirds of public capital social service expenditure is for housing and urbanization and the proportion ranges between 30 and 50 per cent even in Eastern and Western Africa where the degree of urbanization is lower. Moreover, municipal budgets are often larger than those of individual Government Departments. A high proportion of expenditure for urban purposes has sometimes been in conspicuous consumption or in open or concealed subsidies to projects benefiting limited numbers.

The temporary character of the worker's commitment to his job has presented problems for industrialization and urban policy in Africa. During the fifties when labour turnover was high and ties with the home area were strong, the need for a 'permanent' labour force was much discussed both from the standpoint of productivity improvement and from the standpoint of the character and problems of urban provision. Although village links are still important in most countries, the pressure on employment in the towns resulting from net urban immigration (itself the result of increasing pressure of population in some rural areas and the apparent movement in the terms of trade between rural and urban areas in favour of the latter) appears to have been accompanied by lower labour turnover. This change should contribute to productivity improvement and make the aims of urban policy clearer, but does little to alleviate the heavy public financial burden imposed by urbanization.

In the past the migrant character of much of employed labour has also had a considerable bearing on the organization and strength of Trade Unions, which had, in any case, to compete with the numerous other voluntary associations in towns.[1] Nevertheless, the Trade Unions were able to achieve some economic successes, and in some countries they played a significant role in the struggle for independence. More recently they have often been regarded as competitors for power by the ruling party, and have been 'nationalized', controlled or told to 'discipline themselves'. Indeed the new political leaders seem sometimes to have stifled economic pressures on the wages front more than their colonial predecessors (cf. the contributions of Ghana and the Ivory Coast). An appeal for self denial can of course be justified on national grounds, and it is relevant that a generous proportion of available resources is being channelled into urban areas. Nevertheless, exhortation or the takeover of the Trade Union movement will hardly restrain wage demands or reduce high expectations indefinitely unless both the sacrifices and the uses of the resources committed to urban development are seen to be widely and fairly spread.

[1] K. Little, *West African Urbanization*, Cambridge, 1965.

INDUSTRIALIZATION

In most African countries a substantial increase in industrial output, not merely in absolute terms, but also as a share of total production, is seen as a key factor in bringing about the modernization of the economy. At the present time the direct contribution of industrial production to gross domestic product in Africa is still relatively low at about 10 per cent. Its direct contribution to employment is even smaller and currently only 2 per cent of the labour force find employment in industry. By comparison with other sectors however, the industrial sector has been growing at a relatively rapid rate in most African countries in the past ten years. This growth has frequently depended upon the establishment of a few large scale projects. There are so far few signs of the emergence of a balanced size distribution of industrial enterprises such as characterize more developed areas. The tendency in Africa is for a few giant firms (state or expatriate generated) to flourish amongst a large number of very small firms. Moreover these large enterprises tend to remain enclaves. Their linkages with other branches of the economy, either as markets for inputs or as suppliers of output for further processing, tend to be limited. It would be difficult to argue that much if any of the industrial development which has so far taken place has the propulsive character of 'leading sectors'.[1]

Industrial development may be pursued along a number of paths.[2] In the first place it may take the form of the establishment of industries which process primary products for export. Not surprisingly a substantial part of the 'industrial' operations of less developed countries is of this character and is concerned with the preliminary processing of such products. For example, in the area of agricultural products, cotton is ginned, and coffee is hulled locally. The presence of mineral deposits is accompanied by the establishment of concentrators and refineries, as with copper. But in most countries the processing of primary products does not proceed very far. Raw cotton is exported, rather than yarn or cloth, although most countries producing cotton now have a textile factory in which they make some use of their own cultivated cotton for local consumption. Cocoa beans are exported rather than chocolate, and copper ingots rather than copper wire. A number of countries are endeavouring to promote industrial development by moving into later stages of the

[1] The term is Rostow's. See *The Stages of Economic Growth*, Cambridge, 1960, pp. 52–57.

[2] One of the best discussions of industrialization policy is still W. Arthur Lewis, *Report on Industrialization of the Gold Coast*, Accra, 1953.

processing of primary products—for instance by producing groundnut oil rather than exporting groundnuts—but in many cases such a progression is confronted by large difficulties. These range from the very high rates of effective protection enjoyed by similar processing industries in the consuming countries[1] to the accrued advantages of the consuming countries which spring from experience, and from their developed infrastructures. Countries which enjoy associated status with EEC are in a better position in regard to access to markets there than are non-members.

Although processing of primary products for export is the way in which industrial development got under way in most African countries and still represents an important part of total manufactured output today, an increasing part of industrial output rests on a process of import substitution whereby manufactures formerly imported from abroad are instead produced locally for the domestic market. The most important of these are consumption goods and construction goods where local production enjoys a particular advantage because of the availability of local raw materials and the natural protection afforded by high transport costs of imports. Examples of such industries are soft drinks, beer, cigarettes and cement. A more recent feature is the growth of industries which depend heavily on the importation of crude materials or manufactured components and where the local industry performs only the finishing touches to the product. A notable example is provided by the oil refining industry which is now found in most African coastal states. Similarly flat galvanized sheets are imported and corrugated; aluminium sheets are imported and transformed into domestic hollow-ware; cosmetics are imported in bulk and packaged. In many cases the local value added by such industries represents a relatively small part of the total value of production,[2] although it must not be overlooked that sometimes industries of this sort may produce valuable by-products on which other industries may be built. Other local activities classified as industries derive from the need to service equipment; the railway repair and motor repair industries are conspicuous examples.

These two paths represent the main bases of African industrial development up to the present day. Ultimately industrial development may come to rest increasingly on the development of industries producing for export to the world at large, but at present this possi-

[1] See for instance the figures quoted for cocoa and its products on page 55.

[2] In Kenya in 1963 the average ratio of 'domestic' value added to sales value was 28 per cent for the whole of manufacturing industry. (Kenya Census of Industrial Production, 1963.)

bility is remote for most African countries, although there are possibilities of developing markets for their industrial products in other less developed countries, through preferential trading arrangements of the kind discussed in the following section.

Initially, of course, and possibly for a long time, most protected industries in Africa must be expected to be high cost producers. The reasons for this are numerous and well known. In the first place there is the fact of the limited size of markets in most African countries. A. J. Brown has expressed this in a dramatic statistic. 'The money income of the median African country is probably less than that of an English town of 100,000 inhabitants.'[1] Moreover, the market is unlikely to be homogenous. In consequence the chances of operating at efficient scales of output will in many cases be small.

A second factor which sometimes contributes to high costs is the technology employed. Most industries in less developed countries use machines and techniques developed primarily for use in more advanced countries where, normally, long term relative factor scarcities are different. Intermediate technologies which might be better suited to the less developed countries are rarely widely available.[2] But in any case, it must be borne in mind that skilled industrial labour is one of the scarcest of factors in many less developed countries at the present time, a consideration which is most relevant in considering the possibilities of, and economies from, using intermediate technologies. It is usually reinforced by the fact that the employment of the most modern techniques often depends heavily on expatriate staff, who tend to be paid more than in their home countries.

Moreover, even where local staff are employed, the salaries of expatriate staff tend to set the pattern for the salary and wage structure of industry as a whole and provide a continuing externally determined frame of reference against which local salaries are set. Probably just as important in this respect, having in mind the role of the public sector as the pace setter, is the legacy of the salary structure inherited from the colonial services. Here local salaries and terms of service tended to be fixed also by reference to the relatively high ones enjoyed by expatriate administrators. The continued scarcity of skilled and semi-skilled persons after independence has enabled local persons to continue to exploit the structure they inherited and to maintain a

[1] See A. J. Brown, 'Should African Countries form Economic Unions?', in (ed.) E. F. Jackson, *Economic Development in Africa*, Blackwell, Oxford, 1965, p. 180.

[2] The use of intermediate technology is discussed and advocated by the Intermediate Technology Development Group, of which a leading member is Dr E. F. Schumacher.

differential between their salaries and the wages of unskilled workers which is very much greater than elsewhere.

The economic justification for industrialization in the face of the often considerable direct costs involved rests on arguments which look beyond static assumptions. In the first place, in the conditions which prevail in many African countries there is a presumption that the growth of industry under protection, displacing imports, does not merely divert resources from one productive use to another less productive, as may happen when protection is applied in a highly developed economy. It also draws into employment labour which might otherwise be unproductive, brings in capital and skills from abroad and, in general, stimulates economic activity. In the conditions of Africa today it is unrealistic to suppose that such inflows of capital and skill could otherwise be made available for employment in the public sector, or be used to finance private investment in agricultural development. In addition to this consideration, industrial development may generate external economies and also 'dynamic' benefits which, in the longer run, through their impact on attitudes and skills, may be of decisive importance in the process of growth and modernization.

The widespread demand for industrialization in Africa perhaps rests mainly, however, on the simple observation that the rich and powerful countries of the world are those which have a strong industrial base. Industrialization therefore naturally appears to be the means for obtaining riches and power. Although in general terms this conclusion is a correct one, it is often difficult to clothe the general desire with specific and efficient projects. Debate no longer centres on the utility of industrialization *per se*, but on the more practical questions of how much industrial development; at what pace; of which kinds; with what techniques; and employing what forms of organization—statal, para-statal or private enterprise?

There can be little doubt that many failures have occurred in African countries in giving practical effect to the aspirations for industrialization. Given their lack of experienced indigenous entrepreneurs, the undeveloped infrastructure and market uncertainties, this is hardly surprising. In assessing the performance of African countries, it is salutary to bear in mind that the development of industry in countries now advanced was strewn with projects which failed. Indeed, at some stage in the development of most Western economies a high proportion of new enterprises failed in the first few years of their existence and even today the number of bankruptcies is noticeable. In the African context industrial failures may be more serious because of the fact that available resources are so limited.

But what may be even more serious is that in deciding what industries to establish, the balance between high costs on the one hand, and income gains and external benefits on the other, may be wrongly struck so that industries are made viable by a degree of protection which cannot be justified in terms of their contribution to real income and growth. It is usually possible to make an industry viable by protection but it cannot be assumed that industries profitable for this reason necessarily represent well directed investment. A further difficulty in the African context is that when industries turn out to be unprofitable at the level of protection initially assumed to be appropriate, there is often no way, if they are large scale and state supported, of putting an end to their existence. The frequent failure to undertake a realistic appraisal of required levels of protection and of the indirect benefits from particular forms of industrial development is perhaps one of the greatest deficiencies of recent planning practice in African countries. All too often this failure has been encouraged by salesmen of turnkey projects and by the offer of contractor finance which appears misleadingly to offer a painless means of accelerating industrial development. There are now signs that a greater proportion of the scarce economic advice available in African countries is being devoted to such appraisals rather than to the preparation of plan frames and perspectives, as was common in recent years.

The pace, performance and character of industrial development in African countries still for a variety of reasons, leaves something to be desired. Nevertheless, with regard to their general prospects of industrialization historical experience may justify a measure of optimism. Perhaps it is not out of place to conclude this section with Gerschenkron's measured comment: 'In viewing the historical record one cannot fail to be impressed with the ingenuity, originality, and flexibility with which backward countries tried to solve the specific problems of their industrial development. There is no *a priori* reason to suppose that the underdeveloped countries which today stand on the threshold of their industrial revolutions will show less creative adaptation in compensating for the absence of factors which in more fortunate countries may be said to have "preconditioned" the initial spurts of rapid industrial growth. One can only hope that in drafting the maps of their own industrial progress they will be eager to select those paths along which they will be able to keep down the cost and to increase the yield in terms of human welfare and human happiness.'[1]

[1] A. Gerschenkron, 'Reflections on the Concept of "Prerequisites" of Modern Industrialisation', in *Economic Backwardness in Historical Perspective*, The Belknap Press of Harvard University Press, 1962, page 51.

REGIONAL ECONOMIC CO-OPERATION

A major obstacle to accelerating industrial development in African countries is the small size of their local markets—production for export to the world at large though no doubt ultimately desirable being beyond the immediate horizon. Given the importance attached to industrialization as an instrument of modernization it is not surprising that there should be a widespread interest among African states in economic integration in the shape of customs unions, common markets and other forms of close co-operation. Integration is seen as a means of overcoming the disadvantage of small size—the end of colonial rule has led to the creation of a large number of small states—and of making possible a greater rate of growth and development. Of the countries studied in this book, Cameroon, Kenya, Uganda and Tanzania are involved in common markets. Ivory Coast has some loose links with its fellow members of the Entente and is a member of the revived but as yet hardly effective West African Customs Union. Other countries such as Algeria are interested in co-operation projects presently at a formative stage.

From the standpoint of industrialization, integration affords advantages inasmuch as it makes it possible to bring about a given degree or rate of industrialization at lower cost than if it were attempted by separate states. It does this by enabling the countries making up the wider market to take advantage of the economies of scale and specialization. This in turn may result in further benefits inasmuch as it is likely to result in an additional inflow of capital and skills to the area in question. In these ways integration may raise the growth rates of less developed economies directly and in so far as there are 'dynamic' benefits from industry, indirectly too through its contributions to their structural transformation.

At the same time, the operation of a common market is often accompanied by an uneven distribution of costs and benefits. It is not automatic that all of the partners share equitably in any regional gains—any more of course than do all areas of an integrated nation state. Industry tends to concentrate in the more advanced member to enjoy the benefits of its larger markets and of the external economies produced by the existence of other industries and its more developed infrastructure. The members which fail to attract industries suffer because they buy the products of the partners at a higher price than from the outside world, and they do not have the benefits which the more advanced member gets in the form of higher income and employment in industry, the development and growth of external economies and the contribution which industry may make to the structural transformation of the economy. A further difficulty is that since import duties are not imposed on partner country's imports, this convenient source of revenue is lost and alternative means of raising revenue from the bulk of the population are not easy to find.

The countries whose industrial development lags behind that of their partners may of course enjoy some offsetting benefits. In the first place, if labour is free to take employment anywhere in the common market some of the benefits of the industrial development may be transmitted to the lagging members through increased employment and remittances. In the past in Africa this has been very important. Brazzaville and Gabon received workers from the Central African Republic and Chad. Dakar was an urban magnet for the whole of AOF. Malawi's economy was and is supported by remittances from thousands of its nationals working in Rhodesia. All this is becoming less common however, partly because the costs of relying on temporary migrants are increasingly recognized, but more especially because of the political problems involved.

In the second place, the industrializing country may increase its imports from its partner, which may result in additional production and in a faster rate of growth than would have occurred in the absence of the common market. In Africa such 'spread' or 'spill-over' effects seem to have occurred only to a limited extent, because of the structure of the integrating economies. In any case, given the widespread identification of wealth and power with industrialization, few countries forming part of a regional grouping will be satisfied with merely producing primary products for other countries in the area. Hence, the sharing out of industrial projects amongst the member states becomes the crucial issue.

The functioning, achievements and problems of the two principal existing common markets in Africa provide an insight into the possible achievements of projected economic groupings and of the kinds of institutional arrangements which may be necessary if potential benefits from economic co-operation are to be realized.

One of the oldest African common markets, which goes back 40 or 50 years, is the East African Common Market.[1] Under the colonial regime this area enjoyed not only a common market but also a high degree of economic integration in fields other than trade. It included a common currency, and largely similar fiscal systems, so that it possessed many of the characteristics of a full economic union. Within the common market, and partly stimulated by it, a fair amount of industrialization has taken place, mainly in Kenya. It is mainly

[1] Its operation is discussed more fully in P. Robson, *Economic Integration in Africa*, George Allen and Unwin, London.

because of industrialization that exports among the members of the common market have grown more rapidly than total exports in recent years and now amount to about 20 per cent of the total. In this trade Kenya enjoys a large favourable balance with the other two countries (Table 16). As can be seen from the table, the imbalance is mainly in manufacturing products, the trade in agriculture being approximately in balance.

Table 16. *East Africa: intra-regional trade 1965*
(£m)

	Agricultural products	Manufactures	Total
Kenya			
Exports	5·1	24·3	29·4
Imports	5·4	6·3	11·7
Balance	−0·3	18·0	17·7
Uganda			
Exports	3·5	6·2	9·7
Imports	3·7	13·0	16·7
Balance	−0·2	−6·8	− 7·0
Tanzania			
Exports	3·0	2·9	5·9
Imports	2·6	14·0	16·6
Balance	0·4	−11·2	−10·8

Source: East African Statistical Review, Sept. 1966.

Particularly since independence, there has been increasing dissatisfaction in Tanzania and, to a lesser degree, in Uganda, with the working of the common market. There can be little doubt that Kenya has become industrially more advanced than the other two countries, nor that there are disequalizing forces at work in the East African Common Market, although it is extremely difficult to assess the balance of advantages and disadvantages to each member. It is widely accepted—even in Kenya—that there has in the past been some inequity in the distribution of the benefits of the market. A first attempt to deal with this problem was to introduce a measure of fiscal compensation from Kenya to the other two countries, as recommended by the Raisman Commission in 1961.[1] Dissatisfaction continued, however, and Tanzania seems even to have felt that she would be better off outside the Common Market. In 1964 she looked like putting this to the test.

[1] See East Africa, *Report of the Economic and Fiscal Commission*, HMSO, London 1961, Cmnd 1279.

The Kampala-Mbale Agreement[1] of 1965 represented a further attempt to meet Tanzania's claims (and to some extent those of Uganda) by three chief means. First there was to be a reallocation in her favour of production in some firms making beer, cigarettes and footwear which had plants operating in Kenya and Tanzania. Second there was to be the imposition on an agreed basis of some quantitative restrictions on inter-country trade, with the object of stimulating manufacturing production in the lagging countries. Thirdly there was an agreement that certain industries which it was hoped would be shortly established and which needed the whole of the East African market to be viable, would be allocated in such a way that Tanzania and Uganda would get most. The first aspect was implemented, but apart from this the Agreement was ineffective. No steps were taken to make the industrial allocation of new industries effective—though admittedly this would have been difficult. Partly as a result, Tanzania resorted in 1965 and 1966 to unilateral import restrictions against Kenya.

At this point there was a very real possibility that the impressive and useful structure of East African economic co-operation might collapse. In this situation the Philip Commission was set up in October 1965. The Treaty for East African Co-operation[2] which was signed in Kampala on June 6, 1967 is the outcome.

This treaty establishes an East African Economic Community and, as an integral part of this, an East African Common Market. Thus for the first time the common market will have a legal basis. While the aims of the community are broad, its central concern is to preserve the common market and to ensure an equitable distribution of their benefits, in particular of industrial growth.

The main provisions of the Treaty which came into force in December 1967 may be summarized as follows. The headquarters organizations of many of the common services are to be dispersed from Nairobi where they have hitherto been concentrated, in such a way that each country will have two. Quantitative restrictions on inter-territorial trade are to be abolished with exceptions relating to agricultural products and export crops. Nevertheless a country with a deficit in inter-territorial trade in manufactures is to be permitted to impose temporary transfer taxes of up to 50 per cent of the common external tariff on imports from surplus partners, provided that these are imposed on products of industries which the deficit country intends to establish within a short period of time. No attempt is

[1] The text was reprinted in the *East Africa Journal*, Nairobi, April, 1965.

[2] See *Treaty for East African Co-operation*, Government Printer, Nairobi, for East African Common Services Organization, June 1967.

made to reach agreement on the location of industries of which only one can be set up at any time in the region but a country may not impose transfer taxes on the products of such an industry. Thus the transfer tax should offer no hindrance to the continued establishment of such industries. The existing arrangements for fiscal redistribution will be eliminated after a short period of time. A Development Bank is to be established which is intended to influence the location of industry within the region through the allocation of its funds.

In short, although the treaty provides for some moderate interferences with the common market in relation to small scale industries and these will result in some increases in production costs within the region, the treaty if fully implemented would appear to provide a good basis for the continued exploitation of the gains from regional integration.

On the opposite side of Africa there is the Continent's only other major example of a common market in the shape of the Union Douanière et Économique de l'Afrique Centrale (UDEAC).[1] This grouping began life in 1960 as the Union Douanière Équatoriale (UDE), the economic successor to French Equatorial Africa. The subsequent integration of the Federal Republic of Cameroon with UDE at the beginning of 1966 has created a market region with a population of about 10 mn. and a Gross Domestic Product of £400 mn. in an area as large as Western Europe or India.

In the four country UDE area there also occurred a certain amount of industrial development for the home market. Inter-territorial trade (Table 17), in part reflecting this development, grew more rapidly than total trade in the last few years and currently represents about 9 per cent of total imports. As can be seen from the table, Congo enjoys a substantial favourable balance on inter-territorial trade and

Table 17. *UDE: inter-territorial trade 1964*
(million francs CFA)

	Imports	Exports	Balance
Congo	262	2,674	+2,412
Gabon	395	—	−395
CAR	1,077	316	−761
Chad	2,434	1,178	−1,256
Total	4,168	4,168	—

Source: Commerce Extérieure de l'UDE, Brazzaville 1965.

[1] The working of this common market is more fully discussed in P. Robson, *op. cit.*, Chapter 5.

in this way—like Kenya in the East African Common Market—is able to offset part of its external trade deficit. A further parallel is that Congo accounted for the major part (about 80 per cent) of intra-regional trade in manufactures.

From the inception of UDE there has been a small amount of fiscal redistribution from Gabon and Congo to Chad and CAR, designed in part to compensate the latter for their poverty and for the fact that they provided markets for the Congo. The element of true redistribution as opposed to correction of customs attribution was, however, relatively small. Initially there was no attempt to plan industrial location.

With the passage of time some dissatisfaction with the distribution of benefits has emerged in this market too. Unlike East Africa, however, the rate of growth of Gabon, the fastest growing and in *per capita* terms the wealthiest member, has demonstrably not depended on common market induced growth, for up to the present Gabon has exported nothing to its partners. The rates of growth of the other UDE members have not been too dissimilar until recently, when a newly developed diamond industry gave a boost to CAR.

As in East Africa, dissatisfactions in UDE have centred on the distribution of industry serving the local market. The treaty drawn up in 1964 to incorporate Cameroon into the equatorial common market provides that there must be consultation before a location decision is made for any industry serving the common market and that attempts will be made to influence location with the objective of sharing the benefits more equitably. Little emphasis is placed on fiscal compensation as a means of offsetting inequalities in the operations of the market.

Hitherto, despite some dissension, the Equatorial market seems to have operated more smoothly than its counterpart in East Africa. The main reason for this is probably the fact that, so far, industrial development there has been very limited. Moreover, its character has been such that trade diversion has not been important and all countries have benefited from the revenues yielded by the area's principal common market industries through the systems of taxing these industries.

The experience of both African common markets illustrates the determination of their lagging members to be assured of a share of the industrial development facilitated by the common market as a means of sharing the benefits, and a reluctance to rely on fiscal compensation. Even if this is generous, it is not regarded as adequate compensation for the loss of those 'dynamic' influences on growth which are thought to accompany industrial development. There are clearly dangers in attempting to interfere with industrial location, since industries have first to be attracted—and even if such policies are successful they will tend to hinder the development of an optimal locational pattern and so result in a loss of some of the benefits which a common market should make possible. Nonetheless this is almost certainly a price which will have to be paid to maintain existing integrated markets and to make possible the formation of others. The objective must, then, be to ensure that such policies are carried out in such a way as to minimize the additional costs involved.

There can be little doubt that economic integration can create opportunities for the more effective attainment of the economic objectives of many African states. Of course African leaders realize this and some also find further support for integration in the ideology of Pan-Africanism. In these circumstances, the limited extent to which these considerations have been reflected in widespread and close economic links may appear surprising. In part the explanation lies in the fact already emphasized, that although integration is certainly advantageous to the group as a whole, its benefits are not automatically reaped by each member. This consideration is likely to be especially important where integration involves the grouping of countries at somewhat different stages of development for in this situation market forces may direct the benefits of integration mainly towards the more advanced members to the possible detriment of the more backward members. In such conditions bargaining for arrangements to ensure a share of the new industry made possible by integration or for some redistribution of its gains by fiscal means may be a precondition for participation in any form of economic integration. Yet dependable estimates of the effects of integration are difficult to make and divergent assessments on the nature and distribution of gains may render negotiations protracted and difficult. Moreover, while rational considerations based on a promise of prospective benefits are important, they are unlikely to be reflected in policy decisions unless those who make political decisions in the countries in question identify their personal and group concerns with the interests which integration would promote. Furthermore it is necessary for the prospective benefits to be sufficiently large to overcome the obstacles presented by the uncertainties which major changes in economic policy necessarily entail. The lack of fulfilment of these conditions in many cases suggests that although integration may well be a perennial concern of African states for some time to come, it is unrealistic to suppose that its progress will be either smooth or rapid.

* * *

It is a truism that the post-war period in Africa has been one of rapid change. The most dramatic illustration of this is of course the success of the national independence movements leading to the establishment of new states in the place of the former colonial territories. It is salutary to recall that as recently as 1957 there were only four independent states in Africa; now there are more than 40 and only a handful of colonies remain. It is likely that future historians will regard this transfer of power as the essential feature of the era. Since the focus of this book is to be on economic structure and development, this aspect of African development is not emphasized. Nevertheless any fruitful discussion of economic policy and development issues clearly demands that these be placed in their relevant setting of political and social change. In all of the studies in this book their authors have had this in mind.

The achievement of national independence provides a dramatic moment when a country's peoples are brought together in celebration and when ambitious expression is given to the hopes of what can be done with the independence that has been obtained. The work of the day to day struggle for economic development that follows is not so glamorous. Nevertheless all African countries are devoting a large part of their energies to this task. In pursuing this objective, African countries face serious problems, as the contents of this book show. Much has been done, and there is an accumulation of economic experience and knowledge which will be of considerable value in the future. If the results seem modest when set against the size of the problem, it should not be forgotten that the achievement of structural transformation of economies is something which, in countries which are now developed, took a considerable number of years. But it would be idle to claim that development is merely a matter of time or to pretend that there are not many problems for which effective and practical solutions have yet to be found. The contributors to this book will be sufficiently rewarded if it provides a better understanding of what is being attempted and points the way to areas in which improved knowledge may make the immense task of economic development in Africa less intractable.

2

THE ECONOMY OF GHANA[1]

1. INTRODUCTION

The present structure of Ghana's economy is of a transitional nature, embodying in its various aspects a co-existence of the old and the new, the traditional and the modern. It is, therefore, an appropriate starting point to examine the present productive structure against the background of the past development of the economy.

As it entered the nineteen-sixties, the economy of Ghana still largely displayed the structural framework which emerged at the turn of the century.[2] It was in this earlier period that a gold-mining industry and a prosperous and wholly indigenous cocoa sector developed in the forest belt, generating rapid changes in the traditional economy. This framework persisted for almost half a century, although the economy was far from being stagnant. The evidence suggests an annual *per capita* rate of growth of the Gross Domestic Product in real terms of the order of 1·2 per cent between 1911 and 1955, and 1·4 per cent between 1911 and 1960. In the fifties, the rate of growth surpassed the average of the previous decades, and symptoms of change in the structure of the economy began to appear.

The basic demographic and physical data of Ghana, against which the discussion of structural features of the economy will be set, are given in Table 1. They relate to 1960, the last census year, and are presented by the nine administrative subdivisions of the country.

The overall density of population in Ghana in 1960 was 73

[1] Much of the material presented is derived from a larger study in which the authors were engaged, *A Study of Contemporary Ghana:* Vol. I; *The Economy of Ghana*, Allen & Unwin, London, 1966, and they are grateful to the editors of that book, W. B. Birmingham, I. Neustadt and E. N. Omaboe, for permission to use the material here. They wish also to express their thanks to the Central Bureau of Statistics, Accra and the Ghana Academy of Sciences for assistance in preparing this chapter. The present unit of currency in Ghana is the New Cedi (N₵), which was originally equivalent to ten shillings sterling, and was devalued in July 1967 to seven shillings. All values have been expressed in N₵'s.

[2] For a fuller statement of this thesis see R. Szereszewski, *Structural Changes in the Economy of Ghana, 1891–1911*, London, 1965.

persons per square mile, 28 per square kilometer. This is a rather high density by African standards, equal to about three times the estimated continental average. There are, however, large regional differences in density, with the figure for the capital district of Accra some twenty-five times as high as the figure for the Northern region. These differences are related to the rather clear division of Ghana into the forest-clad area of the southern part of the country and the savanna hinterland. The regions of the forest belt, notably Central, Eastern and Ashanti, support substantially denser populations than

Table 1. *Population, area and density in Ghana, 1960*

Region	Population (thousands)			Area (sq. m.)	Density (persons per sq. m.)
	Males	Females	Total		
Accra Capital District	261	230	492	995	494
Western	328	298	626	9,236	68
Central	366	385	751	3,815	197
Eastern	553	542	1,094	7,698	142
Volta	379	398	777	7,943	98
Ashanti	568	541	1,109	9,417	118
Brong Ahafo	309	278	588	15,273	38
Northern	271	261	532	27,175	20
Upper	364	393	757	10,548	72
Total country	3,400	3,327	6,727	92,100	73

Source: *1962 Statistical Year Book of Ghana*, Accra, Central Bureau of Statistics, 1964, Tables 6, 10.

the savanna areas, which include the Northern and Upper regions and large tracts of Brong Ahafo and Volta.[1] The country's economically valuable natural resources are mostly found within the forest-clad part of the country and as a result the dispersion of economic activity coincides to a large extent with the division of the country between forest and savanna land.

Males outnumber females in the population of Ghana, due to the longstanding flow of immigration from neighbouring territories. In 1960, 827,400 people of foreign origin were living in Ghana, 59 per cent of whom were males.[2] Internal migrations affect the regional

[1] The main exceptions to this pattern are the high density of population of certain areas of the Upper region, particularly Frafra country, and the low density in the virgin forests of the Western region.

[2] *1962 Statistical Yearbook*, Table 19.

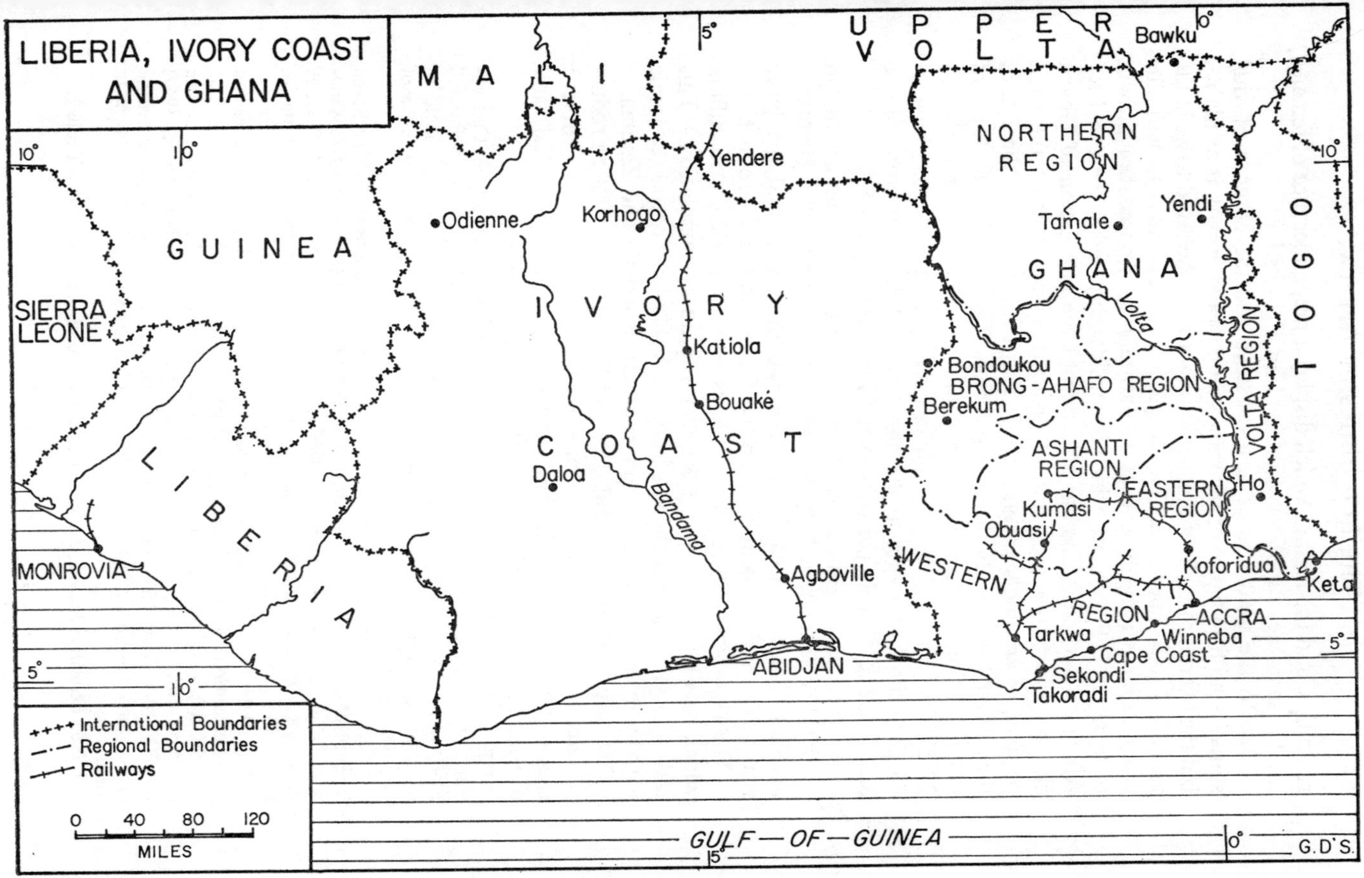
LIBERIA, IVORY COAST AND GHANA
MALI
UPPER VOLTA
GUINEA
SIERRA LEONE
LIBERIA
IVORY COAST
GHANA
TOGO
NORTHERN REGION
BRONG-AHAFO REGION
ASHANTI REGION
EASTERN REGION
WESTERN REGION
VOLTA REGION
Bawku
Yendi
Tamale
Volta
Yendere
Odienne
Korhogo
Katiola
Bouaké
Daloa
Bandama
Agboville
ABIDJAN
Bondoukou
Berekum
Kumasi
Obuasi
Ho
Koforidua
Keta
ACCRA
Winneba
Cape Coast
Sekondi
Takoradi
Tarkwa
MONROVIA
GULF — OF — GUINEA
International Boundaries
Regional Boundaries
Railways
0 40 80 120
MILES
10°
5°
0°
G.D'S.

Map 2.

sex ratios, and the regions which display a preponderance of females are the main net suppliers of internal immigrants.[1]

Due to the weakness of past censuses and the absence of vital statistics no firm figure of the rate of population growth is available, but the overall rate, including net immigration is believed to lie in the range 2·7 to 3·7 per cent.[2] These figures include natural growth plus immigration. Caldwell believes the natural rate of population growth to be about 2·9 per cent, which is considerably higher than that for Africa as a whole.[3] The age structure of the population of Ghana clearly reflects the high rate of growth: 45 per cent of the total population are under the age of 15. This tends to reduce the size of the labour force in the total population. The 1960 labour force of Ghana, defined as people over 15 employed or looking for work, was 2,723,000. Among adults the rate of participation was rather high, at 73 per cent, but owing to the age structure the total labour force amounted to only 40 per cent of the population as a whole.[4]

We turn now to the level and structure of economic activity in Ghana, as summarized by the national accounts. The Ghanaian accounts are estimated from the expenditure side, and the basic magnitude is the expenditure on the Gross Domestic Product.

The 1960 expenditure on the GDP is estimated as N₵ 956 million which was equivalent to US $ 199 per head of population.[5] This indicator gives Ghana the third highest level of *per capita* economic activity in tropical Africa, after Southern Rhodesia and Zambia.

Estimates of the industrial origin of the Gross Domestic Product of Ghana are available only for the seven years 1955–61. Table 2 sets out the data for the two terminal years of the period, and averages for two sub-periods: 1955–57 and 1959–61.

[1] B. Gil and E. N. Omaboe, 'Internal Migration Differentials from Conventional Questionnaire Items—Ghana'. Paper presented to the International Statistical Institute, Ottawa, August 1963. Appendix Table 2. The paper includes an attempt to explain flows of internal migration by differentials in levels of economic activity.

[2] See K. T. de Graft-Johnson, 'Population Growth Estimates and the Seven Year Plan' in *Economic Bulletin of Ghana*, Vol. IX, No. 2 (1965); and J. C. Caldwell in *A Study of Contempory Ghana:* Vol. II; *Some Aspects of Social Structure*, edited by Birmingham, Neustadt and Omaboe, chapters 2 and 4. (We shall call this *Ghana Social Structure* in the following.)

[3] The United Nations *World Economic Survey, 1963*, (Table 2–2) estimates that the population of Africa increased at 2·3 per cent in 1955–60.

[4] For a full explanation of the definitions adopted see *1960 Population Census of Ghana, Advance Report of Volumes III and IV* (Census Office, Accra, 1962) pp. XV–XVI. The difficulties involved in the age-restriction of the potential labour force and in a satisfactory definition of employment should be borne in mind.

[5] *1965 Economic Survey*, Accra, Central Bureau of Statistics, 1966, Table 2.

Table 2. *Gross domestic product by industry of origin at 1960 market prices*

Sector	1955 N₵m.	1955 %	1961 N₵m.	1961 %	1955–57 %	1959–61 %
1. Cocoa	88	12·2	142	14·5	12·9	14·9
2. Agricultural production and distribution (including agricultural exports)	238	32·9	296	30·3	32·5	30·7
3. Forestry and sawmilling	32	4·4	50	5·1	4·8	5·5
4. Mining	32	4·4	40	4·1	4·8	4·4
5. Manufacturing	6	0·8	22	2·3	1·1	2·0
6. Other recorded private industries	116	16·0	158	16·2	16·1	16·2
7. Net rent, personal and other household services	64	8·8	92	9·4	9·1	9·3
8. Government enterprises and public corporations	10	1·4	20	2·0	1·5	1·9
9. General government	36	5·0	52	5·3	5·0	5·1
10. Residual item	102	14·1	104	10·7	12·2	9·9
GDP at constant (1960) market prices	724	100·0	976	100·0	100·0	100·0

Note: Item 6 covers recorded construction, transport and various recorded services. The residual item represents the difference between the total of items 1 to 9 and the expenditure on the GDP. This residual incorporates not only errors and omissions on the previous items but also handicrafts, petty trade (apart from food distribution) and other unrecorded activities.

Source: The Economy of Ghana. Figures slightly revised.

Although the breakdown of Table 2 is not ideal for the purpose of a structural analysis of the economy, a general picture of its sectoral structure does emerge from the table. The largest single element appears to be the complex of activities relating to the production and distribution of agricultural products; this relates almost entirely to local foodstuffs. It is this latter which contains the subsistence element of production. On the basis of household expenditure studies, it is believed that subsistence production of foodstuffs makes up about 40 per cent of total consumption of local foods and 12 to 14 per cent of the total GDP. But one thing must be made clear: there does not exist in Ghana a true subsistence sector in the sense of a large area, or areas, having little or no contact with the market economy. Notwithstanding the importance of subsistence production, there is no part of the country which does not produce for a surplus and market that surplus.

The second sector in order of importance is the omnibus item 6, which covers a variety of recorded private activities in construction, transport and various services. Then follows cocoa, Ghana's principal export. A presentation in terms of *activities* would give a rather different ranking, with services—which are dispersed in Table 2 between items—by far the largest element of activity in the economy of Ghana. An estimate based on an input–output table of the economy for 1960 indicates that 37 per cent of gross value added was contributed by private service activities, with distribution services especially large.[1]

It is tempting to try to identify the traditional and modern elements of the economy from the data of Table 2. This is, however, a rather complicated issue: activities which seem to-day completely integrated in the economic and social fabric, like the cocoa industry, were bearers of the great transformation of half a century ago. A useful distinction for the purpose of a contemporary analysis is rather that between rural and non-rural activities, including food distribution, forestry and sawmilling among the former—this last decision being imposed by the nomenclature of Table 2. We would suggest that *at the present stage of development* non-rural activities are the main vehicles of economic change in Ghana. In 1955 non-rural activities (items 4 to 9) made up 42·4 per cent of the total product of the nine individually identified sectors (i.e. excluding item 10 from the calculation). By 1961 the share of this non-rural part of the economy had risen a little to 44·0 per cent. This was a relatively slight change, but the considerable increase in the weight of manufacturing and Government enterprises and corporations in the Domestic Product is a clear indication of modernization.

The share of non-rural activities increased at the expense of the production and distribution of local foodstuffs. The cocoa industry increased its weight in the Domestic Product, displaying since the mid-fifties a remarkable expansion. This was partly the outcome of new planting in the early part of the decade, but was also attributable to increased yields from older farms in response to improved disease control. The 1955 exports of cocoa beans amounted to 206 thousand tons; in 1961, 405 thousand tons were exported.[2] The fast growth of

[1] *Economy of Ghana.* Chapter 3.

[2] *1962 Statistical Year Book.* Table 122. The 1964–65 crop rose to the new record level of 571,000 tons but this was not maintained in the next two years.

cocoa production was the main factor behind the relative stability of the shares of rural and non-rural activities over the period. It seems unlikely, however, that the rate of growth of the industry will continue over a long period to exceed the rate of growth of the economy as a whole. The government policy of keeping a stable nominal producer price for cocoa when the general level of prices in the economy is rising fast will presumably discourage the continued expansion of the industry.[1] Thus, the increasing momentum of urbanization and industrial development will almost certainly result in more pronounced shifts in the sectoral composition of the GDP.

Three additional features should be mentioned: the regional distribution of economic activity, the weight of foreign transactions in the Gross Domestic Product, and the degree of sectoral interdependence.

The regional problem was alluded to in the discussion of the population figures of the 1960 census. For this same year, an attempt was made to analyse the gross value added which was generated in the economy (GDP at factor prices) in the seven administrative regions into which the country was divided in 1960. The results are presented in Table 3, which shows clearly the degree of concentration of the economic life of Ghana along the coast and in the regions of the forest belt. In the last column the results are given in *per capita* form and it will be observed that the figure for the Northern and Upper region is strikingly smaller than the others. These regional inequalities in value added per head are the consequences of a most

Table 3. *Regional levels of economic activity in Ghana, 1960*

Region	Gross value added N₵ m.	Gross value added %	Gross value added *per capita* (N₵)
Accra	173	20·6	352
Western and Central	187	22·2	136
Eastern	115	13·7	106
Volta	67	8·0	86
Ashanti	150	17·9	136
Brong Ahafo	71	8·5	122
Northern and Upper	78	9·2	60
All regions	841	100·0	126

Source: The Economy of Ghana, Ch. 4.

[1] The justification for a policy of containment of cocoa production would be a marginal export revenue (in terms of foreign exchange) lower than the alternative costs (in terms of export earnings or import substitution) of the absorbed resources. Unfortunately, this vital question has not been studied rigorously so far.

uneven distribution of the country's capital, natural resources and skilled manpower.

The dependence of the economy on foreign transactions is indicated by the shares of exports and imports of goods and non-factor services in the total expenditure on the GDP. In the eleven years 1955–65 the weight of exports in the GDP at current prices ranged between 16 per cent and 30 per cent; that of imports between 21 per cent and 32 per cent.[1] These are remarkably high figures, which stress the degree of dependence of the economy of Ghana on the international economy, and its sensitivity to external movements of prices and incomes. The fact that about two-thirds of Ghana's export earnings are obtained from sales of cocoa complicates the situation, although in this case the price movements are by no means entirely exogenous. Ghana generally supplies more than a third of world cocoa production, and changes in her own output are a most important variable in the behaviour of the international cocoa market.

Next, some words on sectoral inter-dependence. Ghana conforms to the structure of most underdeveloped economies in having a low degree of integration between the sectors of the economy, although not so low as to forbid the construction of meaningful input-output tables.[2] The rural sectors of activity—agriculture, cocoa and forestry—are almost totally independent of locally produced inputs. Significant levels of internal dependence are found in construction, public utilities and electricity, and especially manufacturing. In manufacturing, purchases from other sectors of the economy account for 42 per cent of the value of output at producer prices. On the whole, only 8 per cent of the output of the sectors of the economy consisted of intermediate goods used in the production system. In this respect also Ghana is at present in a transitional stage. The rapid expansion of the industrial sector in the 1960's created a greater amount of inter-dependence in the economy and this change in the productive structure is likely to continue in the future, if at a slower pace.

In order to trace the growth record of Ghana's economy in recent years we utilize official and private estimates of expenditures on the Gross Domestic Product since 1950, in constant (1960) prices, which are set out in Table 4. We wish to emphasize that no high degree of accuracy can be claimed for these figures, especially for the earlier years, and growth rates calculated from them need to be

[1] The weight of exports computed at current prices shows a consistent trend of decline over the period, as a result of declines in the world price of cocoa. At constant (1960) prices this trend is reversed.

[2] *The Economy of Ghana*, Ch. 3.

Table 4. *The gross domestic product of Ghana, 1950–65 at constant (1960) prices*

Year	GDP (N₵ m.)	Index of growth	Year	GDP (N₵ m.)	Index of growth
1950	578	100	1959	890	122
1951	562	97	1960	956	131
1952	582	101	1961	990	136
1953	618	107	1962	1,038	142
1954	630	109	1963	1,074	147
1955	724	100	1964	1,098	151
1956	770	106	1965	1,106	152
1957	790	109			
1958	778	107			

Sources: 1950–54: H. W. Ord (Director of Project Team) *Ghana; Projected Level of Demand, Supply and Imports of Agricultural Products in 1965, 1970, 1975* (US Department of Agriculture, 1965); 1955–58: *Economy of Ghana*; 1959–65 *Economic Survey, 1965*, Table I.

interpreted with caution. Nevertheless, we are satisfied that they give a sufficiently accurate idea of the trend for us to be able to interpret the figures in a meaningful way.

This table requires some words of explanation. The GDP series is broken at two points—1954–55 and 1958–59. In the case of the former we do not have enough information to obtain a 'chained', i.e. continuous, index of growth so we have two index series, one with 1950 as base and one with 1955 as base. In the case of the break between 1958 and 1959 it has been possible to 'chain' the series together and thus to retain continuity in the index series.

Taking the period as a whole, and bearing in mind that we do not know the rate of growth during 1955, the average annual compound rate of growth was 3·7 per cent. Comparing this with the growth of population, which was in the range of 2·7 to 3·7 per cent each year, the resulting growth of the GDP *per capita* was between zero and one per cent. Growth over the period was, however, by no means steady. In two years (1951 and 1958) there was actually a decrease in the GDP and at all times there were strong changes in the yearly growth rates.[1] In spite of this, the nineteen-fifties generally were years of

[1] Take, for example, yearly growth rates (in percentages) since the mid-fifties:

(1955	14·9)	(1959	13·1)	1963	3·5
1956	6·4	1960	7·4	1964	2·2
1957	2·6	1961	3·6	1965	0·8
1958	— 1·5	1962	4·9		

rapid expansion. From 1952 to 1960 the annual average rate of growth in real terms was as high as 5·1 per cent—not withstanding the poor record of 1957 and 1958. By contrast, the nineteen-sixties have witnessed a definite loss of momentum (the average yearly growth rate in 1960–65 was down to 3·0 per cent) and by the mid-sixties the policy-makers were confronted with stagnant, if not declining, *per capita* incomes, severe inflationary pressures and an acute balance of payments disequilibrium. These problems were partly the outcome of the way in which growth was achieved in the earlier years. To elaborate this point we must turn from the aggregate estimates of expenditures on the GDP, to changes in their composition. The composition of expenditures is set out in Table 5, calculated in this case at *current* market prices.

Table 5. *Composition of expenditures on gross domestic product: selected periods*

At current market prices: annual averages of 3-year periods

	1950–52		1954–56		1958–60		1963–65	
	N₵ m.	%	N₵ m.	%	N₵ m.	%	N₵ m.	%
1. Private consumption	360	71	496	73	638	73	1,054	76
2. General Government consumption	28	6	52	8	82	9	168	12
3. Gross Domestic Fixed Capital Formation	64	13	98	14	152	17	236	17
4. Increase in stocks	6	1	4	—	14	2	2	—
5. Export *minus* Imports[a]	46	9	28	4	−12	−1	−73	−5
6. Total Expenditure on GDP	504	100	678	100	876	100	1,386	100

Note: [a] Exports and imports of goods and non-factor services.
Sources: 1950–54: Ord, *op. cit.*; 1955–65: *Economic Surveys.*

Two classes of expenditure on the GDP are distinguishable for their very rapid rise in relation to the total. The fastest-growing was general government consumption which increased in money terms by six-fold and doubled its share in the GDP (from 6 per cent to 12 per cent). The prices of items entering into government consumption went up rather more than prices generally, so that the relative expansion in real terms was not quite so marked; nevertheless even in real terms the expansion was very marked. The second most rapidly expanding item was gross capital formation, which enlarged its share from 13 per cent in 1950–52 to 17 per cent in 1963–65. Gross investment actually claimed 20 per cent of the GDP in 1960 and 1961 but fell again in subsequent years.

In a closed economy the trends just described would have necessitated a decline in the share of personal consumption in the GDP. The experience of Ghana in these years was the opposite: the share of private consumption actually rose from 71 to 76 per cent. It is true that in the 'sixties the apparent rise in this item was largely the result of price inflation in the consumer goods market; in real terms private consumption per head declined in 1960–65. Nevertheless, in the last period of Table 5 the two consumption items together accounted for 88 per cent of the GDP notwithstanding a gross investment ratio approaching one-fifth.

This combination of high consumption and high investment was, of course, only possible at the cost of a deteriorating, and in the last two periods negative, external balance. In the years prior to 1956 Ghana consistently showed a surplus on the current account of the balance of payments, although the surplus tended to decline in size as the decade wore on. The first recorded deficit in 1956 presaged a sequence of deficits that, with the exception of 1958, has continued up to the present. That the deficits could be tolerated was due largely to the excess reserves that had been built up in the surplus years. The country's international reserves at the end of 1955 stood at N₵ 416 million, equivalent to 173 per cent of total imports in that year. By the middle of 1966, however, the reserves were down to N₵25 million, equivalent to 8 per cent of 1965 imports. All excess over current requirements had been used up. A regime of import restrictions and exchange controls was imposed, pushing prices up and slowing down growth. But this was not enough and the Nkrumah government increasingly resorted to the acceptance of suppliers' credits as a way of financing the import surplus. The cost of servicing these debts itself began to add to the strain on the balance of payments and the armed forces deposed Dr Nkrumah in February 1966 at a time when a complete break-down of the country's ability to meet her commitments was imminent. Ghana's inability to meet her obligations was recognized by her major creditors, whose governments agreed to a re-scheduling of medium term loans which, in effect, gave the country a two-year breathing space, until the end of 1968.

A potent factor contributing to the deterioration in the balance of payments after the mid-fifties was a worsening in the commodity terms of trade. The large expansion in cocoa production mentioned earlier was accompanied by (and partly the cause of) a decline in the world cocoa price, so that the 494,000 tons exported in 1965 earned only a trifle more foreign exchange than the 206,000 tons of 1955. But by no means all of the balance of payments troubles could be attributed to the terms of trade. For most of the 'fifties the *volume* of exports was lagging behind the rapidly expanding volume of imports.

The point we wish to stress is that the growth pattern of the nineteen-fifties was too easy, too painless. The simultaneous expansion of the shares in the GDP of private consumption, public consumption and capital formation, made possible by the external inflow of resources, was no doubt extremely welcome after the hardships of the thirties and of the war years, but it could not last. Sooner or later the choice had to be made between having the cake in the form of capital goods, and eating it. With excess reserves gone and foreign capital available only on a limited scale, it was this necessity to choose between consumption and investment that imposed itself in the first half of the 'sixties.

If growth was fairly rapid in the 'fifties, what can be identified as the stimuli of this growth? It was sustained by three main factors: the growth of population, the accumulation of capital, and the combined process of expansion of cocoa-bearing acreage and increased productivity of the cocoa industry—a process equivalent to capital formation though excluded from official computations of investment. The population, and presumably the labour force, grew at a yearly rate of probably over 3·0 per cent. The stock of capital, however, expanded at a much faster rate, sustained by a rate of recorded gross investment which rose from 12 per cent of the GDP in 1950 to over 20 per cent in 1961. The growth of the capital stock of Ghana can be computed from available estimates of the stock, based on the years 1955 and 1961; the estimates are given in two variants, including and excluding the cocoa component.[1] Over the six years the two variants displayed very similar yearly rates of growth: 8·8 and 8·5 per cent. The rate of growth of the GDP over the same years was 5·1 per cent. Thus, in conformity with the standard formulation of the production function under constant returns to scale, output grew at a rate between the rate of growth of the two factors of production; as a result of this process the economy was becoming increasingly capital-intensive, both in terms of the capital-output ratio and the stock of capital per person. Our estimates are that the capital–output ratio of Ghana increased from 2·2 in 1955 (1·7 excluding cocoa from both sides of the ratio) to 2·7 in 1961 (2·2 excluding cocoa) and that by 1965 the ratio excluding cocoa had risen to 2·7. Even the 1955 figures are rather high—certainly high in relation to the typically undercapitalized African economies. This is related to the special com-

[1] *Economy of Ghana*, Ch. 8.

position of the capital stock of Ghana, which is heavily weighted towards cocoa capital and construction. Both these components yield yearly flows of output which are low in relation to their respective investment values. Under-utilization of capital also increased the capital–output ratio. There was a deliberate policy in the 'fifties of creating an infrastructure capable of sustaining levels of economic activity greater than those currently enjoyed. Among other factors making for under-utilization, a shortage of skilled and managerial workers deserves special mention. Table 6 below sets out the estimated stock of capital in 1960, by main components. Table 7 presents the official estimates of the composition of gross fixed capital investment for 1955 and the average of the three years 1963–65; these do not cover capital formation in cocoa.

Table 6. *Estimated capital stock of Ghana, 1960*

Items	N₵ m.	%
General equipment	372	16·0
Vehicles	60	2·6
Construction	1,134	48·7
Cocoa	722	31·0
Other rural capital	34	1·5
Aircraft and ships	8	0·3
Total	2,328	100·0

Note: The stock is estimated for mid-1960 and is net of discard.
Source: *Economy of Ghana.* Ch. 8. Table 8·2.

It will be observed from the record of these tables that over the years a change occurred in the asset-structure of investment, with a proportionate decline in buildings and transport equipment and a particularly rapid growth of investments in equipment. This last reflected the industrialization that had become so prominent a feature of government policies until 1966. An even more drastic change can be observed in the composition of capital formation by purchaser. The share of the Central Government rose rapidly while the relative decline of investment by the private sector was even faster than is implied by the figures for the Central Government. The importance of the public part of 'other public and private purchasers' undoubtedly increased, for a number of private gold mines were taken over by the State Mining Corporation early in 1961 and other public corporations expanded their scale of activities.

The intensification of government investment activities since the mid-fifties was only one facet of the general increase in the importance of government in the economy of Ghana. Between the two periods the share of public consumption mounted from 8 to 12 per cent of the Gross Domestic Product. Along with increasing capitalization, Ghana underwent a process of the socialization of economic activities, on current and capital account—a combined result of increasing welfare commitments, massive development activities and, not least, a conscious desire on the part of the then ruling Convention People's Party to re-shape the institutional structure of the country in a socialist mould.

Table 7. *Gross domestic fixed capital formation, by type of asset and by purchaser, 1955–57: 1963–65*
Yearly averages at current market prices

Type of asset	1955–57		1963–65	
	N₵m.	%	N₵m.	%
Buildings	58	53·7	107	45·3
Other construction and works	22	20·4	58	24·6
Transport equipment	14	13·0	25	10·6
Machinery and other equipment	14	13·0	46	19·5
Total	108	100·0	236	100·0

Purchaser	1955–57		1963–65	
	N₵m.	%	N₵m.	%
Central Government	22	20·4	78	33·1
Other public and private purchasers	86	79·6	158	66·9
Total	108	100·0	236	100·0

Source: Central Bureau of Statistics and 1965 *Economic Survey*.

One further use to which the national accounts may be put is to derive a set of price statistics. Price indices for each of the expenditures items of the Gross Domestic Product are implicit in the ratios between the current and constant-price estimates of the GDP. We confine ourselves to the implicit index of private consumption goods and services. This is presented in graphical form below, re-calculated to a 1950 base.

There were large increases in the cost of living in Ghana in the years immediately after the close of the Second World War and these culminated in the particularly severe inflation of 1950–51, when the index rose by no less than 21 per cent. Apart from a seven-point rise in 1957, the remainder of the decade was marked by a relatively stable price level. One reason for this was the country's ability to increase the volume of imports on a rapid scale as a result of the cocoa boom in the earlier 'fifties and the utilization of excess reserves thereafter, absorbing excess demand for commodities. With the elimination of surplus import capacity at the beginning of the 'sixties, inflationary pressure began to build up, exacerbated by shortages of local food, and consumer-good prices began to rise rapidly again. The index rose by ninety-nine points between 1960 and

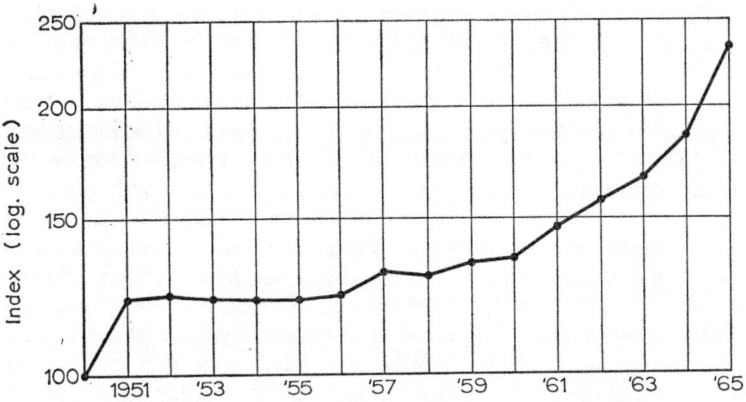

Fig. 1 Index of private consumption prices (1950=100)

1965 and at an accelerating rate during 1964 and 1965. Government fiscal and monetary policies did nothing to provide a disinflationary curb and positively worsened the pressure of demand in the last two years. The only major factor preventing a genuine incomes-prices spiral was a fairly successful but increasingly precarious policy of restraining real wages and real payments to cocoa farmers.[1]

2. DEVELOPMENT PLANNING

Ghana has a claim to be the first developing territory ever to have had a development plan.[2] It was as long ago as 1919 that Governor Guggisberg introduced his Ten Year Development Plan, envisaging a

[1] For a fuller examination of the inflationary pressures in the early nineteen-sixties, see the article by Killick in the *Economic Bulletin of Ghana*, Vol. IX, No. 1, 1965.

[2] For fuller details of the history of planning in Ghana see E. N. Omaboe in *Economy of Ghana*, chapter 18. See also the article by D. K. Greenstreet in *Economic Bulletin of Ghana*, Vol. VIII, No. 1 (1964).

public investment of nearly N₵50 millions, almost entirely on infrastructural projects. It was, moreover, a plan that the Governor intended to be taken seriously. Although a fall in the world price of cocoa (and consequently in governmental revenues) and difficulties in plan implementation enforced a reduction in the scope of the plan, very considerable improvements in the infrastructure of the economy were created in the nineteen-twenties, particularly in the rail and road systems and the Takoradi harbour. Certainly the Guggisberg plan had at least as much impact on the development of the economy as the planning undertaken in later years.

From 1930, the end of the intended period of the Guggisberg plan, there was a long gap before the next attempt at the direction of the economy's development, which came into effect in 1951. Rather misleadingly known as the First Development Plan, this also was intended to cover a ten-year span. It envisaged a total public investment of N₵ 148 millions and once again the main emphasis was on the creation of economic and social overhead capital. Shortly after the launching of the plan, however, the country obtained a measure of self-government and the newly elected Convention People's Party government decided to impart an altogether greater impetus to the country's development by carrying out, in substance, the programme of the ten-year plan in a period of five years. By June 1957 this plan was stated to be 'substantially completed' and the government decided that the following two years—the first after the attainment of complete independence —were to be a period of consolidation. Thus the Second Five Year Development Plan was launched in March, 1959.

This plan, intended to cover the years 1959–64, contained a programme of public investment amounting to no less than N₵ 500 millions plus N₵ 200 millions for the Volta river hydro-electric project. This ambitious investment target was, however, divided into two categories, with a distinction between 'projects for immediate implementation', totalling N₵ 264 millions, and lower-priority projects making up the remaining N₵ 236 millions. Like its predecessors, this too was a plan which placed major emphasis on infrastructural and social investments, with only one-fifth of the planned levels of expenditure being devoted to the productive sectors.

Within two years this plan was abandoned. This was due not to any inability to carry it through but to a fundamental change in the political and economic priorities of the ruling Convention People's Party. An altogether more rigorous and all-embracing style of planning was decided upon, to embody a substantially revised set of policy objectives. The outcome of this new approach was the launching in April 1964 of a Seven Year Development Plan, to cover the financial years 1963–64 to 1969–70.

All the previous plans had been examples of what is nowadays termed 'colonial planning'. They were confined only to those aspects of the economy's development which could be reached by programmes of public investment and were based essentially on an at best imperfectly co-ordinated 'shopping list' of departmental projects. In essence, they were informed by a concept of planning 'which involves little more than longer-period budgeting for the strictly administrative needs of central governments of a liberal-capitalist type'.[1] By contrast, the Seven Year Plan was taken to be a step towards a system of central planning, insofar as that was possible in a mixed economy.[2] In the words of the plan itself,[3] 'The Seven Year Plan represents the first attempt in Ghana to formulate a development plan with a wide concern for the growth of the economy as a whole in contrast to previous planning which has been largely limited to programmes of public works and social development'. For the first time, the plan comprehended investment and production targets for both the public and private sectors, although necessarily intended developments in the private sector were more briefly and generally stated.

The new plan was also built around substantially changed political priorities. In some respects and although it was conceived entirely in the years after the gaining of independence, the Second Five Year Plan showed a clear continuity of policy with the plans of pre-independence days. The Convention People's Party always described itself as a socialist party, but in the earlier years its idea of socialism appeared to have a good deal in common with the social-democratic parties of Western Europe and Scandinavia. Thus Dr Nkrumah described the Second Five Year Plan as having the objective to consolidate political independence and to 'lay the economic foundation to sustain our national independence . . . the implementation and fulfilment of which will give us a solid foundation *to build the welfare state*'.[4]

In many essential features, on the other hand, the Seven Year Plan represented a break with pre-independence policy objectives. By 1964 the 'welfare state' was taking a back seat and the Party had developed a more revolutionary conception of socialism aimed at the compre-

[1] Barbu Niculescu, *Colonial Planning*, Allen and Unwin, London, 1958, p. 180.

[2] See *Draft Programme for Work and Happiness*, Convention People's Party, Accra, 1962, p. 15.

[3] *Seven Year Development Plan*, Government Printer, Accra, 1964, p. 292.

[4] *Second Development Plan, 1959–64*, Government Printer, Accra, 1959, p. i. Our italics.

hensive reorganization of society. The break with the past was emphasized by the opening sentence of the Plan: 'With this first Seven Year Plan Ghana enters upon a period of economic reconstruction and development aimed at creating a socialist society. . . .'

It was therefore inevitable that when an ideologically less committed military Government took control the abandonment of the Seven Year Plan was one of its earliest actions. The two-year period beginning July, 1966 was designated a 'Review Period' and during this time it was intended to 'prepare the ground for a sound economic policy leading to a resumption of a satisfactory rate of growth'.[1] A new development plan was being prepared in this period with the assistance of World Bank and other specialists.

In fact, the formal abandonment of the Seven Year Plan was little more than a recognition of a state of affairs that had existed *de facto* for some time. The inflation and general dislocation of economic activities that were so strongly marked in 1964 and 1965 had quickly rendered the Plan inoperable. It was a document of chiefly historical interest almost from the day it was published. To the economist, however, it remains of value as certainly the most technically ambitious and thoroughgoing attempt to determine the development of the economy. Not least of its virtues was that it sought to view the targets and aspirations for the seven year period in the context of a longer-term strategy of economic development.

In its fundamentals the chosen strategy can be summarized in one word: *industrialization*. Development was seen as necessitating a change from a predominantly agricultural structure of employment and production to one in which non-agricultural activities would be dominant. Starting with simpler manufactured consumption goods, building materials and the local processing before export of primary products, the economy was to progress to basic industries like metals and chemicals and ultimately to the creation of heavy industry and the manufacture of sophisticated products such as electronic equipment.[2] This strategy was subject, however, to a major qualification which was in practice ignored by the Government. It was seen as a pre-condition of even the first phase of industrialization that there must be an increase in agricultural productivity, so that the country could support an enlarged industrial labour force without recourse to large imports of food. Thus (p. 14), 'the most readily available way of raising the national income is by concentrating our efforts in the coming seven years on the modernization of agriculture'.

1 See the March, 1966 budget speech by the Chairman of the National Liberation Council, *Rebuilding the National Economy*, Accra, 1966, p. 5.

2 See *Seven Year Plan*, pp. 32–33.

These, then, were the tasks of the Seven Year Plan—the raising of agricultural productivity, the expansion of the consumer goods fabricating sector and the progressive processing of exported primary products, seen as the first step in a long-run policy of industrialization. To achieve these tasks and to achieve the target growth rate of 5·5 per cent per year an ambitious programme of investment was envisaged, amounting over the seven years to more than N₵ 2,000 millions. About N₵ 950 millions was planned for the Government, N₵ 200 millions as the value of voluntary labour devoted to community development efforts and the remainder was intended as private investment.

By contrast with earlier policies the Seven Year Plan placed a considerably greater emphasis on investment in directly productive activities, as distinct from social overhead capital. This is conveyed by the following comparative figures of the proportions of Government investment to go into agriculture and industry in the three postwar plans.

Table 8. *Share in total Government investment of directly productive investment*
(percentages)

	Agriculture	Industry, construction, mining
First Development Plan	6·5	4·7
Second Five Year Plan[a]	7·9	11·7
Seven Year Plan	14·3	22·9

Note: [a] The figures relate to the respective shares in 'projects for immediate implementation'.

Source: *Second Development Plan*, pp. 1–2.
Seven Year Development Plan, Table 2·2.

In both agriculture and industry the share of Government investment was doubled and this was to be achieved at the expense chiefly of investment in infrastructure and, to a lesser extent, of social services. This latter point is another indication of the shift away from a 'welfare state' concept of socialism, noted earlier.

In retrospect it is clear that the shortcomings of the Plan from the outset reduced the likelihood of its successful completion. While there was much to be said in favour of its overall scheme of development there was lacking a sufficient number of carefully prepared projects, to transform the Plan from a mere statement of aspirations into an operational policy document. To give an example, the planners wished to utilize the great potential of the northern savanna zone to make it the country's granary. But how this was to be done was left vague and in the event no effective action was taken. Or in the sphere of industrialization it is notoriously the case that many new State enterprises were thoroughly misconceived and never subjected to proper economic appraisals. It can validly be objected that this was the fault of politicians rather than planners; it could equally be argued that if the planners had well prepared industrial projects ready on their files it would have been easier to resist the worst excesses of the politicians.

It is true that the political environment at this time was inimical to forward planning. Dr Nkrumah and his colleagues declined to accept the political discipline that serious planning must entail and in consequence the influence of the Seven Year Plan was rarely evident in day-to-day economic policy decisions.[1] Yet this, too, points to a flaw in the planning process. This appeared to be regarded as a task for economic technicians working from a blue-print they had written for themselves. Admittedly the blue-print had been informed by a careful study of a newly formulated statement of party policy, and some attempt was made to draw Ministers into the preparation of the Plan, but these precautions did not meet the need. A development plan cannot fail to be a highly political document and planning must, therefore, be fully integrated into political decision-taking procedures. Lastly, not enough was done to promote the implementation of the Plan. True, various measures were taken to carry it into practice. Financial proposals were supposed to obtain the approval of the Planning Commission before they could reach the Cabinet. Every Government department was supposed to have a high-ranking planning officer to co-ordinate the relevant activities of his department with the rest.

Committees were created responsible, respectively, for the tailoring of the annual Government budgets to the requirements of the plan; for the control of the balance of payments and the availability of foreign exchange; and for the direction of state corporations and enterprises. Actual practices, however, tended to be quite different. The financial procedures were more honoured in the breach, the committees were ineffective, and several departments strongly resisted he supervision which the planners intended to exercise. The Planning Commission itself had neither the power nor the personnel with which to remedy the situation.

The lack of implementation helps to account for the failure of the

[1] A case in point was a decision a few weeks after the launching of the Plan to sign a protocol with an eastern European government for the construction of a N₵ 14 million 'Olympic sport complex'. If this had been carried out it would have been incompatible with the investment programmes of the Plan.

economy to match up to the aspirations of the planners. Against the target growth rate of 5·5 per cent we may set the actual achievements up to 1965. The year-to-year growth rates in 1963 to 1965 inclusive were 3·5, 2·2 and 0·8 per cent respectively, giving a compound rate for the three years of 2·1 per cent. If we exclude from the calculations increases in the volume of cocoa exports, on the grounds that these were offset by corresponding reductions in world prices, the compound growth rate falls even lower to 1·5 per cent. In other words, income per head was declining whereas the Plan was intended to raise it. The trend in the balance of payments and in the public finances was far more adverse than the planners had foreseen, there was little sign of improved agricultural productivity, the expansion of the industrial sector was increasingly hampered by restrictive and poorly administered import controls, and short term attempts to halt inflation necessarily took priority over more slowly maturing development policies.

The authors of the next development plan will be the beneficiaries of past mistakes. They will clearly pay more attention to the task of translating a paper plan into a working design for action by policy makers. They can reasonably hope to be operating in a more rational political climate. But how much difference will this make? What benefits can realistically be expected from development planning in Ghana? To what extent is the economy amenable to planned control?

The amenability of an economy to medium-term planning is a function of the stability of what may be termed its 'key variables'. Which variables are of key importance will differ from one economy to the next. In all cases they would include aggregate investment, government revenues and expenditures, exports and imports, but others may be important in particular instances. To gauge the potentialities of planning it is necessary, therefore, to enquire into the behaviour of these magnitudes. If their movements are moderate and predictable the task of planning will be simplified; if they are liable without warning to fluctuate widely in an uncontrollable manner planning becomes a less meaningful exercise. Planning attempts to will chosen ends and identifies the means by which it is hoped to achieve these ends; but how can realistic targets be set when output is unpredictable and how is it possible to hit the targets with policy weapons impotent to control events? Instability induces a preoccupation with the present while the planner works with a longer time horizon.

When we speak of the stability of the key variables it is useful to distinguish between 'natural' stability and 'contrived' stability. When a variable has no strong tendency to be volatile if left to the free working of economic forces it can be regarded as naturally stable. When a variable is prevented from displaying a natural instability because of deliberate government policies this can be regarded as a contrived stability. The proposition is, therefore, that to assess the amenability of the Ghanaian economy to effective medium-term development planning it is necessary to enquire into the natural behaviour of its key variables and into the ability of the government to impart a contrived stability to otherwise unruly magnitudes.

In Ghana the following can be identified as key variables and we will briefly enquire into their behaviour:

The balance of payments on current account.
The balance of Government revenues and expenditures on current account.
The incomes of cocoa farmers.
Gross investment.

(*a*) *The balance of payments*

The tendency for deficits on current account over the last decade has been described already; it is the unpredictability of the balance which we wish to stress here. This derives largely from fluctuations in export earnings. The country is heavily dependent on the export of a single commodity—cocoa—the world prices of which are subject to large short-term fluctuations. Coppock has calculated instability indices of the unit values of exports of 45 underdeveloped countries which show that in the period 1946–58 only three of the total sample of countries experienced a greater instability than Ghana.[1] The effect of this is partially offset in Ghana by compensating changes in export volumes. Even so, the volatility of the country's total export proceeds is strongly marked and in Coppock's sample of 45 countries Ghana had the tenth-largest index of instability of the total value of exports. It is largely for this reason that the balance of payments itself is markedly unpredictable, as shown in figure 2. Besides portraying the strongly deteriorating trends over the period, this graph demonstrates the very sharp changes that can occur from year to year (consider, for example, 1954–55, 1957–58, 1958–59, 1964–65). The impact of this on the economy overall is all the greater because of the importance of international trade relative to total transactions.

(*b*) *The budgetary balance*

The ability of the Government to use the weapons of fiscal policy to restore stability to the economy, along familiar Keynesian lines, will

[1] J. D. Coppock, *International Economic Instability*, McGraw-Hill, 1962, Table A–2.

be much affected by its success in predicting its revenues and expenditures on current account. As we shall presently describe, taxes on imports and exports are most important sources of government revenue but these are unreliable. As a result budget estimates of current revenues often diverge widely from actual achievements. To give two, admittedly extreme examples, estimated revenues in 1954–55 were N₵ 89 millions and the actual result was receipts as large as

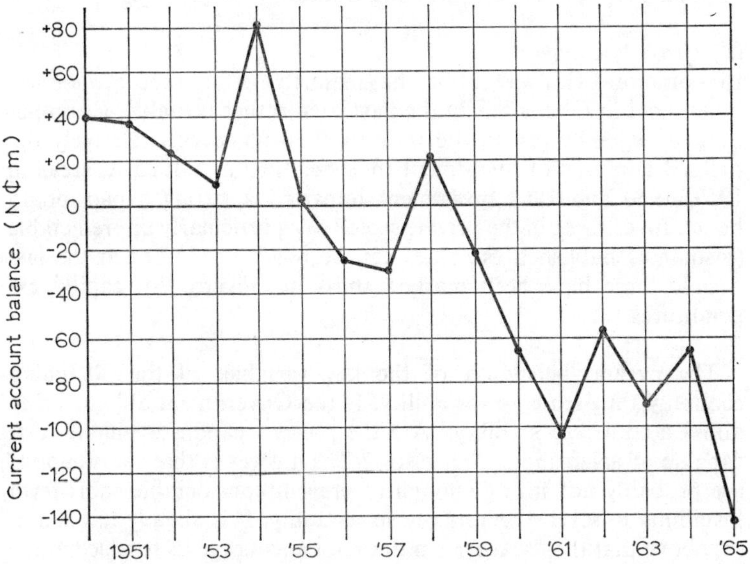

Fig. 2 Changes in Ghana's balance of payments, 1950-65

N₵155 millions and in the following fiscal year estimated and actual revenues were N₵164 millions and N₵ 121 millions respectively.[1] Ability to predict expenditures has been better but far from perfect and the overall result has been to produce budgetary balances on current account bearing little relation to what was originally intended. In the period 1952–53 to 1965 the actually achieved budgetary balance differed from the planned balance by a mean of plus or minus 110 per cent.

(c) *Cocoa farmers' incomes*

The Cocoa Marketing Board endeavours to protect farmers from the sharply varying world price of cocoa by paying a producer price

[1] Fuller details are given in *The Economy of Ghana, op. cit.*, pp. 434–37. See also N. Ahmad, *Economic Bulletin of Ghana*, Vol. X, No. 1, 1966.

which is fixed for the season and is relatively stable between seasons. Unpredictable weather conditions can, however, cause the size of the cocoa crop, and hence total payments to farmers, to vary sharply from one year to the next. There have been a number of years when farmers' incomes changed greatly on their former level and if this did not happen so often in the nineteen-sixties it was only avoided by varying the effective price paid to farmers in a manner contrary to the original purpose of the Marketing Board.

(*d*) *Gross Investment*

In common with probably the majority of market economies, investment in Ghana has in the past been rather unstable. Examination of expenditures on the GDP in 1956–65 reveals relatively depressed amounts of investment in 1958, 1962 and 1965 whereas in 1959, 1960 and 1963 investment imparted a strong expansionary boost. Investment in the private sector was particularly unpredictable (insofar as published estimates can be relied upon) but in the last decade there have been marked shifts in Government capital expenditures.[1]

The natural behaviour of the key variables of the Ghanaian economy thus tends to instability. Is the Government able to bring about a contrived stability? Are the policy weapons available to it capable of achieving such a result? The answer is that the weapons are probably not strong enough to prevent considerable short-term instability in several sectors of the economy. It is already implied in (*b*) above that the fiscal system does not encourage us to place much faith in the use of the budget to maintain a delicate balance in the economy.

There are equally good reasons for doubting the contribution that monetary policy could make to stability. Even in economies with highly developed monetary systems the limitations of monetary policy are today well recognized; for a number of reasons the limitations are much greater in a country like Ghana. It would also be a mistake to pin a great deal of faith on the efficacy of physical controls. There have been import licencing and exchange controls in Ghana since 1961 but the evidence in figure 2 and elsewhere suggests that these have not been altogether successful in preventing unwanted and unpredicted deficits. Similarly, price controls proved quite ineffective in the last inflationary years of the Nkrumah Government. Direct controls certainly have a contribution to make

[1] See Ahmad, *op. cit.*, table 4. This also shows large discrepancies between planned and actual capital expenditures in most years.

but to be effective they need large inputs of administrative skills, reliable and up to date information, a well developed machinery of administration and a strong collective and personal distaste for bribery. None of these conditions is wholly satisfied in present day Ghana.

If the theme of the last paragraphs is accepted it follows that too much should not be expected of development planning for the time being. The failure of past plans to make much impact on events is unsurprising and the transfer of political power from one group to another is by no means a sufficient guarantee that planning will be more successful in future. It may be noted in this connection that the results of a study by the UN Economic Commission for Africa showed generally that planning in the various states of West Africa, with their disparate political systems, had not produced many concrete results.[1]

It also follows from our argument that planners in Ghana should place a premium on flexibility, so that programmes can be readily adjusted to unexpected changes in circumstances. So-called 'rolling plans' have this virtue of flexibility and might, therefore, be appropriate. Present indications are that those now preparing Ghana's new plan are well aware of the shortcomings of overly-rigid plans in the Ghanaian context and are thinking in terms of briefer planning periods than were adopted in the past.

3. FINANCING THE PUBLIC SECTOR

We have referred already to the tendency for Government tax revenues to lag behind Government expenditures. Until the late nineteen-fifties current Government revenues generally exceeded total Government expenditure (current and capital) by a comfortable margin—by no means a necessarily good thing—but since the later fifties the reverse has held true. Surpluses on current account have declined relatively and at the same time capital expenditures have risen. These trends are shown in Table 9, from which it can be seen that Government saving on current account in the early 'sixties was sufficient to finance only a rather small proportion of capital expenditures.

The tax structure has proved unable to tap on an adequate scale incremental additions to income, so that in a period when both Government consumption and development expenditures were increasing faster than the economy as a whole, the proportion of total income going to taxes was rather static. One result of these develop-

[1] UNECA *Economic Survey of Africa*, UN, 1966, p. 167–8.

Table 9. *Current saving and capital expenditure by Government*

Financial year	Revenue on current A/c N₵ m.	Expenditure on current A/c N₵ m.	Current saving N₵ m.	Expenditure on capital A/c N₵ m.	Saving as % of capital expenditure
1957–58	120·0	78·4	41·6	46·6	89·3
1958–59	133·6	91·2	42·4	55·4	76·5
1959–60	129·0	100·6	28·4	87·4	32·5
1960–61	143·8	134·0	9·8	63·0	15·6
1961–62[a]	215·2	202·0	13·2	103·8	12·7
1962–63	180·8	175·6	5·2	118·8	4·4
1963–64[a]	218·2	199·0	19·2	167·6	11·5
1965	282·4	219·8	62·6	174·4	35·9

Note: [a] Fifteen months.
The figures for 1961–62 to 1963–64 have been adjusted to take account of certain tax arrears on the part of the Cocoa Marketing Board.
Source: Economic Surveys.

ments was a tremendous increase in the size of the public debt. Not least of the authorities' problems was to keep track of the growth in government obligations. The following figures are only regarded as provisional, it being thought likely that yet further obligations will come to light. Even so, the estimate of the external debt at the end of 1963, for example, is over double the original figure given in the *Economic Survey* for that year!

Table 10. *Size and composition of public debt, 1959–1963*
(N₵ m.)

Year end	External debt	Internal debt	Total public debt
1959	12	33	45
1960	34	77	111
1961	77	88	165
1962	145	161	307
1963	155	266	422
1964	370	324	693
1965	481	410	891
1966	651	447	1,098

Sources: Bank of Ghana Annual Report, 1965–66, Table 12; *Economic Survey*, 1965, Table 8.

By comparison with high-income countries, a public debt equivalent to about one-half of the GDP is not large; but, firstly, servicing the external debt became increasingly impossible, with the result we have already described, and, secondly, only in a limited way was the government able to expand its internal debt by attracting genuine savings from the community. Much of the expansion of the internal debt took the form of borrowings from the monetary system. Thus, in its transactions with the banking system the government moved from a net credit position of N₵4 millions at the end of 1960 to a net debit position of N₵208 millions by June 1966, including an indebtedness to the central bank (The Bank of Ghana) of N₵133 millions. The effect of this was to cause a very marked monetary expansion which aggravated the inflationary forces already present in the economy.

We have so far been writing in very aggregative terms about the public finances. A more detailed analysis of Government receipts and expenditures in 1965 is set out in Table 11 below.[1] On the revenue side of the table we have counted the cocoa duty as a tax on the incomes of the cocoa farmers, for the incidence of this tax is almost entirely on them. Similarly, the minerals duty is in effect a profits tax and hence is shown as a tax on incomes. Even after these adjustments have been made, the statistics indicate the reliance of the Government upon indirect taxes. Taxes on incomes comprised in this year some 28 per cent of total revenues; indirect taxes were 61 per cent of the total. This dependence on indirect taxes perhaps helps to explain the incapability of the tax system to take off an adequate proportion of increases in income. This dependence has moreover tended to increase. Taxes on income, as defined above, made up 50 per cent of total revenue in 1958–59, for example, and indirect taxes only 30 per cent. This trend is compounded of three major influences. Revenues from the cocoa duty have fallen, relatively and absolutely, under the influence of falling world prices of cocoa in the period. This has, however, been partly offset by an increase in receipts from the income tax proper, which went up from N₵12 millions to a record N₵54 millions during these years. Receipts from import duties have been the main element of expansion in the indirect taxes group, more than trebling between 1958–59 and 1965.

On the side of expenditures, perhaps the most notable feature is the very large amount spent on education—a quarter of the total. Expenditure on general administration and defence between them absorb nearly another quarter of the total. Viewing expenditures over time the main features of note have been a decline in the share devoted to economic services (from 33 per cent in 1958–59 to 17 per cent in 1965) and an increase in the share of expenditure on social services, chiefly education (24 to 38 per cent).

[1] For a survey of fiscal trends in Ghana see the article by Ahmad already cited.

Table 11. *Central Government current account 1965*
(N₵ m.)

Revenue		Expenditure	
1. *Interest, profits and rents*	4·5	1. *Economic services*	
		(*a*) Agriculture and non-mineral resources	20·4
2. *Taxes on incomes*		(*b*) Fuel and power	5·3
(*a*) Income tax	54·3	(*c*) Other mineral resources, manufacturing and construction	3·8
(*b*) Minerals duty	2·0	(*d*) Transport, storage and communication	7·0
(*c*) Cocoa duty	19·8		
(*d*) Other export duties	0·8		
(*e*) Other, including property tax and fines	1·2		
3. *Taxes on production and expenditure:*		2. *Community services*	
(*a*) Import duties	107·5	(*a*) Roads and waterways	6·8
(*b*) Excise duties	21·4	(*b*) Fire protection, water supply and sanitation	4·0
(*c*) Purchase and sales taxes	34·2	(*c*) Other	5·0
(*d*) Other, including royalties and licences	8·7		
4. *Other revenues*		3. *Social services*	
(*a*) Sale of goods and services	24·6	(*a*) Education	56·6
(*b*) All other	3·5	(*b*) Health	18·1
		(*c*) Other	9·6
		4. *General services*	
		(*a*) General administration	32·1
		(*b*) Defence	20·7
		(*c*) Justice and Police	11·6
		5. *Other expenditure*	18·8
Total revenue	282·6	Total expenditure	219·8
		Surplus on current account	62·8

Source: 1965 *Economic Survey*, Tables IV and VIII, and Ahmad *op. cit.*, Table 5.

4. THE AGRICULTURAL SECTOR

Ghana's economy remains a basically agricultural one, as reflected in the industrial origin of the domestic product, in the structure of employment and in the composition of exports. Table 2 shows that cocoa, timber, sawmilling and other agriculture (including the distribution of foodstuffs) accounted for 52 per cent of the GDP in 1959–61. At the time of the 1960 Census of Population the numbers engaged in agriculture, forestry and fishing amounted to 62 per cent of total employment (see Table 12, p. 116). Exports of cocoa and timber alone made up 77 per cent of the country's exports in 1962–65 (see Table 13, p. 120).

The natural vegetation of Ghana, as already intimated, is of two types[1]—forest and savanna—and the distribution of these is strongly influenced by the annual density of rainfall. The luxuriant forest vegetation is sustained by the rich top soil which itself is maintained by the process of decay of plants and leaves. This environment provides the specific ecological conditions required by the cocoa tree. Savanna vegetation, on the other hand, covering the more arid hinterland of Ghana, is typically poor and sparse. It is worth noting, though, that the chemical content of the soil below the top layer is similar in both zones and does not provide any great inherent fertility. The main difference is the combined effect of rainfall, heat and vegetation on the nutrient quality of the top soil. This is a point which is worth stressing: the apparently robust fertility of the forest zone in fact depends upon a very delicate natural balance and attempts to utilize the forest lands for intensive cultivation can only fail if they do not take cognisance of the effects of altering this balance.

The main agricultural products of the forest zone, in addition to cocoa, are cassava, cocoyams and plantains. This is also the home of the timber industry. In the savanna areas yam, maize, guinea corn and millet are cultivated and the rearing of cattle is an important activity.

Except in one or two parts of the country, land has in the past been available in abundance, although it easily becomes exhausted if farmed too intensively. The traditional Ghanaian system of farming, based on the combination of relatively large inputs of land with human labour, is an expression of existing scarcity relationships. Traditionally, the agricultural sector has employed only two factors of production, with almost no application of capital and with the extensive use of land, on the basis of short periods of cultivation followed by lengthy periods of fallow. By demanding only minimal use of fertilizers and other methods of soil improvement, the need for external inputs and capital was very slight. Cocoa farming, which

[1] The vegetation of the narrow coastal strip that runs along three-quarters of Ghana's coast-line is of neither of these types but is of limited economic importance.

developed in this framework, resulted in a large accumulation of capital out of labour and resulted in a much more intensive use of the land. But purchased capital—tools, machines and appliances—did not penetrate Ghanaian agriculture on any large scale and the extensive utilization of land is still evident in all non-perennial crops. Apart from the cocoa areas and limited areas of more intensive cultivation in the 'compound farming' parts of the north-east and north-west, and along the coast, Ghanaian agriculture is based on a system which is best described as 'land rotation'; although it is often loosely referred to as 'shifting cultivation'.[1] Land rotation is a pattern of land use, 'whereby cultivation is carried on for a few years and then the land allowed to rest, perhaps for a considerable period, before the scrub or grass which grows up is again cleared and the land re-cultivated. In such areas, however, the farms or settlements from which cultivation takes place are fixed and the cultivation of the land is the dominant occupation. The secondary growth which is allowed to appear has little or no economic importance.'[2]

This description implies that agriculture in Ghana is overwhelmingly in the hands of small and medium peasant farmers, both for cocoa and foodstuff farming. A number of much larger and semi-mechanized farms were created by the Nkrumah Government but the new administration has reduced the number of these and the remainder are not important in relation to the total agricultural output of the country. Foreign-owned plantations are even more of a rarity.

That land-rotation farming in Ghana makes little use of purchased capital is made abundantly clear from the results of the first phase of the Agricultural Census in 1963—the first of its kind in Ghana. Of a total sample area of 6,225 acres of peasant farms, the Census found that 22 acres were cultivated with the aid of mechanical power, 9 acres with the use of animal power, and 6,194 acres by the use of man power only. The hoe and the 'cutlass' were used over the whole sample area, the axe over two-thirds of it, the plough on only 43 acres. From the estimates of the country's capital stock in 1960 presented on page 91 above rural capital other than the estimated value of the stock of cocoa trees amounted to only 1·5 per cent of the total.

In considering trends in production and productivity, the discussion will be confined to cocoa and foodstuffs.

The output of cocoa remained fairly stable, at around 230,000 tons from the second half of the nineteen-twenties until the end of the

[1] On this see J. B. Wills in Wills (ed.) *Agriculture and Land Use in Ghana*, Oxford, 1962, Chapter 15.

[2] International Geographical Union, 1952 cited by Wills, *op. cit.*, p. 201.

nineteen-fifties. Then within a span of two years production increased sharply to crops above the 400,000 ton size and have remained at this higher level ever since. Indeed, the 1964–65 crop was as large as 571,000 tons but this was not sustained in later years. Export earnings from this product changed only slightly, for the increase in output, which was paralleled in other West African countries, had a depressing effect on the world price of cocoa.

This upward spurt in production was the joint outcome of increases both in the acreage under bearing cocoa and in yields. The increase in the acreage under bearing cocoa was the result of new plantings that had been induced by the high producer prices paid by the Cocoa Marketing Board in the first half of the nineteen-fifties. Since cocoa trees in Ghana have in the past taken seven to ten years to come into bearing,[1] the increase in planting in the earlier 'fifties was not reflected in output until the beginning of the 'sixties. But in addition to this factor there was at the same time a large increase in yields, the result of disease control measures. Tentative estimates suggest that the average yield of mature cocoa in the 'fifties was 200 to 250 lb. per acre and that this went up to around 330 lb. per acre in the early 'sixties.[2]

The output of cocoa is easy to determine because it is entirely an export crop. No such convenience exists for local foodstuff production and hence no series of production figures exists. The national accounts data do not help, for they are based on the assumption of a constant physical consumption of local food per head and not on recurrent estimates of production. There is some evidence, mainly from nutritional studies, that the calorific intake *per capita* does not seem to be changing over time. It has been argued that it was not sustained in the first half of the 'sixties,[3] but the decline suggested is not large and, taking one period with another, the most likely case is that *per capita* consumption has been constant. (Changes in the quantity and composition of imported foods are not significant for the aggregate picture.)

The information about prices is more adequate. The recent price history of locally produced foods falls into three distinct periods. Between 1948 and 1956 food prices rose rapidly and much faster than the prices of other consumption goods and services. Between these years local food-prices in Accra rose by 117 per cent, as against a 30

[1] This period is tending to shorten now, with the introduction of early-bearing Amazonian and hybrid seedlings.

[2] See *Economy of Ghana*. Chapter 10.

[3] F. Stoces: 'Agricultural Production in Ghana, 1955–65', ***Economic Bulletin** of Ghana*, x(3), 1966.

per cent increase in the prices of other items of consumer expenditures. From 1957 to 1960 there was price stability. Finally, from 1961 and through into 1965 food prices rose again, and again rose more rapidly than other prices. Utilizing the data of the new 'national' consumer price index, which has March 1963 as its base, local food prices stood 125 per cent higher by June 1966, compared with a 45 per cent increase in the remainder of the items included in the index. No other category of consumer goods and services had risen in price as much as local foods, in spite of severe import restrictions and the levying of a 110 per cent sales tax on non-food items.

Overall, then, the tendency has been for food prices to rise, both absolutely and in relation to other consumer goods. In other words, the 'barter terms of trade' of food farmers in Ghana show a secular improvement.

The implications of constant *per capita* consumption and rising 'real' prices may be set out, admittedly in a tentative fashion, in the following way.

Aggregate *demand* for local foods is a function of three variables: population growth, real *per capita* incomes, and the level of local food prices relative to other prices. For reasons to be mentioned shortly, population growth has the most important influence. Since we have already shown that the population has been growing, the aggregate demand for food has also increased substantially and continuously.

Supply, on the other hand, tends to lag. Its major determinants are the methods of cultivation, changes in the rural population, and the returns to labour as set by the barter terms of trade of the food farmers. Techniques of cultivation may be taken as practically unchanging. In the rural economy, as in the rest of the country, population is increasing but there is a constant drift to the towns. Stoces has estimated that while total population grew by 14·2 per cent in 1960–65 the agricultural labour force went up by only 1·4 per cent.[1]

If the prices ruling at a given time remained unchanged there would on the one hand be an aggregate demand rising in response to population growth and increasing *per capita* incomes, and on the other hand a total supply that was stagnant or even declining as the rural labour force fell relative to the total labour supply. Inevitably food prices must rise in these circumstances. If the increase is sufficient to cause local food prices to increase more than prices of other consumer

[1] F. Stoces, *ibid.* His estimates make allowance for the reduction in labour resulting from higher school attendance in rural areas. His assumed rate of population increase is probably too low at 2·7 per cent, but this does not affect the above proportions.

goods and services, the consequences will be (*a*) substitution effects tending to reduce demand for foodstuffs or slow down its growth, and (*b*) higher real returns to rural labour, via improvements in the farmers' terms of trade.

Both these consequences have in fact occurred. The barter terms of trade of the food farmers have improved but despite this the agricultural labour force has declined relatively. The substitution effect is also apparent since *per capita* food consumption has remained constant in the face of rising incomes. The relative rise in food prices has elicited a substitution of labour for leisure in the rural economy yielding an increase of food supply just sufficient to keep pace with population growth: or, to look at the situation from the other side, the rise in food prices has limited the growth of demand to the speed with which population is increasing. The rise of prices has been very substantial, but has only maintained the *status quo*. The implication is that, if other changes such as increased food imports are ruled out, the price rise necessary to induce an increase in food production sufficient to raise *per capita* consumption will have to be even greater. This would obviously have serious repercussions on the industrial wage rate, the pace of industrialization and, indeed, of development as a whole.

In the formulation of agricultural policy a basic question which has to be asked is whether it is possible to achieve the desired results on the basis of the present land rotation system operated by a multitude of mainly small-scale peasant farmers? In Ghana a very strong case can be made out for the argument that the system of land rotation will only remain a viable one in future if it is modified in certain respects. The era of a general abundance of land in relation to the population it must support is probably coming to an end in several regions of Ghana. The experts appear to agree that the amount of virgin forest land remaining (outside the forest reserves) is now relatively limited and is being progressively absorbed into the agricultural sector. In the compound farming areas, in the southern fringes of the savanna, and in parts of the forest zone the fallow period is already too short to maintain the fertility of the soil, although there are admittedly large regions in the interior savanna which are virtually unpopulated.

Pressure to secure larger yields from the areas cultivated will tend to disrupt the traditional system of land rotation by shortening the fallow period, leading to declining yields. In this way, a new element of scarcity, in addition to the stagnant methods of cultivation, will gradually make itself felt, intensifying the bottleneck character of foodstuff production.

The system, therefore, will increasingly need modification. More specifically, it will need to be operated in conjunction with larger inputs of capital, in the form of improved seeds and stock, fertilizers, land drainage and irrigation schemes, improved storage facilities, agricultural equipment and also in the 'human capital' embodied in trained agriculturalists. The network of feeder roads, the fleet of transport lorries and the capacity of urban markets also stand in need of improvement and action in this sphere is an essential ingredient of any serious attempt to increase the supply of foods to the markets.

Will the Ghanaian peasant farmer be sufficiently adaptable to be able and willing to cope with such modifications? The answer of the Seven Year Plan seemed to be a qualified No, at least for foodstuff production. For while the country's agriculture would still have remained at the end of the plan period a predominantly peasant agriculture, the public sector (the State Farms and other large-scale farming units) was intended to grow much faster than the private (i.e. peasant) sector as can be seen from the following figures of planned increases in output over the seven years.[1]

	Private sector	Public sector
Cereals	+ 38%	+447%
Roots and plantain	+ 10%	+285%
Legumes and oils	+101%	+880%
Vegetables	+117%	+180%

5. THE INDUSTRIAL SECTOR

The industrial sector, by which we mean construction and manufacturing, is of secondary importance in the present economic structure. Table 2 does not bring this out very clearly, since neither manufacturing nor construction are entirely isolated. A better indication is given by an analysis of the sectoral composition of 'gross value added' in 1960,[2] which shows manufacturing to have contributed 6·3 per cent and construction to have contributed 15·7 per cent of total gross value added in the economy. For all their limited size, however, manufacturing and construction have been major growth-points in the post-war period. From the *Industrial Statistics* published by the Central Bureau of Statistics for 1958 and 1959, it can be seen that of the establishments recorded, about 80 per cent in both manufacturing

[1] Figures calculated from the *Seven Year Development Plan*, Table 4·4.

[2] See *Economy of Ghana*. Chapter 3. The total gross value added in 1960 was calculated at N₵842 millions as compared with GDP of N₵938 millions.

and construction had commenced operations since 1940 and well over half since 1950.[1]

One of the outstanding characteristics of the industrial sector in Ghana is that it comprehends very many different types of activity—from the one-man concern undertaking traditional tasks with the aid of only the simplest equipment, to the large factory or building firm producing goods or buildings of advanced design by capital-intensive methods. This technological dualism is, in fact, one of the most prominent features of the whole economy. It is to be found in mining, where large modern mines co-exist with individual African diamond diggers whose basic piece of equipment is the calabash. It is to be found in the distributive system, with multi-storey department stores within a few yards of street sellers carrying their entire stocks on their heads. It is even to be found, to a limited extent, in agriculture, with the peasant farms on the one hand and the large mechanized State Farms on the other. The Industrial Census held in 1962 revealed some aspects of this diversity. 95,167 manufacturing establishments were counted; about 92 per cent were based on self-employment and family labour only.[2] Of the 6,914 construction establishments, three-fifths had no paid employees.

In spite of the rapid expansion of publicly owned industry in the last years of Dr Nkrumah's Government, manufacturing is still dominated by private endeavour. In the first half of 1966, for example, value added in wholly state owned establishments was only 13 per cent of the national total.[3] No comparable statistics are available for construction but the evidence suggests that the relative importance of public enterprise was rather similar. The two main industry groups of Ghanaian manufacturing are 'beverages and tobacco' and saw-milling. Between them these contributed 59 per cent of value added in manufacturing in 1964.[4]

As we have shown, industrialization was seen by the authors of the Seven Year Plan as the basis for the long term development of Ghana's economy. Industrialization has, in fact, been a consistent element in official policy since the election of the first representative Government in 1951 and there were even some moves in that direction by the earlier colonial administrations. One was the creation in

[1] *Industrial Statistics, 1958 and 1959*, Statistical Reports Series VII, No. 1, February 1962, Central Bureau of Statistics, Accra, Table 64.

[2] It should be pointed out that the Census included many traditional crafts in its definition of manufacturing, therefore presenting a rather inflated picture of industrial activities: see *1962 Industrial Census Reports:* Vol. I—*Industry*, Accra 1965.

[3] Central Bureau of Statistics *News Letter No. 47/66*, Table 6.

[4] *Industrial Statistics, 1962–64*, Accra, 1965, Table 12.

1947 of an Industrial Development Corporation (IDC), having the responsibility of 'securing the investigation, formulation and carrying out of projects for developing industries in the Gold Coast'.[1] For the first few years of its life the IDC operated mainly as a loans agency, lending funds for a variety of privately conceived projects. In 1953 it was decided that the corporation should take a more active part in the encouragement of industry, by the creation of subsidiary companies owned and controlled by the IDC and 'associate' companies operated jointly with private firms. At the time of its dissolution in 1962 the corporation had 22 subsidiary and 9 associate companies. It died—or rather was killed—with a not wholly justified reputation as a failure. Some of the enterprises it created have become successful, well established concerns but some, admittedly, have gone into dissolution or linger on only by the grace of public subsidies.[2]

The disbanding of the IDC in no sense represented an abandonment of attempts to promote government-owned industrial enterprises. On the contrary it is now generally accepted that in the last three or four years of its life the Nkrumah government imposed intolerable strains on the economy by its accelerated and badly planned programme of industrialization. Import restrictions—imposed to permit the creation of yet more factories—badly disrupted industrial production. Indeed, it was estimated at the end of 1966 that modern industrial output was a mere fifth of the single-shift capacity of installed plant!

The policy of the Nkrumah government towards private industry was ambiguous. Officially, private foreign capital was welcomed and in order to encourage potential foreign investors a Capital Investment Act was passed in 1963. This provides, among other things, for a 'tax holiday' of up to ten years; exemptions from tariffs and other indirect taxes; and exemption from property taxes. Guarantees are given of the freedom to repatriate profits and of fair compensation in the 'exceptional circumstances' of nationalization. The Government also showed itself willing to levy protective tariffs on behalf of domestic producers. And at the present time virtually all domestic producers of manufactures receive powerful protection from import restrictions imposed as a result of balance of payments difficulties, sometimes taking the form of total prohibition.

One concrete example of the former Government's anxiety to attract foreign capital is the Volta River Project. This giant scheme consists of a dam across the River Volta for the generation of hydro-

[1] Gold Coast Industrial Development Ordinance, 1947, Section 3 (1).

[2] For a short study of the records of some of the subsidiary companies and of the problems encountered see *Economy of Ghana*, pp. 287–93.

electricity and an aluminium smelter which consumes a large part of the power generated at the dam. The hydro-electric scheme, which cost about N₵120 millions, was financed by the internal resources of the Government and by loans obtained from the American and British Governments and from the World Bank. The N₵86 millions aluminium smelter is owned and operated by two American aluminium companies, led by the Kaiser Aluminium and Chemical Corporation.

Besides introducing new sources of Government revenue and foreign exchange, the project will create an adequate reserve of generating capacity to provide power for the industries intended to grow up in the country. The terms of the Government's agreement with the aluminium companies showed how far it was prepared to go in making concessions for schemes which it was convinced would be of great economic importance. The companies secured a wide range of generous fiscal and other concessions, not least of which was power at cost-price.[1]

Yet in spite of the manifest desire to attract foreign business, there was a good deal of tension between this desire and the socialist objectives of the Convention People's Party, nowhere more clearly seen than in the writings of Dr Nkrumah expressing a profound distrust of foreign capital in Africa.[2] Similarly, Ghanaian private enterprise was regarded with suspicion and the official party policy was that local entrepreneurs should be confined to 'small-scale enterprises'.

No such ambiguity clouded the policy of those taking over from Nkrumah who shared not at all in his ideological distaste for private business. On the other hand, no spectacular resurgence of private industrial activity could be expected until the political future of the country was more clearly defined and until the worst of the economic difficulties had been eliminated. These difficulties have, however, threatened to persist.

6. LABOUR AND WAGES

In Table 12 we set out figures of the industrial structure of employment in Ghana, based on the 1960 Census of Population, which may be regarded as being reasonably complete and accurate. These show that 62 per cent of the employed labour force were engaged in agricultural work and a further 15 per cent in 'commerce'. In man-

1 For a detailed examination of this agreement and of the project as a whole see *Economy of Ghana*, Chapter 16.

2 See, for example, Nkrumah's *Neo-Colonialism*, London, 1965.

power terms commerce is dominated by petty trading, so the aggregate proportion of about 75 per cent may be taken as a reasonable indication of employment in what may be termed 'pre-industrial' occupations.

Table 12. *Total census employment by industry group: 1960*

Industry group	Numbers employed	Percentage of total
1. Agriculture, forestry and fishing, *of which:*	1,578,880	62
Field crops and foodstuffs production	910,460	36
Cocoa growing	522,350	20
Forestry and logging	23,820	1
2. Mining and quarrying	48,430	2
3. Manufacturing	235,240	9
4. Construction	89,370	3
5. Electricity, water and sanitary services	14,110	1
6. Commerce	371,500	15
7. Transport, storage and communications	68,420	3
8. Services	155,090	6
Total	2,561,040	100

Source: Census of Population *Advance Report of Volumes III and IV*, Table 32.

There are no comparable figures for other years but published labour statistics do permit some generalizations about trends in the structure of employment. We have noted earlier the movement of labour out of traditional farming into urban employment. Within the urban sector a number of changes are also apparent. Employment in mining has been on the decline, absolutely and in relation to other sources of paid employment. A number of gold mines have closed in the post-war period, no new ones have commenced operation, and there was also a drop in the number of 'African diggers' in diamond mining. Recorded employment in manufacturing, on the other hand, has expanded fast, as also in public utilities and Government service.

Total recorded employment more than doubled between 1950 and 1964 and it is tempting to use this as an indication of the spread of wage employment. But while there is no doubt that wage employment has increased in importance, the official statistics do not give any firm indication of the extent of this, because of improvements in the coverage of the figures. The best indication of the relative importance of wage labour, but not of the trend, is derived from the results of the 1960 Census of Population. The Census concept of an 'employee'—'Persons who work for a public or private employer and are paid by their employer'[1]—can be taken as synonymous with wage-worker, and adding to the number of employees the number of apprentices (another form of employment status presumably belonging to the wage sector), gives 21 per cent of the employed labour force in 1960 working for wages.

Although there is little direct evidence, it is reasonably clear that returns to labour in the rural economy are substantially below wages in urban areas. In the absence of data on rural earnings, perhaps the best approach is to assume that earnings differentials will be a direct (although not necessarily proportionate) function of productivity differences. From the inter-sectoral study of Ghana's economy referred to earlier[2] the gross value added per worker in the major sectors of activity were found in 1960 to be as follows:—

	N₵
Agriculture (including cocoa and forestry other than logging)	180
Services	448
Construction	958
Mining and Quarrying	934
Manufacturing	684

Average productivities in industrial employments are much higher than in agriculture, and although far more capital per worker is employed in industry it would be surprising if these different productivity levels were not accompanied by substantially different levels of labour earnings.

Wages in the towns of Ghana tend to be 'artificially' high, in the sense that the supply of labour at these wage rates exceeds the number of jobs available. Wage legislation, which covers most wage employment but does not extend to agriculture, decreed until July 1967, a minimum of six and sixpence a day for unskilled labourers (about N₵160 a year, assuming 250 working days a year). Average earnings of wage workers in 1965 were about N₵470 but this figure incorporates also a differential for skilled labour.

A further indication of the superior earning power of urban employment is the large-scale migration of workers, especially from the north to the south and from the villages to the towns—a movement which is reinforced by the spread of education and the superior social

[1] Census of Population *Advance Report of Volume III and IV*, p. xviii.

[2] *Economy of Ghana*, Table 3.3.

attractiveness of urban life. Much of this migration is seasonal but there is also considerable permanent migration. According to the 1960 Census of Population some 57 per cent of the males and 47 per cent of the females in the employed labour force could have been described as migrants at the time of the Census. A good proportion of these were short-distance migrants, working outside the locality in which they were born but within the same Region (21 and 29 per cent respectively). A rather smaller number were long-distance migrants, working outside their Region of birth (19 and 11 per cent). A still smaller—but nevertheless very substantial—number were international migrants (17 and 7 per cent), having been born outside Ghana. The evidence suggests that, while the seasonal migrant workers are largely unskilled, working in cocoa, other agriculture and in the mines, the permanent migrants are much more oriented to the 'modern' sectors of the economy and more often achieve the status of skilled or higher-level workers than non-migrants.[1]

Something must also be said about unemployment. Again, the 1960 Census of Population is the main source of information. The Census figures show that 6·5 per cent of the total male labour force and 5·2 per cent of the total female labour force were unemployed at the time of the Census.[2] However, it is more relevant to express the number of unemployed in relation to the *wage* labour force, since it was to that part of the labour force that the chosen definition of unemployment mainly applied.[3] When expressed in this way the proportions of unemployed rise to 19 and 60 per cent respectively. Unemployment is particularly acute among the young; no fewer than 77 per cent of the total number of unemployed were between 15 and 29 years of age.

The under-utilization of labour in the rural areas largely takes the form of under-employment rather than outright unemployment. By an under-employed worker we mean one who voluntarily or involuntarily engages in work that takes up only part of his work potential. While it is not possible to put any figures to this, observers agree that there is much under-employment in the rural parts of the country, stemming from the largely seasonal nature of agricultural work, the shortage of alternative employments and from insufficient rates of

[1] See *Economy of Ghana*, pp. 131–36 and also the paper by B. Gil and E. N. Omaboe already cited. Caldwell also has an excellent chapter on migration in *Ghana Social Structure*, *op. cit.*

[2] 'Total labour force' here means employed labour force plus unemployed.

[3] An unemployed person was defined as, 'a person who did not work at any time during the reference month and had no fixed job and who was *looking actively* for work by visiting employment agencies, writing applications, etc'. *Advance Report*, p. 16. Original italics.

return obtainable from marginal inputs of labour. The seasonal migration of workers already referred to is itself an indication of this, because for every worker who travels south in search of work during the slack season there are many who cannot or do not make the effort.

The large-scale unemployment that exists is caused in part by a structure of wages that is too high to permit the absorption of the constant influx of young people to the towns. Government policies, however, have endeavoured to restrain trade union attempts to bargain for higher wages and nationally negotiated wage increases have been few since the 1960 minimum wage legislation. Meanwhile prices have been rising fast and an index of real wages for unskilled workers in Accra stood at 63 in October 1966 as compared with 119 in July 1960 and 92 at the end of 1952. To some extent average earnings have gone up while wage rates have stood still, but, even so, there has been a consistent and substantial reduction in real earnings since 1960.

The evident success of the Nkrumah Government in restraining wages had much to do with the centralized trade union structure and system of industrial relations created by the 1958 Industrial Relations Act and later amendments. However, this system did not long survive the change of government and the relationship in which the trade union movement stands to the new structure of political authority remains to be defined.

7. THE PATTERN OF EXTERNAL TRADE

The introductory section of this chapter outlined the balance of payments trends in recent years; this final section concentrates on the pattern and organization of trade. To begin with the composition of trade, set out in Tables 13 and 14 are analyses of the composition of exports of domestic goods[1] and the composition of imports by end use.

The commodity composition of Ghana's foreign trade closely resembles that of most developing countries. Virtually all the country's exports are of primary products and three-quarters of her imports are of manufactured goods. Ghana's export trade also exhibits another feature which is often regarded as typical of developing countries—a high degree of dependence on a single export commodity, with cocoa generally providing around three-fifths of the country's total merchandise export earnings. This is a dependence, moreover, which shows little sign of decline. Whereas in 1962–65

[1] Re-exports are not very important, accounting for under 5 per cent of visible exports.

Table 13. *Composition of exports of domestic goods*
(percentages)

Exports	1952–55	1956–59	1962–65
Cocoa beans	67	59	61
Cocoa butter	—	—	4
Timber (logs and sawn)	7	11	12
Manganese	8	8	4
Diamonds	5	9	5
Gold	10	10	10
Others	3	3	4
Total	100	100	100

Source: Economic Surveys.

cocoa beans made up an average of 61 per cent of exports of domestic goods, in 1935–39 the proportion was 52 per cent.[1] Indeed, looking at all the items of Table 13 the main feature is the stability in the composition of exports. Timber exports have grown substantially; cocoa butter has emerged as a significant item; manganese has declined; but generally speaking the structure of exports has remained relatively frozen.

The statistics of the end-use structure of imports show more fluidity, at least between the late 'fifties and the early 'sixties. In the earlier periods the country's imports were heavily weighted towards consumer goods—considerably more so than most comparable countries.[2] By 1962–65 a marked change had taken place, considering how slowly one would normally expect modifications to occur. This

Table 14. *Composition of imports by end-use*
(percentages)

End-use category	1952–55	1956–59	1962–65
Non-durable consumer goods	48	45	33
Durable consumer goods	8	9	6
Raw and semi-finished materials	24	25	31
Capital equipment	13	15	25
Fuels and lubricants	6	6	5
Total	100	100	100

Source: Economic Surveys.

[1] See article by R. H. Green in *Economic Bulletin of Ghana*, Volume 5, No. 1 (1961), Table 4.

[2] See *Economy of Ghana*, Chapter 14.

was mainly brought about by increased taxation of imported consumer goods and by the import controls imposed at the end of 1961, which were particularly restrictive in the case of consumer goods. Indeed by 1965 total consumer goods imports were down to 34 per cent and producer goods up to 62 per cent of the total import bill. A factor contributing to the changing structure of imports was the creation of plants in Ghana undertaking the final stage of production of consumer and other goods (e.g. putting the wrinkles into corrugated aluminium sheets). The supplies of these plants would be entered as producer goods, although the value added and foreign exchange savings of these activities are rather slight. In this respect also the change of Government brought a reversal of the former trend, and imports in 1966 and 1967 included smaller quantities of capital goods and more consumer goods (including substantial amounts of food aid from North America).

Table 15. *The direction of trade*
(percentage of total exports or imports)

Region or country[a]	Exports 1954–55	Exports 1958–59	Exports 1962–63	Imports 1954–55	Imports 1958–59	Imports 1962–63
Africa	1·1	1·2	3·2	6·4	7·3	7·4
Asia	0·2	0·7	2·5	11·8	12·4	11·8
Centrally planned economies	5·4	1·3	11·3	1·9	3·2	9·3
EEC: France	1·6	1·0	0·6	1·6	1·7	2·1
Other	25·3	34·6	29·1	16·6	19·2	20·5
North America	18·0	19·7	22·1	5·0	6·6	10·0
Sterling Area:						
UK	40·3	33·4	30·1	47·9	41·5	35·0
Other	5·0	4·8	3·7	6·5	6·5	4·9

Note: [a] The regions shown are not mutually exclusive, i.e., the centrally planned economies and the sterling area include countries of Asia and /or Africa.

Source: Statistical Year Books, 1961 and 1962.

Turning to the geographical dispersion of Ghana's trade it will be seen from table 15 that the country's principal trading partners are the United Kingdom, the ex-metropolitan power, and the nations of Western Europe. Over half of total trade was with these countries in 1962–63. North America is very important as an export market but less so as a source of imports. Asia (mainly Japan) is an important supplier of imports and is a growing, if still small, purchaser of Ghana's exports.

As with so many other features of her economy, however, the geographical pattern of Ghana's external trade is in the process of fairly radical change. The relative importance of trade with the United Kingdom and other Sterling Area countries is declining appreciably. It is generally the case that trade between former colonial territories and the metropolitan power falls off after independence. In the second half of the 'fifties trade with the EEC countries was on a rising trend and although this trend failed to maintain itself in the early 'sixties it even so made up about a quarter of the total in 1962–63. Trade with North America has grown slowly but consistently and much the same could be said of trade with other African countries.

The most significant trend of all is probably the growth of trade with the centrally planned economies. Trade with these countries amounted to only about 2 per cent of the total in 1958–59 but by 1962–63 the share was up to 10 per cent. Here again, the administration of import controls contributed significantly to this growth, for they were operated to discriminate in favour of imports from this group of countries. The reason for this, apart from purely political considerations, was that Ghana had been able to negotiate with them low-interest, medium-term trading credits of a large total value (well over N₵200 millions) but was only partially able to make use of these credits because of an inability or unwillingness on the part of importers to discover enough goods which these countries were willing to trade and which would suit Ghana's import requirements. In fact, Ghana tended for a time to experience balance of payments surpluses with the centrally planned countries and in the context of bilateral trade this meant, in effect, that Ghana was a net lender (free of interest) instead of a recipient of credit. If only because of the country's shortage of a foreign exchange and the growing importance of Eastern Europe as a consumer of cocoa, there is no doubt that trade with this group of countries will remain very important to Ghana, notwithstanding the more pro-Western political stance of the present Government.

In relation to the geographical sources of imports, the nature, nationality and traditional business ties of the main importing concerns is of some importance, and we may usefully conclude by saying something about the organization of trade.

In spite of the creation of the state-owned Ghana National Trading Corporation, a large proportion of the import business of the country is still handled by expatriate firms. The most important of these are the British-Dutch United Africa Company (a subsidiary of Unilever), the Swiss Union Trading Company and the French

Compagnie Française de l'Afrique Occidental. In addition to these and other relatively large European-owned trading companies there are numerous smaller and generally more specialized importing concerns, many of which are owned and run by the Levantine community.

The role of the large expatriate trading companies has undergone considerable change in recent years. All of them have effectively withdrawn from retail business, except in the specialized sphere of department stores. They all have tended to place particular emphasis on building-up their technical departments. In some cases, substantial investments have been made in directly productive concerns, such as motor vehicle assembly plants. The Ghana National Trading Corporation, which commenced business only in 1962, has, on the other hand, extended very rapidly into retail/wholesale business and by the middle of 1964 had nearly 200 retail outlets alone.

On the side of exports, the most important institution is the Ghana Cocoa Marketing Board which has the sole right to export cocoa (and certain other agricultural exports), and to buy for export. A subsidiary of the Marketing Board, the Cocoa Marketing Company, handles the delicate business of placing the cocoa on the world market. There is a Diamond Marketing Board which has similar functions in respect of the diamond industry. A Timber Marketing Board was also established but this has since been disbanded and the marketing of timber has virtually reverted to free enterprise.

8. CONCLUSIONS

At the beginning of this chapter we described Ghana's economy as being in a transitional phase, absorbing modern productive techniques, acquiring sophisticated tastes and yet still basically dependent upon the output of industries that have dominated the economy for many years. In concluding we would like to mention some of the stresses in the social and economic structure that are associated with this phase of the country's development. Tensions have appeared between traditional and modernizing social groups, between old and young, between customary chiefs and new-style politicians. Fresh responsibilities and new educational achievements are imposing themselves on the old patterns of status. In the economy, the inability of the country's traditional exports to earn amounts of foreign exchange sufficient to sustain a satisfactory level of economic activity at home is as frustrating to the policy-makers as it is politically hazardous. The inability of foodstuffs production to meet the needs of the growing population has emerged as a major structural weakness.

Shortages of a wide range of middle- and top-level skills add to the frustrations.

Tension exists at yet another level, between the wish for rapid economic development and the ability to achieve it. For all the defects in its policies, Dr Nkrumah's Government was committed to a dynamic programme for development. While better planning and more realistic policies would certainly have created smaller difficulties, the basic point remains that both internally and externally conditions did not, and will not, permit a really rapid rate of economic progress. Growth has proved in the past to depend crucially on the capacity to import. While the cocoa boom lasted and while there were excess sterling reserves, growth was rapid. When static export earnings reasserted themselves as the basic determinant of the ability to import, growth declined. There is little prospect that exports will in the near future exhibit a more dynamic trend. Aid and private capital from industrial countries will help but will supplement rather than substitute for exports.

Meanwhile, the number of mouths to feed and jobs to create are growing apace. The 1980 Census is likely to discover a population not far short of twice the size of the one enumerated in 1960 and, unchecked, this rate of increase will make it difficult to sustain existing living standards, let alone improve them. We do not wish to paint too gloomy a picture. The proven responsiveness of Ghanaians to economic opportunities, the well-developed infrastructure, the high level of domestic saving and the rapid improvement of educational opportunities—all these augur well for the future prospects of the economy. The export and population constraints are neither of them insoluble. Nor is the local foods bottleneck. They are, nevertheless, deeply embedded in the social and economic structure of the country and it will require a high degree of determination and skill to overcome them.

SELECTED READING

General

The major source used for this chapter is *A Study of Contemporary Ghana:* Volume One, *The Economy of Ghana*, edited by Walter Birmingham, I. Neustadt and E. N. Omaboe (George Allen and Unwin, 1966), which is primarily a study of the structure of the economy. For a study of changes in the structure and of the process of growth in an earlier period see R. Szereszewski's *Structural Changes in the Economy of Ghana, 1891–1911* (Weidenfeld and Nicolson, 1965). *A Study of Con-*

temporary Ghana: Volume Two. *Some Aspects of Social Structure* (Allen and Unwin, 1967) contains a valuable study of the demographic features of the country as well as other useful surveys.

Of the considerable body of Ghana Government publications, the annual *Economic Survey*, published by the Central Bureau of Statistics, is an invaluable source of information and comment on current trends in the economy. Valuable also are the *Statistical Year Books* and the *Annual Reports* of the Bank of Ghana.

The Economic Society of Ghana publishes a quarterly journal called *The Economic Bulletin of Ghana:* articles in this journal have over the years contributed much to the study of the economy.

Development Planning

The most important document on this subject is the *Seven Year Development Plan, 1963–64 to 1969–70* (Office of the Planning Commission, 1964). See also the earlier plans referred to in the text.

Financing the Public Sector

The major official source of information on fiscal matters is the annual *Budget* and the accompanying *Financial Statement.* Extraordinarily little unofficial analysis of fiscal data has been published but an article by F. and S. Andic in *Public Finance*, No. 1, 1963 should be consulted, and also that by N. Ahmad in *Economic Bulletin of Ghana*, Vol. X, No. 1, 1966.

Agriculture

By far the most important publication on this segment of the economy is *Agriculture and Land Use in Ghana*, edited by J. Brian Wills (Oxford University Press, 1962), a didactic study drawing on a large number of expert contributors and containing much valuable information. See also Polly Hill's *Gold Coast Cocoa Farmer* (Oxford University Press, 1956).

Labour and Wages

The primary source of information in this field is the reports of the 1960 census of population. Six volumes have so far been published, dealing with demographic, economic and tribal characteristics. The *Survey of High Level Manpower* (Government Printer, 1961) conducted at the same time but independently of the census provides useful supplementary information on its chosen topic.

Industrialization

In 1962 Ghana held a full-scale industrial census which resulted in a great deal of (so far largely undigested) statistics on the industrial sector. The main results of the census are presented in *1962 Industrial Census Report; Volume I—Industry* (Central Bureau of Statistics, 1965). On the basis of the census results the Government has commenced publication of new annual and quarterly series of industrial statistics, of which the *Industrial Statistics, 1962–64* (Central Bureau of Statistics, 1965) was the first. On questions of policy, Prof. W. A. Lewis's well-known *Report on Industrialization and the Gold Coast* (Government Printer, 1953) remains highly pertinent. The *Annual Reports* of the Industrial Development Corporation are also worth looking at.

Trade

P. T. Bauer's *West African Trade* (re-issued London, 1963) remains the only substantial piece of work on this topic, although there is quite a large literature on the operation of the Marketing Boards in learned journals.

3

THE ECONOMY OF NIGERIA

1. INTRODUCTION

By area and population, Nigeria is one of the bigger countries of Africa. In terms of economic potential, it is also usually lauded as one of the most hopeful. Yet in recent times, Nigeria's image of development effectiveness has been criticized unfavourably by some observers at home and abroad. Its pace of recent performance and immediate future prospects were recently characterized, in the words of a Nigerian economist, as a tale of false hope.[1]

This chapter analyses the structure of the country's economy in the decade preceding its political independence up to the early stages of implementing its first national development plan. Its central theme is that both the character of investment and the behaviour of prices provide a useful understanding of the country's economic activities and problems during this vital period. In another dimension, it will also be argued that the foreign trade and public sectors constituted the fulcrum of change and defined the path of overall development. In overall perspective, it will be demonstrated that although the growth path was a positive one, its most characteristic features were those of distortion and uncertainty.

2. RESOURCES

Broadly, Nigeria's resources can be looked at from two standpoints: its physical features and its population. Following the post-independence plebiscite which removed the old Southern Cameroons province to join with the Cameroon Republic, Nigeria has a total land surface of some 357,000 square miles. It lies entirely in the tropics, and displays the characteristic vegetation belts of West Africa moving northward from the swampy southern coast, through the rain forest, derived savannah, open grassland and the southern

[1] Sanmi Olakanpo, 'Nigerian Economy Since Independence,' *African Statesman* Vol. 1, No. 1, October–December, 1965, p. 13. It should be noted that this chapter was completed before the recent armed conflict in Nigeria.

fringes of the Sahara desert. Following this movement, the land's general elevation itself rises gently northwards from the coast to a general height of 2,000 feet in the north. In the central north-eastern part, the Bauchi plateau rises to over 5,000 feet above sea level. Otherwise, the country's relief consists largely of plains, gently rolling hills and, consequently, deep soils.

Nature is generous in both heat and moisture. With small variations, the mean annual temperature is near 80°F. Except in the far-north the mean annual rainfall is over 30 inches and is beneficially divided into two seasons in the Southern belts with their prevailing moist south-west wind current. The two great river basins—Niger and Benue—traverse the country, combine at the confluence in Lokoja, meander powerfully southward and fan out in the large mangrove delta area along the coast. There are scores of other medium and small-size rivers all over the country, providing further drainage for agriculture, fishing and water transportation.

The combination of expansive land surface, deep soil, good heat and adequate moisture provides an excellent basis for successful tropical agriculture. The varying degree in which these factors are combined in the different parts of the country provides for great diversity in the concentration of primary activities. From the mangrove and rain-forest came not only fishing and hunting but valuable hard woods like mahogany, cedar and walnut. The derived savannah generates the cocoa, rubber, palm produce, kola nut and arable crops like yam, cassava, maize and citrus. Conditions in the open grassland are conducive not only to the raising of cattle, other livestock and dairy products, but also the cultivation of grains like guinea corn, millet, rice, cotton, groundnuts, beans and other leguminous crops. The river basins are a natural place for fishing, sugarcane, and various kinds of vegetable.

A further gift of nature consists of the mineral deposits. The geological formation has scattered about a number of very valuable deposits all over the country from the alluvial gold deposits in the Western Region, through the tin mines of the North to the coal, lead-zinc and petroleum in the East and Mid-West. In addition, there are less concentrated traditional iron smelting activity, brass and bronze and the more concentrated iron ore around the Lokoja confluence. There are rare metals like columbite, tantalum, tungsten and radioactive minerals. There are other useful deposits for modern industrial and building activities, in the form of limestone, kaolin, diatomite and clay.

As with material resources, so with human population—varied and extensive. In variety, one writer has put the number of different ethnic

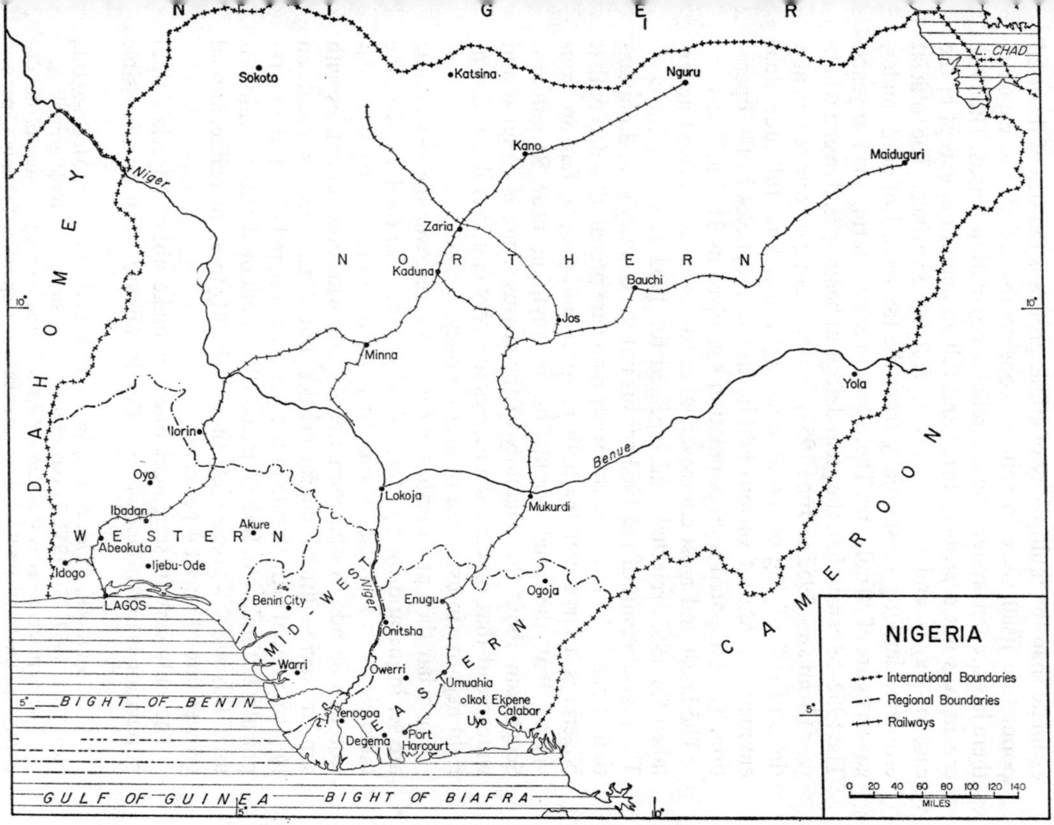

NIGER
L. CHAD
Sokoto
Katsina
Nguru
Kano
Maiduguri
Zaria
NORTHERN
Kaduna
Bauchi
Jos
Minna
Yola
DAHOMEY
Niger
Ilorin
Benue
Oyo
Lokoja
Mukurdi
Ibadan
Akure
WESTERN
Abeokuta
Ijebu-Ode
Idogo
LAGOS
Benin City
MID WEST
Niger
Onitsha
Enugu
Ogoja
CAMEROON
EASTERN
Warri
Owerri
Umuahia
Ikot Ekpene
Uyo
Calabar
Yenogoa
Degema
Port Harcourt
BIGHT OF BENIN
GULF OF GUINEA
BIGHT OF BIAFRA
NIGERIA
International Boundaries
Regional Boundaries
Railways
0 20 40 60 80 100 120 140
MILES
10°
5°

Map 3

E

groups in the country at about four hundred.[1] There are further differences in history, religion and culture. But far more difficult to estimate than the multiplicity of ethnic groups is the size of the total population itself since in spite of considerable effort and expense, there has been no systematic and reliable population census. The 1931 census was not a proper, direct and full enumeration, except in the case of Lagos and some areas in Katsina Province. The official estimate, deriving substantially from the tax record of adult males, gave a figure of 20 millions. There was no census during the war years. The 1952–53 census had the great defects of being spread over a whole year (from July 1952 to June 1953), concentrating on one region at a time, of still relying on group counting rather than full individual enumeration and of various administrative loopholes in the operation. The estimated total population was given as 31·5 millions.

The latest and most controversial census exercise was that undertaken for 1962, rejected, and repeated for 1963 at very great cost. The official result of the 1963 census put the country's total population at nearly 56 millions. But while many are prepared to accept that Nigeria is a large country both in space and people, few are convinced that the total population is anything near 50 millions. Scepticism about the reliability of the census figure is so great and widespread that officials themselves are very cautious if not downright negative in using the result for policy.

For what they are worth, the census figures over the last decade are set in juxtaposition in the following table. On the face of it, the table yields an increase of some 85 per cent in the country's population in a decade. If one compares Nigeria with other countries with similar socio-cultural characteristics but better census data, an implicit annual growth rate of 6·5 per cent in population is demographically unthinkable. If the rejected 1962 result of about 45 millions is used, this will still give a high, though slightly more plausible, annual growth rate of about 4 per cent.[2]

The only certain statement one can make about Nigeria's total population is that nobody knows the right figure within an admissible

[1] G. P. Murdock, *Africa Its Peoples and Their Culture History*, McGraw-Hill, New York, 1959. The 1952–53 census itself listed some 250 ethnic groupings.

[2] The popular belief is that the 1962 result was rejected because of the discovery that the Northern Region would have been responsible for only 47 per cent of the total population of the Federation. In the delicate tri-partite power structure, this was somehow judged to symbolize the end of the dominance of the more conservative but powerful Northern bloc in the federal government. The now officially accepted 1963 figures show that the Northern Region somehow carries about 54 per cent of total—a significant point for the distribution and exercise of political power.

Table 1. *Area and population of Nigeria by regions, 1952/53–1963*

Regions	Area (sq. m.)	1952–53 Population (thousands)	1952–53 Density (Persons per sq. m.)	1963 Population (thousands)	1963 Density (Persons per sq. m.)
Lagos Township	27	267	9,889	665	24,630
West	30,454	4,595	151	10,266	337
Mid-West	14,922	1,492	100	2,536	170
East	29,484	7,215	245	12,394	420
North	281,782	16,835	60	29,809	106
Total Federation[a]	356,669	30,404	85	55,670	156

Note: [a] Total does not include the 1952–53 figure in respect of the ex-Province of Southern Cameroons.
Source: *Annual Abstract of Statistics*, Nigeria, 1964.

margin of error. It is possible that both the 1952–53 and 1963 censuses represent undercounting or overcounting with varying degrees of error. It is unlikely that the earlier census grossly overstated the true figures, but it is not improbable that the 1952–53 figure was slightly understated and the 1963 figure grossly overstated. If we take the less politically charged but rejected 1962 figure and allow even here for subjective errors of some over-zealous census officers, it may not be too wild to suggest that the earlier population was of the order of 33 millions[1] and the latter 42 millions. These figures yield an approximate annual growth rate of 2·5 per cent and a current density of about 118 persons per square mile. Such a growth rate is comparable (for whatever it is worth) with the 2·25 per cent intercensal rate between 1931 and 1952, and slightly more in line with the experience of other underdeveloped countries in a similar stage of demographic transition. In the African context, our guess estimate of total population and density will still rank Nigeria very high in the size hierarchy.

The uneven distribution of population throughout the African

[1] Apart from official admission of undercounting (e.g. the *Population Census of Western Region of Nigeria*, 1952), the actual registration figures for the free primary education scheme showed how wide off the mark the census projection on which the policy design was mistakenly based. In the Western Region, for example, the census suggested a registration figure of 170,000 6–7 years old for 1955 as against the actual enrolment that year of 392,000!

continent is reflected on a smaller scale in the Nigerian pattern. Even allowing for the unsystematic spread of errors in the regional census figures, there is little doubt that the South is more densely populated than the North and that the West has the greatest concentration of urban population. This is a reflection partly of the socio-cultural pattern of the different ethnic groups, partly of the differing incidence of the historic ravaging slavery from European incursions, and partly a consequence of natural forces. The last factor is especially responsible for the continued situation of sparse population in the Middle Belt infested by the debilitating tsetse fly. Other areas of low population density include the arid provinces in the North-East and the swampy Delta area with difficult communication. It does not, however, always follow that population density is well correlated with favourable geographical endowments, as is evidenced by the low density in the potentially rich agricultural areas around the upper Niger basin and the high density on the poor quality soil and rain forest of central Eastern region. But in general, variations in population density within the country reflect real differences in the level, if not the pace, of achievement in economic development.

Other demographic features which bear on the character of the country's economy are the very young age composition of the population and the comparatively small proportion of non-African races. Outside the regional breakdown, no further analysis of the 1963 census data is yet available; but it is unlikely that the age and racial breakdowns would have radically changed from the 1952–53 position. Then, 44 per cent of the population were 14 years or under, only 8 per cent were 50 years or older and only 12 per cent of those of 7 years of age and over were literate in any admissible sense. Only about 0·05 per cent of the country were non-African in origin. Too literal an interpretation should not, however, be given to these figures.

Age is one of the most hazardous things to estimate with any reasonable confidence in a society that has little birth registration record.[1] And it hardly needs restating that the size of a country bears only a tenous relationship with its economic power. Nigeria may be a large country in terms of head counting, but it is far less so in the effectiveness of its economic performance and development policy. This dichotomy between number and power is shared with many other African countries and is a reflection of their semi-colonial

[1] A glimpse of the hazards can be gleaned from the device by Professor J. F. Ajayi and Mr A. A. Igun in their *Population Census of Nigeria, 1963—Lists of Historical Events for Determination of Individual Ages*, The Regional Census Office, Ibadan, 1962 and 1963. Mimeographed.

status. Through foreign aid, ownership of productive assets and the character of public policy, persistent colonial links determine the structure of economic organization and are a basis of possible future conflict in the process of new social formation.

3. BASIC SETTING

A proper understanding of the Nigerian economy today and of its future prospects requires a discussion, no matter how broad, of the historical process which has moulded its activity patterns, production agents and policy makers. After centuries of slavery, the country became systematically exposed to legitimate commerce as an outpost of the growing industrial capitalism of nineteenth century Europe. Steps at formal political control were started in 1861 and completed with the amalgamation edict of 1914. The British firmly controlled both the machinery of government and the character of commerce. Through their determination of prices and money supply, they influenced the size of investment, government expenditure and expansion of domestic income. And since colonies were seen until recently as being primarily an extension of the Metropolitan economy, it is scarcely surprising that Nigeria's economic fortunes should reflect variations in the activity level of the British economy. The two world wars and their aftermath stimulated in general the demand for Nigerian raw material exports. Likewise, the general depression, the collapse of the Korean boom and changes in taste as well as in production techniques in the advanced industrial countries, have led to a general weakening of Nigeria's export earnings; and hence of money, public spending, investment expenditure, and the growth of income.

It is important to stress the foreign orientation of the economy's growth determinants because a questionable contrast is often made between the peasant economies of West Africa and the plantation – mining economies of East and Central Africa.[1] Actually, the distinction is only one of emphasis, not of kind. It is true that the paucity of foreign settlers and the absence of substantial foreign investment in plantation agriculture in West Africa contrast with other parts of the continent. It is also valid to argue that the long

[1] See the ubiquitous Prototypes I and II, long hallowed by United Nations documents on African economies. A fine example is *Economic Survey of Africa Since 1950*, UN Department of Economic and Social Affairs, New York, 1959, p. 12. For earlier formulation, see *Enlargement of the Exchange Economy in Tropical Africa*, 1954; *Scope and Structure of Money Economies in Tropical Africa*, 1955; and *Structure and Growth of Selected African Economies*, 1958.

existence of an active traditional commerce and the peasant structure of agricultural organization confer some buffer against instability in the foreign trade sector. What is doubtful is the implication that these characteristics in any significant way weaken the basic fact that the colonial enclaves, no matter how small, still determine the pace and pattern of the country's economic development. What is important is not number or size, but who controls the leading sectors from the standpoint of saving, investment, money supply and prices. In Nigeria, before the advent of the Marketing Boards, of self-government and of national economic planning, every indication was that the colonial enclaves virtually and openly controlled all the vital determinants of economic growth.

Nor has the situation been materially altered with the achievement of formal political independence; although the control has become more subtle. Economic development is influenced only by the facts of economic power not by the make-belief of political sovereignty. The possession and exercise of economic power, while subject to the constraints of formal political organization even for its own survival, are not necessarily determined by population size or the simple racial characteristic of the government. It depends on the identity or divergence of interests between those who manipulate the machinery of government and those who own and operate the productive assets in the leading sectors of the economy. In the colonial system, the fusion of these interests was complete. In the post-colonial era, the fusion, though less obvious, still persists; hence the attribute of semi-colonialism or neo-colonialism.

We may say, therefore, that a study of the foreign trade, foreign investment, foreign interests and general developments in the advanced industrial countries of Western Europe (and lately of North America), provide a useful point of entry to an understanding of the Nigerian economy over the last decade or two. The act of political independence in 1960 need not affect this basic frame of reference. This does not imply a single-parameter explanation of the country's economic achievements and problems. It only means that both as a starting point and as a reflection of the general socio-political realities, the foreign sector offers a good anchor for economic analysis and evaluation of development strategy. While it is not suggested that public policy has no internal motivation or steam of its own, there appears to be little doubt that both the choice of policy techniques and the effectiveness of their execution are still constrained by the powerful influence the foreign sector exerts on the national economy, out of proportion to its simple statistical magnitude.

4. STRUCTURE OF PRODUCTION

National accounting offers a most valuable framework for discussing the growth and structure of an economy. The defects of compiling such accounting in African countries are well known and Nigeria offers a case study for many of those defects.[1] Estimation errors are especially great if one considers the data for a particular year or a particular sector. But, without implying that the errors are always uniform from year to year, they become less frightening in a consistent time series approach. Whatever their weaknesses and the qualifications necessary for their interpretation, the Nigerian national accounts for the period 1950–1962 have the virtue of being based on the same conceptual and methodological framework. The results for the production approach are set out in Tables 2–5. The economy has been divided into ten major activity sectors—evidently too aggregative for refined analysis but quite useable for a broad discussion of the output structure.

Table 2 gives the current price valuation of the Gross Domestic Product at factor cost. If we relate the total Gross Domestic Product to the total population, we find that the output per head in 1952–53 is of the order of £21, and that in 1962 it remained at best at the same level judging from the official census figure! Since (from Table 4) the general price level rose within the decade by about one-third, the implication is strong that the average Nigerian was becoming steadily worse off through the period. But while there existed signs of what Dr Okigbo calls increasing 'immiseration of the poor',[2] it is unlikely that the *per capita* real living standard fell by anything like one-third during the decade from a level that was already very low even by the standard of the underdeveloped countries. The suspicion is strong that the joker of the pack is the 1963 population census figure. If we use the result of the rejected 1962 exercise, the *per capita* income would have risen to £25; and to £27 if we take our guess estimate (which allowed for a likely upward bias even in the 1962 result). Such a growth in *per capita* income will, even then, just about suffice to wipe off the implicit increase in the general price level, making at best only for a constant *per capita* real income during the period.

One reason for the unspectacular growth in *per capita* real income

[1] See the volume on the subject edited by L. H. Samuels, *African Studies in Income and Wealth*, Bowes and Bowes, London, for the International Association for Research in Income and Wealth, 1963, especially Ch. 12 by Pius Okigbo on 'Nigerian National Accounts, 1950–57', pp. 285–306.

[2] P. C. N. Okigbo, 'Presidential Address', *Nigerian Journal of Economic and Social Studies*, Vol. 7, No. 1, March 1965, p. 8.

Table 2. *Gross domestic product by industry of origin at (factor cost) current prices, 1950–62*
(£m)

Industry	1950	1951	1952	1953	1954	1955	1956	1957	1958	1959	1960	1961	1962
Agriculture, livestock, fishing and forestry	337·4	385·6	381·4	425·1	494·8	530·3	534·7	557·0	594·6	579·0	563·5	657·7	714·5
Mining and oil exploration	5·5	10·7	11·4	11·2	11·0	10·2	8·2	9·4	7·1	8·2	9·9	17·0	22·3
Manufacturing and public utilities	3·3	3·5	4·9	6·4	7·1	8·4	12·2	13·1	26·7	34·0	40·3	44·1	46·7
Building and civil engineering	8·1	12·2	16·8	17·6	28·0	31·4	36·5	43·0	24·4	32·6	33·7	38·9	45·0
Transport and communications	24·7	28·9	31·5	42·9	48·2	56·3	68·1	77·7	33·6	38·5	48·9	54·5	56·2
Banking, insurance and other professions	0·7	0·7	0·9	1·1	1·4	1·8	2·1	2·5	3·4	4·1	5·2	6·3	6·7
Ownership of buildings	5·9	6·2	6·4	7·1	7·5	8·8	8·2	10·3	7·9	8·3	9·5	10·7	12·4
Government	10·8	11·8	14·3	15·0	16·0	21·3	28·7	30·5	29·7	38·8	43·9	47·1	49·1
Services (domestic and miscellaneous)	3·3	3·3	3·7	4·5	4·9	5·6	7·2	7·5	5·0	5·9	7·7	7·7	9·0
Others[a]	112·4	110·3	143·2	134·1	155·3	153·4	164·7	159·0	132·5	153·6	156·3	165·2	185·7
Total	512·1	573·2	614·5	665·0	774·2	827·5	870·6	910·0	864·9	903·0	918·9	1,049·2	1,147·6

Note: [a] Others include crafts, missions, marketing boards, land development, distribution, etc. as well as residual error.
Sources: (1) P. N. C. Okigbo, *Nigerian National Accounts 1950–57*. (2) Federal Office of Statistics.

Table 3. *Gross domestic product by industry of origin at 1957 constant prices, 1950–62*
(£m)

Industry	1950	1951	1952	1953	1954	1955	1956	1957	1958	1959	1960	1961	1962
Agriculture, livestock fishing and forestry	456·8	494·5	503·0	521·4	549·5	564·1	543·6	557·0	620·0	613·1	640·0	665·6	694·1
Mining and oil exploration	7·6	7·6	8·2	7·9	8·1	9·0	9·6	9·4	7·0	6·6	8·4	13·8	18·2
Manufacturing and public utilities	3·9	4·0	5·8	6·3	7·9	8·7	12·0	13·1	25·4	30·6	36·1	39·4	42·2
Building and civil engineering	20·3	25·4	19·4	25·9	37·8	38·3	36·5	43·0	22·9	32·1	33·3	27·5	29·2
Transport and communications	31·3	36·7	38·3	48·3	53·5	62·6	67·7	77·7	32·0	35·4	40·5	46·5	46·5
Banking, insurance and other professions	1·5	1·2	1·3	1·7	1·7	2·1	2·2	2·5	3·0	3·6	3·6	3·8	3·9
Ownership of Buildings	8·9	9·1	9·2	9·4	9·6	9·7	9·8	10·3	7·9	8·6	9·3	10·0	10·7
Government	15·0	16·4	19·9	16·5	17·6	23·4	28·7	30·5	28·4	35·6	34·2	36·7	38·1
Services (domestic and miscellaneous)	5·3	5·5	5·5	5·8	6·0	6·5	7·6	7·5	5·5	6·0	7·7	7·6	8·2
Others[a]	136·5	139·8	182·4	166·6	180·5	173·7	156·4	159·0	147·9	165·3	165·8	163·1	181·2
Total	687·1	740·2	793·0	809·8	872·2	898·1	874·1	910·0	900·0	936·9	978·9	1,014·0	1,072·3

Note: [a] Others include crafts, missions, marketing boards, land development, distribution, etc. as well as residual error.
Sources: (1) P. N. C. Okigbo, *Nigerian National Accounts 1950–57*. (2) Federal Office of Statistics.

Table 4. *Gross domestic product by industry of origin at 1957 constant prices*

Industry	1950	1951	1952	1953	1954	1955	1956	1957	1958	1959	1960	1961	1962
Agriculture, livestock, fishing and forestry	74	78	76	82	90	94	98	100	96	94	88	99	103
Mining and oil exploration	72	141	139	142	136	113	85	100	101	124	118	123	123
Manufacturing and public utilities	85	88	84	102	90	97	102	100	105	111	112	112	111
Building and civil engineering	40	48	87	68	74	82	100	100	107	102	101	141	154
Transport and communications	79	79	82	89	90	90	101	100	105	109	121	117	121
Banking, insurance and other professions	47	58	69	65	82	86	95	100	113	114	144	166	172
Ownership of buildings	66	68	70	76	78	91	84	100	100	97	102	107	116
Government	72	72	72	91	91	91	100	100	105	109	128	128	129
Services (domestic and miscellaneous)	62	60	67	78	82	86	95	100	91	98	100	101	110
Others[a]	82	79	79	80	86	88	105	100	90	93	94	101	102
Total	75	77	77	82	89	92	100	100	96	96	94	103	107

Note: [a] Others include crafts, missions, marketing boards, land development, distribution, etc., as well as residual error.
Sources: (1) P. N. C. Okigbo, *Nigerian National Accounts 1950–57*. (2) Federal Office of Statistics.

is the fact that the bulk of output has always come from the combined agriculture, livestock, fishing and forestry activities; a sector which itself exhibits little progress. Not only has its average growth rate been lower than that of Gross Domestic Product; an important branch of agricultural activity (that producing primarily for domestic use rather than for export) was much worse in performance and in fact relatively declined between 1954 and 1960. Overall, that particular branch of the agricultural sector grew at a rate (2·1 per cent) below our implicit annual population growth rate of 2·5 per cent. Agriculture (with its ancillaries) was obviously not one of the growing points of the economy in any dynamic sense; and yet by 1962 it still accounted for slightly over 60 per cent of the Gross Domestic Product. True, its export component grew much faster than its home-consumption component. But in the second half of the period, the growth in export earning had slackened considerably.

It may be thought that because many of the 'modern activity' sectors continued to grow even after the export down-turning point of 1955, this weakens our thesis that the growth of the economy is substantially determined by activities in the foreign sector. It is true that manufacturing was growing at an impressive average rate of 17 per cent per annum; but at the end of the period it still accounted for only 1·5 per cent of the Gross Domestic Product. It is also true that building and civil engineering, transport and communication, public utilities and government services were all growing at average annual rates of between 10 per cent and 15 per cent; but their financing and operation still derived from stimuli in the foreign sector—through the drawing down of previous accumulated reserves, through foreign direct investment, through external public aid and through the maintenance of an open door foreign exchange policy.

In terms of organization, the economy of course still remains formally in indigenous hands. The peasants still dominate the base of the production iceberg. Nationalist politicians have replaced colonial officers at the controls of the state machinery. But it cannot be said that the growing and economically sensitive points of banking, finance, insurance, mining, manufacturing and high-level manpower are yet effectively controlled by Nigerians for Nigerians. The post-war period witnessed the rise and ascendancy of a small class of bourgeoisie, starting from commerce and the professions, inheriting the state apparatus from the metropolitan power and closely collaborating with foreign capital and skills to dominate the growing points of the economy. As these 'modern' sectors grew (it is more questionable to say developed), they encroached on the predominance of traditional activities like agriculture, livestock, fishing, forestry, handicrafts, petty trading and personal services. The increasing class differentiation and social stratification had important implications for expenditure behaviour, income distribution and the direction of public policy. The increasing ascendency of the 'modern' sectors stimulated the growth of towns and the expansion of commerce. Greater exchange meant the weakening of subsistence and the assimilation of local activities into wider markets.

Nobody really knows the size of subsistence output in Nigeria, whether in absolute value in a particular year or its movement through the years. It is indeed doubtful whether there is a 'subsistence sector' in Nigeria in a clearly defined geographical sense. There is scarcely any pocket of self-sufficiency left in the whole economy. Most of the communities are now exposed to systematic exchange in a complex system of market organization. This does not mean that no producer himself consumes any part of his output. Even after eliminating the dubious intra-household services, subsistence elements are present in simple rural construction, firewood collection and the cultivation of food crops. Inspired guesswork would probably indicate that the share of subsistence in the Gross Domestic Product has moved from something like two-thirds in the late 'forties to about one-third in the early 'sixties. These figures are, however, nothing more than a reflection of the imagination of development economists and the result of a statistical auctioneering exercise by national income accountants. But perhaps it is not necessary to invent any such figures, because it is not clear that the time and money spent on estimating the share of subsistence are worth the practical value of the result, at least from a planning standpoint. In recent years, such requirements of planning have come to determine increasingly the character of national accounting study in Nigeria, replacing earlier preoccupation with an accurate measurement of material welfare for international comparison.

Knowing the size of subsistence in the Gross Domestic Product and of inter-temporal changes therein can be useful from the viewpoint of fiscal policy and general resource mobilization. But the unequal tax burden in Nigeria is already a perverse one, in the sense that peasant agriculture bears a load out of proportion to its relative *per capita* income. By making large grants available for public development, the Marketing Board system has turned out to be the greatest fiscal device in a peasant setting engaged in production for export.[1]

This fiscal operation of the Marketing Boards is relevant for our discussion in this section from two points of view. On the one hand,

[1] See Gerald K. Helleiner, 'The Fiscal Role of the Marketing Boards in Nigerian Economic Development, 1947–1961', *Economic Journal*, September, 1964

it weakens the argument of the need to estimate the movement of subsistence in the Gross Domestic Product from the necessity of raising taxes, although it is obviously of theoretical interest if we intend such knowledge for an evaluation of 'true taxable capacity'. On the other hand, in spite of the high incidence of the export tax, agricultural export production—contrary to the prediction of leading Western economists on Africa (notably Professor P. T. Bauer)—has not fallen. Rather, it has kept on increasing faster than agricultural production for domestic use, in spite of the declining trend in export prices. In the decade 1950–60, the volume of production (valued at constant 1957 prices) increased at an average annual rate of 2·1 per cent for agricultural products that were primarily for domestic use (scarcely enough for the population growth) against a corresponding rate of 5·1 per cent for agricultural products that were primarily for export.

The result above throws an interesting light on the structure of the economy. First, because of the nature of products concerned, the production lag for export crops (e.g. cocoa, rubber and palm produce) is on the average much longer than that for domestically consumed crops (e.g. yams, maize and vegetables). Also production in the agricultural sector is by and large specialized between domestic and export markets, and only few items enter both areas in any significant proportion. Second, it follows from the first point that although supply elasticity is high in the Nigerian economy generally, the responsiveness of producers to price changes would be expected to have a much longer lag for export products. Furthermore, the responsiveness operates more effectively upwards than downwards. This would derive from producers' expectation of the future and the greater investment of time, labour and equipment involved in the long gestation period of the export sector. Third, even though export prices have fallen greatly during the period of our analysis, it should be remembered that they have fallen from the artificial heights of the post-war demand in the advanced industrial countries and especially, the great heights of the Korean boom. The lower levels to which they have fallen were still, in many cases, offering producers a greater rate on their investment and on their variable costs (mostly labour) than the corresponding return on production for the domestic market. Even where the rate of return on export production is not demonstrably greater than on the domestic market, the farmer may still not switch his land and labour from production for export. Apart from possible positive expectation of future price behaviour, alternative opportunities available to him were not great, given his state of knowledge, the economy's general level of development and the character of public policy. Where, as in many cases, his variable costs consist mostly of labour effort and where, again as in many cases, the labour belongs to himself and his household, then his variable costs dissolve in fact into fixed costs and the producer will take—at least in the short run—whatever he can get above a zero rate of return. Finally, the dichotomy between export and non-export production performance is a reflection of a colonial-type agricultural policy which concentrates on increasing labour productivity (and consumers surplus) on crops demanded mainly in the metropolitan countries. The historical organization of international trade and the peculiar nature of trade in primary commodities ensure that the benefits of such increased productivity deriving from public expenditure (ironically financed by export taxes on the peasants) accrue mainly to the consumers. The producers get the backwash effect through a subsequent fall in market price brought about by their increased productivity!

5. OTHER KEY INDICATORS

The structure of output can only tell part of the whole complex story of economic change and development policy. The background implications of the output tables are brought out more clearly in the summary indicators contained in Table 5. In view of our earlier discussion of population statistics, rows 19 and 20 of the table should not be taken seriously beyond the general observation that *per capita* income was very low and that its growth through time was very uneven. Row 18 demonstrates clearly the insignificance of direct taxation, but it does not really tell the whole revenue story, since the figures have not been related to other sources of government revenue (especially taxes on foreign trade). Again, much caution is required in interpreting the government expenditure accounts because of various problems of classification, dating, transfers and stages of auditing. These reservations are particularly strong in relating the current to the capital expenditures.

Otherwise, the following story can be constructed on the basis of Table 5 and of supplementary background materials. From Table 3, we have seen that the economy was growing roughly at an average of 4 per cent per annum before allowing for changes in population, and that this rate was remarkably higher in the first half of the period than in the second half. Exports and re-exports remained generally at between one-fifth and one-sixth of the Gross Domestic Product. In spite of increasing import substitution, the ratio of imports to the Gross Domestic Product was increasing through the period from about one-eighth to one-fifth. These movements indirectly reflect the change from a balance of payment surplus in the first half of the period to a deficit in the second half. The weakening of export earning was not due to a decline in the growth rate of production volume but to the secular fall of prices in the world market. The explanation of the rising pace of imports is to be found not so much in the increased importation of capital goods but rather in the high propensity to consume imported consumer goods. The growth of imports during the decade was several times the growth of *per capita* real income. Given the weaknesses in the export trade, the resulting growing balance of payment deficit meant that the rising imports were increasingly financed by drawing down previous foreign exchange reserves, by foreign direct investment and by external aid. Although fiscal measures, starting in the late 'fifties and early 'sixties aimed at reducing the import consumption propensity, these measures were neither stringent nor consistent with other public policies. For one thing, the public sector was at least as extravagant in import demand as the private sector, without the restraint of self-discipline or of effective public opinion. For another, the maintenance of an open door policy in the use of foreign exchange meant that the imposition of moderate tariffs could not significantly reduce the total import bill.

The ratio of capital formation to the Gross Domestic Product virtually doubled within the decade, although the savings-income ratio remained largely unchanged. In the first half of the period, the savings rate was higher than the rate of capital formation, making for the accumulation of reserves (mainly sterling) abroad. In the second half, the savings rate was in general below the rate of capital formation, the difference being financed from decumulation of previous reserves and capital inflow. The positive savings gap in the earlier period is associated with the economy's low absorptive capacity, given the colonial organization and the post-war shortage of development manpower and physical equipment. The negative savings gap in the latter period reflects the failure of public policy to restrain consumption and the existence of profitable opportunities for foreign investment. The striking combination of a falling growth rate in the Gross Domestic Product and a rising rate of capital formation implies a rising gross incremental capital-output ratio, and hence a changing character of investment.

Changes in the structure of capital formation in fact provide a useful insight into the development of the economy as a whole. A summary view of the breakdown of gross fixed investment is contained in Table 6, where the totals are classified both by operating agents and by type of assets. The public sector and the incorporated

Table 5. *Key indicators of economic growth, 1950–60*

Measure	Units	1950	1951	1952	1953	1954	1955	1956	1957	1958	1959	1960
1. Imports (c.i.f.)	£m	61·9	84·6	113·3	108·3	114·1	136·1	152·8	152·5	166·3	178·4	215·9
2. Domestic exports (f.o.b.)	£m	88·5	116·6	125·1	120·9	146·2	129·8	132·3	124·2	132·8	160·5	165·6
3. Re-exports (f.o.b.)	£m	1·7	3·5	4·4	3·3	3·3	2·7	2·3	3·4	2·8	3·0	4·1
4. Domestic exports and re-exports	£m	90·2	120·1	129·5	124·2	149·5	132·5	134·6	127·6	135·6	163·5	169·7
5. Capital formation (Gross)	£m	36·6	36·3	55·7	52·2	60·0	66·9	78·3	97·2	107·1	120·1	133·5
6. Government capital formation (including Corporations)	£m	12·2	14·7	22·4	22·6	24·1	34·3	43·7	38·2	49·8	61·9	61·6
7. Private capital formation	£m	5·8	8·1	33·4	32·1	42·8	44·1	53·6	61·1	59·4	60·9	67·6
8. Government capital/private capital formation	%	210	182	67	70	56	78	82	63	84	102	91
9. GDP at current (factor cost) prices	£m	512·1	573·2	614·5	665·0	774·2	827·5	870·6	910·0	864·9	903·0	918·9
10. Imports/GDP	%	12·1	14·8	18·4	16·3	14·7	16·4	17·5	16·8	19·4	19·8	23·5
11. Exports and re-exports/GDP	%	17·6	20·9	21·1	18·7	19·3	16·0	15·5	14·0	15·7	18·1	18·5
12. Capital formation/GDP	%	7·1	6·3	9·1	7·8	7·8	8·1	9·0	10·7	12·4	13·3	14·5

13. Mid-year population[a]	million	—	—	—	31·6	32·1	32·8	33·4	34·0	34·6	35·3	35·9
14. Direct taxes[b]	£m	4·8	5·3	6·8	—	5·7	6·7	6·8	6·6	6·7	6·7	6·3
15. Current expenditure[c]	£m	—	30·4	43·7	44·1	55·0	60·7	55·4	62·9	65·7	75·4	81·7
16. Capital fund expenditure	£m	—	—	—	—	—	—	—	12·7	17·1	28·1	35·8
17. Capital expenditure/current expenditure	%	—	—	—	—	—	—	—	20·3	26·1	37·2	43·8
18. Tax revenue/GDP	%	0·9	0·9	1·1	—	0·7	0·8	0·7	0·7	0·7	0·7	0·7
19. GDP *per capita*	£	—	—	—	21·1	24·1	25·3	26·1	26·8	26·0	26·6	27·2
20. Growth rate of GDP *per capita*	%		—	—	—	14·2	5·0	3·2	2·6	−3·0	2·3	2·3

Notes: Rows 1–13 relate to calendar years, rows 14–20 to financial years.

a Based on old estimates worked out by the Federal Office of Statistics. These are 2 per cent and 4 per cent rate of growth for the Regions and Lagos respectively.

b The direct taxes include the native direct tax and the income tax for individuals and companies for 1950–53 and for individual and company income taxes for 1954–60.

c Includes Nigerian Government expenditure, Regional grants and allocations and development grants.

Sources: (1) *Nigerian Trade Report*, 1960.
(2) *Report of the Accountant General* (*Federation of Nigeria*) for the years ending 31st March 1950–61.
(3) *Annual Abstract of Statistics*, 1951–60.

Table 6. *Gross capital formation, 1950–60*

£m

Sectors	1950	1951	1952	1953	1954	1955	1956	1957	1958	1959	1960
A. By purchaser											
1. Government	10·0	11·0	13·6	12·9	14·6	20·3	25·3	26·1	34·9	47·1	49·6
2. Corporations	2·2	3·7	8·8	9·7	9·5	14·0	18·4	12·2	14·9	14·7	11·9
3. Companies	5·8	8·1	7·6	9·5	11·7	11·1	13·3	39·5	40·1	37·9	47·5
4. Voluntary agencies	—	—	—	—	—	—	—	1·5	1·6	1·1	1·1
5. Import of equipment not included in 1–4	—	—	10·0	10·1	9·2	11·5	18·3	12·0	9·4	13·4	10·2
6. Accommodation not included in 1–4	—	—	15·8	12·5	21·9	21·5	22·0	8·0	8·3	8·5	8·8
Total	18·0	22·8	55·8	54·7	66·9	78·4	97·3	99·3	109·2	122·7	129·1
B. By type of Assets											
1. Agriculture, land and mining development	—	1·2	1·9	2·5	3·6	4·4	3·5	10·8	14·2	11·6	11·0
2. Building and other construction	—	13·3	34·1	31·3	43·1	48·8	62·0	53·9	59·5	71·3	73·6
3. Plant, machinery and equipment (including vehicles)	—	8·0	6·6	8·2	8·2	7·8	10·5	26·5	24·0	31·2	33·1
4. Vehicles	—	—	13·1	12·6	12·0	17·4	21·2	8·2	11·5	8·7	11·5
Total	18·0	22·5	55·7	54·6	66·9	78·4	97·2	99·4	109·2	122·8	129·2

Note: There are slight differences in the two sets of totals, arising mainly from rounding of component items.

Sources: (1) Federal Office of Statistics.

(2) *Accountant General's* (*Federation of Nigeria*) *Reports* for the years ending March 31, 1957–60.

private enterprises dominated investment activity, especially at the growing points of the economy. Building and other construction combined, accounted for more than half of total expenditure on fixed assets. Machinery and equipment formed just about one-quarter of total investment expenditure. Although changes in inventories are excluded, it is doubtful if they would have significantly affected the stated figures to derive gross domestic capital formation. The overall pattern is clear. Nigerian capital formation during the periods under reference was heavily biased in favour of residential construction and not much conducive to expanding the true productive capacity of the economy. This fact is worsened by an observed phenomenon, namely that many residential buildings outside the main cities are inefficiently utilized.

And not only was the share of residential construction in gross capital formation substantial, it was rising over the period of our analysis and experienced about the highest price increment of all fixed assets.[1] The building boom itself exerted a more powerful influence on the industrial sector than manufacturing and processing. But apart from the once-over multiplier effect of such impact, its importance for sustained development is doubtful, considering the over-riding need to expand and utilize productive capacity.

6. DEVELOPMENT STRATEGY

The need for sustained development raises the question of capacity utilization and inevitably leads, in the Nigerian context, to a consideration of public policy. While there are many strands to such policy, the most coherent framework in which they can be analysed and appraised is the operation of the development plans or programmes. A sketchy view of the annual expenditure under a series of development programmes between 1951 and 1959 is presented in Table 7. Actually, a national development plan, in any dynamic and integrated sense of the term, came only in 1962—after the main period of our analysis. But there has been no absence of development guidelines in Nigeria, at any rate since the introduction in 1946 of the Ten-Year Development and Welfare Programme.

By and large, Nigerian planning effort has been characterized by a great deal of underspending and weak administrative control. These considerations offer a useful point of reflection on the concept, organization and effectiveness of economic planning in the country.

1 The overall rising proportion of construction in gross capital formation is however to be explained more by a change in volume than by a change in price.

Table 7. *Development plan annual expenditure, 1951–1959*
(£m)

Expenditure heads	1951	1952	1953	1954	1955	1956	1957	1958	1959
Agriculture and veterinary	0·5	0·6	0·8	0·6	1·4	1·9	1·8	2·5	2·8
Irrigation									
Other water development									
Roads	0·7	1·2	1·0	1·1	3·4	6·4	7·5	8·3	13·4
Railways	—	—	1·1	2·2	4·4	4·1	5·8	7·7	7·8
Other means of communications (including harbours and waterways, aviation, posts and telecommunications)	0·2	0·2	3·7	4·4	1·6	3·2	3·8	7·9	11·7
Electricity and power	—	—	3·0	2·8	2·0	1·6	1·8	2·6	4·3
Education	1·4	1·6	3·3	2·7	2·6	3·1	3·4	3·6	5·0
Health	0·8	0·8	0·7	0·5	2·3	2·4	1·7	1·6	3·6
Urban services (water supplies)	0·8	1·2	0·8	0·4	1·2	1·6	1·6	2·7	4·7
Other social services	0·2	0·2	—	—	0·6	1·7	1·8	5·0	2·9
Miscellaneous public works (Public Works Department)	—	—	1·6	1·8	0·8	1·4	1·0	1·1	1·2
Remainder (unclassified)	0·4	0·6	2·5	2·8	5·8	9·4	7·0	14·4	22·4
Total	5·0	6·4	18·5	19·3	26·1	36·8	37·2	57·4	79·8

Sources: (1) *Nigerian National Accounts 1950–57* by P. N. C. Okigbo.
(2) *Accountant General's Reports*, *Federation of Nigeria*, for the years ending March 31, 1956–60.

One big factor in the Nigerian case is the fact of federalism with its intense party political rivalry. Decentralization of power had become such a prominent feature of its political and economic organization that it can be too readily forgotten that Nigeria had a common development programme until the introduction of a regional government system in the early 1950's. The 1946–56 Programme was drawn up under one governmental machinery, even though some of the ideas for welfare facilities were generated in a decentralized manner from the village level upwards through the district, divisional and provincial levels to the government secretariat in Lagos. The four 1956–60 Economic Programmes (one for the Federal Government and one each for the Regional Governments) which followed the report of the World Bank Mission, however, reflected the political spirit of the period; namely, the concentration of effective power and leadership in the regional capitals. The National Economic Council was more a platform of consultation and bargaining than a fulcrum for a cohesive national development.

It is therefore easy to appreciate the difficulties of constructing national statistical tables in an area of policy like planning, where different governments in the country employed different formats of presentation.[1] The preparation of a consolidated functional economic classification of government accounts has proved unusually difficult in Nigeria; and it is not surprising that different authors have come out with different results for particular rows or columns of the consolidated tables. The information in Tables 7–9 is thus to be interpreted with great caution because of the inherent statistical defects in such consolidation. But for whatever it is worth, Table 7 demonstrates two significant points. First, there was a substantial increment in government development expenditure: the figure of £5 millions in 1951 appears insignificant when related to the figure of nearly £80 millions eight years later. This was an unmistakable indication that the task of development was now being faced with greater determination and that the public sector was becoming an increasing instrument of economic intervention. Second, the emphasis on the so-called development infrastructure and social overheads during this period is brought out. Production expansion of agricultural and industrial goods was being encouraged indirectly through public investment in

[1] Even in the post-independence so-called National Plan, it is not easy to derive national sectoral figures by adding up regional components. This is illustrated by the footnote to Tables 5–9 in the plan document, *Federation of Nigeria; National Development Plan 1962–68*, Federal Ministry of Economic Development, Lagos, 1962, p. 41. See also E. O. Obayan: 'The Machinery of Planning in the Federation of Nigeria', *Nigerian Journal of Economic and Social Studies*, Vol. 4, No. 3, November, 1962.

transportation facilities, power, water, education and health programmes.

It is natural to ask why, if public investment as reflected by the figures in Table 8 was increasing by such an enormous magnitude (sixteen times in eight years), the growth in *per capita* real incomes did not show a more impressive performance. The obvious answer is that the long investment gestation period would make the growth in real income lag behind growth in investment. But when we extend the national income data into the 'sixties, the expected growth after some

Table 8. *How plan was to be financed, 1955–62 combined*

	Value (£ m)	Percentage Distribution
Taxation (contributions from revenue reserves) including accumulated surpluses	137·3	40·5
Official internal loans	47·7	14·0
Official external loans (IBRD and UK Government)	25·0	7·4
Grants by marketing boards (internal)	12·8	3·8
External grants	21·1	6·2
Miscellaneous internal sources	5·0	1·5
Gap[a]	27·0	8·0
Statutory bodies	63·3	18·6
Total	339·2	100·0

Note: [a] The gap in the Governments' estimated share in the plan was to be met by entering into contracts for deferred payments.

Source: Economic Survey of Nigeria 1959.

reasonable average lag of say five years still does not reflect impressive performance. Any full explanation must therefore take us back to the character of aggregate capital formation. Table 7 only tells us the financial expenditure totals, not the actual net addition to physical productive capacity. The public sector maintained just about the same proportion of fixed capital formation at the end of the decade as at the beginning, which reflects that the private sector was still the senior partner, accounting for about 70 per cent of total investment expenditure, of which, as we have seen, much consisted of residential construction by households. Neither the private sector as a whole nor the combined public authorities altered to any significant extent the composition of their capital formation throughout the decade. Beyond that, given the political character of government, capital costs in the public sector had increased out of proportion to real addition to physical assets; and, as we have shown, most of these assets were in any case not in the directly productive areas.

A complete evaluation of the impact of public policy on the pace and character of economic development, must take into account the qualitative aspect of governmental intervention. Given the same physical and financial resources in a given country to two governments with different ideological temperaments, we would expect the result of their development planning to be different. The difference would arise from the differing patterns of capital formation deriving from their respective views of the development process. It would also arise from their differing set of policy decisions which might or might not be reflected in the investment figures but which would nevertheless, influence how effectively the economy's productive capacity is utilized. The incidence of capacity utilization would influence their socio-economic development. Government policy (or absence of a policy) in the areas of fiscal-monetary controls, wages and income distribution, price formation and price control, agriculture, industry and commerce, would substantially determine the profitability and efficiency of investment. The sum total of these policies would in turn reflect not only the character of the nation's economic organization but also the quality of its political leadership.

To the extent that one can talk at all of a definite development strategy in Nigeria for the decade before Independence, it can be characterized as diffused and weak public intervention. Potentially, the public sector had the size, resources and opportunity to determine substantially the pace and path of the nation's economic development. The size shows in the usual statistical indicators, but inefficient resource use and valuable lost opportunities do not. No matter how large the public sector even in the area of capital formation, it was really a story of the tail of foreign private enterprise wagging the dog of government's economic policy. The energy of the public sector itself was sapped by a fiercely competitive federalism which prevailed in the absence of a strong, dynamic central political leadership. Moreover, politicians formed a strong alliance with foreign enterprise, which by nature of its history, purpose, resourcefulness and style of operation was able to wield power beyond any magnitude which can be demonstrated by appealing to conventional statistics of investment and growth. Furthermore, the size of the foreign enterprise sector was certainly not inconsequential. Small as was its role in financing capital formation in the early years of the decade, its relative share was becoming increasingly important as Independence approached. Apart from official grants and borrowings, the net inflow of private capital alone tripled within the decade and was directed to the growing and policy-sensitive points of the economy: manufactures, commerce, banking and finance.

The approach to development planning itself was half-hearted. A hindsight developed in later official planning effort has enabled many to see the weaknesses of the earlier plans in a better perspective.[1] One can do little better than quote at length from an authoritative official document on the subject matter:

'These (i.e. the 1945–56 plans, with special reference to the period 1951–56) were not "plans" in the true sense of the word. More accurately, they constituted a series of projects which had not been co-ordinated or related to any overall economic target. Many of the individual schemes proposed no more than an expansion of existing normal department activities and, in large measure, the schemes aimed at building up the social as much as the economic services.

'The main emphasis in these Plans was confined to building up the transport and communications systems. Whilst this in itself was understandable under the circumstances of the time, little provision was made for industrial development whilst, in the agricultural sector, attention was concentrated on a limited range of export crops.

'One major error which was frequently permitted was that entirely new and unrelated projects were readily substituted for the original programmes without proper analysis and co-ordination with other projects. The justification given was "flexibility". This arose because no firm economic targets had been fixed when preparing the Plans. The net effect was that, by the end of the plan period, the results bore little, if any, relationship to the original programmes.

'. . . Understandably perhaps, each Government jealously guarded its own rights and obligations arising from the new Constitution. From the point of view of planning, however, this was inevitably an unsatisfactory situation since it resulted in five separate development programmes (including one for the then Southern Cameroons) . . . there was necessarily considerable overlapping and wasted effort.

'No economic targets were—or could be—fixed for the country as a whole and, although the National Economic Council was established late in 1955 to permit the various Governments to discuss development policies and common economic problems, the programmes had already been formulated by that time. This fact, combined with the relative isolation in which Government programmes were conceived and executed and the infrequent meetings of the Council, meant that

[1] See, for example, Douglas Dosser, 'The Formation of Development Plans in British Colonies', *Economic Journal*, June 1959, pp. 255–66.

although much useful work was achieved on certain specific subjects the problem of reformulating plans to fit into the picture of the overall future of the Nigerian economy could not be undertaken. . . .'[1]

In the statements of the planners (mostly Colonial Civil Service administrative officers), the whole purpose of the Plans was to provide a means of breaking the so-called vicious circle of poverty.[2] The publication in 1946 of the Ten-Year Development and Welfare Plan was supposed to serve as a call to economic progress. But there was neither the grass-root organization nor the central machinery for effective and systematic co-ordination of all sectors of the national economy to give serious meaning to the clarion call. Moreover, there was no coherent underlying philosophy to guide the pace and character of development through public intervention. For the colonial areas in general in their post-war plans, Phyllis Deane had recalled that to the extent that there was any underlying philosophy, 'it was that the government's role in the economy was to spend money in the socially desirable directions neglected by private enterprise'.[3] But even in this vague and limited objective,[4] there was indeed a contrast between lofty statements of principle and the lowly statistics of achievement (even if not of target).

Nigerian planning experience has been characterized from the beginning by persistent underfulfilment. This is only partly accounted for by defects in the Plans' design. More important were the great difficulties in recruitment of skilled staff and supply of capital equipment (both depending substantially on imports), given the general post-war shortage in the colonies. The Public Works Department was seriously undermanned; and private construction firms had not developed. It is easy to appreciate in this circumstance why schemes which depended least on imported materials and technical advice advanced most rapidly and were completed soonest.[5] For example,

1 *National Development Plan, 1962–68, op. cit.*, pp. 6–7, paragraphs 2–5.

2 For the motives behind the Colonial Development and Welfare Acts generally, see Phyllis Deane, *Colonial Social Accounting*, Cambridge University Press, 1953, p. 516. Enlightened self-interest on the part of the colonial power was an unmistakable, strong motive. As the colonial governor, Sir Arthur Richards (now Lord Milverton), also remarked in a speech to the Nigerian Legislative Council on March 5, 1945, the whole exercise was closely related to political development.

3 Phyllis Deane: *op. cit.*, p. 6.

4 *The 1951–52 Annual Report on the Plan* contains (in paragraph 8) the intriguing statement that 'The Revised Plan is not an end in itself, it aims at no single goal since development is a continual goal.'

5 Sometimes, a whole project could depend on one man. For example, work on rural water supplies in Abeokuta Province had to be suspended when the Inspector of Works was on leave (*1949–50 Annual Report on the Development and*

by the end of the 1950–51 financial year, about £34 million of the proposed £55 million for the plan period still remained unspent. It is obvious that within the framework of public policy as reflected in the Plans, the bottlenecks against a more impressive growth of the economy were men and materials, not finance. Indeed, the accumulated reserves were getting so large as the Korean crisis echoed through the early fifties that they were becoming almost a source of embarrassment—an underdeveloped economy with a capital surplus side by side with a rich development potential and a slow growth rate! Evidently, something must be wrong with its economic organization and the content of its public policy.

As the 1950's progressed, the supply position of both manpower and materials eased; but the underfulfilment of plan targets persisted. This raises a presumption of the existence of other intervening variables. An unpublished official report[1] in fact confirmed the existence of widespread weakness in the administrative machinery of development. The Public Works Department, for example, complained that the road tarring programme was delayed, not only by a short supply of bitumen, but also because they had to scatter their resources of men and equipment in an inefficient manner. Apparently, the politicians wanted to show quick results to their electors, and tarred roads were visible achievements of economic progress. The pressure of parliamentary government was stretching thin the economy's already slender absorptive capacity.

7. FINANCING THE PUBLIC SECTOR

The long period of financial surplus combined with a defective administrative machinery deriving from a weak political leadership had created a false sense of opulence. Even when the financial circumstances changed in the latter 1950's, the ingrained feeling of affluence prevented a timely appreciation of the real problems of development. Financial discipline and financial efficiency have not, until very lately, been characteristic features of Nigeria's economic scene. Although within the strategy of development being pursued, finance was still not the most crucial bottleneck, the overflowing financial surplus of the early 'fifties had declined rapidly by the achievement of Independence. The prospect of monetary capital

Welfare Schemes, paragraph 11). A similar story could be written for physical resources: the shortage of dock capacity was very serious and shipping piled up queing to get in, even when shipping conditions eased in Europe.

[1] *Report on the Economic Programmes* by the Federal Economic Adviser, addressed to the Prime Minister, April 1958.

shortage was becoming real, even within the relaxed philosophy of cautious development.

The extent to which the financial picture had been transformed within a short period can be illustrated by comparing the 50 per cent external finance target of the 1962–68 National Plan with the 20 per cent[1] equivalent target of the 1955–62 programmes. Table 9 shows the decisive role that domestic resources were still supposed to play as late as 1955. The bulk of the Programme was to be financed by drawing down the previously accumulated reserves, by official internal loans and by the internal resources of the public corporations. In fact, judging from Table 9 this expectation was confirmed. The most important single source of actual finance of the plans was Taxation and Reserve. But a rough comparison of Tables 8 and 9 shows that official internal loans played a more important role than was anticipated—about two-and-a-half times more than the plan design. The importance of official external loans was also about 50 per cent more than was expected by the time the plan was realized in 1960. However, about 80 per cent of the total costs of the plan still came from the public sector.

A summary analysis of the Federal Government accounts (Tables 10 and 11) brings out the essential features of Nigeria's public finance in the decade before Independence. With only slight modifications, these features are still characteristic of the country's finance today. The crucial importance of taxes on production and on expenditure is well brought out. Import duties are the most important single source of revenue, being in general far more important than the sum total of all taxes on income. Income tax especially was far less important. Total receipts of Government were also rising, over the period even if unevenly; the upward changes being particularly steep in 1960 for personal income tax, import duties and transfers from abroad.

Given the administrative simplicity of duties on external trade (compared with income taxation), it is not surprising that public finance should depend substantially on the foreign trade sector. But since such duties constituted an indirect outlay tax, it is reasonable to presume that the tax structure was regressive.[2] This would be particularly true of the regional governments, who depended far

1 That is if we assume that the bulk of the deferred payment contracts to bridge the 'Gap' is financed from outside. To this, we add the external loans and grants.

2 To the extent that particular trade items can be traced to particular income groups, such taxes need not in principle be regressive. In the Nigerian factual situation, this was either not practicable or it operated in a perverse manner (as in the case of a tax on peasant production.)

Table 9. *How plan was financed, 1950–60*
(£m)

Sources	1950	1951	1952	1953	1954	1955	1956	1957	1958	1959	1960	Cumulative 1955–60	% Distribution 1955–60
Taxation, reserves and balances	2·6	1·8	—	—	8·3	6·9	8·6	13·6	14·2	3·0	—	46·3	43·5
Official internal loans	9·5	0·5	—	—	—	2·0	7·6	6·5	8·9	10·9	1·9	37·8	35·5
Official external loans	—	—	—	—	—	—	—	—	6·9	4·3	0·1	11·3	10·6
Total official loans[a]	9·5	0·5	—	—	—	2·0	7·6	6·5	15·8	15·2	2·0	49·1	46·1
Grants	3·3	4·9	21·1	6·3	6·5	2·0	1·6	5·1	2·2	0·0	0·2	11·1	10·4
Total	15·4	7·2	21·1	6·3	14·8	10·9	17·8	25·2	32·2	18·2	2·2	106·5	100·0

Note: [a] Figures exclude loans from quasi-government institutions to Regional Governments.

Sources: (1) *Accountant General's Reports* (*Federation of Nigeria*) for the years ending March 31, 1950–61.
(2) *Reports of Regional Marketing Boards* 1954–60.
(3) *Reports on Federal and Regional Economic and Development Programmes* (1955–60).
(4) *Regional and Federal Development Finance* 1955–60.

Table 10. *Federal Government Account (current), 1950–60: receipts*
(£m)

Heads	1950	1951	1952	1953	1954	1955	1956	1957	1958	1959	1960
Interest and dividends from outside Federal Government	0·6	1·2	1·5	1·4	1·3	0·6	2·7	3·6	2·6	2·3	8·0
Income tax (individuals)	1·3	1·5	—	1·1	1·1	1·4	1·6	1·7	2·1	2·3	6·6
Income tax (companies)	4·1	5·3	5·8	4·6	5·6	5·3	5·0	5·0	4·6	4·0	4·8
Export duties and excise	4·8	12·6	14·1	17·8	17·6	13·3	13·2	12·7	16·2	16·7	14·6
Other	0·1	0·2	0·2	0·1	0·2	0·2	0·1	0·0	0·0	0·0	2·6
Total taxes on income	10·3	19·6	20·1	23·6	24·5	20·2	19·9	19·4	22·9	23·0	28·6
Import duties	11·7	16·7	17·6	20·8	22·8	27·6	33·2	34·5	35·2	41·2	54·8
Excise duties	1·6	2·6	3·1	3·4	3·4	3·7	4·3	4·3	4·4	5·1	6·2
Royalties	0·9	1·6	1·6	1·3	2·0	1·5	1·6	1·2	0·8	1·2	1·4
Other (licences etc.)[a]	0·5	0·7	0·2	0·1	0·2	0·3	0·1	0·3	0·5	0·6	4·2
Total taxes on production and expenditure	14·7	21·6	22·5	25·6	28·4	33·1	39·2	40·3	40·9	48·1	66·6
Current transfers from abroad	0·4	0·5	—	0·4	0·6	0·5	0·5	1·1	2·2	2·6	7·7
Miscellaneous receipts (other)	6·8	7·8	6·9	5·3	4·8	2·1	2·7	3·1	4·8	6·5	5·6
Total	32·8	50·7	51·0	56·3	59·6	56·5	65·0	67·5	73·4	82·5	116·5

Note: [a] Figures on licences on motor vehicles cover a period of 15 months, which include twice the heaviest quarter for collection.
Sources: (1) *Accountant General's Report (Federation of Nigeria)* for the years ending March 31, 1950–1960.
(2) *Economic and Functional Analysis of Government Accounts (Draft) 1958–59—1961–62.*

Table 11. *Federal Government Account (current), 1950–60: expenditure*
(£m)

Heads	1950	1951	1952	1953	1954	1955	1956	1957	1958	1959	1960
Agriculture, forestry, fisheries, veterinary	0·4	0·4	0·3		0·8	1·0	1·1	0·8	1·7	1·9	0·7
Mines and power	1·2	0·4	0·3		0·8	0·8	0·9	0·6	1·1	0·8	3·2
Other	6·3	5·1	3·9		12·8	10·4	12·7	11·9	14·6	8·9	15·6
Total economic services	7·9	5·9	4·5		14·4	12·2	14·7	13·3	17·4	11·6	19·5
Roads	1·8	2·6	4·0		4·3	5·5	3·5	3·8	4·1	4·9	8·2
Township development	0·8	3·8	4·3		1·4	—	—	—	—	—	—
Other	—	—	—		0·1	0·0	0·0	0·0	0·6	0·5	6·1
Total community services	2·6	6·4	8·3		5·8	5·5	3·5	3·8	4·7	5·4	14·3
Education	0·3	0·4	0·1		0·2	0·5	0·5	0·8	2·5	2·7	5·6
Health	0·7	0·7	0·4		0·7	1·2	1·0	1·0	2·2	2·5	2·3
Other	1·6	1·7	1·9		2·2	2·7	3·9	3·8	4·3	4·6	1·5
Total social services	2·6	2·8	2·4		3·1	4·4	5·4	5·6	9·0	9·8	9·4
Administration, law and order	2·1	2·6	2·4		3·7	4·9	5·2	6·2	7·3	9·4	23·6
Other Services[a]	15·0	27·4	26·5		41·7	34·7	33·4	36·3	35·7	43·9	35·8
Balance (surplus and deficit on current account)	+2·6	+5·6	+6·9		−9·0	−5·2	+2·8	+2·3	−0·7	+2·4	13·9
Total	32·8	50·7	51·0	56·3	59·6	56·5	65·0	67·5	73·4	82·5	116·5

Note: [a] Include statutory appropriations to regional governments.
Sources: (1) *Accountant General's Report (Federation of Nigeria)* for the years ending March 31, 1950–60.
(2) *Economic and Functional Analysis of Government Accounts (Draft) 1958–59—1961–62.*

more on revenue from external trade through transfers from the Federal Government and especially through fiscal manipulations by the Marketing Boards. As the governments were under increasing pressure to find additional revenue to finance expanding services (even more so for current consumption than for capital formation), they turned increasingly to taxes on exports. Although import duties were also being raised, the purpose here had now become associated with reducing the rising balance of payment deficit rather than increasing revenue.[1]

Our concentration on the Federal Government accounts has ignored some interesting differences in revenue structure among different governments of the country. For example, the Eastern Region has for long had a higher proportion of its total revenue from personal income taxation than any other government in the Federation. Before Independence, it was budgeting at times for up to one-third of its total revenue to be derived from direct taxation. And even later, when petroleum royalties came on the scene, almost one-fifth of its total revenue was derived from personal income tax alone. The other regional governments depended less on personal income tax; and the Federal Government depended most on import duties (with the possible exception of the Mid-West Government) and in recent years has depended least on personal income tax (again with the possible exception of the Mid-West). The Western Region in general depended most, of all the governments, on export tax as a proportion of total revenue.[2]

One special source of finance which affected the level of development performance but which cannot be inferred directly from revenue statistics was deferred payment. In Nigeria, since the late 1950's, this has become an increasingly important source of financing capital projects. With constant practice, negotiation for contractor finance and supplier's credit has been developed almost to a fine art. The great pity is that it opened up potential opportunities for political corruption and distortion of capital costs through the varying proportion of contract-kick-backs received by the policy makers. Although the importance of this source of finance was not yet as

[1] Given the high propensity to import, the low price elasticity of demand for imported goods and the normal expansion of import demand for a developing economy, the total yield from import duties was increasing. It would presumably have increased more had the duties not been raised to dampen consumption. Nevertheless, import tax yield had increased faster than total revenue.

[2] For more detailed analysis of the differing revenue structure in the post-Independence period, see Adebayo Adedeji, 'The Future of Personal Income Taxation in Nigeria', *Nigerian Journal of Economic & Social Studies*, Vol. 7, No. 2, July 1965, pp. 159–74.

great as in some other African and Latin American countries, there is little doubt that it had been growing rapidly since Independence and that the opportunities for abuse were already manifestly exploited. As a study on this subject remarked:

'maintenance of national plan priorities is oftener than not, incompatible with short-term credit proposals. In the case of Nigeria, some projects implemented by this method are not even in the National Development Plan 1962–68. Experience has shown that the momentum generated behind a contractor finance project soon develops into an avalanche sweeping overboard all rational considerations!'[1]

However, the increasing reliance on short-term credits (provided mostly by foreign suppliers and contractors) was only an aspect of the increasing general reliance on loans. The financial structure of the public sector had changed in the 1960's from the position of the late 1940's and early 1950's. Far from relying on current revenue with an overflowing reserve, the depleted total foreign exchange reserve was approaching the rule-of-thumb critical minimum level of four months import bill conventionally recommended by international development and loan agencies. Projects were becoming more and more financed as a draft on the future. But by and large, the conservative monetary policy pursued by the Federal Government prevented the tap of Central Bank deficit being turned on beyond the legal fiduciary limit, which had been fixed rather low (in practice if not in law) compared with prevailing levels in some underdeveloped countries.

8. AGRICULTURE

It is commonplace to describe Nigeria as an agricultural country. If by this we mean that the country's long-term comparative development advantage lies in agriculture, the statement is at best of dubious validity if not positively misleading. If we mean that its agricultural potentialities are being developed to the fullest, this is not evident to a careful observer. But if the assertion reflects nothing more than the static fact of occupational distribution and the activity source of national income, it is at once true and trite. At the achievement of Independence, agriculture alone still accounted for about half of the Gross Domestic Product; and when other similar primary activities like livestock, forestry and fishing are added, the share rose to about

[1] A. A. Ayida, 'Contractor Finance and Supplier Credit in Economic Growth'. *Nigerian Journal of Economic & Social Studies*, Vol. 7, No. 2, July 1965, p. 183.

three-fifths of total output. About three-quarters of the population were engaged in all such activities.

But the importance of agriculture to the economy goes beyond such simple aggregative ratios. Mention has been made of the dynamic importance of external trade to the growth of the economy during the period under review. Although only about one fifth of agricultural output was exported, this constituted about four-fifths of total export value. And although only about one-tenth of the Gross Domestic Product derived directly from agricultural export, its contribution to the growth and transformation of the national economy assumes a much bigger proportion when the crucial importance of the Marketing Boards as a fiscal device is recalled. The general impact of government activity as a developmental agency derived significantly during the period under reveiw from the wealth generated from agricultural production.

The character of Nigerian agriculture is of course, a function of its economic geographic features. The dominant vegetation consists of the tropical rain forest and the guinea savanna. Except in the swampy Delta area and the arid far-North, the bulk of the country has a balanced moisture and is well drained; the rain forest gradually thinning up northwards in successive belts of mangroves, clustered trees, scattered woods, tall grasses, open grassland and sandy patches. This vegetation variation not only reflects the varying incidence of rainfall and temperature, but also gives the country its heterogeneous soil composition. The geological foundation, surface physical formation (of terrains and river basins), climatic variation and multiplicity of soil types all combine to give Nigeria its diversity of agricultural products—cocoa, oil palm, rubber, timber and other tree crops; maize, guinea corn, yam, coffee, cassava, rice, groundnuts, millet, cowpeas, citrus fruits and other food crops; cattle, goats, sheep, poultry, bush meat, and other livestock; cotton, tobacco, sugar cane and other agro-industrial raw materials.

Yet only about 10 per cent of Nigeria's 357,000 square miles is under cultivation, and there is a serious deficiency of protein intake. In spite of the large estimated total population, the land-labour ratio is quite high, even given the prevailing hoe and matchet technique of agricultural production. The degree of land utilization is however not evenly spread, as is revealed from the population density pattern indicated in Table 1. The West is the most urban, the East the most intensively cultivated and the North the most sparsely settled. But in general absolute scarcity of land is not the most serious nor even a terribly important constraint on greater expansion of agricultural production. This is still so notwithstanding the existence of large tracts of uncultivable (because geographically and economically as yet unsuitable) land in the Middle Belt and the coastal swamps. There are also large areas of suitable but uncultivated land in many parts of the country; not to mention the enormous government forest and game reserves. The traditional land tenure system is often claimed to be an effective institutional bottleneck against agricultural expansion. But it has not really been demonstrated that land-use availability under the system (as distinct from out-right land ownership) is unresponsive to appropriate economic incentives. On the contrary, there is little doubt that throughout the 1950's a great deal of extra land was brought under cultivation to expand agricultural output, especially the output of food crops in the North and of tree crops in the West and Mid-West.

Indeed, a characteristic feature of Nigerian agricultural organization is that it has been able to develop hitherto without destroying its peasant basis. For how long it could or it should continue to do so in the future, is a question which can only be answered within the total dynamic complex of economic development and social change. Simply as a positive statement, it is not in doubt that the typical unit of agricultural production is the peasant family and that the plantation system is not yet of great relative importance. In spite of government's incentives to private foreign investment in plantation agriculture (mostly tree crops and exportable products) and an expanded programme of farm settlements and similar novel organizations, the peasant farming system still forms the submerged part of the agricultural iceberg—probably still about 95 per cent of total output.

The peasant technique of production is very simple, making much use of unskilled manpower and few implements. There are very small monetary inputs of material (like fertilizers) and of physical equipment (like farm machines). The prevailing form of cultivation, outside areas under tree crops, is the bush-fallow system which makes a heavy demand on cultivable land space. But as long as the land-labour ratio remains high (which is exceptionally not the case in the Eastern region, especially in Annang and Owerri provinces), a shortage of land is not a serious factor in increasing production and productivity. With the available technique of production, the price-cost constellation facing the farmer and the socio-cultural ethos of the farming community, it is believed that the peasant organization in Nigeria has been both efficient and responsive to market incentives.[1] The propagation of improved-quality

[1] See for example P. T. Bauer, *West African Trade*, Cambridge University Press, 1954; and R. Galletti, K. D. S. Baldwin, and I. O. Dina, *Nigerian Cocoa Farmers*, Oxford University Press, 1956, ch. IV.

cotton and tobacco for domestic manufacture—not to mention the quality transformation of Marketing Board products—has been successfully achieved under the peasant system by relying substantially on discriminatory price incentives. Looking to the future, however, and conceiving efficiency in a less static framework, it is doubtful if the bush-fallow system (and hence its complementary production technique) can for long withstand the requirements of faster economic growth. As was recently remarked:

'A stage seems to have been reached in the development of Nigeria and other African countries when a more permanent system of farming must replace the traditional system of shifting cultivation if farms are to produce enough food to meet the needs of an expanding population, and supply in adequate quantities the raw material requirements of growing industries.'[1]

Whatever the direction of organizational changes that may be required in the future, the peasant system has so far performed reasonably well in both the domestic and export markets. In most cases in fact, it is usual to find both export crop and domestic foodstuff being cultivated side by side in the same area and on the same farm unit. Although ecological variations have facilitated some degree of locational specialization by region, there is very little specialization by type of markets. By the same token, there is scarcely an area of the country producing completely for monetary exchange, or another which is producing completely for barter or self-subsistence. Market participation is widespread; which suggests that the familiar thesis of Dualism in the development literature cannot be validly applied to the Nigerian case today. The export sector is not owned (though is manipulated directly or remotely) by a foreign enclave. Production for export is still dominated by peasants. The 'traditional' sector (meaningful only in a technological sense) produces both for the market and for self-consumption; and is well integrated with the 'modern' sector by a complex network of transport, commerce and finance.[2] There is no clear sense in which a 'Subsistence sector' can be said to be isolated from the 'cash economy'. Only in a national

[1] H. A. Oluwasanmi and A. A. Fayemi, 'Costs, Returns and Profitability of Crop Rotation under Peasant Conditions', *Bulletin of Rural Economics and Sociology*, Department of Agricultural Economics, University of Ibadan, Vol. 1, No. 1, 1964, p. 33.

[2] For a recent quantitative analysis of this interesting subject, see A. M. Hay and R. H. T. Smith, 'Preliminary Estimates of Nigeria's Inter-regional Trade and Associated Money Flows', *Nigerian Journal of Economic & Social Studies*, Vol. 8, No. 1, March 1966, pp. 9–35.

accounts sense can one talk of the share of subsistence or non-marketed component of output. And any such share is probably a declining proportion of the Gross Domestic Product; perhaps two-thirds in the early 'fifties compared with about one-third at the end of the decade. But no one really knows the correct magnitude of subsistence output for certain.

As already indicated peasant farmers, although numerous and predominant, do not account for the whole of agricultural output. Indeed, the growing points of the sector are due more to the new forms of organization than to the peasant units. With larger holdings, more sophisticated production techniques, better credit facilities and above all better management skills, there is little doubt that these newer forms of cultivation could be more productive both of land and labour. The simplest (and probably earliest) improvement was from the mixed farming practice in the North, where animal manures were fed into arable land to make possible permanent cultivation of groundnut, cotton and rice. But this by itself did not guarantee large consolidation of peasant holdings, although it made possible higher yields per man-acre. The plantation system proper was to be found on a medium scale in the rubber, cocoa, oil palm and timber farms of the Nigerian middle-class in the Southern regions, and on a large scale in the tree-crop concessions of integrated foreign enterprises (such as the United Africa Company) and in the farm projects of public agencies (such as the various regional Development Corporations). Not only have all these made permanent cultivation possible; they have replaced the harvesting of wild trees by a scientific husbandry which consumes more non-labour inputs but yields greater returns per man-acre.

Most of the plantations produced for the export market, as evidenced by the almost total absence of domestic foodstuff from their composition of output. Some produced for internal industrial processing, as in the case of oil palm, rubber and citrus fruits. But apparently, the plantation system was either not willing or not competitively able to enter the field of domestic food production at the going market prices. And even in the area of export crops, the expansion has not been spectacular over the last two decades. In spite of the intricate land tenure system, it has not been demonstrated that the real constraint on a massive expansion of output is from that quarter. Instead, the blame is often put on the unstable nature of world market prices for primary products and the fiscal operation of the monopolistic Marketing Boards which reduced the freedom of price formation by the plantations. Whether or not this blame is valid, or how far it is valid, a complete view of plantation development in

Nigeria is not possible without looking at the international organizational structure of the foreign concerns. By and large, those concerns were vertically integrated enterprises interested in specific raw materials or semi-finished products for their parent manufacturing firms in the Metropolitan countries. Whether or not they expand, or how far they expand, would therefore depend on a greater number of variables than the mere fact of internal investment opportunities in Nigeria. In any case, with the possible exceptions of rubber and oil palm, it has been demonstrated by agricultural developers that plantations offered the best hope for the transformation of agriculture and the promotion of general economic growth.

A new form of organization which came and spread on the Nigerian agricultural scene during the 1950's was the Farm-Settlement. The inspiration derived from the successful co-operative farming experiment in Israel, the *Moshav*. The transfer of this experiment so far has been confined to the Southern regions. In transporting the concept to Nigeria the operational manifestation, skilled management, joint marketing and supervised credit were all preserved in varying degrees. But the *Moshavim* itself or the composite village organization, its spiritual strength, its 'frontier' social atmosphere and the integrated cultural revivalism associated with Israeli rural life were not in evidence on the Nigerian scene.[1] The Nigerian Farm Settlement scheme was supposed to do varied and slightly different things, all at the same time. These included raising agricultural land-labour productivity, providing employment opportunity for school leavers, stemming the trend of rural depopulation, demonstrating the high profitability of farming and fostering the general pace of economic development. But what about the result? It has certainly not grappled with the unemployment problem. Whatever the scheme has achieved in showing that rural life can be glamorous and profitable, it has not succeeded in spreading the new production technique to the surrounding peasant farms. There are sharp discontinuities between the two systems as to the level of technology, provision of overhead capital, scale of government subsidy and institutional factors affecting social mobility.

Whatever the original attractions and present merits of the Farm Settlement, its usefulness as an approach to massive agricultural transformation in Nigeria is of doubtful validity, at any rate in the

[1] For a discussion of the adaptation experience of Israeli agricultural co-operatives to Afro-Asian countries and particularly to Western and Eastern Nigeria, see Mordechai E. Kreinin, *Israel and Africa—A Study in Technical Co-operation*, Frederick A. Praeger, New York—Praeger Special Studies in International Economics, 1964, Part 11, Chapters 3–4, especially pp. 48–52.

form in which it operates at present. Any realistic approach to rural modernization in the country, as indeed elsewhere in the underdeveloped world, must build on the peasant base of the agricultural iceberg. To replace the traditional system eventually, it must start by modifying it in an evolutionary process, as long as factor endowments (especially capital and skill) for development are short all round. Such an evolutionary process can easily build on a careful appreciation of the existing pattern of peasant farming and rural life. Restating the same problem in the context of optimal investment planning, Dr Wells hinted at the need to study and find alternative forms of modernizing the country's agriculture. He stated:

'Since there has been no thorough analysis of potential agricultural investments which might serve as alternatives to the farm settlement programme, it is not possible to make a definite statement that this constitutes the best programme for achieving the goals of increased agricultural productivity and income, or of retaining competent persons in the agricultural sector. To establish more firmly the place of the farm settlements in the set of possible agricultural investments several alternative programmes should be further explored, and the implications of the programme's personnel requirements need to be considered.'[1]

Considering both the total public expenditure (capital and recurrent) spent on promoting agriculture and the declared public policy that agricultural development is of first priority, Nigerian agriculture did not perform well during the period under review. The growth rate of the sector was not impressive, in spite of increasing population and increasing urbanization. Part of the explanation may be that public development efforts were not directed to the areas that mattered most to effect increased production and higher productivity, for example in the area of extension work for the peasant farmers. Part

[1] Jerome C. Wells, *An Appraisal of Agricultural Investment in the 1962–68 Nigerian Development Programme* (Unpublished Ph.D. Dissertation, University of Michigan, Ann Arbor, 1964), Chapter 4, Section 5.2, pp. 165–66. See also Dr Wells' article, 'The Israeli Moshav in Nigeria: An Estimate of Returns', *Journal of Farm Economics*, May 1966, pp. 279–94; especially his comment on p. 292: 'The tentative judgement which might be drawn from these conclusions is that the Moshav has been imported to Western Nigeria more as a form of organizational structure than a means of creating agricultural change in the region. The benefits of the Moshav form of organization, whatever they may be, do not appear in the form of dramatic increases in productivity which would clearly justify the social overhead component of the investment or which would attract widespread emulation of the form of organization and producing techniques by other farmers.'

may derive from the character of some of the agricultural investment itself, particularly the long gestation period of tree crops and of agricultural research. It was also a period for rehabilitating and replacing old or diseased trees; cocoa and oil palm being notable examples. Furthermore, for some vital works of propagation, funds, materials as well as personnel were not in adequate or timely supply. Not the least important was the declining trend of agricultural prices, and especially the price of export crops. The peak level of 1951–52 export prices accompanying the Korean boom was never attained again throughout the following decade. The period since 1955 has in fact been characterized by stagnant export prices; and this combined with not too favourable weather and pest conditions at home would explain a significant part of the unexciting performance of the agricultural sector.

9. LABOUR AND WAGES

In common with other underdeveloped countries, Nigeria is faced with many problems of statistical concept, definition and measurement.[1] These are well exemplified in the area of gainful employment and cash earnings. There is no doubt that, given the demographic structure of the country, and especially its young age composition, the employable labour force is a smaller proportion of the total population than in the developed countries. But as the size of actual employment is a function of available employment opportunities and as employment opportunities are not (by definition of underdevelopment) plentiful, it is to be expected that the size of wage employment will be very small. Added to these are historical and socio-cultural reasons which militated against an expansion of labour commitment from the supply side. As Dr T. M. Yesufu remarked:

'Wage-earning remains a novelty for many people and, until comparatively recently, it had been found necessary to obtain much of the labour required for public employment by force. Now, however, the acceptance of paid employment is essentially voluntary but there are still wide fields of opportunity for those who cannot or choose not to hire out their labour.'[2]

[1] For a classic exposition of these problems, see P. T. Bauer and B. S. Yamey, 'Economic Progress and Occupational Distribution', *Economic Journal*, December, 1951, pp. 741–55.

[2] T. M. Yesufu, *An Introduction to Industrial Relations in Nigeria*, Oxford University Press, for the Nigerian Institute of Social and Economic Research, 1962, p. 16. For a general discussion of the emergence of wage employment and of motivations behind Nigerian labour supply, see pp. 6–12.

The magnitude of labour employment, according to official statistics, is indicated in Table 12. At Independence, total employment was about half a million, or under 1·5 per cent of the estimated total population. Greater significance should be attached to the relative than to the absolute figure, because of well-known errors and omissions in Nigerian official labour statistics. For one thing, the data covered only establishments employing at least ten persons. For another, there were always gaps in the responses by firms covered in the survey, quite apart from other errors of estimation and computation. But even if generous allowances are made for these errors and the published total figure is doubled, the employed labour force in 1960 would still be only around 2·5 per cent of the estimated total population. The fact is clear: the characteristic feature of Nigerian employable labour force is the dominance of self-account or family non-wage occupation in primary production, trading services and allied activities.

This low ratio of wage employment to total population is only to be expected of an underdeveloped country, given the typical demographic and production structures normally associated with such economies. Part of the explanation lies in the fact that the labour force is counted in units taken regardless of age, skill and similar demographic characteristics. Another part of the explanation is that primary production and service industries necessarily dominate economic activity in an underdeveloped country and are in turn dominated by family labour—a fact which tends to extend the lower and upper ranges of the share of labour force in the underdeveloped versus the developed countries.[1]

The data in Table 12 must, therefore, be interpreted with caution. Apart from deficiencies referred to earlier, there is the problem of inconsistency in errors through time. The errors are not uniformly distributed over the time series, as there are qualitative differences in the data from year to year. Information for 1954 is in any case incomplete; and indeed non-existent for 1955. Adequate allowance was not made for differential coverage and for response gaps from year to year and from sector to sector. But in spite of these limitations, certain broad patterns emerge and can be stated with a reasonable degree of validity. Total recorded wage employment increased from about 300,000 at the beginning of the decade to about 500,000 at the end; that is an increase of about two-thirds in ten years. By and

[1] For further elaboration of the analytical basis of this point, see Simon Kuznets, 'Quantitative Aspects of the Economic Growth of Nations—II. Industrial Distribution of National Product and Labour Force', *Economic Development and Cultural Change*, Vol. V, No. 4, Supplement to July, 1957.

F*

Table 12. *Labour employment by industry, 1950–60*
(thousands)

Number employed	1950 Dec.	1951 Dec.	1952 Dec.	1953 Dec.	1954 Dec.	1955	1956 Sept.	1957 Sept.	1958 Sept.	1959 Sept.	1960 Sept.
Agriculture, livestock, forestry and logging	40·6	54·3	46·6	53·9	68·1	n.a.	36·9	42·7	45·4	45·5	40·1
Mining and quarrying	61·3	61·7	58·7	50·3	68·0	n.a.	58·9	53·6	49·5	41·3	43·1
Manufacturing	15·5	11·7	10·8	14·0	n.a.	n.a.	21·4	31·6	29·7	32·4	32·8
Construction	46·2	38·8	35·4	54·4	47·5	n.a.	101·9	111·2	123·9	102·9	112·7
Electricity, gas and water	2·3	2·5	3·2	3·0	n.a.	n.a.	7·8	8·8	10·1	16·4	8·3
Commerce	14·9	18·0	19·5	35·8	n.a.	n.a.	45·1	56·6	45·7	42·2	40·0
Transportation, storage and communications	36·3	42·9	49·1	45·4	46·3	n.a.	56·8	45·0	48·7	47·6	39·3
Services	101·4	72·4	61·8	66·1	43·3	n.a.	118·5	123·9	122·8	144·4	183·6
Miscellaneous	0·9	1·5	1·7	1·0	n.a.	n.a.	0·1	2·2	2·6	n.a.	n.a.
All industries	319·4	303·8	286·8	323·9	n.a.		447·4	475·6	478·4	472·7	499·9

Note: The Figures represent returns rendered by employers employing 10 or more persons. Many establishments either failed to render returns or rendered them too late to be included for analysis. Figures therefore do not represent either total employment or 100 per cent coverage of establishments with 10 or more workers.

Sources: (1) *Annual Reports of the Department of Labour* 1950–54.
(2) *Report on Employment and Earning Enquiry* (*September*) 1956–59.
(3) *Digest of Statistics* 1960.

large, construction (about 22 per cent) and the service (about 30 per cent) industries dominated the labour market. At least employment-wise, mining and quarrying was a declining industry; and later development of petroleum had not started to have a reviving influence on the general extractive industry during the period under review. Employment level in agriculture (including livestock and forestry) and transportation (including storage and communication) was more or less stable. There was noticeable growth in manufacturing, public utilities and commerce. Elements of fluctuation can also be discovered all round, especially in the service industry.

Other features of the Nigerian labour market included the heavy concentration of unskilled labourers, accounting for at least half of the total labour force; the preponderance of expatriates in the managerial, administrative and professional class; and the very small proportion of women as wage earners (still only about 5 per cent in 1960 in spite of the enormous growth in their number during the decade), most of whom were still employed in the service industry. The public sector still accounted for a lion's share of the employment market—about 57 per cent in 1960—despite the boost given to private enterprise in the 1950's. From a development standpoint, the most characteristic feature of the manpower market was the superabundance of the quantity of unskilled labour, side by side with a serious shortage of high-level and intermediate skills. All round, the quality standard was poor, although there were non-labour intervening variables to explain the low productivity standard.[1] The area of greatest concentration for labour employment was Lagos and the Western Region. Following the general pattern of employment distribution by activity sectors, high-level and intermediate skills were concentrated in the service sector (which is defined to include public service and teaching).[2]

Reference has been made to the distortion of the demand-supply relationship in the Nigerian labour market, that is to say the shortage of high-level skills combined with a surplus of unskilled labour. Ultimately, the distortion can be explained in terms of the pace and character of the general development process. But the proximate factors responsible can be found in the arduous and unattractive life of the rural economy, in the attraction of the city lights with its

[1] Peter Kilby, 'African Labour Productivity Reconsidered', *Economic Journal*, June 1961; and 'Some Determinants of Industrial Productivity in Nigeria', Conference Proceedings of the Nigerian Institute of Social & Economic Research, Ibadan 1960.

[2] For a general discussion of the features of Nigerian labour market, see T. M. Yesufu, 'Nigerian Manpower Problems (A Preliminary Assessment)', *Nigerian Journal of Economic & Social Studies*, Vol. 4, No. 3, November, 1962, pp. 207–27.

attendant rapid rate of urbanization, in the imperfections of the labour market in terms of knowledge and long time-lag for supply adjustment through training, and in the irrationality of public policy in terms of wage policy and educational programme. Since so little definitive is known about the demographic structure of the country, it is difficult to estimate the size of the employable labour force and then deduce the size and characteristics of the unemployed. But one can claim, with good justification, that the unemployment gap (defined as people willing to work but unable to find a paid employment at the going wage rates for their kind of skills) was substantially wider in Nigeria than in the developed countries and that most of them were floating in self-employed or family activities in the services sector.[1]

In recent years, preoccupation with the unemployed has centred increasingly on the so-called school leavers, or more correctly, primary school drop-outs. The importance attached to this category of the unemployed is probably out of proportion to their number relative to the illiterate unemployed or under-employed; although the preoccupation is understandable in terms of the fiscal and other development implications of the money expended on their schooling as well as the inherent political dangers of a growing army of urban unemployed young literates. In a static sense, most of the school-leavers were not immediately employable,[2] although it was not unknown in practice that many children below fourteen years of age were employed against the provision of the Labour Code Ordinance. But it was really the cumulative effect of these children pouring out of the school pipe line into an empty employment market that had become the haunting fear of developers and policy makers in most countries of Tropical Africa.[3]

The foundation of growing unemployment in the Nigerian economy is to be sought in the structural and fundamental aspects of its economic growth. But tentatively, the level and behaviour of wages should contribute at least a partial explanation of the slow pace of expanding employment opportunity. To put it simply, the

[1] This is in contradiction to the strange conclusion by Dr Yesufu in his article on 'Nigerian Manpower Problems', *op. cit.*, to the effect that there was rather an apparent over-employment and not unemployment.

[2] O. Sonubi took this general approach in his 'Note on Nigeria's Youth Employment Problems', *Nigerian Journal of Economic & Social Studies*, Vol. 4, No. 3, November 1962, pp. 228–32.

[3] Archibald Callaway, 'Unemployment Among African School Leavers', *Journal of Modern African Studies*, Vol. 1, No. 3, pp. 351–71. For the Nigerian scene specifically, Dr Callaway had an earlier series of articles on the same subject in *West Africa*, March and April, 1961.

structure of wages and salaries did not reflect relative scarcity of labour skills and productive factors generally. The country was plagued in the early days of nascent party political rivalry by governmental competitive wage bids beyond the normal market mechanism. The urban workers were politically of far greater importance than their relative numbers and constituted a powerful force for securing governmental control through election. Partly out of a humanitarian resentment against the exploiting colonial wage level, but mostly as an economic carrot to woo the urban workers, rival political parties which later gained governmental powers in different parts of the country out-bidded each other successively to raise the minimum wage rates to levels well above the equilibrium rates. An economic rationalization for the political exercise was provided by an intellectual appeal of a Fabian socialist nature to the assumed economies of high wages. But since the private sector was not bound by these promises and the labour market was such that, given the range of demand, unskilled labour supply could be had in almost unlimited quantity, large disparities started to develop between the public and private sectors in the actual wage rates paid since the 1950's. This marked a departure from the earlier tendency of both sets mostly in sympathy, with the public sector playing the role of a leading sector. The distortion was further intensified by the fact that for this category of labour the private sector offered the fastest expansion in employment opportunity. As this was also a period of construction boom and of the replacement of public direct-labour works by private contracting, it opened the way for public financing corruption; not only through contract kick-backs but also by the simple device of calculating the cost of public projects by reference to official wage rates (to which the governments are legally committed) while the actual work was executed by private contractors at the going (much lower) market wage rates.[1]

At the higher echelons of the labour market, a similar situation of earnings above the factor supply price obtained; but for a different set of reasons. Here, the gap was more short-term in nature, as there was (and still is) a serious shortage of high-level manpower supply. So the surplus earning could be regarded as containing a strong element of quasi-rent. What aggravated it was the uncritical acceptance of a colonial salary structure during the process of Nigerianizing posts

[1] Since all the parties involved in such arrangements know the facts, the theoretical opportunity to make huge profits as a result of the wage differentials did not become available in practice to the contractor. A state of perfect knowledge among the players ensured some equitable distribution of spoils; and the contract kick-backs would normally include some of the apparent profits from the wage gaps.

hitherto held by expatriate personnel. For the most part, the salary levels attached to those were irrelevant, whether to the style of living of the Nigerian successors or to the objective requirements of a rational development policy. Albeit, salary rates were irrationally high for the managerial, administrative and professional classes at the top of the labour ladder, and wage rates also irrationally high for the unskilled workers and untested artisans at the bottom of the ladder. The intermediate skills perched uncertainly and unevenly in between the two ridges, discouraging a coherent and smooth pattern of manpower development.[1] But overall, the employed in Nigeria were a very select set, not only by virtue of their great luck in getting jobs at all but by the further fortune of earning well above the objective market rates. What distinguished them from the unemployed can be likened, not just to a breach but to a very high cliff of a great divide.

The real wage rate of unskilled workers in the public sector has increased four-fold since the end of the last world war; and a substantial part of this increment cannot be accounted for by increased productivity. This growth in the real income of workers was well above the general increment in national income indicated earlier in this paper; and was certainly well beyond the movement in the real income of farmers and rural dwellers. This disparity reflects not only the socio-political strength of the urban employed but also the humane and sociological approach of successive Commissions which have influenced wage determination. In the last twenty years about six such Commissions have been appointed to look into one or the other aspect of wages and salaries; and it would be fair to say that none has approached the problem from the viewpoint of general equilibrium planning and dynamic development.[2] Above all,

[1] An editorial comment recently pinpointed this problem while discussing the hangover from the colonial income policy: 'An objective observer looking at the wage structure today might be led to believe that the chief need of the economy is to produce well-paid lower-grade clerks and typists. On the other hand, technicians and good supervisors—both urgently needed—are in the main relatively poorly paid. The consequence of this is that there are many essential positions unfilled because the going wage or salary is not sufficient to induce people to undergo the necessary training'. *Nigerian Opinion*, Vol. 2, No. 3, March 1966, pp. 28–30, at p. 29.

[2] The conflict of approach was demonstrated recently by the minority reports in (as well as the government comments on) the Morgan Commission: Federal Republic of Nigeria, *Report of the Commission on the Review of Wages, Salary and Conditions of Service of the Junior Employees of the Governments of the Federation, and in Private Establishments, 1963–64*, Federal Ministry of Information, Lagos, 1964; and the *Conclusion of the Federal Government on the Report of the Morgan Commission*, Sessional Paper No. 5 of 1964, Federal Ministry of Information, Lagos, 1964.

the official approach had consistently ignored the rural sector and thereby intensified rural depopulation and urban unemployment.

The earnings of the corresponding employed labour force are set out in Table 13. All comments made in respect of Table 12 in terms of the data quality and of the validity of interpretation therefore also apply to the earnings data. Furthermore, it should be stated that certain real incomes were excluded from the definition of 'earnings' under the Employment and Earnings Surveys which formed the basis of Table 13. For example, perquisites like housing, transport, rations, uniforms and other allowances to meet specific expenses were excluded. This omission affects not only the magnitude of total earnings but also the relative magnitudes as between different components of the labour force. Subject to all these limitations, however, some broad conclusions can still be drawn from the earnings data.

The total earning from wage employment of about £6 millions at the time of political independence was an infinitesimal proportion of the national income, being well under 1 per cent of the Gross Domestic Income. However, in spite of the discontinuity in the data in the period 1954–55, it can be stated that the total earning from wage employment was rising in general; but that it is difficult to indicate the magnitude of increase with any reasonable confidence. The pattern of earning by activity sectors follows broadly the corresponding pattern of employment. One would, however, expect that since the skills composition was different from one industry to another, there would not be a one-to-one correspondence between the industrial earnings pattern and the industrial structure of employment. Another factor that would tend to lead to variation in the earnings pattern is the relative strength of trade union effectiveness in wage negotiation. The tradition of wage fixing in Nigeria has been the machinery of collective bargaining, although the large private employers tend in general to follow government wage rates.[1]

10. INDUSTRIALIZATION

Tables 2–4 provide a broad idea of the importance of manufacturing and public utilities in the Gross Domestic Product. Two facts that stand out clearly are that the pace of industrialization quickened from 1950 and that industrial output still constituted at the terminal period a very small proportion of the Gross Domestic Product (Table

[1] Dr Yesufu's book, *An Introduction to Industrial Relations in Nigeria, op. cit.*, contains an exhaustive analysis and evaluation of collective bargaining in Nigeria. He also discusses the well-known factionalization of the trade unions.

Table 13. *Total earnings of labour by industry, 1950–60*
(£ thousands)

Total earnings	1950 Dec.	1951 Dec.	1952 Dec.	1953 Dec.	1954 June	1955	1956 Sept.	1957 Sept.	1958 Sept.	1959 Sept.
Agriculture, livestock, forestry and logging	119·0	180·9	210·8	221·6	304·1	n.a.	210·1	227·0	270·7	319·6
Mining and quarrying	184·1	163·7	235·3	214·2	229·7	n.a.	516·8	432·6	418·8	423·8
Manufacturing	63·4	56·2	72·2	83·8	n.a.	n.a.	195·0	411·8	344·4	404·7
Construction	185·0	159·5	170·1	255·4	215·5	n.a.	815·5	835·8	976·3	854·5
Electricity, gas and water	11·6	13·0	21·3	17·6	n.a.	n.a.	95·8	107·3	125·5	188·8
Commerce	78·6	96·0	125·6	259·9	n.a.	n.a.	722·1	985·8	693·3	635·0
Transportation, storage and communications	265·1	282·5	390·3	437·5	429·5	n.a.	1,061·0	793·9	905·4	786·4
Services	581·7	284·8	301·8	383·3	222·4	n.a.	1,460·9	1,797·7	1,786·8	2,160·5
Miscellaneous	4·4	8·5	15·8	6·1	n.a.	n.a.	2·0	18·5	12·0	n.a.
All industries	1,492·9	1,245·1	1,543·2	1,879·4	n.a.	n.a.	5,079·2	5,610·4	5,533·2	5,773·3

Notes: (1) Wages for certain grades of employees are not given in the sources for certain industries. The 1951 corresponding figures are used to calculate the earnings since the comparison of the 1950 and 1951 wages in those given seems to show little fluctuation in level of earnings in these two years.

(2) Earnings figures are only indicated for certain categories of workers, namely artisans, skilled and unskilled labourers. The comparison of the proportion of the earnings of these groups in all industries with the total earnings of all employees for 1958 and 1959 shows little fluctuation (within a range of 0·05 in most of the cases). The proportion of earnings of these groups for 1958 are therefore used in the computation of total earnings for 1956 and 1957 since the margin of error is very small.

Sources: (1) *Annual Report of the Department of Labour* 1950–54.
(2) *Report on Employment and Earnings Enquiry* (September) 1956–59.
(3) *Digest of Statistics* 1960.

2). Manufacturing alone (i.e. excluding public utilities) grew at an average rate of 17·6 per cent per annum during the 1950's; but still remained only 1·5 per cent of the Gross Domestic Product at the end of the decade. During this period, manufacturing products which dominated the industrial scene were drinks and tobacco. The greatest expansion took place in beer, soft drinks, textiles and, towards the end of the decade, cement.

Groundnut milling and tobacco expanded rapidly at the early stages but slowed down as the decade drew to a close. Metal products had not shown any remarkable progress during the decade. The unmistakable concentration of Nigerian manufacturing industries was in the field of consumer goods and light processing.[1]

There is little doubt that Nigeria has a great industrial potential. Not only is it endowed with good natural resources and a large active population; but also the pace of income growth and the character of social change are conducive to the expansion of an industrial market. Added to these is the impact of public policy on import substitution both through direct investment activities as well as the adoption of various fiscal devices. The general developmental environment during the 1950's stimulated efforts by both the public and private sectors to exploit these industrial opportunities. The range of products in each group of manufacturing has widened considerably since 1950, as importing firms invested in domestic production behind the tariff wall to protect their products or to ward off competition. As the industrial process itself advanced, the range of products became wider still to take advantage of the improving investment environment. This was particularly so in the areas of intermediate products (as in building materials) or complementary products (as in household goods). Partly as a result of the increasing structural interdependence and partly from autonomous accidents of history, other new industries were born with great vigour and promise—notably crude petroleum production and refining. And as the general pace of overall development quickened, the demand for industrial plant, housing, energy, metal products and other producer goods gave an increasing boost to industrial investment and growth. The development of export promotion also started and expanded in this period—especially petroleum, rubber, vegetable oil and plywood. But at the achievement of political independence, the general emphasis (about 68 per cent) was still on light manufacturing for household con-

[1] For further analysis of the country's industrial structure during this period, see the author's book, *Foundation of an African Economy—A Study of Investment and Growth in Nigeria*, Frederick A. Praeger, New York, 1966, ch. 4, especially pp. 133–40.

sumption, deriving largely from import replacement. Examples are food, drink and tobacco, textiles and clothing, shoes and leather, rubber and rubber products, furniture and fittings, flour milling and bakeries, soap and toiletries, plastics and enamelware.[1]

A full appreciation of the importance of manufacturing industry in the Nigerian context cannot be grasped by a simple consideration of its direct contribution to the Gross Domestic Product or to total employment. Its real importance derives from its potential contribution to the process of economic growth and transformation, through its impact on the character and quality of capital formation and the promotion of high-level manpower skill. It constitutes one of the dynamic growing points of the economy, and represents the bridge from primary product and export dependence to a virile self-stimulating and integrated economic system. It offers great promise for a more sophisticated international specialization, wider domestic diversification, increased productivity and greater employment opportunity in quantity and quality.

It is in appreciation of these facts that public policy was designed to accelerate the process of industrial development. Part of the government's active interest in the industrial sector is reflected by the direct and indirect participation in industrial ownership and management. The exchange reserves built up by the commodity Marketing Boards up till 1955 made such participation financially possible, especially at the level of the regional governments and their agencies. Indeed, for many of the industries which government sponsored, it was usual during the period under review for the public sector to provide the financial backing, and for the private sector (typically foreign private interests) to supply the managerial expertise and technical responsibility. Indigenous private capital or managerial service had not played any significant role in the development of medium or large-scale manufacturing industries; although with the recent development of capital market in the country, there are signs of increasing indigenous private financial participation (but still substantially of non-equity types). Private venture capital by Nigerians was to be found mostly in small-scale industries or activities of a short gestation period and simple managerial requirement.

But probably by far the most important way in which the government influenced industrial development was through fiscal incentives in the form of protective tariffs, import duty reliefs, tax holidays, accelerated depreciation, pioneer status certificates, monopolistic

[1] A fuller discussion of the characteristic features of some Nigerian industries is contained in Alan Sokolski, *The Establishment of Manufacturing in Nigeria*, Frederick A. Praeger, New York, 1965, Part III, especially ch. 7.

concessions and discriminatory purchase of manufactured products by government agencies.[1] Efforts were made to improve foreign private investment environment through the establishment of Industrial Promotion Commissions to propagate investment opportunities and offer assistance to prospective industrialists. Declarations were also made to assure private interests against nationalization or expropriation and in favour of free capital and profits repatriation. An open-door policy was maintained with respect to the availability and use of foreign exchange; and government maintained generally a *laissez-faire* ideological posture by adopting in practice the business ethics of international capitalism. It set up industrial estates and provided other infrastructure to minimize private overheads. It engaged actively in the training and provision of indigenous high-level skills, while giving a very liberal effect to the expatriate quota arrangement. All round, it encouraged private enterprise to flourish and to exploit profitable investment opportunities in the country.

However, in fostering industrial growth in this manner, government probably sacrificed more than it needed to have done—not only in terms of current social costs but also with respect to the requirements for future national development. There is reason to believe that some of the protective tariffs (like flour, shoes and textiles) were higher than necessary; and that firms exploited the situation to increase their profits at the expense of domestic prices and of government revenue. Indiscriminate incentives not only generated faulty pre-investment evaluation and excess capacities in some industries; they also sustained inefficient management (possible cases were clinker, cement, woodworking and drinks). The structure of political power and of the public service fostered corruption and irrational considerations in administering the incentives, especially with respect to land acquisition, project evaluation, industrial location pattern, expatriate quota, import restriction and government purchase from approved manufacturers. The quality of administrative supervision could not forestall or prevent dishonest business accounting for tax and other official purposes. Many firms that did not objectively qualify for pioneer status probably got the official certificates and enjoyed the benefits of concession (possible cases included late-comers in metal-working, footware and textiles). Accelerated capital depreciation allowances probably discriminated at the margin against other

[1] That these indirect measures were relatively more important can be deduced somewhat (rather uncertainly) from the fact that total government development expenditure on industry and trade during the period under review amounted to less than 3 per cent of the total development programme. By contrast, the corresponding figure in the current national plan is about 14 per cent.

factors of production, especially against labour. And when the allowances are combined with the pioneer status, much developmental capital must have been lost to the public sector in the intervening period. There were general time-consuming, irritating and cumbersome administrative procedures which had the effect of making the policy incentives discourage rather than encourage some potential industrial investors. The industrial promotion institutions were amateurish, unimaginative and ill-equipped; and it is not altogether evident that their actual results justified their costs. The industrial estates had neither shown much profitability nor demonstrated their effectiveness as a striking force for promoting small and medium-sized industries. With all the foregoing, there was little doubt of the country's need to revise, simplify, streamline and consolidate the set of industrial policy incentives if industrial transformation was to develop faster and more rationally.

As the 1960's progressed, the character of industrial development started to show signs of change. There was the obvious impact of petroleum production and the new opportunities opened for petrochemical and gas-based industries. There was the recognition that unless the great bottleneck in energy supply was eased it would be difficult to maintain the pace of industrial expansion experienced in the 1950's; hence the great expenditure on new sources of electricity in the current national development plan. The great concentration on easy import-substitution industries for long-established markets was also loosening up. Intermediate products and capital goods were coming more to the fore as cement and other building materials were expanding capacity. There was increasing structural interdependence between industry on the one hand and agriculture, transportation, construction and commerce on the other. There was greater mutual connection among different branches of the industrial sector; but the linkages (for example textiles and tobacco) were more in the backward (i.e. towards primary production) than in the forward direction, since most of the manufacturers produced directly for household consumption. There was also an increasing awareness of the need to look over the national borders to neighbouring countries and to explore the possibilities of supra-national planning for industrial development. The need arose out of the recognition that the evolution of an integrated West African economic community could only be based on a co-ordinated system of new products and processes and not on competitive primary production. The recognition was reinforced by some evidence that latent saturation of the domestic market was already showing for certain consumer goods. Internally, there was an increasing pressure to minimize if not eliminate regional rivalries in industrial development and industrial planning, and to reduce the incidence of non-economic factors in industrial policy decisions. Above all, there was an increasing questioning of the fundamental basis underlying the whole industrialization process which the country had passed through since 1950. New tests of social cost and social benefit were being suggested for industrial planning and project evaluation; and a more comprehensive, more dynamic concept of economic development and social change was being applied to the whole complex problem of industrialization.

11. TRADE

Among African countries, Nigeria is widely reputed for its intense trading activity. The reputation is justified both by the size of the country and by the socio-economic history of its peoples. Exchange is the livewire of the Nigerian economy. The fear is even sometimes expressed that the country overtrades, considering the endless chain of distribution from production to consumption and the vast millions of people wholly or partly engaged in commerce. But the complex and intricate trading system reflects the structural and spatial interdependence of the economy.[1]

In measuring the volume of trading, it is difficult if not in fact impossible to account for the relative contributions of domestic goods and imports as there is an imperfect functional specialization by the different units involved. That there is a large traffic of goods continuously moving across the country can be easily appreciated from the various national income studies and other specialized works.[2] However, the problem is reduced in this section as we shall be concentrating for the most part on external trade.

The importance of foreign trade to the growth and transformation of the economy has been demonstrated above in Section 3 as well as in Table 5 under Section 5. Tables 14–17 below provide further information about the level and character of Nigerian foreign trade. The value of exports remained generally around 17 per cent of the Gross Domestic Product between 1950 and 1960, while the corres-

[1] To some individuals and groups, trading has of course become a way of life. Our emphasis on the economic basis of this way of life is not intended to detract from the cultural ethos and psychic satisfaction associated with the trading activity of some people. But surely trading is first and foremost an economic phenomenon.

[2] Of the specialized works, apart from P. T. Bauer's classic work, *West African Trade*, *op. cit.*, a recent solid addition is the article by A. M. Hay and R. H. T. Smith, 'Preliminary Estimates of Nigeria's Interregional Trade and Associated Money Flows', *op. cit.*

Table 14. *Import classification by commodity (SITC), 1950–60*
(£m)

SITC	Commodity groups	1950	1951	1952	1953	1954	1955	1956	1957	1958	1959	1960
Section 0	Food	3·3	5·7	6·8	9·6	12·0	13·0	16·0	18·3	18·2	20·8	23·9
Section 1	Beverages and tobacco	3·0	3·9	4·0	4·4	4·4	5·1	5·3	5·5	5·6	5·8	6·2
Section 2	Crude materials mainly inedible, except fuel	1·3	2·2	2·4	2·1	1·5	1·7	1·9	1·9	2·0	2·1	2·1
Section 3	Mineral fuels, lubricants and related materials	4·0	5·9	6·6	5·7	5·6	6·5	7·3	8·2	8·9	10·4	11·3
Section 4	Animal and vegetable oils and fats	—	—	—	—	0·0	0·0	0·0	0·0	0·1	0·1	0·1
Section 5	Chemicals	2·3	3·1	3·4	3·8	4·8	7·1	7·6	8·0	8·3	10·1	12·2
Section 6	Manufactured goods	31·9	44·7	63·6	54·7	54·2	60·1	65·3	62·8	65·9	65·9	81·1
Section 7	Machinery and Transport equipment	10·9	12·3	18·7	17·9	20·1	27·9	32·3	31·3	39·4	42·7	51·6
Section 8	Miscellaneous manufactured articles	3·6	5·4	5·9	7·4	9·4	12·3	14·2	13·4	15·5	17·8	23·9
Section 9	Miscellaneous transactions and commodities not elsewhere specified	0·0	0·0	0·0	0·0	0·2	2·6	2·7	2·9	2·4	0·4	0·4
	Total	60·3	83·2	111·4	105·6	112·2	136·3	152·6	152·3	166·3	176·1	212·8

Source: *Nigeria Trade Reports*, 1950–60.

ponding ratio of imports rose roughly from about 14 per cent to 20 per cent. In other words, imports grew faster than income and much faster than exports. The benchmark was the year 1955, when the earlier export surpluses turned into larger deficits right on to the year of Independence and beyond. This shift was due basically to real changes in the volume of transaction more than in relative prices.

Tables 14 and 15 present the classification of imports, first by the Standard International Trade Classification System and then by economic areas of origin. The dominance of manufactured goods in total Nigerian imports is unambiguous. The next important commodity group is machinery and transport equipment. It is interesting, however, to observe the general stability of manufactured goods import, especially in the period 1952–59, and the beginning of a fall-off in relative share towards the end, both reflecting the impact of domestic import-substituting industrialization in the area of consumer goods. On the other hand, machinery and transport equipment as well as chemicals showed a definite upward trend. But probably the most striking and bewildering feature (for a vast agrarian country) of the imports classified by commodity is the enormous growth in food items. Food import increased by more than seven times over the period under review. The explanation of this strange phenomenon is to be sought partly in the increasing number of expatriates in the country especially as the foreign private enterprise sector expanded; partly in the growing class of Nigerian middle class who adopted the usual expensive tastes of the managerial, administrative and professional élite; partly in the general if modest increase in *per capita* real income which made possible a qualitative shift (and hence in Nigeria's circumstance a shift towards imports) in food consumption; and partly in the soft open-door trade and payment policy adopted by the government at least with respect to food.

Other features of the import commodity classification (not shown in Table 14) include the following.[1] Non-durable consumer goods accounted for the greater though declining share of import, falling from about 56 to 46 per cent of total within the decade. Durable consumer goods were responsible for between 7 per cent and 10 per cent of total; when these two groups are added, they make Nigeria one of the few countries in the world with half their imports in consumer goods. The share of capital goods increased broadly from about 27 per cent to about 32 per cent during the decade, reflecting both the increased pace of domestic capital formation and the shift

[1] The quantitative evidence for this section can be found in Table 1 of chapter 1 (also pp. 8–10) of the author's book, *Foundation of an African Economy op. cit.* See also chapter 4 of the book, pp. 127–33.

effect of tariff measures on consumer goods imports.[1] Within manufactured goods import, textiles and building materials were becoming relatively less important while metal products of various kinds were gaining ground. If the imported capital goods are further analysed, it would be seen that transport equipment, non-electrical machinery and base metals dominated the scene. For end-use, the greatest concentration was in plant and machinery, construction materials and road vehicles.

Table 15 sets out the commodity imports by areas of origin. The United Kingdom still dominated the trading scene, although it was losing ground as the decade progressed. The most striking feature of the table is the accelerated importance of the European Economic Community countries, and to a lesser extent Asia (mostly Japan) and North America (mostly USA). The relative insignificance, of Africa, Australia, Latin America and the Communist countries is also amply demonstrated. Particular areas further tended to be prominent in the supply of particular commodities—Japan and the United Kingdom for consumer goods, Western Europe and North America for capital goods. Within capital goods, there is evidence that Western European countries substantially increased their share of construction materials, transport equipment and plant and machinery—mostly at the expense of the United Kingdom. North America stepped up its share of construction materials, water and rail transport equipment, and plant and machinery; but it lost ground in the supply of road transport equipment and (since about 1958) in air transport equipment. This changing pattern probably reflects not only competitive cost advantages but also the relative sources of financing capital formation through foreign direct investment and foreign aid.

A factor that tended to reduce effective cost competition among importers was the structure and organization of the trade itself. Reference has been made to the well-known practice of tied finance by financing countries whether public or private. But the international organizational nature of the great trading companies was also a determining influence on the direction of trade, since it was a natural practice for subsidiary companies in Nigeria to place import orders from their parent firms in the Metropolitan countries. And, given the monopolistic or imperfectly competitive basis of industrial

[1] It is, however, not strictly valid to conclude from this analysis that there was a decisive shift towards capital goods at the expense of consumer goods. The time series percentage distribution does not exhibit a firm or uniform trend. The group which has taken over the declining share of consumer goods was really the processing and raw materials, dominated by mineral fuels and lubricants.

Table 15. *Import classification by country or origin, 1950–60*[a]
(£m)

Area groups	1950	1951	1952	1953	1954	1955	1956	1957	1958	1960
African markets	0·7	1·1	1·0	0·8	0·8	1·3	1·4	1·5	1·5	2·3
EEC	5·3	13·6	17·6	18·5	22·1	21·8	26·4	26·1	29·7	42·2
France	0·6	1·2	1·4	0·9	1·7	1·6	2·4	2·0	2·5	4·9
Other EEC countries	4·7	12·4	16·2	17·6	20·4	20·2	24·0	24·1	27·2	37·3
Sterling Area	41·3	49·8	66·1	61·7	61·6	77·0	83·0	78·5	85·9	105·1
United Kingdom	36·4	42·8	57·9	54·7	51·7	63·5	68·3	66·1	72·7	91·4
Other Sterling Area	4·9	7·0	8·2	7·0	10·0	13·5	14·7	12·4	13·2	13·7
Asia	9·4	12·6	17·9	10·3	16·7	25·2	28·4	25·2	27·6	36·3
North America	2·4	4·0	5·7	4·5	6·1	5·9	5·7	8·7	9·9	12·6
Latin America	0·1	0·1	0·0	0·3	0·5	1·6	1·1	2·5	2·2	1·4
Others	7·8	7·8	10·7	15·3	12·6	14·0[b]	17·2	19·5	18·4	21·9
Total[c]	67·0	89·0	119·0	111·4	120·4	146·8	163·2	162·0	175·2	221·8

Notes: [a] Figures for 1959, on the same basis as other years, are not available.
[b] Includes parcel post.
[c] Totals by country of supply exceed totals by commodity because of the duplication of certain markets in either the African and Sterling Area countries or the Asian and Sterling Area countries.

Source: Nigeria Trade Reports, 1950–60.

organization in the Nigerian economy, the sources of supply tended to get specialized for reasons beyond comparative cost advantages. A different kind of imperfect competition is found in the export trade; for while the great commodity Marketing Boards monopolized the staple export crops at home, they had to compete vigorously against other suppliers in the international market for primary products.

A similar analysis has been carried out for export trade and the results are presented in Tables 16–17. Table 16 brings out very clearly the very narrow concentration of Nigerian export commodities. There is no mistaking the dominance of crude materials (mainly inedible), accounting for more than half of total export earnings. The next important group is food, followed by animal and vegetable oils and fats. But two interesting developments in recent years should be noted in Nigeria's export pattern: the rising importance of manufactured goods and the spectacular rise of petroleum as a foreign exchange earner. Beverages, tobacco, chemicals, machinery and transport equipment played a very insignificant part in the country's export activity. As for the direction of trade, again the United Kingdom and the European Economic Community countries were undoubtedly Nigeria's most important markets (Table 17). The degree of concentration in the export trade was greater than the degree of concentration in the import trade.

This high concentration in the export trade both by commodity types and by areas of outlet leads to a consideration of the behaviour of export prices and the role of the Marketing Boards. The incidence of price movement was more important in the export than in the import trade. Fluctuation of export prices and hence of total export earnings (given the fairly high supply elasticity of most of Nigeria's export crops) was a conspicuous feature of the Nigerian economy. The fluctuation in earnings varied of course from crop to crop, depending on variations in acreage and yield, the magnitude of price change in previous years, and the general marketing efficiency in respect of each crop. The overall movement of prices can be divided into two periods—before 1955 and after 1955. The earlier period was characterized by buoyant increases, culminating in the peak of feverish preparation in 1951–52 for the Korean war. Given the general shortage of imported commodities and the limited absorptive capacity of the Nigerian economy for development at the time, the result of rising prices and a brisk export market was the familiar build-up of substantial foreign exchange reserves by the Marketing Boards. After 1955, this trend was reversed. The export market became dull and stagnant, the supply bottleneck for imported com-

Table 16. *Export classification by commodity (SITC), 1950–60*
(£m)

SITC	Commodity groups	1950	1951	1952	1953	1954	1955	1956	1957	1958	1959	1960
Section 0	Food	21·3	34·4	32·0	29·1	44·2	30·5	28·2	31·0	32·2	43·8	43·0
Section 1	Beverages and tobacco	0·0	0·0	0·0	0·0	0·0	0·0	0·1	0·1	0·2	0·2	0·0
Section 2	Crude materials mainly inedible, except fuel	54·1	67·5	73·4	75·1	83·6	80·1	82·0	71·7	79·9	92·2	94·3
Section 3	Mineral fuels, lubricants and related materials	0·0	0·2	0·0	0·0	0·1	0·3	0·3	0·5	1·4	3·1	4·5
Section 4	Animal and vegetable oils and fats	12·4	13·4	18·7	15·4	17·2	16·3	19·0	18·4	16·4	18·4	19·3
Section 5	Chemicals	0·1	0·1	0·1	0·2	0·0	0·1	0·1	0·1	0·1	0·2	0·2
Section 6	Manufactured goods	0·4	0·5	0·5	0·6	1·1	1·2	1·1	1·0	1·2	1·3	1·5
Section 7	Machinery and transport equipment	—	—	—	—	—	—	0·0	0·0	—	—	—
Section 8	Miscellaneous manufactured articles	—	—	—	—	0·0	0·0	0·0	0·0	0·0	0·0	0·0
Section 9	Miscellaneous transactions and commodities not elsewhere specified	0·0	0·0	0·0	0·0	0·1	1·1	1·4	1·4	1·3	1·4	2·7
	Total	88·3	116·1	124·7	120·4	146·3	129·6	132·2	124·2	132·7	160·6	165·5

Source: *Nigeria Trade Reports*, 1950–60.

Table 17. *Export classification by country of destination, 1950–60*[a]
(£m)

Area groups	1950	1951	1952	1953	1954	1955	1956	1957	1958	1960
African markets	0·4	1·3	0·6	0·5	0·6	1·1	1·2	1·6	1·4	2·9
EEC	3·1	5·0	5·9	6·7	20·9	22·1	27·9	32·2	41·9	51·2
France	0·3	1·8	0·3	0·3	2·3	3·2	1·0	5·4	2·0	6·4
Other EEC countries	2·8	3·2	5·6	6·4	18·6	18·9	26·9	26·8	39·9	41·8
Sterling Area	54·5	90·9	101·1	96·7	106·5	91·7	86·3	79·8	76·7	82·5
United Kingdom	54·2	88·6	99·2	96·2	105·4	90·8	85·2	78·3	74·9	79·7
Other Sterling Area	0·3	2·3	1·9	0·5	1·1	0·9	1·1	1·5	1·8	2·8
Asia	0·0	0·0	0·1	0·1	0·6	0·3	0·1	0·1	1·5	3·6
North America	13·3	16·1	15·4	14·7	15·9	12·4	12·9	8·4	8·1	17·1
Latin America	0·0	0·0	—	—	—	—	0·0	0·4	0·7	0·8
Others	17·3	3·8	2·1	2·3	2·6	3·0	4·8	3·1	4·0	10·0
Total[b]	88·6	117·1	125·2	121·0	147·1	130·6	133·2	125·6	134·3	168·1

Note: [a] Figures for 1959, on the same basis as other years, are not available.
[b] Totals of export classification by country of destination exceed totals of classification by commodity because of the double-counting of certain markets in either the African and Sterling Area countries or in the Asian and Sterling Area countries.

Source: *Nigeria Trade Reports*, 1950–60.

modities eased in the industrial countries and the absorptive capacity of the economy gradually improved. The result was a growing deficit in the balance of payments, a depletion of the foreign exchange reserves and a fall in the real incomes of primary producers.

The fact that the producers were not adequately insulated from the fluctuation in world prices has generated many criticisms of the stabilization role of the Marketing Boards. It has been argued[1] that the Boards have achieved neither price stabilization nor income stabilization; and that conceivably the producers, as producers, were worse off under the Boards than under the previous marketing arrangement. A fresh exercise was recently carried out into the whole question of price and income fluctuations under the Marketing Boards and the result indicated the invalidity of trying to generalize for all the Boards or for all the commodities.[2] But whatever the success or failure of the Boards with respect to stabilization of prices and incomes, their importance to the general financing of development during the period under review cannot be denied. And this is really the more crucial problem; for as Dr Helleiner remarked, 'Growth should always have carried greater weight in Nigerian policy formation than stability, and there exists no conclusive evidence that the two are correlated.'[3] In spite of certain misuse of funds, the accumulated reserves were expended largely on beneficial public development projects. And without the existence of the Boards, there is no clear evidence that the same funds would have been collected and expended more rationally from the viewpoint of general economic development. Again, it is useful to recall Dr Helleiner's conclusion on the matter:

'The Marketing Boards' uses of the earnings from their trading operations, while subject to question in some particular instances, notably those involving equity investment in and loans to private companies, have clearly promoted economic development. Such diverse activities as agricultural research and experimentation, the construction of universities, road-building and modern manufacturing have all benefited from the Marketing Boards' support. On balance, it would be difficult not to conclude that the earning and

1 The issue was fiercely contested in the literature in the 1950's—see especially the *Economic Journal*, December 1952, January 1953, June 1953, December 1954 and March 1957. The principal characters involved in the debate include P. T. Bauer, F. W. Paish, Polly Hill, Barbu Niculescu and Arthur Hazlewood.

2 Ayo Ogunsheye, 'Marketing Boards and the Stabilization of Producer Prices and Income in Nigeria', *Nigerian Journal of Economic & Social Studies*, Vol. 7, No. 2, July 1965, pp. 131–43.

3 G. K. Helleiner, 'The Fiscal Role of the Marketing Boards in Nigerian Economic Development, 1947–61', *Economic Journal*, September 1964, p. 582.

subsequent spending of trading (and other surpluses) by the Marketing Boards were beneficial to the economic development of Nigeria.'[1]

The case of the Marketing Boards is only one example, though an important one, of the increasing importance of the State in Nigerian foreign trade since the last world war. The fiscal role of the Boards has since become so vast, penetrating and impressive that the Board's general activities now tend to dominate most discussions of the country's foreign trade. But actually there were other equally if not more important aspects of the role of the State in this sector. There was, for instance, the design and administration of tariff measures. Revenue earnings from import duties had long been the most important single source of government income and, by Independence, still accounted for about 46 per cent of total government revenue (Federal as well as Regional combined). But for our purpose, the interesting feature of the import duties during the 1950's was that they were becoming increasingly a device, not so much to maximize the tax yield, as to influence the pattern of consumption, investment and foreign trade.

To reduce the level of consumption as well as influence the pattern of consumption of different socio-economic groups, successive budgets during the 1950's raised duties on imports and tried to streamline the tariff structure. They also imposed protective duties to help the nascent industrialization of the domestic economy which, as we noted earlier, consisted mostly of import substitution. Import quotas were administered to curb consumption of specific goods which were in short supply or the foreign currency for financing which was scarce. The same device was also used (especially against Japan) as a weapon to alter the direction of trade; although the weapon was not always justifiably applied on rational economic grounds and its administration was not always free from corruption. But by and large, import licences were applicable only to the hard-currency areas, and especially to the dollar countries. Otherwise, the same customs tariff applied to all importing countries. In spite of being a member of the sterling area, Nigeria had not, following a nineteenth-century treaty among European powers in West Africa, given imperial preference to British importers. Lately, however, the recent controversial association agreement with the European Economic Community has introduced a discriminatory element into the Nigerian tariff structure.[2]

1 G. K. Helleiner, *op. cit.*, p. 604.

2 Federal Republic of Nigeria, *Agreement Establishing an Association Between the European Economic Community and The Republic of Nigeria*, Federal Ministry of Information, Lagos, 1966.

But if the extent of state intervention in foreign trade was so pervasive, why then did we assert that government maintained a general open-door policy in the external sector? The key to the apparent conflict lies in a fuller appreciation of the government's ideological posture and economic philosophy. The imposition of tariff measures was not by itself necessarily inconsistent with a free use of foreign exchange. We have to look at the level and content of the tariff measures. In the earlier years, there was little doubt that the measures were luke-warm and half-hearted, designed primarily as a revenue-raising device rather than a positive instrument of controlling foreign trade from a development standpoint. And even in the later years when the tariff walls were gradually raised, other domestic measures simultaneously pursued by the government did little to restructure foreign trade. For example, control over public expenditure was so lax that the resulting indiscipline over spending merely raised the total import bill in spite of the higher tariff. Again, since a soft consumption credit policy was pursued all round, the high tariff wall could do little to dampen the high consumption propensity. This was particularly true of loans for personal cars. Only a small proportion of the total car import, in any case, really felt the brunt of high duties. Moreover, little restriction was imposed on the use of foreign exchange and on the free movement of funds; especially with respect to the Sterling area and to OEEC countries where, as we have noted, Nigeria's trade was massively concentrated. The general trend of policy through the 1950's had decidedly been an increasing liberalization of trade and payments. As an official document puts it:

'In 1958 the system of open import licences was extended, with certain major exceptions, to Japan and early in 1959 to the dollar area. Later the scope of these general licences was still further enlarged and as from July 1, 1959, most goods can be imported freely from any country except that imports from some countries of the Soviet Bloc are still confined to essential commodities. Similarly with exports, all Nigerian products, apart from a few strategic materials, are now freed from control.'[1]

12. CONCLUSIONS AND POSTSCRIPT

We can see from all the foregoing that Nigerian public development policy in the decade before Independence can be described as rather ambivalent and unsure. To the extent that we can discover a central

[1] National Economic Council, *Economic Survey of Nigeria, 1959*, Federal Government Printer, Lagos, 1959, Ch. 12, p. 94. See also the 1962 Budget speech by Chief Festus S. Okotie-Eboh, *The Mobilization Budget*, Federal Ministry of Information, Lagos, 1962, p. 23, for a declaration of the open-economy policy.

theme running through the various public measures, it would be fair to say that there was increasing reliance on private enterprise and private initiative without a clear and coherent leadership from the public sector. In fact, the political and economic power structure was such that a handful of the Nigerian middle class in collusion with powerful foreign interests increasingly gained control of the government apparatus largely for the promotion of their joint interests. It is significant that in spite of all the investment and growth statistics, the Economic Adviser to the Federal Government had come at last to recognize, at least in words, the prospect of an increasing immiseration of the poor.[1]

At Independence, the Nigerian economy had made some quantitative progress, considering its shape at the end of the second world war. But there were still a number of inherent qualitative weaknesses as it faced the future as an independent sovereign nation. The first derived from the fact that it was not truly a cohesive national community. There was a great deal of built-in instability in its tripartite basis of party politics, its delicate game of regional balancing, and the absence of strong, acceptable and effective central leadership.[2] The second derived from the simple truth that Nigeria was not really independent and sovereign. There is of course a sense in which no country is, or can be, sovereign in a world that is closely knit together by mutual political and economic ties. But Nigeria was particularly dependent both in its foreign trade sector and at the growing points of its domestic economy on foreign private initiative and leadership; not to mention the high degree of influence exercised by foreign powers in the formulation and execution of its public policy.

Structurally, considering the magnitude of the problem, little had been achieved to transform the underdeveloped character of the economy. It still consisted largely of a poor, illiterate and diseased rural community. There was growing urbanization unmatched by the slow pace of economic growth and investment opportunities. There was a rising output of unemployed primary school leavers side by side with an increased shortage of manpower with growth-inducing skills. There was expanding capital formation accompanied by a stagnant growth rate in *per capita* real income. There was more economic planning with a more manifest inability to fulfil plans.[3] On the

[1] P. N. C. Okigbo, 'Presidential Address' to the 1965 Conference of the Nigerian Economic Society, *op. cit.*

[2] Henry L. Bretton, *Power and Stability in Nigeria*, Frederick A. Praeger, New York, 1962, Ch. 4.

[3] Federal Republic of Nigeria, *National Development Plan—Progress Report 1964*, Federal Ministry of Economic Development, Lagos, 1965 (especially Ch. 1)

ideological plane, everyone was fashionably one kind of socialist or another; but in practice everybody accepted the ethical basis of capitalism. Appeal only had to be made to ethnic or other group loyalties to rationalize the apparent and real conflicts. In foreign relations, the country stood simultaneously for nationalism, pan-Africanism, negritude, international brotherhood as well as unilateral negotiation as a basis for economic co-operation to gain discriminatory advantage.[1]

Some, probably many, thought that all these aspirations were brilliant and ingenious. A few were sceptical and critical of the tragic implications for the future and pleaded for a more coherent and positive economic policy.[2] Nigeria's foreign friends stood at the sides, cheering and applauding the country's practical good sense and solid stability. But internal inconsistencies in economic policy and incoherent social change have a way of working irresistibly towards collapse. After Independence, there were four years of hurrah followed by two years of tension, strain and synthetic compromise. The logical conclusion came in 1966, when the myth of Nigerian stability exploded and the applauding cheers faded gradually at home and suddenly abroad. The explosion marked the end of the first Republic and the quest for a new political organization and economic philosophy. Meanwhile, the economy continued to plod towards an uncertain future, although many are still conscious of its role as a potential force for African development.

SELECTED READING

1. Aboyade, O., *Foundations of An African Economy: A Study of Investment and Growth in Nigeria* (New York, F. A. Praeger Inc., 1966).
2. Brown, C. V., *The Nigerian Banking System* (London, George Allen and Unwin, 1966).
3. Carter, N. G., *An Input-Output Analysis of the Nigerian Economy, 1959–60: Working Paper* (Cambridge, School of Industrial Management, MIT, Mass., August 1963).

contains a frank discussion of this problem. See also the author's article 'Problems in Plan Revision', *Nigerian Journal of Economic & Social Studies*, Vol. 7, No. 2, July, 1965, pp. 121–30.

[1] If nothing else, the whole history of Nigeria's negotiation with the European Economic Community illustrates this double-talk.

[2] For a sample, see the Selections from 'Nigerian Opinion', *Nigeria 1965–Crisis and Criticism*, Ibadan University Press, 1966.

4. Diké, K. O., *Trade and Politics in the Niger Delta* (Oxford, Clarendon Press, 1956).
5. Dosser, Douglas, 'The Formulation of Development Plans in British Colonies', *Economic Journal*, June 1959, pp. 255–66.
6. Federation of Nigeria, *National Development Plan 1962–68* (Lagos, Federal Ministry of Economic Development, 1962).
7. Federation of Nigeria, *Progress Reports on Nigerian National Development Plan 1962–68* (Lagos, Federal Ministry of Economic Development, 1964).
8. Galletti, R., Baldwin, K. D. and Dina, L. O., *Nigerian Cocoa Farmers—An Economic Survey of Yoroba Cocoa-Farming Families* (London, Oxford University Press, 1956).
9. Government of Nigeria, *A Ten-Year Plan of Development and Welfare for Nigeria, 1946–56* (Lagos, Government Printing Office, 1946).
10. Government of Nigeria, *A Revised Plan of Development and Welfare for Nigeria, 1951–56* (Lagos, Government Printing Office, 1951).
11. Hawkins, E. K., 'The Growth of a Money Economy in Nigeria and Ghana', *Oxford Economic Papers* (New series) (Vol. 10, No. 3, October 1958).
12. Helleiner, G. K., 'The Fiscal Role of the Marketing Boards in Nigerian Economic Development, 1947–61', *Economic Journal*, September 1964.
13. National Economic Council, *Economic Survey of Nigeria, 1959* (Lagos, Federal Government Printer, 1959).
14. *Nigerian Journal of Economic and Social Studies* (Vol. 1, 1959; Vol. II, 1960; Vol. III, 1961; Vols IV–VIII, March, July and November 1962–66, Ibadan, Nigerian Economic Society, Ibadan).
15. Okigbo, P. N. C., *Nigerian National Accounts, 1950–57* (Lagos, Federal Ministry of Economic Development, 1962).
16. Oluwasanmi, H. A., *Agriculture and Nigerian Economic Development*, (Oxford University Press, 1966).
17. Onyemelukwe, C. C., *Problems of Industrial Planning and Management in Nigeria* (London, Longmans, 1966).
18. Perham, Margery, 'The Native Economies of Nigeria', *The Economics of Tropical Dependence*, Vol. 1 (London, Faber & Faber, 1945).
19. Samuel, L. H., *African Studies in Income and Wealth* (London, Bowes & Bowes for the International Association for Research in Income and Wealth, 1963).
20. Stolper, W. F., *Planning Without Facts* (Cambridge, Harvard University Press, 1966).
21. Wells, F. A. and Warmington, W. A., *Studies in Industrialization: Nigeria and the Cameroons*, (London, Oxford University Press, 1962).
22. Yesufu, T. M., *An Introduction to Industrial Relations in Nigeria* (London, Oxford University Press, 1962).

4

THE ECONOMY OF THE IVORY COAST

1. Introduction

In many of its principal characteristics the Ivory Coast economy is strikingly different from other national economies of tropical Africa. Arriving from neighbouring countries one is immediately struck by its relatively high prosperity, and according to two recent studies attempting to measure relative levels of living it ranks at least among the top six or seven tropical African countries. Although it is mainly dependent on agricultural exports for its prosperity and has a significant number of white settlers, African farmers dominate in the production of major cash crops. It has strong economic links with several other African economies. It has no balance of payments problem; there have been no big development schemes in its economic history; the transition from colony to nation was made smoothly and without economic setback; and attempts to attract foreign private investors are a major, and strikingly successful, part of current development policy.

The Ivory Coast economy has always had a strong orientation towards agricultural exports. Prior to colonization kola nuts,[1] exported from what is now southern Ivory Coast to the savanna areas in the north, and palm oil sold to Europe, represented major economic activities and were perhaps as important as the slave trade. Early French administrators, like their counterparts elsewhere in tropical Africa, early introduced exotic crops. They quickly found that coffee and cocoa did well over large areas, and diseases and pests never became serious problems. The economic development of the Ivory Coast until independence in 1960 was largely based on expansion of cocoa and coffee acreage, an expansion that is still in full progress.

Total population was estimated at 3,748,000 in 1964.[2] It is relatively

[1] Cola nitida is a seed resembling a chestnut that is munched as a stimulant and a thirst-quencher throughout West Africa and parts of the Congo Basin; extract of the kola nut is found in *Coca-Cola*.

[2] The first results of the latest Census give a population of about 4 million in 1967.

young (45 per cent of the total is estimated to be under 14); and is thought to be growing at about 2·5 per cent per year (18). Population density is 24·3 persons per square mile, ranging from 9·3 to 40·5 persons per square mile according to region, the south-eastern forest being the most densely populated (Table 1). In 1958 the most densely populated *cercle*,[1] Lagunes, which covered the coastal area around Abidjan, had 87 persons per square mile; but one *cercle*, Tabou, in the extreme southwest had as little as 5 persons per square mile. The median *cercle* had a density of 29·5 persons per square mile (9, pp. 35–36).

Table 1. *Ivory Coast: area and population, 1958*

Region	Population (thousands)	Land area (thousand square miles)	Density (persons per square mile)
Northern savanna	598	38·3	15·6
Southern savanna	786	32·0	24·5
Western forest	871	26·6	32·8
Southwestern forest	83	8·9	9·3
Southeastern forest	750	18·5	40·5
Total	3088	124·3	24·8

Source: Derived from (9), p. 35.

There are about 60 indigenous tribes and probably at least an equal number of foreign tribes represented by bands of immigrants that have established permanent residence since the turn of the century. The largest ethnic groups, the Agni and Baoulé, are closely related to the Ashanti in western Ghana. The European population was officially estimated at 20,000 in 1962 and unofficial estimates put it at 30,000 at the beginning of 1965. Some 3,000 Syrians and Lebanese are found.

Gross Territorial Product[2] more than doubled from 1956 (99·1 billion CFA francs,[3] £143·4 million) to 1964 (216·9 billion CFA francs, £313·8 million). Gross Territorial Product *per capita* is estimated to have grown 6·2 per cent in monetary terms or 2·5 per cent in real terms from 1960–63.

Agriculture accounts for almost half of Gross Territorial Product and commerce accounts for nearly one-third (Table 2). The 'sub-

[1] The *cercle* was the smallest administrative division during the colonial period; it corresponds to the current *sous-prefecture*.

[2] Production intérieure brute—See Introduction, page 27.

[3] The CFA franc exchanges at 50 to the French franc.

Table 2. *Gross territorial product by industry of origin at market prices, 1958 and 1961*

Industry	1958 (billion CFA francs)	1961	1958 (per cent)	1961
Agriculture, forestry, fishing and hunting	53·3	68·8	50·9	46·6
Mining and quarrying	0·5	2·5	0·5	1·7
Manufacture	5·0	9·6	4·8	6·5
Energy and water	2·6	3·7	2·5	2·5
Construction	3·9	6·2	3·7	4·2
Commerce	22·3	43·6	21·3	29·6
Other	17·1	13·1	16·3	8·9
Total	104·7	147·5	100·0	100·0

Sources: Min. Finances, Affaires Économiques, et du Plan, Direction de la Statistique.
(1) *Comptabilité Économique, Résultats Provisoires Concernant l'Année 1961*, and
(2) *Les Comptes Économiques de la Côte d'Ivoire 1958 et 1960.*

sistence' sector was officially estimated to represent only a little over a quarter of the economy in 1958 ((9), p. 5), and it was estimated to have been reduced to 15 per cent of Gross Territorial Product by 1963 ((18), p. 23). Although the definition of subsistence activities is obscure, it is clear that a large proportion of economic activity—even at the village level—is related to market-oriented production. The southern Ivory Coast specializes in production of export crops and the north specializes in furnishing labour and foodstuffs needed in the south, and in conduct of the internal and intra-African international trade of the country.

The amount of capital formation is not known. Estimates made by the government's national income accountants are given in Table 3 but they underestimate the actual volume for the usual reasons.[1]

Role of the State

Government expenditures (current account) varied from 17·6 to 20·6 per cent of Gross Territorial Product between 1960 and 1962, but except for its operation of the port and railway, the State corporation in palm oil processing, and government ownership of 10 to 20 per cent of the stock of two private banks and the development bank for the Ivory Coast, the government's role is indirect in most of the economy. Heavy reliance is placed on private enterprise for develop-

[1] See Introduction.

Table 3. *Gross capital formation 1958 and 1960*

	1958	1960	1958	1960
	(million CFA francs)		(per cent)	
Capital formation by purchaser				
Government	5,168	9,306	36·0	46·1
Business	7,712	9,011	53·7	44·7
Households	1,490	1,855	10·4	9·2
Total	14,370	20,172	100·0	100·0
Capital formation by industry				
Mechanical and electrical	5,444	7,565	37·9	37·5
Construction	8,922	12,597	62·1	62·4
Other	4	10	—	—
Total	14,370	20,172	100.0	100.0

Source: As Table 2, (2).

ment and government regulation is slight compared to that in a number of other African countries—particularly Ghana, Guinea, and Mali with whom it has frontiers.

Some administered prices are found, and government authority is strongly felt at times in some sectors, such as agriculture, where producers can be fined for failure to follow recommended practice and where policy includes obligatory provision of labour by villagers for certain village projects.

Foreign Enterprises

Foreign enterprises are conspicuous throughout the economy and, either directly or indirectly, as pioneering ventures later imitated by indigenous entrepreneurs, have been outstanding in the process of economic development. Successful export crops typically have been introduced by foreigners; the French started cocoa and coffee plantations, as was noted earlier, sometimes forcing African farmers to do the same. Elders in some villages made prosperous by cocoa still remember with amusement initially pouring boiling water on cocoa seedlings they had been forced to plant. Coffee, the leading export, and cocoa, the third most important export, are now produced largely by Africans, but a number of these are African immigrants from neighbouring countries.

Foreign Africans were also important in the development of other cash crops. An early African immigrant from Togo, a tailor named

Gonzague, invested his savings in coconut plantations which for some time the local population thought was pure folly. After other Togolese followed his example and prospered, local Africans began to plant coconuts in areas along the coast that are suitable for the crop and they are now assisted in this by the government.

Pineapples and bananas, recently developed exports, were started by French planters or corporations who are still dominant in production for export, although the share contributed by African farmers is growing rapidly. Initiative to develop rubber, another export crop for which production is expanding rapidly, also came from European investors.

In manufacturing and commerce foreigners have been equally conspicuous. European firms have controlled external trade with Europe since the beginning of the slave trade, and foreign Africans have had a leading, if not dominant, role in the considerable trade with other African countries for as long as there is record. An influx of Lebanese and Syrians in the period between the two world wars resulted in a rapid extension of stores and shops in the interior. Until the last few years this group has controlled the bulk of the domestic distribution of imported goods and the collection of export commodities, although they are now steadily losing ground to African entrepreneurs, of whom many are foreign Africans.

Balance of Payments

The balance of payments of the Ivory Coast have been estimated only for 1963 and 1964, and are, at best, very rough approximations because of the unknown, but according to all evidence sizeable, unrecorded movement of goods and currency across inland frontiers.[1] However, the Ivory Coast seems to have no balance of payments problem and recorded exports have exceeded recorded imports every year during the last decade, often by a considerable margin. Foreign exchange reserves grew by over 5 billion CFA in both 1963 and 1964, reaching a total of about 25 billion CFA by the end of 1964. Total debits and credits with the rest of the world each came to 89 billion CFA francs in 1963 and to 115 billion CFA francs in 1964.

2. THE DEVELOPMENT PLAN AND DEVELOPMENT STRATEGY

Development planning is undertaken by the Ministry of Finances, Economic Affairs, and Planning, directed and largely operated by Frenchmen, and consists of setting forth development objectives and projecting rates of growth and structural changes of the economy.

[1] See Table 4, Note a.

Table 4. *Balance of payments 1963 and 1964*

Item	1963 (Billion CFA francs)[a]	1964
Merchandise	+13·2	+11·1
Other goods and services	− 8·6	− 5·0
Transfers	− 2·4	− 4·5
Private long-term foreign investments	+ 4·7	+ 3·5
Private short-term foreign investments	+ 1·6	+ 0·7
Government foreign loans and securities	+ 1·6	− 1·9
Net errors and omissions	− 4·3	+ 1·2
Additions to foreign exchange holdings	5·8	5·1

Note: [a] The Société Générale de Banques en Côte d'Ivoire estimates net unrecorded payments for imports from neighbouring countries to be at least 2 billion CFA francs in 1963, which if correct would reduce the favourable merchandise balance by 15 per cent. Upper Volta officials believe unrecorded Ivory Coast transactions with Upper Volta alone to come to 2 billion CFA francs annually. In addition to unrecorded commerce in consumer goods, some local observers believe movements of cocoa between Ghana and the Ivory Coast are often fairly large because of differences in the level at which the respective marketing boards set the price of cocoa. Finally, there are large unrecorded monetary transfers to several other African countries by the migrant labourers in the Ivory Coast.

Source: Direction des Finances Extérieures et du Crédit and *Fraternité* June 11, 1965

The current plan covers the whole economy for the 1960–69 period and provides targets for some sectors for 1970–74. Earlier plans emphasized agriculture, transportation, and communications, but the current plan gives first priority to industry (40 per cent), with second priority to transportation and communications (20 per cent). Agriculture is now in third place (12 per cent), while electricity and power as a group and education are in fourth place (7 per cent each).

Part of the explanation of the increase in expenditure in industry is that the current plan includes anticipated private expenditures—principally in industry, and comprising 49 per cent of total development outlays—whereas private expenditures were not included in the earlier plan.

By 1975 domestic savings and investment are expected to be sufficiently large so that no foreign aid will be needed (Table 6). The authors of the plan estimate that savings of businesses and households will be 21 per cent of total value added and more than adequate to finance development towards the end of the plan.

The major structural objective is to achieve vertical and horizontal diversification of production through (1) initiating or expanding in-

Table 5. *Summary of Development Plan*

	Average annual expenditure (billion CFA) 1960–69	1970–74	Percentage expenditure 1960–69
Agriculture, veterinary, irrigation, other water dev.	4·1	7·4	12·2
Roads	4·2		12·4
Railways	0·7	16·5 (Roads to Electricity and power)	2·1
Other communications	1·6		4·7
Electricity and power	2·5		7·3
Education	2·4		7·0
Health	0·5	11·8 (Education to Other social services)	1·5
Housing and urban services	2·9		8·6
Other social services	0·1		0·3
Administrative infrastructure	1·4		4·1
Industry and services	13·3	24·1 (Administrative infrastructure to Other)	39·1
Other	0·3		0·7
Total	34·0	59·8	100·0
Net expenditure			
Private	10·7	18·2	31·5
Public	16·3	30·0	47·9
Capital replacement			
Private	6·2	10·8	18·2
Public	0·7	1·0	2·1

Source: Derived from (19).

dustrial enterprises using locally available resources, and (2) diversifying agricultural exports by addition of new exports and expansion of existing minor exports. Beyond diversification the plan's objectives for agriculture are to make the country more nearly self-sufficient in major foodstuffs—particularly rice—and to reduce geographical disparities in the level of living within the country. Further details are given in the section on agriculture.

Planning suffers greatly from inadequacy of data. Growth rates and structural changes are based on projections of estimates for 1958–60, or, where no data are available for the Ivory Coast, on analogy with other tropical countries. It relies heavily on national income accounts which, at best, are very rough and were considerably less reliable for the 1958–60 period than they are now (see (18)).

The Ministry of Finances, Economic Affairs, and Planning is

attempting to close data gaps mainly through contracts with private French research organizations. The principal studies completed or in progress at July 1965, were four regional studies of commerce, the demographic and social conditions of the major urban areas, and feasibility studies for general development of the south-western corner of the country and for development of irrigated rice and sugar cane of the upper Bandama River.

Table 6. *Financing of the Development Plan*
(billion CFA francs)

Source of financing	Annual receipts 1960	1965	1970	1975
Taxation and reserves	5·3[a]	15·1[a]	22·3[a]	4·5
Official loans	4·0	2·4	4·7	15·9
Grants	4·4	5·0	5·0	0·0
Private sources	5·5	10·4	17·0	19·8
Total	19·2	32·9	49·0	40·2

Note: [a] May include external loans.
Source: Derived from (19).

Despite a considerable increase in research related to economic development since independence, the research effort thus far is weak. Not only is there as yet no attempt to establish crucial parameters—elasticities of demand and supply, for example—but most work is purely descriptive and does not focus on problems of increasing productivity and evoking responses from entrepreneurs and consumers that are appropriate for development. No effort has yet been made to develop a model of the working of the rural economies in a country whose prosperity is based almost entirely on agriculture.

The plan gives little attention to inter relationships between sectors and almost no justification of the priorities given. Except for arguments about the need to diversify agricultural exports, discussion of priorities suggests that they were determined largely by political considerations. The concern over geographical differences in levels of living focuses on the problem of rural exodus with consequent unrest and urban problems, and on the lack of development in agriculture along the borders with Liberia and Ghana. A good deal of the investment in transportation is absorbed by construction of a paved road to the Ghanaian border in the south-east, an area having strong cultural ties with Ghana that was then thought to be coveted by Nkrumah.

Obstacles to implementation are given little attention in the plan.

The planners assume that transmission of superior techniques from research stations to African farmers can be effected simply by formation of farm organizations and a rapid expansion of extension personnel and other government agents. Financing the plan is not treated as an obstacle because government schemes to encourage private investors to plough back profits, and government efforts to attract foreign investors are considered effective.

There is little basis for measuring the achievements of the plan to date. Data on production at the first target date, 1965, were not available at the time of writing. By 1964, the actual rate of growth of Gross Territorial Product from 1960 was 6·2 rather than the 7 per cent per annum planned, but otherwise there is little evidence of difficulty in attaining targets.

3. FINANCING THE PUBLIC SECTOR

Monetary and Fiscal Policy

The Ivory Coast belongs to the West African Monetary Union and jointly with other members (Mauritania, Senegal, Upper Volta, Dahomey, Niger, and Togo) determines the monetary policy to be followed by the common central bank (Banque Centrale des États de l'Afrique de l'Ouest). Members of the monetary union have a common currency issued by the central bank, but each member's holdings can be distinguished by an identifying letter in the serial number.

The central bank has had an unvarying re-discount rate of 3·5 per cent (with a special rate of 3·0 per cent for export bills) since the monetary union became effective (November 1962). The central bank sets re-discount ceilings for each member country and can fix liquidity ratios for commercial banks. In addition, it can, and does, narrow or expand the range of paper it is willing to re-discount. The principal instruments of monetary policy to date have been re-discount ceilings and changes in the scope of paper re-discountable. (For example, private bankers report that in the first half of 1965 the central bank was attempting to encourage inflow of foreign capital by refusing to re-discount loans to companies it considered under-capitalized, some of which had had their loans rediscounted earlier with the same degree of capitalization.)

The Ivory Coast has tried to limit inflation by carefully staying under re-discount ceilings; by restricting the budgetary expenditures (current account), and (1960) not only freezing prices of a number of imported goods at the December, 1959 levels but later (in 1961) even lowering prices of some items. At the same time labour unions have been persuaded—perhaps forced—to settle for small increases in the minimum wage. At the end of 1964 the official price index for a typical African family in the capital city (Abidjan) showed only a 13·7 per cent increase since 1960; that of a typical European family in Abidjan stood at 16·4 per cent above 1960 levels; and average minimum wages were, at the same time, 13·5 per cent above 1960. Some local observers believe that the figures understate the inflation that has occurred.

Expenditures from the government's budget (current) increased only 13·2 per cent between 1960 and 1964, the government consistently running a surplus in the current budget to help finance the development budget.

Table 7. *Current Budgets 1960–64*
(billion CFA francs)

	1960	1961	1962	1963	1964
Receipts	26·6	31·3	28·4	29·6	30·4
Expenditures	22·8	25·5	26·8	29·4	28·7
Surplus	3·8	5·8	1·6	0·2	1·7

Source: Situation Économique de la Côte d'Ivoire, 1962 and *Bulletin Mensuel* of the Chambre de Commerce, January and May 1965.

After administration of regional and local governments, education is the largest single item in the budget with 16 per cent of expenditures in 1964, followed by health services and the presidency which accounted for about 10 per cent each.

Foreign debt of the government—principally loans from France's Caisse Centrale de Coopération Économique—amounted to some 15·6 billion CFA francs in 1964, about half the current budget that year. About 33 per cent of this debt is long-term loans; another 18 to 20 per cent is medium-term deferred payment contracts (public works); and the remainder are loan guarantees of the Ivory Coast Government. The domestic public debt was only about 0·5 billion CFA francs in 1964. Total public debt grew 81 per cent between 1960 and 1964, from 8·7 to 16·1 billion CFA francs. The increase in terms of percentage of Gross Territorial Product was from 6·0 to 7·4.

The current budget is financed largely by duties on imports, other indirect taxes, and export taxes. In 1964 import duties and other indirect taxes accounted for 55 per cent of current budget revenues and export taxes (levied on coffee, cocoa, and diamonds) provided 25 per cent.

Table 8. *Central Government Account* (*current*), *1964*

Receipts	m CFA	%	Payments	m CFA	%
1. Interest and dividends from outside central government	—	—	1. Economic services (*a*) agriculture, forestry, veterinary	1,389	4·6
			(*b*) other	—	—
2. Taxes on income					
(*a*) income tax	2,343	7·7	2. Community services		
(*b*) export duties and cesses	7,802	25·6	(*a*) public works and transportation	1,442	4·7
			(*b*) construction and urban development	1,371	4·5
3. Taxes on production and expenditure			3. Social services		
			(*a*) education	4,947	16·3
			(*b*) health	3,000	9·9
(*a*) import and excise duties	16,804	55·2	(*c*) labour and social affairs	265	0·9
(*b*) other	420	1·4			
4. Current transfers from abroad	—	—	4. Administration, law and order		
			(*a*) defence, armed forces, sports, civic service	2,734	9·0
			(*b*) administration of regional and local governments	4,974	16·3
			(*c*) the presidency	3,143	10·3
			(*d*) Other	5,290	17·3
5. Other	3,058	10·1	5. Public debt	180	0·6
			6. Balance (surplus)	1,692	5·6
Total	30,427	100·0		30,427	100·0

Sources: Derived from *Bulletin Mensuel de Statistique*, January 1965, and Chambre de Commerce de la République de la Côte d'Ivoire, *Bulletin Mensuel*, December 1964.

By 1964 the development budget was 9 billion CFA francs, 30 per cent as large as the current budget. This does not include French subsidies and other foreign aid. Between 1500 and 2000 French technicians, many of whom are teachers, are paid largely by the French Government and several French research organizations contribute directly to the development effort at little or no cost to the Ivory Coast Government. French personnel paid direct by France accounted for 14 per cent of the national wage bill in 1960.

In 1964 aid from Le Fonds Européen de Développement (FED), not all of which was to be used in 1964, came to 6·6 billion CFA francs; that from Le Fonds d'Aide et de Coopération (FAC), was 1·5 billion CFA francs; that from the United States government was 2·7 billion CFA francs; and there were also 3·1 billion CFA francs from West Germany in loans to private companies for development in the Ivory Coast.

In addition to the current and capital budgets there are relatively small municipal budgets, which together came to only 1·7 billion CFA francs in 1962. One third of this came from the Government and the remainder came almost entirely from local taxes and loans.

Promotion of Domestic Savings

The peoples of the Ivory Coast appear traditionally to have largely lacked institutions for the encouragement of savings and their use for productive purposes. There has been little lending of money outside kinship groups, and within such groups money loaned was often not allocated to lenders according to expected rates of return, but simply because the social relationship between the two parties made the loan obligatory. Little has yet been done to create effective credit institutions in most rural areas.

Government efforts to increase domestic savings and their utilization for development purposes consist primarily of devices for putting pressure on foreign investors to invest locally a larger share of profits earned in the country. The Société Nationale de Financement (SONAFI) was created in 1963 to encourage domestic savings and issues 20-year government bonds paying six per cent that are exempt from the tax on securities. Linked with SONAFI and considerably more important is the Fonds National d'Investissement (FNI), a government agency created in 1962 to encourage domestic re-investment of profits. Net business profits are taxed 10 per cent per year and net real estate income 16 per cent per year in the form of compulsory subscription to non-interest bearing certificates, which are redeemable only if the holder produces evidence of new productive investment that is a multiple of the value of his certificates (usually one to four times their face value). Alternatively, such certificates can be converted into SONAFI bonds, providing that an equal amount of SONAFI bonds are purchased outright. By the end of 1963 FNI had collected about 1·5 billion CFA francs through issue of certificates and SONAFI had sold 0·6 billion CFA francs of bonds, only 40 per cent of which represented conversion of FNI certificates.

The agricultural credit agency, Caisse National de Crédit Agricole (CNCA), estimates that rural savings are some 6 billion CFA francs,[1] but they are largely hoarded (and sometimes lost by fire or eaten by termites) because of lack of banks in many areas; unfamiliarity with banking operations; belief that deposits may not be easily or freely withdrawn; and, particularly, fear that bank clerks may be bribed by rapacious relatives to reveal the size of deposits made. In most areas lacking a bank, savings can be deposited at the post office under the postal savings system, and one bank, Société Générale de Banques en Côte d'Ivoire, has recently started a mobile banking unit that reaches a number of communities without a branch bank.

The national agricultural credit agency is making an initial effort to increase use of banking facilities in rural areas by opening branch offices in the interior. Data are not available on the volume of savings deposited, but the number of deposit accounts is growing rapidly, having increased from 291 in 1960 to 3,328 in 1964. Credit is available from several sources for large development expenditures, but is severely rationed for small-scale African enterprises. Credit institutions serving the Ivory Coast and other African countries are the Central Bank, the Ivory Coast branch of the Banque Centrale des États de l'Afrique de l'Ouest, which can provide credit up to five years to finance export industrial production and certain development loans; the West African regional branch of the International Bank for Reconstruction and Development; the Caisse Centrale de Coopération Économique (CCCE), a semi-autonomous French public corporation which makes loans to private corporations as well as the Ivory Coast central government, municipal governments, and public organizations; and, prospectively, the African Development Bank.

Several additional sources serve the Ivory Coast exclusively. The Caisse Autonome d'Amortissement (CAA) created by the Ivory Coast government to handle government debt, to hold part of the country's foreign reserves and to serve as the deposit banker of the marketing board, FNI, the postal system, and the railroad—can make long-term loans to private or public enterprises undertaking development

[1] Total private savings were estimated at 33·9 billion CFA francs for 1963, of which 8·8 billion was thought to be by households and 25·1 billion was by business.

projects. Crédit de la Côte d'Ivoire (CCI), a government institution created in 1959, makes long and medium-term loans mostly to home builders and small to medium scale non-African enterprises. The Banque Ivoirienne de Développement Industrielle (BIDI), established by the United States and Ivory Coast government, the International Finance Corporation, Resources and Development Corporation, and 10 private foreign banks including Chase International Corporation and Lazard Frères, started operations in February 1965. Its purpose is to promote development of medium and large scale industrial enterprises.

Caisse Nationale de Crédit Agricole is about the only source of credit for African farmers, but has made most of its loans to a few individuals or corporations.[1] In 1963, 50 per cent of the 86 million CFA francs it loaned went to five large borrowers and the remainder went to over 1000 small farmers as seasonal loans. From 1961 to 1963, 80 per cent of its loans were short-term (one month to two years) and 20 per cent were 2- to 10-year loans.

In 1962 African farmers accounted for 82 per cent of its loans to individuals, and European planters for the remainder. It has suffered an extremely high, but rapidly falling, rate of defaults partly because it financed an unsuccessful attempt to establish co-operatives throughout rural areas. Cumulative defaults on short-term loans fell from 74 per cent of the cumulative total of loans in 1961, to 24 per cent in 1963. Ninety per cent of defaults considered unrecoverable resulted from loans made in 1959 and 1960.

African farmers claim they can rarely get the credit they need from the agricultural credit agency and must therefore pledge their crops to traders,[2] the major private source of credit in rural areas. Interest-free loans and grants within the extended family are common, but

1 Such loans to corporations may reach a number of African farmers, however. An example is CNCA loans to agricultural corporations who have monopsony privileges and who may use loans received to buy fertilizers, pesticides, etc., which they then provide to African farmers with whom they have contracts. The cost is deducted from the price the corporation pays the farmer at harvest time.

2 The agricultural credit agency's total loans averaged only 793·4 million CFA francs per year from 1960 to 1964, but although this is small compared to the estimated 6 billion CFA francs of rural savings and credit of over 25 billion CFA francs extended by banks largely to urban or non-African populations it may be that farmer opinion also reflects the fact that the agricultural credit agency follows sound banking practices of making loans only if there is good prospect of repayment, as judged by a local committee, and if there is collateral or a co-signer. In any event when loans are made the farmer is never allowed to handle currency, but, instead, must send bills for purchases made to the agricultural credit agency for payment. Payments for labour are handled for borrowers by agricultural agents in the field.

there is apparently very little lending of money at interest. However, advances made between traders, or by traders to producers, and loans within family groups often do, in fact, yield a rate of return to the lender.

Within family groups credit provided for productive purposes is often extended with the understanding that the lender will receive a share of the eventual gains, if any; the lender usually has no protection against loss, however, collateral being apparently as rare as explicit interest. Loans made by traders, whether in buying commodities from producers or in selling them to other traders, almost always involve a more favourable price being paid or received by the lender than when no credit is involved. Thus the equivalent of interest is often implicit in the transaction. Butchers typically receive credit from cattle dealers with the agreed price above that prevailing where no credit is involved. Similar arrangements are common between middlemen in the staple foodstuff trade.

Leasing and sale of land are also part of the money market in that such transactions typically occur only when farmers with rights to land need money they cannot obtain by other means. In the tree crop belt informal leases of various sorts are common (see p. 211 below), and sale of land is not unknown.

For short-term loans of under one year, the country's 30,000 Europeans and 3,000 Syrians and Lebanese, but rarely its Africans, rely on four private banks and three special credit institutions—Société Ivoirienne des Banques, La Banque de l'Afrique Occidentale, La Banque Internationale pour la Commerce et l'Industrie en Côte d'Ivoire, La Société Générale des Banques en Côte d'Ivoire, Crédit Foncier et Immobilier, Côtivoirienne, and Crédit de la Côte d'Ivoire.

The private banks widely believe all Africans to be extremely poor credit risks and rarely loan to them except under political pressure. It is likely that this policy does not accurately reflect the credit worthiness of Africans. Much research remains to be done on utilization of credit by Africans, but data available suggest that Africans apply a different standard of morality to loans made within their social units than to those involving a lender outside the social unit. Experience of government agencies suggests that loans made to villages as units are more likely to be repaid than those made to individuals because loans made to villages are managed through traditional social institutions which ensure that individuals will honour obligations. (Government lending agencies also experience a much lower rate of default on loans made to individual Africans than private credit institutions.)

Credit extended by private credit institutions is mainly for a short term. Short-term loans accounted for about three quarters of credit outstanding in the private sector in recent years. (Total amount outstanding in 1962, 28·7 billion CFA francs.)

Interest rates vary from 4·75 per cent on short-term credit extended by commercial banks to customers with the highest credit rating to 7 to 9 per cent charged by Crédit de la Côte d'Ivoire for purchase of automobiles. The agency for agricultural credit makes loans at 5 to 6 per cent and the same rates apply to most medium and long-term loans made by other lending institutions.

4. AGRICULTURE, FORESTRY, AND FISHING

No satisfactory full or sample census of agriculture has been made. One was begun in 1959, but it was not completed. Production of cocoa and coffee can, however, be reliably estimated by exports, since there is little domestic consumption. For other agricultural exports—principally pineapples and bananas—domestic consumption may be large relative to exports. For the country's major starchy-staples—yams, plantain, taro, manioc, rice, maize, millet, sorghum, and fonio—there is no basis at all for reliable estimates of production. For the purpose of national income accounting lack of price data is equally serious. Prices of staple foodstuffs are published for only four towns and cities and vary greatly geographically and from month to month.

The error in Gross Territorial Product estimates because of yam prices alone may well be several per cent. But although the size of the agricultural sector cannot be accurately estimated, it is clearly large. Nearly 90 per cent of the active population is in agriculture; it generates much of the country's exports (67 per cent in 1964); and it employs most of the labour force (43 per cent of recorded wage-earners and all unrecorded wage-earners[1]).

Export and industry-oriented agriculture accounted for from 11 to 19 per cent of Gross Territorial Product from 1958 to 1963, and non-export food crops, livestock, hunting, and collecting for 21 to 30 per cent. Total agricultural production was estimated to decline steadily in relative importance after 1960 from 49 to 36 per cent of Gross Territorial Product, while the share of forestry has increased from 2 to 6 per cent; fishing is very small and shows no clear trend.

The timber industry and a large portion of the fishing industry—the industrial fleet—are almost entirely foreign enterprises.

[1] These are mainly migrants from Upper Volta and Mali working for African farmers. Some are essentially share-croppers, and those paid a money wage may be hired at piece rates for certain seasonal operations only.

Table 9. *Agriculture, forestry, and fishing in total product* (per cent of Gross Territorial Product)

	1958	1960	1961	1962	1963
Export and industry-oriented agriculture	25·0	19·0	17·0	11·0	15·0
Non-export agriculture, livestock, hunting, and collecting	23·0	30·0	26·0	27·0	21·0
Agriculture	48·0	49·0	43·0	38·0	36·0
Forestry	2·0	2·6	3·2	5·7	6·2
Fishing	0·9	0·7	0·7	1·0	0·9
Total	50·9	52·3	46·9	44·7	43·1

Source: (18) and earlier issues.

European farms and plantations are however, of very little importance in food crop production, although they may participate in production of all agriculture exports[1] and are dominant or as important as Africans in the export production of two relatively new, but minor, crops—bananas and pineapples. The European share of coffee and cocoa, the two major exports, and of kola nuts, a minor but important export is very small.

The relative importance of starchy staple foodstuffs is not precisely known, but certain regional patterns can be outlined. Yams are of primary or secondary importance throughout most of the country, while plantain and taro serve as staples mainly in the south. Maize, millets, sorghums, and fonio appear to be staples only among the

Table 10. *Export crops by race of producer, about 1964*

	Per cent of total exports (value)	Per cent of export production Africans	Europeans
Coffee	46	95	5
Cocoa	15	98	2
Bananas	4	22	78
Pineapples	2	50	50
Kola nuts	2	100	0

Source: See Tables 18–20.

[1] There were European planters in the Ivory Coast as early as 1880, but they were of little importance until 1925 when they were attracted in number by the prosperity of African cocoa and coffee farmers.

northern peoples; manioc and rice are important in urban centres of the south.

The south, because of its prosperous and fairly specialized belt of tree cash crops, its urban centres, and its lack of significant livestock production, runs a sizeable foodstuff deficit filled by the northern region, by imports from other African countries—particularly those to the north—and from overseas (especially rice). A large, but unmeasured, volume of yams, maize, millets, sorghum, rice, fonio, (*Digitaria spp.*) onions, shea nuts (*Butyraspermum parkii*) and shea butter, cattle, sheep, goats, poultry, and dried fish from northern Ivory Coast and neighbouring countries move south, while the major flow north is composed of kola nuts, coconuts, bananas, pineapples, and citrus fruit. Both within the south and the north there is active trade between areas in the east and west because of differences in foodstuffs produced and also because of quality differences in commodities that both areas produce in quantity.

Shifting cultivation and hoe culture prevail among African farmers. The Ministry of Agriculture has been attempting to introduce ploughs and use of oxen for draft power among cattle-keeping peoples in the north of the country, but by 1962 only about 25 teams of oxen had been established and no progress had been made for three or four years. A few of the more prosperous African farmers own tractors.

So far population is not dense enough in most areas to cause land shortage although land is much less abundant than it was 20 years ago. In much of the south there was a great deal of vacant land suitable for coffee and cocoa which attracted migrants when production of these crops began to become widely popular (the 1930's for cocoa and the 1940's for coffee). Most communities now have a fairly large group of immigrant or 'stranger'[1] African farmers.

Most land is held under traditional systems of tenure by which rights to the use of land reside in kinship groups, but traditional tenure is beginning to be displaced by leasing arrangements and some individual ownership. Lease arrangements by which immigrant groups make annual payments of an amount and for a period not well defined, are common in the tree crop belt, and such arrangements sometimes involve permanent transfer of land rights.[2] However, except for some 40,000 hectares leased or owned by European farmers or corporations, few titles have yet been registered.

A form of share-cropping is found in tree-crops under which the

[1] Those called 'strangers' in the rural areas of the Ivory Coast are any not belonging to the predominant ethnic group of the area in which they live; they are not necessarily from other countries. In urban areas the term 'stranger' is reserved for Africans from other countries.

[2] See (20).

person with rights to land, the labourers, and the supplier of non-labour inputs gets shares of the harvest—usually one-third each. Although this sort of share-cropping is fairly common, a large proportion of farmers in the south—probably a majority—hire labour at least part of the year, and farmers frequently cite labour as the limiting factor in determining their scale of operations and their product mix.

Livestock production and inland fish resources are little developed, and the African catch of ocean fish is almost entirely by Ghanaians and Togolese immigrants. Livestock production is found principally in the north and does not meet domestic needs. Recorded imports of live cattle from Upper Volta, Niger and Mali in 1962 were equivalent to 25 per cent of the total domestic cattle production that year, and the additional unrecorded imports may well be large.

According to official estimates, the total livestock population of the Ivory Coast in 1962 was about 1·5 million animals, of which 40 per cent were goats, 34 per cent sheep, 20 per cent cattle, and 6 per cent swine. Poultry numbers are not estimated. There is as yet no livestock feeding industry, but a poultry feeding industry is developing.

Commercial production of eggs and poultry by African farmers, based primarily on purchased feed and regular innoculation of birds to prevent disease, made a vigorous start in 1955 and is expanding rapidly, although it is as yet small and confined to a few areas. Egg imports dropped from 89·2 to 13·0 metric tons between 1957 and 1964, suggesting that the supply has grown enough for the country to be almost self-sufficient in eggs by the end of 1964.

There have been no important resettlement schemes or campaigns to register titles to land. Change of inheritance laws and abolition of polygyny have been the major foci of government land tenure policy. Most peoples of the eastern half of the country are matrilineal, with inheritance being from maternal uncle to nephew rather than from father to son—and among some of the patrilineal groups the lineage head inherits all lineage property—systems that leave the individual little incentive to make improvements on the land he tills (in matrilineal systems sons cultivate their father's land a good portion of their productive years although they do not inherit it). In October 1964 the national legislature passed laws declaring illegal any system of inheritance which denies sons the right to their father's property. At the same time it also passed sweeping legislation abolishing 'bride-price', forced marriages, and polygyny.[1]

[1] 'Bride-price', called dowry by the French, is really a reverse dowry, involving transfer of wealth from the groom's kinsmen to those of the bride as one of the

Abolition of polygyny may also have profound effects on productivity through incentives. Under traditional land tenure systems additional wives were a means of capital accumulation. Women did much of the work in fields and land was allocated partly on the basis of the number of wives a man had and the ability and needs of each (judged by their strength, endurance, and the number of dependent children). Wives gave a portion of their harvests to their husband and worked in his field, if any. Thus taking additional wives meant accumulating a 'bride-price' for each, but gave returns in a larger harvest later.

The labour of wives became increasingly important after introduction of cocoa and coffee (men's crops). These crops were typically planted on food crop fields about to be given the long fallow characteristic of shifting cultivation. Thus a farmer's expansion of tree crops was related to the amount of food crops grown by his women. The new legislation not only provides for monogamy, but makes spouses joint owners of all wealth of the household. If the new civil code is rigorously enforced it will encourage purchase of land and hiring of labour, requiring greater savings or use of credit among farmers. It could result in a reduction in the average size of tree crop groves, possibly adversely affecting productivity, depending on the nature and extent of economies of scale. It could also lead to an increase in the range of individual rural wealth with development of both extremely wealthy and landless farmers, neither of which are now found.

Changes in Agricultural Productivity

Overall trends in agricultural productivity cannot be quantified because of lack of reliable data. However, fertilizer imports—although still at a low level—have increased steadily since 1955 and by 1962–64 had reached 170 per cent of 1955–57 levels, and production of export crops has expanded strikingly in the last few years. Much of this gain came through expansion of European production with relatively efficient methods. There has very probably also been some increase in the productivity of African farmers by the substitution of tree cash crops has expanded strikingly in the last few years. Much of this improved production techniques. African-produced pineapples for export are grown under contracts with the processing firm which have as one of the conditions, provision of technical assistance; and an

conditions of marriage. Sometimes 'bride-prices' involve relatively large sums but under the new legislation only a token gift is permissible. Traditionally marriages were forced in the sense that they were arranged by families without the consent of either bride or groom necessarily being given.

improved banana resistant to Panama disease, *Poyo robusta*, introduced to the Ivory Coast in 1955, has been adopted by the majority of African producers of export bananas. The quality of African-grown coffee and cocoa has been considerably improved in recent years. In 1962 70 per cent of coffee was of 'superior' grade compared with only 18 per cent in 1958; in 1964, 85 per cent of cocoa production was of 'superior' quality, compared with only two per cent in 1955. Many Africans, and an ever-increasing number, own machinery either for processing coffee berries or for grinding dried roots and tubers or grain.

The increase in the volume of exports of tropical woods and the major agricultural exports from 1955–57 to 1962–64 was 455 per cent for timber, 80 per cent for coffee, 54 per cent for cocoa, 345 per cent for bananas, and 850 per cent for fresh, and 460 per cent for canned pineapples; data are insufficient to determine the trend in kola nut exports.[1] Increase in production of cotton, tobacco, and fish for industrial processing plants has also been large in percentage terms, although small in total compared with export production.

Development Policy in Agriculture

Government policy is to encourage diversification of agriculture through rapid expansion of cocoa, bananas, pineapples, rubber, palm oil, and coconuts. The plan ignores the possibility of developing kola nuts, despite the fact that they appear to be at least as important as pineapples as an export.[2]

Production goals of the development plan are the following:

Table 11. *Goals for agricultural production in Development Plan* (thousand metric tons)

	Coffee	Cocoa	Bananas	Pine-apples	Copra	Processed rubber	Palm oil
1960	147·5	62·9	105·0	23·0	1·5	—	22·8
1965	200·0	105·0	156·0	40·0	4·3	4·3	27·8
1970	185·0	175·0	187·5	56·0	13·3	12·5	63·8
1975	180·0	200·0	200·0	69·0	24·4	14·0	194·0
Change (%) 1965–75	−10	+90	+28	+72	+467	+226	+598

Source: (19).

[1] Probably well over half of kola nut exports are not recorded by customs and estimates of total kola nut exports began only in 1961.

[2] Research stations have generally neglected kola nuts throughout West Africa, concentrating on crops better known to Western agricultural scientists, but some

Rubber plantings were started in 1956 and by 1964 had already reached 1970 targets. They consisted entirely of plantations owned by two foreign corporations, Société Africainé des Plantations d'Hévéas (SAPH) and Compagnie des Caoutchoucs du Pakidie (CCP); but the government hopes to start satellite village production around processing plants built by these two companies. Sixty per cent of plantings are in the Dabou savanna, a little-cultivated area near the coast surrounded by forest which was thought to be unsuited to tree crops until experiments were made in the early 1950's.

Oil palm production will be developed by a State corporation, Société pour le Développement et l'Exploitation du Palmier à Huile (SODEPALM) which plans to create a series of plantations of about 1,500 hectares each with satellite zones. It is hoped that many of the coffee growers will convert their coffee groves to oil palms. A loan from Fonds Européen de Développement signed in May, 1965 provides financing for 42 per cent of the 1970 target acreage. Coconut production has been stimulated by distribution of 400,000 seedlings in 1960 and 1961 by Société d'Assistance Technique pour la Modernisation Agricole de la Côte d'Ivoire (SATMACI), but except for this the development of coconut production is to be left to private initiative. Expansion of cocoa, bananas, and pineapples likewise will be left to the private sector.

In both agriculture and industry, policy has been to grant monopoly power as an inducement to foreign investors. For example, Compagnie Agricole et Industrielle des Tabacs Africains (CAITA) and Compagnie Française pour le Développement des Fibres Textiles (CFDT) have protected monopsonies in the purchase of tobacco and cotton, respectively. They supervise production of these crops by African farmers, provide technical assistance, and pay producers a fixed price from which charges for assistance are deducted. Prices paid must have government approval. CFDT also has a monopoly of cotton-ginning and there is only one firm, Ets. Gonfreville, in textile production. Manufacture de Tabac de la Côte d'Ivoire (MTC) has a protected monopoly on manufacture of tobacco products. Three pineapple canning companies have protected monopsonies in the areas around their plants. The largest of these firms, La Société Alsacienne de la Côte d'Ivoire (SALCI) buys from African producers under contracts which fix the producer price and stipulate supervision of production techniques and supply of needed fertilizers, insecticides, and hormones (used to increase yields) by SALCI.

The government continues to emphasize exploitation of unused

observers argue that kola nut yields could be greatly increased if this crop were given more attention.

resources and has engaged the Resources and Development Corporation to determine the productive potential of the isolated, sparsely inhabited southwestern corner of the country.

Imports of rice and sugar more than doubled from 1955–57 to 1962–64 and Government development policy for staple foodstuffs emphasizes development of their production. The government has received a loan from West Germany and 18 technicians from Nationalist China to improve and expand rice production. The number of Formosan technicians is to be increased to a total of 160 in 1966. Sugar production is expected to increase somewhat later, with expansion of sugar cane acreage following the development of irrigation on the Bandama River. Planned production is 17·6 thousand metric tons of refined sugar by 1970.

The development plan underscores the importance of expanding extension services because of the large discrepancy between yields attained by research stations and by most African farmers. For oil palms, coconuts, bananas, pineapples, cotton, and peanuts, potential yields with known techniques are estimated to be at least twice those commonly found in peasant agriculture.

Government policy calls for formation of producer organizations to facilitate dissemination of improved techniques; expansion of the number of demonstration agents living in villages with producers; and creation of communal village gardens to which each adult male will be required to donate one day of labour per week. In addition, young men serving in the Civic Service are given agricultural instruction during their military training.

The policy with respect to co-operatives is not clear. After independence a vigorous effort to establish producer and consumer co-operatives was made but they have, on balance, been a failure, even though a few successful ones still survive. In most areas mismanagement of funds by co-operative officers has led Africans to associate co-operatives with fraud and they have no interest in participating in them.

5. LABOUR AND WAGES

Wage earners seem unlikely to represent more than 20 per cent of the active population. The great majority of the economically active population are self-employed or work in family enterprises without fixed rates of compensation.

In towns and cities a large proportion of the women—perhaps 90 per cent—regularly earn income from selling in markets, as hawkers, or by sale of foods or foodstuffs in or near their homes. Such earnings are typically kept separate from the husband's income and sometimes give women a great deal of financial independence. A considerably smaller proportion of men regularly participate in trade but commerce seems frequently to be at least a supplementary source of income at one time or another during the year for most men except some of the skilled workers. If wage employment becomes distasteful workers can readily turn to full-time trading, little capital or experience being required to begin trade in many commodities. The majority of workers still have rights to land in rural areas, and thus are only weakly committed to wage employment.

There is a conspicuous seasonal influx of labour, workers from northern Ivory Coast and neighbouring countries migrating south to the tree crop belt during the harvest (October to January). A 1959 study by the Ivory Coast statistics service estimated migrant labourers to number at least 140 thousand—64 per cent of employed labour.[1]

Since the development of coffee and cocoa exports the country has consistently had a labour shortage filled, but never over-filled, by migrant labourers.

Non-voluntary unemployment is not yet a problem, although data from the 1963 census of Abidjan would appear disquieting if the social context in which unemployment occurs were not taken into account. According to this sample census, 40 per cent of the active labour force reported no regular employment during the past two years, and 14·7 per cent of the men had no job or profession at the time of the interview. However, most urban Africans still have rights to land in rural areas, and can escape if urban conditions become unbearable. Further, all urban Africans have urban kinsmen who are obligated to give them assistance without repayment, and it is not uncommon for townsmen to receive money or shipments of foodstuffs from relatives in rural areas. It is not surprising then, that rapid growth of the Ivory Coast urban centres has not yet been characterized by a rapid increase in crime or urban discontent, as it well may in the future if there is substantial change in African social structure and land tenure systems.

The rapid rate of urban growth is shown in Table 12, page 218. A large part of this urban growth represents rural exodus and immigration. In 1963 only 31 per cent of the residents of Abidjan had been born there and 29 per cent of the total were from foreign countries (mainly Upper Volta and Mali). Immigration is estimated to account for two-thirds of Abidjan's 9 per cent annual growth from 1955 to 1963. Abidjan also has a striking seasonal influx of

[1] Min. Finances, Affaires Économiques, et du Plan, Direction de la Statistique, *Situation Économique de la Côte d'Ivoire 1960* (1961).

Table 12. *Growth of selected towns*
Population (thousands)

	1931	1945	1958	1962	1963	1962 or 1963 as per cent of 1945
Abidjan	10·0	46·0	155·0	—	254·0	552
Bouaké	5·0	22·0	45·0	—	53·0	241
Man	—	2·8	17·3	22·9	—	818
Gagnoa	—	2·0	15·0	19·5	—	975
Daloa	—	5·0	13·3	18·2	—	364

Source: (9), and United Nations, *Demographic Yearbook 1963.*

temporary labourers numbering up to 25,000 at the peak of the harvest season.

The number of salaried workers in the Ivory Coast increased 23 per cent between 1958 and 1964 according to official statistics. The largest gains were in manufacturing, transportation, and construction, while there was a decline in the number of employees in commerce, banking, insurance, and professions. Figures are in Table 13.

In 1962 there were about 10,000 managers, technicians, master craftsmen, and foremen, 72 per cent of whom were non-Africans, mainly Frenchmen. French workers are also conspicuous in less

Table 13. *Employees by industry*
(thousands)

Industry	1958	1962	1964
Agriculture, forestry, fishing, and hunting	85·0	84·7	90·3
Mining and quarrying	2·0	2·1	3·0
Manufacturing and processing[a]	7·7	18·6	22·1
Construction and public works	13·2	21·3	16·5
Transportation	10·7	14·1	16·9
Commerce	16·5 (Commerce and Banking and insurance combined)	11·0	10·9
Banking and insurance		1·5	2·0
Public administration	25·9	29·1	30·0
Other	9·0	14·0	17·2
Total	170·0	196·4	208·9

Notes: [a] Includes electricity.
In 1960 the total wage and salary bill was 24·3 billion CFA francs. 3·6 per cent of employees were non-African and 46·0 per cent were Africans from other countries.

Sources: Mainly (9), and République de la Côte d'Ivoire, *Ivory Coast Republic, 1964.*

skilled positions—as clerks, drivers, and, sometimes, even as waiters. According to the 1963 census of Abidjan, 34 per cent of the men, and 27 per cent of the women, of the non-African population were employed in relatively unskilled positions.

Workers are guaranteed a minimum wage, *salarie minimum interprofessionnel garanti* (SMIG), that varies geographically and by skill and industry. The Labour Advisory Committee, with equal representation of labour and employers, bases recommendations for changes in the minimum wage on changes in the cost of living. The minimum wage more than tripled between 1950 and 1960, but rose only 13·5 per cent between 1960 and 1964. Many workers receive a wage above the minimum as a result of collective bargaining agreements or government action.

In 1961 there were some 190 labour unions, but only about one-fifth (19 per cent) of salaried workers were union members. Since independence there have been no strikes and little publicized agitation for higher wages, labour unions concentrating on education of their members and on securing wider employment compliance with existing legislation on working conditions and benefits due to employees.

Employers are required to contribute to a government family allowance scheme and to insure their employees against illness and accidents related to their work. Workers must be paid at higher rates for overtime and must be given paid annual leave of one day per month worked. Firms with more than 100 employees are required to have a medical centre directed by a trained nurse and to give free medical care to workers and their families.

6. INDUSTRIALIZATION

Total gross revenues of industrial firms increased nearly six times from 1954 to 1964—from 4 to 23·3 billion CFA francs. Food, tobacco, and matches, chemicals and fats and oils, wood processing, and textiles together accounted for from 78 to 85 per cent of gross industrial revenues from 1960 to 1962 and continue to grow rapidly, their gross revenues increasing 49 per cent between 1960 and 1962 (from 8·5 to 12·6 billion CFA francs). Completion of projects in progress in 1964 is expected to expand gross revenues of this group[1] to 23 billion CFA francs by 1967, i.e. to 70 per cent above 1960 levels.

In 1962 industry accounted for only 7·8 per cent of Gross Territorial Product but its share in 1958 was only 4·8 per cent and it appears to be the most rapidly growing sector of the economy. Industrial enterprises include two breweries, industrial bakeries, a tuna

1 Preliminary estimates of turnover for 1966 are 34·2 billion CFA francs.

cannery, fruit canning, margarine manufacturing plants, cocoa butter and instant coffee plants, soap factories, plants for extraction of palm oil, a Renault assembly plant, a bicycle factory, and factories for production of metal drums, steel frames, cans, metal beds, nails, household utensils, corrugated aluminium sheets, liquid air, plastics, and chlorine. Eleven of the thirteen types of industrial enterprises for which data are published had more than 50 per cent growth in value added between 1960 and 1963, and eight of these had their annual value added doubled. Value added was at least 40 per cent of the value of production in nine of the groups (see Table 14).

The bulk of the increment in industrial production is expected to be absorbed locally. Exports to other members of the West African Customs Union and abroad together amounted to only about one-fifth of total sales in 1961 and 1962.

Table 14. *Value added in industry*

Type of enterprise	Value added 1960 (million CFA francs)	Index of value added (1960 = 100) 1958	1961	1963	Value added as per cent of production (1961)
Grain and flour processing	343	99	118	152	34
Coffee, tea, cocoa processing	176	—	125	262	30
Drinks and ice	714	99	156	127	69
Misc. food enterprises and tobacco	517	80	243	300	81
Construction materials	242	66	225	217	74
Wood processing	857	84	129	277	48
Chemicals, etc.	96	—	133	541	63
Manuf. of rubber and plastic articles	37	27	100	491	17
Processing of fats and oils other than butter	1,062	76	91	135	28
Metal working, repair and assembly of machines and electrical equipment	558	—	100	217	48
Assembly and repair of vehicles	1,198	—	140	204	45
Manuf. of textiles and leather goods	1,153	49	116	189	49
Other industrial enterprises	197	76	123	170	69

Source: Mainly (18).

Development Policy in Industry

The development plan provides for virtually all of industrial development to come from the private sector,[1] relying on tax exemptions and protected markets to attract the volume of capital and the technical skills needed. By legislation in 1959, firms undertaking 'priority' investment can apply for long-term benefits. The following six categories are considered as 'priority' enterprises for development:

(1) Housing and urban construction;
(2) Plantations producing such crops as sugar-cane, rubber, and oil palm fruit and doing related processing;
(3) Enterprises engaged in processing local agricultural and forest products;
(4) Manufacturing and assembling enterprises of 'mass consumer goods', e.g., textiles, construction materials, tools, fertilizers, paper and plastics;
(5) Firms engaged in mining, oil prospecting, or refining;
(6) Firms producing power.

Applications for exemptions go to the Ministry of Finances, Economic Affairs, and Planning which makes recommendations to the Cabinet. By January 1964, 30 enterprises with investments totalling some 13 billion CFA francs had been given benefits as 'priority' enterprises and an equal number, representing investments of about 12·5 billion CFA francs were under consideration.

Benefits granted are (1) a ten-year exemption from duties and import taxes on needed raw material imports; (2) a five-year exemption from taxes on profits and a similar exemption for licenses; (3) an exemption from real estate taxes for a period to be determined for each firm separately; and (4) a ten-year reduction of export taxes of as much as 50 per cent on products produced.

In addition, firms whose investments are considered particularly important for economic development may be allowed to come under long-term fiscal regulations which guarantee existing tax rates and provide for exemption from new taxes created during the period. These benefits may be given for as much as 25 years and firms receiving them may be also allowed to sign agreements with the government guaranteeing the 'economic, fiscal and judicial conditions' of their operations for a period not longer than that for which special long-term fiscal regulations extend.[2]

1 The government has provided part of the capital for a petroleum refinery in Abidjan and there is a State corporation for development of palm oil production —discussed above under agriculture—which will be engaged in processing, as well as production, of palm fruit, hence will be engaged in industrial activity.

2 See (6) for details of the investment code.

7. TRADE

The values of exports and imports have both more than doubled during the period 1958 to 1964: but measured in terms of proportion of Gross Territorial Product the trend is not so spectacular. As mentioned already exports have been larger than imports, in some years very much so.

Table 15. *External trade aggregates*

	Imports		Exports	
	billion CFA francs	% of GTP	billion CFA francs	% of GTP
1958	22·8	21·8	31·5	30·1
1960	29·6	21·9	37·3	27·5
1961	41·8	28·3	43·6	29·6
1962	38·5	23·8	47·7	29·4
1963	41·9	23·0	56·8	32·0
1964	60·5	28·0	74·5	34·6

Source: (21).

During the 1960–64 period 92 per cent of exports were food, drink, tobacco, or animal and vegetable raw materials, and 73 per cent of imports were finished or semi-finished goods. Imports are primarily (about four-fifths) from Common Market countries, mainly from France although her share has declined somewhat since 1960—from 71 per cent then to 61 per cent in 1964. About three-fourths of exports go to the Common Market, but France accounts for a considerably smaller share of exports than imports—only 44 per cent of total exports for 1960–64.

The detailed figures in Tables 16–21 speak for themselves. Of particular note is the quadrupling of the value of imports of equipment, etc., for industry; and the increase in imports of food, drink and tobacco has matched the rate of increase in total imports. On the export side, the increases in exports of tropical woods and of bananas are remarkable.

During 1964, primarily in an effort to find new outlets for coffee, the Ivory Coast expanded barter deals with eastern bloc countries to 0·8 billion CFA francs. This represents a ten-fold increase although it remains a small proportion of total trade.

Total trade with other African countries averaged only 8·8 per cent of total exports and 7·6 per cent of imports in 1963 and 1964. Recorded trade with other members of the West African Customs Union—Mauritania, Senegal, Mali, Upper Volta, Niger and

Table 16. *Imports by major commodity groups, 1957–64*
(million CFA francs)

Commodity group	1957	1958	1959	1960	1961	1962	1963	1964
Food, drink, tobacco	3,596	4,040	5,303	5,030	7,746	7,502	6,959	10,031
Power, lubricants	1,130	1,488	1,867	1,748	2,004	2,014	2,155	2,724
Animal and vegetable raw materials } Mineral raw materials	397	406						
Animal and vegetable raw materials			360	525	843	840	834	1,144
Mineral raw materials			111	122	236	144	239	242
Semi-finished goods	2,938	3,151	3,352	4,550	5,624	5,410	6,039	9,260
Finished goods for agriculture	144	194	274	298	341	213	301	441
Finished goods for industry	4,148	4,724	6,612	6,587	9,137	8,867	11,109	16,643
Finished goods for consumers	7,159	8,826	10,408	10,751	15,859	13,544	14,272	20,024
Total	19,513	22,827	28,287	29,611	41,790	38,534	41,908	60,509

Source: (21).

Table 17. *Main import items 1964*

Item	million CFA francs	Item	million CFA francs
Milk products, eggs	1,014	Other cloth	1,165
Rice	1,959	Articles made of cloth	1,951
Refined sugar	1,310	Common metals	2,766
Wine	1,067	Miscellaneous metal products	1,718
Cement and road surfacing compounds	1,085	Hardware goods and household articles	1,254
Petroleum products	2,717	Machines and equipment	4,635
Miscellaneous chemical derivatives	1,182	Electrical appliances	3,366
Tyres	1,078	Automobiles	1,450
Paper, cardboard, paper products	1,694	Trucks	1,703
Unprinted cotton cloth and blanket	1,697	Automobile parts	1,649
Printed cotton cloth	3,455	Other transport equipment	5,363

Source: (21).

Table 18. *Imports by country of origin*
(million CFA francs)

Supplier	1955	1956	1957	1958	1959	1960	1961	1962	1963	1964
France	12,483	12,595	12,252	14,491	18,558	20,868	26,673	24,134	27,662	37,777
Senegal	n.a.	n.a.	n.a.	n.a.	n.a.	n.a.	3,578	2,166	1,560	1,528
Morocco	721	598	766	831	775	782	820	1,033	966	1,270
Other Franc Zone	1,063	495	1,051	612	998	757	1,051	742	1,442	2,292
Total Franc Zone	14,267	13,688	14,069	15,934	20,331	22,407	32,122	28,075	31,630	42,867
Great Britain	594	428	517	612	543	616	909	831	839	1,037
Ghana	252	244	182	308	298	260	53	4	6	14
Other sterling area	229	291	312	664	936	567	1,127	1,456	1,230	1,369
Total sterling area	1,075	963	1,011	1,584	1,777	1,443	2,089	2,291	2,075	2,420
USA	1,216	1,024	949	916	1,122	1,073	1,472	1,642	2,020	5,702
Venezuela	125	123	146	175	96	505	889	914	836	1,147
Germany	709	720	935	1,197	1,301	1,248	1,742	1,554	2,176	2,771
Belgium[a]	194	193	343	330	312	287	479	548	561	1,501
Italy	274	324	450	502	570	444	729	611	730	1,189
Netherlands	400	318	419	617	498	592	829	1,044	732	892
Other Countries	745	1,064	1,202	1,572	2,280	1,612	1,439	1,855	1,148	2,020
Total	19,005	18,417	19,524	22,827	28,287	29,611	41,790	38,534	41,908	60,509
Common Market Countries	n.a.	n.a.	n.a.	n.a.	22,207	24,099	35,119	30,916	34,158	46,985

Note: [a] Includes Luxembourg from 1962.
Source: (21).

Dahomey—was about 3 per cent of imports and exports. Actual trade is certainly larger. Senegal accounts for nearly all of Ivory Coast's recorded imports from other members of the West African Customs Union (supplying mainly wheat and wheat flour, salt, and cloth), and takes about half of its recorded exports to Customs Union members (receiving mainly kola nuts).

Table 19. *Exports by major commodity groups, 1957–64*
(million CFA francs)

Commodity group	1957	1958	1959	1960	1961	1962	1963	1964
Food, drink, tobacco	21,723	26,912	28,375	29,382	32,992	34,341	41,029	51,879
Power, lubricants	—	3	1	—	—	9	11	2
Animal and vegetable raw materials	2,422	4,129	4,693	7,090	8,833	10,556	13,449	19,417
Mineral raw materials			457	414	939	819	637	681
Semi-finished goods	105	201	73	229	657	697	666	867
Finished goods	175	247	222	214	182	1,271	1,026	1,655
Total	24,425	31,492	33,821	37,329	43,603	47,693	56,818	74,501

Source: (21).

Algeria, Tunisia, and Morocco are the principal African trading partners outside the West African Customs Union, in the main supplying wine, petroleum, and sugar and receiving principally coffee and cocoa in exchange. North Africa will probably continue to account for the bulk of trade with other African countries. Except for kola nuts, dried fish, and livestock there is little basis at the moment for trade between the Ivory Coast and other tropical African countries—they have little need for her coffee, cocoa, and bananas and can offer neither the manufactured goods nor the industrial raw materials imported by the Ivory Coast.

The organization of trade is fairly complex and varies greatly according to commodity. A few large foreign companies do almost all importing from overseas and sell directly through their own retail outlets or to wholesalers, the majority of whom are non-Africans. Wholesalers may sell directly to retailers, but not infrequently will also sell at retail themselves. Retailers include shopkeepers, open-air vendors with a stand of fixed location, and peddlers. All of these may depend on wholesalers, but peddlers and those operating stands often buy from other retailers.

Vendors with small stands are the most numerous of all sellers for most of the commodities that they sell, and survive because each one

Table 20. *Main exports*
(Qu: 000 metric tons; V: million CFA francs)

	1955		1958		1961		1964	
	Qu.	V.	Qu.	V.	Qu.	V.	Qu.	V.
Coffee	84·8	11,957	112·5	18,780	153·8	20,348	204·3	31,724
Tropical woods	169·4	1,274	401·2	3,316	792·6	8,529	1,526·1	17,858
Cocoa	75·2	11,058	46·3	6,415	88·5	9,816	124·3	14,530
Bananas	27·0	379	46·1	1,274	91·5	2,105	125·9	3,120
Canned pineapple	0·8	56	2·2	177	4·4	325	10·7	797
Kola nuts[a]	n.a.	n.a.	n.a.	18	0·3	901	17·3	668

Note: [a] Almost certainly a gross underestimate. Kola nuts have been exported to countries north of the Ivory Coast for as long as we have written record, but most of the trade is never recorded. J. Tricart in his *Étude Géographique des Problèmes de Transports en Côte d'Ivoire* (République de Côte d'Ivoire, Min. des Travaux Publics Paris, 1963), estimates on the basis of a sample of transporters surveyed that kola nut exports were 42,500 metric tons in 1958. The official estimate of kola nut trade in 1963 was originally 9,253 metric tons, based largely on customs records from ports; after an attempt to estimate exports across inland borders, the official estimate was raised to 21,425 metric tons for the same year. The published estimates for other years should probably be revised upwards considerably, but it is difficult to determine how much. My interviews with kola nut traders strongly suggest kola nut prices can fluctuate wildly and that kola nut traders are very sensitive to price changes. Traders in the Grand Bassam area of the Ivory Coast report that kola nut prices in foreign markets to the north increased from 25 to 35 CFA francs per kilogram from January to March, 1965 while in the previous year the increase was from 20 to 80 CFA francs per kilogram over the same period.

Source: (21).

is more convenient for a group of customers than the nearest store; and because they are willing to sell the smallest unit which consumers desire. As a rule consumers prefer to buy only enough for immediate needs since they are obliged to share whatever they have with friends and relatives.

Foodstuffs (both local produce and those imported from neighbouring African countries) are marketed through a network of

Table 21: *Exports by country of destination*
(million CFA francs)

Destination	1955	1956	1957	1958	1959	1960	1961	1962	1963	1964
France	11,840	13,644	14,083	18,807	17,635	19,560	22,540	22,148	26,615	26,720
Algeria	2,404	2,750	2,965	3,174	3,257	3,342	3,492	3,280	2,485	3,140
Senegal	n.a.	n.a.	n.a.	n.a.	n.a.	n.a.	1,781	1,787	759	1,031
Morocco	592	780	295	302	282	768	825	621	713	798
Other countries	152	101	163	790	307	238	1,924	1,426	1,189	1,825
Total franc zone	14,988	17,275	17,506	23,073	21,481	23,908	30,562	29,262	31,761	33,514
Great Britain	83	86	179	125	155	331	888	664	761	2,263
Other countries	36	50	48	122	75	332	433	657	668	434
Total sterling area	119	136	227	247	230	663	1,321	1,321	1,429	2,697
USA	4,685	5,062	3,740	5,143	5,411	5,615	6,228	6,883	7,812	14,902
Netherlands	3,153	1,801	1,181	1,027	2,414	2,253	2,993	2,480	3,755	5,933
Germany	1,253	669	628	462	782	1,443	1,978	2,609	3,633	5,451
Belgium[a]	64	126	132	124	162	440	507	585	843	1,554
Italy	668	713	559	571	880	1,566	2,095	3,126	5,107	4,991
Other countries	655	558	451	845	2,461	1,441	1,434	1,427	2,478	5,459
Total all countries	25,585	26,340	24,424	31,492	33,821	37,329	47,118	47,693	56,818	74,501
Total Common Market Countries	n.a.	n.a.	n.a.	n.a.	25,375	28,762	37,226	37,382	44,336	50,476

Note: [a] Includes Luxemburg from 1962.
Sources: République de la Côte d'Ivoire, Min. Finances, Affaires Économiques, et du Plan, Direction de la Statistique, *Bulletin Mensuel de Statistique*, various issues; and *Ibid.*, *Statistiques Douanières, Exportations*, various issues.

weekly and daily open-air markets. Producers or importers may sell directly to consumers in market places or may sell to middlemen who sell to other middlemen or to consumers.

Most of the larger urban centres have foodstuff wholesalers who are supplied either by rural markets or by middlemen buying directly from producers (who may have pledged crops against cash advances). Urban wholsesalers, in turn, sell not only to local retailers but also to surrounding rural retailers and to wholesalers in other towns.

Except for bread, foodstuff processing is principally a cottage industry in which probably a majority of African women in towns are active, buying foodstuffs from producers, from wholesalers, or even at retail in the market place and processing them into dishes that are hawked or sold in the market place, at home or at roadside. Many towns have modern mechanized bakeries which make French bread of good quality, and all towns have small African bakers operating simple home ovens.

Commodities exported to overseas countries may be purchased directly by agents of the few large foreign trading companies which handle most of external trade, or may first pass through the hands of two or three African middlemen and a Syrian or Lebanese trader. All of the export bananas and pineapples are sold through producer co-operatives.

The prices of two of the major exports, coffee and cocoa, are regulated by a government marketing board[1] which operates through exporters and does not itself take possession of commodities, although it not only attempts to regulate prices paid to producers but specifies the terms of sale of these commodities abroad, designating countries of destination, shipping lines, and export release price. Like many marketing boards it has followed policies which have resulted in accumulation of large surpluses which by the beginning of 1965 were said to be about half of the country's foreign exchange reserves.

Export of kola nuts, coconuts, and some re-exports of manufactured goods to other West African countries are handled entirely by African traders. These traders typically import foodstuffs from the countries they sell to, indeed sometimes they have no choice, being forced to barter because of difficulties of currency conversion in Guinea and Mali.

The distribution of imports from overseas is characterized by the dominance first of non-African firms as importers and wholesalers and secondly of foreign African traders and storekeepers below the wholesale level.

[1] There is also a marketing board for cotton purchased for domestic mills.

Table 22. *Concentration of importing, 1961–62*
(per cent of imports)

Firms	All imports	Food, food-stuffs, drinks	Tobacco	Textiles and Clothing	Hardware and drugs	Equipment and appliances
1st 3	29·6	29·8	44·8	45·2	27·2	31·0
1st 10	54·4	67·9	80·4	72·3	63·4	64·7

Source: (22).

In 1961–62 the three largest importers accounted for over a quarter, and the ten largest for over half, of all imports.

The sales in Abidjan of the 15 largest import firms accounted for 63 per cent of their total sales and thus provide some guide to the pattern of activity in the Ivory Coast as a whole. Two thirds of their sales to wholesalers and one third of their sales to retailers were to Syrians and Lebanese. Two fifths of their sales to retailers but only one quarter of their sales to wholesalers were to Africans.

Table 23. *Patterns of distribution*
(per cent of purchases from 15 largest firms)

Type of merchant	Total sales	Food and drink	Tex-tiles and cloth-ing	Hard-ware	Per-fumes etc.	Tob-acco	Con-struc-tion mater-ials[a]	Equip-ment and appli-ances[a]
Wholesalers								
African	25·5	51·5	12·5	19·9	26·5	24·5	70·2	—
Syrians and Lebanese	67·4	38·2	83·1	58·1	57·8	75·5	13·2	38·5
Other non-Africans	7·1	10·3	4·4	19·9	15·7	—	16·1	61·5
Total	100·0	100·0	100·0	100·0	100·0	100·0	100·0	100·0
Retailers								
African	44·4	40·5	53·4	25·5	71·5	42·0	34·5	42·0
Syrians and Lebanese	35·4	29·4	41·0	41·5	25·8	50·3	33·1	3·0
Other non-Africans	20·2	30·1	5·6	33·0	2·7	7·7	32·4	55·0
Total	100·0	100·0	100·0	100·0	100·0	100·0	100·0	100·0

Note: [a] Based on data known to be of questionable reliability. In some columns the totals do not add to 100.

Source: (22).

The Syrians and Lebanese have gained and held their dominant position by (1) knowing African tastes better than their European competitors—they mix more with Africans and learn their languages; (2) extending credit to Africans as European firms usually do not; (3) working longer hours; (4) operating in isolated communities lacking amenities Europeans consider essential; and (5) reportedly by their skill in negotiation, sometimes supported by collusion. The Syrians and Lebanese compete successfully with Africans mainly because of greater experience in bookkeeping and store management and greater access to capital.

A 1961–62 survey in Abidjan showed that foreign Africans outnumber local Africans considerably. Some observers assert that foreign Africans—particularly northern Moslems—control practically all internal commerce not handled by non-Africans. There seems little reason to doubt this for some commodities—e.g. kola nuts, livestock, dried fish from the Niger River, textiles and African bread, but it is clearly not true for the major starchy-staples, vegetables, fruits, and drinks.

The amount and kind of competition found varies considerably. Besides the fairly high concentration at the import level already discussed, seller concentration is also fairly high among merchants with stores in rural areas. In 1961–62, 12 of 47 communities surveyed had eight or less independent stores, and many had a branch of one or more of the three national retail chains. In any community the large proportion of stores owned by Syrians and Lebanese usually practice tacit if not overt collusion because of their economic and social solidarity, hence oligopolistic behaviour arises with a larger number of sellers than would be expected otherwise.

The numerous peddlers and sellers with stands that are found in every town[1] may provide limited competition to stores, but they deal only in a few commodities—principally cloth and matches, soap, kerosene, candles, canned fish, cigarettes, sugar, cooking oil, and soft drinks. Most of them however, provide no threat either because they are working for one of the stores in the community or because lack of capital or credit forces them to procure supplies from the local stores. The few existing or potential sellers with larger amounts of capital still have considerably less than Syrians and Lebanese and cannot get the same discount for quantity purchases.

Other clear departures from competition are the monopolies and

[1] The number of stands has been estimated at one per 40 inhabitants in Agboville in 1961–62; one per 200 inhabitants around Man in western Ivory Coast in 1961; and one per 4,098 inhabitants in Abidjan in 1957–58. See (22).

monopsonies granted by the government as part of its development policy, the marketing boards, and the formal cartels among middlemen in fresh ocean fish and among transporters throughout the country. Sale of domestically produced commodities is sometimes fairly competitive at the retail level, but it is rarely, if ever, that anything more competitive than monopolistic competition is found, even in large markets. The belief that Western African market places are characterized by pure competition is groundless.

In the first place, commodities that look similar often have important quality differences. For instance, palm oil fruit recently harvested, can be used for cooking or for soap making, but as the fruit ages, it becomes progressively less suitable for cooking. Moreover, special services, including the provision of credit, are often part of the transaction, and have the effect of tying customers to particular suppliers.

In the second place, even if the total number of sellers for a similar commodity in a market is large, sellers seem rarely to be informed on the prices of those of their competitors who are out of sight. Moreover, a large proportion of sellers may in fact be working for someone else so that the number of decision takers is typically rather less than the number of persons offering the goods for sale. Finally, even in market places, the number of sellers of any commodity may in practice be quite small. For instance, there were typically less than 8 sellers for 15 of the 37 major commodities sold in the market place of Grand Bassam, a town of about 12,000, between May and the end of October 1965. With numbers as small as this, the likelihood of collusive behaviour is high. To take another example, it is rare for a town to have more than two butchers, although there may be a number of vendors who are given meat on credit by the butcher on the condition that they follow the price he sets.

Indeed, rigidly enforced price agreements are characteristic of some commodities in at least the urban markets of the southern part of the country. Among sellers of plantains and grains, major starchy-staples of the area, and among operators of push carts a seller caught cutting prices must pay a stiff fine to the other members of the agreement or else be driven out of the market place by them. Milder forms of price agreement are found in palm oil, palm fruit, and soap; with these commodities fines are not levied, but individuals are pressured by the other sellers acting in unison, to follow the agreed price.

Well-organized restrictive arrangements are also found among middle men. The first echelon of middle men in the ocean-fish trade operate a well-organized cartel; and cartels among transporters tightly regulate rates charged and allocate market shares by forcing each driver to wait his turn. Drivers who do not co-operate run the danger of having their vehicles damaged.

Trade associations are also common among middle men, and although their function is partly mutual aid, they sometimes serve as vehicles through which prices are fixed. Price agreements are enforced by control of supplies (achieved mainly through credit extended to producers); by refusing to give aid to sellers breaking agreements; and by pressure exerted through the social structure.

Restrictions on foreign trade include customs, a fiscal duty, a statistical tax, a special import duty, a 'tax on value added' (which is a misnomer merely being a final surtax calculated on c.i.f. plus all other taxes), import quotas, and exchange controls. Revenue duties of up to 50 per cent are levied on almost all commodities, and an additional customs duty of as much as 75 per cent is added for commodities coming from countries outside the West African Customs Union and other parts of the Franc zone.

Minimum tariffs vary from 0 to 75 per cent, by commodity, with most goods being in the 5 to 25 per cent range. Common Market countries pay 40 per cent of the minimum tariff; the full minimum tariff is levied on commodities from countries with which the Ivory Coast has trade agreements and on some commodities from other countries; and the general tariff—three times the minimum applies to all other commodities.

Import quotas are fixed for the Common Market countries other than France, for bilateral commercial agreements, for the Soviet-bloc, and for all other countries as a group. Such quotas specify total foreign exchange for each group of countries and allocate exchange within groups by commodity. Firms making export sales of certain commodities to non-traditional markets—e.g. coffee to East Germany—may be given supplementary import quotas of equal value.

In the past the import quota system has been used to ensure that a high proportion of the imports of the Ivory Coast came from France. In return for this favoured treatment France purchased the bulk of Ivory Coast's coffee and bananas at higher prices than those obtainable elsewhere on the European market. Under the Yaoundé Convention of 1964 which applies to the EEC countries and their associated African states, of which the Ivory Coast is one, the Ivory Coast is obliged gradually to abolish discriminatory duties and quantitative restrictions on imports from Common Market countries.[1] At the

[1] The Yaoundé Convention provides, however, that quotas or quantitative restrictions may be retained or new ones introduced to meet development or balance of payments needs.

same time the Convention will result in a loss of the Ivory Coast's favourable prices for its main products in the French market. As an associated state the Ivory Coast enjoys duty free access to the European Common Market for its primary products and it also benefits in aid from the European Development Fund.

8. CONCLUSIONS

The character of the Ivory Coast economy both during the colonial period and since independence has favoured rapid economic growth. Early colonial policies of development through introduction and spread of export crops succeeded well. A large proportion of the Ivory Coast has a physical environment favourable to coffee and cocoa, crops suited to development by African farmers.

French colonial economic policy was principally to encourage export crop production through coercion and dissemination of planting material in early years and by developing transportation, assisting in recruitment of labour, and paying premiums for expansion of tree crop acreage in later periods. White settlers participated in development of export crops but were never dominant. The limit of coffee and cocoa acreage had not been reached by the end of colonial rule, and there was little, if any, evidence of failure of foodstuff supplies to keep pace with demand, hence there was little pressure for increasing productivity—policy focussed on expansion of acreage rather than improvement of yields. To a considerable extent the Ivory Coast specialized in production of export crops and became dependent on neighbouring countries for labour and foodstuffs.

Since independence industrialization has been strongly encouraged by the relatively high and well-distributed African prosperity based on cash crops; by the country's political stability; by investment incentives offered by the government and its heavy reliance on private enterprise for development; and by the government's ability to control inflationary pressures.

The prospects for continued attraction of large amounts of foreign capital and for control of inflation are good. The government appears committed to continuation of a budgetary surplus, and economic development expenditures may well exert little inflationary pressure. A sizeable share of development expenditure is used for imports, and the government's success in convincing labour unions that wage increases are not in the interest of economic development, plus a large reservoir of migrant labour from neighbouring countries have served to keep wage increases small. Increases in demand have come largely through expansion of the number of wage-earning labourers, but appear to have increased the cost of living among Africans little because prices of many imported goods are administratively controlled and because of the high elasticity of foodstuff supply in major urban areas. Whether it is expansion of domestic foodstuff production or increases in imports that has dominated in increments of foodstuff supply cannot be determined from data available, but the Ivory Coast has had no problem in provisioning her cities despite their strikingly rapid growth.

Government agricultural policy since independence basically has been to accelerate development of unused resources with continuation of the expansion of export crop acreage and by development of import-substitute industries, especially sugar and rice. Most successful development projects have involved mainly the solution of technical problems at the initiative of foreign entrepreneurs with foreign technicians and management. Where the success of development efforts has hinged on an understanding of the nature of the rural economies, efforts have been severely hampered by lack of knowledge. Until higher priority is given to agrarian research (both economic and technical) it is likely that failures, such as those with co-operatives and development of animal draft power, will be more numerous than successes.

For a while development based on exploitation of unused land may continue to be fairly impressive. Whether economic expansion can continue at a rapid pace once the sparsely populated southwest has been settled and land suitable for export crops becomes scarce, when increases in agricultural production will be dependent mainly on increases in agricultural productivity, depends to a large extent on government policy. The Ivory Coast has not yet had to face most of the more difficult development problems.

SELECTED READING

1. Thompson, V. and Adloff, R., *French West Africa* (Stanford University Press, 1958).
2. Miège, J., 'Les cultures vivrières en Afrique Occidentale. Étude de leur répartitoire géographique, particulièrement en Côte d'Ivoire', *Cahiers d'Outre-Mer*, VII, No. 25 (1954), pp. 25–50.
3. Tricart, J., 'Les échanges entre la zone forestière de la Côte d' Ivoire et les savanes soudaniennes,' *Cahiers d'Outre-Mer*, IX, No. 35 (July–September 1956), pp. 209–308.

4. Foreign Areas Studies Division, Special Operations Research Office, The American University, *US Army Area Handbook for the Ivory Coast* (Washington, DC, December 1962).
5. Ambassade de France, Service de Presse et d' Information, *The Republic of The Ivory Coast, Hour of Independence* (New York, November 1960).
6. 'The Ivory Coast Market', *Marchés Tropicaux et Mediterranéens*, June 15, 1963.
7. 'The CFA Franc System', *IMF Staff Papers*, Vol. X, No. 3, November 1963, pp. 345–96.
8. Abdel-Rahman, A., 'The Revenue Structure of the CFA Countries', *IMF Staff Papers*, Vol. XII, No. 1, March, 1965, pp. 73–118.
9. Ivory Coast, Min. Finances, Affaires Économiques, et du Plan, Direction de la Statistique, *Inventaire Économique et Social de la Côte d'Ivoire, 1947–1958* (Abidjan, 1960).
10. Tricart, J., *et. al.*, *Étude Géographique des Problèmes de Transport en Côte d'Ivoire* (République de la Côte d'Ivoire, Min. des Travaux Publiques, Paris, 1963).
11. Zolberg, A. R., *One Party Government in The Ivory Coast* (Princeton University Press, 1964).
12. Meilliassoux, C., *Anthropologie Économique des Gourou de Côte d'Ivoire* (Mouton & Co., Paris, 1964).
13. Köbhen, A., 'Le Planteur Noir', *Études Éburnéennes*, V (1956).
14. Ivory Coast, Service de la Statistique et de la Mécanographie, Enquéte agricole par sondage dans le cercle de Bouaké, Juillet 1954–Janvier 1955 (Abidjan, n.d.).
15. Paulme, D., *Une société de Côte d'Ivoire et aujourd'hui: les Bété* (Mouton & Co., Paris, 1962).
16. Tricart, J., 'Le café en Côte d'Ivoire', *Les Cahiers d'Outre-Mer*, X, 39, July–September 1957, pp. 203–33.
17. Dupire, M., 'Planteurs autochtones et étrangers en Basse-Côte d'Ivoire', *Études Éburnéennes*, VIII, 1960, pp. 9–234.
18. Berthelot, Y., République de Côte d'Ivoire, Min. Finances, Affaires Économiques, et du Plan, Direction de la Statistique, *Comptabilité Économique, Comptes Économiques 1962–63, Retrospective 1960–63, Perspective 1964*.
19. Min. Finances, Affaires Économiques, et du Plan, *Perspectives Décennales de Développement Économique, Social et Cultural 1960–70* (Abidjan, September 1964).
20. Köbben, A., 'Land as an object of gain in nonliterate society', in D. Biebuyck (ed.), *African Agrarian Systems* (Oxford 1963).
21. Min. Finances, Affaires Économiques, et du Plan, Direction de la Statistique, *Bulletin Mensuel de Statistique*.
22. Haik, G., Guillard, R., and Le Masson, C., *La Distribution en Côte d'Ivoire* (Paris 1963).

5

THE ECONOMY OF CAMEROON FEDERAL REPUBLIC

1. THE ECONOMY: AN INTRODUCTORY SKETCH[1]

The development over the last half-century of the present Cameroon economy has hinged on expansion of primary exports. These export crops were initially produced mainly on plantations but increasingly they are produced by African commercial farmers. The expansion of output was based on the utilization of previously unused land and labour and on the introduction of new products (largely tree crops) employing labour intensive techniques. A limited volume of transport, commercial, and administrative infrastructure was built up mainly in the southwestern sixth of the territory. A typical 'opening up' export boom was interrupted by World War I but started again afterwards in the East under French colonial development policy. In the West, plantations (largely privately owned German ones in the interwar period and state owned ones later under the Cameroon Development Corporation) remained dominant and the sketchy British mandatory administration and the Lagos–Accra centred commercial interests failed to stimulate any very substantial growth in African production or in public revenue.

Economic achievement under the export oriented production structure in Eastern Cameroon was substantial—although it was never as dramatic as that of the parallel but somewhat earlier development in the then Gold Coast. During the 1930's and early 1940's although the physical volume of production rose, real income almost certainly fell substantially because of export price trends and wartime transport bottlenecks. The late 1940's and the first half of the 1950's saw a resumption of growth without significant structural change as primary export prices regained remunerative levels and output continued to rise. After independence, more energetic

[1] Dr Green wishes to emphasize that all analyses presented, and views expressed are his personal responsibility and are not necessarily those of the Tanzania Treasury to which he is Economic Adviser.

investment and export promotion programmes raised the real growth rate of domestic product to 5 per cent in the East Cameroon. West Cameroon's economy, by contrast, has continued to stagnate continuously since 1914, and probably its real GDP *per capita* has not risen over the past half-century.

Cameroon's economy today is in many respects highly typical of the less underdeveloped coastal African states. National product in 1965 was of the order of 166 billion CFA francs[1] for a population of 5 million or 33,000 francs *per capita*. Exports and imports are in near balance at just over 30 billion francs giving a ratio of total external trade to national product of nearly 40 per cent. Nearly 10 per cent of GDP is stated to originate in manufacturing, but two-thirds of this represents initial processing of raw materials for export and only one-fifth manufacturing for the domestic market. The wage labour force (including agriculture) is less than 5 per cent of the total, and 10 per cent of the economically active population.

Relationships between sectors of production and between geographical regions within the economy are limited. Further growth within the existing productive structure is restricted by the poor prospects of several key exports (cocoa, coffee, bananas, cotton), world duty structures which hinder further processing (e.g. of logs), and the lack of adequate transport links from the interior to the coast. Production for the local market is hampered by its small and fragmented nature and by the limited availability of high level manpower and technical capacity. Accumulated capital—both physical and human—is low absolutely and relatively to production and to population.

Dependence is a pervasive aspect of the economic structure in trade outlets, supplies of manufactured goods, investment funds, and for advisers, teachers, technical personnel and commercial managers. This limits Cameroonian ability to control the economy. Economic nationalism, discontent, and analysis combine to produce dissatisfaction with the existing economic pattern and doubts as to its future desirability or viability.

2. THE SETTING: GEOGRAPHIC, DEMOGRAPHIC, POLITICAL

The area of the Cameroon Republic is over 183,000 square miles with a 425 mile base at 2°N narrowing to a point offshore in Lake Chad at 13°N, 700 miles away. About 60 per cent of the area lies in a

[1] Values are expressed in terms of the local currency, the CFA (Communauté Financière Africaine) franc. 50 CFA = 1 French franc and £1 = 690 CFA. (The rate after the 1967 sterling devaluation is £1 = 592 CFA.)

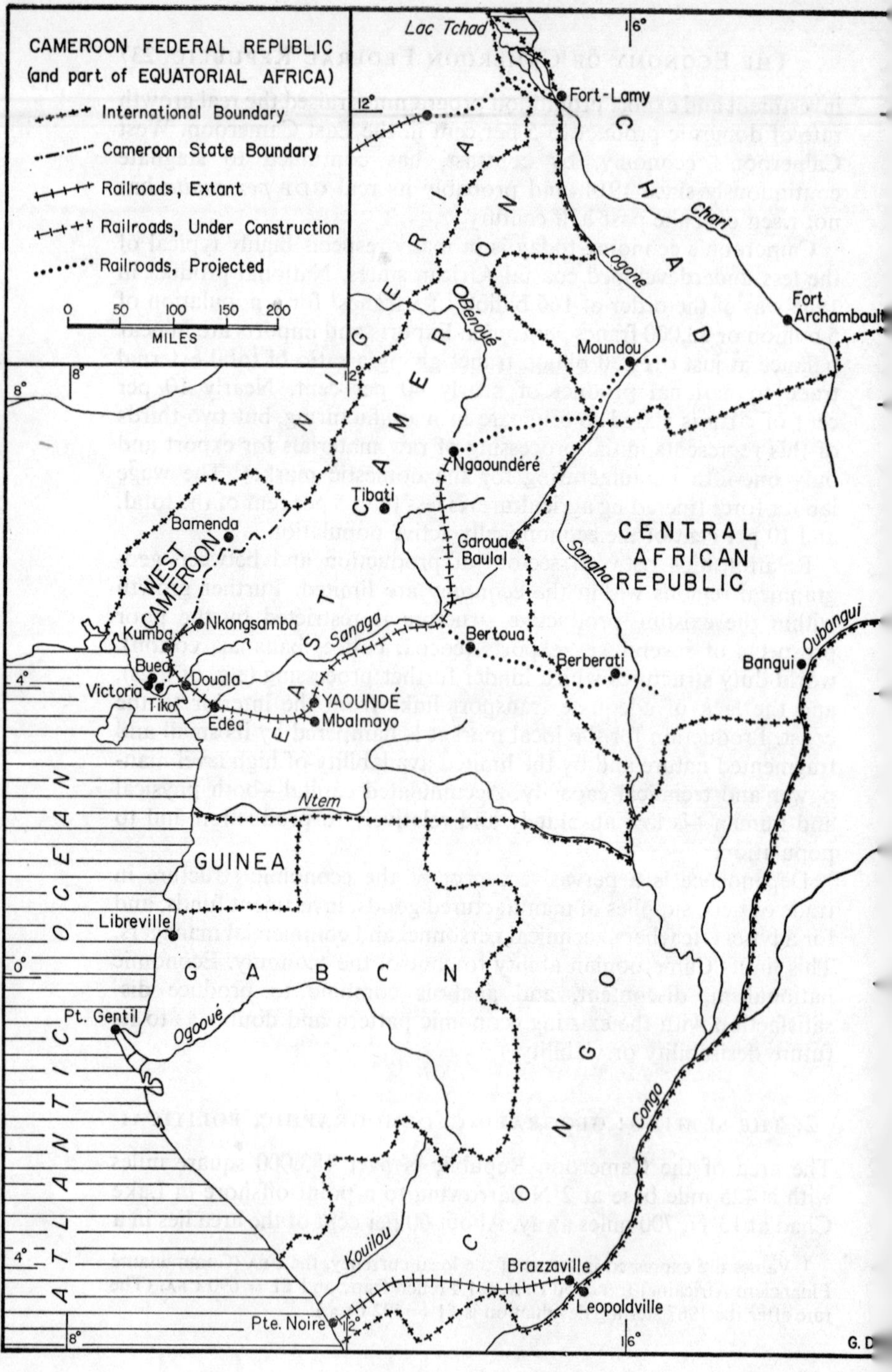
CAMEROON FEDERAL REPUBLIC
(and part of EQUATORIAL AFRICA)
International Boundary
Cameroon State Boundary
Railroads, Extant
Railroads, Under Construction
Railroads, Projected
0 50 100 150 200
MILES
Lac Tchad
Fort-Lamy
CHAD
Chari
Logone
Fort Archambault
Moundou
NIGERIA
Bénoué
EAST CAMEROON
Ngaoundéré
Tibati
Garoua Baulal
Sangha
CENTRAL AFRICAN REPUBLIC
Bamenda
WEST CAMEROON
Nkongsamba
Kumba
Buea
Victoria
Tiko
Douala
Edéa
Sanaga
YAOUNDÉ
Mbalmayo
Bertoua
Berberati
Bangui
Oubangui
Ntem
GUINEA
Libreville
GABON
Pt. Gentil
Ogooué
ATLANTIC OCEAN
CONGO
Congo
Kouilou
Brazzaville
Leopoldville
Pte. Noire
8°
12°
16°
4°
0°
G. D

Map 4

250 by 400 miles quadrilateral at the base, and the rest in a 450 mile long triangle. In the southern quadrilateral the main rivers are the Sanaga, Wouri and Nyong which are all important power sources—actual or potential. In the north the Logone drains into Lake Chad and the Maya Krebi-Bénoue system leading through Nigeria to the sea is navigable to Garoua for six weeks of the year. Douala is the port for the East and Victoria is the major port for the West.

Five rough geographical zones can be distinguished in the Federal Republic:

(*a*) the mountain area of the south and the west which runs from Mount Cameroon through the Manengouba, Bambouta and Mbam massifs and north into the Mandara hills near the Bénoue:

(*b*) the coastal forest plain, a hot humid belt of 10–50 miles between the coast and the forest plateau;

(*c*) the forested central plateau which rises precipitously from the plain to an altitude of about 2,000 feet and extends to the Adamaoua highlands.

(*d*) the Adamaoua savannah zone with an average elevation of 3,600 feet and a dry temperate continental climate;

(*e*) the northern scrub-grass plateau stretching to Lake Chad which becomes increasingly hot and arid as it progresses toward the Sahara.

Demographic Features

The population of the Federal Republic was about 5 millions in 1965. Between 20 and 25 per cent of the population is in West Cameroon (10 per cent of the area) and between 75 and 80 per cent in East Cameroon.

No single tribal group is numerically dominant. In both states political power rests in the hands of the interior savannah populations. Economically the Bassa, Beti-Pahouin (Yaoundé area), and—above all—the Bamiléké are key groups. Over 100,000 Bamiléké are migrants especially to Yaoundé and Douala where they are coming to dominate African commercial and, increasingly, public sector posts.

Urbanization is about 10 per cent and is a product of the modern economy rather than of pre-colonial society. 430–450,000 Cameroonians live in towns of over 5,000, (380–400,000 in towns of over 10,000) with Douala (200,000), Yaoundé (110,000) and the Victoria-Buéa-Tiko combination (50–60,000) the largest. For the country as a whole population density is about 27 per square mile, but in the West the density is twice as high. The range by department is from over 260 in Wouri (which includes Douala) to 1·3 in Boumba Ngaro in the northeast. In certain of the south and western highlands—especially the Bamiléké—population density and land tenure patterns encourage migration and create growing discontent.

Table 1. *Population*

	Population ('000) 1962–63	1965
East Cameroon		
Littoral	446	500
West	705	700
South Central	973	1000
East	240	215
North	1258	1335
Sub total	3621	3750
West Cameroon		
Littoral	114	150
Forest	316	380
Savannah	590	720
Sub total	1020	1250
Total Cameroon Federal Republic	4641	5000

Sources: 1962–63 *Annuaire Statistique*, Yaoundé (Ministère de l'Economie Nationale), and Buéa, (Ministry of Education). 1965, Author's estimates. A later official estimate puts the total for that year at 5,300,000.

The crude birth rate is estimated at 40 to 45 per 1,000 and life expectancy is in the low or middle 30's. This produces a population structure of which 40 per cent are under 15, 55 per cent are between 15–59, and only 5 per cent are 60 and over. The rate of population growth has been variously estimated from 1·0 to 2·1 per cent. Considering that Cameroon nutrition and health standards are at least comparable to those of Nigeria and the birth rate may well be understated, a rate of growth of 2–2·25 per cent rising to 2·5 per cent by 1970 appears more realistic.

Political Patterns

As in most African states, political power leads to the good life and to success in economic activity more often than the reverse. The solution to breaking the circle of limited resources—limited output and growth—limited resources is widely seen to lie in a strong centralized state. Thus at the individual, communal and the national level, concern with economics leads logically to the primacy of politics.

Today the Cameroon Federal Republic is a one party state (Cameroon National Union—UNC[1]) with one dominant leader—President Ahmedu Ahidjo. A one party state has been created partly because those in power cannot afford to lose its fruits and the (many) 'carpet-crossers' are unable to resist accepting a share; but also because, in the absence of an extensive skilled bureaucracy, the 'parti unique' is seen as a means to using less technically trained men to further national union, partly by appeals to Cameroonian solidarity and partly through the distribution of benefits.

Cameroon's political pattern takes the form of a semi-open elite in which political power is concentrated in Northern hands but civil service and technical positions are held largely by expatriates or Southerners (especially Bamiléké). Political loyalty is a prerequisite for public employment, but within this framework ability appears to be critical in promotion.

Control by a Northern party has greatly influenced Cameroonian politico-economic decisions. Technically and educationally weak *vis a vis* the South, UCAM's Northern leaders have nonetheless been forced to depend on Southern civil servants whilst relying on political means (e.g. breaking alternative Southern parties) and a continued French technocratic presence to maintain its control. Coming from a poor area with few opportunities for economic advance Northern leaders are also deeply committed to retaining office and to making political power yield personal economic gain. At the same time they wish to see their area catch up, and this is reflected in their emphasis on the Trans-Cameroon railway, on road construction and on improvements in education and health in the north. As a modernizing, and increasingly a national, élite, UCAM has also pursued policies of building Cameroon oriented élites throughout the country and seeks to increase freedom of manoeuvre *vis à vis* France through broader foreign contacts and the economic regionalism now formalized in UDEAC.[2]

1 UNC results from a 1966–67 merger of UCAM—the East's *parti unique*—and the parties of the West.

2 The operation of this economic union is briefly discussed in the Introduction, pp. 71–77.

3. STRUCTURAL PATTERNS IN THE CAMEROON ECONOMY

Table 2 sets out Gross Domestic Product estimates in a form deriving from the familiar UN System of National Accounts. Table 3 presents for 1962–63 resource and use data utilizing the framework developed for national accounting by the French.

In 1962–63 GDP was 142·7 thousand mn. fr. CFA equivalent to about 28,000 fr. *per capita*. The primary sector—mainly agriculture—

Table 2. *Gross domestic product 1951–65*
(thousand million fr. CFA)

	1951	1957	1959	1962–3	1965
East Cameroon[a]					
Primary	37·0	44·7	45·8	49·8	52·6
Secondary	4·4	8·2	9·3	14·5	19·1
Tertiary	17·2	27·7	31·4	45·9	57·6
General Govt.	2·7	7·0	8·3	10·9	12·8
Domestic service	0·3	1·2	1·3	2·0	2·3
Total	61·6	88·8	96·1	123·1	144·4
West Cameroon[b]					
Primary	7·7	9·0	8·2	11·4	12·4
Secondary	0·8	1·4	2·0	1·4	1·8
Tertiary	2·5	3·9	4·9	5·2	5·9
General Govt.	0·4	0·8	0·8	1·1	1·2
Domestic service	0·2	0·3	0·4	0·5	0·5
Total	11·6	15·4	16·3	19·6	21·8
Total Cameroon					
Primary	44·7	53·7	54·0	61·2	65·0
Secondary	5·2	9·6	11·3	15·9	20·9
Tertiary	19·7	31·6	36·3	51·1	63·5
General Govt.	3·1	7·8	9·1	12·0	14·0
Domestic service	0·5	1·5	1·7	2·5	2·8
Total	73·2	104·2	112·4	142·7	166·2

Notes: [a] 1951–57 and 1957–59 are not fully comparable, especially as to sectoral breakdown.

[b] Approximate calculations based on incomplete Nigerian regional accounts for 1951, 1957. Non-comparability may account for 1957–59 shifts in sectoral contributions or 1959 calculations (made in 1964) may have been allocated inconsistently.

Source: Comptes Économiques 1963 & 1965: *Nigerian National Accounts 1962* (for West Cameroon).

Table 5. *Federal Cameroon resources and use flows 1962–63*
(thousand million fr. CFA)

	SUPPLIES					USES						
		Domestic Production					Consumption			Investment		
							Households					
	Imports	Commercialised	Non-commercialised	Margins[a]	Total	Intermediate Inputs	Monetary	Own products	State	Enterprises	State	Exports
Animal and vegetable goods (unprocessed)	1·0	25·1	23·9	11·6	61·6	5·7	13·4	23·9	0·1	—	—	18·5
Processed foodstuffs	5·1	11·1	3·9	8·7	28·8	1·6	20·8	3·9	0·4	—	—	2·1
Fuel and power	1·9	1·7	4·0	2·8	10·4	3·6	2·0	3·7	1·1	—	—	—
Semi-processed goods	4·4	9·9	1·0	5·0	20·3	10·3	0·1	—	0·1	—	—	9·8
Industrial goods (machinery etc.)	7·8	6·3	—	7·3	21·4	8·2	3·3	—	1·2	6·8	1·2	0·7
Textile and leather products	5·0	2·7	0·5	5·0	13·2	1·5	10·6	0·5	0·5	—	—	0·1
Misc industrial products	4·5	3·2	0·1	5·0	12·8	3·2	7·8	0·2	1·1	—	—	0·5
Construction[b]	—	10·2	4·4	—	14·6	0·7	1·0	4·4	1·8	3·2	3·5	—
Services[c]	—	20·7	—	—	20·7	11·1	7·6	—	1·5	—	0·5	—
Total goods and services	29·7	90·9[d]	37·8[d]	45·4	203·8	45·9	66·6	36·6	7·8	10·0	5·2	31·7
Net Remuneration wage—salary labour	—	33·8	—	—	33·8	19·3	2·5[e]	—	12·0[e]	—	—	—
Total	29·7	124·7	37·8	45·4	237·6	62·2	69·1	36·6	19·8	10·0	5·2	31·7

Notes: a This column represents gross operating revenues (net of cost of goods sold) of commercial sector.
b Maintenance and most replacement are treated as consumption.
c Excludes commerce, administration and domestic service.
d The total domestic production after minor tax-subsidy corrections (—0·5) is equal to Production Intérieure Brute.
e 'Non-production services'. Represents the difference between Production Interieur Brut (128·2) and Produit Intérieur Brut, i.e. Gross Domestic Product (142·7).

Source: *Comptes Économiques* 1962–63.

was responsible for more than two fifths (43 per cent) of this. The secondary sector comprising industry, crafts, construction and power, accounted for 11 per cent; and the remaining 47 per cent (that is almost one half) was contributed by the tertiary sector (commerce, transport, etc.) and government.

Since 1951 the figures reveal a shift toward a more 'modern' and economically advanced structure. During this period the proportionate share of secondary production has virtually doubled as has that of government. The contribution of primary production has, on the other hand, fallen from three fifths to two fifths of the total. In addition goods and services sold as inputs for further stages of production total substantially over one third of value added. The proportion of imports to GDP fell from 26 per cent in 1951 to 22 per cent in 1962–63, whilst that of exports rose from 19 per cent to 23 per cent.

The progress of East and West Cameroon has been very different over this period. Taking 1951 as 100, *per capita* income in 1962–63 was of the order of 140 in the East compared to only 90 in the West. But comparisons in absolute terms between the East and the West are extremely difficult to make because of the very considerable differences in the general price levels which have existed in these two areas until recently. Part of this difference in the post war period was due to the overvaluation of the CFA franc. It is certain that the difference between the price levels in the two areas narrowed over the period and they are likely now to be fairly close together although striking differences in prices of domestic market foodstuffs remain. In making comparisons between the West and East it is wise to concentrate attention on the differences in the rates of change and in structural alterations which have occurred in the two areas rather than to make direct comparisons between absolute levels of consumption and income. The 'modernizing' of the economic structure referred to above has taken place largely in the East, where it has been accompanied by a more complex system of linkages between agriculture and exports, agriculture and urban consumption and industrial cash markets.

From 1951 to 1957 the East maintained a 6·3 per cent growth rate which was generated partly by the 6·6 per cent (see table 10) export growth rate, but also by the increase in government consumption and in private as well as government investment, both directed to re-establishing and broadening the export oriented strategy of the 1930's. Throughout the period, a substantial but declining trade gap was bridged by French budget subsidies and a net private capital inflow (largely for the new aluminium refinery at Edea, based on imported bauxite from Guinea). Deflating by price and population changes yields a 3·1 per cent rate of growth of *per capita* GDP purchasing power (in 1959 prices).

1957–59 saw the fruition of the early post-war export investment and exports leapt by over 30 per cent. But with slackened public and private investment (private investment actually fell with the completion of Edea) the rate of growth of GDP fell to 4 per cent, roughly equal to combined population and price increase rates.

From 1959 to 1962–63 government expenditure on recurrent account and both public and private investment once more grew rapidly and a 7·4 per cent GDP growth rate was attained. Allowing for price increases and population growth, *per capita* purchasing power rose at a rate of 2·7 per cent. Some slackening in growth occurred from 1962–63 to 1965 but real *per capita* GDP continued to increase by nearly 2 per cent annually.

West Cameroon's economy has been much less dynamic, although weaker statistics make computed magnitudes subject to wider margins of error. From 1951 to 1957 a 4·8 per cent growth rate of GDP was secured, but this was more than matched by price increases and population growth, so that the outcome was an annual *decline* of 1·5 per cent in *per capita* GDP purchasing power in 1959 prices. During 1957–59, the growth rate was lower, but prices did not rise as rapidly as before, and GDP *per capita* probably fell only by about 1 per cent a year. Since then GDP has grown by about 5 per cent a year but this has been almost entirely offset by price and population increases so that GDP *per capita* has remained stationary.

Capital Stock and Investment

Capital stock in 1962–63 was estimated to be 370 thousand mn fr. (equivalent to 75,000 francs *per capita*). Over one half of this is construction (of which one sixth is 'traditional' housing), about one third is rural investment (mainly in tree crops), and the remainder consists of transport equipment and machinery. The domestic capital–output ratio is 2·6. In the commercialized sector alone the ratio is 3·2. These data do not support the view that the Cameroon economy is basically non-capital using. Its ratio is within the 'normal' range for industrialized economies, and its capital stock *per capita* is nearly 60 per cent of that in Japan.

The divergence between the level and composition of the capital stocks of East and West Cameroon is marked. In the first place the East has a better infrastructure than the West. This is particularly noticeable in the case of modern buildings and installations. Investment by peasant farmers, particularly in tree crops and livestock, is about 40 per cent in the East compared to about 60 per cent in the

Table 4. *Capital stock 1962–63*

Asset type	East Value	East %	West Value	West %	Federal Value	Federal %
Infrastructure	87·5	27·7	11·25	19·4	98·75	26·5
Buildings and works	91·0	29·0	18·50	31·9	109·50	29·4
Rural investment	91·5	29·0	24·25	41·8	115·75	31·0
Vehicles, machinery and equipment	45·0	14·3	4·00	6·9	49·00	13·1
Total	315·0	100·0	58·00	100·0	373·00	100·0

Note: Values in thousand million frs. CFA.
Source: Adapted from *Comptes Économiques* 1959, 1962–63.

West, although absolutely the Eastern stock is much larger. These differences partly explain the West's lower *per capita* production and its *higher* capital-output ratio, since the inadequate infrastructure hampers the use of productive investment, including that in the direct labour category. This needs access to markets as much as any other type of investment.

Both gross and net investment totals are hard to estimate. *Comptes Économiques* figures exclude direct labour and reproduction investment (except for rural housing which is lumped into household consumption) and list a substantial share of public replacement investment under consumption. A gross ratio of investment to GDP of about 15 per cent (excluding replacement direct labour investment) is the best estimate that can be made.

4. CAMEROON'S INTERNATIONAL ECONOMIC RELATIONS: THE STRUCTURES OF TRADE, RESOURCE TRANSFERS AND ECONOMIC DEPENDENCE

Tables 5–7 provide a summary of statistics relating to the external trade of Cameroon. The economy is externally dependent not only for markets and manufactured products, but also for the finance of domestic investment and the supply of domestic high level manpower requirements. Within this framework substantial growth has been attained, and attempts are now being made to reduce the degree of dependence. Since growth prospects for Cameroon's exports (even including additional processing) are decidedly poor, maintenance of a high growth rate is not compatible with the present import content of consumption and investment.

The dependence of Cameroon is not satisfactorily expressed merely in the ratio of exports and imports to GDP. Although this ratio of 40 per cent (60 per cent if monetary GDP alone is considered) is high, it is not much above that of several of the smaller industrial economies or indeed of the United Kingdom. A number of additional indicators given in Table 8 illuminate the full extent of the economy's external dependence.

Table 5. *Federal Cameroon external trade 1951–62*

	thousand m fr. CFA		Index 1959 = 100	
	Imports	Exports	Imports	Exports
1951	18·8	14·2	71	44
1953	17·2	17·5	65	55
1955	22·0	19·8	84	62
1957	22·7	19·4	87	61
1959	26·3	32·1	100	100
1960	27·5	29·7	105	93
1961	30·0	29·7	114	93
1962	30·2	29·9	115	94
1963	31·9	33·3	121	104

Notes: Imports: Based on recorded East Cameroon imports and West Cameroon data adjusted to include imports through Nigeria.
Exports: Includes 'New Series' West Cameroon data with extrapolation for 1951, 1953.
Growth rates (percentage annual cumulative) are as follows:

	Imports	Exports
1951–57	3·3%	5·3%
1957–59	7·2%	28·5%
1959–63	5·0%	0·8%

Sources: Trade Statistics, Cameroon; UN *Trade Statistics.*

The outstanding aspect of dependence is the predominance of economic relations with France. In 1963 50 per cent of Cameroon's exports were to France and 50 per cent of its imports came from this source. A further 41 per cent of exports and 23 per cent of imports resulted from trade with the rest of the EEC, UK and USA. Cameroon is limited in its choice of markets by preferential EEC duties tied to its reciprocal provision of preferences for (often high cost)[1] French and EEC exports, and by its hopes of substantial capital transfers from the same countries. These effects are reinforced by the institutional dominance of French firms whose preferential treatment (now shared by other EEC countries) is guaranteed under the Yaoundé Convention.

Cameroon net domestic investment is heavily dependent on foreign

[1] cf. F. Bloch-Laine, *La Zone Franc*, Presses Universitaires de France, 1956, for data on these differentials which appear to have averaged at least 10 per cent and much higher on consumer durables, construction inputs, and machinery-transport equipment.

Table 6. *Federal Cameroon exports by class 1951–1963*
(million fr CFA)

Classification	1951	%	1957	%	1959	%	1960	%	1961	%	1962	%	1963	%
Non-monetary gold	43	—	9	—	8	—	2	—	5	—	38	—	11	—
0. Food/live animals	10,400	75	14,100	73	20,625	64	17,800	60	16,785	56	16,450	56	19,075	57
Bananas	2,500	18	3,320	18	2,125	7	2,445	8	2,730	9	2,390	8	1,870	6
Coffee	1,510	11	3,255	18	5,650	18	5,410	19	5,815	19	5,865	19	6,525	20
Cocoa	6,230	45	6,450	35	10,770	33	8,825	31	7,010	23	7,040	23	8,970	27
Cocoa products	—	—	684	3	872	3	864	3	862	3	1,008	3	1,381	4
1. Alcoholic bevs./tobacco	95	1	178	1	264	1	161	1	242	1	463	2	450	1
2. Crude inedible	2,600	19	3,650	19	5,725	18	5,715	19	6,530	22	6,030	20	6,955	21
Oilseeds	1,290	9	741	4	1,341	4	899	3	924	3	886	3	1,305	4
Rubber	712	5	604	3	1,092	3	1,381	4	1,284	4	1,180	4	1,327	4
Cotton	8	—	783	4	968	3	1,047	4	1,445	5	1,684	6	2,043	6
Wood: logs	452	3	1,001	5	1,771	5	1,927	6	2,262	8	1,850	6	1,785	5
Wood: shaped	120	1	234	1	229	1	289	1	261	1	342	1	299	1
3. Mineral fuels	—	—	—	—	—	—	4	—	7	—	9	—	14	—
4. Vegetable oils (Palm, cotton, g'nut)	510	4	408	2	483	2	490	2	475	2	459	2	401	1
5. Chemicals	—	—	—	—	—	—	28	—	22	—	29	—	30	—

6. Mfg. by material	—	—	100	1	4,350	14	4,752	16	5,063	17	5,592	19	5,700	17
Plywood-veneer	—	—	—	—	—	—	—	—	125	—	147	—	150	—
Aluminium	—	—	—	—	4,147	13	4,402	15	4,798	16	5,294	18	5,400	16
7. Machinery/transport equipt.	—	—	400	2	500	2	531	2	416	1	600	2	500	1
8. Miscellaneous mfg.	—	—	—	—	—	—	158	1	130	—	161	1	150	—
9. Other	153	1	500	3	102	—	11	—	10	—	7	—	3	—
Total	13,800	100	19,350	100	32,050	100	29,650	100	29,700	100	29,850	100	33,250	100
							thousand m. tons							
Bananas	127		187		130		123		138		134		122	
Coffee	9		19		33		34		40		42		44	
Cocoa	51		58		61		65		66		66		80	
Cocoa products	—		3		2		5		6		8		10	
Oilseeds	34		26		35		25		30		26		39	
Cotton	—		6		7		7		10		13		15	
Rubber	4		5		7		7		10		8		9	
Wood: logs	67		122		246		263		265		230		213	
Wood: shaped	12		18		14		19		16		19		16	
Aluminium	—		—		39		42		46		51		52	

Sources: *Trade Statistics, Cameroon;* UN *Trade Statistics.*

Table 7. *Federal Cameroon: distribution of trade*
(values in million fr CFA)

	Exports								Imports	
	1951	%	1957	%	1959	%	1963[a]	%	1963[a]	%
France	6,857	50	8,639	46	14,159	45	16,553	50	15,524	50
Total Franc Area	7,230	52	9,790	52	15,700	50	17,880	54	19,222	61
Other EEC	2,579	19	3,319	18	6,117	19	9,207	28	3,456	11
Total EEC	9,436	68	11,958	64	20,276	64	25,742	77	18,980	64
United Kingdom	2,575	19	3,367	18	3,291	10	2,632	8	2,282	7
Total Sterling Area	2,758	20	3,457	19	3,393	11	3,216	9	3,004	10
Continental EFTA	335	2	260	1	250	1	176	1	753	2
Total EFTA	2,910	21	3,627	20	3,541	11	2,808	8	3,035	10
United States	608	4	984	5	2,757	9	1,766	5	1,588	5
Curacao-Venezuela	—	—	—	—	—	—	—	—	1,068	3
Japan	—	—	—	—	16	—	217	1	1,197	4
Total, Africa	660	5	1,290	7	1,720	5	1,900	6	3,801	13
UDE	125	1	739	4	729	2	685	2	114	—
Ex-UDAO	48	—	123	1	173	1	15	—	2,775	9
Nigeria[b]	169	1	60	—	95	—	543	2	297	1
Mahgreb	200	2	287	2	614	2	600	2	590	2
All countries	13,800	100	18,686	100	31,804	100	33,343	100	30,953	100

Notes: [a] For West Cameroon the figures included relate to 1962–63.
[b] West Cameroon exports to Nigeria not included before 1962–63.

Sources: *Cameroon Trade Statistics*, UN *Trade Statistics*.

Table 8. *Indicators of External Dependence, 1962–63*

	East	West
1. Exports as % of GDP		
(*a*) Total GDP	22·2	21·9
(*b*) Commercialized GDP	29·9	31·6
2. Imports as % of GDP		
(*a*) Total GDP	21·0	22·4
(*b*) Commercialized GDP	28·4	32·4
3. Export concentration		
(*a*) % value to leading market	57	51
(*b*) % to 5 leading markets	91	93
(*c*) % value of leading commodity	33	24
(*d*) % value of 5 leading commodities	85	90
4. Import concentration		
(*a*) % value from leading source	57	43
(*b*) % from 5 leading sources	79	73
5. Relative economic size of trading partners (ratio of GDPs)	130:1	
6. National savings as % domestic investment	20	
7. Foreign aid source concentration		
(*a*) % capital from leading source (France and EEC)	78	
8. Foreign high level manpower source concentration		
(*a*) % from leading source	85	
9. Proportion of high level manpower met from local sources	About one third	

Notes: Item 5: average trading partner GDP's weighted by their share in Cameroon exports or imports.
Item 6 excludes profits (remitted or reinvested) of foreign owned concerns. Excludes traditional construction but includes tree crops. Recurrent Budget contribution to capital budget and Administration investment total included in numerator and denominator respectively.

Sources: Calculated and estimated from UN, Cameroon Trade, GDP, Employment and Aid Statistics.

resource transfers. For the 'administration' sector these transfers appear to finance approximately two thirds of investment. Exact data are not available for the private and autonomous corporation sector but the autonomous corporations do not generate significant surpluses available for new investment and, except for tree crops, private investment comes almost entirely from France, mainly from very large corporate groups who have a wide choice of locations for their projects in Africa and which are therefore able to extract favourable terms from government. Four fifths of foreign capital aid comes from France and the EEC European Development Fund. As to manpower only about one third of Cameroon's high level requirements are met by its own nationals. Of the foreign personnel 80–85 per cent come from France. It seems clear that while Cameroon public sector development plans and objectives can be, and increasingly are being, proposed in Yaoundé and Douala, they are still ultimately disposed in Paris and Brussels.

The lack of flexibility of the economy is finally indicated by the structure of external trade. Cocoa, coffee and aluminium account for two thirds of exports, most of the remaining third being made up of cotton, bananas, timber, rubber and oilseeds. About half the imports[1] in 1962–63 were of consumer goods (textiles, clothing, and footwear being the most important items), over a quarter were machinery, equipment and materials for construction, and the remainder were intermediate goods.

A comparison of import and domestic production patterns reveals a substantial overlap in food, tobacco and beer, and aluminium household ware; significant overlaps in soap, clothing and footwear; but very little in other consumer goods, or construction materials, fuel or machinery and equipment. Among the major exports only timber products have a significant local market, if one separates bananas for export and local consumption. An amount equivalent to nearly half of cotton export volume is 'reimported' in the form of textiles and clothing, and both rubber and (basic form) aluminium imports are significant.

The dichotomy between the character of imports and domestic production for local use and between local demand and export production reduces the flexibility of the economy. It is not feasible with the present structure of production to shift exports to meet local demand or to substitute at the margin between domestic production and most key imports. Nevertheless, the nature of imports taken jointly with the local raw materials available (cotton, tobacco, rubber, vegetable oils, meat and fish, potable alcohol, sugar, rice, timber, limestone, potentially bauxite and aluminium, hydro-electric power) and the existing market size suggests opportunities for fairly extensive import substitution based on expansion of both commercial agriculture and industry. Mass market consumer soft goods, furniture and furnishings, construction materials, assembly of machinery and transport equipment, and some component manufacture, offer possibilities for creating additional industrial incomes and, in many cases, for domestic input production, ultimately leading to a lower recurrent import content and a higher domestic multiplier.

Despite the restrictions on freedom of action resulting from this pattern of dependence, external trade has been an extremely im-

[1] East Cameroon figures only.

Table 9. *Long term external trends 1930–63*
(1930 = 100 rounded to nearest 5)

	East					West				
Year	Export volume	Commodity terms of trade	Income terms of trade[a]	Real *per capita* domestic import capacity[b]	Real *per capita* imports[d]	Export volume	Commodity terms of trade[c]	Income terms of trade[a]	Real *per capita* domestic import capacity[b]	Real *per capita* imports[d]
1930	100	100	100	100	100	100	100	100	100	100
1938	200	70	140	120	80	—	—	—	—	—
1946	200	65	135	85	70	85	65	55	35	35
1951	370	150	540	320	380	100	150	150	90	90
1959	680	150	1020	565	345	155	150	230	120	170
1963	875	125	1100	565	390	135	125	170	80	135[e] / 160[f]

Notes: [a] Income Terms of trade is the export earnings index divided by the import price index (i.e. commodity terms of trade index times export volume index) and represents an index of real import capacity sustainable from export earnings.

[b] Real *Per Capita* Domestic Import Capacity equals the Income Terms divided by the index of population.

[c] East series. West and East export mixes are similar. Some discrepancy has almost certainly been introduced by different price movements in the relevant (UK, France) preferential markets and sources of supply.

[d] This series is particularly fragile. To a 1951 base the values are 100, 190, 150/175. The 1930 extrapolation is based on the assumption (roughly valid for Nigeria and Gold Coast) that 1930 and 1946–51 ratios of imports to exports were of the same order of magnitude. An additional source of error is the very approximate nature of West Cameroon import estimates.

[e] Excluding East Cameroon goods which replaced Nigerian imports.

[f] Including East Cameroon goods which replaced Nigerian imports.

Sources: Adapted and estimated from United Nations, Cameroon and Nigeria trade and population statistics.

portant generator of development, but once again there are marked differences between East and West Cameroon (see Table 9).

In East Cameroon, real export volume in 1963 was 875 (1930 = 100) and the income terms of trade (a measure of domestic import capacity) rose even more rapidly, although there was some falling off in 1959–63 when import capacity per head probably fell slightly. Commodity terms of trade have behaved erratically, falling to 65 in 1946 but recovering to 150 in the 1950's before falling to 125 in 1963 (base 1930). Real *per capita* imports also fluctuated, falling to 70 in 1946, exploding to 380 in 1951, declining to 345 in 1959 (after reaching a peak at about 400 in 1958), and recovering to 390 in 1963.

In the short run, the association between import levels and GDP appears closer than that with exports. Investment in advance of export increases has given rise to high and rising imports as well as to rapid growth of GDP but the 1957–59 export boom, resulting in much higher remittances (both household and corporate) and net private capital outflow, was accompanied by a slackening in growth. The 1959–63 recovery in investment and resource inflows led to a rapid growth of GDP and of imports even though export revenue actually remained below 1959 until 1963.

In West Cameroon economic performance, by contrast, is dismal. 1963 export volume stood at 135 (1930 = 100) a fall from the 1959 figures of 155, and real *per capita* imports were about the same level, that is little more than one third higher than they were in 1930. (The underlying statistical data is, however, very weak.)

Balance of Payments

Cameroon's balance of payments statistics, summarized in Table 10 are of doubtful value but for the East several facts stand out clearly. The first is the large and continued public transfer inflow, equal to a quarter of export receipts, which helps to finance general recurrent expenses, public investment, and technical assistance personnel. The second is a somewhat larger outflow of personal remittances and profits running in recent years at 6–7 per cent of GDP. Net inflows of new private capital—as opposed to reinvested profits—were substantial only in 1951. Finally, since 1957, East Cameroon has in most years reduced its foreign debt and/or increased its overseas reserves.

In West Cameroon, there appears to have been a substantial deficit on goods and services account plus a significant flow of remittances by Nigerian workers and small businessmen, offset roughly by public recurrent and capital subsidies, and the depletion of net foreign assets of marketing boards and of the Cameroon Development Corporation.

Table 10. *Cameroon: balance of payments*
(thousand m fr CFA)

	1951	1957	East 1959	1962–3	Federal 1962–3
Exports	11,300	16,600[b]	29,100[b]	27,300	31,300
Public Transfers:					
Administration	} 3,800				
Capital		7,600	8,500[d]	8,200	8,600
Private transfers	300	—	—	—	—
Private capital inflow	8,800	1,800	—[e]	1,800	1,800
Foreign borrowing:					
reserve depletion	—	2,000	—	—	—
Total	24,200	28,000	37,600	37,300	41,700
Imports	16,500	19,300[c]	26,100[c]	25,600	29,700
Overseas state expenses	400	—	300	—	—
Private remittances	600	2,000	3,000	2,200	} 9,000[f]
Private capital payments:					
Dividends	} 5,600	700	} 700	} 6,100	
Other profit flows		4,000	5,500		
Other transfers	800	—	—	—	—
Debt repayment:					
reserve additions	[a]300	2,000	2,000[e]	3,400	3,000[f]
Total	24,200	28,000	37,600	37,300	41,700

Notes: [a] Increase in individual (household) assets abroad.
[b] Includes unofficial exports: 1957—1,100; 1959—2,300.
[c] Includes unofficial imports: 1957—1,000; 1959—6,000 (?). Last appears incredible.
[d] The figure is given as 8,400 current and 100 capital, but this is a fiscal accounting *not* a resource use division.
[e] Apparently 2,000 net private capital outflow. Private balance of transfers capital given as 11,200.
[f] Net. West Cameroon includes CDC loss and repatriation of reserves as well as state use of overseas General and Development Fund assets.

Sources: Computed and adapted from *Comptes Économiques*: 1951, 1957, 1959 from *Comptes* (1963), 1962–63 from *Comptes* (1965).

5. THE EVOLUTION OF ECONOMIC DEVELOPMENT AND PLANNING STRATEGY

Neither planning nor a government strategy for economic growth is a recent innovation in the Cameroon Republic. Nevertheless, an attempt to establish comprehensive national planning and to formulate an economic strategy aimed at development of Cameroon's economy as a separate unit (rather than as a segment of the France–Outre Mer economic unit) did not begin seriously before East Cameroon attained independence in 1960.

French colonial economic policy in Cameroon was neither strictly *laissez faire* nor fully private sector oriented, but involved the use of administrative and fiscal coercion as well as transport development and law and order to raise Cameroon's exports and revenues. Policy towards the private sector involved agreements with large private units—especially the members of the SCAO (Commercial Company of West Africa) and CFAO (French West Africa Company) groups. Tariffs, concessions, and administrative policy were designed to favour French investment and trade connections, even more in the 1945–60 period than in the inter-war years. To this extent the general lines of Cameroon's growth were planned, but as part of the French economy. Three limitations characterized post-war planning prior to pre-independence.

(1) No overall macro goals were set, nor was any structural analysis of the economy conducted on which to base a co-ordinated macro-plan;
(2) Project selection was explicitly in terms of current Franc zone interests—especially easing of France's foreign exchange stringency—not long term territorial development;
(3) Planning—especially decentralized consultation—was carried out in France.

In the West Cameroon British economic policy was far less interventionist. Although the Cameroon Development Corporation emerged as the leading plantation producer after 1945, this came about not as a result of any general policy of public ownership but simply from the 1939 re-seizure of German holdings. The CDC, which is an autonomous body, has played little overall development role. The expenditure of the Government itself on development certainly increased, but its approach remained an extreme example of the 'shopping list' plan and compared either with Nigeria or French Cameroon its effect was limited.

At first, after independence, Cameroon national development strategy and its approaches to planning and to institution creation continued to be dominated by official French thinking, especially by its emphasis on 'animation rurale' via 'investissment humain'. Direct labour investment, in transport and public works as well as in massive agricultural renovation, was designed to absorb up to a third of the investment in the process of a doubling of *per capita* income over the period 1960–80. This concept of 'animation rurale' originated with

French agricultural civil servants, and springs on the one hand from the historical pattern of direct 'labour tax' (corvée) construction, and on the other from a reaction toward widely based agricultural education and extension and away from large capital intensive (and unprofitable) state projects.

In the event several conceptual and procedural errors have operated to limited the extent to which these objectives were implemented.

(1) the need for considering production changes in the context of overall rural socio-political institutional patterns and of their alteration was ignored, or underestimated;
(2) the need for mass understanding of and enthusiasm for any programme based on local action to succeed was never faced;
(3) The degree to which direct labour could be used effectively without intensive technical and monetary capital support was overestimated.

Partly as a result the entire 'animation rurale' programme proved impracticable and a new rural development strategy based on administrative and land reform, intensive popularization and agro-training, and the concentration of personnel and funds on selected areas was developed for the Second (1966–71) Plan period. More recently the development strategy of independent Cameroon has evolved away from the French Colonial model in other respects. But the caution with which the strategy has been altered is related to Cameroonian economic dependence; and the continuation of certain key elements from the past and other factors such as the 'opening up' of the interior, the Trans-Cameroon Railway and economic regionalism, blur the real extent of the changes.

Perhaps the most important of these is that Cameroonian development strategy is now seen as a way of obtaining Cameroonian socio-political goals and is firmly centred on the Cameroon Republic, whereas in the colonial era development strategy was ultimately bound up with the economic and political interests of France and of the Franc Zone. The change in outlook demands rapid development and the paramountcy of Cameroonian interests where possible. The main elements of present Cameroonian development strategy can be summed up under six headings:

(1) Creation of a more nationally integrated Cameroon economy with lower relative dependence on primary exports and greater national control over economic decisions and forces;
(2) Encouragement of industrial development on a broad front

linked to increased processing of exports and national production of agricultural raw material imports;

(3) Construction of the Trans-Cameroon Railway as a means to national and regional economic integration and expansion of effective industrial market size;

(4) Continued 'animation rurale' based efforts to build up agricultural productivity but with a broader attack on problems of institutions and participation, a strengthened technical base and a more limited geographic coverage;

(5) Expansion of export earnings in order to allow the implementation of other elements of the strategy through greater pre-export processing, opening up of new fields of production, e.g. Tibati bauxite-aluminium, southwest forests, and building regional industrial outlets, as much as through general expansion of present smallholder exports.

(6) Diversification of international economic contacts both to increase resource flows and to broaden the range of choice in economic decision making.

Nevertheless, the influence of French ideas on planning continues to be very marked. The first two plans (1947–53, 1954–59) were part of overall French and Overseas-Franc Zone plans. They were characterized by: public sector concentration on infrastructure (particularly transport) largely in support of export expansion; the absence of any coherent set of macro-targets; isolation of a few selected sectors, e.g. cotton, tree crops, and the Edéa aluminium complex; and provision of incentives to and the promotion of private sector activity. This emphasis reflects the immediate post-war French strategy which concentrated on key targets and eschewed more complex macro target patterns and consistency tests until more adequate statistics could be built up.

The 1961–66 Plan was more elaborate and more Cameroon centred but was still grounded on data prepared in Paris or by Paris-based institutions and teams. Tables 11 and 12 summarize some of the salient data. A series of overall economic goals were set for the 1960–80 period, among them the doubling of GDP *per capita* but, despite the preparation of national accounts by sector for 1951, 1956, 1957, 1959, no co-ordinated set of five year plan targets was set and no formal tests of consistency or efficiency of investment allocation could be carried out. The main goals included:

(1) Use of the plan to forge national unity, including provision of special gains in income to economically lagging or politically

Table 11. *East Cameroon: actual growth between 1959 and 1962–63 compared with planned growth in 1961–65 Plan*

	1959	1962–3	Index	Annual growth rates 1959–62–3	Plan 1961–65 projected growth rates
Population ('000)	3,630	3,900	107·4	2·1	1·5–2[a]
Gross Domestic Product	96·1	123·1	128·1	7·4	5·5[a]
Marketed goods and services	57	77·8	136·5	9·3	—
GDP *per capita* at constant 1959 purchasing power[b]	26,470	28,950	109·6	2·7	3·5
Value added:					
Primary	45·8	49·8	108·7	2·4	—
Secondary	9·3	14·5	155·9	13·5	—
Tertiary	31·4	45·9	146·2	11·5	—
Other[c]	9·6	12·9	133·3	8·6	—
Consumption	83·6	108·3	129·5	7·7	(2·9)[d]
Consumption at constant 1959 purchasing power	83·6	99·3	120·0	5·4	(2·9)[d]
Investment	10·3	13·1	127·2	7·1	(10–11)[d]
Gross entrepreneurial incomes	54·8	62·4	113·8	3·8	—
Trade surplus	3·0	1·7	56·6	—	—
Investment rate	10·7	10·6	99·1	−0·25	(5·8)[d]
Tax rate	10·7	18·0	168·2	16·0	—
Food output (real)[e]	—	—	(112–114)	(3·3–3·8)	4·6
Cocoa ('000 tons)[f]	53·4	57·7	108·1	2·3	8·5
Coffee ('000 tons)[f]	29·5	40·7	138·0	9·6	11·2
Cotton ('000 tons)[f]	7·0	14·7	210·0	23·7	4·6
Groundnuts '000 tons)[f]	6·6	9·3	140·9	10·2	14·9
Palm Kernels ('000 tons)[f]	22·6	4·9	52·7	—	9·9

Notes: [a] 1960–1980.

[b] Assumes a 2½% annual decline in purchasing power of CFA franc in terms of weighted average of local and imported goods and services.

[c] General government and (paid) domestic service.

[d] Implicit. Plan investment totals are net. These rates are obtained by adding depreciation and administrative overhead investment (3·5 in 1961 to 4·5 in 1965) and assuming 10·3 as the 1960 investment estimate of planners.

[e] The share of food in primary production rose from 19·5–19·8 to 24·1–24·4. 1962–63 deflated by 2½% per annum price increase.

[*Continued overleaf*

discontented regions (in large part by improved transportation facilities and commercialization of agriculture);

(2) Mobilization of potential national investible surplus, especially underutilized labour time both rural and urban, to implement plan programmes and to create a communal-cooperative rural structure;

(3) Creation of stronger planning (including both data collection and analysis and implementation) institutions;

(4) Training of high level manpower, i.e. extension of education (no manpower plan has been drawn up to date);

(5) Concentration on additional output of coffee, cocoa, oil palms, rubber, cotton, timber, livestock, and rice (the first five for export, rice for import substitution, livestock for domestic and export markets);

(6) Extension of industrialization in the context of plan harmonisation with the states of former French Equatorial Africa.

The detailed project list for 1961–66 totalled 53,000 m. fr. (£79 m). including 18,000 m. fr. 'Direct labour'; 13,000 m. fr. local investment of which 4–6,000 m. represented reinvestment of foreign firms profits; and 22,000 m. fr. external public and private (at most one quarter private). The plan covered only East Cameroon.

The results except for the direct labour field, have been impressive. Real Territorial Product in the East per head rose 3 per cent per year between 1959 and 1962–63, sharply above 1956–59 results. Investment in 1960–61 through 1964–65 will probably exceed 50,000 m. fr. with the 1964–65 level in excess of 15,000 m. Expansion of education, of transport facilities, and of selected key commodities has proceeded in reasonable congruity with the Plan.

Industrial advance has averaged 18–20 per cent annually for 1959–65. The adoption of the UDEAC treaty in 1965 and the steady advance of the TransCameroon Railway will improve both the organizational and physical possibilities for regional market production and plan harmonization. The creation of CIDEP (Centre d'Information, de Documentation et d'Études du Plan), the strengthening of the Direction du Plan and Service Statistique staffs, and the attempts to create additional technical and advisory councils at

---

[f] Exports and export targets. Actual production and planned growth rates of total production would differ from these figures because of local consumption of these products.

Sources: Premier Plan Quinquennial; Bulletin Trimestriel d'Information, 5 ("Rapport Général sur l'Execution"), *E.C.A. Statistics; Cameroun and OMACE Trade Statistics.*

Table 12. *1961-65 East Cameroon Plan: investment details*
(million fr CFA and percentages)

Breakdown by Category		
Studies	2,399	4·5
Production:		
Tourism	182	0·3
Agriculture	9,598	18·0
Livestock	899	1·7
Forestry	1,200	2·3
Industry	3,577	6·7
Co-operatives	950	1·8
Total production	16,406	30·9
Infrastructure:		
Roads and bridges	11,784	22·2
Ports and harbours	3,135	5·9
Aerial	584	1·1
Railways	9,380	17·6
Posts and telecommunications	395	0·7
Total infrastructure	25,278	47·5
Social overhead:		
Health	3,564	6·7
Education[a]	3,460	6·5
Urbanization and environment	2,075	3·9
Total social	9,099	17·1
Total plan	53,182	100·0
Estimated administrative overhead investment[b]	6,000	11·3
Estimated replacement investment[b]	14,000	26·3
Estimated total gross investment	73,182	137·6

national, regional and departmental levels strengthened the ability to prepare, obtain public support and implement both the 1961–65 Plan (which has been 'extended' to mid-1966) and its successors.

The most serious shortcomings of the Plan which have been clearly seen by the Direction du Plan were:

(1) the unrealism of the original direct labour and 'animation rurale' programmes and the delay in working out a more viable rural development scheme;

Table 12—*continued*

Breakdown by Category	
Implicit estimated increase in GDP over plan period[c]	30,000
Implicit capital/output ratio, gross	2·44
Implicit capital/output ratio, net[d]	1·97
Actual Outcome	
1960–62/3	
Investment	41,500
Direct primary and traditional	8,500
Replacement investment in current public budget	7,500
Total investment	57,500
1959–62/3	
Increase in GDP	27,000
Capital/output ratio (gross)	2·13
Change in capital stock	35,000
Capital/output ratio (net)	1·30

Notes: [a] Of this 1,460 m. frs. represents investment in the standard educational system and 2,000 m. frs. the informational and educative aspects of '*cadre formation*' and '*animation rurale*'.
[b] Author's estimates.
[c] Assumes base year (1960–61) GDP of 100,000 million frs. CFA and 5·5 per cent growth rate.
[d] Includes administrative overhead investment.

Sources: Plan Quinquennial de Développement Économique et Social, Ministère des Finance et du Plan, Yaoundé 1961. *Comptes Économiques* 1951, 1956–1957–1959, Ministère de la Coopération, Paris 1963.

(2) the lack of effective public support and the related absence of effective departmental development committees;

(3) the failure to act effectively in West Cameroon after 1962 and the resultant low rate of growth in that region;

(4) the absence of an overall set of sectoral and macro targets with consistency and allocational efficiency tests;

In addition, three problems arise in French style planning in states such as the Cameroon Republic:

(1) extensive decentralization of planning (including data provision and analysis) involving thousands of government, private interest and expert committee members is technically

impracticable in an under-developed economy: centrality in the technical aspects of formulation at least is essential;

(2) interest group members, who in the case of business are predominantly foreign, do not have as convergent interests either with each other or with the state as in France, and are far less willing or able to participate in plan formulation and goal resolution;

(3) indirect financial controls based on credit rationing are of doubtful efficiency in providing controls or incentives for large overseas firms and the limited role assigned to state productive investment participation seems inappropriate.

The 1966–71 Plan will be based on the revised strategy discussed above and particular attention is to be given to overcoming the four shortcomings noted. A more coherent set of sectoral studies was begun in 1963, and regional and CIDEP activity came into full swing in 1965. Detailed consultations and inter-communication with advisory committees and with specialized study groups has been undertaken, and consistency tests have been carried out based on projections from the 1962–63 Federal and Regional National Accounts.

6. GOVERNMENT REVENUE AND EXPENDITURE

Consolidated recurrent expenditure accounts for 1962–63 for Cameroon Federal, Regional, and at least half of Local Authorities, total 22,226 mn. fr. (£32 mn.) or 15·5 per cent of Gross Domestic Product. The corresponding proportion for 1951 and 1959 is estimated at 10 per cent and 13·75 per cent.

Table 13. *Recurrent expenditure*[a]
(m fr CFA)

	1961	1961–62 (adjusted[b])	1962–63	1964–65
Federal		13,800	14,503	15,055
East	18,746	5,850	6,243	7,187
West	2,424	1,520	1,480	2,000
Total	21,170	21,170	22,226	24,242

Notes: [a] Excludes recurrent budget allocations to capital budgets.
[b] Approximate re-allocation on basis of the 1962–63 division of functions.

Sources: Budgets—Cameroun Fédérale, Orientale and Occidentale.

Table 14. *Analysis of recurrent expenditure 1964–65*
(values in million fr CFA)

	Federal		East		West		Consolidated	
	Value	%	Value	%	Value	%	Value	%
1. *Administration etc.*								
Administration[a]	2,588	17·2	2,327	32·4	304	15·2	5,219	21·5
Justice, Police etc.	657	4·4	769	10·7	301	15·1	1,727	7·1
Armed Forces	3,678	24·4	—	—	—	—	3,678	15·2
Other	1,139	7·6	—	—	—	—	1,139	4·7
Total	8,062	53·6	3,096	43·1	605	30·3	11,763	48·5
2. *Social services*								
Education	1,526	10·1	1,519[b]	21·1	453	22·6	3,498	14·4
Health	2,145	14·2	—	—	—	—	2,145	8·8
Other	177	1·2	87	1·2	28[b]	1·4	293	1·2
Total	3,848	25·6	1,606	22·3	481	24·0	5,936	24·5

3. *Economic services*								
Agriculture etc.	149	1·0	192	2·7	292	14·6	632	2·6
Transport, mines and communications[c]	1,275	8·5	789	11·0	110[d]	5·5	2,173	8·9
Finance, Plan, National Economy	1,597	10·5	394	5·5	90	4·5	2,082	8·6
Community development	—	—	618	8·6	44	2·2	662	2·8
Total	3,021	20·0	1,993	27·8	536	26·8	5,549	22·9
4. *Miscellaneous*	124	0·8	492	6·8	378	18·9	994	4·1
Total	15,055[e]	100·0	7,187	100·0	2,000[f]	100·0	24,242	100·0

Notes: [a] East includes 700 mn. fr. in transfers to local government. A greater share of West local government is handled directly and does not appear in State accounts. Works/PWD (a residual of non-transport works) is predominantly administration. Adjusting for local government transfers and works the figures would be East 2,000 mn. fr., West 660 mn. fr. This, however, relatively overestimates the Western share for administration because of the different treatment of educational, agricultural and other non-administration building; most of this is directly allocable in the East but not in the West.

[b] Includes social welfare.

[c] Excludes main railway and ports expenditure which arise in para-statal corporations.

[d] Includes 50 per cent of expenditure of Ministry of Works and Transport.

[e] Excludes transfers: 1,386 mn. frs. to East.
1,200 mn. frs. to West.
909 mn. frs. to Development Budgets.

[f] Excludes transfer of 200 mn. frs. to Development Budget

Sources: *1964–65 Budgets—Cameroun Fédérale, Orientale, Occidentale.*

Examination of 1961–62 (the last pre-union year), 1962–63 accounts and 1964–65 Budget Estimates (see Table 13) suggests that Union has not greatly affected either the overall level or distribution of expenditures. From 1961–62 to 1964–65 there has been a steady growth in expenditure of slightly under 5 per cent a year (less than GDP). However, allowing for services transferred to the Federal Government, Regional Expenditure in the West has risen nearly 10 per cent[1] a year, reflecting a higher level of Cameroonian Federal subsidization than of previous British grants. Expenditure in the East has risen by about 8 per cent a year, and Federal expenditure by 3 per cent. Because of the elimination of the pre 1962–63 French and British recurrent subsidies then running at 20 per cent of recurrent expenditure, growth of domestic revenues substantially exceeded that of expenditure in 1959–63. Expenditures are set out in detail in Table 14 for 1964–65.

Of consolidated recurrent expenditure, approximately one half is spent on administration (21·5 per cent), security (22·3 per cent), foreign affairs (2·9 per cent) and debt service (1·8 per cent). Social services account for about a quarter of Federal and Regional expenditure. The amount spent on social services is understated as approximately 1,225–1,300 mn. fr. (or 20 per cent of budget figures) is financed by FAC and the US Peace Corps in the form of teachers, doctors, scholarships and institutional equipment and material. Health is a Federal responsibility, while education is a Federal responsibility at the lycée, technical and university levels, and a Regional responsibility at the primary and secondary.

Economic services represent about one fifth of the Federal and somewhat over one fourth of Regional budgets. Transport and communications (8·5 per cent), finance-planning-national economy (8·5 per cent), and rural and agricultural (5·5 per cent) are the dominant areas. Agriculture-livestock-forestry and rural development are Regional responsibilities (except for research financing), transport is shared, whilst communications and planning and national economy are essentially Federal.

Overall recurrent expenditurres *per capita* are about 4,850 fr. (£7) of which 3,000 fr. is Federal and 1,850 fr. Regional (1,920 East, 1,600 West). Assuming equal Federal expenditure *per capita* in each region, total *per capita* expenditure in the East would be 7·5 per cent higher than in the West. In fact Federal expenditure *per capita* is still

[1] In the Eastern Region prefectural and local revenues are largely received from or through the Regional Government. This is not true in the West. Correction of local revenue collection might raise the total to 23,000 mn. fr.; i.e. by less than 4 per cent.

skewed to the East for historical reasons, but the total *per capita* divergence is unlikely to exceed 20 per cent.

The level and structure of revenues is shown in Table 15 for 1964–65. Consolidated revenue estimates total 24,115 mn. fr. (£35 mn.). Of this 17,900 mn. fr. or virtually three fourths is Federal, 5,656 mn. (or slightly under one quarter) Eastern, and 559 mn. (less than one fortieth) Western. Federal transfers to the East total 1,386 mn. fr. or about 25 per cent of Eastern revenue, and to the West 1,400 mn. fr. or 250 per cent of Western resources recorded in this Table. (The direct treatment of much of the West's Local Government referred to in the notes to Table 14 affects these proportions.)

Direct taxes are basically regional, and indirect taxes basically Federal. Tax revenues amount to 85 per cent of consolidated revenues. Licences and fees at about one sixth are significant sources of Regional revenues. Rents and interest and services and sales contribute a third of Western revenue. The tax system is fairly severe, but is regressive and non-buoyant. Tax revenue as a proportion of monetary GDP is 30 per cent. The various import duty levies average nearly 30 per cent and are distinctly higher on consumer items. Turnover tax is 6 per cent (East only) and excises plus 'tax unique' amount to perhaps 9 per cent on a comparable basis. Both are progressive for very low income groups but regressive thereafter.

Company tax at 27·5 per cent is low. The wage and salary tax at a flat 3 per cent is low and progressive only to the extent that wage and salary earners as a group have above average incomes. The progressive income tax (super-tax) comes to only 0·2 per cent on a single man with an annual income of 2 mn. fr. (£2,900). Export duties certainly bear on the higher income group but are not progressive within it.

Over time tax revenues at constant rates tend to rise less rapidly than domestic product. This lag is accentuated as the share of production for the national and regional market rises and as capital and intermediate goods form a growing proportion of imports. Assuming a 3 per cent rate of increase in external trade, a 6 per cent increase in GDP (3 per cent subsistence, 7½ per cent market), and an annual increase of 1 per cent in the capital—intermediate goods share of imports, the elasticity of revenue with respect to income appears to be of the order of 0·6. The basic causes of its low elasticity are the unprogressive nature of all the important taxes and the fact that over 60 per cent of total revenues (70 per cent of taxes alone) derive from the export–import sector (if relevant company tax and concession-licence fees are included).

The 1960–65 increase in revenues collected locally from 12,000 mn.

Table 15. *Analysis of revenue 1964–65*

	Federal		East		West		Total—Net of Federal/State transfers	
	m fr CFA	%	m fr CFA	%	m fr CFA	%	m fr CFA	%
Direct taxes:								
Income	—	—	2,552	45·1	38	6·8	2,590	10·7
Poll	—	—	—	—	60	10·7	60	0·3
Company	—	—	1,050	18·6	48	8·6	1,098	4·6
Transactions[a]	2,100	11·7	—	—	—	—	2,100	8·7
Other	—	—	118	2·1	3	0·5	121	0·5
Total direct taxes	2,100	11·7	3,720	65·8	149	26·6	5,969	24·8
Indirect taxes:								
Export duties[b]	3,042	17·0	—	—	106	18·9	3,147	13·1
Import duties[c]	9,896	55·3	—	—	—	—	9,896	41·0
Excises and tax unique	896	5·0	95	1·7	—	—	991	4·1
Turnover	—	—	540	9·5	—	—	540	2·2
Miscellaneous	32	0·2	—	—	—	—	32	0·1
Total indirect taxes	13,866	77·5	635	11·2	106	18·9	14,606	60·6
Total taxes	15,966	89·2	4,355	77·0	255	45·5	20,576	85·4

Licences and fees	133	0·7	992	17·5	96	17·1	1,220	5·1
Rents and interest	40	0·2	177	3·1	91	16·2	308	1·3
Services and sales[d]	1,696	9·5	33	0·6	97	17·5	1,827	7·6
Miscellaneous	65	0·4	99	1·7	20	3·6	184	0·8
Total own revenue	17,900	100·0	5,656	100·0	559	100·0	24,115	100·0
Federal transfers	—	—	1,386	24·5	1,400[e]	250·4	—	—
Caisse Centrale loans	650	3·6	145	2·6	—	—	795	3·3
Total budgeted income	18,550	103·6	7,187	127·1	1,959	350·4	24,910	103·3
Uncovered Deficit	—	—	—	—	240	43·0	240	1·0
Total allocations	18,550	103·6	7,187	127·1	2,200	393·4	25,151	104·4

Notes: a Although classified by the Cameroon as a direct tax, the Federal transactions levy would in English terminology be viewed as an indirect (turnover) tax.

b Includes produce levies on exported primary products.

c Includes all fiscal levies on imports. The structure of import charges is very complex.

d A heterogeneous category. In the Federal case over half represents posts, and telecommunications, and in the West over half is inspection service charges.

e The budgeted Federal transfer is 1,200 mn. fr, but the Western budgeted receipt is 1,400 mn. fr.

Sources: *1964–65 Budgets—Cameroun Fédérale, Orientale and Occidentale.*

fr. to 22,750 mn. fr. has been forced by the increase in expenditure and the reduction of aid. The increase was achieved by drastic rate increases and tax additions. The apparent buoyancy of the initial revenue structure over the period was about 0·7, bolstered by 8 per cent and 7 per cent annual increases in imports and exports.

Cameroon's foreign debt in July 1965 stood at 625·5 mn. fr. (£0·9 mn.). Foreign assets totalled 9,529 mn. fr. (£14 mn.) in July 1963 of which 2,200 mn. fr. was marketing board reserves (a steadily declining item), 4,685 mn. fr. deposits with the French Treasury (partly undrawn aid), and over 1,500 mn. fr. the working account balance of the Banque Centrale. At 30 per cent of imports, these reserves appear adequate but allow little leeway either for financing a more ambitious investment programme or for ameliorating any serious export slump.

7. SELECTED SECTORS: AGRICULTURE, MINING, POWER, COMMUNICATION, MANUFACTURING AND PROCESSING

Agriculture directly generates 35 per cent[1] of the domestic product and provides 75–80 per cent of the population with both occupations and income. Moreover it provides the basis for perhaps two-thirds of Cameroon's processing and manufacturing, for 80 per cent of exports (including value added in processing), and for the modern transport and commerce system. On the other hand, about half of total agricultural production and four-fifths of domestic food output are self consumed. Over 35 per cent of total agricultural output and 70 per cent of marketed agricultural production represents exports. Except for a decreasing share of bananas and cocoa the export producers are African farmers.

Income and productivity levels are low throughout the agricultural sector, but are substantially higher for cash crop farmers, especially the coffee and cocoa-growers of the south. Overall output *per capita* in agriculture is about 15,000 fr. CFA (c.f. a national average of 32,000 fr. (£46)), of which two-ninths is monetary. For cocoa growers the estimated income level is 44,000 fr. (£64), for cotton growers (North Cameroon) 25,000 fr. (£36), and for pure subsistence farmers 6,000 fr. (£9). Production levels per acre in cocoa and coffee appear to compare with those of Ghana and Nigeria and of the Ivory Coast respectively, and cotton productivity at 535 lbs per acre is well above African non-irrigated averages; rubber yields are above those of Nigeria though below those of Liberia.

Land tenure and cultivation patterns have altered only slowly.

[1] Including livestock (5 per cent) and fishing (2–3 per cent) but excluding forestry (5 per cent). All figures in these two paragraphs refer to 1962–63.

Rotation with a long fallow, remains characteristic of the coastal, plateau forest, and agricultural savannah areas. The real agricultural problem is not a general shortage of land nor overall land impoverishment but the low output *per capita* attainable on the basis of present techniques. Land tenure systems are usually based on extended family or lineage ownership, with guaranteed access for lineage members and firm tenure (plus ownership of improvements, e.g. tree crops) for cultivators. Land tenure problems have arisen not from any general non-adaptability of the system but from fragmentation under conditions of overpopulation and from the abuse of land allocating powers by local notables in their attempts to control tree crop wealth, particularly in the Bamiléké country.

Bananas, plantains and starchy roots together with tree export crops dominate the coastal and forested plateau areas. To the north, cotton, groundnuts, millet, sorghum, and livestock are produced. As aridity increases, crops tend to thin out and livestock assumes greater importance. Only maize and chickens are common to both rural patterns. Trade, except in cattle (from the North) and fish (in both directions), is limited, since the cost of storage and transport on the one hand and acquired tastes on the other interact to create consumption patterns almost as divergent as those of production.

In the early 1950's agricultural output, sparked by export crops, grew at perhaps 6 per cent a year. After 1955 it fell to perhaps 2–3 per cent and the 1959–63 Plan implementation estimates give 2·4 per cent for that period.

Agricultural research and extension are limited and concentrated on export crops in at least one of which—cotton—they have been notably successful. More comprehensive research and extension work is now being developed. Any expansion of agricultural output in the central and northern regions will demand both cheaper transport and better market opportunities. Cotton and groundnuts for industrial and export markets and livestock for sale in the south appear the most promising crops, but maize is a possibility if markets can be found. In the south the most suitable tree crops are rubber, oil palm, and cocoa; of industrial crops fibres, and among annual food crops perhaps sugar and rice, vegetables, and (if a bakeable flour based on it can be developed) cassava. In the south, higher net yields per man year (and in the more densely settled areas per acre) are particularly needed to allow rising incomes. Research directed at seeds, pesticides, fertilizers, hand tools, and timing of productive operations, together with improved storage facilities, intensive extension work and probably some land consolidation appear the most fruitful avenues for action.

Transport

Improvements in transport are critical for extending Cameroonian development. Interior trunk routes (road or rail) would also be vital to providing Chad and the CAR with access to regional (UDEAC) and to export markets. Not surprisingly investment in transport has assumed a central role in Cameroon development strategy.

Since 1958 the East Cameroon's road system has been rapidly extended and improved. In 1964 there were 540 miles tarred, 2,590 miles of gravel and laterite main routes, 3,130 miles of earth roads, and 1,060 miles of tracks. In 1964 over 2,000 mn. fr. (£2·9 mn.) was spent on roads and bridges (50 per cent FAC, 20 per cent FED, 30 per cent State funds). 2,220 miles of roads exist in the West, of which perhaps 45 miles are tarred, and 235 miles of others are comparable to Eastern main routes. The remainder are earth roads. Although they have improved since union, West Cameroon roads (even key routes) are among the worst in West Africa.

Railroads total 342 miles of mainline track which run from Douala to Yaoundé and Mbalmayo and from Douala to Nkongsamba. A 21 mile link from Mbanga to Kumba in the West is now complete and the first 390 miles of the Trans-Cameroon Railway to Ngaoundéré are under way. The completion of the Trans-Cameroon Railway is scheduled for 1968. Further extensions to Chad (Ngaoundéré-Moundou-Fort Archambault) and to the CAR (Mbalmayo or Bertoua-Berbereti-Bangui) are under study. The line to CAR would open up large forest reserves in both countries. Both routes would provide shorter and less costly routes from interior centres of production to the coast in all three states. Given present and plausible projected volumes of production (groundnuts, cotton, cattle, timber) these rail extensions appear potentially viable.

Power

Most of the East Cameroon's electric power is utilized in producing aluminium for export; of 1,072 mn. Kwh produced in 1962, 1,004 (93 per cent) went to ALUCAM's Edéa smelter. A mere 61 mn. Kwh. was consumed by the rest of the economy—43 mn. Kwh. in Doula, 12 mn. in Yaoundé, and 6 mn. elsewhere. Installed capacity amounts to 160·5 Mw of hydroelectric and 10·6 Mw of diesel. The most critical of the power issues centres on locating a cheap source for smelting the bauxite deposits of the Tibati region (near the line of the Trans Cameroon Railway, 47 miles south of Ngaoundéré). It appears most economical to convert from bauxite to aluminium on the spot to reduce railing costs. Alternative sites are at Bakou on the

Njerem (Upper Sanaga) and Nachtigall (250 miles southwest but a better dam-site).

Manufacturing and Processing

Gross industrial output for 1962–63 was 31,100 mn. fr. (£45 mn.). Value added was 9,800 mn. fr. of which about 40 per cent represented aluminium smelting. The increase from the 5,700 mn. fr. value added in 1959 was an impressive achievement. Industrial employment in 1963 was 6,800 (1,000 in the West) which gives a value added per worker of 1·44 mn. fr. (£2,090). Excluding aluminium smelting the value added per worker would be 0·91 mn. fr. (£1,320).

A listing of major industries in 1963–64 gives a total capital of about 25,500 mn. fr. of which one third (8,200 mn. fr.) was the Edéa complex. This would yield a capital/value added ratio of 2·6 (or 3·1 excluding aluminium). Unfortunately these figures lump some forestry and plantation operations (rubber, palm oil) with manufacturing proper. However, the capital adjustment involved is probably at most 2–3,000 mn. fr. leaving 22,500–23,000 mn. fr. in industry, and adjusted capital/value added ratios of approximately 2·4 and 2·7.

Including aluminium smelting, nearly 60 per cent of value added and of capital but only 30 per cent of the strictly industrial workers are employed in export processing. The share of value added in 1962–63 originating from domestic market production can scarcely have exceeded 4,000 mn. fr. and the gross value 12,000 mn. fr. Imports of industrial goods were 19,100 mn. fr. with perhaps 1,800 mn. fr. in fuel, semi-processed and raw material imports for domestic market manufactures. The total Cameroonian industrial goods market appears to approximate 31,000 mn. fr. (£45 mn.) of which the domestic share is about 10,200 mn. fr. or one third. The share is distinctly higher in food, drink, tobacco, textiles–clothing, wood products and repairs in all of which it exceeds one half.

French colonial and business thinking on industrialization was cautious and pessimistic. Production, other than initial processing for export, was seen as uneconomic, because of lack of skilled labour, infrastructure and raw materials and the small size of market. Thus only a very limited range of small consumer goods industries plus lumber and plywood, cement, and flour milling were proposed in the 1960 SEDES (Société d'Études pour le Développement Économique) statement of the pre-independence French position.

This point of view has been increasingly rejected by the Cameroon government. Even the first Plan laid more emphasis on industry than the SEDES report would justify. Cameroon's involvement with

UDEAC has been stimulated largely by a desire to secure access to export markets for its industry thereby increasing possible plant sizes and thus the range of economically viable industries. Major industrial projects under construction or firmly scheduled totalled over 9,500 mn. fr. (£14 mn.) in mid-1965. Cement and concrete products, an integrated textile complex, leather footwear, flour milling and biscuit manufacture, sugar milling, meat tinning, sawmilling and match-making account for about 90 per cent of the investment total. Growth projections for industry and other major sectors are set out for 1962–63 to 1975 in Table 16.

The projected growth rate of industrial value added for 1962–63 to 1970 is 16–17 per cent overall and over 20 per cent outside processing. This is not radically out of line with the overall 1959–63 experience nor the tentative 1962–65 estimates. If 6–7 per cent annual growth rates are attained in the Cameroon-UDEAC area (again a moderate improvement on the 4–5 per cent in 1960–65) the growth of demand should be adequate to sustain industrial development on this scale. Difficulties are more likely to centre first on securing capital and relations with foreign firms and their governments and second on the success of UDEAC and the Cameroon-CAR-Chad transport link proposals.

8. HUMAN RESOURCES: NUTRITION, HEALTH, EDUCATION, LABOUR AND EMPLOYMENT

The Cameroon economy is marked by low levels of output by the vast majority of its participants and, as a corollary, by low levels of consumption and of human investment. These in turn hamper efforts to raise productivity. Standards of nutrition, health and education are clearly dependent on available resources and therefore, ultimately, on output per head; but present deficiencies limit the physical, mental and technical capacity of most Cameroonians to achieve higher levels of output.

Nutrition

On an aggregative basis both the present *per capita* gross calorie levels available (2,500–2,750) and the trend in food production (3·5 per cent annual growth rate over the decade 1952–53–1962–63 and about 2·5 per cent of 1959–60–1960–65) are satisfactory. The former safely exceeds the commonly employed *per capita* minimum standard (adjusted for age structure) of 1,800–2,200 and the latter the population growth rate of about 2 per cent. Even allowing for serious errors of estimation, the Cameroon does not appear to suffer from a

Table 16. *Growth projections of value added: East Cameroon 1962–75*
(thousand million fr CFA)

	Primary	Secondary					Tertiary		Total
		Mining[a]	Industry	Energy	Construction[b]	Total	Transport	Total	
1962–3	49·8	—	9·0	1·0	4·5	14·5	5·9	45·9	110·2
1965	52·1	—	12·7	1·1	5·2	18·9	10·6	56·6	127·6
1970	65·8	1·2	24·9	1·3	7·7	35·1	15·0	86·4	187·4
1975	79·3	6·2	49·1	1·6	11·5	68·3	21·2	131·8	279·4
Increase 1962/3–75	29·5	6·2	40·1	0·6	7·0	53·8	15·3	85·9	169·2
			percentage distribution						
1962–3	45·2	—	8·2	0·9	4·1	13·2	5·3	41·6	100·0
1975	28·4	2·2	17·6	0·6	4·1	24·4	7·6	47·2	100·0

Notes: a ECA estimates are zero throughout. The figure here assumes the establishment of a local cement industry by 1970 and the probable exploitation of Tibati bauxite by 1975.

b ECA estimates for 1970 and 1975 are only 6·8 and 9·5 thousand mn. frs. The implied declining share of construction is inconsistent with a 7·5–7·7 per cent growth rate.

Sources: Adapted from ECA projections based on East Cameroon data and plan targets.

present overall food shortage or from an imminent inability of food supplies to keep pace with population increases.

If regional, seasonal and dietary factors are taken into account, however, the position is seen to be far less satisfactory. The Kirdi face endemic malnutrition and recurrent severe food shortages. The grassland and savannah area and probably the densely populated Bamiléké-Bamoun semi-forest area as well, comprising over half the population, encounter pre-harvest 'hungry seasons' of varying intensity.

The most serious national problem probably lies in dietary composition. Cereals (maize, millet, sorghum, wheat, rice) account for perhaps 50 per cent of calorie intake and root crops and plaintains perhaps 40 per cent. Protein and vitamin deficiencies are severe, reflecting the low consumption of meat, fish, beans, green vegetables and citrus fruits.

Health

Medical statistics are fragmentary and because of the wide disparity of services available, both between East and West and between urban and rural areas, are rather misleading. There appear to be 160–180 doctors and dentists (1: 25–30,000) of which two-thirds or more are in Yaoundé, Douala and Buea—Victoria. Nurses and assistant nurses number 2,000–2,500 (1: 2,000–2,500). Hospital and clinic beds total 14–16,000 (1: 300–350). For doctors and fully qualified nurses these are about 1/10th of levels thought desirable but substantially exceed levels in interior West and Central African states, parallel or exceed those of Nigeria and are distinctly inferior only to those of Ghana and those Francophonic states which have relatively much larger European populations (e.g. Gabon, Côte d'Ivoire, Senegal).

Endemic diseases include malaria, worm infestations, bilharzia, river blindness, and protein deficiency maladies. Probably 75–80 per cent of the population suffers from one or more of these recurrently.

Education

Statistics on education are summarized in Table 17.

Primary educational enrolment has reached perhaps 60 per cent of the 7–14 age group. One problem is its uneven distribution geographically and by sex. Final year primary enrolment is only one quarter (in the West one sixth) of the initial year; and of them only one third in the East and one half in the West pass the primary leaving examination.

Total secondary enrolment is only 5·8 per 1,000 population (2·0 in West) and is not more than 5 per cent of the 14–19 group. Of these, three quarters of the pupils are boys. Regional distribution is more unequal than for primary schools. Final year enrolment—including two year and longer programmes—is 40–45 per cent of initial enrolment.

Table 17. *Education: total enrolments 1963–64*

	East	West	Total
Primary	551,900	106,100	658,000
%	95·2	97·3	95·5
Secondary	26,600	2,610	29,210
%	4·6	2·4	4·2
Tertiary	(1,370)[a]	(330)[a]	1,700
%	0·24	0·30	0·25
Total	579,870	109,040	688,910

Stocks of educated manpower

Category	Number	% of population
Some primary education[b]	1,500,000–1,750,000	30–35
Completed primary education	300,000– 400,000	6–8
Some secondary education	50,000– 60,000	1·0–1·2
Completed some secondary course	20,000	0·4
Some tertiary qualification	2,250– 2,750	0·04

Notes: [a] Estimated.
[b] Of the 1,200,000–1,400,000 with incomplete primary education, a high proportion is likely to have reverted to illiteracy.

Sources: Calculated and estimated from Cameroon Orientale and Occidentale and ECA publications and statistics.

In 1963–64, tertiary enrolment was about 850 with a similar number of Cameroonian students abroad. By 1965–66 it probably stood at 1,600–1,800 in the Cameroon and 1,000 abroad with an annual completion of 600. However, over two-thirds of Cameroon enrolment is in two year programmes.

No sound estimates of stocks of educated manpower exist but apparently about one-third of the population has had some primary education and perhaps one-fifth remain literate. Only about 1 per cent appear to have any secondary education and perhaps two-fifths of them completed their secondary school programme. The total stock of tertiary qualification holders (end 1965) is probably 2,250–2,750 (far higher than usually assumed) but of these a substantial proportion (over 10 per cent) have remained in France for political or economic reasons.

Labour Force, Employment, Wages[1]

The Cameroon labour force in 1962–63 (see Table 18) was of the order of 2,165,000 (10 per cent of the 0–14 age group, 75 per cent of the 15–59 age group, 46 per cent of total population). The wage and salary earning section was about 340,000 (16 per cent of total labour force, under 7 per cent of population). Between 1959 and 1962–63 employment (wage and salary) probably grew by 10–12 per cent and the self-employed 6 per cent. The labour force probably grew 7 per cent overall parallel to population.

Table 18. *Federal Cameroon: estimated labour force 1959*

	Employed[a]		Self-employed		Total[b].	
	000s	%	000s	%	000s	%
Primary	155	51	1,267	74	1,422	71
Secondary	48	16	145	8	193	9
Tertiary	50	16	306	18	356	17
Administration	42	14	—	—	42	2
Household service	12	4	—	—	12	1
Total	307	100	1,718	100	2,025	100

Notes: [a] Estimated from *1959 Comptes Économiques* and W. African labour statistics (particularly Ghana Census 1960).
[b] Labour force calculation (total):
10% of population 0–14 (40% of total)
+75% of population 15–59 (56% of total)
For division by category see note (*a*).

About half of wage and salary employment is in primary production (counting employees of cash crop farmers), one sixth in secondary activity (perhaps 3 per cent industry, 4 per cent crafts and repairs, 6 per cent construction, 3 per cent utilities and mining), one sixth in tertiary services and one sixth in general government. Three quarters of self-employment is in agriculture, perhaps a sixth in services (basically small trading) and a tenth in crafts and construction.

Some 70 per cent of the total labour force is engaged in primary production and 10 per cent in secondary, with 18 per cent in tertiary, 2·4 per cent in general government and 0·6 per cent in (paid) domestic services. During 1959–1962–63 there was a slight drift to

[1] All data in this section are estimates subject to error of ± 10 to 15 per cent. No plausible official data exists except on minimum wages and earnings of recorded employees.

secondary and tertiary employment, especially in the East which has a rather more modern labour force pattern.

No unemployment estimates exist except unofficial 25 per cent sample survey estimates for Douala and Yaoundé. Unemployment in the wage sector is probably of the order of 50–75,000. Regional under-employment is high in the southern plateau areas (especially the Bamiléké country). Seasonal unemployment is high throughout (especially in the north) with the probable exception of cash crop cultivators having food farms and also land to expand their tree crop plantings.

Minimum wages and salaries (fixed in seven zones) range from 31,200 to 72,000 fr. (£45–105). They are probably effective for recorded wage and salary employment (35 per cent of total estimated employment). Average wage incomes for recorded employment are of the order of 85,000 fr. (£125) in the East and 60,000 fr. (£88) in the West. Non-recorded wages and earnings are substantially lower and —especially for farm labour—are paid mainly in kind and are based on more irregular employment.

Effectively, the wages floors are set by the States. Variations above them reflect employers' policies with respect to maintenance of low turnover and absence rates and productivity inducements, etc., and also their ability to practise selective hiring. Higher level manpower salaries range from 500–900,000 fr. (£720–£1,300) for middle and senior civil servants and junior and middle level African managers to 1,860,000 fr. (£2,700) for the highest civil servants (African doctors are at 1,300,000–1,500,000) and perhaps 2,000,000 fr. for private sector African senior positions. Senior political salaries include Deputies 900,000 fr. (£1,300—part-time job), Ambassadors 1,000,000–1,500,000 fr. (£1,500–£2,200), Ministers 3,240,000 fr. (£4,700) and the President 4,800,000 fr. (£7,000). These are usually augmented by business and other 'quasi-official' incomes. Expatriate earnings probably average 1,500,000–2,000,000 fr. (£2,200–£2,900) and expatriate employment is about 7,000–7,500.

The Labour Departments are active in regard to wages, conditions, safety, health and dispute settlement in the recorded employment sector but their effective coverage seems to be declining. Trade Unions exist in both East and West but in the former they appear of negligible importance at present although the Edéa (aluminium) and the railway and port unions had some impact in the 1950's.[1] In the

[1] The now outlawed mass radical party—UPC (Cameroon Peoples Union) had some union support and backed UGTAN (Guinea based Francophonic African international). UGTAN affiliates are unlawful and the whole idea of independent and, indeed, strong unions is distrusted by UNC.

West, unions are more active and appear to have some influence on the Department of Labour. The Cameroon Development Corporation plantation union has in the past been of real significance but appears less so today. West Cameroon unionists express misgivings that the East Cameroon pattern (which they view as overt repression of unions) will be duplicated in the West and have attempted to maintain unofficial ties with AATUF (the radical All African Trade Union Federation) although they—like some Eastern unions—are officially, if tenuously, members of AATUC (All African Trade Union Congress, the moderate counter to AATUF, largely a paper body) and to ICFTU's (International Confederation of Free Trade Unions) African regional organization.

9. TOWARD FEDERAL AND SUBREGIONAL ECONOMIC UNION

The Cameroon Federal Government is deeply concerned with the need for large markets and trade flows to support its planned industrial transport, and commercial sectors. Since Federal 'reunion' in 1961 this concern can be seen in the form taken by economic relations between the two states, and accounts for the greatly heightened interest in economic union with the former UDE states (Congo-Brazzaville, Gabon, Chad, Central African Republic).

Fifty years (1916–1961) of separate rule created virtually totally unlinked economies in the East and West Cameroon, not only in trade patterns but also in the labour market. Perhaps two-fifths of Western migrant and semi-migrant plantation and urban labour force, as well as many of the lower civil servants, teachers and small businessmen, came from Nigeria. This division was reinforced after 1946 by the dichotomy between the relatively low price-wage anglophonic West African economy as compared with the high price-wage francophonic African area resulting from the valuation of the CFA frame at 2 (old) French francs.[1] Not only did this system protect French colonial export markets (which, given the exchange rate, paid well above world prices for their French imported goods), but it also effectively halted legal trade between francophonic and anglophonic African states. Some illegal trade—with the CFA franc valued at about 2/3 the official rate—did take place but in the case of the two Cameroons it was not significant. Physically, the division of the two Cameroons

[1] In terms of European goods their purchasing power was probably about equal. Assuming a 30–40 per cent margin of West African over European prices this over-valuing of the CFA fr. vis a vis the West African pound came to 50 per cent in 1946. It was somewhat eroded by subsequent more rapid price increases in Ghana and Nigeria compared to the CFA area.

was strengthened by separate transport, communication, commerce and port facilities. Institutional factors reflected in the dominance of British (Holt, United Africa Company) and French (CFAO, SCOA) commercial houses with extensive metropolitan connections, and of metropolitan bank branches, worked in the same direction.

Since reunification, the Federal Republic has tackled economic integration pragmatically and aims to create a unified economy by 1975. The difficulties centre on the West's established trade patterns, the separate institutional and transport systems, the basic stagnation of the economy of West Cameroon and the different initial 'real' price levels. All but the third have proved to be partially self-eroding, justifying the somewhat leisurely pace of action in 1961–65, followed by more rapid action marked by complete tariff union and the initiation of the first Federal Development Plan.

For the West, the loss of Commonwealth Preference and the acquisition of EEC preference (though *not* of adequate quotas for its bananas) has led to a somewhat altered export pattern but in 1965 half of its total exports still went to the UK. The EEC share is about 40 per cent, and that of France about 5 per cent. With import and quota unification there has been less progress. Partly this results from lack of familiarity with non-British goods in the West, but more from a desire to prevent rapid price increases through imposition of the higher Federal (East) duty levels and the substitution of higher cost EEC sources of supply. Nevertheless, by 1965 UK imports (direct and via Nigeria) had declined from at least 75 per cent at reunion to 40 per cent. EEC however supplies less than 20 per cent (France approaching 10 per cent). Until 1966 the old Nigerian tariff (by then much lower than the extant Nigerian) rather than the UDEAC one was applied to most UK imports. Nigeria lost substantially; its cement, plastics, and rubber goods faced discriminatory tariffs in favour of EEC members and its cigarettes and beer were displaced by the products of East Cameroon. In the labour market Nigerian workers have been largely squeezed out, especially in the public sector and Nigerian traders now barred by the tariff from their traditional sources in Eastern Nigeria have been partially replaced by traders from East Cameroon.

In commerce, French firms have substantially replaced British ones though this has not yet occurred in banking. The federal government has established in the West branches of its major financial development agencies and of some physical operative arms but most ministries are not yet fully integrated in practice. Until 1966 the Western development budget was only partly integrated with that of the East and the Federation and even now represents an *ad hoc* addition to, rather than an integral part of, the Federal Development Plan. Road mileage had been raised from 1,131 in 1959 to nearly 3,000 in 1965 including better links (especially in the mountain and plateau areas) with the East and the Mbanga-Kumba (Western highlands) rail link has been completed.

The stagnation of the Western economy was not greatly affected during the early years of Union. The decade-long slump of wage employment was certainly halted but mainly because of sharp increases in government personnel. There was no export expansion and the Tiko-Victoria area lost part of its trade with inland areas to Douala, a logical shift and one aided by the road and rail development. No major projects industrial or otherwise were located in the West, although negotiations were begun within the framework of the 1965 Plan. Civil service enthusiasm at the economic effects of merger was offset by business doubts.

Price and wage level differences between East and West narrowed somewhat during 1961–65 but even for local foodstuffs, Victoria prices appeared to be at least 15–20 per cent below Douala in 1965. Wages were, on the whole, less than 10 per cent apart in terms of minimum rates but probably somewhat more in terms of total earnings, suggesting moderately comparable low and middle employee purchasing power.

On the whole, the 1961–65 economic unification policy appears to have laid the foundations of fuller union without entailing costs to the West which would have endangered the quite evident growth of a Cameroonian national feeling there. The framework of the second plan suggests that a serious attempt is to be made to inaugurate Western development in the framework of the Federal State.

On a wider front Cameroon development strategy is keyed both to becoming the main commercial outlet for the CAR and Chad and also to creating an industrial sector aimed at wider regional markets, and since 1961 it has been among the most active proponents of functional economic co-ordination in Africa. While focussing largely on the Union Douanière et Économique de l'Afrique Centrale (UDEAC) this policy has also dominated Cameroon's attitudes toward the successive Francophonic African bodies (Brazzaville Group, UAM, OAMCE, OCAM) and to the African regional units of the UN (especially ECA).[1]

[1] In 1968 Chad and the CAR appear to have withdrawn from UDEAC, but the result may be a UDEAC–Congo (Kinshasa) trade area.

10. RETROSPECT AND PROSPECT

Since 1951 the Cameroon economy has demonstrated both the possibilities and the limitations of primary export centred growth in mid-20th century Africa. Although less spectacular than the 1950–60 Ghana and 1954–64 Ivory Coast export-fuelled spurts, its growth from 1951 to 1959 was rapid and sustained. Since 1959 the pattern has changed and exports have become sluggish (indeed below 1959 in 1960–62) but growth has continued under the impetus of a development programme directed toward structural change as well as export expansion.

One indicator of the task confronting the Cameroon economy is the relatively small change in the structure of output achieved between 1959 and 1965. Despite the relatively rapid growth of the secondary sector it still accounts for barely one seventh of output and only one tenth of employment. Moreover though the process of commercialization proceeded rapidly enough for over 90 per cent of additions to GDP to be in the monetary sector, it still represented slightly under three quarters of output. Despite substantial growth of production based on import substitution (and massive duty increases) the share of imports in GDP declined only marginally.

If the 1959–65 pattern of development could be maintained for a decade however, substantial changes could be anticipated in the structure and level of the economy. These could include not only a doubling of GDP per head to 55–60,000 fr. but also an increase in the country's autonomous capacity for development and a decrease in its external dependence. For this development to become a reality, a variety of constraints will need to be overcome or at least reduced.

In the first place, the ratio of gross investment to GDP will almost certainly need to be raised from perhaps an eighth to a fifth or a quarter. A related need will be to raise the domestic (and the domestically owned) investible surplus from perhaps a fifth to one half of total investment. This arises from the virtual impossibility of securing the additional funds abroad and from the severe limitations which even the present ratio of foreign to total investment places on development choices.

For the State this will imply continued tax reform building on the 1959–63 leap which created domestic revenue cover for recurrent expenditure to the extent of a current surplus of five per cent of GDP. In a context of national and regional import substitution, this will demand large increases in the income tax and an augmentation of turnover and transactions taxes designed not only to secure additional revenue in the short run but also to secure a tax structure buoyant with respect to national product.

The 1959–65 export stagnation can not be allowed to recur. Regional industrial exports are necessary both to broaden the manufacturing base and to participate in regional (UDEAC) import substitution. Extra-regional exports will have to rise steadily—and hopefully by at least five per cent a year—if the necessary imports to support seven to seven-and-a-half per cent growth are to be achieved. The prospects for success here are not bright, but concentration on expanded forestry and cotton production, fuller processing of timber and cocoa before exports, and the exploitation of the Tibati bauxite deposits could enable the target rate to be achieved.

Even with a five per cent growth of exports and a substantial development of the industrial sector, the trade balance can be expected to be substantially negative for most of the next decade. Unless the reinvestment rate continues its 1959–65 rise, increased foreign capital earnings will cause the substantial present current account deficit to become ominously large. Expanded long term loans (or grants) as well as foreign private investment will therefore be needed.

The present pattern of concentrated external dependence (France-EEC) tends to tighten both the export and the aid-investment constraints. While the enjoyment of EEC Associate status is a step towards broader international economic contacts, further diversification is needed. So long as both trade and aid are tied to France and heavily French influenced bodies such as FED, Cameroon's freedom of choice and bargaining power will continue to be limited particularly when its economic interests diverge from the policies France would prefer.

In high level manpower as in physical capital, Cameroon needs to increase both the absolute supply and the domestic share in it and to reduce its dependence on French sources. While the Federal University is already making a significant general contribution it is not clear that this is equally so in the fields of technology and science.

As the economy approaches the end of the 'easy' stage of import substitution in mass consumed soft consumer goods, internal market size will increasingly become a constraint both to growth and to changes in the structure of production. Even on favourable assumptions, GDP by 1975 will be only of the same order of magnitude as those of Ghana, the Sudan or East Africa in 1965. The first step toward market broadening—and one whose consolidation can be critical for Cameroon's growth—is UDEAC. But UDEAC's domestic product and demand for manufactures is only slightly over twice that of Cameroon itself. This suggests the need to explore the possibility of broader industrial development based on trade expansion agreements with the Congo (Kinshasa) and/or Nigeria. Existing trade with the Mahgreb countries might also furnish a basis for a limited but significant set of agreements.

Internally, the retarded development and lagging growth of West Cameroon and of the interior pose challenges for national development. Although the Transcameroon Railway may stimulate development in the East, the integration of the Western state into the process of structural development and the greater involvement of the North in the commercial economy are less readily solved by single massive programmes. For the North the effective implementation of the Lake Chad Basin development programme offers a hopeful approach towards creating growth nuclei. For the West, an industrial location policy designed to break the Tiko-Victoria stagnation by industries geared to the needs of the Federation (and possibly of UDEAC) appears imperative.

To suggest that these constraints will in fact be relaxed would be highly optimistic. Nevertheless, the fact that it is possible to pose the problem of Cameroonian development in terms of constraints to the fulfilment of a national development strategy which appears inherently viable is, in itself, a ground for cautious optimism. Possible lines of development do exist, and realistic policies have been formulated both in terms of goals and routes. Continuation of the 1959–65 growth and development rates and trends would by 1975 provide a basis for a bright future. Cameroon would not even then be a wealthy economy, but if it can attain a sustained *per capita* growth rate of four to five per cent, while achieving considerable autonomy (and regional interdependence) in its economic structure, a breakthrough to Japanese consumption standards may by then be a realizable medium run objective.

SELECTED READINGS

1. Ardener, E., Ardener, S., and Warmington, A., *Plantation and Village in the Cameroons* (Oxford, for Nigerian Institute of Social and Economic Research, 1960).
2. Banque Centrale des États de l'Afrique Équatoriale et du Cameroun, *Bulletin Mensuel* (Paris).
3. Berrill, K., *The Economy of the Southern Cameroons under United Kingdom Trusteeship* (Cambridge, 1960, mimeoed).
4. Economic Commission for Africa, *Report of the ECA MISSION for the Economic Co-operation in Central Africa* (Addis Ababa, 1966).

5. Gardiner, D. E., *Cameroon: United Nations Challenge to French Policy* (Oxford, for Institute of Race Relations, 1963).
6. Gonidec, P. F., 'Les Institutions Politiques de la République Fédérale du Cameroun', *Civilizations*, XI, 1 (1962).
7. Le Vine, V. T., 'The Cameroun Federal Republic' in G. Carter (Ed.), *Five African States* (Cornell, 1963).
8. Le Vine, V. T., and M'Ballah, H., 'Education in the Federal Republic of Cameroun' in H. Kitche, (Ed.), *The Educated African* (Praeger, 1962).
9. République Fédérale du Cameroun, *Comptes Économiques 1951–1957–1959*, Ministère De La Co-opération (Paris 1963).
10. République Fédérale du Cameroon, *Comptes Économiques 1959, 1962–63*, Centre d' Information, de Documentation et d'Études du Plan (Yaoundé, 1965).
11. République Fédérale du Cameroun, *Bulletin Trimestriel d'Information*, Ministère des Finances et du Plan (Yaoundé, irregular).
12. République Fédérale du Cameroun, *Note Trimestrielle Sur La Situation Économique*, Ministère de l'Économie Nationale (Yaoundé). *West Cameroon Digest of Statistics, Ministry of National Economy (Buéa)*
13. République Fédérale du Cameroun, *Budget Fédérale*, Ministère des Finances et du Plan (Yaoundé); *Budget, Cameroun, Orientale*, Secrétariat d'État aux Finances (Yaoundé); *West Cameroon Budget*—Ministry of Finance (Buéa).
14. République Fédérale du Cameroun, *Premier Plan Quinquennal de Développement Économique et Sociale*, Ministère des Finance et du Plan (Yaoundé, 1961).
15. République Fédérale du Cameroun, *Plan—Travaux Préparatoires* (3 volumes), Société Generale d'Études et de Planification (Paris, 1960).
16. Robson, P., 'Economic Integration in Equatorial Africa', in A. Hazlewood (Ed.) *Studies in African Integration and Disintegration* (Oxford, for RIIA, 1967).
17. Rudin, H. R., *Germans in the Cameroons 1884–1914* (Jonathan Cape, 1938).
18. Warmington, A., *A West African Trade Union* (Oxford, for NISER, 1960).

6

THE ECONOMY OF LIBERIA

1. INTRODUCTION

Liberia is the fifth smallest country in Africa with a population of about one-million persons, an area of 43,000 square miles, and a density of 23 persons a square mile. Some of its economic, political and social features are not shared by other African countries because Liberia was never a colony of a European power. It became an independent republic in 1847 at the initiative of a small colony of several thousand free Negroes from the United States (Americo-Liberians) who claimed sovereignty over a hinterland of some twenty tribal groups. For the most part, tribal persons were little affected by European commerce and culture until well into the twentieth century.

The salient characteristics of Liberian economy are the recent start of private and governmental development activities, the unusual extent to which new lines of production are undertaken by foreign firms, the extreme concentration of activities in primary production for export (rubber and iron-ore), and the relative absence of systematic national planning to transform traditional sectors of the economy and initiate other structural changes. In short, Liberia is a prime example of a 'dual' economy and an 'enclave' economy. It has one of the highest rates of output growth on record because of heavy European and American investments in iron-ore mining and rubber, but remains largely undeveloped otherwise.

The national income figures presented here were the first ever compiled for Liberia. With few exceptions the largest components of output and income in 1960 represent lines of production begun since 1950 and types of government expenditure initiated after 1955. Tables 1 and 2 show that gross domestic income (which includes income from subsistence agriculture) in 1960 was almost triple the figures for 1950. The rate of growth of gross domestic money income since 1957 has been about 15 per cent per year. Aggregate growth figures for Liberia reflect increasing rubber production and the growth in iron-ore mining begun in 1951. (The value of iron-ore produced yearly will continue to grow into the 1970's as the mining concessions reach full production.) The relative importance of subsistence agriculture has declined sharply, from 38 per cent of gross domestic income in 1950 to 10 per cent in 1960, reflecting the growth of new activities by foreigners rather than a mass exodus from subsistence agriculture by tribal Liberians.

Table 1. *Gross domestic product at market price by industry of origin*[a] (million dollars)

Industry	1950	1960
Agriculture, forestry, fishing, hunting		
(*a*) Subsistence	22·2	18·1
(*b*) Peasant money	1·8	7·3
(*c*) Large scale commercial	21·0	31·4
Mining and quarrying	0·1	31·1
Construction	} 7·4	28·0[c]
Electricity, gas and water		2·4
Ownership of dwellings		12·1
Others not elsewhere specified (i.e. distribution, transport and manufacture)		19·3
Public Administration and defence	3·0	18·1[b]
Services (including banking and insurance)	2·6	5·0
Total	58·1	172·8

Notes: [a] Indirect taxes were $15·7m (1960) and $2·8m. (1950).
[b] Includes interest ($4·5 m) on productive government debt.
[c] A very rough estimate only.

Source: R. W. Clower *et al.; Growth without Development; an Economic Survey of Liberia*, Northwestern University Press, 1966. (This is the source of most statistics cited in this chapter.)

Little is known for certain about Liberian population growth. In 1953 an American geographer estimated the population at 750,000 on the basis of a hut count made from aerial photographs and checked by samples on the ground. In 1961–62 a census was attempted for the first time, but its findings were not made public. The Department of Justice has recently estimated that the population is about one million, of whom about 30,000 are foreigners.

In 1960 government revenue (see Table 3) was about 20 per cent of gross domestic money income. The role of the State in Liberian economic growth is conveniently described under three headings: (i) The Liberian government's most important economic policy was initiated by President Tubman on taking office in 1944. His 'open door' policy invited American and European firms into Liberia prin-

K

Table 2. *Domestic income components, 1950–60*
(million dollars)

	1950	1951	1952	1953	1954	1955	1956	1957	1958	1959	1960
Wages, salaries, plus pay of the armed forces	11·5	14·0	16·5	19·0	22·0	25·6	30·2	31·6	35·6	41·2	46·9
Net money income of tribal households (other than wages)	1·8	2·2	2·7	3·0	3·4	3·9	4·5	4·8	5·5	6·3	7·3
Gross business surplus (including interest, rent, depreciation)											
(*a*) Concessions	16·2	18·3	19·6	21·7	19·1	30·5	32·9	29·1	27·4	44·6	53·3
(*b*) Other (including govt.)	3·5	5·1	8·1	8·2	9·8	12·1	14·2	16·1	18·7	22·5	29·8
Indirect taxes	2·8	6·1	5·7	6·5	6·2	7·0	7·9	9·3	9·9	15·5	15·7
Gross domestic money income at market prices	35·8	45·7	52·6	58·4	60·5	79·1	89·7	90·9	97·1	130·1	153·0
PLUS subsistence agriculture not entering money sector	22·2	21·7	20·9	20·0	18·8	18·4	18·0	17·0	17·5	17·8	18·1
Gross domestic income at market prices	58·0	67·4	73·5	78·4	79·3	97·5	107·7	107·9	114·6	147·9	171·1
LESS net property income paid overseas	9·8	11·1	13·2	14·2	10·6	17·1	19·0	16·3	16·6	28·9	34·6
Gross national income at market prices	48·2	56·3	60·3	64·2	68·7	80·4	88·7	91·6	98·0	119·0	136·5
LESS indirect taxes	2·8	6·1	5·7	6·5	6·2	7·0	7·9	9·3	9·9	15·5	15·7
Gross national income at factor cost	45·4	50·2	54·6	57·7	62·5	73·4	80·8	82·3	88·1	103·5	120·8

Source: '*Growth without Development*'. Appendix 2A (pp. 41–61) consists of a detailed discussion and presentation of the National Income (1950–60) and the Social Accounts (1960) calculations made by the authors.

Table 3. *Government economic accounts: 1960*
(million dollars)

Government Current Revenue and Expenditure a/c

Receipts		Expenditures	
Direct taxes on income:		Current expenditure:	
(*a*) Rubber concessions	7·0	(*a*) Wages and salaries	8·8
(*b*) Iron ore concessions	6·4	(*b*) Travel and transport	1·3
(*c*) Other	1·9	(*c*) Other goods and services	8·3
Customs and external trade taxes	14·5	(*d*) Transfers	2·0
Public utility revenues	0·8	(*e*) Depreciation	0·8
Other revenues and fees:			
(*a*) Hut, health and development taxes	0·7		
(*b*) Other taxes and fees	1·0	Surplus on current account	11·0
Total	32·3	Total	32·3

Government savings—investment a/c

Receipts		Expenditures	
Surplus on current account	11·0	Gross fixed capital formation	4·9
Sales of government property	0·1	Transfers to local government	0·9
		Transfers to business sector	4·9
		Balance	0·4
Total	11·1	Total	11·1

Source: Growth without Development.

cipally to create large-scale rubber plantations and to extract iron-ore. On a smaller scale several other commercial, extractive, and processing activities were also undertaken by foreign concessions. The result has been the very rapid growth of primary production for export, and the sharp rise in government revenues from $4 million in 1950 to $50 million in 1967. (ii) The growth in government revenues enlarged the scope for fiscal policy and increased the creditworthiness of the Government. Its borrowings in 1955–63 were large and were running at over $20 million a year in the early sixties. It has also received rather generous amounts of foreign aid and technical assistance from American and European governments, and from international agencies. (iii) However, there persist social and economic policies which, carried over from the early settler community, impede and even prevent development. The retention of unchanged, traditional modes of procedure and organization are the most important obstacles to economic development, and largely account for Liberia's failure to develop the whole economy and the policy of renting enclaves for foreigners to exploit. We shall have occasion in the sections that follow to relate these aspects of government policy to each sector of the Liberian economy. In general, Liberia's political, social, and economic institutions have changed little, and the opportunity cost of foregone development has been high.

Capital formation figures are difficult to obtain. It has been estimated[1] that total private foreign investment (the bulk of private activity) averaged about seventy to eighty million dollars annually from 1959–63, whilst public investment was probably over twenty million dollars a year over the whole period. As foreign investment is so high, public activities are a lower proportion of total capital formation than in most African countries. This situation still appears in fields such as electric power where the US AID financed hydro-electric project of some twenty-four million dollars is overshadowed by an investment of more than twice that size by LAMCO (Liberian-American-Swedish Minerals Company). Nevertheless, public expenditure was high absolutely (over $20 a head or more than 10 per cent of *per capita* GDP) and the accumulation of short and medium term debt by which it was financed brought about a serious crisis in 1963. The fiscal operations of Government leading to this situation are summarized in Table 4.

Balance of payment figures for Liberia are fragmentary but in any case they do not have quite the same significance as they have for other countries. There is no Central bank and until 1963 the United States dollar was the official and exclusive money in use; it still remains the principal currency, although Liberian coins are now in circulation. Thus there were no problems of exchange rates or exchange control; neither was there any control over the free movement of capital, profits or money. Moreover, a large proportion of imports, especially since 1955, were capital and consumption goods purchased directly by foreign concessions for their internal use rather than for re-sale, and were divorced, so to speak, from the rest of the Liberian economy. Primary production for export constituted more than half the value of gross domestic money product.

It should be noted that about 20 per cent of income earned within

[1] M. A. Qureshi, Y. Mizoe, and F. d'A. Collings, The Liberian Economy, *IMF Staff Papers*, XI(2), July, 1964.

Table 4. *Fiscal operations of the government,[a] 1959/60–1962/63*
(million dollars)

	Fiscal Years, October 1–September 30			
	1959–60	1960–61	1961–62	1962–63
Current revenues	28·9	32·7	35·5	36·2
Expenditures				
Budgeted nondebt expenditures	30·7	28·9	32·6	33·7
Debt service	5·6	9·7	11·7	9·0
'Prefinanced' expenditures outside the budget[b]	12·5	17·1	14·4	20·4
Total	48·7	55·6	58·7	63·0
Over-all deficit or surplus	−19·8	−22·9	−23·2	−26·9
Financing				
Eximbank loans	3·2	5·8	2·3	4·0
Prefinancing credits	12·5	17·1	14·4	20·4
Commercial bank credit (net)	4·0	0·5	6·6	−0·5
Purchases from IMF	—	—	—	2·5
Other, including use of cash balances[b]	0·1	−0·5	−0·1	0·5

Notes: [a] Estimated on the basis of utilization of credits.
[b] Arrived at as a balancing item.

Source: M. A. Qureshi, Y. Mizoe, and F. d'A. Collings, 'The Liberian Economy' *IMF Staff Papers*, XI (2) July, 1964.

Liberia is remitted to firms and persons resident in other countries. This may be regarded as the annual (net) cost of importing capital for Liberian development and has of course to be deducted from domestic income to arrive at national income (see Table 2).

2. THE DEVELOPMENT PLAN AND DEVELOPMENT STRATEGY: FINANCING THE PUBLIC SECTOR

Up to 1962, there was no development plan or development strategy in Liberia, as these terms are understood by economists. There was no systematic scheme to transform subsistence agriculture, to train and educate large numbers of Liberians to undertake new lines of production or more highly skilled jobs in accordance with development needs, or to analyse various sectors of the economy and project the requirements for structural improvement.

Government intervention in the economy took the form of general policy preferences reflected in the contractual terms under which foreign concessions operate, in budgetary outlays, and in the occasional acceptance and implementation of specific projects suggested by foreign advisers. Until 1962 there was no designated agency of economic planning within the government. The Secretary of the Treasury, with the approval of the President, negotiated the terms of agreements with foreign concessions, several of which required the foreign firms to build roads or harbours, or to provide other facilities or services to enlarge commercial activities in their regions. The government had no policy of giving preference to those foreign concessions which would initiate lines of production especially valuable for economic development (e.g. manufacturing or processing); nor did the contract oblige the foreign firms to train specified numbers of Liberians in skilled jobs.

The most important developmental policy undertaken by the Liberian government itself had been the large expenditures, already mentioned, which were used for social capital, principally public building, roads and facilities to provide utility services (electricity, water, etc.) A functional classification of budgetary outlays for 1960 indicates the absence of priority given to expenditures for development purposes (Table 5.) Almost as much was spent on diplomacy as on education; more than one-fourth of total outlay was for general administrative expenses, and expenditures of all kinds were heavily concentrated in the county containing the capital city of Monrovia.

In 1962 there were very few Liberians in the higher echelons of government with training in economics, statistics or other skills relating to economic planning for development. However, Liberia is exceptionally well served in having access to foreign economic advisers and other technical experts concerned with development. The AID branch of the United States government had an establishment of one hundred and sixty persons in residence. Agencies of the United Nations provided several kinds of technical assistance as did several European governments.

IMF advisers were brought in to formulate a plan to cope with the serious financial situation that existed in early 1963. The Government owed over one hundred million dollars principal—about half of which was short term, arising almost entirely from contractor finance—and over thirty million dollars in interest payments to maturity. The Debt Rearrangement Plan, which was accepted generally, rephased the repayments of debt and interest over fifteen years taking into account likely increases in revenue, particularly the increased payments expected from LAMCO and LMC (Liberian Mining Company) in 1969. Government expenditures for purposes other

Table 5. *Functional classification of Government expenditures: 1960* (million dollars)

Function	Current expenditure	Capital expenditure	Total expenditure	Percent of total expenditure
General services				
General administration	5·7	0·7	6·4	19
Foreign affairs	2·7	—	2·7	8
Defence	1·4	0·1	1·5	5
Justice and police	1·1	—	1·1	4
Subtotal	10·9	0·8	11·7	36
Community services				
Roads, waterways and Fire protection	2·0	3·0	5·0	15
Water supply	0·2	0·3	0·5	1
Other	0·3	0·1	0·4	1
Subtotal	2·5	3·4	5·9	17
Social services				
Education	2·9	0·6	3·5	10
Health and welfare	2·7	0·3	3·0	9
Other	0·1	0·1	0·2	1
Subtotal	5·7	1·0	6·7	20
Economic services				
Agriculture	0·6	0·1	0·7	2
Fuel and power	0·2	0·3	0·5	1
Mineral resources, Manufacturing	—	4·8	4·8	14
Transport and Communication	0·6	—	0·6	2
Other	0·1	0·1	0·2	1
Subtotal	1·5	5·3	6·8	20
Unallocable				
Transfers and subsidies	0·8	0·2	1·0	3
Misc. contingencies	1·1		1·1	4
Subtotal	1·9	0·2	2·1	7
Total all functions	22·5	10·7	33·2	100

Source: Growth without Development.

than debt re-payments were to be allowed to rise by five per cent a year from the 1963 level.

The forecasting procedures required to produce the Debt Rearrangement Plan have had repercussions on planning. There is now a Liberian National Planning Council of Cabinet Ministers, a Department of Planning and Economic Affairs, and a five-year plan. It is too soon, however, to assess how far these moves will affect the underlying situation.

3. OBSTACLES TO ECONOMIC DEVELOPMENT

Liberia enjoyed none of the benefits of European colonization which in some measure were conferred on most other African countries. It received neither the tangible benefits of roads and schools, nor the more important but less tangible benefits of trained administrators, and a civil service ethic of performance, efficiency and honesty in the public service. Instead, the traditional practices and values of Americo-Liberian society were carried into the post-war period.

The most formidable obstacles to economic development in Liberia come from its political and social organization: the retention of traditional politics and society in the new economic environment of massive iron-ore mines and rubber plantations. The opportunities for nation-wide development provided by the rapid growth in primary production undertaken by foreigners, had not yet been seized.

Some of the traditional institutional arrangements which are detrimental to development may be cited briefly. In 1962, about one-fourth of the wage earning labour force was recruited involuntarily, principally to work on rubber farms owned by foreigners and Liberians. The effect was to keep wage rates down, to increase the turnover of labour, and, in effect, to put a regressive tax on tribal workers so recruited by reducing their income in kind from rice production. Similarly, the administration of the hinterland provinces continued on a colonial pattern of indirect rule, with District Commissioners representing the central government, and Paramount Chiefs, responsible for everyday matters, serving under their jurisdiction. With regard to taxation, land-tenure, control over residence and movement, marriage and divorce, legal jurisdiction, obligatory labour service to local authorities (without pay), labour recruitment (forced labour with pay,) extra-legal exactions of money, rice, and services, tribal Liberians in the hinterland were subject to a different socio-legal system from Americo-Liberians.

4. AGRICULTURE

There are three distinct agricultural sectors in Liberia: (i) foreign plantations, principally in rubber; (ii) independent rubber farms (the largest owned by Americo-Liberians); (iii) and tribal agriculture, principally rice and cassava grown for direct self-consumption, and cash crops of palm kernels, coffee, cocoa, piassava, and rubber. (In 1960 tribal agriculture produced $7·3 million worth of cash crops).

In 1960, agriculture accounted for a little more than one-third of gross domestic product (about $60 million out of $170 million). Between 1950 and 1960, the proportion of total exports attributed to agriculture declined from 95 per cent to less than 60 per cent because of the rapid growth in iron-ore mining. Less than one-quarter of the income generated in the money sector is attributable to agriculture, although agricultural employment accounts for nearly half the employment in the money sector. Similarly, less than one-sixth of total income is generated in the subsistence agriculture sector, although it accounts for nearly half of total employment. The differences in value product per man-year among the sectors are striking[1]: $2540 in the non-agricultural sector compared to $507 in agriculture; and within agriculture $878 in foreign plantation agriculture (rubber) compared with $611 in private Liberian commercial farming (principally rubber), and only $339 in the subsistence sector.

The variation in labour productivity is clearly due mainly to the varying capital-labour ratios in different industries; the capital intensive technology used in iron ore mining, for example, is largely responsible for the high productivity in the non-agricultural sector. But it is also true that in those industries which employ a proportionally high capital per worker the labour force is on the average of a higher quality, both physically and in terms of technical and educational qualifications than the labour employed in agricultural pursuits.

One foreign plantation (Firestone) accounted for more than 80 per cent of all rubber produced in 1960. Five other large foreign plantations began to produce rubber between 1963 and 1965 and are expected to produce by 1967 20 million pounds a year (about as much as is currently produced by independent Liberian farmers). Plantation cultivation of crops other than rubber has been tried with bananas, but the venture failed because Panama disease decimated the crop.

Independent rubber farms (those owned by Liberians) increased

[1] By value product per man-year is meant simply the total dollars worth of output divided by the labour input.

in number from about 500 in 1941 to more than 2500 in 1960. The principal causes of growth were the price rises during the second World War and the Korean war, Firestone's stimulation of rubber production through its provision of marketing, credit, and technical services to Liberian producers, and new roads built since 1955 which made areas in the hinterland accessible for commercial agriculture and reduced transport costs to the local market provided by Firestone. However, the productivity per acre of independent farms is markedly less, on the average, than Firestone's.

The transformation of subsistence agriculture in the tribal hinterland has hardly begun. The reasons we suggest must be put tentatively because no systematic enquiry into subsistence agriculture has ever been undertaken.

The wage-earning labour force almost tripled between 1950 and 1960 thereby increasing the market demand for rice. There was increased trade in rice but there was no marked increase in domestic rice production. Improved growing procedures have not been adopted. Upland rice grown on dry land was still the principal growing method despite the fact that wet rice yields on demonstration farms were three or four times as much per acre (and there are many marshy areas suitable for growing wet rice without irrigation equipment). Moreover, after some ten years of sustained agricultural advice, the American AID establishment curtailed its agricultural programme in 1962 because of disappointing results. Imports of rice grew to fill the food gap and cost 5·5 million dollars in 1963. The principal obstacles to transforming subsistence agriculture seem to be 'institutional' rather than 'economic' or 'technological': traditional land tenure arrangements, traditional tribute demanded of tribal communities, traditional forced labour, etc. Aside from hut taxes and forced labour tours, tribal Liberians in the hinterland are subject to extra-legal tribute payments of rice, money, and labour services to a variety of governmental employees. Similarly, there is no guarantee that land which is turned to commercial production and thereby made more valuable, will not be appropriated by highly-placed Liberians, or rented to foreign concessions by the central government. There is little incentive for tribal persons to abandon subsistence agriculture as long as they believe they will be allowed to retain little if any of the higher income from expanded commercial production. When new roads are built in the hinterland a not infrequent reaction of tribal communities is to move away from the road so as to become less accessible to tribute demands.

The only clearly successful development in agriculture undertaken by Liberians has been in rubber produced by independent farms.

But here the conditions have been very special. Apart from high wartime prices, the success is largely attributable to the services (and demonstration effect) provided by Firestone, and to the fact that by far the largest proportion of rubber produced is on farms owned by highly-placed and educated Americo-Liberians rather than tribal persons. Firestone has provided effective extension work concentrating on a single tree crop. Its services to private growers have been effective because Firestone has a financial stake in knowing how much private farms produce (to ensure that the rubber it buys does not come from its own trees), because practical advice is given to

Table 6. *Annual production of independent rubber farms*

Year[a]	Production ('000 lbs)	No. of farms
1941	475	150
1950	2,716	477
1955	7,805	991
1960	13,926	2,312

Note: [a] Year is from November 1st of previous year to October 31st in current year. Production refers to thousands of pounds of dry rubber content.

Source: Firestone Plantation; see Growth without Development.

Liberian producers on all aspects of rubber farm management, and because most of the farmers assisted are literate and commercially-minded. Because Firestone was the sole buyer of rubber in Liberia, it was able to impose quality standards on Liberian producers by using price differentials for different grades of rubber. But, above all, Firestone was able to introduce profitable farming to chiefs and other influential persons. They depended on Firestone and Firestone could count on their support. If conditions of the kind that characterize rubber production could be created for other cash crops, the success of Firestone's programme of research and extension services might be duplicated. However, the problems are formidable. Unlike rice, palm kernels, sugar cane and most other agricultural commodities grown in Liberia, rubber has no domestic use and only one domestic market outlet. It is likely that if rubber could be eaten, demanded as tribute, or stolen and sold with impunity, rubber production would be rather less profitable.

To be successful, a plan for agricultural development in Liberia would have to reach a much larger group of farmers than any scheme has managed to do so far. Only the half-dozen foreign plantations and fewer than one hundred of the independent rubber farms can be regarded as efficient establishments with growth prospects.[1]

Liberia's most serious and intractable agricultural problems arise in connection with tribal farms and farmers; some 150,000 shifting subsistence farms, occupying one-third of Liberia's land area, operated at low levels of efficiency. As elsewhere in Africa, tribal agriculture is not so much a technique for producing food as a way of life. Low productivity is not only a matter of inferior skill and equipment, but also of ingrained cultural habits, and political and social institutions unreceptive to improved technical performance. Agricultural extension services for tribal farmers seemed to be ineffective because they were not accompanied by changes in the social and economic institutions of hinterland communities. The traditional policies of control and levy exercised by agencies of central government would have to change to assure tribal farmers that they may retain a substantial share of higher income resulting from increased output. Similarly, land tenure arrangements would have to change to guarantee firm title to improved land.

Under Liberian law, only citizens and charitable institutions may own land in fee simple. All undeeded lands, including those occupied and used by tribal people, are part of the public domain and can be sold to private individuals only by the Government of Liberia. In law, there are safeguards against private encroachment on tribal holdings: 'Each tribe is entitled to the use of as much of the public land in the area inhabited by it as required for farming and other enterprise', and 'shall have the right to the possession of such land as against any person whomsoever'. Provision is also made for surveys to delimit tribal territory, for the conversion of surveyed lands into communal holdings, and, 'if a tribe shall become sufficiently advanced in civilization', for the division of tribal land into family holdings of 25 acres each. In practice, these safeguards are frequently ignored. Land is still a free good in most of the hinterland areas of Liberia, and dispossession of tribal people has not so far imposed operative limits to land areas available for tribal cultivation. However, individual tribal farmers have been dispossessed from lands on which they have planted coffee, cocoa, and rubber trees, entire communities have occasionally been swallowed up in government grants to foreign concessions, and large tracts of public land along newly constructed roads have been sold to nontribal individuals for business, farming, or speculative purposes. Dispossession may or may not be accompanied by compensation, depending

[1] Of some 2,500 independent rubber farms in Liberia, the 70 largest accounted for 60 per cent of the rubber grown by independents in 1960.

on the social and political position of the buyer and the tribal group affected. These practices make tribal people suspicious of any governmental programme for improving agricultural output as long as tribal land tenure is insecure.

5. LABOUR AND WAGES

Many of the characteristic features of the modern sector of the Liberian economy can be illuminated by a study of the labour situation. Out of the population of one million, over 80,000 were full-time wage or salary employees in 1960 (see Table 7). This represents a significant increase over previous years. In 1950 the wage earning labour force was probably not more than 30,000, some 20,000 of whom were employed by one firm (Firestone).

Table 7. *Average full-time employment in money sector of Liberian economy by principal activity of employer*
(number of equivalent man years)

	1955[a]	1958[a]	1960[b]
Agriculture:			
Concessions	22,000	23,500	24,500
Independent farms	5,000	6,500	8,400
Forestry and fishing	200	400	600
Construction	5,000	6,300	9,100
Mining	2,900	4,200	8,000
Trade	2,500	3,000	4,000
Manufacturing	300	500	1,100
Services	7,000	8,000	11,200
Transport and communication	2,100	3,200	3,500
Government	9,500	10,400	11,600
Total	56,500	66,000	82,000

Notes: a Based on US Foreign Service Report No. 71, Monrovia, 1958.
b Based on a sample census of employment conducted in 1960 by the Bureau of Economic Research and Statistics, RL. The statistics were processed for *Growth without Development*.

Most of the labour force were unskilled, low-paid, illiterate, and of tribal origin. More than two-thirds were unskilled workers who earned about fifty cents per day (excluding wage supplements). Almost half of all employees worked for foreign agricultural concessions or Liberian farmers (primarily in rubber). If we exclude government employees, about 80 per cent of Liberian wage workers were employed by foreign-owned firms. Roughly one-third of a million people derived the bulk of their livelihood in the money economy; about two-thirds of a million earned the bulk of their livelihood in subsistence agriculture. Non-African foreigners employed in Liberia occupied more than half of all salaried positions in private enterprise. About 5,000 women and 5,000 children under 17 worked for wages. About 15 per cent of all wage and salary workers and nearly 50 per cent of all female workers were employed by the Liberian Government.

Recruitment for both government and private employers was carried on legally by requisitions on tribal chiefs, resulting in a considerable amount of involuntary employment. In 1960, some 20,000 unskilled labourers (almost a quarter of the wage-earning labour force) were so recruited, largely for rubber plantations and local government service in the interior.

Those employees with skills exhibited a wide range of productivity. Interviews with employers cited the following reasons for the low productivity of Liberian labour: (1) deficiencies in cultural background and elementary education (especially illiteracy); (2) absence of training in and commitment to commercial and industrial work methods; (3) poor physical fitness; (4) high rates of absenteeism and labour turnover. There was unanimous agreement among employers and labour experts that constant supervision of Liberian labour was necessary to elicit tolerable levels of productivity.

There was a seasonal shortage of unskilled labour, especially at independent rubber farms paying less than market wage rates. Skilled and professional Liberian personnel were extremely scarce. Non-Liberian Africans as well as Europeans, Americans, and Lebanese, comprised an unusually large proportion of professional manpower and highly skilled labour (e.g. motor mechanics, carpenters, masons, electricians, etc.) More than 90 per cent of all Liberians with professional and technical training worked for the Government of Liberia.

Wage bill figures are given in Table 8. The 60,000 unskilled workers, received cash wage rates which ranged from 25 cents per day in the interior to 80 cents per day in Monrovia (1961–62). About 30,000 unskilled employees, or half of the total, were employed on rubber farms. Firestone was the largest employer of unskilled labour, employing about 20,000. Independent rubber farms employed 8,000–9,000, other rubber producers (new foreign concessions establishing their plantations) employed 2,000–3,000.

Information on foreign concession employment is given in Tables 9 and 10. These employers made their unskilled workers substantial wage supplements which amounted to between one-fourth and one-

Table 8. *Wage bill by industries (1960)*
(thousand dollars)

Industry	Non-African	African	African supplements
Agriculture, Forestry and Fishing	2,800	6,300	2,200
Mining	2,400	2,200	1,000
Manufacturing	80	190	80
Construction	3,100	3,000	1,100
Commerce and Banking	1,600	900	300
Transport and Communication	630	1,900	100
Services	500	1,000	—
Domestic servants	—	2,500	—
Total for private sector	11,110	17,990	4,780
Government (including overseas consular representation)		8,760	
Total	11,110	26,750	4,780

Source: Growth without Development.

third of the annual African money wage bill. The supplements on large concessions took the form of free housing, medical care, elementary education, and subsidized food. The older concessions, such as Firestone, usually have incentive wage schemes, such as turnout bonuses and automatic wage-rate increases with longevity.

The low level of wage rates is reflected in the wage share of National Income going to Africans.[1] For 1960, African wages and

Table 9. *Foreign concession employment (number on payroll) in thousands August 1961*

Sector	Total Employment	Skilled	Unskilled	Foreign
Mining	7·9	1·4	6·0	0·5
Rubber	27·0	3·4	23·4	0·2
Other	1·1	0·2	0·9	—
Total	36·0	5·0	30·3	0·7

Note: 'Employment' refers to the number on the payroll at the end of the month of August 1961. This exceeds the number of man years in 1961. Non concession foreign firms, e.g., Lebanese stores, are excluded.

Source: Growth without Development and Economic Survey of Liberia Staff.

[1] A small proportion of African wage income, not more than 1 per cent, accrues to non-Liberian Africans.

Table 10. *Estimate of foreign concession payments for wages, salaries and supplements, average number on payroll, 1960*

Sector	Africans		Non-Africans		Total
	Amount ('000$)	Number ('000)	Amount ('000$)	Number ('000)	Supplements ('000$)
Mining	3,400	7·4	2,800	0·50	900
Rubber	5,470	26·8	1,860	0·20	2,028
Other	260	1·1	245	0·04	25
Total	9,130	35·3	4,905	0·74	2,953

Source: Growth without Development.

supplements amounted to over 30 million dollars, about 20 per cent of total Gross Domestic Income. Assuming that families of wage workers average three persons, the average family income of Africans is about $130 per head for the 85,000 families in the money sector.

Table 11 shows the number of skilled and semi-skilled workers in employment. There was a Liberian shortage of skilled labour in two senses: a large proportion of skilled workers were not Liberians, but were from other African countries, Europe and America; many firms had skilled jobs to offer which remained unfilled for lack of qualified personnel.

Table 11. *Estimated number of skilled and semi-skilled workers (Liberian, other African, and non-African) employed in selected occupations, 1969*

Occupation	Skilled	Semi-skilled	Total
Mason	375	475	850
Carpenter	516	516	1032
Plumber	76	110	186
Electrician (including radio)	105	124	229
Auto mechanic	257	309	566
Heavy duty vehicle mechanic	146	78	224
Welder	100	60	160
Machine operator	57	113	170
Heavy duty vehicle operator	276	140	416
Driller; blaster	95	—	95
Painter	51	65	116
Total	2054	1990	4044

Source: Dr Hans Baritsh, ILO. '*Survey on the Present Vocational Training Facilities and the Future Vocational Training Moods of Liberia*', *April 1961.*

Wage statistics indicate a second distinguishing characteristic of skilled labour in Liberia: an unusually wide range in wage rates is paid for workers in the same job class, reflecting wide variations in the degree of skill of different workers. Table 12, which shows wage rates paid to several job categories by three large firms is of particular interest. It appears that the range paid has tended to widen rather than narrow over the years in the more highly skilled categories (e.g. labour overseer, carpenter).

Table 12. *Comparison of wages and salary rates. Large foreign firms, 1961*
(rate per day in dollars)

	1949	1954	1958	1961
Firm A				
Common labourer	0·20	0·25	0·35–0·40	0·40
Carpenter	0·25–1·50	0·50–1·75	0·40–2·90	0·50–2·75
Truck driver	0·25–1·50	0·50–1·75	0·40–2·30	0·60–2·85
Labour overseer	—	0·60–2·25	0·80–2·75	0·50–3·50
Firm B				
Common labourer	0·25–0·35	0·32–0·40	0·32–0·56	0·80
Carpenter	1·25–1·50	—	0·96–2·80	1·04–2·72
Truck driver	0·96–1·44	1·28–2·40	0·96–2·80	1·04–2·48
Typist[a]	2·27–2·50	1·51–4·55	1·51–3·31	0·88–3·12
Firm C				
Labourer	0·56–0·80	0·56–0·80	0·56–0·80	0·80
Carpenter	1·52–2·00	1·44–2·00	1·28–3·20	1·44–3·84
Truck driver	1·09–1·36	1·14–1·59	1·36–1·82	1·82–2·73
Account clerk	2·95–4·55	4·55–6·81	4·55–8·86	1·92–8·80
Typist	1·82–2·27	2·05–2·27	1·82–3·14	3·20–6·00

Note: [a] Monthly rates converted to daily rates assuming 22 working days a month.
Source: US Embassy, Monrovia.

Traditional agricultural patterns strongly influence the supply of labour to the wage-earning sectors of the economy. The land is cut, cleared and burned between March and May and the main upland rice crops are harvested between July and September. It is during these periods that tribal people leave their wage-earning jobs in order to return to traditional farming activities.

To explain the high rate of seasonal return to subsistence rice production, we compare the cash wages plus material benefits paid by rubber farms to the imputed value of alternative real earnings in subsistence agriculture. A tribal family of five people typically cultivates a three acre farm, two acres planted in upland rice, one in other crops. The male head of the family spends about 15 days per acre clearing and burning the land, and about an equal amount of time during the harvest. His total labour time, per season, comes to about three months on the family farm. The wife does the sowing and weeding during the growing season. She sows around 140 pounds of seed rice on the two acres, for a gross yield of 2,000 pounds of rice in husks 60–65 per cent of which is clean rice, or some 1,250 pounds. Deducting the 140 pounds of seed sown, the net yield in clean rice is about 1,100 pounds, which at $6·50 per hundred pounds, has a market value of $71·50. We may attribute this net value product entirely to the man, as long as tribal women have almost zero cash-earning opportunities.

This $71·50 in rice income from farming may be contrasted with three months earnings as a rubber tapper at $0·45 per day, a total of some $40. Wage rates on rubber farms would almost have to be doubled to make it materially worthwhile for the man to give up rice farming during the planting season. Indeed, if we count the other crops grown on the third acre, and the non-material benefits of returning to the farm, perhaps $0·90 per day would be close to the mark. On the other hand, at a wage rate of $0·55 per day, an unskilled worker can earn in a year an income somewhat larger than that presently yielded by three months of rice farming and nine months of rubber tapping.[1] This calculation suggests why enterprises paying $0·55 per day and more did not experience great difficulty in finding unskilled labourers. It also suggests that those persons who have had some contact with the money economy are better calculators of long term income prospects than is commonly supposed.

Rubber workers return to rice farming not only for the material income it yields directly, but also to maintain rights in tribal land (rights which are based on usage) and to fulfil social obligations to assist kinsmen in farming and other pursuits. Even at a wage rate of $0·55 per day, unskilled labour might well have been in short supply were it not for labour recruitment. As a result of the minimum wage legislation and a strike in 1963, the Firestone plantation claimed that tappers were subsequently costing 1·20 dollars a day. Costs on

[1] The return from 90 days of rice farming plus 250 days of rubber tapping is $71·50 + (250× ·45) = $71·50 + $112·50 = $184·00. From 360 days of unskilled labour at $0·55 per day, the comparable return is $198·00.

private plantations were, however, still little more than the 55 cents used in the analysis here of the situation at the beginning of the sixties.

There are three kinds of female labour in Liberia: (1) literate and trained women (e.g. secretaries and schoolteachers); (2) illiterate and untrained women in the interior; (3) illiterate and untrained women in Monrovia and other cities. There is no problem in employing literate and trained woman seeking employment. Such women are regarded in Liberia as they are in Europe and America, and conventionally occupy positions in offices, schools, and hospitals. But there are even fewer literate females in Liberia than literate males. In the interior, females have been occasionally employed for wages with success on some rubber concessions. Liberian men have no objection to wives earning money if it is done at some familiar task (petty marketing, weeding gardens) which is 'women's work' and does not interfere with household and family-farm work. Women are seldom employed as tappers in Liberia (men's work) and there are no jobs for illiterate women in other commercial production lines undertaken in the interior; road construction, iron ore mining, timber cutting.

Disguised unemployment of female labour is apparent in Monrovia. Indigenously, tribal women work extremely hard, both in household tasks and farming. When they come to live in Monrovia with their husbands or relatives, they have no farming tasks to do. Since there is no urban employment for illiterate and untrained females, other than petty marketing, one sees hundreds of women putting in very long hours. Most of them probably earn less than twenty-five cents for a twelve to sixteen hour day.

Such facts reinforce the need for more literacy and vocational training in Liberia. Indeed, one aspect of economic development is the continuing decline in the proportion of unskilled to total labour force. Skills and literacy require training and education, which, at the same time as they increase labour productivity, also weaken tribal allegiance: even moderately educated men and women invariably leave the confined orbit of tribal society.

With regard to child labour, little can be said. In tribal surroundings, children work at light farming tasks to aid family effort and to learn proper procedures and performance of duty. It is not uncommon for boys under 12 to be employed as spare tappers on independent rubber farms. In urban situations they frequently work as yard boys, newspaper sellers, and petty marketeers. In Monrovia, a few perform car-watching services which—for a small fee—protects owners from the vandalism of the watchers.

The salient characteristics of professional and managerial personnel in Liberia can be listed as follows:

(1) At least 90 per cent of all Africans with professional and managerial skills are employed by the Government of Liberia. Of this group, about one fourth are Negro immigrants (from other African countries, the United States, West Indies, Haiti). The government also employs several hundred Europeans, Americans and Asians.

(2) Managerial and professional positions at foreign concessions and other foreign firms are almost wholly occupied by Europeans, Americans and Lebanese.

(3) It is not uncommon for Liberian-owned establishments (e.g., large independent rubber farms, trucking companies) to be managed by foreigners.

It is only a slight exaggeration to say that the professional, managerial, and entrepreneurial labour force in Liberia is divided into two groups: Liberians work for government, are absentee owners (for the most part) of rubber farms, transport facilities and buildings,[1] provide legal services, and to a small extent medical and commercial services. Foreigners are overwhelmingly predominant in staff positions in iron ore, rubber and timber. Where Liberians are employed by concessions, they most frequently act as advisers in law, public relations and advertising.

A sample survey concerning skilled and professional labour was carried out by questionnaire in the summer of 1961 amongst the largest firms in Liberia: its results are summarized in Table 13. The firms and government departments in the sample employed about 60 per cent of all wage and salary earners in Liberia and about 80 per cent of all professional and managerial persons. An increase of 25 per cent in total employment of such persons was expected by 1966. Industries in which employment is expected to grow most rapidly in the sampled establishments were Government, 54 per cent; Trading Companies, 33 per cent; Construction Firms, 32 per cent. Three of the establishments estimated a future decline in employment caused by a transition from a construction or development to a production phase of activity. Three other establishments predicted no change in their future employment levels. All other establishments estimated gains in the future ranging from 2 per cent to 450 per cent.

The estimated future growth in wage employment is a continuation of the gains reported since 1958. With but three exceptions, all

[1] Under Liberian law, foreigners cannot own land or commercial transport facilities.

Table 13. *Currentand estimated employment in sampled firms*
(number of persons)

	August 1961	Estimated 1966	Net Change
Civil engineer	78	88	10
Electrical engineer	23	32	9
Mechanical engineer	57	66	9
Mining engineer	10	16	6
Chemical and metallurgical engineer	4	9	5
Surveyor	53	44	−9
Geologist	14	17	3
Agronomist	37	55	18
Forester	55	72	17
Economist	7	17	10
Statistician	18	34	16
Accountant and auditor	180	266	86
Teacher, secondary school	253	668	415
Teacher, primary school	1926	4448	2522
Draftsman	51	73	22
Physician and surgeon	68	127	59
Dentist	8	12	4
Nurse, professional	211	340	129
Pharmacist	4	9	5
Medical technician	72	80	8
Science and eng. technician	260	314	54
Dresser, medical	125	181	56
Administrative and managerial	503	657	154
Secretary and stenographer	221	324	103
Typist	336	498	162

Source: William Langbehn, '*A Pilot Study of High-Level Manpower in Liberia*', August 1961.

surveyed firms reported substantial gains in employment for the period 1958–61. Of those three, only one reported a net decline, and that was of less than 10 per cent of the firm's total work force. However, there are problems arising from the large numbers of workers becoming unemployed simultaneously when large construction works are completed. Thus about 10,000 workers were laid off in 1963 when major LAMCO projects were completed.

In mid-1962, there were approximately 2,500 non-Africans employed at professional, managerial, and highly technical jobs, which Liberians—if qualified—could fill.[1] If the Government pursues a

[1] This figure excludes such positions as those with diplomatic and missionary organizations, and family firms owned by Lebanese.

policy of 'Liberianization' it must identify the types and numbers of positions available, and direct its scholarship programme toward external training for these positions. Moreover, there would have to be created some sort of staff training programme to give educationally qualified Liberians entrance into and experience at junior-level professional and managerial occupations in the private sector of the economy. The tradition of highly trained Liberians seeking jobs exclusively with the Government[1] would have to be changed, as larger numbers of trained Liberians become available for private employment.

In developed Western countries, trade unions are distinguished by three characteristics: (1) Union leaders regard the interests of their rank and file membership as primary, and leaders are independent of government and employers. (2) Unions engage in periodic collective bargaining, the results of which are set forth explicitly in contractual rights, obligations, and stipulations concerning wages, other income benefits, and work conditions. (3) Union bargaining power is made effective through the right to strike.

All three features of Western trade unionism were absent in Liberia: union leaders were independent of neither the government nor employers;[2] there was no collective bargaining in Liberia—no written wage contracts periodically negotiated; strikes were illegal in Liberia if they occurred before the legal processes of arbitration and court decision are exhausted. (All strikes known to have occurred in Liberia from 1949 through 1961—some 12 to 15 strikes—were illegal).

Strikes have been partly successful in the sense that wage increases have followed several of them. In 1961 there were more strikes and

1 Some of the reasons why professionally trained Liberians traditionally prefer government employment even at distinctly lower salary scales are these: (1) government employment often requires the employee to be 'on the job' only a few hours per week, which allows civil servants to carry on private enterprises on government time: (2) although government salary scales are lower than those of resident foreign firms, there is frequently a higher real income to be earned when one counts perquisites of office—free housing, automobile, travel outside the country, supplementary emoluments of the kickback system, and private use of government property.

2 The head of the CIO (which has no affiliation with the American CIO) is the President of Liberia's son, who, before becoming a union head in mid-1960 was a public relations consultant for the Liberia Mining Company. In 1962 he was still a public relations consultant for Lamco, the second largest private employer and the biggest mining venture in Liberia. At the time of his investiture as CIO head in 1960, the government of Liberia gave the CIO a gift of $5,000. The head of the other trade union, Col. Dupeigny-Leigh, is the President of Liberia's social secretary and a former member of the House of Representatives.

more workers involved in strikes, than in all previous strikes taken together. Although there were strikes in Liberia as early as 1949, 1961 marks the first time that a strike occurred in a wholly Liberian-owned enterprise (a large rubber farm); before 1961 all strikes took place in large foreign firms. With the exception of a strike in September 1961,[1] none of the strikes known to have occurred between 1949 and 1961 was initiated by union action.

The weak, indeed, almost non-existent role of unions in Liberia can be explained by the economic and social structure and the traditional institutional complex of Liberia. Most Liberian wage workers were illiterate, unskilled, and of tribal origin. Relatively few were permanently committed to wage employment. About half of all wage workers did unskilled jobs in commercial agriculture (mostly rubber farms owned by foreign concessions and Liberians): wage employment is relatively new for most Liberians. These factors work against the successful establishment and functioning of effective unions. There was an absence in Liberia of experience with democratically controlled voluntary associations. There were no analogues in Liberian society to associations controlled by the rank and file whose leaders act primarily in the interests of the membership.[2] In addition, many top echelon government officials are themselves large employers (rubber farms, trucking companies) and had no wish to relinquish to unions their traditional paternalistic control over labourers.

The extremely weak position of unions was partly due to the absence of a concern with increasing the real income of rank and file workers. For example (1) official tolerance of labour recruitment (which acts to keep wages from rising in response to market forces); (2) labour legislation (as of 1962) which exempts half the wage-earning labour force—the lowest-paid half, in commercial agriculture and domestic service—from the minimum wage rate of four cents an hour. Sensitivity to foreign criticism has deterred the government from eliminating unionism. Liberia has been publicly castigated by the ILO for allowing unsavoury labour practices. Moreover, Liberia would lose prestige in the eyes of other African countries if trade unions were legally disallowed. The government of Liberia's position on unions may be fairly stated as follows: unions should exist but should remain ineffective. Although official policy

[1] It started when the Head of the Union was out of the country. Since then there has been a major organized strike at Harbel in 1963.

[2] There are two newspapers published in Liberia. One is wholly owned by the government of Liberia, the other gets a small government subsidy. One of the radio stations in Liberia is government owned, the other is owned and operated by a Protestant Mission.

is to tolerate the existence of unions, President Tubman on several occasions has emphasized that Liberian economic development must not be impeded or jeopardized by strikes. Indeed, Col Dupeigny-Leigh, head of a union (Labour Congress) is on record as not favouring strikes.

The dominance and control of the fragile trade union movement by government is not institutionally unique in Liberia. No potential focus of political opposition, no organization which criticizes government policy or exists for purposes which might conflict with governmental aims, is allowed to flourish. The government interpret strikes as evidence of political disloyalty and foreign subversion, rather than economic discontent. Such a view effectively hobbles union officers, since they can be arrested and jailed without trial under the President's emergency powers. Not being free to criticize the Government of Liberia or private Liberian employers (many of whom are upper level government civil servants), union spokesmen confined their criticism to foreign employers, even though wage rates and supplements are almost invariably higher in foreign than in Liberian-owned firms.

In summary, the reasons for the lack of success of trade unionism in Liberia can be listed as follows:

Structure of economy and labour force: two thirds of the wage-earning labour force was unskilled, and largely illiterate, many of whom retained tribal identification and a semi-tribal way of life; there was high labour turnover and a seasonal return to subsistence agriculture. Agricultural employment (which even in developed countries is less amenable to union organization) accounts for a large fraction of the wage earning labour force.

Structure of government and society: there was an absence of independent voluntary associations and of overt political opposition; there was the fear of an independent trade union movement becoming a focus of political opposition (the present—and tolerated—union leadership is obviously loyal to the administration). Political leaders as private employers are opposed to wage increases and to losing control over their workers. Union officials were subject to arrest under the President's emergency powers.

6. INDUSTRIALIZATION

In 1962, industrial processing of primary commodities for export was done exclusively by foreign concessions. Latex rubber was processed into crepe, and crude iron-ore was beneficiated so as to reduce transport costs by exporting a less bulky, more refined product.

Manufacturing and fabrication of finished goods for domestic consumers and producers markets was just beginning. Here too the few new lines of production were being undertaken principally by foreigners: automobile tyre re-capping, milk reconstitution, beer and soft drink manufacture, soap and furniture.

There was no industrialization plan. As with the granting of foreign concessions to rubber and iron-ore mining firms, the Government of Liberia played a passive role: European and American firms would take the initiative to get contractual approval from the government to undertake a specific line of production. Here too, Liberians supply unskilled and some skilled labour, and the European management supplied the required entrepreneurial and professional labour, and capital.

Import duties provide some encouragement for manufacturers to set up manufacturing or processing plants in Liberia to avoid the duty. For example, the duty imposed on boiled sweets has stimulated an English manufacturer to examine the feasibility of local manufacture. But the limited market in Liberia means that 'infant industry' protection can only be successful if there are no great diseconomies of small plants. Unfortunately this is true of only very few commodities. If, and it is an enormous if, West Africa ever develops a common market these disadvantages may be overcome. Specialization within the region could provide a viable market for many industries.

7. TRADE

Some of the components of imports and exports have been described in earlier sections. Figures for 1959 to 1962 are given in Table 14. Rubber and iron ore exports which together comprised about 85 per cent of all exports in 1962, were not sold in free markets abroad. The direction of export trade is roughly indicated by the nationality of the foreign concessions resident in Liberia (selling mainly in their home countries). Firestone sells its rubber to its parent company in the United States, and much the same is true for the European iron ore mines. About 40 per cent of imports and exports were the result of trade with the USA.

Two points in particular may be noted. First, much of the imports of machinery, vehicles, and manufactured goods during the period shown were required and financed by the iron ore mining companies. Secondly, iron ore is becoming increasingly important as the figures in Table 15 show. Production has more than quintupled over the last 6 years and the output forecast for 1970 is 20 million tons.

Table 14. *Exports and imports 1959–62*
(million dollars)

	1959	1960	1961	1962
Exports				
Rubber	30·7	39·1	25·5	25·7
Iron ore	28·2	34·6	29·4	32·4
Diamonds	2·1	2·3	2·2	4·5
Palm kernels	2·3	2·0	1·1	0·8
Cocoa	0·5	0·5	0·2	0·2
Coffee	0·6	0·5	0·4	0·6
Other	2·5	3·6	3·1	3·4
Total	66·9	82·6	61·9	67·6
Imports				
Food, beverages, tobacco	7·8	11·0	14·1	17·0
Machinery and vehicles	10·4	23·3	35·0	53·7
Manufactured goods	18·7	26·2	31·5	47·1
Chemicals	2·7	4·7	4·3	5·8
Fuels and lubricants	2·8	2·9	3·4	4·3
Other	0·5	1·1	2·4	3·7
Total	42·9	69·2	90·7	131·6

Source: M. A. Qureshi, Y. Mizoe, and F. d'A. Collings, 'The Liberian Economy' *IMF Staff Papers*, XI (2), July 1964.

In 1960, import duties yielded the Government of Liberia almost one-third of its total revenue. Aside from import duties, a small export tax on rubber, and control over the import of firearms, pharmaceuticals and used clothing, foreign trade is entirely free from quota restrictions. There were no marketing boards in Liberia. Traditional export crops, such as palm kernels and piassava, and the more recent export crops such as cocoa and coffee, are purchased directly from small scale peasant farmers by Lebanese merchants.

Table 15. *Exports (quantity) of main commodities*

	1959	1960	1961	1962	1966[a]
Rubber (m lbs)	97·9	106·7	90·8	100·1	115
Iron ore (m long tons)	2·6	2·9	2·8	3·7	15
Diamonds ('000 carats)	638·0	967·0	1095·0	854·0	n.a.

Note: [a] Production figures.
Source: M. A. Qureshi, Y. Mizoe, and F.d' A. Collings, 'The Liberian Economy' *IMF Staff Papers*, XI (2), July 1964 and *Africa Research Bulletin*, Vol. 4, Nos. 3 and 6.

The Government has not attempted to control or influence imports and exports in order to stimulate development. Tariffs and export duties have been imposed in order to raise revenue rather than to stimulate industrial development, to finance government expenditure rather than to provide incentives for import-substitute industries.

8. CONCLUSIONS

Despite its historical association with the United States, its rich resource base relative to population, and generous external assistance by foreign governments and international agencies, Liberia must be placed among the least developed countries in Africa. In 1962, less than 10 per cent of the population was literate, the quality of its educational establishment was low, the traditional divisions between tribal Liberians and the Americo-Liberian descendants of the colonial settlers remained in force, and traditional governmental procedures and preferences had not been appreciably revised to serve development needs.

The great burgeoning of rubber and iron-ore production by foreigners since 1950 has had relatively little developmental impact: the unskilled labour force working for wages has almost tripled, but the enlarged receipt of money wages has not induced appreciably more production for the domestic market; rather it has increased the effective demand for imported consumption goods. The enlarged governmental revenues (which increased eightfold between 1950 and 1960) and enlarged borrowing from abroad—both of which are direct consequences of the rapid growth in primary products for export—for the most part have not been spent in ways which increase the productive capacity of the nation. Most professionally trained Liberians worked for the Government. The uneducated mass of tribal Liberians grew subsistance and traditional cash crops and worked as unskilled labourers on rubber farms. A few had acquired vocational and clerical skills. Only in rubber production has there been marked growth in an economic activity undertaken by Liberians.

In 1962 there was nothing that could reasonably be called developmental planning. Neither effective plan nor personnel existed. Liberia's principal tasks in research and in developmental planning are to transform subsistence agriculture (and especially to increase production of marketed rice, and its protein staple, fish), to reform its educational establishment to supply the growing demand for skilled and professional labour, and to undertake feasibility studies for new lines of processing and manufacture. Its most tenacious problems are institutional and require policies to reform traditional social and political organizations; to abolish forced recruitment of labour, to reform traditional land tenure arrangements, to reform the traditional administration of the tribal hinterland in ways which provide incentives for tribal persons to enlarge their production for sale, and to allow them access to higher education and political expression.

SELECTED READING

1. Clower, R., Dalton, G., Harwitz, M., and Walters, A. A., *Growth without Development:* An Economic Survey of Liberia (Evanston, Northwestern University Press, 1966).
2. Clower, R., Dalton, G., and Walters, A. A., 'Statistics and Development Policy Decisions', *Development Digest* (National Planning Association), Vol. 1, No. 1, July 1962, pp. 65–74.
3. Dalton, G., 'History, Politics, and Economic Development in Liberia', *The Journal of Economic History*, December 1965, pp. 569–91.
4. Qureshi, M. A., Mizoe, Y., and Collings, F. d'A., 'The Liberian Economy', *IMF Staff Papers*, X1, No. 2, July 1964, pp. 285–326.
5. Adelman, I., and Morris, C. T., 'Factor Analysis of the Inter-relationship between Social and Political Variables and Per Capita Gross National Product', *The Quarterly Journal of Economics*, November 1965, pp. 555–78.
6. Liebenow, J. G., 'The Republic of Liberia', in Gwendolen M. Carter (Ed.), *African One-Party States* (Ithaca, Cornell University Press, 1962).
7. Liebenow, J. G., 'Liberia', in James S. Coleman and Carl G. Rosberg Jr. (Eds.), *Political Parties and National Integration in Tropical Africa* (Berkeley, University of California Press, 1964).
8. Robinson, E. A. G. (Ed.), *Economic Development for Africa South of the Sahara* (New York, St Martin's Press, 1964).
9. Samuels, L. H., (Ed.), *African Studies in Income and Wealth* (Chicago, Quadrangle Books, 1963).

7

THE EAST AFRICAN ECONOMIES

1. INTRODUCTION

The East African economies afford an interesting special case in Africa because they form to some degree an inter-dependent economy at the same time as operating as three separate states. Although the arrangements which form the basis for this interdependence have been modified in recent years, their existence has meant that the three countries in some ways form more of an interdependent economic unit than many unitary states.

This interdependence is combined with some similarities in the lines of development of the three countries, but there are also striking economic contrasts. The patterns of development of the three countries during the colonial period were quite different, resulting in differences in industrial structure, in income distribution and in the form of their integration with the world economy.

In examining these three economies we take as our starting point a description of these contrasts. In particular, the differing roles of the non-African communities has been a crucial factor in creating the diversity of development in the East African countries. This is important because of both its economic and political significance.

The contrast is put most clearly when it is seen that before independence the level of *per capita* income of East Africa was highest in Kenya, lowest in Tanganyika,[1] with Uganda in between. However, as far as can be ascertained from the available data, the picture was quite different for the levels of African *per capita* income. Kenya had the lowest performance with Tanganyika slightly higher, whereas Uganda enjoyed African income levels considerably above the other two countries. Put another way, towards the end of the 'fifties, Africans claimed two-thirds of the monetary Gross Domestic Product

[1] Tanganyika united with Zanzibar in 1964 to form the United Republic of Tanzania. Many of the statistics quoted are available for Tanganyika (or mainland Tanzania) only, and the word is retained in this chapter for this and other relevant purposes. Tanzania is used when the current situation is discussed, or in other contexts where it appears natural and appropriate.

of Uganda, half of the Tanganyika product and only one-third of the Kenya product.[1]

From the point of view of economic analysis a systematic account of the differences in structure of the three countries should draw attention to the differing roles of agriculture as compared with other forms of economic activity, to the differing importance of the non-African element, to the differing importance of exports and of the differing role in the three countries of intra-East African economic relationships.

In all three countries agriculture forms the occupation and the source of income for the predominant portion of the population. Its role as a source of monetary income, however, differs substantially in the three countries. Whereas value added in cash agriculture in Kenya plays a fairly minor role in total domestic product for a country of that level of development, the Tanzania and Uganda cases are more in line with experience elsewhere. The Kenya economy has developed service and manufacturing sectors well in excess of what would normally be expected for an economy with such a low *per capita* level of income. This was for two reasons:

(*a*) the economy partly provides services and, to a lesser degree, processing facilities for the other two East African countries.
(*b*) the non-African community represents an enclave with income levels not only much higher than the rest of the population but also higher, in the case of the Europeans, than average levels of income in the United Kingdom. This sector has a high demand for services and imported commodities, generating incomes in commerce.

Uganda has never had a large commercial community composed of Europeans, but a highly prosperous African agriculture has developed, based on coffee and cotton production. In this comparison, as in many others, Tanzania lies somewhere between the two.

The difference is not only one of the balance between agriculture and other forms of economic activity, it also involves the structure of the agriculture sector as such. In considering agriculture in East Africa it is important to distinguish a number of different types. In addition to purely agrarian methods of classification it is useful to distinguish types of agricultural activity on the basis of the form of their economic organization in the following way:

[1] Dharam P. Ghai, 'Some Aspects of Income Distribution in East Africa', *East African Institute of Social Research*, discussion paper series EDRP, No. 52, 1964.

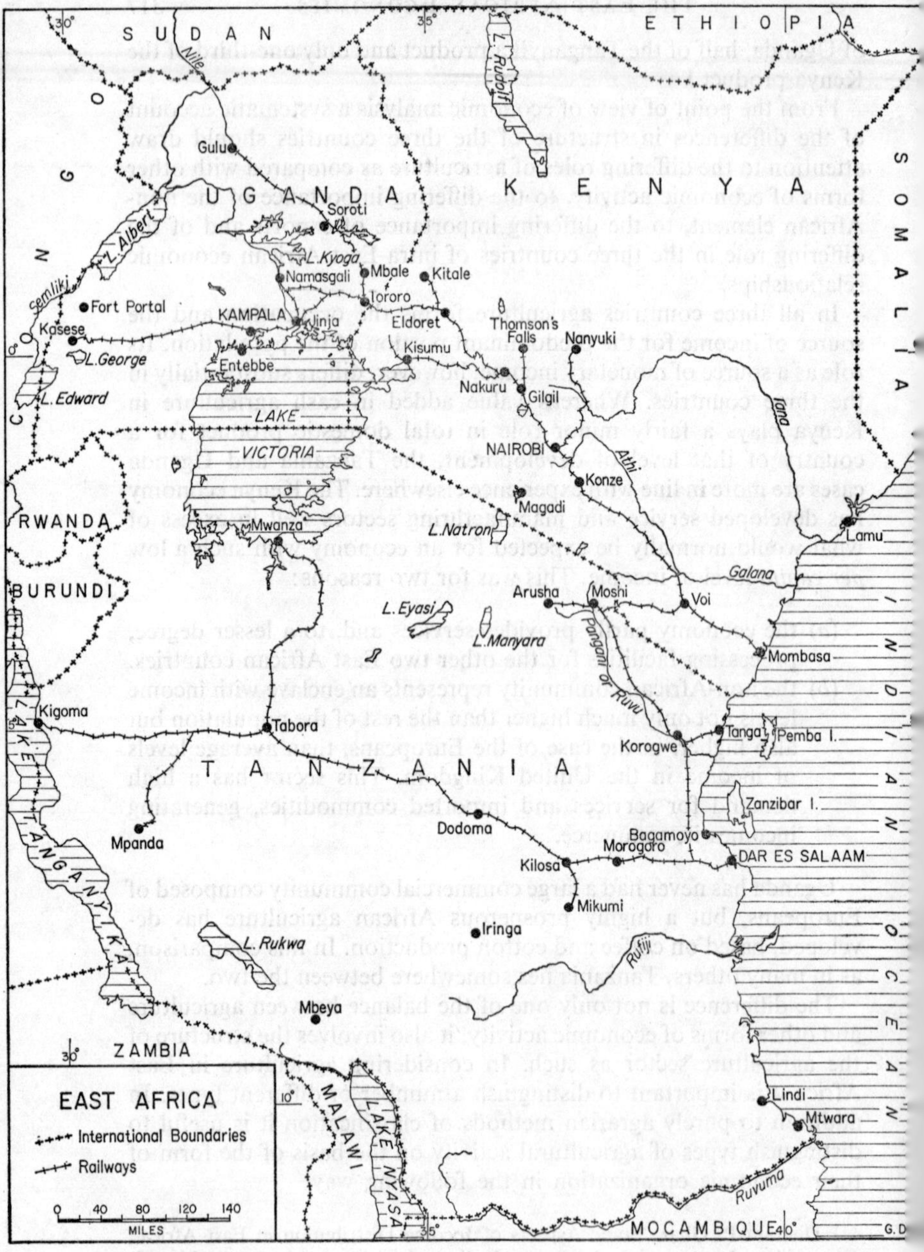
EAST AFRICA
International Boundaries
Railways
0
40
80
120
140
MILES
SUDAN
ETHIOPIA
SOMALIA
UGANDA
KENYA
TANZANIA
RWANDA
BURUNDI
ZAMBIA
MALAWI
MOCAMBIQUE
INDIAN OCEAN
CONGO
30°
35°
40°
10°
0°
5°
Nile
L. Rudolf
L. Albert
Semliki
L. Kyoga
L. George
L. Edward
LAKE VICTORIA
L. Natron
L. Eyasi
L. Manyara
L. Rukwa
LAKE TANGANYIKA
LAKE NYASA
Tana
Athi
Galana
Pangani or Ruvu
Rufiji
Ruvuma
Gulu
Soroti
Namasgali
Mbale
Kitale
Tororo
Fort Portal
KAMPALA
Jinja
Kasese
Entebbe
Eldoret
Thomson's Falls
Nanyuki
Kisumu
Nakuru
Gilgil
NAIROBI
Konze
Magadi
Mwanza
Lamu
Arusha
Moshi
Voi
Mombasa
Kigoma
Tabora
Tanga
Pemba I.
Korogwe
Zanzibar I.
Mpanda
Dodoma
Bagamoyo
Morogoro
DAR ES SALAAM
Kilosa
Mikumi
Iringa
Mbeya
Lindi
Mtwara

Map 5

(*a*) so called subsistence agriculture, that is, the output of African peasant farmers which is not recorded as generating a cash market transaction;
(*b*) African peasant cash production, both for export and for local food consumption;
(*c*) non-African mixed farming;
(*d*) non-African ranching and plantation farming.

It is interesting to note that in East Africa activity involved under classification (*b*) is probably as export oriented as (*c*). The development of African cash farming, as elsewhere in Africa, was heavily dependent on the expansion of the export trade to overseas markets. Export production sprang up alongside the subsistence production of the African farmer, providing an economic link with the most remote world markets. By contrast, a substantial proportion of the cash agriculture of the European mixed farmers found a market supplying local food needs.

Using this classification, we see that in Uganda agriculture predominantly falls under categories (*a*) and (*b*) with the exception of the important sugar and tea plantations which fall under category (*d*).[1] There was no significant development of non-African mixed farming and only a very minor development of non-African cultivation in the major cash crops, such as coffee.

By contrast, throughout most of the colonial period in Kenya African involvement in export agriculture (and even in recorded market output for local consumption) predominantly took the form of employment as wage labour on farms or plantations falling under categories (*c*) and (*d*). Nevertheless the majority of Africans spend their time engaging in economic activity which would be located in the social accounts under (*a*). This structure has been changing radically in recent years. Land transfer programmes have transferred more than a million acres of European mixed farms to African ownership on smallholder settlement schemes.[2] In addition to official programmes, which aimed to transfer about one-fifth of the total European mixed farming over to African smallholder occupancy by 1967, there were also considerable private purchases by Africans of European owned lands. Even more important in influencing the structure of the Kenya economy has been the very high expansion of

[1] D. J. Parson, *The Systems of Agriculture Practised in Uganda*, Uganda Department of Agriculture, Kawanda, 1960.

[2] C. P. R. Nottidge and J. R. Goldsack, *The Million-Acre Settlement Scheme, 1962–1966*, Department of Settlement, Nairobi, 1966.

cash crop production over the past decade in the traditional African smallholding areas (the former trust lands).[1]

All four elements are significantly represented in Tanzanian agriculture. The very important sisal export industry has been almost entirely a plantation industry in the past. There has been small but significant European owned mixed farming activity and there have been major export crops, in particular coffee, which have been produced both by non-African and African farmers. Cotton, a major export crop, has been grown exclusively by African farmers. There have also been a wide range of minor crops which, combined, form an important source of export earnings, and which have been predominantly the concern of the African farmer.[2]

Relatively good data on the structure and growth of gross product is available from the early 1950's and are summarized in Tables 1 and 2. From the available official data it is possible to gain a clear picture of the evolution of the economies in recent years. The aggregate data is not without inevitable inadequacies, however, and must be handled with care. The estimates distinguish between output which is marketed ('monetary' output) and output consumed in the household of the producer ('subsistence' output); but the breakdown between subsistence and monetary output is inevitably arbitrary, and it is likely, therefore, that there is a much higher level of welfare in rural areas, and a higher proportion of total output derived from rural activities, than is suggested by these figures.

As a result of the development of successful peasant export agriculture in Tanzania and Uganda and the development of plantation export agriculture in Tanzania, these two countries ship sufficient exports to the rest of the world for external trade to play the major role in determining the level of their income. By contrast, the economy in Kenya has been much less dependent on overseas export earnings as a source of income while at the same time it has been much more heavily dependent on imports from outside East Africa as a source of goods for local use.

The dependence of Uganda and Tanzania on agricultural export earnings has made both countries susceptible to the effects of short-term commodity fluctuations. For example, the sharp fluctuation in

[1] Hans Ruthenberg, *African Agricultural Production Development Policy in Kenya 1952–1965*, African Studies Center of the Ifo-Institute, Study No. 10, New York, 1966.

[2] For a full description of Tanganyikan agriculture see Hans Ruthenberg, *Agricultural Development in Tanganyika*, African Studies Center of the Ifo-Institute, Study No. 2, New York, 1964; and N. R. Fuggles-Couchman, *Agricultural Change in Tanganyika: 1945–1960*, Food Research Institute, Stanford University, Stanford, 1964.

Table 1. *Gross domestic product at factor cost*
(£m)

Industry	Kenya		Tanganyika				Uganda	
			1954–56	1961–63 (new series)				
	1954–56	1961–63	(old series)	Private	Public	Total	1954–56	1961–63
Agriculture, forestry, fishing and hunting								
Total	77·3	100·3	91·6	123·3	2·4	125·7	95·1	103·9
Non-monetary	46·5	59·3	53·9	72·6	—	72·6	37·7	47·1
Monetary	30·9	41·0	37·7	50·7	2·4	53·1	57·5	56·8
Mining and quarrying	1·2	0·9	4·9	4·9	0·1	5·0	1·0	2·6
Manufacturing	16·6	23·4	3·9	7·3	0·3	7·6	6·4	6·4
Construction	7·9	6·5	4·9	3·0	3·1	6·1	4·5	3·7
Public utilities	1·5	3·2	0·8	1·2	0·3	1·5	0·9	2·5
Transport and communication	14·2	22·7	8·5	4·0	5·1	9·1	4·1	6·0
Commerce	26·3	34·5	7·4	24·5	—	24·5	12·7	15·8
Rents	5·3	8·6	2·7	4·0	4·8	8·8	1·7	3·6
Services	9·6	14·6	4·0	8·2	15·0	23·2	6·2	11·7
Government	17·3	28·0	8·6	—	—	—	4·2	7·0
Total	177·2	242·6	137·3	180·4	31·1	211·5	136·8	163·0

Sources: *Annual Statistical Abstracts* for the three countries; *The Real Growth of the Economy of Uganda 1954–62*. The industrial classification methods used in the three countries are not strictly comparable. See the explanatory notes to Table 2.

L

Table 2. *Structure of GDP by major sector*
(percentages)

	Kenya 1961–63	Tanganyika 1961–63	Uganda 1961–63
Agriculture, forestry, fishing and hunting	41·3	59·4	63·7
Mining and quarrying	0·4	2·4	1·6
Total primary	41·7	61·8	65·3
Manufacturing	9·6	3·6	3·9
Construction	2·7	2·9	2·3
Total manufacturing and construction	12·3	6·5	6·2
Services	46·0	31·7	28·6
Total	100·0	100·0	100·0

Notes: Detailed comparisons based on these data should be handled with care. The three countries use significantly different methods of estimation. The two series available for Tanganyika also differ considerably.

The Uganda Gross Domestic Product estimates include separate estimates for coffee curing, cotton ginning and sugar refining as an industry group. In this table these activities have been incorporated under agriculture, although in the Tanganyikan accounts they are included under manufacturing. Miscellaneous services, in the Uganda estimates, include among other things public educational and medical services.

The old series produced for Tanganyika for 1954–62 included estimates for non-monetary product in rural hut building. These figures have not been included here because of the desire to improve comparability of the data.

Detailed presentation of the estimation techniques is available in the following basic sources:

Domestic Income and Product in Kenya, Government Printer, Nairobi, 1959.

The Gross Domestic Product of Uganda: 1954–1959, East African Statistical Department, Uganda Unit, April 1961.

The Gross Domestic Product of Tanganyika: 1954–1957, Government Printer, Dar es Salaam 1959.

The National Accounts of Tanganyika 1960–1962, Central Statistical Bureau, The Treasury, May 1964.

sisal prices during the period 1962 to 1965 was one of the major influences determining the buoyancy of the Tanzanian economy.[1] Similarly, over the years Uganda has been strongly affected by the fluctuations in the price of her coffee exports and from instability in cotton output resulting from climatic factors. Such fluctuations make a direct impact on disposable private incomes and also, through

[1] See Tanzanian *Background to the Budget 1965–66*, Government Printer, Dar es Salaam, 1965; and *Background to the Budget, 1966–67*, Government Printer, Dar es Salaam, 1966.

their effect on available public finance, induce fluctuation in government spending. Kenya, although less dependent on overseas export crops, is still susceptible to changes in the prosperity of the agricultural sector and also finds her economic fate inextricably involved with that of the two neighbouring countries.

Kenya has undoubtedly reaped considerable advantage from the special character of her industrial and agricultural structure. That important part of Kenyan agricultural output which is sold in Kenya markets enjoys substantial guaranteed price stability through a complex of specialized marketing arrangements. Her industry, likewise, has received substantial protection in the East African market. The Kenya economy therefore has been far less sensitive to terms of trade effects and to externally induced fluctuations than the other two countries.

Further insight into the structure of the economy is to be gained from detailed consideration of the estimates of income distribution in the three countries given in Table 3.[1] Although the roughness of some of the approximations required in making these estimates is admitted, the general picture emerging is reliable. The comparison between Uganda and Kenya is most striking. The most important source of African incomes in Uganda is the marketing of the produce of the peasant farmer; employment income generated only one-sixth of total monetary income in 1954 and less than one-third even in 1962, despite rapid growth in wage levels and a major agricultural setback. The position was substantially reversed in Kenya, where African marketed produce still formed only one-fifth of total monetary incomes at the end of the period. The reason for the existence of such a considerable peasant agriculture in Uganda, compared with its stunted growth in Kenya is of considerable historical interest, but lies beyond the boundaries of this discussion. However, the contrast has resulted in the economies being faced with very different social and economic problems currently. The Tanzanian income structure lies somewhere between the other two, with marketed produce providing Africans with about two-fifths of monetary incomes and employment about one-half.

The difference in the role of the non-Africans in the three countries has had widespread implications. In Kenya more elaborate systems of administration, commercial and financial institutions, and processing industries were developed than elsewhere in East Africa. This difference in the pattern of growth was both a cause and effect of the larger European and Asian minority groups and resulted in a much more complex economy than would be expected from the overall

[1] Dharam P. Ghai, *op. cit.*, EDRP.

Table 3. *Distribution of income between Africans and non-Africans*

	Kenya		Tanganyika	Uganda	
	1954	1962	1962	1954	1962
1. Gross Domestic Product	£158·0 m	£244·1 m	£211·4 m	£128·7 m	£156·7 m
2. Monetary GDP	£112·5 m	£180·9 m	£136·8 m	£92·8 m	£107·9 m
3. Subsistence sector	£45·5 m	£63·2 m	£74·6 m	£36·0 m	£48·7 m
4. African employment income	£24·5 m	£44·9 m	£36·5 m	£10·7 m	£23·2 m
5. African marketed produce	£6·6 m	£11·7 m	£30·0 m	£48·2 m	£40·0 m
6. Non-agricultural African enterprises	£2·4 m	£4·5 m	£9·4 m	£4·5 m	£8·1 m
7. Total African monetary income	£33·5 m	£61·1 m	£75·9 m	£63·4 m	£71·3 m
8. Total African income	£79·0 m	£124·3 m	£150·5 m	£99·4 m	£120·0 m
9. (8) as % of (1)	50·0	50·9	71·2	77·2	76·6
10. (7) as % of (2)	29·8	33·8	55·5	68·3	66·1
11. African population ('000)	6,572	8,325	9,419	5,682	6,920
12. African *per capita* income	£12·0	£14·9	£16·0	£17·5	£17·3
13. African *per capita* monetary income	£5·1	£7·3	£8·1	£11·2	£10·3
14. Non-African Income	£72·4 m	£108·0 m	£52·3 m	£25·4 m	£27·9 m
15. (14) as % of (2)	64·4	59·7	38·2	27·4	25·9
16. Non-African population ('000)	215	270	141	67	96
17. Non-African *per capita* income	£337	£400	£371	£379	£291

Source: Dharam P. Ghai, 'Some Aspects of Income Distribution in East Africa', *East African Institute of Social Research*, discussion paper series, EDRP, No. 52, 1964.

average level of *per capita* income. The inter-industry connections are still not complex but it is possible to distinguish a number of forms of economic activity which have substantial backward and forward linkages with other domestic industries. Industries based upon the processing of agricultural produce and upon the production of the inputs of the construction industry have played an important part in the growth of an industrial sector.

The institutional structure of industry and commerce is complex, with a mixture of small and medium scale local entrepreneurs alongside subsidiaries of overseas firms and large companies of local ownership. The role of the Asian community is particularly important in commerce and industry in all three East African countries.[1]

Economic relations between the three countries have, over the years, been the subject of debate and disagreement from time to time, but very substantial practical achievements have been fashioned through various forms of economic co-operation over the years.[2] In the first place, there has been a *de facto* common market, with a common external tariff. In the second place a wide range of public services has been operated jointly on an East African basis. These have included the railways, airways, posts and telegraphs, a number of research activities and the East African Customs and Excise and Income Tax Departments. In addition there has been a monetary union. Although in recent years the free trading arrangements have been under some stress, and in 1966 the three countries adopted separate currencies and initiated three Central Banks to replace the East African Currency Board, the range of economic integration confirmed by the Treaty for East African Co-operation is impressive.

Inevitably, as the three countries pursue more aggressive national development strategies co-operative arrangements will continue to be under stress. The pattern of future economic integration will emerge as an end result of conflicting forces: the underlying economic momentum for existing links to be strengthened; the growth of existing common service organizations and the buoyant expansion of trade between the three countries; and the assertion of national interests and the needs of the separate planning strategies of the three countries.

The evolution of payments flows between the three countries is

[1] Dharam P. Ghai, (ed.): *Portrait of a Minority; Asians in East Africa*, Oxford University Press, 1965.

[2] Joseph Nye, *Pan-Africanism and East African Integration*, Cambridge, Harvard University Press, 1965. See also C. Leys and P. Robson, *Federation in East Africa*, Nairobi, Oxford University Press, 1965.

not fully documented because of the lack of detailed quantitative evidence on invisibles and capital transactions. The evidence regarding the balance of trade is, as was suggested above, clear. Kenya has maintained a favourable balance of trade with Tanzania and Uganda which has enabled her to maintain a less favourable balance with the rest of the world. The balance between Kenya and Uganda has been more equal than that between Kenya and Tanzania, notably because of the export of sugar and the recent growth in manufactured exports from Uganda to Kenya. However, recently even this gap has been widening with a decline in Uganda's surplus sugar production. The balance on invisible account is also in Kenya's favour, because of its geographical position.

In considering the population the significant characteristics are the size and growth of the non-African population and the geographical distribution of the population. The most recent censuses provide a good guide to the size of the African population and reliable estimates of its rate of growth. The data are not conclusive, because of the difficulties of working with only two censuses, but it has been estimated that the rates of growth of population are of the order of 3·0 per cent per annum in Kenya, 2·5 per cent in Uganda and 2·1 per cent in Tanzania.[1] However, it seems likely that with reductions in the mortality rate throughout East Africa the rate of population growth will rise still higher, even in Kenya.

The relative importance of the non-African communities is clearly indicated in Table 4. The European community firmly established its dominant economic and political role in Kenya in the inter-war period and then grew at a high rate in the years following the Second World War, but at its height it still made up less than 1 per cent of the total population of Kenya. The European communities in Uganda and Tanganyika are relatively much less important. Since Independence there has been substantial emigration by non-Africans, particularly by Europeans leaving Kenya.

The location of population is largely determined by climate, soil and land tenure rights. In Kenya and Tanzania there is a heavy concentration of population in limited areas with very large areas extremely sparsely populated. In Uganda population is more evenly distributed, but even so there is a striking regional contrast in the extent of pressure of population on land. The degree of urbanization is extremely low throughout East Africa and especially so in Uganda. There is also an absence of a developed system of villages in the traditional patterns of rural living. A characteristic of many rural

[1] J. G. C. Blacker, 'Population Growth in East Africa', *Economic and Statistical Review* of the East African Statistical Department, No. 8, September, 1963.

Table 4. *Population*

	Tanzania (mainland)		Kenya		Uganda		Total East Africa (not including Zanzibar and Pemba)	
Areas and population density								
Land area ('000 sq. miles)	341		220		75		636	
Water and swamp ('000 sq. miles)	21		5		16		42	
Total ('000 sq. miles)	362		225		91		678	
Population density (persons per sq. mile of land area in 1965)	29·8		42·6		101·0		40·0	
Estimated population by race (thousands)	1960	1965	1960	1965	1960	1965	1960	1965
African	9,099	10,046	7,847	9,097	6,586	7,452	23,532	26,595
European	22	17	61	41	11	9	94	67
Indo-Pakistani	87	86	169	186	75	86	331	357
Arab	24	26	34	37	2	2	60	65
Other	4	4	4	4	2	2	10	10
Total	9,237	10,179	8,115	9,365	6,677	7,551	24,029	27,095

Total population of towns over 15,000 by race	Tanzania 1957	Kenya 1962	Uganda 1959
African	148,582	327,460	43,884
Non-African	53,451	200,222	32,592
Total	202,033	527,682	76,476

Estimated Population by Race of Zanzibar and Pemba (thousands)	1960
Indigenous inhabitants (Arabs, Mainland Africans, Comorians)	287·8
Asian (excluding Arabs)	18·9
European	0·6
Somali and other	0·4
Total	307·7

Source: *East African Economic and Statistical Review*, No. 18, March 1966. The figures are estimates derived by applying growth assumptions and migration data to census information.

areas of East Africa is that the individual farmer lives on his smallholding. This does not mean that he is isolated, because he is surrounded by similar small scale farmers.

Looking at the population map as a whole there are three types of area with heavy concentrations of population, (1) the Coast, (2) the areas around Lake Victoria and (3) the Highland areas of the three countries. In the case of Kenya a peculiar distribution of population developed as a result of the regulations controlling the use of the land in the Kenya Highlands. As a result of these regulations, towards the end of the Colonial period there was a heavy concentration of African population around the edges of the area designated as scheduled areas (i.e. the so-called White Highlands).

Except for the Coast, large towns no longer existed in East Africa at the end of the nineteenth century; this provides a striking contrast between East Africa and West or Northern Africa. Although this contrast may be of considerable importance for economic development, its effects will in large part be felt through the resulting cultural differences and response to economic stimuli which it is difficult to evaluate in a survey of this type. In addition this distribution of population will have other direct implications for economic development. The dispersion of population throughout the countryside renders it difficult to provide services. On the other hand, the considerable degree to which the population of East Africa maintains its link with the countryside and lives for at least a part of the time on the land, provides an important social security system and an element of stability in the lives of East Africans. This stability and the importance of such a social security system becomes evident when for one reason or another some group becomes landless.

In Tanzania the distribution of population presents special problems because the main congregations of population are located at considerable distances from each other. It has sometimes been represented as a country rather like a saucer, with the population concentrated around the edges and with the areas of lowest potential in the middle.

The population distribution is changing. The towns are growing much faster than the total population. There are also considerable movements of rural population, although much slower than would be the case in the absence of strong tribal attachments to and claims over particular areas of land.

The considerable concentration of population in all three countries around Lake Victoria suggests the possibility that the Lake area could become an increasingly integrated economic unit in the future. Although this may be a geographical possibility, its evolution in practice depends on the future development of the Common Market.

Industrial Structure

For the purpose of analysing the industrial structure, three major groups of industry will be identified: agriculture; manufacturing, mining and construction; and services. Mining will be dealt with separately sometimes, for, as an export oriented primary producing industry it can be regarded for some purposes as having much in common with agriculture.

The estimates of Gross Domestic Product show the division of product according to the values added by these industrial groups. The initial impression is sharp. Throughout East Africa, the manufacturing, mining and construction group is a minor source of product, although it is considerably more developed in Kenya than in the rest of East Africa. What is most striking, however, is the variation in the degree of dependence on agriculture and services. Kenya has a highly developed service sector and, for a country in which the vast majority of the population is still rural, a surprisingly low dependence on agriculture. The contrast with Uganda is sharp. Half of monetary domestic product in Uganda originates in agriculture, while less than two-fifths is derived from services, whereas in Kenya nearly three-fifths of total monetary product is derived from services and little more than one-fifth from agriculture. Tanzania lies somewhere in between.

Kenya presents an interesting example from an international viewpoint. Chenery notes that the non-agricultural component of Kenya's product is relatively more developed than would be expected from the *per capita* income levels,[1] and Kuznets' findings lead to the same conclusion.[2] The ranking of Kenya amongst developing countries is higher when the criterion is the proportion of non-agricultural product to total GDP than if *per capita* income is chosen as the basis of comparison.

What is the explanation of this variation in structure? Part of it is undoubtedly due to differences in definition of the boundaries between sectors and variation in completeness of the coverage. But even if allowance is made for such differences there is still a wide variation and the contrast between Kenya and the rest of East Africa

[1] Hollis B. Chenery, 'Patterns of Industrial Growth', *American Economic Review*, Vol. L, No. 4, September 1960.

[2] Simon Kuznets, 'Industrial Distribution of National Product and Labor Force', *Economic Development and Cultural Change*, Vol. V, No. 4, (Part II), July 1957.

is still readily apparent. The explanation for this remaining difference lies in two directions.

The economies of Uganda and Kenya are closely interrelated. Uganda is a considerable purchaser of services from Kenya. This is a necessary result of physical relationship between the countries, reinforced by the development of Nairobi as the commercial centre of East Africa. H. W. Ord[1] has suggested that through the period 1951–58 Uganda had a negative net invisible balance with the rest of East Africa of £6–7 million, while Kenya had a corresponding favourable balance of £7 million. Although approximate these estimates suggest, that Uganda's consumption of Kenya services is large enough to have a noticeable influence on the structure of the two economies.

Uganda's purchase of services from Kenya consists of transport of Uganda's exports and imports via Mombasa, wholesale profits of Kenya importers distributing to the Uganda market, and commercial and other services supplied to Uganda residents. Because of the past location of the Common Services headquarters in Nairobi the transfer of services even extended to the public service field through the incomes of headquarters staff of East African wide organizations.[2]

In Kenya, a higher proportion of product is derived from services, even after the provision for the needs of its two neighbours has been allowed for. This is related to the income structure described in the previous section. Income structure, the degree of urbanization, and the importance of services are all reflections of the same underlying phenomenon, the special role of the non-African communities in Kenya.

The non-African communities of Kenya created, by their very existence and their control over development, an economic enclave characterized by a high degree of urbanization; a heavy concentration of incomes; and a high demand for services, itself providing a source of income and employment for many of the members of these communities.

Throughout East Africa there is a heavy concentration of non-African population in the cities and the larger non-African population of Kenya has resulted in a greater degree of urbanization. Further, there is a heavy concentration of non-Africans in services;

[1] H. W. Ord, 'Social Accounting and Inter-Territorial Transactions in East Africa', *East African Economic Review*, Vol. 9, No. 2, December 1962.

[2] David Walker, *et. al.*, in *African Studies in Income and Wealth*, L. H. Samuels, ed., London: Bowes & Bowes, 1963, contains a discussion of the division of the product of the common services between the three countries in their national accounts.

correspondingly, services contribute proportionately more to total value added than they do to total employment. Detailed estimates of value added and employment in the Kenya service sector provide an additional opportunity to distinguish between the contribution of commerce and the entrepôt trade on the one hand and the high demand for services resulting from the presence of the high income non-African community on the other. About half of the service sector consists of commercial and transport activities. Some part of the product of transport and of banking, insurance and real estate represents direct consumption activities. Electricity, water, rents, government and miscellaneous services may be viewed as predominantly consumption items (i.e. as not being generated by local commerce or entrepot trade). The growth of urban communities not only results in an expansion in the demand for services, but also an increase in the likelihood that such activities will be recorded in official data. This is most apparent in the case of rents, but may also be true of public utilities and the provision of personal services.

A further interesting contrast is provided by a comparison of the output and employment figures in each of the countries. Examination reveals a contrast between the degree to which agriculture provides opportunities for paid employment in the three countries. Although Uganda's agriculture generated more product, both in absolute value and as a proportion of total domestic product, it resulted in less than a quarter and less than a third of the wage employment in the agricultural sectors of Kenya and Tanganyika respectively. This is the result of the contrast between self-employed peasant agriculture, the most usual form of organization in Uganda, and the much more extensive development of European controlled plantation and mixed farming in Kenya and Tanganyika.

The same figures also indicate that whereas value added in Kenya manufacturing and construction was more than 50 per cent greater than in Uganda and 40 per cent greater than in Tanzania this difference was not reflected in employment levels. In fact, African employment was greater in those activities in Tanzania than in Kenya. The much higher proportion of non-Africans employed in these activities in Kenya is associated with a higher skilled workforce and also the likelihood that more capital equipment was in use.

Manufacturing industries are little developed in any of the three countries. Although such activity is still only of limited importance, there is interest in examining it in some detail, if only because of the widespread expectation that its future growth is likely to be faster than in other sectors. In particular, there is some interest in discussing the interindustry relationships within manufacturing. The process of

Table 5. *Industrial structure: censuses of industrial production*

Tanganyika, 1961

Industry	Value added[a] £'000
Sisal	9,455
Sugar (including jaggery)[c]	845
Tea	1,090
Total agriculture	11,390
Dairy products	27
Grain mill products	536
Bakery products	56
Miscellaneous foods	616
Beverages[c]	390
Tobacco[c]	94
Textiles	63
Ginning	902
Footwear	66
Tailoring	62
Sawmilling	479
Woodworking	214
Printing and publishing	302
Rubber products	32
Oil milling and soap	130

Uganda, 1963

Industry	Persons employed	Value added[b] £'000
Cotton ginning	13,000	2,437·8
Coffee processing	4,700	2,871·0
Tea processing	1,255	710·1
Total agriculture	18,955	6,018·8
Meat and fish industry	265	128·4
Grain milling	385	205·0
Bakery and confectionery	634	155·4
Miscellaneous food preparations	174	62·3
Sugar and tobacco	2,550	2,923·5
Beverages	857	927·8
Textiles, footwear and apparel	3,250	1,779·1
Sawmilling and plywood	2,411	460·8
Miscellaneous wood products	135	30·0
Furniture	560	119·0
Printing and publishing	1,005	353·2
Rubber products	159	213·0
Basic industrial chemicals	389	13·8
Oils and fats	957	335·1
Soap and other chemical products	366	122·2

Kenya, 1963

Industry	Persons engaged	Value added[b] (£'000)
Meat products	2,068	1,171
Dairy products	881	1,124
Canned fruits and vegetables	994	307
Grain mill products	1,973	2,257
Bakery products	1,086	536
Sugar	1,500	755
Confectionery	87	
Miscellaneous foods	535	153
Spirits	35	2,679
Beer and malt	2,023	
Soft drinks	752	1,651
Tobacco	702	
Cordage, rope and twine	2,233	655
Textiles	1,820	463
Clothing	704	1,121
Footwear	1,177	
Sawn timber	5,299	894
Other wood products	320	93
Furniture and fixtures	1,218	497
Paper and products	706	639
Printing and publishing	2,977	2,225
Tanning and leather	503	207

Brick, block and		Structural clay products	450	110·7	Rubber products	276	189
tile	54	Glass, cement and concrete			Basic industrial		
Metal products	157	products	1,422	650·9	chemicals	1,561	1,475
Engineering and		Metal industries and			Paints	246	207
repairs	186	engineering	1,868	1,157·9	Soap	788	1,116
Electrical repairing	12	Repair of motor vehicles	1,350	538·3	Miscellaneous chemicals	864	1,185
Motor vehicle		Motorcycles and bicycles	33	10·9	Clay and concrete products	533	170
repairing	336				Glass and products	307	1,713
Jewellery and					Cement and other minerals	921	
goldsmiths	24				Metal products	2,870	1,819
Miscellaneous	521				Non-electrical machinery	711	323
					Electrical machinery	251	153
					Shipbuilding and repairing	2,107	663
					Railway rolling stock	6,392	1,012
					Motor vehicles	464	213
					Motor repairs	1,454	602
					Miscellaneous	491	313
Total manufacturing	5,259	Total manufacturing	19,220	10,293·5	Total manufacturing	49,829	28,580
Electricity	782	Electricity	1,550	2,410·2	Electricity	2,194	3,433
Grand total	17,701	Grand total	39,725	18,722·5	Grand total	52,023	32,013

Notes: [a] Value-added is categorized as net output in the Census of Industrial Production for 1961.
[b] Value-added is gross output less consumption of fuels, materials and other costs.
[c] Net output excludes excise duty.

Sources: *Census of Industrial Production in Tanganyika—1961*, Appendix, Table 1.
Uganda: Survey of Industrial Production—1963.
Kenya: Statistical Abstract 1965, p. 74.

development not only involves changes in the size of the major sectors but also is associated with an evolution of a web of connections between the domestic producers and consumers of manufactured intermediate inputs. As higher levels of income and industrialization are achieved the interdependence between domestic industries is increased, with growing specialization in the intermediate stages of manufacture. The achievement of a fully fledged industrial economy, in which most of the manufactured industrial inputs are domestically produced and in which a high proportion of the domestic needs for manufactured goods are met by the products of local industry, is at best a distant goal in the East African case. The evidence to date relates to the first steps in the development of manufacturing.

A complete picture of industrial activity is much easier to obtain in the case of Kenya than for the other two East African countries because of the existence of a series of industrial surveys. To demonstrate the limited degree of industrial development, it is appropriate to use the Kenya data, for the conclusions derived from the most elaborate industrial development in East Africa, should apply *a fortiori* for the rest of East Africa.

Table 5 presents a synopsis of the results of the 1963 Kenya Census of Industrial Production together with available information for Tanzania and Uganda. Just under one-half of the material and other costs incurred in Kenya industry were borne by the food, drink and tobacco industries. In previous censuses this ratio was slightly higher. There was a certain amount of interdependency within this group, but the major backward linkage was to agriculture, while the products either flowed directly to the consumer or to the export market. Agricultural products also formed the major material inputs into soap, miscellaneous chemicals and leather and leather goods. Furniture, timber and other wood products form another group with some interdependency within the group and linkage back to primary production (i.e. forest products).

Another group mainly uses imported inputs in the production process. It includes machinery, transport equipment, rubber products, printing, paper and metal products. In most cases the imported inputs were already at a fairly advanced stage of manufacture.

Textiles, clothing and footwear form a potentially important group. Here important consumer products are being produced, already with some degree of domestic interdependence. This group is still very small, generating less than 10 per cent of the net product of manufacturing in 1963, but is growing faster than the rest of manufacturing. It is of much greater relative importance to the small

Uganda manufacturing sector, through a fully integrated cotton textile industry. Its potential importance lies in the size of the current import bill; in 1965 £23 million of textiles, clothing and footwear were still being imported into East Africa. Cement and clay and concrete products, along with metal products, mainly produce intermediate goods for the local construction industry. Part of the output of the paper and textile industries are also intermediate goods in the form of packing materials.

In summary, whereas the most important domestic source of inputs for Kenya manufacturing is agriculture, followed by other primary activities, the most important domestic purchaser of intermediate products at this stage is the construction industry.

The Tanganyika 1961 Census of Industrial Production results indicate the more limited degree of industrial development. Indeed, this would appear even more if cotton ginning, which is so close to the primary stage was to be considered as part of agriculture rather than manufacturing.

Mainly through the agency of the Uganda Development Corporation, there has been a more substantial growth of large scale industry in Uganda than in Tanganyika, although the impact of this development was not great enough for Uganda to rival Kenya industrial development. Large scale factory operations were already under way by 1961 in cotton textiles, cement, copper smelting (all in part UDC operations), beer brewing, and cigarette manufacture.

2. AGRICULTURE

As in most African countries, the major part of agricultural activity is directed to production for subsistence or for purely local marketing. This is demonstrated by the Gross Domestic Product estimates, which indicate that in 1964 subsistence production in agriculture, forestry and livestock production was £195·5 million for East Africa as a whole as compared with market output from the same industries of £191·4 million. As subsistence production is valued at producer prices and as the estimates may well underestimate levels of output achieved, it may be supposed that the production covered in the so-called subsistence sector exceeded by a substantial margin that in the monetary sector. Much of the so-called subsistence production may well enter into local market transactions. Since part of the estimated monetary production of agriculture is sold for consumption in the local market it is clear that the agricultural sector has had as its primary function the feeding of the local population.

Nevertheless, it is very easy to view agricultural activity mainly in terms of the export products. Exports are crucially important from the point of view of government policy and planning and have played an important role as the determinant of past growth. Further, far more is known about the levels of output and the techniques of export production. Exports are accurately and fairly exhaustively recorded in the available trade data; in many cases they are grown with considerable supervision and attention from agricultural experts and are purchased through a sophisticated marketing mechanism. This is not to say that there has been no research on subsistence crop production for there has been some notable work on its problems. However, it is fair to comment that in most economic surveys and policy documents the dominant concern is with the major export crops and those food crops for which there are centralized marketing arrangements.

This concentration of attention on exports can be dangerous for two reasons. Ultimately the concern of economic policy must be the welfare of the mass of the population. In East Africa the most immediate determinant of economic welfare for the vast majority of the population is their ability to provide themselves with food from their own holdings or immediately local sources of supply. If the ability to expand such subsistence food production does not match the growth in the population then this will not only have unfortunate welfare implications but will also have serious consequences for other aspects of economic policy. A forewarning occurred in 1965 when the Kenya government had to take emergency measures at considerable cost to provide an emergency maize supply to meet a shortfall in local production.

Subsistence food production is also a crucial influence on the organization of smallholder farming. It is impossible to understand the behaviour of a peasant farmer or the operation of any smallholder farming system without a detailed understanding of the role of subsistence crop production in the farming economy. But staple food production can vary greatly from district to district according to ecological conditions and traditional food habits. It is therefore difficult to make any simple generalizations, and such generalizations as are possible will provide little guidance to the conditions in any particular area.[1]

Traditionally, the East African grain crops were finger and bulrush millet and sorghum. The other major traditional staple food crop is the banana which is still predominant in much of Uganda. The two major root crops are cassava and sweet potatoes. Cassava was

[1] A good survey is provided in A. M. O'Connor, *An Economic Geography of East Africa*, London, G. Bell & Sons, Ltd., 1966, see chapters 2–4.

spread partly through the efforts of the government during the colonial period as a famine reserve crop. It still largely fulfills that function. Sweet potatoes are of relatively minor importance but are widespread in distribution. Although of American origin they were widespread in East Africa before the arrival of Europeans.

The most important development in the history of food crop production in East Africa over the period for which we have detailed knowledge has been the emergence of maize as a major staple. In Kenya it has become the major food crop. In Tanzania, although millet and sorghum have not been displaced to the same extent as in Kenya, it is the staple food crop in a number of districts and has been steadily expanding in relative importance in most parts of the country. In Uganda the picture is somewhat different. Although maize is grown and consumed extensively, the banana reigns supreme as the major staple in the most populous parts of the country. In addition to these major food crops, there are numerous other crops of importance such as beans and peas, potatoes, ground-nuts, sesame, coconuts, sugarcane, rice and wheat.

Livestock also play an important part in the subsistence economy. Cattle are kept in all parts of East Africa not infested by tsetse fly where there is sufficient water. Although many tribes are traditionally pastoral and some tribes still specialize to the degree that they engage in little cultivation, the nonpastoral cultivating tribes also generally keep livestock.

In addition to the local livestock there was a considerable development in Kenya of grade cattle, which were high grade stock developed from crosses of exotic and local animals. The European owned herds consisted of nearly one million head of cattle at the peak in 1959 and were the major source of East Africa's highgrade milk and dairy products. European farmers also kept exotic sheep and pigs.

Subsistence consumption and local trade in meat and milk are clearly an important factor in the diets of East Africans. Most estimates of meat production are based upon recorded sales of hides and skins, or upon assumptions of offtake applied to estimates of the total herds. Estimates as high as two million cattle and six million goats and sheep a year have been made. An alternative indication of the importance of livestock production is that in 1965 exports of hides and skins from East Africa amounted to £4·5 million. Exports of meat and meat preparations also exceeded £4·5 million in 1965. This was mainly the output of meat canning factories in Kenya and Tanzania. Uganda is now also entering the meat canning industry with the establishment of a new packing plant at Soroti.

An important element in the development efforts of all three East

African governments is the attempt to improve the quality of local livestock by cross-breeding and by improved methods of animal husbandry.

Fishing, particularly in the inland lakes, is also important as a source of food supply. In Uganda in 1964 the fisheries department estimated the value of the total catch at £3 million. Inland fishing in Tanzania is estimated to produce a similar amount, but Kenya's production is estimated to be less than one-quarter this. Marine fishing is of importance in some coastal areas, in particular, on Zanzibar and Pemba islands. However, estimates of production suggest that the tonnage of the marine fishing catch is less than one-fifth of the total fresh water production.

The picture of food production is highly complex. Much of the rural population is largely dependent on the output of the small-holding. There is also considerable local trade and barter, and even interregional trade, left unrecorded except for rough estimates in the official statistics. Also there is considerable interregional specialization, with the Kenya mixed farming sector providing the rest of the Kenyan economy and the other East African countries with high-grade meat products and dairy products. The mixed farming economy has also been a supplier of wheat and maize. Over the years food production has presumably grown along with expansion in population. It would be highly desirable if food production could claim greater prominence in research priorities in the future.

The story of export agriculture is much more simple. Three crops dominate the picture. Three-fifths of East Africa's exports to the rest of the world are accounted for by coffee, cotton and sisal. As noted in the introduction to this chapter, cotton is entirely a peasant crop, sisal a plantation crop, and coffee divided between African peasant farmers and expatriate owned farms. In addition to the three major export crops there is a highly diverse range of minor crops which together make a major contribution to total exports. Some of these crops, such as tea, cashew nuts and meat products are growing rapidly. Both Kenya and Tanzania are fairly fortunate in the diversity of their exports. In addition to the crops already mentioned, pyrethrum, wattle, pineapples, and various beans and peas all make significant contributions to total exports.

East Africa is particularly vulnerable to fluctuations in coffee prices, as all three countries have coffee as a major export. In the light of coffee market prospects and the operation of the International Coffee Agreement all three countries will need to achieve increasing diversification of their agricultural exports if they are to achieve substantial export growth. They are likely to do this particularly through expansion in tea, meat products, and various nuts. The temperate products of Kenya mixed farming have in the past been marketed predominantly in East Africa. In future surplus production from this type of agriculture may increasingly seek markets abroad, possibly in adjacent tropical areas.

The role of agriculture in the economy and the importance of the differences in its structure in the three East African countries has already been outlined. These differences of structure were one of the main determinants of the political and social life of the countries during the colonial period. Now considerable changes are under way. This is particularly so in Kenya where the land issue was one of the great subjects of debate. In all three countries the impact of the development plans will ultimately change the pattern of agriculture considerably since agricultural diversification is, as noted below, one of the key features of the plans of East African countries.

Of particular interest from the point of view of innovation in methods of agricultural organization are four different programmes. (1) The programme of land settlement (with the objective of concentrated 'Agricultural Transformation') in the Tanzanian Five-Year Plan. (2) The massive programme of land settlement undertaken during the last five years in Kenya for the purpose of transferring land from European to African owners. (3) The growing programme of land consolidation and registration in the peasant farming areas of Kenya. (4) The experiments in group farming in Uganda.

In addition to these experiments in new forms of organization and land tenure there are continuing efforts to improve the level of productivity and the range of products within the peasant farming sector. There has also been some expansion in estate farming although this is, by and large, becoming a relatively less important sector. Programmes of improvement through extension, the spread of insecticides, the encouragement of the use of fertilizers and the provision of improved seed strains, are of major importance because they involve a much larger section of the population than concentrated exercises in transformation and because they affect a larger share of agricultural output. However, irrespective of their quantitative importance, the experiments in rural reconstruction are of considerable interest for the insight they provide into potentialities in the rural sector. The settlement programmes in Tanzania and Kenya and the group farm programme in Uganda have in common the objective of achieving high increases in agricultural productivity through the concentration of services and effort within a limited geographical area.

In Tanzania it was hoped that through concentrating populations into new villages and through the planned development of new areas a breakthrough from the traditional patterns of peasant farming would be achieved. The origins of this programme may be seen both in the special ideological commitments of the Tanzanian leadership and also in the technical advice emanating from the World Bank report on Tanganyika (1959).[1] Recently, however, the ambitious programme in the Five-Year Plan has been severely curtailed. Initial experiments did not generate returns sufficient to justify continued expansion at the rate originally envisaged. Tanzania has unusually limited supplies of technical resources and also extremely limited local capital. Moreover, there was lacking in Tanzania a widespread and pressing demand for new areas for land settlement, of the kind which provided the background to the programme in Kenya. The opportunity costs of concentrating heavily on limited areas were especially high. These factors combined with the absence of sufficiently enthusiastic and able settlers and the limited availability of planning and technical resources meant that investment in this programme generated far lower returns than had been hoped for.

In addition, there is some evidence that the scale of investment in social overhead capital within the schemes made it extremely difficult for them to prove profitable. Efforts are now concentrated on consolidating those elements of the programme which have been more successful and studying the experience gained for the purpose of designing future programmes.

The land settlement programme in Kenya was on an altogether more ambitious scale.[2] In the period since 1960 more than a million acres of land have been involved while the financial costs of the programme have been more than £23,000,000. This programme shared with that of Tanzania the ambition to create cash income peasant farming with a high level of technique. But it was primarily a means of transferring land from European ownership in the former scheduled areas (i.e. the so-called White Highlands) to African ownership. Its objectives were (1) to create a viable market for land in a period of considerable economic and political uncertainty. This was as much in the interest of the European farming community, both those wishing to liquidate their assets to leave and those wishing to shift the location of their activities within Kenya, as it was in the interests of the African acquiring the land. (2) To contribute to providing for an orderly process of social change and suitable foundation for economic and political stability. (3) To provide a basis for

[1] International Bank for Reconstruction and Development, *The Economic Development of Tanganyika*, Baltimore, Johns Hopkins Press, 1961, Chapters 4–6.

[2] Nottidge and Goldsack, *op. cit.*

the maintenance of output levels in those areas transferred. (4) To provide for additional economic opportunities to unemployed and land hungry members of the African community.

The concept of land hunger is necessarily ambiguous. It clearly exists when there is a rural landless unemployed. However, in part the settlement programme in Kenya provided an opportunity for the acquisition of land to a section of the population who were not in any sense economically destitute but who wished to become land holders. For example, those successfully employed in the city would often view the acquisition of a plot of land as a means of providing economic security against old age.

The implementation of the programme of land settlement presents a complex picture. Within the total programme there were a number of alternative methods of land transfer involving not only settlement proper, but also co-operative farming and assisted purchase of large-scale farms by individual African owners.

The major part of the programme consisted of two types of schemes known as 'High Density' and 'Low Density' schemes. The High Density schemes were financed entirely by the United Kingdom Government whereas the finance for the development side of the Low Density schemes was provided by the World Bank and the Commonwealth Development Corporation, with additional finance coming from the West German Government. The finance provided by the United Kingdom Government provided land purchase terms favourable to the seller, but with a grant element to finance the difference between the value of the assets on the farm as purchased and the probable value of the land in the alternative use to which it would be put. There was also a substantial grant element to cover the administrative costs of the programme.

High Density schemes were intended to provide family plots which would generate cash incomes, net of subsistence and allowances for debt repayments, of the order of £25 to £40 per annum. On the other hand, the Low Density schemes were intended to provide net cash incomes of the order of £100 per annum. There were some schemes lying between these totals and there was one case of a scheme involving target incomes of £250 per acre (a so-called Yeoman Farmer scheme). Development loans were provided to cover the cost of simple housing, initial land preparation and certain aspects of farm development. The schemes were provided with budgets designed to generate the desired levels of income. In practice the schemes have been heavily dependent on three major sources of cash income, namely dairy products, pyrethrum and maize. There have also been some schemes in which tea has played an important role in the budgets, while there is a specialized group of settlement schemes involving sugar production, and a number of ranching schemes with beef cattle. Schemes involving sisal and wheat proved unsuccessful.

The schemes have engendered a certain amount of controversy.[1] Critics argue that they surrendered economic efficiency to political expediency. However, it is too early to judge the economic success of the programme because of the time it will take for them to achieve full operation. It seems likely that the Low Density schemes will prove successful and that in many cases the High Density schemes will eventually generate satisfactory levels of cash income. Moreover, it is quite possible that the programme as a whole will result in a more intensive degree of land use than was previously achieved and higher levels of total output.

The Group Farm programme in Uganda aims, through bringing together of numbers of peasant farmers to pool at least part of their land in a common area, to provide mechanical services on a more efficient basis than would otherwise be possible. The economic rationale of the project is the existence of certain critical manpower constraints limiting output at certain times of the year, giving rise to the possibility that despite the low cost of labour there may be considerable returns to mechanization at certain stages of the productive process (e.g. at planting time).

There is, as yet, little published evidence on the success of the Uganda Group Farms. The application of the mechanized services to peasant agriculture raises considerable administrative and financial problems. In particular, it has proved difficult to use equipment (i.e., mainly tractors) sufficiently to carry depreciation costs with a reasonable margin of profitability. Nevertheless the Uganda Government is pursuing its experiment on a fairly ambitious scale although some critics have already raised a warning note regarding the efficacy of the programme.[2]

Land consolidation and registration in Kenya presents an alternative method of tackling the problem of rural transformation. The programme is part of an attempt to raise the level of productivity and technique in the traditional African farming areas. Although it originated in an earlier period it received its major impetus from the East African Royal Commission Report 1953–55 and from the Swynnerton Plan. This aspect of Kenya development is now fairly well documented in readily available sources. The objective is (1) to

[1] Notably the series of articles by Leslie Brown in the *Kenya Weekly News*, entitled, 'The Settlement Schemes', July, 1965—October 1965.

[2] D. Forbes Watt. 'Work for Progress and the Recent Design of Agricultural Development Policy in Uganda', *E. A. Econ. Rev.* 2(2), December 1966.

consolidate land to provide a usable unit for development; (2) to provide title to land as a means of engineering greater credit facilities and commercialization in general; (3) to follow this up with a programme of extension, credit facilities and a cash crop policy which will enable the small farmer to achieve a high level of income.

Agriculture throughout East Africa involves literally millions of decision-making units and vast numbers of different cash crops. Within a general survey such as this, it is not possible to touch on all the problems of marketing and production throughout East Africa. However, there are certain issues in relation to marketing, particularly the use of marketing boards and co-operatives, which require comment.

Over the years, a complex set of agricultural marketing institutions has developed. In Uganda in the post-war period marketing boards were established to handle cotton and coffee exports. In Kenya, government marketing boards were not developed in the same fashion for the export trade, but a complex of arrangements in the form of public marketing boards and other highly centralized marketing arrangements were established to serve the European mixed farming economy, for products which were being produced predominantly for local markets.

In Tanganyika the situation was more complex than in Uganda because of the more diversified nature of the agricultural activity. A Lint and Seed Marketing Board was established with similar functions to that of Uganda. There were also a number of growers' associations (sisal, coffee and tea) which represented the interests of and provided services to the European owned estates. There were also official boards for coffee, cashew nuts, tea, pyrethrum and seed, but these boards had mainly advisory and mediation roles.[1] Since independence there has been an expansion of public marketing activities. The coffee board extended its functions into actual marketing in 1962. New boards were established to control the marketing of wheat, sugar and papain. In 1963 a National Agricultural Products Board was established to handle the marketing of maize, paddy, oilseeds, cashew nuts and copra.

The historical function of some of the marketing boards has been to stabilize the price received by the grower. During the early 1950's the Coffee and Lint Marketing Boards in Uganda and the Lint Marketing Board in Tanganyika accumulated large reserves as a result of the high world prices. In subsequent years considerable funds were used to subsidize the prices received by the farmers. It

[1] Ruthenberg, *op. cit.*, Appendix B, pp. 187–90.

seems unlikely that such activities can be continued in the future. In Uganda the Lint Marketing Board has maintained a subsidized price to the grower in the 1965–66 season despite the exhaustion of price stabilization reserves. Such a policy could only continue if the Uganda Government were willing to allocate considerable sums of scarce fiscal resources to maintain the prices paid to the farmers.

Possibly the most important role of many of the marketing boards for the future will be as representatives in the world market place. The coffee marketing boards, for example, have strategic advisory and representation tasks in relation to the International Coffee Agreement. The future share of the world quota market, the crucial determinant of the value of coffee exports, will be dependent upon the skill of those participating in negotiations.

The existence of the marketing boards inevitably renders commodity pricing one of the key issues of government policy. On the one hand, this introduces an additional instrument of policy-making into the range of available tools. On the other hand it introduces an arena for considerable potential conflict between the interests of particular groups of growers and the achievement of the more general objectives of economic policy. The spread of the explicit use of export taxes, described in the fiscal section of this chapter, has eliminated the possible need for marketing boards as taxation instruments. But they could play a taxation role in the future (by maintaining a differential between export and producer prices) if explicit export taxes were abandoned and implicit taxation procedures adopted.

At the local level, the most interesting questions relating to agricultural marketing arise from the role of the co-operatives. Historically, a key link in the extension of agricultural marketing facilities to the individual farmer in the countryside was provided by Asian middlemen. Although they continue to play an important role in all three countries they have been steadily displaced by the expansion of co-operatives over the past fifteen years.

Before the Second World War the most notable development of co-operative marketing arrangements was that developed by the European farmers of Kenya to serve their needs. The Kenya Farmers' Association provided a wide range of marketing services, both as a purchaser of agricultural products and a supplier of farm inputs. Similarly the Kenya Co-operative Creameries is the major distribution channel for milk products.

Among African producers, the most notable example of successful co-operative development in the inter-war period was the foundation and development of the famous Kilimanjaro Native Co-operative

Union, by the Chagga coffee farmers of Tanganyika. By the outbreak of the Second World War, the KNCU was handling over 2,000 tons of green coffee a year.

The major expansion of co-operatives, however, came in the post-war period. In Tanzania the number of co-operatives expanded from 79 in 1949 to over 1,000 by 1963. In Kenya, a new Co-operative Societies Ordinance in 1945 provided for the establishment of co-operatives among African smallholders. By 1964 there were over 500 active societies. In Uganda there was an even more impressive expansion. By 1960 there were over 1,500 registered societies, most of which were affiliated to co-operative unions. In recent years, the cotton co-operatives have received official encouragement in pursuing a vigorous programme of extending their activities into cotton ginning, previously largely the preserve of Asian businessmen.

In all three countries, co-operation is recognized by the Governments as the most desirable direction in which agricultural marketing should develop. Co-operatives are likely to play an increasingly important role, not only as marketing organizations but also as channels for the distribution of credit and as investors of accumulated surpluses. The success or failure of the co-operatives will therefore be an important influence on future rural development.

The co-operative movement is, however, facing a number of difficulties in all three countries. A period of very fast expansion has inevitably been followed by administrative difficulties as management problems exceed the experience and training of the officers and staff of the societies.[1] In some cases they have proved to be a very inefficient means of marketing both in terms of costs, so lowering the price received by the farmer, and the level of service provided. Also, a number of commentators have questioned whether the co-operatives are likely to make sensible investment decisions in disposing of the surpluses which come under their control, and have criticized the levels of efficiency achieved in such ancillary activities as cotton ginning. In fairness, however, it should be stressed that co-operatives have passed through a period of fast growth. Only now are the governments of East Africa becoming aware of the magnitude of management training requirements if the co-operative is to play the key role assigned to it in rural development. The regulations governing the co-operatives and their form of organization are still substantially those derived from the co-operative legislation introduced by the colonial governments in the 1940's. This is an area where further probing and experimenting will be needed to define the

[1] See especially—*Report of the Presidential Special Committee of Enquiry into Co-operative Movement and Marketing Boards*, Dar es Salaam, 1966.

appropriate role and the most effective manner of organizing the co-operatives, in the circumstances of independence.

3. TRADE

It was noted in an earlier section that foreign trade has played and continues to play an extremely important role in the development of East African economies. The most important influence on the determination of national income in all the three countries is the level of export earnings: this is especially true of Uganda and Tanzania where, for instance, in 1964 exports outside East Africa amounted to about 45 per cent and 40 per cent respectively of monetary GDP.[1]

The trade patterns of East African countries (summarized in Tables 6–8) display features typical of the developing countries relying heavily on external trade. But there are at least two respects in which their experience is somewhat unusual. Firstly, mainly because of the existence of the common market in East Africa, trade among the three countries plays an important role in their economies. This is especially true of Kenya where exports to Uganda and Tanzania amounted to well over one-third of her total exports in 1964. Secondly, Uganda and Tanzania are unusual among developing countries in having a surplus in their balance of trade. The surplus in external trade is especially large for both countries but is reduced somewhat by the deficit in interterritorial trade.

East African exports consist for the most part of agricultural commodities. As was pointed out above, cotton, coffee and sisal have in recent years accounted for well over three-fifths of the total export earnings. Of the three countries, Uganda has the least diversified export base with cotton and coffee alone accounting for over three-quarters of total export receipts. Kenya and Tanganyika exports are less narrowly based, and are generally more favourably placed than the majority of tropical African countries. In all three countries the export base has tended to widen over time.

The import pattern again is typical of developing countries: manufactured goods, machinery and transport equipment, and chemicals account for about 80 per cent of total imports. The relative importance of manufactured consumers' goods has tended to diminish somewhat over time. There are some territorial differences with respect to structure of imports from overseas. Manufactured goods

[1] For a general discussion of the role of trade in East African development see Philip Ndegwa, *The Common Market and Development in East Africa*, (East African Studies No. 22) East African Institute of Social Research—East African Publishing House, Nairobi, 1965.

Table 6. *Balance of trade*
(£m)

Year	Net imports			Exports					Balance		
	External	Inter-territorial	Total	External	to Kenya	to Uganda	to Tanganyika	Total	External	Inter-territorial	Total
					(a) Kenya						
1961	68·9	7·0	75·9	41·7	—	7·0	8·9	57·7	−27·2	+ 9·0	−18·2
1962	69·5	7·3	76·8	45·1	—	7·3	10·0	62·5	−24·3	+10·0	−14·4
1963	73·7	9·2	82·9	51·0	—	9·4	10·4	70·8	−22·7	+10·6	−12·1
1964	76·6	11·5	88·0	53·5	—	12·6	13·3	79·4	−23·0	+14·4	− 8·6
1965	89·0	11·7	100·7	52·0	—	15·3	14·1	81·5	−37·0	+17·7	−19·3
					(b) Tanganyika						
1961	39·7	10·6	50·3	50·6	1·8	0·4	—	52·9	+10·9	− 8·4	+ 2·6
1962	39·8	11·7	51·5	53·6	2·0	0·4	—	55·9	+13·7	− 9·3	+ 4·4
1963	40·4	12·4	52·8	65·2	2·9	0·5	—	68·6	+24·8	− 8·9	+15·9
1964	44·0	15·7	59·7	71·4	4·1	1·0	—	76·5	+27·4	−10·6	+16·8
1965	50·0	16·7	66·7	64·1	4·6	1·3	—	70·0	+14·0	−10·8	+ 3·3
					(c) Uganda						
1961	26·5	7·4	34·0	41·3	5·2	—	1·7	48·1	+14·7	− 0·6	+14·1
1962	26·2	7·7	33·9	41·0	5·4	—	1·7	48·0	+14·7	− 0·7	+14·1
1963	30·9	9·9	40·9	54·5	6·2	—	2·0	62·7	+23·6	− 1·7	+21·9
1964	32·8	13·6	46·4	66·4	7·3	—	2·4	76·2	+33·6	− 3·8	+29·8
1965	40·9	16·7	57·6	64·0	7·1	—	2·6	73·7	+23·1	− 7·0	+16·1

Source: *East African Trade Reports.*

Table 7. *Major East African exports*

(values in £m, quantities in 'ooo tons)

		Kenya			Uganda[a]			Tanganyika			East Africa		
		1957	1960	1963	1957	1960	1963	1957	1960	1963	1957	1960	1963
Coffee	Value	10·8	10·3	11·0	21·6	17·0	27·2	7·6	7·3	6·8	40·0	34·6	45·0
	Quantity	22·3	27·8	36·8	84·1	116·8	145·3	18·5	25·1	26·0			
Cotton	Value	0·4	0·8	0·4	17·5	15·9	14·3	7·2	8·8	10·7	25·1	24·6	25·5
	Quantity	1·4	3·5	1·9	60·1	58·9	58·8	27·2	38·9	47·8			
Sisal	Value	2·1	4·6	7·5	—	—	—	10·3	15·4	22·7	12·4	20·1	30·2
	Quantity	39·6	57·0	63·7	—	—	—	181·8	207·2	214·4			
Tea	Value	2·9	4·4	5·7	1·1	1·5	2·0	0·6	1·2	1·6	4·6	7·0	9·3
	Quantity	7·2	10·7	14·7	2·8	3·4	5·4	2·2	3·2	3·9			
Total exports	Value	26·4	35·2	43·8	45·9	41·6	51·5	41·7	54·8	63·6	114·0	131·6	152·2

Note: [a] Uganda exports are valued at the port of exit from East Africa, which is usually Mombasa, Kenya. The figures shown therefore overvalue Uganda's exports, including transport and other costs incurred in Kenya.

Source: *East African Trade Reports.*

form a higher proportion of imports in Uganda and Tanganyika than in Kenya and this conclusion is reinforced if we take account of interterritorial trade. This pattern is, of course, a reflection of the relatively more developed manufacturing sector in Kenya.

As far as the amount of imports is concerned, it is noteworthy that Kenya's imports from outside East Africa nearly equal the combined imports of Uganda and Tanzania. There are several reasons for this. Firstly, Uganda's imports are underestimated because they exclude the transport costs between Mombasa and the Uganda border. Secondly, a great many of the commercial concerns and EACSO agencies that serve the whole of East Africa have their headquarters in Nairobi, with the result that their imports are attributed to Kenya: for example, aircraft purchased by East African Airways will be shown as Kenya imports. Thirdly, because the Kenya population contains larger numbers of Europeans and Asians who are in the higher income groups, together with the generally higher level of total incomes, the average propensity to import is higher than in the other two countries.[1] Lastly, it was noted earlier that both Uganda and Tanzania rely relatively more on interterritorial imports. This reduces their demand for imports from outside East Africa.

United Kingdom remains the principal trading partner, accounting for nearly one-third of East African imports and one-fifth of its exports. In recent years Japan has emerged as the second most important source of East African imports, followed by West Germany, USA and India. The principal markets for East African exports are UK, USA, West Germany and India in that order. These four countries together purchase over half of East African exports. In recent years, EEC countries have accounted for about 20 per cent of exports and about 17 per cent of imports, as compared with EFTA countries 28 per cent and 36 per cent respectively.

Trade with other African countries is negligible. East African exports to the rest of Africa amount to less than 5 per cent of exports, while imports from African countries account for less than 2 per cent of imports. The bulk of this trade is with the immediate neighbours such as Sudan, Congo, Somalia and Mauritius. During 1966 there was a sharp increase in trade with Zambia which, if continued, could make her a significant trading partner.

The above trading relationships have emerged largely as a result of economic forces and the informal effects of colonial political ties. For the most part the East African countries have refrained from the discriminatory use of tariff policy. In part this was due to their adherence to the Congo Basin Treaty which laid down the principle of

[1] See, 'East African Trade', in *UN Economic Bulletin; Africa,* Vol. II, No. 1.

Table 8. *East African international trade relationships: 1965*
(a) imports by major SITC classification
(£m)

Countries	SITC section 0	1	2	3	4	5	6	7	8	9	Total
United Kingdom	1·8	0·6	0·3	0·6	0·1	7·0	12·9	28·5	5·0	0·4	57·1
Japan	—	—	0·3	—	—	0·2	12·8	3·3	1·2	—	17·8
West Germany	0·2	—	0·2	0·1	0·3	2·8	2·8	6·9	0·9	—	14·1
USA	3·9	0·1	0·1	0·5	0·6	0·9	1·9	4·0	1·2	—	13·3
Italy	0·2	0·1	0·4	0·1	—	0·6	2·6	3·3	0·4	—	7·8
India	0·3	—	0·1	—	—	0·2	6·1	0·4	0·4	—	7·5
Netherlands	1·3	—	—	0·1	0·3	1·4	0·9	1·0	0·3	—	5·5
France	0·1	0·2	0·1	—	—	0·3	1·7	2·7	0·3	—	5·5
Iran	—	—	—	4·9	—	—	—	—	—	—	5·0
China (Mainland)	0·4	—	—	—	—	—	2·4	0·3	0·5	—	3·7
Belgium	0·1	—	—	—	—	0·7	1·5	0·6	0·1	0·1	3·2
Total Imports	14·9	1·4	2·7	12·0	3·1	15·3	55·5	53·9	13·7	7·5	180·0

(b) Imports and exports: selected areas and countries

Countries	Imports	Exports	Countries	Imports	Exports
Sterling Area	78·0	73·7	EFTA (inc. UK)	63·5	45·9
United Kingdom	57·1	40·8	Dollar Area	14·1	26·6
Australia	1·8	3·0	Canada	0·9	5·9
Hong Kong	2·4	6·7	USA	13·3	20·7
India	7·5	9·9	Other countries	38·5	35·8
EEC	36·2	35·6	Japan	17·8	5·0
Belgium	3·2	9·7	China (Mainland)	3·7	11·2
France	5·5	2·4	Postal packages	6·7	
West Germany	14·1	14·1	Ships' stores		3·3
Italy	7·8	3·3			
Netherlands	5·5	6·1	Grand total	180·0	180·0

non-discrimination in the trading relations among signatories to the treaty. In the early postwar years, in common with other Sterling Area countries, exchange restrictions and import licensing were used to control imports from the Dollar Area, Japan and Eastern European countries, but most of these restrictions were abandoned by early 'sixties.

The existence of the common market has necessitated the co-ordination of commercial policy by the East African countries and has limited the freedom of individual countries to manipulate commercial policy to influence the rate and pattern of economic growth. Inevitably this has led to friction and conflict of interest. This has been the case, for example, over the signing of trade agreements by individual East African countries with the planned economies, trade with whom was restricted by licence in the colonial days. In the years to come increasing pressures of divergent interests and desires for greater autonomy in economic policy may lead to increasingly important departures from a common foreign trade policy.

The structure of import duties has been designed with the twin objectives of raising revenue and providing protection to local industry. The former objective has been the predominant one, but increasingly the import duty structure is being modified to accord protection to rapidly expanding domestic manufactures. Nevertheless, import duties remain the single most important source of tax revenue to East African governments. Therefore most imports, with the exception of certain raw materials and capital equipment, are subject to duty. The rates vary a good deal, the most common being 75 per cent *ad valorem* (the rate on luxury goods), 37 per cent (the protective rate), 30 per cent (the standard rate), and 15 per cent (the general assisted rate). The general level of import duties has risen substantially over the last six years.

A remarkable feature of the East African economies is the important role played by interterritorial trade. This trade has expanded at a very rapid rate in the postwar period; interterritorial exports have jumped from a little over £6 million in 1949 to a little under £41 million in 1964. This rapid expansion has been made possible in large measure by the existence of the common market in East Africa. Other contributory factors have been the existence of the common currency, a reasonably efficient transport network linking the three countries and, until 1961, the administration of the three countries by the same colonial power.

What is more, this expansion has been relatively free from the fluctuations experienced by East African exports to the outside world. The reason for this is to be sought in the commodity composition of interterritorial trade. Although in the early postwar years, trade among the three countries was largely dominated by agricultural produce, there has been a progressive increase in the importance of processed and manufactured goods. This is especially true of Kenya's exports to Uganda and Tanzania where manufactured goods accounted for well over half of total exports.

The rapid growth of interterritorial trade has not been without its problems, however. There were complaints from Tanganyika and Uganda in the late 'fifties that Kenya had reaped most of the benefit from the expansion of the manufacturing industry stimulated by the common market. These protests resulted in the appointment of the Raisman Commission to study the working of the common market and common services.[1] Its recommendations led to the creation of the 'distributable pool' mechanism for fiscal redistribution from Kenya to Uganda and Tanganyika. Tanganyika did not consider this adequate compensation for its continuing and increasing deficit with Kenya, and its renewed sustained pressure led in 1964 to the negotiation of the 'Kampala Agreement' which made important in-roads into the working of the common market in East Africa. Under this agreement, the deficit countries were permitted to impose quota restrictions on imports from the surplus countries in the common market. Tanzania, and to a lesser extent Uganda, made immediate use of this provision to impose restrictions on a wide range of imports from Kenya. This had the effect of slowing down the expansion of interterritorial trade, as is clearly shown by 1966 trade figures.

However, in June 1967, the three heads of states signed a new Treaty for East African Co-operation. This Treaty was the culmination of eighteen months work by the Philip Commission, which had been appointed by the three heads of states to review the entire range of economic relations among the East African countries. Among the important provisions of the Treaty, which came into operation in December 1967, are the replacement of quantitative restrictions on interterritorial trade by transfer taxes under specified conditions, the creation of an East African Development Bank to promote equitable distribution of industry in the three countries, the decentralization of common services, and the establishment of a number of councils to assist the working of the common services and the common market.

Finally, it is necessary to say something about the balance of payments position of the East African countries. Although there are still many gaps in our knowledge, the general picture is clear. Uganda

[1] *Report of the Raisman Commission* (East Africa: Report of the Economic and Fiscal Commission, Cmnd. 1279, 1961).

has had a persistent surplus on current trading account, Kenya a persistent deficit, while Tanzania has alternated between a small deficit and a small surplus. The favourable position enjoyed by Uganda and, to a lesser extent, Tanzania is unusual among developing countries and has largely been made possible by the vigorous expansion of peasant cash production. Both of these countries are now launched on ambitious programmes of industrialization which can be expected to swell their imports in the short-run. Thus, unless commodity prices hold up well, these surpluses are likely to disappear.

The balance of payments statistics for East Africa as a whole compiled since 1956 show a progressive improvement in the trade balance from a deficit in 1956–57 of about £20 million to a surplus in 1963–64 of almost £28 million. The East African balance of payments on current account have also shown a significant surplus in the last few years. The combination of current surplus and a substantial net capital inflow on public account should have led to a significant rise in the external reserves of East Africa. That this did not happen is due entirely to a massive capital outflow on private account between 1961 and 1965. Restrictions on transfer of capital from East Africa to the Sterling area were introduced only in June 1965. They should have a considerable beneficial effect on the external reserves of the East African countries.

4. EMPLOYMENT AND WAGES

The structure of recorded paid employment is a straightforward reflection of the industrial structure described above. The available statistics summarized in Table 9, underestimate employment, particularly casual employment, both in agriculture and in services in those parts of the economy dominated by African small-holdings. There may also be bias over time, resulting from an underestimation of paid employment in petty services in the towns; the considerable gap between the high rate of growth of urban population and the apparent stagnation in urban employment, would be consistent with this contention. Nevertheless the figures represent the degree of involvement of the population in particular types of fairly organized and stable employment situations. They provide some index, therefore, of the degree of division of labour and the pervasiveness of medium and large scale organizations in the society.

The small size of the employed work force in East Africa, even in Kenya, is clear. The comparative size of the employment opportunities in the three countries reflects the differing sizes of the manufacturing and services sectors; and the differing structure of agriculture. Although the rough estimates in the Uganda data of employment in small scale agriculture may well underestimate the extent of employment in that sector, the contrast between Uganda and the other two countries is still very real. Uganda has undoubtedly a much lower proportion of her population in paid employment. Despite this, Uganda employs a higher proportion of migrant African workers (from Kenya and Ruanda particularly) than the other two countries.

The picture of employment growth is interesting, although it is not uncommon in the less developed world. The notable feature is that employment growth has, for more than a decade, lagged behind both the growth in output and the growth in population. It is evident that for all three countries there have been substantial periods of employment stagnation.

The causes for the failure of employment to expand at a faster rate have not been conclusively established. Although there must have been some substitution of capital for labour, as by and large investment embodies the current techniques of the developed world, it would be dangerous to assume that this was the dominant factor. The period in which average labour productivity grew most was not characterized by high rates of capital formation. It is probable that in this sort of economy, when there is a low rate of growth of output and employment there is an automatic tendency for productivity to increase due to the increasing average experience of the work-force. Such evidence as there is suggests that over the past decade, while employment has stagnated, the stability of the work-force has increased considerably. Whereas it was still possible in the early 1950's to characterize a large part of the work-force in Uganda as temporary members, today turnover rates in industry are typically low and membership of the non-agricultural work-force represents a permanent commitment.

A further reason for the failure of employment to expand faster may be the impact of the increased wages for the unskilled and semi-skilled resulting from minimum wage regulations. It is likely that minimum wage regulations were more important as a means of exposing the existence of concealed under-employment in the work-force than in inducing the choice of more capital intensive techniques.

The governments of East Africa are becoming increasingly aware of the need to expand employment opportunities and are likely to view it in the future as a policy objective competing with that of the growth of output as such. At the same time, however, they are subject to pressures to increase minimum wages and to extend enforcement over wider sectors of the economy—policies which will become increas-

Table 9. *Industrial distribution of employees*[a]
(thousands)

Industry	Kenya 1954–56	Kenya 1961–62	Tanganyika 1954–56	Tanganyika 1961–62	Uganda[b] 1956	Uganda[b] 1961–63
Agriculture and forestry	235·4	248·8	n.a.	201·8	63·3	57·1
African	233·8	246·6	208·8	199·6	62·0	55·8
Non-African	2·2	2·1	n.a.	2·2	1·3	1·3
Mining and quarrying	7·5	3·7	n.a.	10·4	5·7	5·6
African	7·2	3·4	14·8	10·0	5·4	5·2
Non-African	0·2	0·2	n.a.	0·8	0·3	0·4
Construction	25·8	15·2	n.a.	41·5	38·8	28·7
African	22·3	13·1	13·9	40·4	37·1	27·7
Non-African	3·6	2·2	n.a.	1·1	1·7	1·0
Commerce	35·0	43·0	n.a.	17·3	6·9	14·0
African	22·1	26·6	10·7	12·8	5·3	10·4
Non-African	12·9	16·4	n.a.	4·5	1·5	3·6
Transportation and communications	12·7	15·3	n.a.	22·4	9·7	10·2
African	10·3	11·8	6·7	19·9	8·9	9·4
Non-African	2·4	3·4	n.a.	2·4	0·8	0·8
Educational and medical	n.a.	n.a.	n.a.	n.a.	21·4	27·9
African	n.a.	n.a.	n.a.	n.a.	20·2	25·6
Non-African	n.a.	n.a.	n.a.	n.a.	1·2	2·3

Table 9. *Industrial distribution of employees (continued)*

Industry	Kenya 1954–56	Kenya 1961–62	Tanganyika 1954–56	Tanganyika 1961–62	Uganda[b] 1956	Uganda[b] 1961–63
Manufactures	53·5	43·9	n.a.	27·2	27·4	27·7
African	44·2	37·1	19·2	24·4	24·8	25·0
Non-African	9·3	6·8	n.a.	2·8	2·5	2·7
Miscellaneous Services	51·5	47·9	n.a.	53·2	13·2	13·9
African	48·0	41·6	12·7	49·2	12·2	12·9
Non-African	5·1	6·4	n.a.	4·0	1·0	0·9
Not Stated	—	—	n.a.	n.a.	—	—
African	—	—	8·0	n.a.	—	—
Non-African	—	—	n.a.	n.a.	—	—
Public Services	164·0	167·6	n.a.	n.a.	50·8	44·3
African	144·7	147·2	100·8[c]	n.a.	49·8	43·3
Non-African	19·3	20·4	n.a.	n.a.	1·1	0·9
Total Employment	585·4	585·1	n.a.	394·8	237·0	229·5
African	530·4	527·1	395·5	376·0	225·7	215·4
Non-African	55·0	58·0	n.a.	18·8	11·4	14·1

Notes: [a] Over time the coverage in all three countries has changed. The figures cannot therefore be used as a simple basis of comparison. Coverage should be somewhat more complete in the later period, however, so that the impression of stagnating employment is essentially correct.

[b] It was estimated that in 1956 there were 13,000 domestic employees and 50–60,000 employees in peasant agriculture not covered by the Annual Enumeration. By 1962 these estimates had been increased to 20,000 and 85,000 respectively.

[c] For 1954–56 all workers employed in public service are included in this group and have not been allocated to the industry in which they are engaged. In 1961–62, workers were allocated to individual industries; the figures for the two are not comparable because of changes in the method of estimation.

Source: *Statistical Abstracts* and *Annual Enumeration of Employees* for the three countries.

ingly inconsistent with a high employment objective. Nevertheless, the introduction of minimum wages has not been without beneficial side effects. Industrial development requires both the creation of a permanent and disciplined labour force and the spread of basic skills. To achieve these ends it is necessary that the worker shall be able to gain a certain minimum level of well-being while the manager should not view the worker as an almost free good. High levels of disguised under-employment are not conducive to the creation of an effective labour force.

It is interesting to note the change in the perspective of commentators on employment problems in East Africa. Prior to the Second World War there was considerable concern with the target income worker, with a widely held view that the local work-force was characterized by behaviour consistent with the model of a backward sloping supply curve for labour. By the early and mid 1950's, Elkan's study of the Uganda labour market distinguished a much more complex situation.[1] He saw the labour force as containing a mixture of substantially permanent members, particularly drawn from the tribes resident around the two major towns, and migrants of varying degrees of permanency in commitment to their employment. Yet although he saw the labour force in a process of evolution, he nevertheless identified major problems as arising from the impermanency of much of the labour force, particularly for those industries requiring semi-skilled labour of the kind created by experience on the job within the particular industry.

More recent comment is much less concerned with problems of migration. Experience of industrial plants suggests that a high degree of stability with low rates of turnover is achievable.[2] Even where a permanent commitment to urban living is not made, the worker may still spend the major part of a normal working lifetime in urban employment. Further, the permanent urban dweller, with wife and children maintained in the town, is becoming an increasingly familiar element in all the East African towns. The dominant concern of contemporary commentators is the problem of generating sufficient job opportunities for those seeking employment outside agriculture.

The unemployment problem is particularly noticeable in relation to the need to provide opportunities which meet the aspirations of

1 Walter Elkan, *Migrants and Proletarians: Urban Labour in the Economic Development of Uganda*, London, Oxford University Press, 1960.

2 A. Baryaruha, *Factors Affecting Industrial Employment. A Study of Ugandan Experience 1954–1964*. Nairobi, Oxford University Press, 1967, on behalf of the East African Institute of Social Research, Occasional Paper 1.

those completing primary education. This is a problem not only of supplying additional job opportunities but also of gearing educational programmes more closely to preparing the young to take advantage of those opportunities which are likely to exist, particularly in the rural environment.[1]

For the future, the employment problem will undoubtedly loom increasingly large as a challenge to East African policy-makers. The problems are most obvious in Kenya. The 3 per cent annual growth in total population, 6 per cent annual growth in town population, rapid expansion in educational opportunities, and a more widespread shortage of land than in the other two countries will create a more urgent demand for jobs. A sustained and high rate of output growth of the kind envisaged in the three East African development plans would undoubtedly transform the dismal performance of the past decade. With the pressures for social change and the omnipresent effects of high population growth, employment must grow well over 3 per cent annually over the long period if a critical social situation is to be avoided.

In relation to the wage structure, four characteristics are of some interest. First, amongst the reported employed, minimum wage regulation has resulted in bunching of large numbers of employees at the minimum wage level. This makes for a highly skewed distribution of wage earners.

Secondly, wage rates have been rising at a very lively rate in all three countries in recent years, under the influence of minimum wage controls and trade union pressures. Thirdly, the wage share is not the major income source that it would be in most developed economies. Finally, in the upper ranges of the wage scale, the salary structure was determined in the past by the role of the expatriates. Both within the public service and the large foreign firms, salaries in administrative and professional posts were determined by the rates prevailing in Britain at the end of the colonial period. Where the posts were filled by expatriates there was the usual overseas allowance in addition to the basic scales, but the basic scales were themselves in line with British civil service rates.

With the localization of the public service and the introduction of Africans into administrative posts in the private sector, the persistence of this salary structure has been of strategic social significance in defining the style and expectations of a new class of African officials. The inherited salary structure has not, however, been out of line with

[1] See J. R. Sheffield, (ed.), *Education, Employment, and Rural Development.* Nairobi, East Africa Publishing House, 1968.

the existing supply and demand situation for scarce skills. The East African governments would only be able to lower administrative salaries, narrowing the wide differentials within the wage structure of the public services, if they were able to direct manpower into public service jobs. The scarcity of local graduates means that the governments must compete with the private sector who already find it worthwhile to offer rates somewhat above existing public service scales. In the future, however, the supply of trained manpower will grow faster than demand, and employers should be faced with more of a buyers' market. Although there is likely to be rigidity in the level of money wage rates at the upper levels, real salary levels are likely to decline with increases in the price level.

5. DEVELOPMENT PLANS

Although development planning has many antecedents in the colonial period the past three years has seen the emergence of more elaborate forms of planning, which can lay some claim to being comprehensive in character.[1] The Tanganyika First Five-Year Plan (1964–69), Uganda's Second Five-Year Plan (1966–71), and the Kenya Six-Year Plan (1964–70) with its revised version (1965–70) have all, in principle, incorporated a comprehensive view of the pattern of development expected in the three countries.[2]

Before this round of plans there was a considerable history of colonial public development expenditure plans, plus some interesting isolated efforts at longer term and more comprehensive planning, such as the Worthington Ten-Year Plan for Uganda in 1946.[3] In each of the East African countries there was a comprehensive survey of development prospects and problems by the World Bank just previous to independence.[4] The Uganda First Five-Year Plan was largely

1 For a discussion of many of the issues involved in East African planning see Paul G. Clark, *Development Planning in East Africa*, (East African studies No. 21) East African Institute of Social Research—East African Publishing House, Nairobi, 1965.

2 Uganda Government, *The First Five-Year Plan, 1961–62–1965–66*, Entebbe 1961. Uganda Government, *Work for Progress* (Uganda's Second Five-Year Plan, 1966–71), 1966. Tanganyika Government, *Five-Year Plan for Economic and Social Development, 1st July, 1964–30th June, 1969*, 1964. Kenya Government, *Development Plan, 1966–1970*, 1966.

3 E. B. Worthington, *A Development Plan for Uganda 1946–1956*, Uganda, 1946.

4 International Bank for Reconstruction and Development, Tanganyika, *op. cit.*, International Bank for Reconstruction and Development, *The Economic Development of Kenya*, Baltimore, the Johns Hopkins Press, 1963; International Bank for Reconstruction and Development, *The Economic Development of Uganda*, Baltimore, The Johns Hopkins Press, 1962.

based on the World Bank report.[1] There had also been in each of the countries reports of many public committees and commissions which had influenced public policy.

Although there is this history of colonial policy making, the Tanganyika First Five-Year Plan had some claim to being the first attempt to provide a programme of phased development, with investment and output targets for all sectors, set in an aggregative national income accounting framework and directed at a strategy of structural change. The Tanganyika Plan was important for the rest of East Africa because of this, even if in implementation it has, so far, fallen short of the initial conception.

The three plans now in operation and summarized in Tables 10 and 11 have many similarities in strategy, targets and methodology. In certain aspects, however, they present a striking contrast. The plans may be conveniently analysed by first examining the basic similarities, then exposing the evident contrasts and finally by evaluating the implementation difficulties faced in the three cases.

The first similarity is in the aggregate growth of targets chosen in the three plans. The Tanganyikan Five-Year Plan aimed to achieve a rate of growth in the period from 1960–62 to 1970 of 6·7 per cent per annum in total GDP. This was to be made up of rates of growth of 8·5 per cent in the monetary sector and 2·1 per cent in subsistence production. The subsistence growth rate was based upon an expected growth in population of 2·1 per cent per annum. The Uganda Plan aimed at achieving an overall rate of growth of 6·3 per cent per annum in the period 1966 to 1971, made up in this case of a rate of growth of 7·2 per cent for monetary output and of 3·2 per cent for subsistence production. The Revised Kenya Plan set a target rate of growth over the period 1964 to 1970 of 6·3 per cent in total GDP made up of a 7·1 per cent rate of growth in monetary activities and of 3·2 per cent in the subsistence sector.

The considerable degree of similarity in aggregate growth targets is partly accounted for by the comparable underlying economic conditions in the three countries, particularly in relation to export prospects. Also, they represent something of a common view emerging amongst professional planners regarding reasonable growth targets for this type of economy, in the light of their past performance. Further, while the growth targets represent a reasonable aspiration from the point of view of a professional economist, they also represent a minimum aspiration for the society, particularly in the light of population growth and demands for expanding employment opportunities.

[1] Uganda Government, *The First Five-Year Plan, op. cit.*

Table 10. Plan targets: gross domestic product growth targets

Kenya 1964–70	Compound annual rate of growth %	Tanganyika 1960/62–70	Compound annual rate of growth %	Uganda 1966–71	Compound annual rate of growth %
Monetary		*Monetary*		*Monetary*	
Agriculture	6·8	Crop husbandry	7·5	Agriculture	5·1
Fishing and hunting	22·6	Livestock	6·8	Cotton ginning, coffee curing, sugar manufacturing	5·6
Forestry	10·2	Forest products	4·3	Forestry, fishing and hunting	6·0
Livestock	3·5	Fishing	5·5	Mining and quarrying	6·6
Construction	18·3	Mining and quarrying	4·7	Manufacture of food	10·8
Mining and quarrying	8·2	Processing and manufacturing	14·8	Miscellaneous manufacturing	12·6
Banking, insurance, and real estate	8·0	Public utilities	12·3	Electricity	9·8
Manufacturing	8·0	Construction	12·7	Construction	11·3
Other services	7·5	Transport and communications	7·8	Commerce	7·0
Transport, storage and communications	7·0	Distribution	8·0	Transport and communications	8·5
General government	7·0	Rents and royalties	8·7	Government administration	8·2
Electricity and water	6·7	Public administration and defence	7·9	Local government	7·0
Wholesale and retail trade	6·0	Other services	9·0	Miscellaneous services	9·3
Rent (including ownership of dwellings)	3·5			Rents	7·4
Total monetary	7·1	Total monetary	8·5	Total monetary	7·2
Non-monetary	3·2	Non-monetary	2·1	Non-monetary	3·2
Total	6·3	Total	6·7	Total	6·3

Sources: *Kenya Development Plan 1966–1970*, p. 83.
Tanganyika Five-Year Plan 1964–1969, p. 10.
Uganda: Work for Progress Plan 1966–1971, p. 21.

M*

Table 11. *Plan targets: capital formation by industry* (£m)

Kenya 1965/66–1969/70	Total
Agriculture	47·7
Livestock	7·4
Forestry	6·0
Fisheries	2·5
Mining and quarrying	1·3
Manufacturing	61·7
Electricity and water	27·7
Transport and communications	63·3
Hotels and restaurants	7·0
Education	
Health	22·1
Other social services	
Non-residential buildings	12·7
Housing (not included elsewhere)	[b]17·2
Security and defence	3·7
Unallocable investments	19·6
Private cars	25·0
Total	325·0

Uganda 1966–71	Total
Agriculture and livestock	21·0
Cotton ginning, coffee curing and sugar manufacturing	8·0
Forestry, fishing and hunting	1·0
Mining and quarrying	3·0
Manufacture of food products	6·0
Miscellaneous manufacturing	31·0
Electricity	23·0
Construction	8·0
Commerce	14·0
Transport and communications	40·0
Government (administrative and miscellaneous)	
Local government	50·0
Miscellaneous services	
Rents	25·0
Total	230·0

Tanganyika 1964–69[a]	Total
Agriculture and livestock	25·5
Forestry	1·0
Water irrigation	10·0
Game and preservation of wildlife	0·4
Processing industry	10·8
Manufacturing and construction equipment	40·6
Mining and quarrying	4·9
Geological mapping and mineral surveys	0·4
Distribution	15·2
Other commerce	17·9
Lands and surveys	2·0
Trunk roads	6·0
Feeder roads	7·8
Aerodromes	1·2
Railways and harbours	15·5
Posts and telegraphs	1·0
Civil aviation and meteorology	1·5
Power	7·1
Housing & township development	41·7
Community development	2·3
Labour	0·4
Education	18·1
Health and welfare	6·2
National culture	0·3
National service	0·7
Law and order	2·9
Defence	2·3
External affairs	0·3
Information services and broadcasting	0·4
Government buildings	1·9
Total	246·0

Sources:

Kenya Development Plan 1966–1970, p. 111.
Tanganyika Five-Year Plan 1964–1969, p. 91.
Uganda Work for Progress Plan 1966–1971, p. 21.

Notes: [a] Excluding uncompleted Government projects from 1961–64 Plan which were estimated to be £7 million at time of publication.
[b] Total £7·8 million elsewhere.

The capital targets in the three plans show rather more variation. The Tanganyika Plan has a five-year growth capital formation target of roughly £246 million. However, there was also an additional total of £7 million which was carried over from the previous plan. In the event the carryover of investment from the previous plan was somewhat higher than the £7 million which was expected. Because of the lack of information regarding the level of domestic product from which the planners were projecting for the year prior to the plan it is difficult to translate this figure into a capital output ratio. Taking the increase in output from the level achieved in 1964–65 to the target for 1969–70 or from 1963–64 to 1968–69 the resulting gross capital output ratio is 2·9. In the Uganda case a gross capital formation target of £230 million is to be compared with an output increase from 1966 to 1971 of £82 million resulting in a gross capital output ratio of 2·8. The Kenya Plan seems to allow for somewhat more extensive use of capital. In the Kenya Plan an increase in output from 1964 to 1970 of £109 million is to be compared with a target for gross capital formation in the five remaining years of the Revised Plan for £325 million plus the investment achieved in the first year of the Six-Year Plan. The implied gross capital output ratio in the Kenya Plan is therefore 3·2. However, it should be noted that in the Kenya case a very high rate of growth of capital formation is assumed over the Plan. As a result of this the implied capital output ratio in the Plan will be greatly affected by the assumption made as regards the lag between capital formation and the resulting expansion in output capacity. The capital formation achieved in the past is recorded in Table 12 for comparison with the plan targets.

In relation to employment the three plans have some similarities but also significant differences. All three plans are very concerned with the necessity of increasing the proportion of the population in wage employment. However, in the Tanganyika First Five-Year Plan the problem is discussed in the long-term context of the perspective plan. In the Kenya Plan there is a much more detailed treatment of employment targets over the Plan period. The employment problem is, as indicated earlier, more obviously a critical and immediate concern of the Kenya government. Also, the period intervening between the publication of the Tanganyika First Plan and the publication of the Revised Kenya Plan saw a heightened awareness among policy makers in East Africa of the importance of the employment problem. The Kenya Plan not only attempts to set out explicit targets for wage earning opportunities in full time employment in those areas covered by existing employment statistics but also makes an ambitious attempt to estimate the increased economic opportunities outside the reported employment sector. In the Uganda Plan targets are limited to projections for the employed sector as covered by existing statistics, with the addition of income opportunities in smallholder outgrowing schemes.

The Kenya Plan justifies its employment targets by offering explicit assumptions about productivity change in the major sectors. Based upon these assumptions, the aim is, during the six-year period from 1964 to 1970, to achieve a rate of growth of wage employment and self-employment outside agriculture of 5 per cent per annum. Such an achievement would be satisfactory for long-term objectives, in the light of the overall population growth of 3 per cent per year. It does, however, assume that in aggregate terms the rate of growth of productivity will be lower than that experienced in the recent past.

In the Uganda Plan the employment targets are justified in terms of assumptions regarding overall productivity, but an interesting further step is taken. An attempt is made to render the employment and output objectives consistent with the overall resource allocation proposals through a proposed income policy. This income policy consists of a set of guidelines for the rates of growth of income over the plan for various income groups. In addition to achieving the balance required between incomes and outputs in the plan, there is also an attempt to incorporate social objectives as regards income distribution. Thus the guideline for wage rates increases for those in the income group over £600 per year is stated to be zero per cent per year. It is pointed out, however, that the rigid stabilization of wage rates in the higher salary levels has to be evaluated in the light of the fact that those in this category will receive substantial income increases over the Plan through rapid promotion. At the other end of the scale the objective is that wage rate increases should be at the rate of 3·5 per cent per annum for those earning under £90 per year at the beginning of the Plan. The intervening levels receive somewhat lower increases than this. Although these guidelines as set out in the Plan are an interesting first step towards an income policy, there is as yet no firm idea expressed as regards the method of implementation of such a policy.

In the Tanganyika Plan there is also a considerable concern about social justice in relation to income distribution. In particular, this resulted in a concern to develop the co-operative movement and to expand and improve training programmes to increase the skill and productivity of the labour force. The Kenya Plan is concerned less explicitly with income distribution problems, although the background paper on African Socialism which preceded the Plan treats income distribution as one of its major themes.

Table 12. *Gross capital formation*

(£ million)

Kenya	1954–56 Average	1961–63 Average
Residential buildings		
Government	1·46	2·11
EACSO (trading services)	0·91	0·12
Large scale agriculture[a]	0·87	0·44
Private	4·49	0·64
Total	7·73	3·30
Non-Residential Buildings		
Government	2·22	1·67
EACSO (trading services)	0·49	0·21
Large scale agriculture[a]	0·59	0·32
Private, other	3·42	1·50
Total	6·72	3·70
Construction and other works		
Government	4·60	5·21
EACSO (Trading services)	2·70	1·00
Large scale agriculture[a]	1·04	1·91
Private, other	0·80	1·84
Total	9·14	9·96

Kenya (contd.)	1954–56 Average	1961–63 Average
Transport equipment		
Government	0·52	0·67
EACSO (trading services)	2·28	0·35
Large scale agriculture[a]	0·85	0·66
Private:		
Cars	3·67	3·52
Commercial vehicles	2·50	1·94
Air	0·03	0·31
Total	9·84	7·45
Machine and Other Equipment		
Government	0·76	0·66
EACSO (trading services)	0·94	0·34
Large scale agriculture[a]	1·20	0·84
Private, other	5·25	5·71
Total	8·16	7·56
All Assets		
Government	9·55	10·33
EACSO (trading services)	7·33	2·03
Large scale agriculture[a]	4·55	4·16
Private, other	20·16	15·36
Total	41·59	31·88

[*Continued overleaf*

Table 12. *Gross capital formation* (continued)

(£million)

Tanganyika

By Sector	1954–56 Average	1961–63 Average
Private		
Building	4·9	5·2
Construction	—	1·3
Machinery and Equipment	8·2	7·0
Total	13·0	13·4
Public		
Building	7·1	2·7
Construction	—	5·7
Machinery and Equipment	3·0	1·2
Total	10·1	9·6
Para-Statal Organizations[b]		
Building	—	0·5
Construction	—	0·7
Machinery and Equipment	—	0·9
Total	—	2·1
Total	23·2	25·1

Uganda

By Sector	1954–56 Average	1961–63 Average[c]
Central Government	5·2	
Local Government	1·3	
East African High Commission	2·3	
Uganda Development Corporation and Uganda Electricity Board	5·8	
Other	6·5	
Total	21·2	
Building and construction		10·1
Plant and equipment		6·4
Vehicles		2·0
Total		18·6

By Asset		
Building		
Residential	3·7	3·7
Non-Residential	3·4	4·7
Construction		
Water Supplies	0·8	1·1
Communications	1·7	1·6
Railways and Harbours	1·6	2·1
Other	0·7	2·8
Equipment		
Transportation	6·6	2·7
Machinery and other	4·6	6·4
Total	23·2	25·1

By Asset	
Central Government	
Buildings and construction	4·7
Plant and equipment	0·4
Vehicles	0·1
Total	5·2
Remainder	
Urban Building	2·4
Rural industrial building and construction	1·7
Plant and equipment	6·5
Vehicles	1·7
Total	12·3
Total	17·5

Notes: [a] Regarded as non-African agriculture.

[b] Para-statal organizations are composed mainly of National Housing Corporation, Tanganyika Electric Supply Company and Williamson Diamonds. In the earlier figures the National Housing Corporation did not exist and the investment of the other two organizations was included under private.

[c] Uganda figures classified by sector were published on a provisional basis for the period 1961–63. These investment estimates have been revised subsequently and are not now available in a sector breakdown. The earlier unrevised estimates which will give a correct general impression indicated that Central and Local Government accounted for 31 per cent, the Uganda Development Corporation and Electricity Board for 16 per cent, East African Common Services for 6 per cent and 46 per cent for 'other'.

Sources: *Kenya Statistical Abstract*, 1965, p. 102.
Tanganyika Statistical Abstract, 1959, p. 126; 1964, p. 137.
Uganda Statistical Abstract, 1961, p. 91; 1965, p. 80.

Although these questions of employment and income distribution are clearly of great concern to the East African governments, and output objectives are incorporated in the Plans which are consistent with long-term goals for changing the structure of employment towards greater employment opportunities, there is as yet little attempt to introduce employment generating criteria into detailed project analysis.

An interesting development in all three countries has been the attempt to co-ordinate educational policies, labour policies and employment policies through the development of manpower planning. This has perhaps evolved most in Tanzania but major efforts have been made in all three countries. The educational policies in the plans are related to manpower projections. In the Tanzanian case manpower planning has been carried to the point of controlling through a system of bonding the allocation of university graduates in the period immediately following the completion of their studies.

The overall strategic views presented in the three plans have much in common. The three countries are, at the moment, pursuing fairly balanced strategies, with import substitution as a means of developing manufacturing sectors, along with widespread programmes of agricultural development to ensure the diffusion of well being through the rural sector and to maintain the buoyancy of export earnings. In none of the three plans is there, for example, an emphasis on industrialization at the expense of severe neglect of the agricultural sector.

The output targets in both the Tanganyika Plan and the Uganda Plan require a higher rate of structural change than those in the Kenya Plan. In particular, the Tanganyika and Uganda industrial sectors are projected to grow at rates much higher than the over-all growth of the economy. In the Tanganyika Plan the rate of growth of processing and manufacturing aimed at is 14·8 per cent per year compared with 6·7 per cent growth in total GDP over the period 1960–62 to 1970. In the Uganda Plan miscellaneous manufacturing is intended to grow at 12·6 per cent per annum, twice the rate of growth of total GDP. In the Kenya Plan, on the other hand, manufacturing is expected to grow at only 8 per cent per annum compared with a rate of growth in total GDP of 6·3 per cent per annum. At first sight this represents a striking difference in strategies of structural change in the three plans.

However, the difference does not necessarily represent a striking difference in view between these three countries. Both Uganda and Tanzania have a smaller manufacturing base from which to begin development and therefore might be expected to achieve higher rates of growth more readily. Also Kenya has a very favourable balance of trade with the other two countries, particularly in relation to manufactured goods. It is reasonable to suppose that if Kenya is to retain a substantial market in the other two countries then this balance will have to be evened to some degree in the current Plan period. A further important point is that the Kenya government has a fundamental problem of structural change within the agricultural sector on which it must concentrate its energies. The structure of the Kenyan economy has been fundamentally different from the other two countries. In the past opportunities for smallholder cash crop production were severely limited. The main contributions to cash agriculture were European mixed farming and plantations. The most important structural change taking place currently in the Kenyan economy is the rapid expansion in smallholder cash production in areas outside the former European owned farming areas, and the transfer of land from European mixed farming to African smallholder farming in the so-called White Highlands. This has meant that much finance and administrative energy has had to be concentrated upon problems of reorganization within agriculture. The restructuring of the agricultural sector will by itself represent a major achievement in economic reorganization.

There are differences in view represented in the balance of the programmes as between public and private sector and domestic and foreign sources of finance. The Uganda Plan has only 39 per cent of its capital formation targets allocated to the private sector, whereas the Tanganyika Plan allocated 47 per cent and the Kenya Plan 55 per cent. An important contributing factor to this difference is the greater relative importance of publicly owned corporations, such as the Uganda Development Corporation, in the Ugandan economy. It is also to some small degree the result of the greater relative importance of private smallholder investment in Uganda, which is not covered by existing estimates of capital formation and not included in planned targets. However, there is a very real difference in plan strategies, in that the Kenya Plan relies upon much higher levels of investment from the private sector than is expected in the other two cases. The Kenyan planners may have some justification in making such projections, in that in the past a much higher proportion of total capital formation has been generated within the private sector in the Kenya economy than in the other two countries. However, the periods of investment boom during the 1950's were in political circumstances which are quite different from those currently existing. Recent investment performance has certainly suggested that the private sector can still be relied upon in the right circumstances to

Table 13. *Finance of the Plans*
(£m)

	Private sector			Parastatal sector			Public sector			Total gross capital formation		
	Domestic	Foreign	Total	Domestic	Foreign	Total	Domestic	Foreign	Total	Domestic	Foreign	Total
Kenya (1965/66–1969/70)	105	75	180	22	31	53	31	61	92	158	167	325
Uganda (1966/67–1970/71)	75	15	90	40	20	60	50	40	90[a]	155	85	240
Tanganyika (1964/65–1968/69)	76	20	96	9	29	38	32	80	112	117	129	246

Notes: [a] Including £10m. development spending which is not counted as capital formation in national accounting terms.
Kenya will also receive £14 m. in foreign aid to finance the land transfer programme which is not included in these totals.

Sources: *Kenya Development Plan, 1966–1970.*
Tanganyika Five-Year Plan, 1964–1969.
Uganda Work for Progress Plan, 1966–1971.

generate high levels of investment. Nevertheless, the very considerable achievements which are expected of private investment during the period of the Revised Kenya Plan may well prove to be one vulnerable point in the overall strategy.

There is also a striking contrast in assumptions about the possible contributions of foreign investment. Whereas the Uganda Plan assumes that the foreign contribution will only be 35 per cent of total capital formation, in both the Tanganyika and Kenya Plans this figure rises to just over one-half. The Uganda Plan makes a much more cautious assumption about the likely availability of foreign finance for the public sector on the one hand as compared to the Tanganyika Plan, while it also makes a more conservative assumption about the relative role of foreign capital in the private sector than that contained in the Kenya Plan. Information on the balance of payments of the three East African countries is inadequate for assessing the role private foreign capital played in the past. However, it seems evident that even the cautious assumptions of the Uganda Plan about the availability of external support for public sector activities still leaves the expected level of foreign support for the Central Government development budget much higher than previous achievement. The assumption in the Kenya Plan that 40 per cent of private sector capital formation will be externally financed indicates that the Kenya strategy is not only one of heavy dependence on private investment but will, if achieved, also imply a considerable element of private foreign ownership in the Kenya economy in the future.

It is difficult to offer a firm judgment on these strategic decisions in the plans, as foreign support is so subject to uncertainties, particularly of a political character. Certainly the degree to which the Tanganyika Plan was dependent upon external support for the public sector, and the Kenya Plan has been based upon a heavy foreign involvement in both public and private sectors, render both subject to decisions and uncertainties outside the direct control of the governments concerned. On the other hand, the assumptions in the Uganda Plan require much higher local savings, particularly by the Central government. Thus although the Uganda Plan is, in principle, not so vulnerable to the whims of foreign private investors or aid donors, it is dependent upon the ability of the Uganda government and the Uganda public to achieve high levels of domestic savings during the Plan period, and this may be subject to severe political constraints. In devising ambitious plans intended to raise rates of investment above levels previously achieved it is inevitable that ambitious targets must be chosen either for domestic savings or for foreign capital investment or for some combination of the two. The advantage of choosing to place a large proportion of the burden on the domestic economy is that, at least in principle, this area is subject to instruments of policy available to the domestic government. Dependence on foreign sources in economies already excessively vulnerable to international economic influences carries obvious dangers.

The proof of a Plan is in its implementation rather than in its consistency. At the time of writing the Kenya and Uganda Plans have just been published. It is therefore too early to attempt to evaluate their implementation. The Tanzanians have had two years experience with their Plan which has indicated some difficulties which will have to be more explicitly treated in any future plans. The Plan documents of all three countries set out five-year targets and suggest paths along which investments should expand in order to achieve the levels desired at the end of the Plan and the cumulative totals over the Plan. In the case of Tanzania four main areas of difficulty have emerged which are also likely to arise in the other two countries.

The first of these is that implementation is made difficult by any severe fluctuation in export earnings. Such instability is fully recognized in all three plans in a strategic sense, in that it is one of the objectives of the Plans to reduce the dependence of the three economies on such external influences. However, it cannot be said that the tactical significance of instability has yet been fully incorporated into the planning methods of the three countries. Progress in the East African economies can never be a smooth affair and will always be subject to severe instability while the three economies remain so dependent on primary export earnings. In Tanzania the implementation of the Plan was impeded by the severe decline in sisal prices during 1965. Such experiences are likely to be shared in the future by the other two East African countries.

The three countries are also vulnerable to the interpretation foreign investors and aid donors give to political policies. Tanzanian experience has indicated that political independence can only be achieved at economic costs and Tanzania sacrificed economic aid to pursue independent policies in relation to both the West German and British governments.

A third major problem is that if a fast rate of expansion of investment is achieved then unforeseen bottlenecks may appear. When investment expanded at a fast rate in 1964 and 1965 difficulties in the construction industries quickly appeared, resulting in delays in building programmes and sharp rises in construction costs.

A fourth difficulty which has arisen is that the expansion in investment in all these plans is being attempted whilst the public services are extensively substituting local personnel for expatriate officials. This has meant a high rate of turnover in the public service. Moreover, the manning of the service has been below establishment, with a considerable number of vacancies in strategic technical posts which are difficult to fill by reallocation of manpower resources. For many of the officers in the public service the current period is a critical learning time, during which the new recruits are familiarizing themselves with current procedures. They can expand their activities into new areas only to a very limited degree. There are therefore delays in implementation within the public sector, both in undertaking projects for which finance is available and in carrying projects to the point of design and planning at which foreign finance can be sought.

The development plans still tend to place most emphasis on capital investment targets and project design. Areas of policy such as commercial policy, wage regulation, trade union policy and commodity pricing policy are all areas in which government decisions have a major impact on the performance of the economy. The achievement of the target rates of growth depends on effective and rational decision-making, not only in relation to the development projects of the three countries but also in devising detailed government policies during the implementation of the plans. The individual ministries in the three countries will need to develop a greater economic awareness of the policies within their control, and the planning ministries will have to co-ordinate the economic activity of the public sector more effectively than in the past.

To meet such needs, all three countries are developing a more sophisticated planning machinery. The location and organization of the planning function has changed considerably in recent years in all three countries. At the time of writing all three countries have separate ministries of planning with ministers who are members of the Cabinet. Each of these ministries is still highly dependent upon foreign technical assistance at the professional level. Small planning units have also been set up in some of the major implementation ministries. By 1970 the considerable experience which will have been gained with implementation in all three countries will enable more realistic experiments in plan organization and implementation to be made.

5. FINANCING THE PUBLIC SECTOR[1]

The public finances of the East African countries in recent years have been characterized by considerable fluctuations in tax receipts, relatively heavy dependence on external loans and grants, and relatively little reliance on domestic loans from the public or the banking system. Until the mid-'fifties current revenue was increasing at a faster rate than the current public expenditure, thus enabling the three countries, especially Uganda, to finance a part of capital expenditure from surplus on current account and to enhance their reserves.

This favourable situation was reversed in the late 'fifties and early 'sixties; government expenditures continued to increase at a rapid rate while tax receipts lost their earlier buoyancy due to falling commodity prices. The resultant gap between expenditure and current receipts was filled partly by increasing the tax burden, partly by drawing on reserves accumulated in earlier years and increasingly by external assistance. The contribution made by loans either from the general public or the banking system remained relatively small. Revenue and expenditure figures are given in Table 14.

Table 15 shows the Central government tax structure in the three countries. In common with other developing countries, taxes on foreign trade play a dominant role in the tax structures of East African countries. This is especially true of Uganda where import and export taxes have tended to account for well over 60 per cent of total tax receipts. Kenya and Tanzania have recently introduced export taxes in their tax systems but the revenue derived from them is relatively modest.

Import duties are the most important source of revenue in all the three countries. The relatively greater importance of income taxes in Kenya's tax system is to be explained by its more extensive commercial and industrial sectors and by its larger high income immigrant population. The uniformity of income, import and excise tax structures in the three countries required by the common market limits the use of fiscal policy to influence the pattern and rate of growth of the economy. Any important changes in these taxes are discussed and agreed in advance by the finance ministers of the three countries. Considering the severe limitations this must impose on the flexibility of fiscal policies in individual countries, the joint approach

[1] Dharam P. Ghai, *Taxation for Development: A Case Study of Uganda* (East African Studies No. 23) East African Institute of Social Research—East African Publishing House, Nairobi, 1966. L. Schnittger, *Taxation and Economic Development in East Africa*, African Studies Center of the Ifo-Institute, Study No. 8, New York, 1966.

Table 14. *Government finance*

(*a*) *Summary of Revenue and Expenditure* (*not including appropriations-in-aid*)

(£m)

Financial Year	Kenya Recurrent Revenue	Kenya Recurrent Expenditure	Kenya Development Revenue	Kenya Development Expenditure	Uganda Recurrent Revenue	Uganda Recurrent Expenditure	Uganda Development Revenue	Uganda Development Expenditure	Tanganyika Recurrent Revenue	Tanganyika Recurrent Expenditure	Tanganyika Development Revenue	Tanganyika Development Expenditure
1956–57	32·8	34·7	5·2	8·2	19·0	18·3[a]	5·5[a]	6·6	17·5	18·2	5·3	5·3
1957–58	33·4	33·3	6·8	7·9	18·8	19·2	3·7	6·3	18·8	18·7	5·5	5·5
1958–59	33·5	32·8	6·8	9·2	20·2	20·3	3·9	5·4	19·4	19·5	5·2	5·2
1959–60	32·4	31·7	8·1	9·7	20·6	19·6	1·3	5·3	22·1	21·2	3·9	3·9
1960–61	34·2	34·3	8·8	9·2	20·6	21·8	1·8	5·1	21·4	21·3	5·7	5·6
1961–62	35·0	33·3	8·9	9·3	17·6	20·3	1·6	4·8	21·9	24·7	3·4	7·3
1962–63	36·1	35·6	11·1	11·1	21·9	21·4	3·1	4·8	25·0	23·9	6·1	5·7
1963–64	48·3	45·6	12·9	14·9	36·6	33·8[a]	3·5[a]	6·5	28·3	27·8	5·3	7·3

Note: [a] In Uganda in 1956–57 and 1963–64 £0·9m. and £1·5m., respectively, were transferred from recurrent to development account, increasing both recurrent expenditure and development revenue by those amounts.

Source: *East African Economic and Statistical Review.*

Table 15. *Central Government Accounts, 1963–64*
(£'000)

Receipts

Item	Kenya[a]	Tanganyika[a] (not including appropriations in aid)	Uganda
1. Taxes			
Income tax	13,231	6,018	3,739
Personal tax	148	1,016	—
Export duties	—	907	7,866
Import duties	13,694	10,408	8,945
Excise tax	6,019	3,894	3,812
Other	3,674	1,454	942
Total	36,766	23,697	25,304
2. Sales of goods and services	4,540	1,704	2,271
3. Loan charges, interest, dividends and profits	2,035	872	896
4. Miscellaneous			
Reimbursement from other administrations	1,083	—	—
Aid from UK government	8,970	—	—
Transfers from abroad	—	—	1,823
Other	2,172	1,991	1,828
Total	12,225	1,991	3,652
5. Capital accounts[b]	—	—	1,165
6. Total receipts	55,567	28,265	33,289

Notes: [a] Includes revenue received direct by regions.
[b] Includes loans and sales of capital equipment.

Table 15—*continued*

(£'000)
Expenditures

Item	Kenya	Tanganyika (not including appropriations in aid)	Uganda
1. General services			
Defence	1,163	924	909
Law and order	7,858	3,354	3,645
Other	4,772	3,623	2,073
Total	13,793	7,901	6,626
2. Community services (roads, water, supplies, bridges, etc.)	2,423	1,157	851
3. Social services			
Education	6,961	4,941	3,549
Health	2,895	2,256	2,302
Other	941	469	551
Total	10,797	7,666	6,403
4. Economic services			
Agriculture, veterinary, forestry	4,802	2,542	1,813
Other	1,379	342	1,030
Total	6,181	2,884	2,843
5. Recurrent financial obligations			
Pensions and gratuities	10,008	1,988	3,525
Other	7,831	2,170	6,486
Total	17,839	4,158	10,011
6. Unallocable expenditure	3,008	3,351	2,794
7. Total expenditure	54,041	27,115	29,529

Sources: *Kenya Statistical Abstract 1965*, pp. 91, 93.
Tanzania Statistical Abstract 1964, pp. 111, 113, 114.
Uganda Statistical Abstract 1965, pp. 64, 65.

to fiscal problems has worked remarkably well. Part of the reason for this lies in the fact that responsibility for assessing and collecting these taxes is vested not in the individual governments but in the East African Common Services Organization. This undoubtedly results in substantial economies in costs of collection and contributes significantly to the smooth working of fiscal co-ordination in the three countries.

Since 1961 there has been a measure of fiscal compensation to Uganda and Tanzania to offset the unequal territorial distribution of benefits flowing from the existence of the common market. According to the scheme, 40 per cent of the proceeds of income tax charged to companies on profits arising from manufacturing and finance, and 6 per cent of the annual revenue collected in the three countries from customs and excise duties are paid into a 'distributable pool.' One-half of the total receipts of the pool are distributed to the East African Common Services Organization to finance its non-self-contained services, while the other half is shared in equal parts among the three countries. This results in a redistribution of revenue from Kenya to Uganda and Tanzania of about £0·8 million or so.

With the development of planning and the increased role of the state, fiscal policy will assume a more important role as an instrument of general economic policy. This will bring into even sharper focus than hitherto the potential conflict between political sovereignty and economic interdependence inherent in the East African situation. Already there have been some departures from common tax policies, especially in the use of development levies and excise taxes. It is likely that with the modification in the working of the common market and with differing rates of economic growth and different development plans in the three countries, fiscal policies will tend to diverge increasingly in the future.

Before attempting an evaluation of the tax systems of the East African countries it is necessary to say something about the base and rate structure of individual taxes. The import tax structure has been designed so as to tax relatively heavily the importation of consumer goods and to tax lightly or admit duty-free raw material and capital equipment imports. In particular a fairly narrow range of imported goods, such as textiles, fuels, beverages and tobacco, are responsible for a high proportion of total import tax receipts.

Export taxes, with all their alleged drawbacks, are perhaps the best instrument for taxing a large number of peasant farmers scattered all over the country. Uganda has made extensive use of taxes levied on exports of coffee and cotton, the rates varying with the export prices. Although reliance on export taxes has contributed to a considerable instability in the fiscal system, it is difficult to see how the Uganda government could otherwise have raised so high a proportion of GDP in taxes. It is interesting to see that in their search for additional revenue and with the increased importance of the peasant cash sector both Kenya and Tanzania have moved nearer to the Uganda position by levying export taxes on coffee and sisal.

The existence of large scale agriculture in Kenya and Tanzania and of relatively larger commercial and industrial sectors in Kenya has enabled both these countries, especially Kenya, to raise a substantial proportion of revenue through income taxes. Both individual and corporate income tax are based on the British system. The individual income tax is levied on persons and partnerships and is characterized, despite recent changes, by relatively large allowances, the most important ones being marriage, children and insurance contribution allowances. Consequently only a very small fraction of the total working population is subject to income tax. On the other hand, the tax rates are high and rise steeply.

The company tax has risen steadily in the last ten years and is now levied at a rate of 8 shillings in the pound. It contains generous provisions for investment and accelerated depreciation allowances for various classes of capital expenditure. These allowances may have aided the trend towards more capital-intensive techniques of production in recent years in East Africa.

Excise taxes are levied at specific rates on domestically produced beer, sugar, tobacco, cigarettes and soft drinks. The last few years have seen a progressive increase in most rates.

On the local government side, the most important tax sources are graduated personal tax in Kenya and Uganda, personal tax in Tanzania, tax on urban property and cesses on agricultural produce. The graduated personal tax is a kind of local income tax, adapted to circumstances in East Africa. It is levied on income, actual or presumed, from all sources, including land and other assets used for subsistence. The widespread use of this tax extends the principle of direct taxation to virtually all persons.

Although no systematic thought has been given to the use of fiscal policy to force the pace of development, the tax system does embody some provisions designed to encourage investment and savings, such as generous depreciation allowances and exemption of life insurance premiums from taxation. One of its main weaknesses lies in its equity implications. Although there has been no comprehensive study of the incidence of benefits and burdens of government expenditure and taxation in East Africa, there are indications that the overall tax system in East Africa tends to be regressive.

Another potential defect of the East African tax system is that it is unlikely to be sufficiently income elastic to meet the revenue requirements of the East African countries in the years ahead. Recent experience indicates that lack of revenue is already an important constraint upon development in East Africa. One of the urgently needed reforms in the tax structures, therefore, is to increase their revenue potential. This can be achieved, *inter alia*, by a reduction in personal allowances, higher rates of indirect taxes on consumption of luxury goods, and by an extension of the taxation of domestically produced goods and services through such devices as sales tax. There has been some progress along these lines in recent years and some surpluses have been generated in the current budget to finance development expenditure.

Apart from tax receipts, income from property and departmental earnings, the only other important domestic source of revenue is local loans. Although in the past they contributed relatively little to government revenue, major efforts are now being made by all three governments to raise substantially larger amounts through local loans. The practice of government short-term borrowing through Treasury Bills is now well-established. Attempts are also being made to mobilize small savings through the issue of development premium bonds, lotteries, and other low-denomination securities. These attempts may have psychological value in involving wide groups in the developmental process, but their revenue yields have, so far, been relatively small.

In many developing countries the banking system is a significant source of domestic finance for governments. This source has been relatively unimportant in East Africa. In order to understand why this has been so, it is necessary to say a few words about the monetary institutions in East Africa. An important element in the pattern of common East African institutions was, until July 1966, the existence of an East African Currency Board, which served the three East African countries plus Aden. This situation has now changed with the creation, in 1966, of separate Central Banks for the three countries.

In the colonial period, the operation of the Currency Board was essentially similar to that of the currency boards operating in other British colonies in Africa. In recent years it evolved from an essentially passive role of note issuer, backing the currency completely with sterling asset holdings, to a position in which it was willing to hold substantial quantities of East African governments' debt. Nevertheless it did not attempt to develop a role as an implementor of an active monetary policy. It did, however, attempt to provide seasonal liquidity to the three economies for the finance of crop movements.

The commercial banking system has been almost entirely dominated by branches of international banks. Barclay's Bank, DCO, the Standard Bank and National and Grindlays have been particularly prominent. In the past these banks operated on an East African basis in handling their liquidity situation, shifting reserves from country to country. When faced with short-term drains on their liquidity, as in 1960–61 when there was a substantial outflow of liquid assets from East Africa, the commercial banks have been able to call on their head offices overseas for support. Conversely, in times of great liquidity they have accumulated substantial balances in London. Thus the head offices have in a sense, fulfilled one of the functions o a central bank in cushioning the East African monetary system from monetary fluctuations resulting from sharp fluctuations in the Balance of Payments.

In the past the commercial banks have been subject to criticism for their limited willingness to provide finance for industrial development activities. At the same time they have refrained from holding government securities to any significant extent. The establishment of the three Central Banks may make the commercial banks more willing to hold government securities. It is possible that the Central Banks may themselves finance government expenditure to a greater degree than did the Currency Board, but the nature of the East African economies places sharp limits on the degree to which deficit financing could be resorted to without endangering price stability and external solvency. An important change occurred in February 1967, when Tanzania nationalized the private commercial banks and a number of other industrial and commercial enterprises. It is too early to say how this will effect monetary policy there.

The three new Central Banks have maintained convertibility between the three new currencies and, indeed, the notes of all three countries continue to circulate throughout East Africa. As the constitutions of all three Central Banks suggest that the monetary policies to be pursued are likely to be cautious, if not conservative, the operations of the Banks as such should not place any strain on convertibility or freedom of exchange between the three countries. However, if widely divergent balance of payments situations, arising from other causes, should lead to great differences in external exchange control policies, serious strains are bound to arise.

One effect of the break-up of the unified monetary system will be that both in terms of official reserves and the liquidity situations of the commercial banks there will no longer be any pooling effect. This is likely to make all three East African countries more vulnerable to the effects of Balance of Payments instability.

6. CONCLUSION

The three East African countries are undergoing a period of social transformation in which expatriate administrators are being displaced by local personnel and increasing economic opportunities are being made available to the local populations in all the sectors of the economy. The governments of East Africa have set more ambitious targets for growth and structural change than they have attempted or achieved before. These plans are being implemented in a period during which the East African economies are as subject as ever to externally induced fluctuations and in which experience will be gained in using new political and administrative tools. Prediction in such circumstances is subject to great uncertainty.

The implementation of the Treaty for East African Co-operation will go a long way to maintain and extend the already close economic ties binding the three countries and, in the longer run, make a major contribution to the industrialization of the region.

The efforts to diversify the economies are certain to achieve some success in expanding manufactured consumer goods production, particularly in the textile range. In the near future, however, the three countries will have to consider embarking on a range of products which will be much more difficult to introduce in a market of the East African size. The advantages of economic integration, possibly extended beyond the existing common market, are therefore likely to become increasingly important during the 1970's.

Export diversification is likely to be limited in its immediate impact. East Africa will remain heavily dependent on coffee, cotton and sisal, although tea will compete with these for importance in the 1970's.

Expansion of the education system and population will make employment an increasingly critical issue in public policy during the coming decade, even if the current development plans are substantially successful. The seriousness of the problem will depend on the success of peasant agriculture in sustaining or accelerating the growth in physical output achieved in the past. From this point of view, the research area with the highest priority is, perhaps, agriculture and ancillary economic activities. Too little is now known of the systems of small-holder farming and the sources of past output growth.

SELECTED READING

1. Clark, P. G., *Development Planning in East Africa* (East African Studies No. 21), East African Institute of Social Research—(East African Publishing House, 1965).
2. Elkan, W., *Migrants and Proletarians: Urban Labour in the Economic Development of Uganda* (Oxford University Press, London, 1960).
3. Fuggles-Couchman, N. R., *Agricultural Change in Tanganyika:* 1945–60, Stanford Research Institute (Stanford University, Stanford, 1964).
4. Ghai, D. P., *Taxation for Development: A Case Study of Uganda* (East African Studies No. 23) East African Institute of Social Research (East African Publishing House, 1966).
5. Hazlewood, A., *Rail and Road in East Africa* (Blackwell, Oxford, 1964).
6. International Bank for Reconstruction and Development, *The Economic Development of Tanganyika, 1960; The Economic Development of Uganda, 1961; The Economic Development of Kenya 1962.*
7. Kenya Government, *Economic Planning and its Application to African Socialism, 1965.*
8. Kenya Government, *Development Plan, 1966–70,* 1966 (Government Printer, Nairobi).
9. *East African Royal Commission 1953–55 Report,* 1955.
10. *Report of the Economic and Fiscal Commission* (*Raisman Report*) (HMSO London, Cmd. 1279, 1961).
11. Newlyn, W., and Rowan, D., *Money and Banking in British Colonial Africa* (Oxford University Press, 1954).
12. Ndegwa, P., *The Common Market and Development in East Africa* (East African Studies No. 22) East African Institute of Social Research (East African Publishing House, 1965).
13. O'Connor, A. M., *Railways and Development in Uganda* (East African Studies No. 18) (Oxford University Press, 1965).
14. Robson, P., and Leys, C. (Eds.) *Federation in East Africa; Problems and Opportunities* (Oxford University Press, 1965).
15. Ruthenberg, H., *Agricultural Development in Tanganyika,* African Studies Centre of the Ifo-Institute, Study No. 2 (New York, 1964).
16. Ruthenberg, H., *African Agricultural Production Development Policy in Kenya 1952–1965,* African Studies Centre of the Ifo-Institute, Study No. 10 (New York, 1966).
17. Tanganyika Government, *Five Year Plan for Economic and Social Development, 1964–69* (Government Printer, Dar es Salaam).
18. Uganda Government, *Work For Progress,* Uganda's Second Five-Year Plan, 1966–71 (Government Printer, Entebbe).

8

THE ECONOMY OF CENTRAL AFRICA

1. INTRODUCTION

This chapter deals with the area of Central Africa which formerly made up the Federation of Rhodesia and Nyasaland. Discussion is focussed on the ten year life of the Federation which terminated on December 31, 1963. Since that time substantial changes in finance, money, trade and economic policy have taken place. Nevertheless, the basic economic structures remain substantially unchanged and the fundamental economic problems which faced the former federation have been inherited by Rhodesia, Zambia and Malawi.[1] This chapter provides a brief review of the economic structure of the area and focuses attention on the role of the former federal government in economic policy. Its aim is not merely to examine a particular historical era but also to furnish statistical and economic data on a country basis which provides a background for an understanding of present day development in Rhodesia, Zambia and Malawi.

The three countries which make up Central Africa have a total area of 475,000 sq. miles. Zambia, with an area of 288,000 sq. miles accounts for more than half the total. Rhodesia covers 150,000 sq. miles whilst Malawi with 37,000 sq. miles is the smallest. Reliable estimates of total population are lacking for most of the decade in question although the non-African population was well documented. The first territorial Census of Africans in Rhodesia took place as late as 1962 and it made clear that earlier estimates had understated the African population by 20 per cent. A similar census undertaken for Zambia in 1963 suggests that the relevant precensus estimate was too small by 35 per cent and the earlier figures for Malawi are also substantially in error. Table 1 summarizes the estimates for mid-1963 showing a total population of over 11 m. Throughout the area Africans constituted the dominant racial group. Europeans, Asians

[1] In this chapter the countries are referred to by their present names; Southern Rhodesia is Rhodesia; Northern Rhodesia is Zambia; and Nyasaland is Malawi. It should be remembered that discussion of Government policies and actions concerns the earlier Colonial administrations.

and persons of mixed parentage accounted for little more than 3 per cent of total population. However, markedly different ratios of Africans to non-Africans prevailed in each country. Whereas for the area as a whole there were over 30 Africans to each non-African, the corresponding ratios for Rhodesia, Zambia and Malawi were 15, 39 and about 150 respectively.

Table 1. *Area and estimated population, mid 1963*

	Area ('000 sq. miles)	Population ('000)	Density (persons per sq. m.)
Rhodesia	150	4,010	27
Zambia	288	3,496	12
Malawi	37	3,753	101
Total	475	11,259	24

Source: UN Demographic Year Book, 1964.

Comparison of areas and population indicates that population densities in Central Africa are fairly light. The average density was about 24: in Rhodesia it was 27 and in Zambia 12. In Malawi, it was much higher at 101, and it is several times as great in the densely populated southern part of that country. The pressure on land resources there is reflected in the importance of labour migration to Rhodesia and South Africa.

The rate of population growth of the African population was high and increasing. In Rhodesia the yearly rate of natural increase of the African population was estimated to have increased from 3 per cent in 1954 to 3·5 per cent in 1962. In Zambia the rate is believed to have been of the order of 2·5 per cent in 1954 and to have increased to 3 per cent by 1962. No reliable estimates were available for Malawi but official projections assumed a rate of growth of 2·2 per cent.

The rate of natural increase of the European population was fairly steady throughout the period at 2 per cent per annum. However, natural increase accounted for only a fraction of this increase, the rest being accounted for by immigration, which was considerable. In 1956, for instance, there was a net immigration of non-Africans amounting to 18,500 persons, equivalent to an additional population increase in that year of 6·8 per cent. This was the peak immigration year. Subsequent figures were much lower and in 1961 there was a net migration of non-Africans from the area.

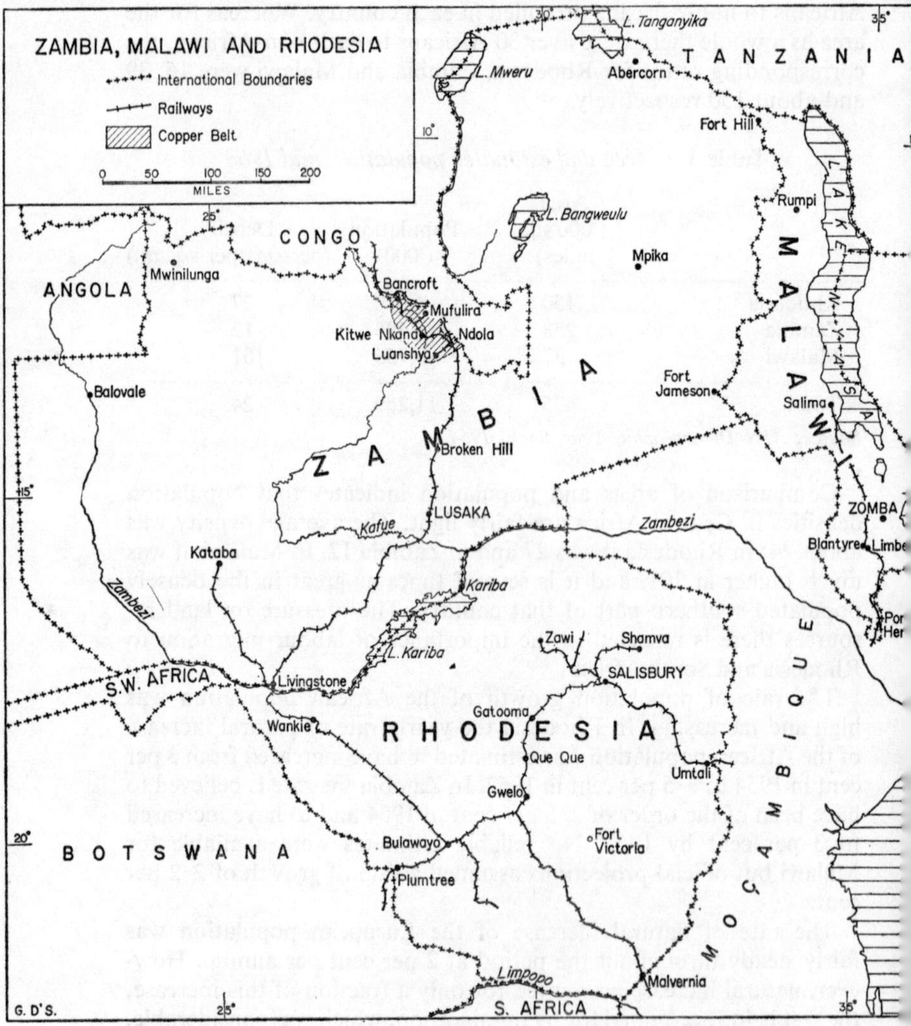
ZAMBIA, MALAWI AND RHODESIA
International Boundaries
Railways
Copper Belt
0 50 100 150 200
MILES
L. Tanganyika
L. Mweru
Abercorn
TANZANIA
Fort Hill
Rumpi
L. Bangweulu
CONGO
Mpika
ANGOLA
Mwinilunga
Bancroft
Mufulira
Kitwe Nkana
Ndola
Luanshya
LAKE NYASA
MALAWI
Fort Jameson
Salima
Balovale
ZAMBIA
Broken Hill
LUSAKA
Kafue
Zambezi
ZOMBA
Blantyre
Limbe
Kataba
Zambezi
Kariba
L. Kariba
Zawi
Shamva
SALISBURY
S.W. AFRICA
Livingstone
Gatooma
Wankie
RHODESIA
Que Que
Umtali
Gwelo
Fort Victoria
BOTSWANA
Bulawayo
Plumtree
MOCAMBIQUE
Limpopo
Malvernia
S. AFRICA
G. D'S.
10°
15°
20°
25°
30°
35°

Map 6

Although non-Africans constituted a very small proportion of the area's total population, in terms of their contribution to the output and economic development of the area they were a most important and influential minority. Industry, commerce and agriculture were all controlled and dominated by Europeans. Although African traders were growing in numbers and African farmers were increasingly participating in the cash sector of the economy through sales of surplus produce, Africans were mainly either subsistence workers or, where employment could be found, paid workers. Apart from obstacles of education and resources, legislation hindered the rise of an African entrepreneurial and capitalist class, especially in agriculture.

In terms of Gross Domestic Product Rhodesia was the richest of the three countries and Malawi the poorest (Table 2). In 1963 Rhodesia contributed 55 per cent of the area's GDP, Zambia 37 per cent and Malawi 8 per cent. *Per capita* GDP amounted to £76·4 in Rhodesia, £59·3 in Zambia and £12·5 in Malawi.

The economy of the area was based on agriculture and on mining. In 1954 roughly one-fifth of the GDP originated in agriculture and nearly three-tenths in mining. The three countries differ greatly however in their economic structures. The data are summarized in Table 3. Zambia's economy is dominated by the copper mining industry which is located on the Copperbelt, and in 1954 mining accounted for nearly three-fifths of its GDP. Half the European population and half of the Africans in employment are found in the Copperbelt. In the same year, agriculture generated less than 10 per cent of GDP. Malawi by contrast is basically agricultural, and more than 55 per cent of GDP originated from this section. Rhodesia's economy was rather more diversified. About a quarter of the GDP originated in agriculture which was the largest productive sector, but there is also a large mining industry producing mainly asbestos, chrome and gold. In 1954, about 10 per cent of the GDP originated in this sector. Rhodesia also had an important manufacturing sector which produced about one-eighth of GDP in 1954. In Zambia and Malawi manufacturing generated less than 5 per cent of GDP and in Malawi this sector was concerned mainly with the processing of agricultural production.

The economy of Central Africa, like that of all African economies, contains a mixture of traditional production activities, involving both subsistence and cash activities on the one hand, and production employing modern methods and techniques on the other. According to official estimates, in 1954 the subsistence part of the Rural Household Sector produced goods and services worth £41·5 m, and mar-

Table 2. *Gross domestic product*

	Rhodesia				Zambia			
	GDP		GDP *per capita*		GDP		GDP *per capita*	
	at current factor cost (£ m)	at 1954 market prices (£ m)	at current factor cost (£)	at 1954 market prices (£)	at current factor cost (£ m)	at 1954 market prices (£ m)	at current factor cost (£)	at 1954 market prices (£)
1954	161·5	169·6	54·0	56·7	138·8	140·1	51·0	51·5
1955	180·7	184·9	58·5	59·8	169·5	136·9	60·8	49·1
1956	206·8	212·6	64·8	66·6	188·1	153·1	65·5	53·3
1957	231·2	227·2	70·1	68·8	155·2	159·6	52·4	53·9
1958	241·4	232·1	70·8	68·1	141·0	155·8	46·4	51·3
1959	256·9	247·4	73·0	70·3	188·1	187·6	60·3	60·1
1960	274·7	259·4	75·5	71·3	207·4	202·7	64·6	63·1
1961	290·4	275·3	77·2	73·2	200·6	202·7	60·8	61·4
1962	295·0	281·0	76·0	72·4	198·2	200·0	58·3	58·8
1963	306·3	279·5	76·4	69·7	207·5	204·7	59·3	58·5

	Malawi				Central Africa			
	GDP		GDP *per capita*		GDP		GDP *per capita*	
	at current factor cost (£ m)	at constant 1954 market prices (£ m)	at current factor cost (£)	at constant 1954 market prices (£)	at current factor cost (£ m)	at constant 1954 market prices (£ m)	at current factor cost (£)	at constant 1954 market prices (£)
1954	29·7	30·5	10·0	10·2	329·8	340·0	37·9	39·1
1955	31·7	31·0	10·4	10·1	382·0	352·8	42·7	39·5
1956	34·1	33·6	10·9	10·7	429·0	399·3	46·6	43·4
1957	35·9	35·0	11·1	10·9	422·3	421·8	44·5	44·5
1958	38·1	36·3	11·5	11·0	420·6	424·1	43·1	43·5
1959	39·9	37·6	11·8	11·1	484·9	472·3	48·3	47·1
1960	42·1	38·6	12·1	11·1	524·2	500·7	50·8	48·5
1961	43·5	40·5	12·2	11·4	534·5	518·5	50·3	48·8
1962	45·3	40·5	12·4	11·1	538·7	521·3	49·3	47·7
1963	46·7	39·8	12·5	10·6	560·5	524·1	49·8	46·5

Source: National Accounts and Balance of Payments of Northern Rhodesia, Nyasaland and Southern Rhodesia, 1954–63. Central Statistical Office, Salisbury, 1964.

Table 3. *Central Africa: gross domestic product (at factor cost) % by industry of origin*

	1954						Central Africa	
	Rhodesia		Zambia		Malawi			
Sector	£m	%	£m	%	£m	%	£m	%
1. Agriculture, forestry and fishing								
(*a*) Subsistence	10·9	6·7	11·6	8·4	11·0	37·0	33·4	10·1
(*b*) Peasant money	3·7	2·3	1·5	1·1	2·1	7·1	7·3	2·2
(*c*) Large scale commercial	23·5	14·6	2·6	1·9	3·3	11·1	29·2	8·9
2. Mining and quarrying	13·7	8·5	80·3	57·9	...	0·1	93·8	28·4
3. Manufacture	20·7	12·8	4·6	3·3	1·4	4·8	26·9	8·1
4. Construction and building	13·2	8·2	8·9	6·4	1·1	3·9	23·3	7·1
5. Electricity and water	4·0	2·5	0·4	0·3	0·1	0·3	4·5	1·4
6. Transport and communication	12·5	7·7	4·9	3·5	1·4	4·6	18·7	5·7
7. Wholesale and retail trade	22·0	13·7	9·2	6·6	3·0	10·3	34·3	10·4
8. Banking, insurance, finance and real estate	5·0	3·1	1·0	0·7	0·1	0·4	6·2	1·9
9. Ownership of dwellings	4·8	3·0	0·7	0·5	0·2	0·6	5·7	1·7
10. Public Administration and defence	6·5	4·0	3·1	2·2	1·2	4·0	10·7	3·2
11. Education	3·3	2·0	1·2	0·9	0·5	1·7	5·1	1·5
12. Health	1·5	0·9	0·7	0·5	0·3	1·0	2·6	0·8
13. Other services[a]	16·1	10·0	7·8	5·6	3·9	13·1	27·8	8·5
Total	161·5	100	138·8	100	29·7	100	329·8	100

[*Continued overleaf*

keted goods worth £7·3 m. On this basis, subsistence output represented one-eighth of Central Africa's GDP in 1954, but there was a substantial difference in its relative importance in the three countries. Whereas in 1954 the monetary economy represented about 90 per cent of GDP in Rhodesia and Zambia respectively, in Malawi its share was only just over one-half.

If the subsistence sector is not, overall, important in terms of output, it is of major importance in terms of the numbers of persons who find occupation in the sector. In Rhodesia for instance, the 1962 Census showed that about one half of the total African population were living in the Tribal Trust Lands. A further small proportion of

Table 3—*continued*

Sector	1958 Rhodesia £m	%	Zambia £m	%	Malawi £m	%	Central Africa £m	%
1. Agriculture, forestry and fishing								
(*a*) Subsistence	13·0	5·4	14·6	10·4	12·1	31·8	39·7	9·4
(*b*) Peasant money	3·7	1·5	1·0	0·7	2·8	7·3	7·5	1·8
(*c*) Large scale commercial	29·6	12·3	3·1	2·2	3·3	8·7	35·9	8·5
2. Mining and quarrying	16·4	6·8	52·6	37·3	...	0·1	69·1	16·4
3. Manufacture	35·6	14·6	7·8	5·5	2·4	6·2	45·8	10·9
4. Construction and building	22·0	9·1	14·3	10·1	2·1	5·5	38·2	9·1
5. Electricity and water	6·6	2·7	4·2	3·0	0·3	0·7	11·0	2·6
6. Transport and communication	19·1	7·9	7·6	5·4	2·2	5·9	29·3	7·0
7. Wholesale and retail trade	33·7	13·9	10·8	7·7	4·4	11·7	49·2	11·7
8. Banking, insurance, finance and real estate	10·0	4·2	2·7	1·9	0·2	0·5	12·9	3·1
9. Ownership of dwellings	7·9	3·3	1·2	0·9	0·4	1·1	9·5	2·3
10. Public Administration and defence	11·0	4·6	5·9	4·2	1·7	4·6	18·7	4·4
11. Education	6·0	2·5	2·3	1·6	0·8	2·1	9·1	2·2
12. Health	2·3	1·0	1·4	1·0	0·5	1·3	4·1	1·0
13. Other services[a]	24·3	10·2	11·5	8·2	4·7	12·4	40·5	9·6
Total	241·4	100	141·0	100	38·1	100	420·6	100

the African population is found in the Native Purchase Areas where Africans hold title to the lands they use and are at a transitional stage in the process of moving from the subsistence to the cash economy. For the Federation as a whole it has been estimated[1] that 80 per cent of African population resided in the rural areas and were associated in some degree with agricultural production.

Throughout the decade 1954–63 the Federal economy expanded substantially. GDP (in current prices at factor cost) expanded from £330 m to £560 m or by 70 per cent which represented a growth rate of 6·1 per cent per annum. This growth however, did not occur

[1] M. Yudelman, *Africans on the Land*, Harvard University Press 1964, p. 7.

Table 3—*continued*

Sector	1961–63—Annual Average Rhodesia £m	%	Zambia £m	%	Malawi £m	%	Central Africa £m	%
1. Agriculture, forestry and fishing								
(*a*) Subsistence	15·8	5·3	16·0	7·9	13·5	29·9	45·3	8·3
(*b*) Peasant money	3·7	1·2	2·8	1·4	3·8	8·4	10·4	1·9
(*c*) Large scale commercial	43·4	14·6	5·6	2·8	3·9	8·6	52·8	9·7
2. Mining and quarrying	16·1	5·4	95·9	47·5	...	0·1	112·0	20·6
3. Manufacture	48·6	16·4	11·4	5·6	2·7	6·0	62·8	11·5
4. Construction and building	14·9	5·1	8·3	4·1	1·8	4·0	25·1	4·6
5. Electricity and water	12·4	4·2	3·9	1·9	0·5	1·1	16·9	3·1
6. Transport and communication	26·4	8·9	10·2	5·0	2·7	6·0	39·4	7·2
7. Wholesale and retail trade	40·3	13·6	15·3	7·6	5·7	12·6	61·3	11·3
8. Banking, insurance, finance and real estate	10·5	3·5	4·2	2·1	0·3	0·7	15·0	2·8
9. Ownership of dwellings	9·9	3·3	1·4	0·7	0·5	1·1	11·8	2·2
10. Public Administration and defence	14·6	4·9	8·8	4·4	2·5	5·5	26·0	4·8
11. Education	8·8	3·0	3·7	1·8	1·1	2·4	13·6	2·5
12. Health	3·1	1·0	1·6	0·8	0·6	1·3	5·3	1·0
13. Other services[a]	28·7	9·7	12·9	6·4	5·4	11·9	47·0	8·6
Total	297·2	100	202·1	100	45·2	100	544·5	100

Note: [a] Includes African rural household services (subsistence) as follows:

	1954	1958	1961–3 (ann. av.)
Rhodesia	2·6	2·8	3·5
Zambia	2·9	3·6	3·9
Malawi	2·7	3·0	3·3
Central Africa	8·1	9·3	10·7

Source : As for Table 2.

smoothly. During 1954–56 very rapid growth of over 14 per cent occurred. In 1957 there was a slight fall, followed by a further slight fall in 1958. Substantial growth again took place in 1958–60 but the rate then slackened.

In real terms the growth rate of GDP was less rapid. Over the period 1954–63 GDP in terms of 1954 market prices increased from £340 m to £524 m or by 54 per cent equivalent to an annual growth rate of 4·9 per cent. Real growth rates also varied during the period. Particularly notable is the striking difference in rates experienced before and after 1960. From 1960 to 1963 indeed, the growth rate was only 1·5 per cent per annum, which was well below the rate of growth of population.

Examination of the figures for the separate countries reveals that the fall in product at current price was mainly accounted for in 1957 and 1958 by the fall in Zambia's GDP[1] which followed the sharp reduction in the price of copper. Rhodesia's output rose uninteruptedly from £161 m in 1954 to £306 m in 1963. Malawi's output rose from £30 m to £47 m. In Zambia by contrast domestic product fell from £188·1 m in 1956 to £155·2 m in 1957 and £141·0 m in 1958 before rising again to £200 m in 1960–63. The rapidity of growth in the federal economy was very much bound up with the price of copper, which during the decade ranged from a high point of £437 per long ton, reached in March 1956, to a low point of £160 per long ton in February 1958.

The substantial growth of GDP over the period was not accompanied by any dramatic structural change in the economy of the region as a whole as measured in the industrial origin of GDP. Perhaps the most notable change to occur was the increased contribution of manufacturing industry to output. This increased from £27 m in 1954 to £65 m in 1963, and its relative share of GDP rose from 8 to 12 per cent in the region as a whole. In Zambia, manufacturing output more than doubled over the period and in Malawi too a substantial increase occurred, but at the end of the period the combined manufacturing output of the two northern countries was still less than one-third of the output of Rhodesian industry. A further important feature of development during the period was the growing importance of infrastructure—electricity and water, and transport and communications, in the GDP. In the area as a whole the contribution of large scale farming more than kept pace with the overall growth of GDP. This was also the case in Rhodesia. In Malawi its contribution lagged, although it increased in absolute terms. In Zambia the output of this sector more than doubled and its relative contribution had increased by the end of the period. The contribution

[1] The Zambian figures in terms of 1954 market prices rise fairly smoothly but to assess their significance it would be necessary to correct for changes in the terms of trade. This factor was much less important in the other countries during this period.

of mining, the largest single component of GDP varied over the period as the price of copper fluctuated but its contribution throughout was dominant. Even in 1961–63, a time of relatively low prices, 20 per cent of GDP in the area as a whole originated in this sector.

Data on the external account is summarized in Table 4. It can be seen that except for the years 1957 and 1958 the balance of visible trade was positive. The fall in copper prices which reached a low point in February 1958 was accompanied by a swing from surplus to deficit in the trade balance and a sharp deterioration in the current account balance of payments. The high level of imports also contributed to this change. Throughout the period up to 1962 any favourable balance on visible trade was more than matched by the deficit on invisible trade. The major debit item was for remittances of corporate earnings and the size of this item reflected the high level of past foreign capital investment in the area. Payments for transport and for insurance of merchandise were also substantial. In 1957 and 1958 the deterioration in copper prices turned a formerly modest current account deficit into a very large one. In 1956 there had been some drawing down of external assets and in the following years as can be seen, a very large withdrawal was necessary to balance external payments. The current account did not become positive until 1963. The change was associated with increased export earnings and decreased imports, the latter reflecting both the impact of import substitution and a lower level of investment demand. Throughout the period there was a large inflow of new capital into the area. It rose from £27 m in 1954 to a peak of £54 m in 1958. Thereafter it fell, and in 1962 there was an outflow; but in the final year an inflow, albeit small, recurred.

From the institutional point of view the single most important feature of the economy of Central Africa lay in the federal arrangements themselves. Federation came into effect partly because of its anticipated benefits to the region as a whole. Although the force of the purely economic case for Federation may be disputed[1] the framework of economic policy was certainly profoundly affected by the character of the federal arrangements adopted. In particular both the manner in which responsibility for measures affecting the economic development of the territories was shared among the Federal government and the three territorial governments, and the revenue

[1] See *Nyasaland, The Economics of Federation*, by A. Hazlewood and P. D. Henderson, Oxford, 1960, for an interesting discussion of arguments for federation. The economic arguments for federation and its problems are similar to those of any scheme for regional economic integration. See Introduction, pp. 71–2 for a discussion of these.

Table 4. *Balance of payments*

(*a*) Balance of payments on current account (£ m)

	Rhodesia			Zambia			Malawi			Central Africa		
	Visible	Invisible	Total	Visible	Invisible	Total	Visible	Invisible	Total	Visible	Invisible	Total
1954	−22·0	−4·6	−26·6	33·6	−20·8	12·8	−1·0	0·9	0·1	35·2	−49·5	−14·2
1955	−30·8	−4·7	−35·5	46·0	−24·0	22·0	−3·0	1·3	−1·7	40·3	−55·7	−15·4
1956	−34·3	−4·8	−39·1	36·6	−30·0	6·6	−5·2	1·2	−4·0	27·8	−64·3	−36·5
1957	−30·7	−9·5	−40·2	−8·9	−18·6	−27·5	−6·5	1·7	−4·8	−13·1	−59·5	−72·5
1958	−41·8	−8·5	−50·3	4·1	−9·8	−5·7	−7·5	1·3	−6·2	−12·4	−49·8	−62·2
1959	−15·0	−8·5	−23·5	30·4	−18·9	11·5	−4·3	1·0	−3·3	45·8	−60·9	−15·0
1960	−4·4	−8·1	−12·5	37·6	−24·5	13·1	−8·5	1·9	−6·6	61·1	−67·2	−6·1
1961	2·5	−14·7	−12·2	30·1	−22·6	7·5	−9·0	2·5	−6·5	62·8	−73·9	−11·0
1962	17·1	−16·3	0·8	24·1	−24·3	−0·2	−8·2	2·7	−5·5	74·1	−78·9	−4·8
1963	26·8	−20·6	6·2	37·4	−24·8	12·6	−9·9	5·4	−4·5	95·7	−81·4	14·4

(*b*) Balance of Payments on capital account (£ m)

	Central Africa Private capital inflow	Central Africa Public capital inflow	Central Africa Change in external assets (+ = decrease)		Central Africa Private capital inflow	Central Africa Public capital inflow	Central Africa Change in external assets (+ = decrease)
1954	11·0	16·0	−12·8	1959	16·2	18·2	−19·4
1955	22·2	9·8	−16·6	1960	19·1	6·5	−19·5
1956	23·9	4·3	+8·2	1961	5·1	12·9	−7·0
1957	27·6	5·9	+39·1	1962	−5·5	0·8	+9·5
1958	28·8	25·0	+8·4	1963	2·1	−0·2	+12·5

Notes: Net exports of goods and services are derived from the National income approach by comparing the Gross Domestic Product from the respective income and expenditure sides. The exercise involved a considerable amount of estimation and the results must be treated as very approximate.

There are two serious omissions in the territorial estimates: the first is the inter-territorial transfers of Company profits, interest and dividends and the second is the net transfers between territories on Federal Government accounts. According to A. G. Irvine, 'The Balance of Payments of Rhodesia and Nyasaland, 1945–1954' (OUP 1959), Inter-territorial Corporate income payments were negligible in 1953, but this position would not obtain in later years considering the number of branches, particularly in Zambia, which have been set up since 1953, and which were under the control of Companies resident in Rhodesia.

Source: *National Accounts and Balance of Payments of Northern Rhodesia, Nyasaland and Southern Rhodesia, 1954–1963*, Central Statistical Office, Salisbury, Tables 143, 98, 54 and 184.

allocation itself were to have a major influence on the possibilities of development policy, on the allocation of resources, and finally on the costs and benefits of Federation to the respective countries.

The division of responsibilities as between the Federal government and the territorial governments in respect of matters directly affecting economic development was briefly as follows. In relation to social services, non-African and higher education and health were federal responsibilities but African primary and secondary education were a territorial responsibility. As to agriculture, the Federal government took responsibility for non-African agriculture in Zambia and Rhodesia whereas the territorial governments had responsibility for African agriculture. In Malawi the territorial government was responsible for all agriculture, African and non-African. Commerce and industry, including responsibility for external trade and trade agreements, were in federal hands, as was currency and banking.

On the revenue side, fiscal power lay predominantly with the Federal government. The two main sources of tax revenue in the area were income tax and customs and excise duties, of which the first was more important than the second. The right to levy these taxes was reserved to the Federal government, although the territories were empowered to levy and receive the proceeds from a surcharge of up to 20 per cent on the basic income tax levied by the Federal government. The whole of the proceeds from customs and excise duties (except on motor spirit) was retained by the Federal government. The proceeds of the income tax on the other hand were divided up among the four governments, and formed the major source of revenue of the territorial governments. Other territorial revenues were derived from the supplementary income tax, poll taxes, licences, and in the case of Zambia, from mineral royalties. The structure of revenue is illustrated for 1963 in Table 5.

Initially the Federal Constitution provided for the following shares of the basic income tax to be paid to the territories: Rhodesia 13 per cent; Zambia 17 per cent; Malawi 6 per cent. These shares were fixed so that each territory would be in a position to maintain the facilities for which it retained responsibility at their existing (pre-federal) level. Initially agreed revenue allocation arrangements in a federation rarely remain satisfactory with the passage of time. In Central Africa provision was made for a Fiscal Review Committee to reconsider the allocation from time to time. In 1957, on its recommendation the shares of basic income tax were revised from July 1, 1957, so that Rhodesia and Zambia each received 1 per cent more; Malawi's share remained unchanged.

It is arguable that even after this revision the relative growth of shared revenues failed to match the responsibilities of the various levels of government so that for instance, too much was spent on Federal services and too little on matters for which the territorial governments were responsible. The issue is a complex one, which not only raises questions concerning the impact of the Federal financial system on the welfare of non-Africans for which the Federal government was responsible, as opposed to Africans whose welfare was directly affected mainly by the operations of the territorial governments, but also issues of resource allocation and strategy in relation to economic development. In the following section we turn to a discussion of some aspects of development policy at the Federal level.

2. DEVELOPMENT PLANS AND DEVELOPMENT STRATEGY

Throughout the decade the role of government in economic development was seen mainly as to provide satisfactory conditions for the operation and development of private enterprise which was itself regarded as the driving force for economic growth. Federal expenditures for development therefore took the form mainly of building up an adequate infrastructure with the object of promoting foreign investment. During the decade a series of four year development plans were published covering the periods 1954–57, 1955–59, 1957–61 and 1961–65. Each plan was reviewed and revised after two years. The 1957–61 Plan underwent revision after a year because of the change in the financial position which followed the drastic fall in the price of copper. These plans were admittedly not attempts to plan for the economy as a whole with detailed policies designed to achieve particular rates of growth, but means of planning the Federal Government's capital expenditure on a co-ordinated basis having regard to the needs of the private sector. A Development Planning Group of officials obtained information on a voluntary basis about these plans and the level of government expenditure was determined in the light of those intentions, but the government had no means of compelling the submission of information on planned activities, nor of seeing that the plans of the private sector were implemented. The role of Government and the functions of the plans are well expressed in the following quotations:

'The Federal Government's development plan does not represent a comprehensive blueprint for the economic progress of the Federation during the period July 1, 1957, to June 30, 1961. The plan is an allocation of capital expenditure between those sectors of the economy for which the Federal Government is directly responsible,

Table 5. *Current account of Central Governments 1963*

Revenue (£m)

	Rhodesia		Zambia		Malawi	
	Federal revenue	Territorial revenue	Federal revenue	Territorial revenue	Federal revenue	Territorial revenue
1. *Interest and dividends, rents and profits*	6·8	3·7	2·1	4·5	0·4	0·5
2. *Taxes on income*						
Income tax	13·0	9·7	16·4	11·6	−1·2	2·9
Poll tax	—	3·0	—	0·1	—	1·1
Services etc.	—	1·3	—	—	—	—
3. *Taxes on production and expenditure*						
Customs and excise	11·9	4·6	4·9	0·3	1·2	0·4
Licences etc.	—	3·2	—	0·7	—	0·4
Royalties	—	0·4	—	2·7	—	—
4. *Current transfers from abroad*	—	—	—	0·4	—	5·6
5. *Other*	—	1·0	—	0·2	—	—
Net reimbursement from other governments	−2·0	2·0	−0·6	0·6	−0·7	0·7
	29·7	28·9	22·8	21·1	−0·3	11·6

Table 5—*continued*

Central Africa: Total federal revenue	Central Africa: Grand total federal and territorial revenue		Expenditure (£m): Rhodesia	Zambia	Malawi	Federal	Total Federal and Territorial expenditures
		1. *Economic services*					
9·3	18·0	Agriculture and non mineral resources	1·0	2·3	0·9	4·0	8·2
		Mineral resources, manufacturing and construction	0·4	0·6	0·1	0·6	1·7
		Transport, storage and Communication	—	—	0·2	0·9	1·1
		2. *Community services*					
28·2	52·4	Roads and					
—	4·2	waterways	3·0	1·0	0·1	—	4·1
—	1·3	Water supply,					
		sanitation and fire	0·1	0·4 }			
		protection			} 0·1	—	0·5
		Other	0·4	0·6 }		0·5	1·6
		3. *Social services*					
		Education	5·5	3·4	1·5	7·9	18·3
18·0	23·3	Health	0·3	0·1	0·3	7·5	8·2
—	4·3	Other	2·2	0·5	—	0·3	3·0
—	3·1						
—	6·0	4. *General services*					
		General Administration	3·1	3·1	1·6	3·7	11·5
		Defence	—	—	—	10·5	10·5
		Justice and Police	5·0	4·0	1·3	1·3	11·6
—	1·2	5. *Other*	6·3	5·7	2·9	13·9	28·8
-3·3	—						
52·2	114·1		27·3	21·7	9·0	51·1	109·1

Source: 'National Accounts and Balance of Northern Rhodesia, Nyasaland and Southern Rhodesia 1954–1963'. Central Statistical Office, Salisbury.

having regard to the availability of finance and to the expansion which is expected to occur in the private sector'.[1]

'It is the policy of the Federal Government to ensure that private enterprise participates in the economy over as wide a field as possible and to focus the economic activity of Government on the creation of the best possible climate for expansion, including the provision of basic services.'[2]

The other notable aspect of Federal development expenditure policy concerned what was termed 'less productive expenditure'—Government services in the social and non-economic field. Here the intention was that this type of expenditure should not be permitted to rise at a rate faster than the national income.[3] This emphasis on infrastructure expenditure and the small role assigned to social services is illustrated in the 1959–63 Development Plan summarized in Table 6. It can be seen that of the total planned expenditure of £77 m, £57 m or 74 per cent of the total was to be used for economic services compared with £9·5 m or 12 per cent of the total for social services.

The provision of adequate infrastructure is, though important, hardly an adequate basis for a development policy in African conditions. The Federal Government explicity recognized this in its statement of economic policy.[4] In this statement the fundamental obstacles to the achievement of a high rate of economic growth were identified as:

(i) the continued existence of the subsistence sector;
(ii) the shortage of capital and skills within the economy;
(iii) the existence and mounting severity of unemployment and restrictions on the use of land.

To the extent that this was so, it is evident that one limitation on the development of an effective Federal development policy lay in the allocation of functions between the territorial government and the Federal government which necessarily prevented the Federal government from doing much about some of these problems, either through its expenditure policy or through other policy measures. As we have seen, the responsibility for African agriculture and for the subsistence

[1] Federation of Rhodesia and Nyasaland, *Economic Report*, 1960 Ministry of Economic Affairs, C. Fed. 151.

[2] *Federal Government Development Plan, 1962–65*, Ministry of Economic Affairs, 1962, C. Fed. 217.

[3] 1959–63 Development Plan, p. 7.

[4] *Federal Government Economic Policy: Principles*, 1962, C. Fed. 218.

Table 6. *Summary of the Development Plan, 1959–62*[a]
(£'000)

(*a*) *Annual expenditure by financial years*

	1959–60	1960–61	1961–62	1962–63	Total
Economic services					
Roads and bridges	1,829	2,130	1,681	1,410	7,050
Railways	4,908	2,909	2,128	797	10,742
Other transport	193	113	222	285	813
Posts and telecommunications	1,650	1,491	1,461	1,358	5,960
Electricity and power	18,422	7,897	3,017	1,691	31,027
Agriculture	204	124	70	61	459
Land and agricultural bank	100	100	100	100	400
Kariba Lake development	348	158	—	—	506
Subtotal	27,654	14,922	8,679	5,702	56,957
Social services					
Health	772	954	1,324	963	4,013
Education[b]	1,491	1,618	996	1,115	5,220
Other	126	78	92	38	334
Subtotal	2,389	2,650	2,412	2,116	9,567
General administrative services	1,067	1,003	764	656	3,490
Miscellaneous					
Contingency provision	650	400	1,600	1,800	4,450
Estimated development expenditure on revenue votes	500	500	500	500	2,000
Add net estimated underspending brought forward	—	100	100	100	300
Subtotal	1,150	1,000	2,200	2,400	6,750
Grand total	32,260	19,575	14,055	10,874	76,764

[*Continued overleaf*

sector lay with the territorial governments. Similarly, restrictions on the use of land remained a territorial responsibility. The shortage of skilled manpower was directly related to the adequacy of educational provisions at all levels, but a major base, African primary and secondary education, was a territorial responsibility. The Federal Govern-

Table 6—*continued*

(*b*) *Annual finance by fiscal years*

	1959–60	1960–61	1961–62	1962–63	Total
Revenue provision for development	1,000	—	—	—	1,000
Development expenditure on revenue votes	500	500	500	500	2,000
Loan recoveries	900	1,000	1,375	1,400	4,675
Special project finance	960	1,631	1,395	1,100	5,086
Kariba Project finance	16,841	6,391	1,721	434	25,387
Development resources of public corporations	677	682	637	637	2,633
	20,878	10,204	5,628	4,071	40,781
Less: Loan repayments	1,106	90	90	90	1,376
	19,772	10,114	5,538	3,981	39,405
Add: Net balance from 1958–59	677	—	—	—	677
	20,449	10,114	5,538	3,981	40,082
Amount to be borrowed	11,811	9,461	8,517	6,893	36,682
Total	32,260	19,575	14,055	10,874	76,764

Notes: [a] This plan refers only to those sections of the economy for which the Federal Government was responsible.

[b] Education includes expenditure on an African Agricultural College.

Source: Development Plan, 1959–63, Ministry of Economic Affairs (C. Fed 122) Schedules A and B.

ment was of course, in a position to play a very important role in relation to policies for overcoming the shortage of capital and skills. Through its control over non-African and higher education and immigration it was certainly able to influence the supply of skilled manpower, but as has been seen, the relative weight placed on education in the Federal plan was modest. Likewise, the Federal Government was in a strategic position, through budgetary, monetary and exchange policies, to influence capital supply. Some aspects of its financial policies, which of course also had other purposes, are discussed later. But the major responsibility for implementing policies designed to overcome some of the more fundamental obstacles of development lay with the territorial governments, and demanded for their solution institutional and political changes.

Table 7. *Sources of investment finance*
(£m)

	1954	1955	1956	1957	1958	1959	1960	1961	1962	1963	Total 1954–63
Personal savings	7·6	11·4	22·7	20·3	25·0	31·1	23·6	29·6	26·6	26·5	224·4
Government savings	15·0	25·7	31·3	32·9	21·4	11·0	16·4	20·8	17·6	9·9	202·0
Corporate savings	41·8	55·9	54·0	23·4	25·8	62·5	84·1	62·1	54·4	62·7	526·7
External	14·2	15·4	36·5	72·5	62·2	15·0	6·1	11·0	4·8	−14·4	223·3
Gross domestic investment	82·7	116·6	147·1	158·3	135·3	112·0	127·4	128·9	102·5	88·1	1,189·9
Total domestic expenditure	333·8	391·0	453·6	498·3	487·2	489·9	523·2	544·8	534·5	541·5	4,797·8
Investment % of domestic expenditure	25	30	32	32	28	23	24	24	19	16	25

Note: Differences between the total of available finance and gross domestic investment are due to errors and omissions.
Source: *National Accounts and Balance Payment of Northern Rhodesia, Nyasaland and Southern Rhodesia, 1954–63*, Salisbury 1964.

Evidently the Development Plans of the Federal Government did not provide a strategy for overcoming the fundamental problems of growth, but many of these problems lay outside its competence. Nor were the plans designed to control the private sector, and it would be inappropriate to evaluate them by reference to these objectives. It is possible to argue that the Federal view of the human factor in economic development was inadequate and that its provision for manpower development was at fault. Apart from this, two principal comments are suggested by a review of Federal Planning. First, even as planning documents for the public sector they left much to be desired. The financial analysis was of a rudimentary nature. The discussion of resources consisted merely of a statement of available finance. This sum was then deducted from planned expenditures and the balance presented as amounts to be borrowed. The form and nature of the borrowing was not specified, nor was availability assessed. Only capital expenditures were considered. Moreover the plans were purely financial documents and no attempt was made to assess the availability or otherwise of the real resources required. Nevertheless, within their very limited sphere—in part chosen, in part imposed, Federal development expenditure policy may be said to have successfully overcome a variety of physical constraints to the development of private enterprise, most notably in relation to power and transport facilities.

3. FINANCIAL POLICY AND INVESTMENT

Investment was a major engine of growth in the decade. During the early years of the Federation it amounted to one-third of domestic expenditure. It reached its peak in the years 1956–58. Thereafter it declined steadily until at the end of the period it had fallen to £88 m, 56 per cent of its peak level, and representing only 16 per cent of domestic expenditures. Its development over the period and its financing are shown in Table 7. The character of Gross Fixed Capital Formation is shown in Table 8.

External finance played as can be seen, a major part in supporting the high rate of investment which underpinned the growth of income during the decade. Over the period, of a total gross investment of £1200 m, some £223 m, or one-fifth, was provided from external sources. The most conspicuous example of foreign investment was the Kariba Hydro-electric project. Of the £79·4 m which the first stage of the scheme cost, £46·6 m came from external sources, of which the World Bank provided £28·7 m.

A substantial part of the external contribution to investment arose

Table 8. *Central Africa: gross fixed capital formation*
(£m)

	1954			
	Rhodesia	Zambia	Malawi	Central Africa
1. *By purchaser*				
Federal Government	1·6	1·2	0·3	3·1
Territorial Government	3·6	6·5	1·1	11·2
Local authorities	2·7	2·1	0·1	4·9
Government enterprises	4·2	1·2	0·1	5·5
Public corporations	10·5	3·6	0·2	14·3
Private enterprise	24·2	22·9	1·3	48·4
Total	46·8	37·5	3·1	87·4
2. *By type*				
Building and Works	24·6	18·3	2·2	45·1
Transport equipment				12·5
Plant, machinery and other equipment	20·7	17·0	0·8	26·0
Land improvement	0·7	0·2	0·1	1·0
Mine development	0·8	2·0	—	2·8
Total	46·8	37·5	3·1	87·4
3. *By industrial use*				
Agriculture	5·0	1·2	0·4	6·6
Mining	5·0	14·3	—	19·3
Manufacturing	4·3	1·2	0·4	5·9
Building and construction	1·5	1·1	0·3	2·9
Electricity and water	6·7	4·0	0·2	10·9
Transport and communications	10·4	4·2	0·4	15·0
Distribution	2·1	1·4	0·2	3·7
Banking, insurance, finance and real estate	5·0	5·1	0·6	10·7
Public administration	1·7	2·8	0·4	4·9
Services	1·0	0·8	0·2	2·0
Unallocated	4·1	1·4	—	5·5
Total	46·8	37·5	3·1	87·4

Table 8—*continued*

	1958			
	Rhodesia	Zambia	Malawi	Central Africa
1. *By purchaser*				
Federal Government	4·6	3·1	0·9	8·6
Territorial Government	5·8	5·0	2·5	13·3
Local authorities	5·3	3·6	0·3	9·2
Government enterprises	10·0	1·6	0·1	11·7
Public corporations	19·8	10·0	0·5	30·3
Private enterprise	39·0	20·7	2·2	61·9
Total	84·5	44·0	6·5	135·0
2. *By type*				
Building and Works	50·2	25·0	4·7	79·9
Transport equipment	}			15·1
Plant, machinery and other equipment	}32·2	14·9	1·7	33·7
Land improvement	1·4	0·2	0·1	1·7
Mine development	0·7	3·9	—	4·6
Total	84·5	44·0	6·5	135·0
3. *By industrial use*				
Agriculture	7·4	1·0	1·0	9·4
Mining	3·2	14·2	—	17·4
Manufacturing	12·6	1·1	0·4	14·1
Building and construction	1·1	0·7	0·2	2·0
Electricity and water	22·6	9·5	0·4	32·5
Transport and communications	15·4	6·3	1·4	23·1
Distribution	4·4	0·4	0·4	5·2
Banking, insurance, finance and real estate	7·8	4·6	1·1	13·5
Public administration	3·3	2·9	1·1	7·3
Services	2·8	2·0	0·5	5·3
Unallocated	3·9	1·3	—	5·2
Total	84·5	44·0	6·5	135·0

Table 8—*continued*

	1963			
	Rhodesia	Zambia	Malawi	Central Africa
1. *By purchaser*				
Federal Government	2·4	1·0	0·5	3·9
Territorial Government	5·3	5·6	3·6	14·5
Local authorities	2·9	2·2	0·3	5·4
Government enterprises	3·5	0·8	0·1	4·4
Public corporations	5·3	2·9	0·3	8·5
Private enterprise	26·5	20·5	2·1	49·1
Total	45·9	33·0	6·9	85·8
2. *By type*				
Building and Works	24·6	14·5	4·3	43·4
Transport equipment				12·2
Plant, machinery and other equipment	19·5	13·3	2·3	22·9
Land improvement	1·3	1·2	0·3	2·8
Mine development	0·5	4·0	—	4·5
Total	45·9	33·0	6·9	85·8
3. *By industrial use*				
Agriculture	8·9	1·8	1·0	11·7
Mining	2·8	14·1	—	16·9
Manufacturing	8·5	1·3	0·1	9·9
Building and construction	0·1	0·1	—	0·2
Electricity and water	4·7	2·1	0·6	7·4
Transport and communications	9·0	3·7	1·3	14·0
Distribution	2·6	1·4	0·3	4·3
Banking, insurance, finance and real estate	3·0	1·9	0·7	5·6
Public administration	1·9	2·5	1·6	6·0
Services	3·0	3·6	1·3	7·9
Unallocated	1·4	0·5	—	1·9
Total	45·9	33·0	6·9	85·8

Note: Difference between Central African totals here and Gross Domestic Investment figures in Table 7 due to omission of stock charges here.
Source: As Table 7

directly from borrowing undertaken by the four Governments. In Central Africa all loans, external and internal, were normally raised by the Federal Government on behalf of the four Governments. Under the Constitution external loans had to be approved by the Loan Council consisting of one member from each of the four Governments. The Federal Constitution originally provided that, in the absence of unanimous agreement on some other share, the proceeds of such loans should be allocated in the following proportions: Federal Government, 64 per cent; Rhodesia 13 per cent; Zambia 17 per cent; Malawi 6 per cent. Following the recommendations of the Federal Review Committee these proportions were changed with effect from July 1, 1957 so as to reduce slightly the Federal Government's share and to increase the shares of the Rhodesian and the Zambian Governments.

Throughout the period stated domestic savings formed a very high proportion of GDP, ranging from 17 to 25 per cent, and as can be seen from Table 7, they provided £966 m, in total of the finance for investment. However, £527 m of this sum consisted of undistributed profits and depreciation provisions. Much of this was accounted for by externally controlled firms so these estimates of domestic savings therefore overstate the contribution of internally controlled savings.[1]

The size of domestic savings nevertheless reflects the importance of financial policies designed to encourage and facilitate domestic savings. In the monetary field this partly took the form of the provision of savings facilities. The European population had a wide range of facilities, and savings among the African population were successfully promoted through the Post Office Savings Bank. Emphasis on the promotion of personal savings was reflected in the relatively low rates of income tax in the Federation.[2]

Perhaps the most interesting aspect of financial policy in Central Africa was the developing use of monetary policy and institutions as a means of keeping the economy in balance through the establishment of the Central Bank and the later creation of a local money market. The use of monetary policy in the Federation went well beyond what had been attempted hitherto in tropical Africa. When the Federation was established in 1953, control over the money supply continued for the time being to be in the hands of the existing Central African

[1] *Economic Development for Africa, South of the Sahara*, (*Edited* E. A. G. Robinson, Proceedings of a Conference held by the International Economic Association), W. L. Taylor, *Problems of Economic Development of the Federation of Rhodesia and Nyasaland*, Macmillan, London, 1964, pp. 228–29.

[2] For comparative data on taxation rates in English-speaking African countries at this time see J. E. Due, *Taxation and Economic Development in Tropical Africa*, MIT Press, 1963.

Currency Board. The Board was responsible for the issue of currency which, in the established fashion, was required to have 100 per cent backing in foreign currency, and there was no monetary policy. In 1956 the Bank of Rhodesia and Nyasaland was established and took over the assets and liabilities of the Currency Board. The Bank assumed responsibility not only for currency issue but also for controlling the money supply as a whole. As instruments of policy the bank was empowered to fix reserve ratios for the commercial banks, and a discount rate was established. The Bank was required to maintain reserves in the form of gold, sterling or foreign assets convertible into gold or sterling equal to at least 25 per cent of its public liability. In 1959 a money market was created with the setting up of the Discount Company of Rhodesia Ltd., and the British and Rhodesian Discount House Ltd. The discount houses operated on the basis of call money from the banking and financial institutions. These funds were employed to buy Government and commercial bills. The development of the money market not only facilitated the retention of local money in the Federation but it also provided a flexible mechanism through which the government could exert influence over the level of credit and of demand in the economy.

During the early booming years of the Federation, monetary policy was designed to restrict credit in order to limit domestic demand.[1] The restrictive measures of 1956 were directed towards controlling the speculative acquisition or construction of real estate, and limiting non-essential imports. The later restrictive measures of 1958 were particularly aimed at imports and were reinforced by restrictions on hire purchase transactions in connection with imported consumer durables. This early credit squeeze was brought about not so much by technical measures, but mainly through moral suasion. It depended for its success on the authority and respect which the Bank had established for itself among the financial institutions.

In March 1957 the Bank assumed responsibility for exchange control which at that time was applied only to countries outside the sterling area. In February 1961 in response to the marked deterioration on external capital account, exchange control was extended to the sterling area. This change supplemented an upward revision which had already occurred in the interest rate structure, with the object of keeping investment funds in the country, but which did not have sufficient effect. The Bank's first discount rate, quoted on August 1, 1957 was 4½ per cent. It remained at this level until August 3, 1960 when it was raised by ½ per cent. In June 1961 it was further increased to 5½ per cent. The introduction of exchange control

[1] See *Annual Report*, 1961, Bank of Rhodesia and Nyasaland.

eventually made it possible to reduce the rate to 5 per cent in 9 May, 1962 and in January 1963 it was further reduced to 4½ per cent.

Apart from these measures, the Bank also influenced the money supply by open-market operations. With the growth of the money market there was a concomitant growth in the supply of Treasury Bills to the market, which reached a peak in August/September 1962 with six successive weekly issues of £3 million each. The size of the issue fluctuated directly with government's seasonal demands for short-term finance. The Bank itself held varying quantities of Treasury Bills which meant that the market holdings of Bills fluctuated more than the total issue. Thus, the Bank through its holding of Bills was able to control the supply of money to the market.

The growth of the money market eventually enabled the Bank to employ a series of fairly flexible controls over the economy, in support of the policy of maintaining internal monetary stability. In addition, the growth of the money market enabled the government and other financial institutions to make use of the available short-term money supply.[1] These were not inconsiderable achievements. Initially there had been some hesitation by the Banks about the likely efficacy of orthodox monetary policies within the area's unsophisticated money market. For example:

'As in other countries, the level of the bank rate exerts an influence on other rates and it is therefore likely to affect the level of credit throughout the financial system. However, it cannot be so effective an instrument of control as in more highly developed centres, and on several occasions, therefore, the Bank has relied more on moral suasion reinforced by the powers to fix statutory deposits and liquidity ratios'.[2]

Nevertheless this initial hesitancy as to the effectiveness of Bank Rate was not converted into inertia. As has been seen, Bank Rate was frequently changed in attempts to influence conditions, but the liquidity ratios, initially set at 3 per cent for time liabilities and 8 per cent for demand liabilities were also varied from time to time.[3] In

[1] For a comprehensive treatment of the Federation's money markets see V. P. Romilly, 'The Money Market in the Federation of Rhodesia and Nyasaland', *The Bankers' Magazine*, December, 1962, pp. 401–07.

[2] Bank of Rhodesia and Nyasaland, *Annual Report*, 1961.

[3] These were implemented in August 1957 and resulted in the amounts held by the commercial banks with the Central Bank rising from working balances totalling £131,709 at the end of December 1956 to an overall amount of £8,798,585 at the end of December 1957.

February 1960 in response to a shortage of internal credit, the demand liability ratio was reduced to 6 per cent and both ratios were subsequently maintained at these levels.

In this section on financial policy, monetary policy has been deliberately emphasized, since it was an innovation in the Federation, and moreover it has been little used in other tropical African countries. Central African experience should therefore be of particular interest.[1] The role of fiscal policy in the period should not of course be underrated, but its methods were basically similar in scope, method and achievement to those of other English speaking African countries.

4. AGRICULTURE

Agriculture is a major industry in Central Africa, both in terms of output and employment. Throughout the decade, except in 1954 and 1963 about 20 per cent of the area's output originated in this industry. As already indicated, its relative importance was very different in the three countries however. In 1963 it accounted for 47 per cent of GDP in Malawi, 20 per cent in Rhodesia and 12 per cent in Zambia. In the area as a whole the industry accounted for 32 per cent of recorded employment in 1963. Figures of recorded employment of course greatly understate the numbers occupied in the industry since these figures relate only to the modern commercial agricultural sector. In fact the greater part of the population finds its occupation in the rural household sector and is engaged in producing agricultural products partly for self consumption and partly for the market by traditional methods. Fruitful analysis of the area's agricultural sector demands that a distinction is drawn between these sectors, which correspond largely to the distinction between European farming and plantations on the one hand and African farming on the other.

The character of the two sectors has been considerably influenced by land allocation policies. In Rhodesia land was allocated on a racial basis under the Land Apportionment Act. Of the total area about one half is assigned to Europeans, mainly in the High Veld. About two-fifths is reserved for African use, but the bulk of the African population is in reserves which comprise about a quarter

[1] Since this chapter was written, a full length study of monetary policy in the Federation has been written to which the reader is referred. See R. A. Sowelem, *Towards Independence in a Developing Economy: An Analysis of the Monetary Experience of the Federation of Rhodesia and Nyasaland, 1952–1963*, Allen and Unwin, London.

of the total area. In Zambia there was a similar basis of land allocation, but the European area was confined to less than 6 per cent of the total area, mainly found along the line-of-rail. In Malawi 5 per cent of the land is held by Europeans. European holdings in Central Africa averaged in 1959 approximately 5,000 acres. The average size of African holdings is not known, but they were very much smaller than European holdings, and with existing techniques, pressure on the land has become acute in many areas in Rhodesia and Malawi.

Over the decade output from the European sector increased from £29·1 m in 1954 to £53·7 m in 1963 so that its share of GDP rose from 8·9 per cent in the earlier year to 9·6 per cent in 1963. Of the absolute increase 1 per cent originated in Malawi, 88 per cent in Rhodesia and 11 per cent in Zambia. Output was partly for domestic consumption and partly for export. The composition of sales (gross output) is shown for 1963 in the following table.

Table 9. *European agriculture. Value of gross output 1963*

	Rhodesia		Zambia		Malawi		Total Central Africa	
	£ m	%	£ m	%	£ m	%	£ m	%
Tobacco	32·2	53	2·9	43	1·4	25	36·5	50
Maize	7·5	12	1·7	25	—	—	9·2	13
Sugar	6·3	10	—	—	—	—	6·3	9
Livestock	7·3	12	1·8	27	0·1	2	9·2	13
Tea	0·4	1	—	—	3·5	64	3·9	5
Other	6·9	12	0·3	5	0·5	9	7·7	10
Total	60·6	100	6·7	100	5·5	100	72·8	100

Source: Agricultural Production in Southern Rhodesia, Northern Rhodesia and Nyasaland, 1963.

The sources of the increased output which occurred mainly in Rhodesia and Zambia are of some interest. Over the period the acreage under crops expanded by only 10 per cent so that an expansion in acreage could not account for more than part of the increase. Increased labour inputs are also insufficient to account for much of the total increase in output—employment of Africans increased by only 15 per cent and that of non-Africans by 45 per cent. The available evidence suggests that the increased output has been achieved mainly by a higher degree of capital intensity and improved technology. Thus expenditure on fertilizer and insecticide increased by almost

125 per cent and on vehicle repairs and spares by 85 per cent.[1] The relatively large increase in non-African employment points in the same direction. These changes were associated with a change in the structure of crop production; maize acreage declined by 8 per cent and the acreage devoted to Viginia flue-cured tobacco increased by 30 per cent.[2]

The changing role and composition of African agriculture in the period is broadly indicated in Table 3. Over the period to 1961–63 total GDP increased by about 65 per cent. The agricultural output of the African Household Sector increased from £40·7 to £55·7 m, an increase of about 37½ per cent. Thus whereas at the beginning of the period its share of GDP was 12·3 per cent by the end of the period it was 10·2 per cent. At the beginning of the period the share of monetary output in the total output of African agriculture was about 17½ per cent. At the end of the period it was somewhat higher, perhaps approaching a quarter. Nevertheless, the rise in African money incomes in agriculture did not keep pace with the rise of income in the economy as a whole. No substantial improvement is discernible in the movement from the subsistence economy to the cash economy, which is normally a condition of substantial agricultural improvement. It must be emphasized that the estimates of production for the subsistence sector are not reliable. Given the techniques generally in use the maintenance even of existing productivity became an increasingly doubtful hypothesis for Rhodesia and parts of Malawi as the decade wore on.

It should be borne in mind that estimates of the shares of the cash and the subsistence sectors must be treated as no more than a rough esimate since the figures for subsistence output are little more than guesses. In addition the figure for sales is possibly understated because of unrecorded sales within the Rural Household Sector. Nevertheless, there is little evidence of major improvements in this sector over the period. Indeed there are grounds (which are mentioned later) for thinking that productivity may have fallen as a result of increasing under-employment in the rural areas. Agricultural improvement in the traditional sector represented a major challenge for policy in Central Africa.

The responsibility for action in this area rested, as already noted, with the territorial governments. Each territory approached the problem of transforming the largely subsistence basis of the agricultural sector in somewhat different ways. The major instrument

[1] *The Input/Output Accounts for European Agriculture in Southern Rhodesia and Northern Rhodesia*, Supplement to the Monthly Digest of Statistics, October 1963, Central Statistical Office, Salisbury, Southern Rhodesia. [2] *Ibid.*

for agricultural improvement in the traditional sector in all three countries was, of course, extension work designed to bring about improvements in productivity by spreading knowledge of improved techniques and changing the character and methods of production of traditional farmers, and by promoting production for cash. Initially these attempts to bring about changes in techniques were not accompanied by any attempts to change the structure of the land tenure system. In Rhodesia from 1926, under the direction of E. D. Alvord, an American missionary, Africans received training in particular methods of farming which they were then expected to demonstrate to peasant farmers. In 1928 this approach was supplemented by a policy of encouraging the use of one specific area in the neighbourhood of a village for the production of crops. The potentialities of irrigation were realized and several small projects were undertaken. The scale of the effort before 1951, however, was small, and traditional methods involving shifting cultivation continued. Even by 1954, when extension services for African agriculture had undergone a major expansion, only 25 per cent of African farmers were believed to have been 'influenced by demonstrators'.[1]

Further, an effective improvement policy for traditional agriculture requires measures on a variety of fronts, not merely extension work. Marketing methods need to be improved. Above all, policies are needed to ensure that land is allocated efficiently and that cooperating factors of production can be made available. In particular these issues raise the problem of land tenure and the provision of credit. Policies in these areas were developed only after 1945.

The principal changes occurred in Rhodesia. Here the Native Land Husbandry Act of 1951 (which was not implemented until 1955) was the instrument devised for bringing about further improvements in the productivity of African farmers. Its most important single innovation was to enable a cultivator to receive rights to farm a fixed piece of land. This right was negotiable but the piece of land could not be fragmented. This innovation cut right across the traditional methods of land allocation. Grazing rights permitting an individual to graze a limited number of stock were also instituted. Finally the Act provided for the observance of certain farming practices. If these were not followed the owners of the land could be compelled to sell their title rights.

The Act had two immediate effects. In the first place it created a market in land rights and grazing rights. This market is performing an important economic function since increasingly land is allocated not according to tribal tradition but more in accordance with con-

[1] See *Report of the Chief Native Commissioner*, Salisbury 1954, page 4.

siderations of efficiency and productivity. The Act's second important effect was to create a landless group. An allocation of land was made only to those elegible persons who were present in each area at the time of allocation. Thus absentees, who were mainly migratory workers in the money economy, were dispossessed of their traditional tribal land rights. If they became unemployed they could no longer as of right return to the tribal areas where they could obtain a subsistence income. One of the objectives of the Act was to create stable urban and rural communities by abolishing the basis of the system of migratory labour. Not surprisingly it was unable by itself to achieve this objective. The former system of land tenure provided an ultimate security for African workers, but no such security system was provided in the money economy. The continuous decline in the employment of African workers in the early 1960's was consequently accompanied by pressure to make additional land available. An amendment to the Act made provision for grazing land to be made available temporarily for cultivation. Thus, in spite of the Act, unemployment in the money sector continued to be exported to the traditional farming areas where it became under-employment.

Thus the question whether the Act has led to increased productivity is not easy to answer. Available statistics do not permit firm conclusions to be drawn. But whether or not the productivity of African farmers has increased, several preconditions for economic development have certainly been created. The individual producer is freed of tribal obligations, is subjected to the forces of competition for land, and is unable automatically to fall back on the tribal structure for security, though family obligations inevitably weaken the force of this sanction. Land has become a negotiable asset although the producer was not able to mortgage his land to secure working capital.

The problem of credit is perhaps the major problem still confronting the African commercial farmer. A small scale attempt to deal with this problem has been made by the African Loan and Development Company which also aids traders, but its funds are very limited. One of its problems has been that the demand is for small loans. The cost of servicing these loans has been high and the rate of interest has had to be set correspondingly high.

In Zambia and Malawi there were no comparable attempts through such a measure as the Southern Rhodesian Land Husbandry Act to bring about forced institutional changes in the African agricultural economy. Nevertheless population pressure, soil exhaustion, and changes in the market for wage labour were destroying the basis on which traditional agricultural practice rested, and the transition to new systems presents intractable problems.

5. EMPLOYMENT AND EARNINGS

The salient facts about employment, the wage bill and earnings in Central Africa are set out in Table 10. In 1954 the employed labour force was about 1 million of which 91 per cent was African. By 1962 employment had scarcely increased and was estimated at 1,106,000, of which 88 per cent was African. Over the period African employment increased by 6 per cent and non-African by 37 per cent. The main employment sectors in the area as a whole were agriculture, domestic service, manufacturing, mining and building and construction. Employment in building and construction fluctuated during the period and although in 1963 it was the least important of the major sectors in terms of employment its share in peak years had been second only to that of agriculture.

One of the most striking features of the employment situation was the slow rate of growth exhibited by the employed labour force, by comparison with total output and total population. Over the period 1954–62 output increased by over 60 per cent and total population by about 30 per cent. Over the same period the proportion of the population in employment fell from 11·6 per cent to 9·8 per cent. This phenomenon has been analysed in detail for Rhodesia by D. S. Pearson,[1] but his findings seem to be applicable to the area as a whole. He considers employment trends and prospects in terms of the growth of demand in the economy, and the elasticity of demand for labour as an input with respect to output, in different sectors of the economy. He finds that the sectoral elasticities of demand for labour in mining, manufacturing and agriculture had been less than unity and that they might be expected to continue to be below unity. This phenomenon is explained in terms of an inherent tendency towards more capital intensive methods of production in the three leading sectors of the Rhodesian economy, due to factors in the financial and institutional framework. These factors include technology, interest rates, and, except in agriculture, a notable upward pressure on wages coming from the institutional side which produced an increase in the relative cost of labour, most notably in manufacturing industry. The implication of the analysis is that wage employment may be expected to continue to decline as a proportion of the total population. The wider significance of this trend evidently depends much on the extent to which the alternative to wage employment for the bulk of the population, namely peasant agriculture, can

[1] D. S. Pearson, 'Employment Trends in a Developing Economy: The case of Southern Rhodesia', *East African Economics Review*, June, 1964, Vol. II, No. 1.

Table 10. *Employment and earnings*

(*a*) 1954

Numbers employed ('000)

	Rhodesia		Zambia		Malawi	
	Afrs.	Non Afrs.	Afrs.	Non Afrs.	Afrs.	Non Afrs.
Agriculture	218·0	3·2	39·0	0·5	48·0	0·3
Mining and quarrying	62·4	2·9	44·1	6·8	0·4	—
Manufacturing	62·5	11·0	16·1	1·7	13·6	0·5
Building and construction	51·0	7·5	56·0	3·2	19·0	0·4
Electricity and water	5·2	1·2	2·4	—	1·0	—
Wholesale and retail trade	24·8	14·0	12·2	4·1	10·9	1·2
Banking, finance and insurance	0·8	3·2	0·2	0·6	0·1	0·1
Transport and communication	12·1	6·7	6·8	2·2	3·3	0·4
Government administration	13·4	5·9	14·3	2·0	8·0	0·5
Education	10·8	2·6	4·5	0·9	5·5	0·2
Health	2·9	1·8	4·1	0·6	2·5	0·2
Private domestic services	76·1	0·2	29·6	0·1	11·5	—
Other services	13·9	4·4	11·1	2·1	5·8	0·6
Total	554·0	64·4	240·0	24·8	130·0	4·3

(*b*) 1962

Numbers employed ('000)

	Rhodesia		Zambia		Malawi	
	Afrs.	Non Afrs.	Afrs.	Non Afrs.	Afrs.	Non Afrs.
Agriculture	243·9	4·5	38·7	0·7	52·6	0·5
Mining and quarrying	44·1	2·7	41·1	8·3	0·4	—
Manufacturing	73·4	15·8	17·4	2·9	12·4	0·7
Building and construction	36·8	6·1	23·9	1·9	15·0	0·4
Electricity and water	5·6	1·3	2·4	0·3	1·3	0·1
Wholesale and retail trade	33·0	18·4	14·8	5·6	13·4	1·5
Banking, finance and insurance	1·8	5·4	0·5	1·2	0·2	0·1
Transport and communication	16·6	10·2	9·6	3·1	6·0	0·7
Government administration	20·4	9·1	21·0	4·1	10·9	0·7
Education	14·2	5·2	9·5	1·6	5·6	0·5
Health	6·2	2·4	5·6	0·8	2·6	0·3
Private domestic services	95·2	0·3	36·2	0·1	8·7	—
Other services	20·4	7·2	10·1	2·7	6·0	0·7
Total	612·0	88·6	231·0	33·3	135·0	6·2

Table 10—*continued*

(*a*) 1954

	Average earnings (£)					
	Rhodesia		Zambia		Malawi	
	Afrs.	Non Afrs.	Afrs.	Non Afrs.	Afrs.	Non Afrs.
Agriculture	48	833	41	803	24	1,251
Mining and quarrying	83	1,169	132	2,120	36	694
Manufacturing	65	973	76	1,080	35	960
Building and construction	65	1,022	74	1,094	35	1,018
Electricity and water	71	1,118	65	1,179	54	891
Wholesale and retail trade	88	637	73	743	25	635
Banking, finance and insurance	87	896	86	793	77	927
Transport and communication	94	1,042	86	1,024	56	935
Government administration	79	923	76	990	73	1,114
Education	100	858	122	798	62	651
Health	79	722	73	783	70	696
Private domestic services	71	358	56	540	32	523
Other services	79	800	62	701	48	661
Total	64	884	78	1,237	35	853

(*b*) 1962

	Average earnings (£)					
	Rhodesia		Zambia		Malawi	
	Afrs.	Non Afrs.	Afrs.	Non Afrs.	Afrs.	Non Afrs.
Agriculture	61	1,166	64	1,230	38	1,604
Mining and quarrying	109	1,512	296	2,563	49	919
Manufacturing	164	1,297	142	1,342	79	1,269
Building and construction	122	1,289	127	1,420	68	1,234
Electricity and water	147	1,391	130	1,830	94	1,580
Wholesale and retail trade	158	1,031	149	991	51	849
Banking, finance and insurance	184	1,215	165	1,104	228	1,073
Transport and communication	209	1,302	194	1,384	114	1,163
Government administration	156	1,256	157	1,392	125	1,446
Education	200	1,137	192	1,142	103	929
Health	150	825	120	1,124	118	1,290
Private domestic services	102	480	90	659	68	330
Other services	135	986	114	948	74	794
Total	107	1,183	151	1,548	65	1,111

Table 10—*continued*

(*a*) 1954

Total earnings (£m)

	Rhodesia		Zambia		Malawi	
	Afrs.	Non Afrs.	Afrs.	Non Afrs.	Afrs.	Non Afrs.
Agriculture	10·5	2·7	1·6	0·4	1·1	0·4
Mining and quarrying	5·2	3·3	5·9	14·5	—	—
Manufacturing	4·1	10·7	1·2	1·8	0·5	0·4
Building and construction	3·3	7·7	4·1	3·5	0·7	0·4
Electricity and water	0·4	1·3	0·2	—	0·1	—
Wholesale and retail trade	2·2	8·9	0·9	3·0	0·3	0·7
Banking, finance and insurance	0·1	2·8	—	0·5	—	0·1
Transport and communication	1·1	7·0	0·6	2·2	0·2	0·4
Government administration	1·1	5·4	1·1	2·0	0·6	0·6
Education	1·1	2·2	0·5	0·7	0·3	0·2
Health	0·2	1·3	0·3	0·4	0·2	0·1
Private domestic services	5·4	0·1	1·7	—	0·4	—
Other services	1·1	3·5	0·7	1·5	0·3	0·4
Total	35·7	56·9	18·8	30·7	4·6	3·7

(*b*) 1962

Total earnings (£ m)

	Rhodesia		Zambia		Malawi	
	Afrs.	Non Afrs.	Afrs.	Non Afrs.	Afrs.	Non Afrs.
Agriculture	14·9	5·2	2·5	0·8	2·0	0·6
Mining and quarrying	4·8	4·0	12·2	21·4	—	—
Manufacturing	12·0	20·5	2·5	3·9	1·0	0·9
Building and construction	4·5	7·9	3·0	2·7	1·0	0·5
Electricity and water	0·8	1·8	0·3	0·5	0·1	0·2
Wholesale and retail trade	5·2	19·0	2·2	5·5	0·7	1·3
Banking, finance and insurance	0·3	6·6	0·1	1·3	—	0·1
Transport and communication	3·5	13·3	1·9	4·3	0·7	0·7
Government administration	3·2	11·4	3·3	5·7	1·4	1·1
Education	2·8	5·9	1·8	1·8	0·6	0·4
Health	0·9	2·0	0·7	0·9	0·3	0·3
Private domestic services	9·7	0·1	3·3	0·1	0·6	—
Other services	2·8	7·1	1·2	2·6	0·4	0·5
Total	65·5	104·8	34·8	51·5	8·8	6·8

Source: *National Accounts and Balance of Payments of Northern Rhodesia Nyasaland and Southern Rhodesia, 1954–1963*, Central Statistical Office, Salisbury, 1964.

provide incomes comparable to those to be earned in the employment sector.

The facts about the structure of earnings and their increase over the period have already been set out in Table 10 above. The institutional background which contributed to the situation displayed will now be briefly outlined. In Rhodesia prior to 1960 the Industrial Conciliation Act in force made the formation of African trade unions illegal. In 1960, however, a new Industrial Conciliation Act was enacted which recognized the rights of all employed persons to enter into trade unions. Under this legislation any union formed had to be non-racial in character, although the establishment of separate, racial branches of the union was permitted. The Act imposed a variety of limitations on the functions of the unions and limited the membership of each to the workers of a single industry. Limitations were also imposed on the disposal of union funds especially with regard to contributions to political parties. Industrial Councils and Boards were established composed of representatives of workers and employers and chaired by a civil servant. Their purpose was to lay down minimum wages for each industry, but in a number of industries they went further and laid down graduated wage and salary scales. The difference between an Industrial Council and an Industrial Board lay in the fact that in the case of Industrial Councils the workers' representatives were trade unionists, but in those industries where there were no trade unions and, therefore, no elected workers' representatives, an Industrial Board was formed, composed of individuals nominated by the Minister to represent the workers. Neither in agriculture nor in domestic service, two large employers of African labour, were Industrial Councils or Boards established and there was no minimum wage legislation for these industries.

In Zambia and Malawi during the period there was no minimum wage legislation. The mining industry in Zambia was however heavily unionized, and the unions played a major role in the determination of wage and employment policies. These unions did not come under the jurisdiction of the Industrial Conciliation Act and were organized on racial lines. Initially, occupational categories were created which were exclusively African or European but for different reasons neither the African nor European mining unions wished this categorization to continue. The African unions held that many of the so-called European jobs could be filled by Africans at lower rates of pay. On the other hand, the European unions maintained that when job classifications were transferred to open categories the existing rates of pay for the job should continue. This conflict of views is, in essence, the traditional argument concerning dilution of a skilled occupational group by unskilled workers, claimed to be less efficient. Transport was the only other industry in Zambia where trade unions played an important role, and here only in regard to the Rhodesia Railways which performed an inter-territorial function and did not come under the jurisdiction of the territorial governments.

Over the period 1954 to 1963 average earnings for Africans increased by 84 per cent and for non-Africans by 34 per cent. The increase recorded in different industries varied greatly. Among Africans for instance, average earnings increased by 47 per cent in agriculture; in mining and quarrying average earnings doubled, and in manufacturing the increase was 173 per cent. In the four major employment sectors in 1962 the average wage level was highest in mining and quarrying, followed by manufacturing, domestic service and agriculture. This order corresponds closely to the strength of the trade union movement in each sector and country, although wage differences also, of course, reflected skill differentials.

The supply of African labour to the labour market in Central Africa rests on migration. This occurs within each territory, between territories, and there was also an inflow of labour from outside. Data from the Rhodesia Census of 1962 will be used to indicate its character and extent. Of the African population employed at the time of the Census, 53 per cent was born in Rhodesia, 23 per cent came from Malawi, 7 per cent from Zambia and 11 per cent from Portugese East Africa. An analysis of the sex ratio in different groups of the African population provides insight into the nature of the migration. For the African population as a whole the sex ratio was 106 males to 100 females. In the indigenous African population the ratio was 95 to 100 whereas in the foreign born population it was 280 per 100. Furthermore there were differences between the sex ratios in the African rural areas, the European farming areas and the urban areas. For the indigenous populations the respective ratios were 84: 100, 104: 100; and 142: 100. These figures suggest that male labour migrated into Rhodesia and that within Rhodesia there was a migration of male labour from the rural areas to the towns. The situation in Zambia was basically similar, but in Malawi the migration was mainly from that country to Rhodesia and South Africa. These statistics of course reflect the established patterns in which workers move to urban areas but leave their families behind in the rural areas since they do not intend to become permanently urbanized. In recent years, however, there has been a tendency for periods of residence in the urban economy to become longer relative to the sojourn in the rural area. W. J. Barber explains the pattern of labour migration in Central Africa by suggesting that it was inversely related to the real income of any area, and directly related to the population pressure in the area.[1]

In view of the importance attached to differentials between urban wages and rural incomes in relation to the labour supply and from other standpoints, this section on labour and employment will be concluded by a brief discussion of incomes in the traditional agricultural sector. Information of this kind is not directly available. The statistical method often employed to estimate it normally assumes a standard consumption of real goods in the rural area, which is then converted to a money equivalent and the result multiplied by the estimated *de facto* population of the rural areas. To this figure is added the estimated value of domestic household services and the value of income from sale of produce. At best, this method is hazardous but on its basis the following estimates of African incomes have been presented.

'In the African area (in 1958) the average gross value of output was less than £80 per holding and average gross money incomes were less than £15 per year. Average money outlays for current expenses in African agriculture are unknown, but samples indicate an average of £3 per holding, leaving a net income of £12 per family holding. If an imputed cost is charged for labour, seed, compost, transport and rent, then the average returns for management must be very close to zero if not negative'.[2]

This statement relates to Rhodesia where, in 1958, the average earnings of employed labour were £85 per annum. In agriculture, the lowest paid sector, the average was £75. In comparing these figures it must be borne in mind that a family holding, which on the basis of Yudelman's estimates would have produced £77 per annum, normally employs at least one adult, sometimes more, and that children provide some labour. Taking this into account it seems that the return per occupied person in the traditional sector was certainly lower than the average return from employment and probably below that in agriculture.

A different conclusion has however been reached by R. W. M. Johnson, who argues that the output of the rural areas should be valued at its cost of purchase. This, in the case of maize, the major output, was substantially higher than the selling price. This approach leads Johnson to conclude that the real income of rural Africans was close to that of the urban sector and substantially higher than that of

[1] W. J. Barber, *The Economy of British Central Africa*, Oxford University Press, London, Chapter 4. [2] Yudelman, *Africans on the Land*, p. 90.

agricultural employees.[1] This conclusion refers to the situation in Rhodesia, where the indigenous African employee works in the higher paid sectors, whereas the migrant worker from outside Rhodesia works in the lower paid sectors, especially agriculture. Although the position in the two northern territories has not been independently examined using Johnson's method, it is likely that a similar result would be obtained. Such an outcome might appear overall to offer no incentive for migration; but although the average return in both the subsistence and money economies may have been equal, a distribution on either side of the mean will have existed, and workers would have a motive to move from the less affluent areas of the subsistence economy. Further, increases in the labour supply arising through population growth could act to depress average returns and thus provide grounds for a continuing migration.

6. INDUSTRIAL DEVELOPMENT

A feature of economic development during the decade was an impressive growth of industry. Manufacturing output not only expanded substantially in absolute terms but also increased its relative contribution to GDP. The value of manufactured output rose from £26·9 m in 1954 to £65·4 m in 1963, and its share of GDP rose from 8·1 per cent to 11·7 per cent. The highest rates of growth were achieved by industries which started with a relatively small gross output. Among the rapidly growing sectors which accounted for a substantial proportion of gross output were the clothing and shoe industries, chemicals and chemical products, and a variety of engineering industries covering ferrous and non-ferrous basic industries, metal products and machinery, and the repair and manufacture of transport equipment. If industry is defined more broadly to include the mining sector and the supply of water and power, the industrial sector of the area assumes a much greater importance. By itself, the mining and quarrying sector was one of the most important in Central Africa, but although in absolute terms its output formed a consistently high proportion of total output its relative contribution to GDP declined over the period.

An examination of the pattern of development of manufacturing industry suggests two comments. Firstly, although growth occurred in operations related to the processing of foodstuffs (especially meat and dairy products) the linkage effects in this industry were not as

[1] R. W. M. Johnson, 'The Economics of Subsistence', Technical Paper in *Agricultural Economics No. 1*, Department of Economics, University College of Rhodesia and Nyasaland.

great as in other industries. Secondly, during the period there was a marked structural change in the composition of manufacturing, involving a move away from its dependence on the processing of agricultural products towards a more sophisticated structure based increasingly on the engineering and allied industries. There was thus established an industrial structure with a considerable growth potential on which further industrial development could rest.

The territorial distribution of industrial growth over the period in terms of size and character is of considerable interest. In terms of contribution to GDP, manufacturing industry expanded in Zambia between 1954 and 1963 from £4·6 m to £12·6 m. In Rhodesia over the same period the increase was from £20·7 m to £50·2 m. Malawi's industrial output was very much smaller. Over the period it increased from £1·4 m to £2·5 m. Thus in terms of rates of growth, Zambia's manufacturing industry developed fastest, but in absolute terms however, industrial expansion in Rhodesia was much greater. Malawi's industry lagged behind both. These territorial differences cannot be explained entirely by the differences in the increase, measured in terms of purchasing power, of the respective territorial markets over the period. In Rhodesia industry grew much more rapidly than might have been expected on the basis of its own market. In the other countries industry grew considerably less. It seems clear that these differences reflect the advantages which the already well established industrial base of Rhodesia could afford to new industries set up to serve the area as a whole. Not only did the two larger territories differ in the shares of industrial growth which they succeeded in attracting during the period. There was also a marked difference in the character of the industries which developed. In Zambia the main growth occurred in the food processing and textile industries. In Rhodesia, on the other hand, a more diverse pattern of industrial development took place, in which the engineering and allied industries played a major role. The industries which developed in Zambia, largely to serve its internal market, were basically less sophisticated and had a smaller growth potential than those which grew up in Rhodesia. This territorial pattern of development confirms that industry tends to become centralized within a market area, and that the forces working to this end may be particularly strong as technology becomes more complex.

Except for the provision of power and water facilities which came under direct governmental control and direction, governments in Central Africa did not participate directly in the industrial sector on any scale. There are however, a few instances in which government established a particular industry and guided it through its first years. For instance the Rhodesian Government established an iron and steel plant at Que Que and a cotton spinning plant at Gatooma, both of which were subsequently sold off to private enterprises. The same government also established a jute processing industry but this proved unsuccessful and was closed down. Governments also participated directly in the processing and marketing of a number of major agricultural products through such statutory bodies as the Cold Storage Commission, the Dairy Board and the Grain Marketing Board. In addition the Rhodesian Government operated an Industrial Board, and the Federal Government established a private development body known as the Industrial Promotion Corporation. In general however, industrial promotion policy took the form of providing encouragement and inducements for private enterprise. The provision of protective tariffs for newly established industries was, at the Federal level, an important aspect of this policy. External trade agreements, in particular those with South Africa, also had an important impact on the development of certain industries, such as textiles and clothing.

Apart from these measures, the formation of the Federation, by creating a larger and more unified market, must itself be expected to have had an influence on the pace of industrial development during the period. This influence however, must not be exaggerated. Already before the establishment of Federation, Rhodesia and the most prosperous and accessible areas of Zambia constituted an area within which trade was in effect free. Federation led to the inclusion of the north-eastern part of Zambia and Malawi in the free trade area, and to that extent enlarged the market; but the poorness and inaccessibility of those areas meant that the effective expansion in the size of the market was small. However, Federation also gave the Federal government control over tariff rates and enabled it to adopt tariff policies which could stimulate industrial development and the increased protection afforded in the market area must have accounted for part of the industrial growth of the period.

7. TARIFFS AND EXTERNAL TRADE

The common external tariff which was introduced for the Federation in 1955 was a four column tariff. Column D applied to the United Kingdom and Colonies, column C applied to other Commonwealth countries, column B applied to a number of other countries which were accorded 'most favoured nation status' and column A applied to all other countries. The tariff rates were highest in column A and decreased to the lowest rates in column D. The tariff itself reflected, and was supplemented by, certain special arrangements affecting trade with the major trading partners of the Federation. For instance the Federation not only gave, but also received Commonwealth Preferences. These were most important in encouraging the production of tobacco for export to the British market, the chief outlet for the country's tobacco exports. Special agreements were concluded with South Africa. Earlier, both Zambia and Rhodesia had been partners with South Africa in separate Customs Union agreements. With the introduction of the Federal tariff these agreements were replaced by a Trade Agreement which also brought Malawi into a special trading relationship with South Africa.

The 1955 Trade Agreement granted preferential, and in some cases duty free entry of certain Federal goods into South Africa, and also provided for a quota of 2 million lbs of Federal tobacco. In return, certain specified South African goods entered the Federation under column C and at 90 per cent of column D. There was also provision for duty free trade (under import licence) in specified agricultural products. The Agreement was revised in 1960. It extended the duty free and preferential entry of Federal goods in to South Africa and placed all goods, other than specified agricultural products of South African origin into the Federation at column C rates, i.e. at the normal Commonwealth preference rate. The main advantage of these two Agreements for the Federation was that they provided an incentive and an assured market for certain made-up textiles.

Little attempt was made to control imports directly, except in the case of certain agricultural imports which were only imported under licence where the policy was that the licence was only granted to cover any deficit between local supply and demand at the usual price levels. In general, for non-agricultural products, control was exercised through tariff protection.

A basic characteristic of the economy of Central Africa is its dependence on foreign trade.[1] Throughout the decade exports and imports amounted to a high proportion of GDP.

Table 11. *Exports and imports in Central Africa*

	1954			1958			1962		
	R	Z	M	R	Z	M	R	Z	M
Exports as % of GDP	27	68	24	20	53	19	25	60	23
Imports as % of GDP	40	43	27	34	28	39	14	36	41

[1] During most of the Federal period the trade of the three countries was not separately identified, but in 1963 there was published the result of an attempt to allocate trade by territory of origin and destination for the period 1954–62. The country figures in this section are taken from this publication. It should be borne in mind that the figures are estimates.

Table 12. *Exports to countries outside Federation*
(£m)

	1954			
	Rhodesia	Zambia	Malawi	Central Africa
0. Food and live animals	2·3	—	3·4	5·7
Meat	1·8	—	—	1·8
Maize	—	—	0·4	0·5
Tea	—	—	2·8	2·8
1. Beverages and tobacco	21·3	1·2	2·8	25·2
Tobacco (unmfd.)	20·9	1·2	2·8	24·9
2. Crude materials	11·5	0·8	0·8	13·1
Groundnuts	—	0·2	0·2	0·4
Asbestos	6·5	—	—	6·5
Copper ore	0·1	—	—	0·1
Chrome ore	2·6	—	—	2·6
3. Mineral fuels and lubricants	0·2	—	—	0·2
4. Animal and vegetable oils and fats	0·1	—	0·1	0·3
5. Chemicals	0·4	—	—	0·4
6. Mfd. goods classified by materials	3·5	91·5	—	94·9
Copper and products	—	86·5	—	86·5
Lead, zinc, and cobalt	—	5·0	—	5·0
Iron and steel and products	0·4	—	—	0·4
7. Machinery and transport equipment	0·6	—	—	0·6
8. Misc. manufactured articles	3·2	0·2	—	3·4
Clothing	2·6	—	—	2·6
9. Misc. transactions	—	—	—	—
Subtotal	43·0	93·7	7·1	143·8
Net gold sales	6·5	—	—	6·5
Total	49·5	93·7	7·1	150·3

It has already been pointed out that, except in 1957 and 1958, there was a favourable balance of visible trade. Copper played the major role in determining the size of export receipts and its price fluctuations were probably the biggest single factor determining the area's international trading position. The positions for the individual countries are depicted in Table 4.

Table 12—*continued*

	1958			
	Rhodesia	Zambia	Malawi	Central Africa
0. Food and live animals	3·3	0·1	3·2	6·6
Meat	1·0	—	—	1·0
Maize	1·6	—	—	1·6
Tea	—	—	3·0	3·0
1. Beverages and tobacco	24·0	1·1	3·3	28·4
Tobacco (unmfd.)	23·4	1·1	3·3	27·8
2. Crude materials	14·0	1·3	0·7	16·0
Groundnuts	—	0·2	0·3	0·6
Asbestos	7·4	—	—	7·4
Copper ore	1·7	—	—	1·7
Chrome ore	3·0	—	—	3·0
3. Mineral fuels and lubricants	0·6	—	—	0·6
4. Animal and vegetable oils and fats	0·1	—	0·1	0·2
5. Chemicals	1·7	0·5	—	2·2
6. Mfd. goods classified by materials	2·9	71·7	—	74·6
Copper and products	0·2	67·7	—	67·9
Lead, zinc, and cobalt	—	3·9	—	3·9
Iron and steel and products	1·1	—	—	1·1
7. Machinery and transport equipment	0·8	—	—	0·8
8. Misc. manufactured articles	1·9	0·1	—	2·0
Clothing	1·5	—	—	1·5
9. Misc. transactions	—	—	—	—
Subtotal	49·4	74·7	7·3	131·4
Net gold sales	6·8	—	—	6·8
Total	56·1	74·7	7·3	138·2

The domestic exports of Central Africa are shown in Table 12. It can be seen that they consisted almost entirely of primary products and some of these were processed only to a small extent. For the area as a whole a very high proportion of total proceeds came from two products—copper products and tobacco which together accounted for three-quarters of total export proceeds in 1962. Price fluctuations occurred for both of these commodities but were especially severe for copper. Fluctuations in the export proceeds from copper

Table 12—*continued*

	1962 Rhodesia	Zambia	Malawi	Central Africa
0. Food and live animals	10·6	0·8	4·0	15·5
Meat	3·4	—	—	3·4
Maize	5·8	0·5	—	6·3
Tea	—	—	3·6	3·6
1. Beverages and tobacco	35·1	2·7	4·0	41·8
Tobacco (unmfd.)	34·3	2·7	4·0	41·0
2. Crude materials	12·8	2·7	1·8	17·2
Groundnuts	—	0·9	1·5	2·4
Asbestos	7·6	—	—	7·6
Copper ore	0·2	—	—	0·2
Chrome ore	2·6	—	—	2·6
3. Mineral fuels and lubricants	0·5	—	—	0·5
4. Animal and vegetable oils and fats	0·1	—	0·3	0·4
5. Chemicals	1·2	0·1	—	1·3
6. Mfd. goods classified by materials	9·1	113·2	—	122·3
Copper and products	3·0	108·8	—	111·7
Lead, zinc, and cobalt	—	4·2	—	4·2
Iron and steel and products	4·2	0·1	—	4·3
7. Machinery and transport equipment	1·3	—	—	1·3
8. Misc. manufactured articles	1·9	0·1	—	2·0
Clothing	1·4	—	—	1·4
9. Misc. transactions	0·3	0·1	—	0·4
Subtotal	72·8	119·6	10·2	202·6
Net gold sales	6·8	—	—	6·8
Total	79·7	119·6	10·2	209·5

Source: Supplementary Statistics on Merchandise Trade of the Federation of Rhodesia & Nyasaland, CSO, Salisbury 1963.

arose both from price fluctuations and from changes in the industry's output. Export concentration for the individual countries shows a rather different pattern. Nine tenths of Zambia's exports in 1962 came from copper. In Malawi, three quarters of total export proceeds came from tobacco and tea, with tobacco accounting for rather more than half of this share. Rhodesia's exports were rather more diversified, 47 per cent came from tobacco, 10 per cent from asbestos, 8 per cent from maize and 6 per cent from iron and steel products. The import structure of Central Africa is shown in Table 13.

In terms of origin and destination the area's foreign trade was concentrated in the sense that a large portion of trade was done with a small number of countries. In 1963, of total exports, about 40 per cent went to the United Kingdom, a quarter to countries of the European Economic Community, 8 per cent to South Africa and 6 per cent to Japan. In the same year the United Kingdom provided a third of imports, South Africa nearly 30 per cent, EEC 10 per cent and the United States and Canada 8 per cent. The geographical pattern of external trade was however changing during the decade. In particular, both Japan and EEC became more important markets at the expense of the UK's share. Similar changes in the import pattern are also discernible.

Inter-territorial trade is normally a most important part of trade within a federal area and one of the economic objectives of Federation is to encourage it. The costs and benefits of Federation to its members were influenced by this trade although other factors were of considerable relevance too. Despite its importance, satisfactory inter-territorial trade statistics are rarely provided in a Federation unless tax attribution makes the recording of inter-territorial trade important. Central Africa was no exception to this. No accurate data exist on the magnitude of inter-territorial trade flows during the decade. However, in 1962 an enquiry was undertaken by the Central Statistical Office into trade between Rhodesia, Zambia and Malawi. The output of those responding in Rhodesia was about two-thirds of total manufacturing sales as recorded in the 1961 Census. It would clearly be inappropriate to gross up the recorded sales since a significant proportion of the non-respondent firms would certainly be producing for the Rhodesian market only, especially in the furniture, paper and printing and transport equipment groups. However, such a grossed up figure should provide a probable upper limit for the size of the sales to Zambia and Malawi. Table 14 summarizes the aggregate data.

On this basis, inter-territorial exports of local products amounted to between 10 and 16 per cent of domestic exports for the area as a whole, (lower and upper limits respectively). The importance of such exports was however very different for each of the members. For Rhodesia the ratio would have been between 25 and 40 per cent; for Zambia 1 per cent and for Malawi 12 per cent. The commodity composition and the relative importance of inter-territorial sales in relation to domestic sales is obviously of interest. For Zambia's exports no breakdown by commodity was released since it would

Table 13. *Imports by commodity and country of supply, 1963*
(£m)

	SITC Sections										Total	
	0	1	2	3	4	5	6	7	8	9	£ m	%
United Kingdom	1·3	0·6	0·3	0·1	0·1	2·6	9·3	22·8	5·4	0·8	43·3	32·2
Africa	5·7	0·4	2·1	2·5	0·2	5·7	12·1	8·5	4·6	0·2	42·0	31·2
Republic of S. Africa	4·2	0·3	0·8	1·3	—	5·6	11·9	8·5	4·5	0·2	37·3	27·7
EEC	0·4	0·2	0·4	0·1	—	3·2	2·5	5·5	1·3	0·3	13·8	10·3
Germany	—	—	0·2	—	—	1·4	0·8	3·0	0·5	0·1	6·1	4·5
Asia	0·5	—	0·5	—	0·1	0·1	5·9	0·8	1·0	—	8·9	6·6
Japan	—	—	—	—	—	—	3·5	0·7	0·5	—	4·9	3·6
N. America	0·6	—	0·9	0·2	—	1·2	1·7	5·1	0·8	0·1	10·5	7·8
USA	0·2	—	0·2	0·2	—	1·2	1·4	4·5	0·7	0·1	8·6	6·4
Latin America	—	—	—	—	—	—	—	—	—	—	0·1	0·1
Other	3·3	0·1	0·3	6·2	0·3	0·5	1·8	1·5	0·7	—	14·6	10·8
Australia	3·0	—	—	—	0·1	—	0·1	0·2	0·1	—	3·5	2·6
Iran	—	—	—	4·3	—	—	—	—	—	—	4·4	3·2
Parcel Post	—	—	—	—	—	—	—	—	—	1·4	1·4	1·1
Total	11·8	1·3	4·4	9·2	0·8	13·3	33·2	44·2	13·8	2·8	134·8	100·0
Per cent	(8·8)	(1·0)	(3·2)	(6·8)	(0·6)	(9·9)	(24·7)	(32·8)	(10·3)	(2·1)	(100·0)	—

Source: *Annual Statement of External Trade, 1963*, CSO, Salisbury.

Table 14. *Recorded inter-territorial trade*[a] *1962*
(£m)

	Imported by: Rhodesia	Zambia	Malawi	Total
Exported by:				
Rhodesia (i) Lower Estimate	—	14·8	3·6	18·4
(ii) Upper Estimate	—	23·4	5·7	29·1
Zambia	1·6	—	([b])	n.a.
Malawi	1·3	([b])	—	n.a.

Notes: [a] Excluding Kariba power, unmanufactured tobacco from Zambia sold on the Salisbury and Limbe auction floors, and Rhodesia Railway stores.

[b] For 1953, the last year for which information is available, exports of the produce of Malawi to Zambia was £660,000 and exports of the produce of Zambia to Malawi was £15,000.

disclose confidential information. Malawi's recorded inter-territorial exports were solely of agricultural produce, and more than 50 per cent consisted of cotton lint. The most detailed information was provided for Rhodesia. Table 15 summarizes some aspects of this information. The extent to which the industries shown separately in the table depended on inter-territorial sales is particularly noticeable.

Table 15. *Recorded inter-territorial exports of Rhodesia*

Product	Per cent of Rhodesian inter-territorial sales[a]	Per cent of Rhodesian Output represented by inter-territorial sales
Tobacco	9	37
Fuels	7	39
Toilet Preparations	6	41
Transport Equipment	10	29
Clothing	12	35
Rubber Manufactures	5	38
Other	51	15
Total	100	20

Note: [a] 100% = £18,415,000.
Source: Inter-territorial Trade Enquiry, 1962.

8. CONCLUSION

Central Africa achieved an impressive rate of growth of aggregate GDP over the decade, supported by its excellent mineral and agricultural resource base. But although the overall rate of growth was high, and particularly so during the earlier part of the period it fell off towards the end. Expansion had been fueled to a considerable extent by capital inflow, but with growing uncertainty about the future of the Federation, this fell off markedly. Moreover, although an impressive aggregate growth rate had been achieved, in relation to population growth, performance appears less satisfactory and the character of the growth itself raised doubts about the adequacy of the area's economic progress. As has been shown, paid employment opportunities did not increase, with the result that, in terms of employment structure, the economies became more peasant based, and increasingly in the subsistence sector, despite the impressive urban super-structure. Under-employment if not unemployment became a growing problem. The general technical level of farming among the African population showed no marked improvement. The structure of the economies remained fundamentally unchanged.

The extent to which Federation contributed to economic growth in the area as a whole has never been adequately assessed, but it certainly affected the three countries unevenly. Throughout the period the debate on the costs and benefits of Federation to its members mounted and in the end economic dissatisfactions with its operation played a part in its dissolution. The end of Federation left each of the three countries responsible for dealing with the fundamental problems of long run growth and the task of raising living standards and in much altered positions for doing so. In financial terms Zambia became substantially better off even allowing for the cost of the services she took over from the Federal Government. Malawi's financial position however suffered a deterioration. Both were placed in a position to use tariff policy to aid their separate development in the new situation. Rhodesia was left with a potentially unbalanced industrial base as a result of the break up of the tariff area, although as a result of a trade agreement with Malawi, and the *de facto* continuance of the common market arrangement *vis a vis* Zambia, the need for adjustments was postponed for some time.

With their well developed mineral bases and overall adequacy of agricultural land supplies Rhodesia and Zambia possess bases for development which are at least as good as those of most other tropical African countries, and better than many. Malawi's economic base is perhaps less happy to the extent that it lacks minerals, and it is already encountering population pressures reflected in the importance of emigrant labour. Most of the long run economic problems of Central Africa are not unique to it but are shared by many other African countries although some, as in Rhodesia are specific to the political and social structure. Of these problems agricultural improvement, employment opportunities and education are interrelated and dominant. It is in the effectiveness of their response to these problems that the programmes of the successor states will be judged.

SELECTED READING

Books

1. Barber, W. J., *The Economy of British Central Africa* (London, 1961).
2. Irvine, A. G., *The Balance of Payments of Rhodesia and Nyasaland* (London, 1959).
3. Taylor, W. L., *Problems of Economic Development of the Federation of Rhodesia and Nyasaland*, in *Economic Development for Africa South of the Sahara*, International Economic Association, edited by Professor E. A. G. Robinson (London, 1963).
4. Yudelman, M., *Africans on the Land* (London, 1964).

Articles and Pamphlets

5. Cole, R. L., and Pearson, D. S., The Tobacco Industry of Central Africa, *East African Economics Review* (December, 1965).
6. Johnson, R. W. M., *The Labour Economy and the Reserves*, Occasional Paper No. 4, Department of Economics, University College of Rhodesia and Nyasaland (October, 1964).
7. Phoenix Group, *Planning for Progress* (Salisbury, Rhodesia, 1962).
8. Phoenix Group, *Break-up: Economic Consequences of the Dissolution of the Federation of Rhodesia and Nyasaland* (Salisbury, Rhodesia, 1963).
9. Robson, R., Growth in Southern Rhodesia, '*Productivity Measurement Review*', No. 33 (OECD, Paris, May 1963).
10. Taylor, W. L., Economic Possibilities in Southern Rhodesia, '*Optima*' (June, 1962).
11. Taylor, W. L., *Reflections on the Role of Education in Developing Countries*, Inaugural Lecture, University College of Rhodesia and Nyasaland (Oxford University Press, 1964).
12. Taylor, W. L., and Pearson, D. S., *The Requirements and Supplies of High Level Manpower in Southern Rhodesia*, 1961–70, University College of Rhodesia and Nyasaland, Department of Economics, Occasional Paper No. 2 (Salisbury, 1964).
13. Taylor, W. L., and Pearson, D. S., *The Requirements and Supplies of High Level Manpower in Northern Rhodesia, 1961–70*, University College of Rhodesia and Nyasaland, Department of Economics, Occasional Paper No. 3 (Salisbury, 1964).

14. Tow, L., *Manufacturing Industry in Southern Rhodesia*, National Academy of Science, National Research Council (US, 1960).

Official Publications

15. Official Publications of the Central Statistical Office, Salisbury, Rhodesia; especially useful are the annual presentations of the *National Accounts* and the *Balance of Payments*.
16. Southern Rhodesia, *Report of the Advisory Committee on the Development of the Economic Resources of Southern Rhodesia*, (*the Phillips Report*): Salisbury, 1962.
17. United Nations, *Report of the UN/ECA/FAO Economic Survey Mission on the Economic Survey Development of Zambia, October, 1964.*

9

THE ECONOMY OF SUDAN

1. INTRODUCTION

In area, Sudan is the largest country in Africa. It covers nearly one million square miles and extends between latitudes 3°N and 22°N and longitudes 22°E and 39°E. The country displays a wide range of geological and climatic features which much influence the structure of the economy and the course of its development. One third of the area consists of barren desert. Unfortunately it is these vast unproductive parts that lie close to the Red Sea coast, whereas the more productive regions are separated from the sea by distances which range between 500 and 1,500 miles. Their remoteness was a major factor retarding the development of the economy until the beginning of the present century when a network of railway and steamer lines was developed. Roads are still poor and undeveloped. Outside the towns there is only one short stretch of tarmac from Khartoum to the northern Gezira. The problem of relatively high transportation costs remains a major obstacle to a faster rate of economic growth and to a more even geographical distribution of development efforts.

According to the first (and so far only) Population Census carried out in the Sudan, the population of the country was estimated at about 10·26 millions in January 1956. This gives an average density of only ten persons per square mile. When the unproductive parts are excluded the effective density is of course much higher. Nearly one quarter of the population live in the three southern provinces of Bahr-el-Gazal, Equatoria and Upper Nile. These are the least developed areas and their *per capita* income is less than half of the average for the country as a whole. Another quarter of the population lives in the two western provinces—Kordofan and Darfur—which though more developed than the southern provinces still lag well behind the more developed regions of eastern and northern Sudan, which contain the remaining half of the country's population.

The rate of growth of population is estimated at 2·8 per cent per annum. The birth rate is high and the population is young, with 43 per cent under 15. The population is expected to double itself in less than 25 years. For 1963, it was estimated at 13 million. The masculinity ratio is 51 per cent. This ratio varies widely for various age groups and more significantly, for various regions. In the less developed regions of the South, West and extreme North the ratio is well below 50 per cent which reflects the fact that more men than women migrate to the centres of development. Detailed figures are given in Table 1.

Table 1. *Area and population 1956*

Province	Males ('000)	Females ('000)	Total ('000)	Land area (sq. m)	Density (persons per sq. m.)
North and East					
Northern Province	422	451	873	236,200	3·7
Khartoum	273	232	505	5,700	88·5
Kassala	503	438	941	134,450	6·9
Blue Nile	1,066	1,004	2,070	54,775	37·7
West					
Kordofan	888	874	1,762	146,930	11·9
Dafur	632	697	1,329	138,150	9·6
South					
Upper Nile	455	434	889	92,270	9·6
Bahr el Chazal	505	486	991	82,530	12·0
Equatoria	443	461	904	76,495	11·8
Sudan	5,186	5,076	10,263	967,500	10·6

Source: Economic Survey 1957, page 53.

The economy is basically agricultural and pastoral. Nearly 90 per cent of the country's population live in rural areas and over 85 per cent of its labour force are engaged in primary activities. In 1964–65 farm products contributed about one-third of the GDP, and animal and forestry products contributed one-fifth. Transport and distribution constitutes a fairly large sector which grew rapidly in the 'fifties but has recently remained at a steady proportionate level (above 15 per cent). Industrial production contributes only about $2\frac{1}{2}$ per cent to GDP, and almost all the modern industrial firms are less than ten years old. Mineral production is insignificant. Although surveys and prospecting indicate that several minerals exist, their exploitation has been prevented by several obstacles, especially high transportation costs.

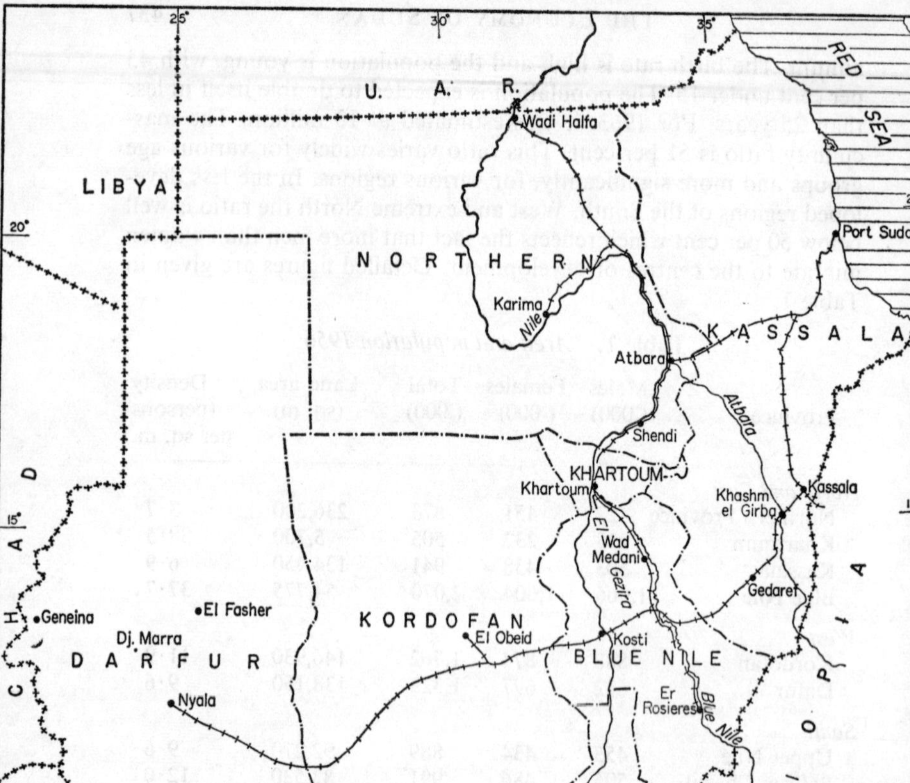

U. A. R.
Wadi Halfa
RED SEA
LIBYA
Port Sudan
NORTHERN
Karima
Nile
KASSALA
Atbara
Atbara
Shendi
KHARTOUM
Khartoum
Kassala
Khashm el Girba
El Gezira
Wad Medani
Gedaref
CHAD
Geneina
El Fasher
KORDOFAN
Dj. Marra
El Obeid
Kosti
DARFUR
BLUE NILE
Nyala
Er Rosieres
Blue Nile
ETHIOPIA
CENTRAL AFRICAN REPUBLIC
Malakal
White Nile
UPPER NILE
BAHR EL GHAZAL
Wau
SUDAN
International Boundaries
Provincial Boundaries
Railways
EQUATORIA
Juba
KENYA
CONGO REPUBLIC
UGANDA
L. Rudolf
0 40 80 120 160 200
MILES
G. D'S.
25°
30°
35°
20°
15°
10°
5°

Map 7

Subsistence production still occupies an important place in the Sudan. Indeed in much of the country, this form of production is dominant in the sense that peasants' efforts are almost wholly devoted to the production of goods directly consumed within the household or, at most, within the village. The role of subsistence production goes well beyond these districts, however, and as mentioned already a substantial part of the production of the modern sector consists of goods directly consumed. This is mainly because of the manner in which modern agricultural schemes are organized in the Sudan. For example, in the two million acre cotton growing schemes in the Gezira, the area of land devoted to the production of food and fodder crops is compulsorily equal to that devoted to cotton, the objective being to shelter tenants from the effect of price fluctuations for cotton exports.

Estimates of the subsistence sector are not regularly produced in Sudan but the Department of Statistics has made crude estimates and a private estimate[1] puts its share for 1956 at 44 per cent. The most usual basis of classifying production however is according to technique, distinguishing between sectors using modern methods of production on the one hand and those using traditional techniques on the other. These bases of classification overlap. Much of the output produced by traditional techniques is for the market, and in Sudan, as noted, much agricultural output produced in the modern sector is for subsistence. National income statistics compiled for the first time in 1955–56 put the share of the traditional sector, including its production for the market and the erection of traditional buildings, at about 56 per cent of the GDP. Since then its share has declined somewhat but it still represented just under 50 per cent in 1964–65.

Gross Domestic Product statistics are summarized in Table 2. For 1955–56 GDP was estimated at £S284 m and *per capita* income at £S28.[2] In 1964–65 GDP in current prices was £439 m and the *per capita* figure £32. This level is low compared even with many other developing countries. The period since 1956 exhibits a number of important features. There has been a relatively rapid growth of the government sector and the relative importance of the manufacturing sector has more than doubled although its share is still very low. A particularly notable feature is the instability exhibited by construction (modern) and agriculture (modern). Over short periods the rate of growth of GDP is of course much affected by the wide annual fluctua-

[1] P. F. M. McLoughlin, 'Income Distribution and Direct Taxation; an Administrative Problem in Low Output African Nations; A Case Study of the Sudan', *Economia Internazionale*, 1959, No. 3.

[2] All figures in this chapter are in Sudanese pounds. One pound sterling = £0·975 Sudanese pounds.

Table 2. *Gross domestic product at factor cost, 1955–65*

	1955–56 £Sm	%	1960–61 £Sm	1961–62 £Sm	1962–63 £Sm	1963–64 £Sm	1964–65 £Sm	%
Agriculture:								
Traditional			70·9	74·3	77·6	81·1	84·7	19·3
Modern			45·1	74·5	55·9	44·8	61·9	14·1
Total	105·6	37·1	116·0	148·7	133·5	125·9	146·6	33·4
Livestock:								
Traditional			33·2	34·7	36·3	38·0	39·8	9·1
Modern			4·1	4·3	4·6	4·8	5·1	1·2
Total	32·3	11·4	37·3	39·0	40·9	42·8	44·9	10·3
Forestry:								
Traditional			31·1	32·5	34·0	35·6	37·2	8·5
Modern			0·5	0·7	0·7	0·8	0·5	—
Total	28·3	10·0	31·6	33·2	34·7	36·4	37·7	8·5
Fisheries, traditional	6·5	2·3	7·5	7·8	8·2	8·6	9·0	2·1
Mining	0·2	—	0·3	0·2	0·3	0·3	0·3	—
Manufacturing	2·8	1·0	5·7	6·4	8·0	9·2	11·0	2·5
Crafts	9·8	3·4	11·3	11·8	12·4	12·9	13·5	3·1

Construction:								
Traditional			11·2	11·7	12·2	12·8	13·4	3·1
Modern			11·7	9·9	13·6	20·2	12·0	2·7
Total	16·2	5·7	22·9	21·6	25·8	33·0	25·4	5·8
Transport and distribution	37·6	13·2	52·0	58·5	62·7	68·7	62·7	14·3
Government[a]	17·2	6·1	28·0	34·0	36·6	38·6	45·1	10·3
Other services:								
Traditional			17·0	17·8	18·6	19·3	20·3	4·6
Modern			7·2	8·3	9·2	10·2	10·5	2·4
Total	19·5	6·9	24·2	26·1	27·8	29·5	30·8	7·0
Ownership of dwellings	8·2	2·9	10·0	10·4	10·8	11·2	11·6	2·6
Subtotals:								
Traditional	160·7	56·5	182·2	190·5	199·3	208·3	217·9	49·7
Modern	123·5	43·5	164·6	207·2	202·4	208·7	220·7	50·3
Total	284·2	100·0	346·8	397·7	401·7	417·1	438·6	100·0

Note: [a] Provisional figures for 1961–62—1964–65.
Source: Department of Economic Planning, Ministry of Finance and Economics.

tions in agricultural output which is due mainly to the unreliability of rainfall which affects yields both for the rainland cultivation areas and the artificially irrigated lands. For example, GDP increased 12·7 per cent from 1961 to 1962 but only 1·5 per cent from 1962 to 1963. Nevertheless, taking the whole period 1956–57 to 1962–63 it is estimated that the rate of growth in terms of constant 1961–62 prices was about 4 per cent per annum.

The low income level is due mainly to the low productivity of agriculture. The large amounts which are invested in agriculture every year are devoted to capital intensive projects for water supply—dams, canals, and pumping machinery. Despite this high and relatively successful series of investments, traditional rainland agriculture, using little and locally made equipment is still predominant and currently accounts for about two-thirds of the value of agricultural production. Its productivity tends to be low, partly because of unreliable rainfall. Transportation difficulties, imperfect marketing channels, and inadequate supply of credit are other obstacles which hinder its expansion and improvement.

The key factor in the country's development and prosperity since the 1920's has been the production of cotton, mainly of long-staple varieties. Cotton and cotton seed accounted regularly for two-thirds of the country's exports, and one-fifth of the income generated within the economy. Gum arabic and groundnuts are the other main exports. Wide year-to-year fluctuations in average yields of cotton per acre and in its world price subject the whole economy to considerable instability. Besides causing fluctuations in the incomes of the farmers and in the country's foreign exchange earnings, the prosperity of the cotton sector is the major determinant of all business activity.

The role of the public sector in the economy is indicated by the fact that Government revenue accounts for a little under one-fifth and Government expenditure for about one-fourth of the Gross Domestic Product. These proportions would be more than doubled if revenue and expenditure are related only to that part of the GDP which is produced in the modern sector. The share of the public sector in fixed Gross Domestic Capital Formation in the monetary sector has normally been well above one-half except for a short period in the second half of the 1950's when there was an upsurge in private investment in buildings and manufacturing industries. The 1961/62—1970/71 Plan required public investment to rise again and, in the first years of the plan, to become more than two-thirds of the total. Apart from investment in transport and other public utilities and social services, the government also plays a dominant role in the extension of irrigated agriculture through the construction of dams, canals and the provision of assistance to mechanized pumping schemes. Government investment in industry has also increased considerably in recent years and has led to the establishment of two large sugar factories, a tannery and several other smaller factories.

Table 3. *Capital formation*
(annual averages in £Sm)

	1955-56–1956-57	1960-61–1962-63
1. *Capital formation by sponsor*		
Government (Central + Local)	7·7	26·5
Public corporations	4·3	12·6
Private enterprise	11·1	20·1
2. *Capital formation by type*		
(*a*) European and African-style building	12·7	20·7
(*b*) Civil engineering	3·6	10·2
(*c*) Transport equipment	1·7	9·6
(*d*) Other machinery and equipment	5·1	15·4
3. *Capital formation by industrial use*		
(*a*) Agriculture	3·7	15·2
(*b*) Transport and distribution	3·8	10·8
(*c*) Mining	0·2	—
(*d*) Manufacturing	0·5	9·3
(*e*) Water and electricity	1·3	2·3
(*f*) Building and civil engineering	0·5	2·0
(*g*) Banks	0·2	0·5
(*h*) Non-Government education	0·2	0·7
(*i*) Miscellaneous services	—	0·2
(*j*) Government	4·5	10·7
(*k*) Ownership of buildings	8·0	8·0

Note: European and African-style building includes dwellings as well as office building and industrial premises.

Source: National Income of Sudan 1961/62—1962/63, Department of Statistics, Khartoum, pp. 44, 43 and 46.

Apart from directly undertaking productive investment, the government also plays an active role in promoting private investment. Private investment in manufacturing is stimulated by the provision of assistance under the Approved Enterprises Act of 1956 and by finance from the Government-owned Industrial Bank as well as by other less direct though effective measures. Investment in agriculture also receives much help through the Agricultural Bank and technical and advisory services. Government also attempts to remove other obstacles which slow down the growth of the modern sector; for example, by alleviating the shortage of skilled personnel by training programmes.

Until the middle of the 1950's Sudan enjoyed on the whole a favourable balance of payments. Proceeds from exports were, at the high export prices of the early 1950's, sufficient to pay for the country's imports and to permit the accumulation of substantial foreign reserves. Since then the decline in prices of primary products and pressure on the government to accelerate its development efforts, has led to an almost continuous, and sometimes a substantial, deficit on current account. An inflow of foreign capital, mainly borrowed by the Government from several countries and International lending agencies has helped to bridge the gap between total foreign receipts and payments, but the major impact was felt by the foreign reserves.[1] Net foreign assets underwent a dramatic decline from about £50 m at the end of 1962 to just over £10 m at the end of 1966. This represents less than 2 months imports which is well below the level normally considered safe.

Table 4. *Export fluctuations and balance of payments 1947–65* (£Sm)

	Trade balance	Balance on current a/c	Capital movements	Changes in reserves[a]
1947–51	61·7	50·1	−12·9	−38·4
1952–54	−26·7	−36·9	−1·2	31·8
1955–56	28·3	12·5	−2·0	−11·2
1957–58	−27·4	−34·3	16·7	17·6
1959–62	−2·6	−7·6	36·5	−31·0
1963–65	−31·5	−62·8	26·7	35·7

Note: [a] Minus sign indicates increase in reserves.
Source: A. Mahhouk and F. Drees 'Domestic Policies and Payments Problems of the Sudan, 1947–62', *IMF Staff Papers* XI (1), March 1964, 1959–62 figures adjusted by later information and *IMF Balance of Payments Year Book*, from which 1963–65 figures were also obtained.

In its dependence on the fortunes of a small number of agricultural products, the Sudan is like most other less developed countries, but in one respect it differs from many of these. It has a shortage of labour, not only of the high level man power which is generally short in

[1] A. Mahhouk and F. Drees, 'Domestic Policies and Payment Problems of the Sudan, 1947–1962'. *International Monetary Fund Staff Papers*, March 1964.

Africa, but also of unskilled or semi-skilled agricultural labour. The problem of labour shortage is bound up with the country's sparse population in relation to its natural resources, and also to some extent with social customs. The ease with which subsistence peasant farming and animal breeding can be undertaken by nomadic and semi-nomadic people limits their incentive to shift to the modern economy. As a result, many of the new agricultural schemes find it difficult to induce enough people to take up tenancies. There is also a particular problem of meeting the high seasonal demand for labour during the cotton picking season. The seasonal shortage is bound up with the apparent unwillingness of those already in the modern sector to supply more of their own labour. In the Gezira and elsewhere, for example, tenants apparently prefer to devote a large proportion of their cash incomes to employing casual labour.[1]

This characteristic of the labour supply in the Sudan partly explains the fact that, according to the population census, nearly 5 per cent of the inhabitants are foreigners or of obvious foreign origin. Most of these are immigrants from Central and West Africa, who are attracted into the country by the higher incomes they can earn in the new agricultural schemes and their presence has eased the labour shortage caused by the reluctance of Sudanese to shift to areas of high demand for labour. Most immigrants become successful permanent tenants in the agricultural scheme as soon as they qualify for Sudanese nationality.

Greeks, Armenians, Syrians and Lebanese also occupy an important place in the modern sector of the economy though they are of course in number a much smaller group than the immigrant Africans. Excluded by law from the ownership of agricultural schemes, their efforts are concentrated in the field of trade, manufacturing, banking and insurance and services. Nevertheless, particularly since political independence in 1956, Sudanese are well represented in all kinds and levels of private enterprise, although Europeans dominate export and import business, banking and insurance. Since political independence in 1956, Sudanese entrepreneurs including Sudanese public companies are steadily entering these key positions of commercial activities. Examples include the establishment of a Sudanese Commercial Bank, the part nationalization of a European bank and the setting up of two Sudanese insurance firms and two large trading firms. The manufacturing sector is still dominated by foreign firms but the share of Sudanese firms is steadily growing. The government has recently stepped up its demands for 'Sudanization' of foreign

[1] See, for instance, G. Brausch, P. Crooke and J. Shaw, '*Bashaqa Area Settlement 1963*', University of Khartoum 1964, pp. 90–93.

firms, and are entrusting the importation of essential consumer goods to Sudanese public companies only.[1]

2. THE TEN YEAR PLAN 1961–62—1970–71

The present Ten Year Plan is not the first attempt at development planning in the Sudan. It was preceded by three development programmes for the periods 1946–51, 1951–56 and 1956–61. The present

Table 5. *Summary of the development plan, 1961–62—1970–71*

Sectors	Private (£S m)	Public (£S m)	Total (£S m)	In % of Total
1. Agriculture, livestock, forestry and fishing[a]	30·0	90·1	120·1	21
2. Industry, including public utilities and building and civil engineering, and mining	65·0	41·9	106·9	19
3. Transport and distribution[b]	32·0	63·0	95·0	17
4. Social services, including housing, health care, education and general administration, others[c]	60·0	90·0	150·0	27
Total	187·0	285·0	472·0	84
Replacement investment	41·4	52·0	93·4	16
Total gross fixed investment	228·4	337·0	565·4	100

Notes: [a] Irrigation is included in agriculture and amounts to £S66·4 million—p. 85.

[b] Railways are included in Item 3 and amount to about £S25·1 million. Roads amount to just over £S1 million.

[c] Education and health are included in Item 4 and amount to about £S36·6 million and £S8·4 million respectively. Private Sector investment in Item 4 is mainly housing.

Source: The Ten-year Plan of Economic and Social Development 1961–62—1970–71, p. 65.

plan differs from these primarily in its more ambitious nature and in the fact that, for the first time, an attempt is made to include the private sector.

The central objectives of the plan are:

1. A substantial increase in real income per head.
2. Diversification of the structure of production.

[1] Minister of Finance and Economy in Budget Speech, January, 1967.

Table 6. *Proposed growth of GDP and population; 1960/61—1970/71*

	1960–1	1961–2	1962–3	1963–4	1964–5	1965–6	1966–7	1967–8	1968–9	1969–70	1970–1
1. *GDP (factor cost)* (£S m)											
(*a*) Traditional	187·2	193·3	199·7	206·3	213·1	220·1	227·4	234·9	242·7	250·7	259·0
(*b*) Modern	170·0	191·8	190·6	200·7	213·6	227·3	241·9	260·5	280·6	302·2	325·5
(*c*) Whole	357·2	385·1	390·3	407·0	426·7	447·4	469·3	495·4	523·3	552·9	584·5
2. *Population* (thousands)	11,928	12,264	12,610	12,966	13,332	13,733	14,120	14,518	14,927	15,348	15,781
3. *GDP per capita* (£S) (whole economy)	29·9	31·4	30·9	31·4	32·0	32·6	33·2	34·1	35·1	36·6	37·0

Source: *Ten Year Plan.* Table 24, p. 42.

3. A considerable increase in exports and in import substitution.
4. Improvements in social conditions, education and training and increased opportunities for productive employment.
5. The maintenance of a stable price level.

During the period covered by the Plan GDP was expected to rise by 65 per cent or 5 per cent annually. *Per capita* income was expected to rise by 25 per cent or approximately 2·25 per cent per annum, so that by 1970–71 it would amount to approximately £37. Details of the calculations are set out in Table 6. They are at constant prices and consequently imply corresponding real increases.

The plan envisages total gross investment of £565 million. Net investment was planned to be £472 m of which £285 m (60 per cent) is in the public sector. This total is to be distributed as shown in the following table:

Table 7. *Net public investment, Ten Year Plan*

	(£Sm)	% of total
1. Agriculture and irrigation	85	29·9
2. Industries, mining and public utilities	42	14·6
3. Education, health, housing and other social services and general administration	85	29·9
4. Transport and communication	63	22·1
5. Miscellaneous, including central reserve fund	10	3·5
Total	285	100

Source: The Ten Year Plan, page 7.

The central economic objectives of the plan are all bound up with the development of agriculture. The focal point of the plan is its emphasis on the development of the irrigated areas. Three major irrigation programmes are included in the plan. The first is the Roseires Dam on the Blue Nile, the construction of which is designed to make possible an extension of the Gezira area, intensification of cropping on the Gezira, and the development of new pump schemes on the Blue and White Niles. Altogether the scheme should enable an increase in the irrigated area by 1,200,000 feddans.[1] The second is the Managil extension of the Gezira scheme which will make possible the expansion of production of long stapled cotton and durra. The third is the Kasm el Girba Dam on the Atbara river which will make possible the development of an additional 500,000 feddans. These three schemes together were estimated in the Plan to cost about £65

[1] A feddan is 1·038 acres.

million or about three quarters of the cost of the whole agriculture and irrigation programme. In addition to these schemes which lie in the already better developed central belt of the country, the plan also included projects for pump schemes in the Upper Nile, and schemes for the development of the Jebel Marra massif in the extreme west of the country as well as for the development of coffee and tea in the south. In pursuit of the objective of diversification, efforts are to be made to increase the production of other agricultural commodities such as groundnuts and oilseeds for export, castor, durra, wheat and kenaf.[1] As part of the programme of import substitution, sugar, wheat, rice and coffee are also to be expanded, as well as the production of short stapled cotton which is needed as an input for the new local textile factories. In consequence it is hoped that subsistence farming and pastoral activities will become relatively less important and also that export proceeds will be less vulnerable than hitherto to fluctuations.

The projects for industrial expansion and import substitution include a sugar factory at Khasm el Girba to complement the existing one at El Guneid. Other planned public sector industries are cement, fruit canning, milk powder and cardboard. In addition to these developments in the public sector, a wide range of industrial development projects are expected to be undertaken in the private sector which should indeed provide the bulk of investment in industry. If the projected industrial changes materialise it is estimated that the industrial sector will by 1970 account for 10 per cent of GDP.

From this brief summary of the Plan it is clear that its main economic emphasis is on large scale irrigation projects and on the development of industry, mainly processing. This emphasis largely explains the regional distribution of investment, which is concentrated on the central area around Khartoum and the adjoining area to the east and south east. It is always an issue in development policy whether to concentrate resources on a limited number of projects which may pay off better, though benefitting only small numbers, or to spread them more widely in the interests of a more equitable distribution of income, and above all, of political stability. This is clearly a serious problem in the Sudan; but in the current plan the first alternative seems to have been chosen, despite the professed desire to spread development more widely and to effect a diversification of production, which if carried very far would surely imply ultimately the accelerated development of the South and West.

The introduction of the Ten Year Plan was accompanied by the establishment of more elaborate planning machinery. In 1961, there

[1] Kenaf is a vegetable fibre which is used with jute and sisal for bag-making.

was established an Economic Council, a Development Committee, a National Technical Planning Committee, and a Planning Secretariat. The Economic Council under the chairmanship of the Prime Minister is the highest policy-making organ. It is composed of selected ministers and its main function is to formulate general economic policy and to approve the long-term plans and the annual development budget. The Development Committee, under the chairmanship of the Minister of Finance and Economics consists of all Ministers who are not members of the Economic Council. Its functions are to consider the recommendations of the Technical Committee, the annual budgets and the reports on the progress of the Plan and to submit its own recommendations to the Economic Council. The National Technical Planning Committee is under the chairmanship of the Governor of the Bank of Sudan. It consists of almost all heads of government and semi-government departments. Its responsibilities include the assessment of the country's resources and needs, and formulation of development plans and annual development budgets, the preparation of progress reports and submissions of general recommendations to the Development Committee on all matters relating to or affecting development planning. The Planning Secretariat is located in the Ministry of Finance and Economics and is headed by the Under-Secretary for Economic Planning.

These planning authorities were not properly associated with the formulation of the Ten Year Plan since it was already at a fairly advanced stage when the new organization was set up and there was a considerable degree of commitment to most of its major projects. The cumbersome nature of the new organization and its internal difficulties later hindered it from making an effective contribution even to the oversight and revision of the Plan. Among other difficulties, the very size of the Technical Committee limited its effectiveness. Moreover the membership of the Council and of the Planning Committee has been based rather on political considerations than the departmental functions of the Ministers concerned. Finally, the Planning Secretariat itself was weak and inadequately staffed to enable it to evaluate projects, to influence investment decisions, to provide advice. Weakness of planning in the Sudan has been reflected in the undertaking of a number of patently uneconomic projects and in a failure to synchronise the completion of complementary projects. In some cases, as with the Roseires Dam, this has resulted in irrigation capacity being completed while the related works, canalization etc., have been much delayed. Recently the limitations of the original planning organizations have been increasingly recognized and a number of important changes have been made. These include the

Table 8. *Planned finance and expenditure*
(£S m)

	1961–62	1962–63	1963–64	1964–65	1965–66	1966–67	1967–68	1968–69	1969–70	1970–71	Total
Planned Finance											
Public Sector:											
Investment[a]	29·6	44·7	37·8	34·9	32·0	30·2	30·9	31·6	32·3	33·0	337·0
Savings	16·1	26·0	20·7	20·5	20·1	20·3	21·6	23·3	24·6	26·5	219·7
External Sources[b]	13·5	18·7	17·1	14·4	11·9	9·9	9·3	8·3	7·7	6·5	117·3
Private Sector:											
Investment	18·7	16·0	16·1	18·1	20·5	22·8	25·7	27·9	30·1	32·5	228·4
Savings	9·1	15·5	14·6	16·2	18·0	20·1	22·8	24·6	26·6	28·7	196·2
External Sources	9·6	0·5	1·5	1·9	2·5	2·7	2·9	3·3	3·5	3·8	32·2
Actual Expenditure											
Public Sector	40·8	48·5	58·7	34·0	32·0						
Private Sector	21·8	17·0	22·3	17·7	13·0						

Notes: [a] Includes £S52 Million for replacement and renewals.
[b] Does not include provisions for repayment of foreign debt.
Source: *The Ten-year Plan*, p. 75.

strengthening of the Central Planning Bureau and the establishment of planning units in major ministries and in the regions. If staff can be found these changes should enable the planning organizations to make a more useful contribution than in the past. A more effective planning staff will increasingly be needed if, as seems likely with the completion of the present major irrigation projects, the emphasis of expenditure moves in the direction of a more diversified and balanced programme of expenditure, and perhaps large numbers of smaller schemes.

The Progress of the Plan

Table 8 shows that in the early years of the Plan expenditure, particularly in the public sector, was greater than provided for. From 1961–62 to 1965–66 expenditure was £148 m against a plan for £102 m. In the first year, particularly, part of this increase was due to hasty execution of projects resulting in increased costs.

Partly because of this higher investment, there was in the first two years generally higher economic activity than was foreseen in the Plan. In 1961–62 national income was above the plan target by £13·5 m or 3·8 per cent and in 1962–63 again the target was surpassed by £12·4 m or 3·2 per cent. But this higher performance was not all the result of higher private and Government investment expenditure; it was due in 1961–62 to higher average yields and to a higher average price of cotton than assumed in the plan.

Higher than planned development expenditures were partly responsible for the financial difficulties experienced by the Government during the second year of the Plan, though factors which affected Government revenue such as the decline in cotton output and a rise in sugar prices also played an important part. These difficulties led in December 1963 to a variety of measures aimed at a reduction of current expenditure. In addition steps were taken to increase revenue. These included a vigorous search for more foreign funds, the promotion and encouragement of domestic savings through the sale of government bonds, an increase in the rates of some indirect taxes and the introduction of new direct taxes.

Further financial difficulties were caused by the decision of the Government to maintain a high minimum reserve price in the face of a fall in cotton prices. This resulted in the accumulation of cotton stocks, for which finance had also to be found.

The attempt to maintain development expenditure in the face of these adverse developments, and the need to finance stocks led later to heavy borrowing from the Central Bank, which ultimately resulted in the spectacular decline in the foreign reserves, already alluded to.

During 1964–65 to 1965–66 as part of the measures to restore the situation, development expenditure was kept to approximately the levels indicated in the Plan by cutting and deferring of projects. The whole Plan is now under review.

3. FINANCING THE PUBLIC SECTOR

Since the beginning of modern Sudan at the dawn of the present century, the Government has played a key role in the development of the economy. Until 1956 Government took the form of an Anglo-Egyptian Condominium, whose members both contributed to the supply of capital needed for early development projects. During the first decade of the century, Egypt supplied capital in the form of free grants and soft loans for the construction of a network of railway lines, harbours and river steamers and setting-up of a modern system of administration. This aid was in addition to generous subsidies to the annual civilian and military budgets. The economy responded favourably to this early investment in infrastructure and the Government was enabled to float sufficient loans in the London Capital Market, in the inter-war years, to extend the railway lines and to establish the one-million-feddan Gezira Cotton Growing Scheme.

Until 1958, the Government felt no need for any other financial help. Its financial policy was designed to produce sufficient annual budget surpluses to finance its other development projects and it was successful in this objective. These projects, admittedly, were not of any significant magnitude until after the end of the Second World War when the series of 5-year development programmes were launched. Funds accumulated during the War years and the considerable growth in Government revenue due to the rise in export prices, enabled the Government also to finance these early programmes which cost nearly £100 million from its own internal resources.

After political independence in 1956, pressure on the Government to speed up the development of productive projects and social services, combined with the sharp decline in Government revenue and supply of foreign exchange caused by the decline in the prices of primary products this time from a wider variety of sources, forced the Government to resume borrowing in an effort to maintain its Development Programme.

The International Bank for Reconstruction and Development and the International Development Agency have been the leading sources having provided between 1958 and 1964 just over £30 m for the extension and improvement of the railways and for new irrigation

Table 9. *Central Government account* (*Current*)

Revenue	1961–62 £S'000	1961–62 %	1962–63 £S'000	1962–63 %
Indirect taxes				
Import duties	25,777	42·7	29,787	40·1
Sugar monopoly	1,558	2·6	1,451	2·0
Other indirect	8,667	14·4	10,718	14·4
Total indirect taxes	36,002	59·7	41,956	56·5
Direct taxes	2,003	3·3	2,223	3·0
Participation in enterprises (Gezira Board and others)	6,220	10·3	13,200	17·8
Interest and dividends	1,471	2·4	721	1·0
Fees and charges	5,838	9·7	7,120	9·6
Reimbursement and inter-departmental services	5,370	8·9	5,687	7·7
Others	3,434	5·7	3,274	4·4
Total	60,338	100·0	74,181	100·0

Expenditure (functional basis)	1961–62 £S'000	1961–62 %	1962–63 £S'000	1962–63 %
Economic Services				
(*a*) Agriculture and animal resources	5,555	9·2	5,025	6·8
(*b*) Irrigation and hydro-electric power	1,747	2·9	2,112	2·8
(*c*) Mineral resources	476	0·8	430	0·6
(*d*) Communication	3,820	6·3	5,016	6·8
(*e*) Others	4,025	6·7	4,356	5·8
Total economic services	15,623	25·9	16,939	22·8
Social Services				
(*a*) Education	4,547	7·5	4,986	6·7
(*b*) Health	4,323	7·2	4,787	6·4
(*c*) Information and Labour	1,009	1·7	1,167	1·6
Total social services	9,879	16·4	10,940	14·7
General administration, security and others	26,109	43·3	29,562	39·9
Surplus	8,727	14·4	16,740	22·6
Total	60,338	100·0	74,181	100·0

Source: *Economic Survey 1963*, Ministry of Finance and Economics. Khartoum.

schemes. Loans from Governments during the same period included £9·7 m from Western Germany, £8 m from Yugoslavia, £7·7 m from the Soviet Union, £7 m from the Kuwaiti Government and £4·9 m from Britain. In addition to these loans, the United States Government provided about £20 m under various items of its Aid Programme. These loans were chiefly negotiated for specific development projects, mainly in the fields of irrigation and transport, but some industrial projects were also financed in this way, including the Guneid sugar factory.

The current ten-year plan assessed the total need for foreign finance at £149·5 m but experience during the first three years of the Plan was disappointing. During this period only £33·1 m of foreign capital was attracted against the Plan target of £49·3 m. More recently, as has been indicated, resort was had to deficit financing in an effort to meet the shortfall in finance from this and other sources. The Government has also tried to mobilise domestic savings starting with an issue of £1 m of five-year bonds in 1956.

Recurrent expenditure is of course financed from ordinary revenue which depends heavily on indirect taxation, chiefly on imports. From 1961–65 indirect taxes contributed annually about 60 per cent of the revenue while the share of direct taxation was only 3–5 per cent. Business profits tax accounts for nearly four-fifths of direct taxes. Personal Income Tax was introduced in 1964 and it was restricted to high income earners (of over £1350 per annum). In 1966, the minimum income subject to tax was brought down to £300. Revenue from Income Tax has risen from about £200,000 to about £1 m but this is still less than two per cent of the government revenue.

Until recently, substantial revenues were derived from government participation in agricultural enterprises, mainly representing profits on the Gezira scheme. Latterly, the decline in cotton prices has considerably reduced this contribution which fell from £17·7 m in 1962–63 to £4·63 m in 1964–65. Direct taxation of the traditional agricultural sector is limited to local taxation which finances purely local services. Over the period 1960 to 1965 the contribution from the recurrent budget to the development programme fell from about £10 m to nothing, and in 1966–67 the recurrent budget is in deficit.

4. AGRICULTURE

As has been shown, the economy of the Sudan is basically agricultural and pastoral. Farm crops alone contribute 36 per cent of the Gross Domestic Product. Cotton accounts for one-third of this and the remaining two-thirds come from the production of food crops mainly

Durra (*Sorghum Vulgare*) which is the staple food of the people. For Sudan agriculture, the method of water supply is of considerable importance and the sector is from this point of view conveniently classified into three different types, these are: Flood Agriculture, Rainland Agriculture, and Irrigated Agriculture.

Flood Agriculture is undertaken in areas watered annually by the flood of the Nile and its tributaries. The flood renews the fertility of these lands annually by heavy silt brought down from the Ethiopian Plateau, and the soil is considered among the most fertile in the world. This type also includes the areas watered by the two seasonal streams of Gash and Baraka in Eastern Sudan. The main problems of this type of cultivation include the wide fluctuation in its area and the relative shortness of the season which limits the variety of crops that can be produced. Apart from long staple cotton produced in the Gash and Baraka basins, various food and fodder crops are produced, mostly for subsistence.

Rainland Agriculture is feasible in well over 100 m acres, of which not more than 5 per cent have so far been utilized. This sector suffers from many problems such as the unreliability of rainfall in Central Sudan and bad drainage and transportation difficulties in Southern Sudan. Most of the crops have until recently consisted of food crops and oil seeds. Latterly the production of short staple cotton is rapidly increasing. The predominant mode of production is still traditional, but in recent years rain cultivation schemes on a mechanized basis have steadily increased partly as a result of an effort to overcome labour scarcity. The rainlands sector also make a substantial contribution to the economy in the field of animal production which itself contributes about one-tenth of the Gross Domestic Product.

The productivity of rainland agriculture is not easy to measure because estimates of both area and output are only very approximate and because of wide fluctuations in area and yield. Nevertheless, its productivity measured in terms of labour or land is certainly extremely low. A major explanatory factor is probably the abundance of land so that peasants do not have to pay attention to its productivity. However, the mechanized rainland cultivation schemes which now cover over one million feddans, use mostly direct-wage labour rather than crop-sharing tenants. This arrangement provides their owners with incentive to use efficiently capital invested in the clearing and levelling of the land and in machinery.

Irrigated Agriculture is the back-bone of the modern sector of the economy. Although the total area cultivated is much smaller than the area under rainland cultivation, this sector enjoys a much greater stability in area and average yield and in volume of output. It produces almost all the long as well as some of the short staple cotton and accounts for over 75 per cent of the country's cotton exports.

Three methods of irrigation are in use in the Sudan. The first method employs the traditional devices of the *Sagia* and the *Shaduf*. The Sagia is a water wheel worked by oxen; the Shaduf is a kind of see-saw, manually operated by the use of counter weights. These instruments have been a characteristic feature of the rural landscape of the Nile Valley for hundreds of years, but are now gradually disappearing.

The second method of irrigation employs mechanized pumping, which is expanding rapidly to replace the traditional methods and to cover the new riverain lands. Pump schemes extend mainly along the two banks of the main Nile and its tributaries. In size they vary considerably from 10 feddans to 18,000 feddans.[1] As a result of the high prices of agricultural products and the availability of capital, the number of these schemes grew rapidly from 372 schemes irrigating 170,000 feddans in 1944 to 2,229 schemes irrigating 777,000 feddans in 1957. Expansion continued after 1957 but at a much slower rate owing to the sharp decline in agricultural prices. Most of the area under pump schemes is in the long-staple cotton growing region of the Blue Nile Province.

Pump schemes are controlled by the Government since the utilization of the Nile waters, available to Sudan, is fixed under international agreement and must be supervised. All schemes are licensed on a short concession basis. This has enabled the Government to enforce a tenancy system. The system in the Blue Nile cotton-growing schemes is modelled on that of the Gezira Scheme. The tenant is allocated a 15 feddan tenancy of which one-third is under cotton, one-third under food and fodder crops and one-third is left fallow. The tenant receives 40 per cent of the proceeds of cotton and all the food and fodder crops. The Northern Province schemes produce mainly food crops and although a tenancy system is enforced by law, no system for the sharing of the proceeds has yet been devised. In some schemes water rates are paid in cash by tenants while in others a crop-sharing system is practised. Apart from these private schemes which are owned by private companies, partnerships, individual owners or co-operative societies, the Government itself also operates a few large schemes in the Blue Nile and Northern Province. These are long-established schemes, set up in the 1930's to provide productive employment for the local population.

1 O. M. Osman, 'Some Aspects of Private Pump Schemes', *Sudan Notes and Records*, Vol. XXVII, 1956.

In the last few years the economics of pump schemes have come under a considerable degree of scrutiny with the object of increasing the contribution they make to the national economy. One of their current limitations is that there is normally no means by which the more vigorous or enterprising tenant can increase his holding. Another problem (which has a bearing on the problem of development generally) is that tenants seem to wish to spend a large part of their incomes from cotton on casual labour to pick the crop instead of themselves undertaking the task, preferring to take their higher incomes in the form of increased leisure. This also appears to be a problem in the Gezira Scheme which is discussed below.

In 1967 the Government announced its intention of forming an Agricultural Reform Corporation to take over the administration of private schemes as their licences expire. It is proposed to form co-operative unions for each scheme to take over the management as soon as they have acquired the necessary technical experience. About 400 schemes are affected immediately by this new policy. Compensation is to be paid. The Corporation will also supervise those private schemes whose licences have not yet expired and will be responsible for the development of land not at present under cultivation.

The third method of irrigation relies on gravity to produce the flow of water. Of the large-scale gravity irrigation schemes, the Gezira is the oldest and best known. The scheme is irrigated by the flow of water raised by the Sennar Dam. The original scheme covers one million feddans and there are 800,000 feddans in the new Managil extension which was completed in the 1957-60 period. Tenancies are of 40 feddans in the original scheme and 15 feddans in the Managil Extension. The rotation system in the original scheme devotes 10 feddans to long staple cotton and 10 feddans to food and fodder crops. In the new extension 5 feddans are devoted to cotton and 5 feddans to food and fodder crops. The rest of the tenancy is left fallow to rest.

The Gezira involves a tripartite partnership scheme between Government, tenants and Management. Government's role has been to provide water by constructing the Dam and canals and regulating its flow. The tenants provide labour for the sowing and harvesting of the crops. Management supervises the cultivation and harvest, sells the cotton and distributes the proceeds in addition to providing technical and social services to tenants. From 1924 to 1950, management was entrusted to a British Company. This was replaced at the end of its concession by a Government-controlled Board. In 1966 the Government received 42 per cent of the proceeds of cotton, the tenants 46 per cent and the Board 12 per cent. In addition to his share of cotton proceeds the tenant gets all the food and fodder crops, which helps to shelter him from the effects of wide fluctuations in the average yield or in the price of cotton.

On the whole the Gezira Scheme has operated satisfactorily. This owes much to the manner in which its organization has combined the advantages of public ownership and large-scale units with those of private ownership and small units. Although the land remains in the nominal ownership of the original private owners who receive an annual nominal rent, it is compulsorily leased to the Government for a period of 40 years, open for extension. The original owner, who is in most cases a tenant of the Scheme, enjoys the satisfaction of ownership although in practice, this merely entitles him to priority in securing the tenancy. Basically he is rewarded for his labour services, yet he has the satisfaction of the feeling that he is utilizing his own property. The decision to nationalize the use of land in the Gezira was taken mainly to enable the Government to design the lay-out of the Scheme in the most convenient and efficient manner; to avoid the problems of land fragmentation caused by the Muslim system of inheritance and to place the tenant under a sufficient degree of agricultural control—he can be evicted if he does not fulfil his functions properly even if he is the owner of the land. Within flexible and broad boundaries of control the tenant enjoys a wide degree of freedom and is provided with incentive to devote himself to the management of his tenancy. Large scale public ownership placed Government in a favourable position to provide the water by constructing the Dam and the network of canals and also facilitated the provision of services such as technical advice, crop spraying, marketing, social services and mechanized ploughing which are best handled by one centralized body such as the Management Board.

The most notable benefit of the Scheme is that it has greatly expanded the output of long staple cotton in the Sudan. In doing so, it has also provided the Gezira tenant with a much higher standard of living than is enjoyed in any other rural area in the country and perhaps higher even than that which is enjoyed by a large proportion of the urban population. Also the Scheme has until recently contributed substantially to the finance of the capital development programme. Nevertheless, its success is not unalloyed and recently as the Scheme's contribution to development finance has fallen and cotton prices have fluctuated, concern with some aspects of its progress has mounted. In the first place, the productivity of the Scheme over the last thirty years has been virtually static. During 1934–43 average yields in kantars[1] per feddan were 4·07. During the period 1954–63

[1] A kantar is approximately 100 lbs.

they were 4·50, a very slow increase despite substantial research inputs and increased inputs of other factors over the period.[1]

Physical factors partly explained this unsatisfactory state, but part of the explanation may be that under the present system the tenant has an incentive to devote any additional efforts to the production of crops other than cotton, since he receives the proceeds from these other goods in full. The whole policy of encouraging the growth of subsistence crops is now being questioned and it has been argued that it would be better to encourage the growth of more cash crops (groundnuts have been suggested).

This debate might raise some doubt about the return to investment in the schemes which are being newly set up on the Gezira pattern in other parts of the country. However, a recent study by the World Bank has indicated that even at present very low prices of cotton, the return to Government capital in such new schemes exceeds 10 per cent. These new major gravity-irrigation schemes include the construction of the Khasm el Girba Dam on the Atbara River which will bring another 500,000 feddans under cultivation. Of this some 150,000 feddans have so far been utilized mainly by people displaced by the Egyptian High Dam. The remaining area is intended to be utilized in the immediate future although the likelihood of attracting sufficient additional tenants and seasonal labour does not seem, at present, promising. The Roseires Dam on the Blue Nile which was completed in 1965 should enable the Gezira Scheme to use more water, to change the existing crop-rotation system and to expand the area under other cash crops such as wheat and groundnuts. The New Dam will also bring under cultivation a further 1·8 million feddans in the Kenana area to the South of the existing Gezira Scheme.

Productivity in irrigated agriculture is certainly higher than in rainland agriculture because of the high capital investment which provides a more reliable water supply and the greater fertility of land. A feddan in the irrigated schemes produces, on the average 4 kantars of seed-cotton, whereas less than one kantar of much lower quality of cotton is produced in rainland conditions. Compared with other countries such as Egypt which use the same techniques of cultivation and produce the same type of cotton, productivity in the Sudan is considerably lower. This may be due to the less intensive methods of cultivation and the smaller use of fertilizers and insecticides. However, there are indications that the average yield of rainland agriculture is gradually improving, but this is reflected in a re-

[1] '*The Development of Agriculture in the Main Gezira Area*', Interim Report by the Working Party, Ministry of Agriculture, May 1965, pp. 16–18.

duced frequency of low-yield seasons rather than an increase in maximum yield.

5. LABOUR AND WAGES

The 1956 Census estimated the country's labour force at 4·8 m or 47·3 per cent of the population. The Census included in the definition of labour force all persons considered as being 'economically active' rather than 'gainfully employed'. The rather high percentage is explained mainly by the fact that a substantial proportion of the population consists of nomad and semi-nomad tribes whose children become economically active, as shepherds, at a very early age.

At the time of the Census nearly 86 per cent of the labour force was engaged in agricultural and pastoral activities and almost two-thirds of these were engaged in subsistence production of low productivity. The industrial sector which includes handicrafts, maintenance workshops and factories employed about 5 per cent of the labour force, leaving another 5 per cent for services including Government and 2 per cent for commerce.

Table 10. *Industrial distribution of labour force in 1955–56*

Sector	Numbers ('000)	%
Agriculture, livestock production, forestry and fishing	4,154	85·6
Manufacturing[a]	248	5·1
Construction	31	0·6
Commerce	100	2·1
Transport	31	0·6
Services	223	4·6
Unskilled and unclassified	64	1·3
Total Sudan all sectors	4,851	100

Note: [a] Manufacturing includes hand-crafts, work-shops and factory employment as well.

Source: Economic Survey, 1964, p. 75.

The Census indicates that nearly one-third of the labour force is in wage employment. This proportion is likely to have increased during recent years as a result of the expansion in modern agricultural schemes, industry, Government services and commerce, but no later estimates are available.

Nine-tenths of the labour force is male. It is also very young; almost 20 per cent of the labour force is under the age of 15, and nearly 50 per cent is under the age of 20. Most of the wage labour is in the urban areas. There is considerable temporary and seasonal migration to towns involving a high turnover of labour.

No reliable information is available about the level and structure of wages. There is no legal minimum wage rate, perhaps because the Government has always been the largest employer of labour and could therefore set the standard for other employers to follow. In addition a need for fixing minima has not been felt because labour has on the whole enjoyed a seller's market. The Government fixes the wage rate for its own employees. For the lowest paid employees the standard is the reasonable subsistence need of an average family estimated in 1952 at £5·7 per month. The wage rate then increases according to skill and responsibility to a maximum basic rate which was £37·5 in 1952. Female workers are paid four-fifths of this rate except in a few occupations, such as nursing. To maintain the real value of wages a cost-of-living allowance is paid which is periodically adjusted with changes to the cost-of-living index. These wage levels set the pattern for wages in the economy at large. On the whole, real wages appear to have been rather stable since 1956.

A substantial proportion of workers is organized in trade unions in accordance with the 1948 Trade Unions Ordinance which is modelled on the lines of similar British laws. The right of collective action is guaranteed by the 1948 Regulation of Trade Disputes Ordinance. Apart from this, the 1952 Wages Tribunal Ordinance provide for negotiations between representatives of employers and workers to fix minimum wages and other conditions of employment. This is confined to categories of workers such as domestic servants who are not, or cannot, be conveniently organized in a trade union. The Trade Union movement is not strong or well organized, and it was completely suppressed for a period under the military regime of 1958–64. Three other laws define minimum working conditions and terms of employment. The Workshop and Factories Ordinance enforces minimum standards of safety and hygiene. The Employers and Employed Persons Ordinance defines minimum terms of employment, other than wages, such as the length of working day, leave and gratuity payments and over-time payments. The 'Workmen's Compensation Ordinance' regulates compensation of workers for any injuries suffered while performing their work.

6. INDUSTRIALIZATION

Industrial activity was unimportant in the economy of the Sudan until after independence in 1956. Factories employing 50 persons or more were few in number and most of the industrial undertakings which existed then were of the cottage-type engaged in oil-pressing, hand-weaving, domestic glass-ware and consumer goods to satisfy the needs of local markets. The year 1955–56 witnessed a spurt in industrial production which has continued to grow at an average annual rate of 15 per cent and is planned to increase to 20 per cent during the Ten-year Plan period.

Several factors have contributed to the recent rapid expansion. The availability of capital from internal sources due to agricultural expansion and higher agricultural product prices in the early 1950's and from external sources was naturally a major factor. The decline in the profitability of agricultural schemes in the second half of the 1950's also encouraged a redirection of resources to industrial investment. There was also an obvious improvement in the supply of skill and entrepreneurial factors, and the policy emphasis of the new National Government was of great importance. Indirectly the Government has encouraged industrial growth by the progressive raising of import duties, undertaken mainly to increase revenue, and also by restricting imports of consumer goods to conserve the continuously diminishing foreign exchange reserves.

Direct measures to promote industrial expansion have also played an important role. The Approved Enterprises Act of 1956 empowers the Minister of Commerce, Industry and Supply to offer generous assistance to new enterprises, approved by the Industrial Advisory Committee. The assistance includes the provision of industrial sites at a nominal price, exemption from import duties on machinery, equipment and raw materials and exemption from Business Profit Tax for a period of up to five years.

In addition, the Government established in 1962 the Sudan Industrial Bank to help in the finance of new and existing industrial undertakings and to provide technical assistance and advice and to carry out feasibility studies. A Government sponsored industrial Research Institute is expected to begin its activities in 1966 and has the objective of undertaking technological and economic research to help industrial expansion.

The Government also takes an active role in the industrial field by promoting its own undertakings. To manage these enterprises and to undertake the establishment of new ones, the Government in 1965 set up the Industrial Development Corporation. The Corporation is also empowered by law to help private industrial firms by carrying out investigations and by offering them advice and generally to co-ordinate the activities of the industrial public sector with those of the private sector.

Enterprises so far operated by the IDC include the two sugar factories at Guneid and Khasm-el-Girba, a tannery in Khartoum, a cardboard factory based on cotton stalks at Aroma, and several fruit canning factories. Operating experience has been mixed, but it seems clear that several undertakings were established without proper feasibility studies, and have run into economic difficulties. In some cases, as in food processing, the problems are of an agricultural, rather than an industrial, nature in the sense that the difficulties have arisen because of inadequate and irregular supplies, in some cases of poor quality.

An indicator of the industrial expansion, which has taken place, the Gross Value added by manufacturing industry increased from £2·76 m in 1955–56 to £6·6 m in 1961–62. Although all types of manufacturing expanded, the relative share of various types underwent considerable change. The share of food manufacturing declined from 54 per cent to 49 per cent and beverages and tobacco from 37 per cent to 33 per cent while the share of paper and printing increased from 3 per cent to 5 per cent, rubber and chemicals from 6 per cent to 9 per cent and tiles, cement and glass from 9 per cent to 10 per cent.

7. TRADE

Cotton has dominated the exports of the Sudan for nearly 40 years, and accounted on the average for over 65 per cent of the value of domestic exports. Although other exports rose steadily in volume and value, cotton retained a high share because of the steady expansion in Government and private cotton-growing schemes. Gum-arabic exports, which account for over 80 per cent of total world consumption, continued to occupy the second place although its relative share continued to decline steadily. Livestock exports fell to fifth place, towards the middle of the 1950's losing the third place to groundnuts, and the fourth place to sesame.

The projection of exports in the Ten-year Plan shows cotton maintaining its dominant place although its relative share may decline by 1970 to about 60 per cent. The share of gum arabic is expected to drop to the fourth place leaving the second and third places to groundnuts and sesame respectively.

The character of imports has changed considerably in recent years.

Table 11. *Foreign trade*
(£S m)

	Exports							Imports			
	Cotton lint and seed	Gum Arabic	Ground-nuts	Sesame	Cattle and hides	Others and re-exports	Total exports	Total imports	Consumer goods	Raw materials	Capital goods and building materials
1950	24·8	2·7	0·2	—	1·8	3·6	33·1	27·3	18·8	4·3	4·2
1951	49·3	3·5	0·8	0·4	2·0	6·8	62·8	42·0	28·0	8·2	5·8
1952	31·5	2·5	1·1	1·3	1·3	5·1	42·8	61·7	39·1	12·5	10·1
1953	30·0	3·0	2·0	1·5	1·6	6·3	44·4	50·8	29·5	8·7	12·6
1954	24·9	3·8	1·1	1·6	2·4	6·6	40·4	48·5	30·8	7·6	10·1
1955	33·8	4·7	2·4	1·8	1·9	5·9	50·5	48·8	30·4	8·4	10·0
1956	46·9	5·4	3·8	2·1	2·6	6·1	66·9	45·2	28·4	8·8	8·0
1957	28·8	4·7	4·7	3·0	3·1	7·1	51·4	67·6	40·1	12·7	14·8
1958	23·8	5·2	3·4	2·2	2·4	6·4	43·4	59·5	27·5	12·5	19·5
1959	45·0	5·1	3·6	2·8	2·2	8·1	66·8	57·0	33·2	11·2	12·6
1960	36·3	7·0	4·4	4·6	2·5	8·9	63·7	63·0	33·4	12·4	17·2
1961	34·7	6·1	5·4	4·2	2·5	9·3	62·2	81·5	40·4	14·1	27·0
1962	48·5	4·6	6·7	5·6	1·8	11·7	78·9	89·3	39·5	19·1	30·7
1963	49·4	5·5	5·9	4·8	2·3	10·7	78·6	97·6	45·8	23·2	28·6
1964	33·6	6·5	9·2	6·5	1·7	11·1	68·6	93·2	44·7	20·1	28·4
1965	33·1	7·2	8·6	4·8	3·2	11·1	68·0	72·3			

Source: *The Ten Year Plan of Economic and Social Development 1961/62—1970/71* and *Economic Survey 1964*, Ministry of Finance and Economics, Khartoum.

Between 1950 and 1963 the share of consumer goods declined from 70 per cent to 46 per cent while the share of raw materials increased from 15 per cent to 24 per cent and the share of capital goods and building materials increased from 15 per cent to 30 per cent. The Ten-year Plan projection put the share of consumer goods in total imports (before import substitution) by 1970, at 57 per cent, raw materials at 20 per cent and capital goods and building materials at 23 per cent. Import substitution is expected to reduce total imports by

Table 12. *Sources and destination of foreign trade*
(£S'000)

	Sources of imports		Destination of exports	
	1960	1965	1960	1965
Sterling Area				
United Kingdom	17,344	16,918	16,473	6,198
India	7,675	6,490	6,539	4,210
Uganda	826	2,190	6	—
Kenya	429	715	61	48
EEC				
France	1,840	1,562	3,055	2,937
W. Germany	5,210	3,835	3,983	7,121
Belgium, Luxemburg	1,252	1,570	1,028	1,970
Netherlands	1,251	2,571	1,583	4,447
Italy	3,339	2,497	4,313	6,997
USSR	2,287	2,583	2,007	—
UAR	5,339	2,815	3,022[a]	1,890[a]
Japan	1,622	6,819	1,789	2,708
China	772	2,283	3,275	—
USA	1,826	4,728	2,003	2,040
Other Countries	11,986	14,713	11,513	26,572
Total	62,998	72,289	60,650	67,138

Note: [a] Excluding camels on the hoof.
Source: Yearbook of International Trade Statistics, United Nations; *Foreign Trade Statistics of the Sudan, Khartoum.*

about 24 per cent; its effect will be mainly on consumer goods and to a lesser degree on imports of building materials.

The direction of trade has also undergone significant changes during the last decade. Although Britain has continued to occupy first place as supplier and purchaser, its relative share declined considerably. Comparing the 1949–51 and 1962–63 periods, Britain's share in Sudan exports declined from 65 per cent to 15 per cent while its share in Sudan imports declined from 37 per cent to 28 per cent.

The drop in Britain's imports from the Sudan was compensated by new customers in EEC (mainly West Germany) whose share increased from 8 to 28 per cent and members of Socialist countries whose share increased from 0·5 per cent to 14 per cent. India's share also increased from about 10 per cent to 12 per cent. As for Sudan imports, the share of the Common Market countries increased from 7 to about 19 per cent and that of the Socialist countries from 5 to 10 per cent, while the share of India dropped to about 7 per cent.

The export trade of Sudan over the period since 1945 is characterized by extreme fluctuations. Sudan ranks number six in the order of instability calculated by Coppock comprising 83 countries.[1] The following periods can be distinguished: an export boom culminating in 1951, two cycles from 1952–56 and 1957–63, followed by a fairly steady period for the three succeeding years. The value of exports rose from £16·9 m in 1947 to £79·6 m in 1951, when the balance of trade reached a peak surplus of £38 m. In the following year, 1952 both the quantity exported and the price of cotton decreased and by 1954 total exports were down to about £40 m. They recovered to about £70 m in 1956 but dropped back in 1957 and 1958. In 1962 and 1963 exports ran at about £79 m a year, but still did not exceed the 1951 record. Since then exports have been running at about £70 m annually. A notable feature has been the way in which imports have lagged about a year behind exports, so that the trade balance has oscillated violently: a surplus of £38 m in 1951 being followed by a deficit of £14·5 m in 1952, a surplus of £23·5 m in 1956 by a deficit of £18·1 m in 1957. Since 1961 there has been a deficit every year ranging from £7 m to £30 m, and these wide fluctuations have made it extremely difficult for the Government to follow a consistent fiscal policy.

Export trade in the Sudan is completely in the hands of private trading firms, most of which are foreign or run by immigrant businessmen. Government exercises little control except over the sale of cotton produced in Government controlled schemes. Even here its role does not go beyond agreeing with the Gezira Board on its cotton auction arrangements, especially the fixing of minimum prices to which reference has already been made. In recent years the Government has also shown some interest in the marketing of gum arabic with a view to guaranteeing minimum prices for local producers. Import trade also is largely in the hands of foreign trading firms but it was announced in 1967 that these are to be completely Sudanized within 5 years. The Government role in imports has been confined to the purchasing of Government's own supplies which account, on

[1] J. D. Coppock, *International Economic Instability*, New York 1962.

the average, for about 25 per cent of the value of imports, including the import of sugar which has always been monopolized by the Government. In future it will also import jute, insecticides and fertilizers.

Preferential trade arrangements exist only with the United Arab Republic, which was, until political independence in 1956, in a form of currency and customs union with the Sudan. Currently the preferential reductions of import duties between the two countries range from 20 per cent to complete exemption. In addition there is a trade and payments agreement. As the balance of payments tends always to be against UAR, the Sudan Government favours importation of some commodities which are subject to import licence from UAR. Bilateral trade agreements have also been concluded between Sudan and several Eastern European countries.

Sudan's import policy tends on the whole to be liberal. For control purposes, imports are divided into two categories: (1) goods which may be imported under an open general licence and (2) goods which require an import licence. The first category can be imported freely but importers must complete registration forms for record purposes and for the allocation of foreign exchange. The second category can only be imported on licence if and when the Ministry of Commerce makes an announcement calling for applications. The Ministry sometimes specifies the prices and the countries from which imports can be obtained. The criteria for drawing the line between the two categories are not clear but are evidently influenced by such factors as the protection of local industries, the preservation of foreign exchange reserves and by the need to support bilateral trade agreements. There is much flexibility in the determination of the variety of imports which are subject to control but the general tendency is to restrict these to as few commodities as possible.

The Sudan has not seriously considered establishing any special relationship with the EEC, though trade relations with its members are close and growing. A major reason for lack of interest in association is that the Sudan has hitherto had little to gain, mainly because Sudan exports to the Community dominated by cotton and gum arabic, are exempted from custom duties. Moreover, Associate Members of the Community are not likely to be serious competitors of the Sudan as far as the existing exports are concerned. However, in the future association could well yield benefits in the light of the plan to expand the production and export of seed-oils. The Community's import duties on seed oil are considerable whereas imports of oil-seeds are exempted from duties.

8. CONCLUSIONS

In spite of the remarkable economic, social and political transformation of the Sudan during the past sixty years, the economy remains basically agricultural and pastoral. Judged by average income per head in the whole country, the Sudan is still amongst the poorer half of the developing countries. That this is so in spite of its potentially vast agricultural resources, may be attributed to the predominance of subsistence production, traditional techniques and nomadism. Essentially the Sudan consists of two distinct sectors which are geographically separated. The modern exchange sector occupies largely the north-eastern quarter of the country, while the western and southern parts are predominantly subsistence and traditional. Government development strategy has hitherto concentrated on the more developed districts and has left the remaining districts to grow slowly at a rate which is not much higher than the rate of growth of its inhabitants. The slow expansion of education and transportation improvements are virtually the only stimulants received by these poorer regions, and the spread effect from greater growth in the north is negligible. The effect of this approach has, at least in political terms, shown signs of being disastrous; and has resulted in the continued unrest in the three Southern Provinces and of other regional political groupings which, at present, agitate for more attention.

On political grounds there are strong reasons for thinking that, especially after the return of democratic rule, the Government should modify the emphasis of its development policy and spread its efforts more widely, even if the result is initially a slowing down of the overall rate of economic growth. It may be however, that even on economic grounds a more generalized development effort is called for. In the first place it may help to overcome the shortage of labour which has been encountered in the development of agricultural schemes in the north and east. In the second place it seems likely that it is only through such a change of emphasis that diversification which is a major objective of economic policy, will be able to make headway in the forseeable future. Moreover, a fuller utilization of the country's vast agricultural resources entailing a progressive modernization of methods of agricultural production must in any case be the basis for any substantial improvement of the living standards in the Sudan. In this connection it deserves emphasis that Sudan is one of the few countries in Africa which seems likely to be capable of producing a substantial food surplus for export in the 1970's.

SELECTED READING

1. Wahab, A. A., 'The Financing of Economic Development in the Sudan—The Public Sector', *Proceedings, Institute of Public Administration of the Sudan* (Khartoum, 1962).
2. Kubinski, Z. M., *Public Finance for Stability and Growth in an Underdeveloped Economy*, a case study of the Republic of the Sudan (International Bureau of Fiscal Documentation, Amsterdam, 1961).
3. *The Ten Year Plan of Economic and Social Development 1961–62–1970–71* (The Economic Secretariat, Ministry of Finance and Economics, Khartoum).
4. *Capital Formation and Increase in National Income in Sudan in 1955–59* (Department of Statistics, Khartoum, 1961).
5. 'The Population of the Sudan'; in *Report on the Sixth Annual Conference* (Philosophical Society of Sudan, 1958).
6. *Agricultural Development in the Sudan* (The Sudan Agricultural Society, The Thirteenth Annual Conference, Khartoum, 1965).
7. Wells, F. A., 'Economic Development in the Sudan', *The Three Banks Review*, No. 61, March 1964.
8. Harvie, C. H., and Kleve, J. G., *The National Income of the Sudan* (Department of Statistics, Khartoum, 1959).
9. Shaw, D. J., 'A Note on the Sudan's Ten-Year Plan of Economic and Social Development', *Agricultural Economics Bulletin for Africa* No. 3, June, 1963.
10. Tothill, J. D., *Agriculture in the Sudan* (Oxford University Press, London, 1948).
11. Gaitskell, A., *Gezira: A story of Development in the Sudan* (Faber and Faber, London 1959).
12. Mahhouk, A., and Drees, F., 'Domestic Policies and Payments Problems of the Sudan, 1947–62', *IMF Staff Papers* XI (1), March 1964.

10

THE ECONOMY OF ALGERIA

1. INTRODUCTION

An analysis of the economy of Algeria today is bound to be fragmentary. Statistics cover only a few of the principal events which have taken place since 1959 and 1960, the last years for which comprehensive data are available. In the course of the last few years fundamental changes have taken place in the whole Algerian society. Thus, although a fairly exact picture of the Algerian economy in 1959 or even 1960 can be drawn, a picture of Algeria today can contain quantitative assessments of only some of the fundamental aspects of the economic structure of the country; for others only qualitative descriptions are possible.

The Historical Background

Algeria was administratively a part of France until the summer of 1962. Its way to independence was long and cruel. The French government did not recognize Algeria as a political unit which—like Morocco and Tunisia—was under temporary French control. On the contrary, the official French attitude was that an Algerian state had never existed, and that the Algerian departments simply were parts of France like the departments in France itself. The basis for this political philosophy was that no unified Algerian state existed when France occupied the country in 1830. In 1954 the FLN (The National Liberation Front) started an armed uprising against the French rule. This soon developed into a guerilla war which lasted until the cease fire of March 19, 1962, agreed in Evian between representatives of France and the FLN. At that time the French military forces in Algeria numbered 500,000 and heavy losses had been inflicted on both sides, but particularly on the Moslem population which may have suffered many hundred thousand casualties.

The war lasted so long for another reason: the French government became for a while the prisoner of the European minority in Algeria. This minority, which only partly consisted of people of French origin, controlled the economic and social life of the country. In the whole of Africa its position could be compared only with that of the European population in South Africa. Until about 1930 there were more non-Moslems than Moslems in the Algerian towns. Up to Independence the capital Algiers had barely a Moslem majority and the next largest city Oran had a European majority. At the same time most of the modern farming was in the hands of Europeans, and in the cities and towns they held almost all skilled jobs. The European community was not only against an independent Algeria under Moslem leadership, but also against a French policy which meant equality between Moslems and Non-Moslems in Algeria. They sabotaged progressive policy measures initiated by France after the Second World War. When the French electorate in 1956 chose a government which aimed to defeat the Algerian uprising through a policy of justice, the Europeans in Algeria threw rotten fruit at the new prime minister and frightened the government into sterner military actions rather than political steps. Even this was not enough, and in 1958 the Europeans in Algiers started the movement which toppled the Fourth Republic and brought de Gaulle to power. Later on two occasions they tried to force de Gaulle's hand or bring him down, but without success. Finally came the most ugly of all efforts to maintain European superiority and control in Algeria—the OAS (Organization of the Secret Army), a terrorist movement which killed thousands of innocent Moslems in Algeria, and held Paris in terror for some time through bomb explosions and murders in 1962.

The violence of the years before Independence led in turn to dramatic changes in the social and economic structure. During the war about one-quarter of the Moslem population migrated—2 million were 'regrouped' by the French authorities, and a large number migrated temporarily to Tunisia or Morocco.

The return of peace led to renewed movements amongst the Moslem population, which were dwarfed, however, by the mass exodus of the non-Moslem population. This was estimated at one million in 1960 in Algeria other than Sahara. About 140,000 of this population were Israelites, but the great majority were French citizens. Most of the European population had directly or indirectly supported hard French policies against the Moslems, and what was worse, the OAS terrorist movement, and they feared the revenge of the winning Moslems. Moreover, they felt that they had no economic future in a country in which they no longer were undisputed masters. The European part of the non-Moslem population therefore left. At the end of 1963 there were only 60,000 French citizens left in Algeria,

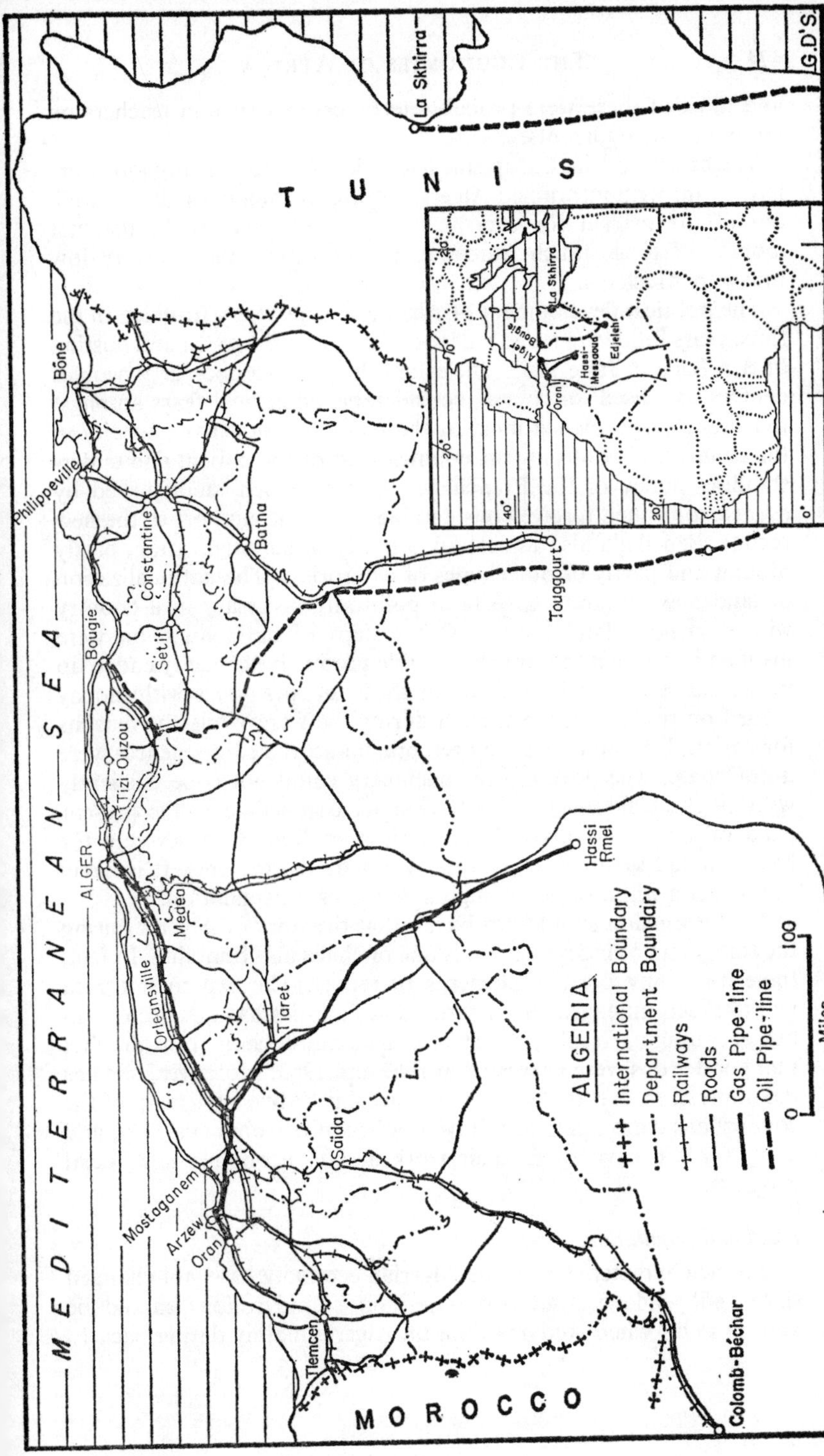

MEDITERRANEAN SEA
TUNIS
MOROCCO
G.D'S.
La Skhirra
Bône
Philippeville
Constantine
Batna
Bougie
Setif
Tizi-Ouzou
ALGER
Medea
Orleansville
Tiaret
Mostaganem
Arzew
Oran
Saida
Tlemcen
Touggourt
Hassi Rmel
Colomb-Béchar
ALGERIA
International Boundary
Department Boundary
Railways
Roads
Gas Pipe-line
Oil Pipe-line
0
100
Miles
La Skhirra
Alger
Bougie
Hassi-Messaoud
Edjeleh
Oran

Map 8

and most of these were probably technical experts and teachers on temporary assignments.

The exodus of the Europeans had a double effect: many jobs were left vacant without trained Algerians to fill them and the bottom fell out of the market for consumer goods and services. In the first months of panic much European property was sold for very low prices to Moslems.

The political development of Algeria was also very troubled in the three years following independence ending with the arrest and ousting of Ben Bella in June 1965. The establishment of a one-party peoples democracy raised, of course, considerable additional fears amongst the French who owned most of the modern productive capacity in the country. This was in part counteracted by the patient and understanding policy of the French government which, undisturbed by events, continued to give considerable economic support to the new regime. Ben Bella also undertook a policy of nationalization, partly of land and partly of other types of enterprises. The nationalization of land may certainly have been politically necessary in a country with enormous land hunger. Other steps of nationalization were justified by the fact that much valuable productive capacity ended up in the hands of Moslems who bought it for low prices with money earned on trade with the French during the war. While the reasons for nationalization may have been pragmatic, the consequences were unfortunate. The government machinery could not cope efficiently with all the tasks on its hands. Colonel Boumedienne, the present head of state, and his followers criticized Ben Bella severely for having failed to solve the country's economic problems. It is likely that Algeria will now go through a period of consolidation.

The impression should not be left that the story of Algeria during the four years of independence is one of chaos and fumbling. In fact, there are many positive elements to report. The experiment with workers' self management of farms and factories has not been without encouraging results, which *inter alia* can be seen from the fact that good crops were harvested in 1962 and 1963. Moreover, one has the impression that the political and administrative leadership of the country has determined to follow a policy of personal austerity, and that they are devoted to their work and to economic and social progress.

Land and population

The basic characteristics of the Algerian economy have not changed since Independence, but two important considerations should be kept in mind when studying data on Algeria mainly dating back to

1959 and 1960. The non-Moslem population has fallen by at least four-fifths since 1961, and its role in the economy has to a great extent been taken over by the state or by Algerians; and due mainly to the mass exodus of non-Moslem consumers (i.e. former European residents in Algeria plus half a million French soldiers) and partly to the effects on production of this mass exodus, the output of secondary and tertiary industries has fallen drastically.

Algeria falls into two distinct parts: first the wide belt of land 600 miles long and 200 miles wide between the Mediterranean and the Sahara; secondly the Sahara itself. Some of the land included in the old 13 departments of Algeria stretched into the Sahara, while parts of the Sahara proper belong to neighbouring countries in West, South and East. Including the Sahara, Algeria has an area which is about as large as that of Congo Kinshasa, and Sudan is the only African country that is larger. In population, however, Algeria holds only the eighth position in Africa.

The Sahara constitutes a most valuable part of Algeria due to its vast mineral resources of which petroleum and natural gas are exploited intensively. In discussing the economy of the country it is useful to distinguish between the Sahara and the rest of Algeria.

Two mountain ranges run parallel to the sea and in general only the narrow plains and the hillsides close to the sea get more than 16 inches of rain annually. There are small areas between the mountain ranges which get reasonably adequate rainfall. Western Algeria gets less rain than Eastern Algeria and even at the coast in the West, annual rainfalls of below 16 inches are normal.

Most of the population lives in this relatively fertile area within 60 to 125 miles from the sea. Four of the departments listed in Table 1 are landlocked. These are the four most sparsely populated ones, all with a density of population of 39 per sq. mile or less, (Medea, Tiaret, Saida and Batna). They have a population of 1·8 million or 18 per cent of the total, and an area of below 70,000 sq. miles or 60 per cent of the land area.[1] Adjustments of the figures, show that more than 85 per cent of the population is concentrated in regions with a relatively high density of 185 persons per sq. mile. While this is not high compared to most Asian or European countries, it is for a country which still is basically a nation of farmers and herdsmen, and in which climatic and soil conditions are difficult.

[1] We get a more correct picture of the distribution of the population if we use the figures for "arrondissements" (i.e. districts within the departments) instead of departments. This gives us the following figures: about 1·4 million people lived in thinly populated areas with a total area of 69,000 sq. miles. These areas had an average density of 21 persons per sq. mile while the rest had a density of 185.

The last line of Table 1 shows that the exodus of the European population during the period 1960–64 has been offset by the natural growth of the Moslem population and to some extent the return from the neighbouring countries of war refugees. It is likely that the outflow of Europeans has led to some changes in the urban/rural distribution of the population, but the changes are possibly not significant, except in the case of Oran, because of the continued migration of Moslems to the cities.

Table 1. *Area and population*

	Population (thousands)				Density
	Moslems	Non-Moslems	Total	Area (sq. miles)	(per sq. m)
Departments (1960):					
Alger	925	415	1,340	1,300	1020
Tizi-Ouzou	885	14	899	2,250	401
Orleansville	680	31	711	4,750	150
Medea	680	17	697	19,450	36
Oran	685	307	992	6,350	155
Tlemcen	350	31	381	3,150	122
Mostaganem	595	56	651	4,400	147
Tiaret	280	17	297	10,000	28
Saida	200	10	210	23,200	8
Constantine	1,195	82	1,277	7,700	165
Bone	735	52	787	9,800	80
Setif	1,065	30	1,095	6,700	162
Batna	575	13	588	14,850	39
Algeria without Sahara (1960)	8,850	1,075	9,925	113,900	88
Sahara (1954)	475	15	490	(805,800)	0·6
Sahara (1960, crude estimate	(525)	(25)	550	(805,800)	0·7
All-Algeria (1960)	9,375	1,100	10,475	(919,700)	11·5
Algeria (1964)	10,230	60[a]	10,290	(852,700)	12·0

Note: [a] Europeans only.

Sources: Figures for 13 Algerian departments 1960, (1), pages 98–100, for the Sahara, area 1954, 1960(1), page 128, population 1954 (1) page 19, population 1960, estimate by the present author.

Figures for 1st January 1964—(13), page 447. Some of the borders in the Sahara are rather undetermined, which perhaps explains the difference between the two figures for the total area.

In 1962, 400,000 Algerian Moslems lived in France[1] of whom 250,000 were workers. The present figure is probably somewhat higher. Severe unemployment in Algeria forces a large part of the labour force to seek employment elsewhere, and as France lacks manpower and still accords relatively free entry of Algerian workers into France, the result is that a significant proportion of the Algerian population lives and works abroad.

Figures on the rate of population growth in Algeria are still somewhat uncertain. Obviously no conclusions can be drawn from comparisons between the figures for the total population at different dates, since both migrations and war losses influence these figures heavily. Estimates made by the statistical office in Algiers in 1960 suggest that the natural rate of growth was around 2 per cent per annum during the period 1955 to 1960 (birthrate slightly below 4 per cent, death rate—excluding deaths caused by the war—close to 2 per cent.)[2]

During the period 1936 to 1948 the Moslem population of Algeria increased by 1·8 per cent per year but between 1948 and 1954 the rate of increase was only 1·6 per cent.[3] The estimated rate of increase is not high by comparison with other less developed economies. This is explained by a relatively high death rate combined with a birth rate which is much lower than elsewhere.

The dual economy

To some extent the dual economy of Algeria as it was in 1960 is a thing of the past, but its effects are not eliminated in the course of a few years. A description of the past situation is therefore still highly relevant, although we must keep in mind that the then modern sector of the economy which on the whole was owned and managed by non-Moslems of European origin, is now to a large extent nationalized and under Algerian management.

In 1958 the average income *per capita* in Algeria was £90 which was about five times more than in India or Pakistan or about twice that of Tunisia. One tentative estimate of the income distribution between Europeans and Moslems shows, however, that this relative prosperity of Algeria only benefited a small minority. The average income of the European population in 1954 was estimated at 360,000 old francs per head (£365 on the basis of the then prevailing exchange rate), against 29,000 old francs (£29·5) for the Moslems. A comparison between Algeria and France shows that the Europeans in Algeria had an income which was one-third higher than the average income of the French in France, while it was twelve times higher than

[1] *Source:* (3), page 15. [2] *Source:* (1), p. 21. [3] *Ibid.*, p. 219.

the average income of the Algerian Moslem population, in spite of the fact that many benefited from job opportunities in a prosperous, urban European community.[1] In agriculture income per head was only a little above £23, which meant that the agricultural population in Algeria was not much better off than the people in the poorest countries in the world.

The background to the poverty of the Moslem population was partly the stagnation of traditional agriculture and partly that in the modern economy Moslems had to be satisfied with the lowest paid jobs. These two facts hang together, of course. The population pressure in the rural areas made it unnecessary to entice Moslems to towns with high wages—job opportunities in themselves were sufficient to move more than enough Moslems to the towns. Urban unemployment was, in fact, very high.

The stagnation and the poverty of the Moslem agriculture can be illustrated by a few examples. Although between the period 1911–15 and 1955–59 the output of the three major grains increased from 1·88 million tons to 2·04 million tons, this increase was more than fully accounted for by increased output of hard wheat, 40 per cent of which was produced by European farmers. The output of barley which was mostly grown by Moslems, actually fell. Between 1906 and 1959 the rural Moslem population increased from 3·6 to 6·8 million. No data are available which can show exactly how much the output of the Moslem agriculture changed during this period, but the few figures quoted here suggest that if any change took place output is more likely to have fallen than to have increased. The base period for these estimates was a favourable one, but whatever period is chosen as base and whatever estimates are made of the distribution of grain output between Moslems and non-Moslems, the rural population certainly grew much faster than the Moslem output of food. This stagnation of agricultural output on Moslem owned farms may have had several reasons among which may be mentioned the backwardness of the peasants, who did not manage to raise the yields on their land, and extensive land erosion which reduced the potential output. It has been estimated that 250 acres of land is washed away every day in Algeria.

Statistics on various aspects of the dual economy in Algeria can be summarized as shown opposite.

In evaluating these figures, account must be taken of the fact that the total cultivable land plus vineyards and fruit plantations amounted to about 16·6 million acres in Algeria without Sahara[2] while the land included in the statistics above amounted to 24·2 million acres.

[1] *Source:* (5), p. 143. [2] *Source:* (1), p. 128.

Table 2. *Duality in Algeria's economy before Independence*

	Moslems	Non-Moslems
Algeria excl. Sahara, 1958		
Number of farms	543,310	21,674
Average size of farm (acres)	32·4	307·7
Sahara, 1958		
Number of farms	87,422	363
Average size of farms (acres)	6·2	140·3
Gross agricultural income 1957		
(*a*) Billion old francs	109·0	164·9
(*b*) £ million	111·2	168·3
Sale of agricultural produce 1957		
(*a*) Billion old francs	63·8	160·2
(*b*) £ million	65·1	163·5
Total non-ag. labour force: Males 1954	546,200	245,500
of whom unemployed	130,500	12,900
Per cent of male labour force in agric., 1954	74·0	10·6
Income per head, £ (pre-Independence)		
Agriculture	20·5	735[a]
Other activities	47	330[a]
Total population	29·5	365[a]

Note: [a] Europeans.
Sources: Land ownership (1), page 129; agricultural income (1) pages 132 to 135; labour force (1), pages 26, 27; estimate of income distribution, (6), page 143.

European farmers mostly owned cultivable land, vineyards and fruit plantations, or probably at least about one-third of all such land in Algeria. Thus 22,000 non-Moslem farmers owned about half as much fertile land as almost 550,000 Moslem farmers. Furthermore about one-quarter of the total registered area was farmed by 6,400 non-Moslem farmers (and companies) who owned as much as 90 per cent of the land under non-Moslem ownership. These large farms and some smaller vineyards and fruit plantations were the mainstay of the commercialised Algerian agriculture.

In 1957 non-Moslems produced about 60 per cent of the crops, 90 per cent of the wine and 40 per cent of the cereals. Similar data on fruit and vegetable production are not available, but it is likely that about 80 per cent of this came from non-Moslem owned farms. Thus the dominant position of the non-Moslem agriculturist rested on four types of products: wine, citrus fruits, fresh vegetables for export, and wheat growing on large, mechanized farms. Wine, fruit and fresh vegetables accounted for about five-sixths of the total non-Moslem crop production while cereals and dried pulses accounted for about two-thirds of the Moslem output of crops. These figures suggest the main reason for the key position of non-Moslems in Algeria's agriculture: European farm enterprises exploited the favourable aspects of climatic conditions for development of farm enterprises based on exports. Well developed business acumen, combined with superior financial resources, and helped by knowledge of agricultural technology permitted Europeans to develop a very profitable agriculture on Algerian soil while the Moslem peasants remained miserably poor, and indeed, became even poorer.

There is no clear evidence that these differences are due to the Europeans having acquired all the best land in Algeria. Vineyards can be very successful under soil and climatic conditions which do not favour other forms of cultivation; the same is the case for some types of fruit, while vegetable gardens can be created out of arid land with the help of irrigation. Data of wheat yields in various parts of Algeria do not suggest that non-Moslem farmers settled in departments which have better conditions for wheat than departments in which the Moslems farmers own most of the land. The gap between yields on Moslem owned and non-Moslem owned land is not larger than can reasonably be expected between the yields in traditional and modern agriculture. It seems safe to conclude that, in spite of widespread soil erosion on Moslem owned land, the large difference in agricultural income between Moslem and non-Moslem cultivators was on the whole caused by differences in farm methods and choice of crops.

Income earned per head in Moslem owned agriculture was, of course, very low. If it is assumed that a significant part of the income from Moslem owned farms accrued to large land-owners and owners of modern enterprises, the average annual income of the bulk of the Moslem peasants at the end of the 1950's cannot have been more than about £68 per active worker,[1] or £13½ per family member. Some 150,000 farm labourers worked on non-Moslem owned farms and their income was little higher—maybe somewhere between £85 and £125. By contrast, the income per *head* (*not* per active worker) of non-Moslems in Algeria's agriculture has been estimated at £735 per year during the same period.

The dual character of agriculture is only one aspect of the dual

[1] Family members excluded.

character of the entire economy. Section 5 below gives a striking picture of the degree to which non-Moslems dominated skilled and well paid positions in the non-agricultural sectors of the economy in 1954.

Table 2 shows the rather abnormal distribution of the labour force between agriculture and non-agricultural occupations. Thus, only slightly more than 10 per cent of the non-Moslem labour force worked in agriculture while the non-Moslem owned agriculture in 1957 contributed close to 20 per cent of the Gross Domestic Production. That about three-quarters of the male Moslem (and total) labour force worked in agriculture is normal for a less developed country. But the structure of the agricultural labour force followed distinct racial and religious lines, with the non-Moslems owning or managing the efficient farms, while Moslems, with few exceptions, were peasants on small farms, farm workers or landless casual workers.

As will be seen from Table 11 in the section on labour and wages, this dual employment pattern was present in non-agricultural activities as well. Firstly, unemployment amongst Moslems was both in absolute and in relative terms higher than amongst non-Moslems (about one-quarter against 5 per cent). Secondly, liberal professions and top management jobs were completely dominated by non-Moslems who also held the majority of jobs as skilled workers. Thirdly, the occupational structure amongst non-Moslems was atypical in the sense that the ratio of skilled to unskilled workers was much higher than in the countries of origin of the non-Moslems. Thus, in 1954 there were in Algeria three times as many people in top management and professional jobs as there were university graduates, while in France at the same time the number of such jobs corresponded only to 78 per cent of the number of university graduates.[1] The very low participation of women in the non-Moslem labour force (with only 700 women holding unskilled jobs) also reflected the relative affluence of the Algerian non-Moslems. Fourthly, only 6½ per cent of the non-agricultural labour force were Moslem women. While this may largely be attributed to traditional attitudes amongst Moslems, it also reflected lack of suitable employment opportunities. Fifthly, unequal job opportunities were not only the result of a 'colour-bar', but also of a serious 'education gap'. Thus in 1954 there were four times as many non-Moslems as Moslems in secondary schools and more non-Moslems than Moslems in technical and professional schools. At the university level the gap was even larger.[2]

The fundamental difference between the earning capacity of Moslems and non-Moslems in pre-Independence Algeria is illustra-

[1] *Source:* (3), pp. 77–79.

[2] *Ibid.*, pp. 52–53.

ted by the figures in the bottom part of Table 2. The extreme prosperity of the European farmer and the equally extreme poverty of the Moslem peasants and land-workers are perhaps the two most striking features brought out by the figures. But the fact that the non-Moslems in non-agricultural activities earned seven times as much as the Moslems in these activities is equally significant.

The dualism of the economy was strongly reflected in the regional income distribution. A calculation of income *per capita* in different departments[1] shows that there was a very close correspondence between income per head and proportion of non-Moslems in the different departments. Income per head ranged between £245 in Alger with 2 Moslems for each non-Moslem to £25 in Batna with 71 Moslems for each non-Moslem. Tizi-Ouzou, with a population of 81 Moslems for each non-Moslem would have been at the bottom of the list with an income of £23 per head, if it had not been for the fact that emigrant workers contributed £10 *per capita* of the resident population, i.e. this income constituted 30 per cent of total income in that department. In the Setif department wages from abroad accounted for almost one-quarter of total income.

The main aspects of the dual economy in pre-Independence Algeria may now be briefly summarized: modern agriculture was mainly in non-Moslem hands, and as the supply of labour was ample, the large number of Moslem wage earners on European owned farms were paid very low wages. Traditional agriculture, the source of living of the large majority of the Moslem population, has stagnated or perhaps even declined during the last 50 years. This is not only due to traditional farming methods, but also to the severe risk of soil erosion, unless modern methods of soil protection are used. Urban activities, except small scale retail trade and traditional craftsmanship, were owned and staffed by non-Moslems. Moslems were mostly recruited to unskilled jobs, The number of Moslems who received secondary, technical and higher education was until recently far below the number of non-Moslems who did so. The problems created by the dual economy survived Independence and the exodus of the Europeans. The traditional agriculture in the 'bled' remained as poor as before, and the serious decline of economic activities which followed the exodus of the Europeans and the withdrawal of half a million French troops meant a sharp fall in employment opportunities in non-agricultural activities. In order to get the economy on the move again, the Algerian government had to revive the modern sector of the economy, and was faced with the problem of filling the posts which were left empty after the non-Moslem employees had

[1] Based on (1), page 112 for income, and page 98 for population.

left. As educated Algerians become available to fill these jobs, many more of them become privileged members of the modern part of the dual economy. The programme of nationalization and self-government in Algeria must partly be seen against this background. A large number of foreign owned enterprises, including very many formerly European owned farms, have been nationalized and handed over to the workers for management. The success or failure of this policy depends on how good the management is. If output in the modern farm sector could be maintained and raised, it would be possible to raise the income of the workers/owners on the farms without reducing the profit of the enterprises so much that nothing was left for investments. Data on the non-Moslem agriculture suggest that profits were so high that re-distribution of income should be possible. In non-agricultural activities, however, there may be far less scope for income re-distribution.

Whatever system of ownership and management is retained for the modern sector of the economy, it will need skilled staff at different levels, and even though the Algerian government has followed a far more austere policy of salaries in the public sector than most other newly independent countries, income differentials are unavoidable. Yet new industries in a country on its first steps towards industrialization cannot afford very high wages to the majority of its workers if they are to compete successfully with foreign enterprises or deliver quality goods at reasonable prices to the consumers. The dilemma of the dual economy cannot be overcome as long as the modern sector remains an island of prosperity in the midst of a sea of very poor peasant farmers. This is why the independence movement during the Algerian war and many others asked for first priority for development of the traditional Algerian agriculture. The scope for such development will be discussed in a later section.

The national income and its distribution among sectors

During the war Gross Domestic Product rose very rapidly. Part of the increase was, of course, due to rising prices. Between 1954 and 1958, the last year for which an estimate in constant prices is available, GDP at current prices rose by 78 per cent and at constant prices by 42 per cent. Thus about 55 per cent of the apparent growth was real during that period.

Between 1954 and 1959 the growth in current prices was no less than 105 per cent, and at constant prices it must have been well above 55 per cent. This growth took place in spite of a fall in the output of agriculture. (6 to 7 per cent between 1954 and 1959 according to FAO's index).

Table 3. *Industrial origin of gross domestic product*

	Million dinars (current prices)			Per cent			Per cent (excluding administration)		
	1954	1959	1963	1954	1959	1963	1954	1959	1963
Agriculture, forestry, fishing	1,994	2,685	2,686	30	19	27	34	24	34
Mining, energy	310	341	634	5	4	6	5	5	8
Manufacturing, construction	1,301	2,519	1,483	19	18	15	22	23	18
of which:									
Manufacturing	n.a.	1,520	1,210	n.a.	(11)	(12)	n.a.	(14)	(15)
Construction	n.a.	999	273	n.a.	(7)	(3)	n.a.	(9)	(3)
Services	2,306	5,536	3,472	34	39	35	39	48	42
Algerian administration	514	1,215	1,350	8	8	14	—	—	—
French and other administration	363	(1,800)	(375)	5	13	4	—	—	—
Total	6,788	(14,000)	(10,000)	100	100	100	100	100	100
of which subsistence	—	—	—	(6)	(4)	(5)	—	—	—

Notes: 1 dinar = 100 old or 1 new franc. The French national accounts system which was used in Algeria does not include a figure for government product (i.e. government salaries etc.) in their figure for Gross Domestic *Production.* The figures used for administration are therefore estimated by the present author. *Figures in brackets in this and succeeding tables are crude estimates.*

Sources: 1954: (1), pages 61 and 65; 1959: (1), page 61, (2), page 429, and (12); 1963: (12).

Table 3 shows that between 1954 and 1959 income from services increased much faster than income from production of goods. Private services increased their share by 4 per cent of the GDP, while government services increased its share by 8 per cent. Most of this increase was compensated by a fall in the share of agriculture, but both mining (including oil production) and manufacturing and construction lost part of their share of the Gross Domestic Product as well. This change was a result of the war. The growth of direct French Government expenditure is reflected partly in the fast growth of the government product and partly in the sharp increase in government consumption shown in Table 4. The indirect effects of this growth were partly much higher output of transport services, and of other services, notably trade, but also banking, personal services etc., as well as construction services.

Local manufacturing benefited also to some extent from this additional demand which did not only originate from the Government, but also from the vastly increased number of military and other personnel in Algeria. Output in agriculture did not respond to this additional demand, partly because war operations in themselves hampered agricultural output, and as the Algerian manufacturing industries were concentrated on some few lines of production, most of the added demand for *goods* was met by imports. In addition imported goods had to be transported and marketed by local service industries, which explains the extraordinary fast growth of services industries in Algeria during this period of war.

A war boom is always artificial and the decline of demand which follows the end of a war, will always lead to a painful process of reconversion. But it is difficult to find any more striking example of a war boom which left so few lasting beneficial effects as the one in Algeria. The results of a war boom are manifold. In general, it will lead to some strengthening of the infrastructure—railways, harbours, roads, telephone and telegraph network, airfields, electricity supply—which may be extended to areas which did not have such facilities before (while, on the other hand, existing facilities may be run down because of the exigencies of the military forces). The most important effect, though, will in general be the development of new industries which supply goods to the military forces, and which, after the end of the hostilities, can substitute for imports on the domestic market or even find other outlets. In Algeria very little of this happened in the manufacturing field as a result of the war. The changing structure of manufacturing industries is discussed in section 6 on industrialization. But some striking developments can be noted in the present context. The food industries which represented 22 per cent of the output in manufacturing proper in 1954 more than doubled their output between 1954 and 1959, but one main reason for this rapid growth was the expansion of the output of beer from 0·35 m hl to 1·2 m hl, mainly in response to demand by the French armed forces. As the great majority of the Moslem population are teetotallers and beer was not an export product, the expansion of that industry was of no lasting value. Similarly, the expansion of the metal working industry which in 1954 was of the same size as the food industries, reflected mainly higher repair activities. While its output had grown by more than 50 per cent between 1954 and 1960, it fell by almost 20 per cent in 1961 only, when the European population began to depart and the business climate changed. Also the expansion of the construction industry and the closely linked progress in the building materials industries can to a large extent be attributed to the war effort, although also civilian projects under the Constantine Plan added to construction activities during the period 1959 to 1962. In 1963 the construction volume had fallen to about one-quarter of what it had been at its peak in 1960.

Table 3 shows that between 1959 and 1963 GDP at current prices fell by about 28 per cent. In constant prices the GDP fell probably even more. Thus, income in agriculture must have fallen considerably, in spite of excellent crops of cereals. The output of wine, however, only reached 65 per cent of the 1959 level. While GDP originating in agriculture in 1963 was the same as in 1959, at constant prices it must have been at least 5 to 10 per cent lower.

The effects of the strong growth of the product between 1954 and 1959 and the sharp fall in the early 'sixties can be seen in Table 4.

Between 1954 and 1959 rapidly growing public expenditure was the driving force of demand, though the investment boom also contributed strongly to growth. It should be noted, though, that a very large part of the increased amount of investment, represented investment in the Sahara oil industry which has less direct influence on the Algerian economy than investment in Algeria itself. Investment in Algeria proper did not increase by more than 800 million new francs between 1954 and 1959, and at constant prices it probably rose only by about 40 per cent. In the two years that followed the launching of the Constantine Plan however, investments outside Sahara rose by another 900 million francs. There is no doubt that the increased spending by the French army and other parts of the French administration was the major driving force in the growth of Algeria's national income between 1954 and 1959. Between 1959 and 1961, however, capital formation in Algeria proper was the major stimulating factor.

Exports did not contribute at all to the growth. While the value of exports of goods rose from 1,403 m to 1,805 m dinars during this period, its volume fell by 23 per cent.[1] The average unit value for exports rose by about two-thirds, and increased export prices therefore overcame the effect of the fall in volume. But even so exports rose much more slowly than other elements of demand.

Table 4. *Expenditure on the gross domestic product (at market prices)*

(Million dinars, current prices)

	1954	1959	1963
Gross domestic product	6,788	(14,000)	(10,000)
+ Imports of goods and services	2,249	5,950	(4,000)
Total resources	9,037	(19,950)	(14,000)
Used for:			
Private consumption	4,612	9,150	(7,700)
Public consumption	1,141	4,865	(2,300)
Gross capital formation	1,720	4,000	(1,400)
Exports of goods and services	1,564	2,000	(2,600)

Sources: The figures for 1963 are very approximate estimates made by the author. Figures for exports and imports of *goods* are available for 1963 but no such figures are available for services. (Since apparently only a small part of the income from exports of petroleum is included in the Gross Domestic Product, only half of the export of petroleum in exports has been included). A figure for gross capital formation is given in source (2), but figures given there for earlier years are lower than those used in the national accounts, and the 1963 figure has therefore been rounded upwards. Similarly, no information is available on the purchase of goods and services other than wages, by the Government.

The consumer price index rose by about 30 per cent from 1954 to 1959, but personal consumption at constant prices rose by about 50 per cent, implying a substantial increase in average consumption per head. Greater employment opportunities for Moslem workers in non-agricultural activities meant that at least part of the increase in consumption per head reflected a better living standard amongst the masses of the Algerian population. Also the minimum wage for land workers was increased substantially during this period, between 75 and 85 per cent depending on region of the country.[2] On the other hand, the output of cereals on Moslem owned farms dropped sub-

[1] *Source:* (1), pp. 197 and 200.

[2] *Ibid.*, p. 39.

stantially during the same period, and while the deliveries of meat rose, it is probable that the income of the small farmers fell rather than rose, during this period. It should be noted that the consumption by French soldiers and government servants also is included in the figure for total personal consumption, and accounts for some of the increase in consumption.

Between 1959 and 1963 the development from 1954 to 1959 was reversed. The sharp fall in investment and in public consumption (a fall that perhaps was even more marked than the table shows) was bound to have a very distinct effect on the Gross Domestic Product, and thereby cause a fall in private consumption which again would reinforce the fall in GDP.

It is debatable whether national income fell because of fall in demand, or whether the productive capacity shrunk so much due to the exodus of the bulk of the non-Moslem population that output would have fallen drastically in any case. But there is hardly any doubt that the actual level of the output in most sectors of the economy was limited by demand, and not by productive capacity. Agriculture which could export its surpluses abroad, did certainly decline due to shortage of skilled management in some cases and the influence of climatic conditions in others. But it is unlikely that the output of the buildingand construction industryfell to below one-quarter of its peak level in 1960–61 merely because of shortage of management, technicians and skilled manpower.

Without specific information on the changes in cost of living it is not possible to determine whether the average standard of living fell or rose between 1959 and 1963. 1959 personal consumption can be broken down as follows: Moslems 4,970 million dinars, non-Moslem civilian community 3,050 million dinars and French military forces, 1,250 million dinars. If we assume that the consumption by the two last groups fell by 75 and 80 per cent respectively between 1959 and 1963 and that the consumption by Moslems should rise by about 11–12 per cent, total personal consumption in 1963 at constant 1959 prices should have reached 6,550 million dinars. The estimate of 7,700 million dinars in Table 11 is about 18 per cent higher. If prices did not rise by more than twenty per cent, and if in fact the consumption of the non-Moslem community fell by more than 75 per cent—which is possible—consumption per head amongst Moslems will have risen somewhat between 1959 and 1963. This is an astounding conclusion, but there is some other evidence in support of it. Thus the output of hard wheat—75 per cent of which normally was produced in Moslem owned farms—rose from 850,000 tons to 1,450,000 tons. Supplies of food grain amongst Moslem farmers were therefore considerably larger than 4 years earlier, and this might possibly have raised the level of consumption of the Moslem farmers, and thus helped to offset some of the effects of unemployment amongst the urban workers. Moreover, employment in public administration rose, and the Algerian army certainly also helped to raise the level of consumption. What is certain however, is that the relief offered by a good crop of cereals and the building up of a national administration and a national army were special phenomena, and that other factors of demand, notably public and private investment, will have to be raised in the future in order to maintain a growth in private consumption.

2. DEVELOPMENT PLANNING AND DEVELOPMENT STRATEGY

The independent Algerian republic has not yet published a comprehensive development plan, and very little is known about its development programme. Development planning must therefore be reviewed mainly on the basis of pre-independence information.

In 1960 France published the so called Plan de Constantine which was to have been the blue print for the development of Algeria during the period 1959 to 1964.[1] This plan was dependent on a massive injection of French capital and manpower, and was based on the philosophy that in the course of some years the standard of living of the Moslems in Algeria should be raised to the level of people in France itself. This represented France's attempt to win the war in Algeria by social and economic means. The programme envisaged *net* investments of 19,400 million francs during the period 1959 to 1963 (or 140 per cent of the GDP in 1959), plus 5,520 million francs in investments by the petroleum industry, 2,700 million francs in replacements and 2,280 million francs in investments outside the plan. Thus, the total planned gross investments amounted to 29,900 million francs spread over a five year period. This sum is about 215 per cent of the GDP in 1959. A plan of this magnitude could not have been carried out without enormous amounts of foreign aid.

So far as concerns its strategy the Constantine Plan was a realistic expression of what was possible on the basis of an injection of extremely large amounts of foreign aid in the midst of a war. Rural development could not be pursued much more vigorously, because many very backward rural areas were battlefields, and the population (between 1 and 2 million persons) had in many instances been moved away from their homes. Urban housing, on the other hand, was

[1] Source for all information on the Constantine Plan, (2) unless otherwise stated.

an easy way of mobilizing manpower, and reducing unemployment while at the same time reducing incidence of urban slums.

The calculated effect on the Gross Domestic Production (i.e. GDP less government product) of the Plan was that it should increase from 11,100 million francs in 1959 to 19,555 million francs in 1964, or by 76 per cent, i.e. by 12 per cent per year. If the petroleum industry was excluded, the annual growth rate would still be 9·7 per cent or 58 per cent for the whole period.

During the plan period the aim was to absorb 60 per cent of the urban unemployment, and to employ the natural increase in the male labour force and 75,000 women. To reach this target, employment would have to grow by about 475,000. The Plan estimated that 145,000 new jobs would be created in the construction industry, 113,000 in manufacturing industries etc., 80,000 in services, 50,000 in public service and 2,500 in the petroleum industry, or in total 390,000 new jobs. 20,000 new jobs should be created in agriculture due to specific works, but the plan disregarded these in assessing how the employment estimate compared to the need for new jobs. The authors of the Plan concluded that there would be a short fall of 80,000 jobs which would have to be compensated by migration of workers to France.

The Constantine Plan was criticized by many French observers and by the Algerian nationalists for its concentration on urban activities, but it is not fair to say that the rural development was neglected altogether. The Plan included provisions for an increase of agricultural extension workers from 400 to 2,950, for land reform on 600,000 acres, for land improvements affecting 1·3 million acres, for strengthening of agricultural co-operatives, and agricultural schools and for professional training of adults. Two-thirds of the large number of additional primary school places were to be in rural areas, almost all educational social centres were to serve them, and 90,000 new houses were to be built in rural areas. As pointed out before, war conditions made it difficult to set very much higher targets. Manufacturing was projected to grow by 88 per cent over the five year period and be responsible for 19 per cent of the growth of the total GDP. The French strategy was partly to encourage a large number of smaller projects through tax facilities, credits etc., and partly to establish a couple of larger complexes, such as a steel mill in Bone and a chemical complex in Arzew, at the end of the gas pipeline from Sahara. But Algerian industries were not to be protected against competition from French industries, and critics of the plan argued with considerable plausibility that the industrial targets could not have been reached, even if the political climate had been more favourable.

The Constantine Plan was carried out energetically by the French authorities, and between 1959 and 1960 gross capital formation rose from 3,700 to 4,650 million francs, which though below the planned average of 6,000 million was still a long step in the right direction. Many of the specific programmes included in the Plan were carried out according to schedule. According to the Evian agreement France was to continue to support Algeria's development programme, and considerable sums have been transferred from France to Algeria after Independence. But the independent government lacked the administrative capacity to pursue development as vigorously as during the last year of French rule.

In 1963 the independent government produced its own development budget from which the following figures are drawn (Table 5). From this it can be seen that the Algerian planners hoped to maintain

Table 5. *Public development budgets*
(percentages)

	Constantine Plan: Public Funds: 1959–63	Algerian Govt. New Authorizations 1963	Estimated Govt. Expenditure 1963
Agriculture, water development, rural programmes	29	46	36
Industry	9	17	17½
Infrastructure, transport, public utilities	18	8	22½
Education	10	15	10
Health	3	3	2
Housing, urban development etc.	25	8	6
Public Administration	5	3	4
Miscellaneous	—	—	2
Total	100	100	100
Million francs	12,230	2,650	2,200

the rate of public development expenditure under the Constantine Plan, but had decided to change the emphasis very considerably. Since the third column was influenced by contractual obligations to finalize work under progress a comparison between the two first columns of the table is particularly illuminating. Expenditure under two headings were planned to increase very considerably—agriculture and rural development, and industry. The first change in emphasis reflects the general criticism that the Constantine Plan gave too little emphasis to rural development. In the Draft Plan much more money was to be allocated to soil protection and similar works in rural areas which could be carried out by mobilizing under-employed rural manpower. The stronger emphasis on industry in the government budget was partly due to the need to stimulate certain forms of industrialization through the building of state enterprises and partly to a switch away from a liberalistic to a socialistic view of the role of the state in the industrialization process. The emphasis on education was also further strengthened. Two expenditure headings were reduced drastically in order to permit these increases for rural development, industry and education: infrastructure which was cut below half and housing which was cut down to about one-third. The reduction in the expenditure on housing is explained partly by the fact that Algeria 'inherited' housing from almost one million non-Moslems who had left, and partly by a deliberate decision to replace 'unproductive' investments by those of a more directly productive character. Finally, the reduced allocation to infrastructure must also be seen against the background of the good infrastructure which had been built in the country under the French rule. The most pressing need in this sphere in Algeria was, and probably still is, to build access roads from isolated rural communities. Many such access roads will be included under rural development rather than under infrastructure.

It has unfortunately not been possible to find exact information on what the Algerian government actually has spent on development during the last few years. One estimate puts total capital formation in 1963 in Algeria at 677 million dinars; another suggests 726 million dinars out of public funds only.[1] According to the most recent information the Algerian government has raised the development budget from 800 million dinars in 1965 to about 2,260 million in 1966.[2] The figures suggest that during the period 1963 to 1965 public investments were below one-third of the planned annual average during the Plan de Constantine, while the 1966 budget represents an effort to bring the development programme up to a level close to what it was in the last full year of the French rule.[3]

It is, of course, impossible to describe the development efforts undertaken in Algeria on the basis of the scattered information quoted in this section. What is evident is that during the last few years investment outside the petroleum industry has fallen well below 10 per cent of the Gross Domestic Product (the figures in Table 4 suggest 7–8

[1] *Source:* (2) and (3), p. 134.

[2] *Source: Le Monde* 19–20 June 1966, article by J. Ben Brahem and a report on the Algerian Budget.

[3] In 1961 public investments reached 2,314 million francs (*Source:* (3), p. 134).

per cent of GDP, taking into account that investments in Sahara amounted to 672 million dinars). Such a low rate of investment will not permit any significant increase in the Gross Domestic Product. Only if the 1966 budget is implemented more or less fully will Algeria once more enter a period of rapid and planned economic growth.

3. FINANCING THE PUBLIC SECTOR

The information available on the Algerian budget does not permit a very detailed analysis of either sources of revenue or the way in which the resources are being spent. Table 6 summarizes available information.

Table 6. *Government of Algeria, recurrent budget*
(million francs or dinars)

	1954–55	1959	1963 (revised)	1964
Revenue				
Direct taxes	215	479	585	563
Indirect taxes	589	1,617	1,699	1,808
of which:				
Customs duties	32	66	105	118
Enterprise income etc.	106	274	122	144
Extraordinary income	—	—	98	—
Other	106	275	291	261
Total recurrent revenue	910	2,371	2,575	2,632
Expenditure				
Debt services	(106)	324	223	58
Current operations	n.a.	1,344	1,712	1,935
of which:				
Personnel expenditure	(469)	991	1,354	1,494
Goods and services	(133)	210	232	329
Miscellaneous and maintenance	n.a.	143	126	112
Subsidies etc.	n.a.	525	1,112	637
Other	n.a.	154	6	2
Global adjustment	—	—	−480	—

Source: (1) pp. 210–12; (3), p. 84.

According to recent information the recurrent expenditure in 1965 reached 3,050 million francs and is budgeted at 3,200 million francs for 1966.[1]

[1] *Le Monde, op. cit.*

The revenue structure in the Algerian budget is fairly typical of a less developed country. Indirect taxes contributed about two-thirds of recurrent revenue in the four years listed in the Table. However, before Independence custom duties represented only about 5 per cent of total indirect taxes, and even after Independence that figure is barely higher. This is a result of free trade with France which was and is Algeria's main supplier of imported goods. Algeria has therefore, in principle, an untapped resource of recurrent income. The practical effect may not be very large because other indirect taxes are so high that introduction of custom duties may merely result in a lower combined income from duties and excise taxes on many products.

Between 1959 and 1963 the tax revenue increased somewhat in spite of a fall in the Gross Domestic Product. Without detailed information on the composition of the indirect taxes it is not possible to trace the reason for this, i.e. whether the tax incidence in general is higher, whether taxes on certain products have been raised, or whether revenue from taxation of the oil companies explains the increase.[1]

The expenditure figures cannot be properly compared over time, partly because the classification of expenditure was changed between 1954–55 and 1959, and partly because the figures for 1963 include a negative item of 480 million francs, which represents an overall reduction of expenditure the distribution of which between expenditure headings is not known. The apparent substantial increase in expenditure on personnel and on goods and services after Independence has one obvious explanation—the independent government of Algeria has a wider range of expenditure than the colonial government which did not have any military expenditure, or expenditure on the foreign service. The sharp increase in 'public interventions' which are subsidies and other contributions, reflects most probably extraordinary expenditure to keep the economy and certain social organizations going under very difficult conditions.

Due to the very conflicting information which is available on the financing of the public sector investment programme it is not possible to attempt an analysis of the Government capital budget for the time being.

[1] Estimates of income from the petroleum industry vary. One source puts royalty income at 250 million dinars in 1963 ((19), p. 160), while another source estimates Government revenue at 300 million dinars, of which 160 million come from taxes and 140 million from royalties ((17), p. 270).

4. AGRICULTURE

Some of the more important data on Algerian agriculture have been mentioned above. In this section some data on the development potential of agriculture will be examined.

Table 7 shows the predominant position of wine in the Algerian agriculture. Both in 1954 and in 1957 wine accounted for more than 40 per cent of total gross income. Typical export products (wine, fruit and fresh vegetables) represented more than half of the gross income. The strategy of agricultural development in Algeria will necessarily have to put considerable emphasis on more production for home consumption, including better food standards amongst the farmers themselves.

Table 7. *Gross income in agriculture broken down by products—million dinars*

	1954	1957	1960
Cereals	625	667	624
Pulses etc. (dried)	33	21	17
Wine	1,375	1,119	952
Fruit	244	221	290
Industrial crops	67	48	70
Fresh vegetables	203	212	352
Subtotal	2,547	2,288	2,305
Animal products, total	580	558	744
Total	3,127	2,846	3,049

Note: 1 dinar = 100 old or 1 new franc.
Sources: (1), pp. 133–135; data for 1960 (6), pp. 94 and 95.

24 million acres belonged to individual farm units. Another 5·4 million acres were owned collectively in the form of so called 'arch' or 'sabega'.[1] Of the cultivable land many acres are usually fallow. Thus, in 1959, 7,400,000 acres were fallow out of a total of 16,470,000 acres (including vineyards, fruit gardens etc.). The Constantine Plan included a long term plan to reform land use—it was estimated to take about 15 to 20 years to improve the land to extend the land utilization to areas which are not cultivable at present.

The strategy was to reduce the monoculture of cereals, and thereby make it possible through crop rotation to reduce the area which on the

[1] *Source:* (5), p. 12.

Table 8. *Agricultural land use*
('000 acres)

	Algeria without Sahara	Sahara
Cultivable land	15,260	42
Natural meadows	80	—
Vineyards	905	—
Fruit plantations	490	62
Pastures and bushland	23,730	71,960
Unproductive land	775	6
Total land used by agriculture	41,240	72,070
Land covered by alpha grass	9,820	—
Forests	7,520	10
Misc. land	14,300	(443,500)
Total land area	72,880	515,600

Source: (1), p. 128.

average is fallow. Fodder crops and to a lesser extent pulses etc. would have to be introduced on a large scale. The other remarkable aspect of the Constantine Plan was the programme for plantations of fruit trees and widespread planting of other trees. By bringing partly or fully eroded land under crops or tree plantations, the authors of the Plan expected to be able to retain more rain water and control the flow of water in streams and rivers better. They concluded that

Table 9. *Potential land use (Constantine Plan)*
('000 acres)

	1959	Potential use
Cereals	7,240	6,400
Pulses	175	690
Other annual cultures	75	195
Vineyards	890	980
Fruit gardens	490	4,400
Fruit trees in 'half forests'	0	3,700
Fodder crops	195	5,950
Fallow land	7,410	750
Total	16,470	23,050

Note: The figures above do not include 500,000 to 750,000 acres of land that can be irrigated (of which about 250,000 were wholly or partially irrigated in 1959). *Source:* (2), p. 262.

if such a programme were carried through, it should be possible to raise the net output from agriculture by 3 to 4 times in the course of 30 to 35 years.

From a purely economic point of view, there are reasons to believe that the proposed pattern of land use is unrealistic. The following alternative land use pattern is therefore suggested, subject to closer analysis of the need to reserve larger areas for forests.

The main differences between the figures in Table 10 prepared by

Table 10. *Potential land use, yields and crops*

	Area ('000 acres)	Potential Total output ('000 metric tons)	Potential Yield per acre (metric tons)	Present yield per acre (metric tons)
Cereals	6,900	4,200	0·60	0·25
Pulses	750	300	0·40	0·20
Industrial cultures	250	—	—	—
Vineyards	750	—	—	—
Fresh vegetables	750	4,500	6·00	4·00
Citrus fruits	750	1,200	4·80	4·80
Other fruits, intensive culture	1,000	—	—	—
Other fruits, extensive culture	2,400	—	—	—
		Mill FU	FU	FU
Fodder crops, irrigated	750	2,400	3,200	n.a.
Fodder crops, dry crops	4,200	3,400	800	n.a.
Pastures	24,750	4,000	160	56
Total	43,250			
of which:				
Arable land	18,500			

Notes: Data on present yields (except for pastures) derived from (1), p. 81. The estimate of the present yield of pastures is based on minimum feed requirements for the normal livestock in Algeria, less other available feed. FU (feed unit) equals the equivalent of one k.g. of barley. (2·2 lbs.) 1 metric ton = 0·984 long tons.

the present author and the potential land use in accordance with the Constantine Plan is the sharp reduction of the fruit plantations and 'half-forests', and the slight increase in the area allocated to cereals. Both these changes were motivated by demand considerations—how would it be possible to sell fruit from almost 4·5 million acres of gardens and in addition also fruit from more than 3·5 million acres of 'half-forests'? On the other hand, the total demand for cereals will probably double in 20 to 30 years, and 6,900,000 acres will probably be needed to produce enough foodgrain. From the point of view of the ecological consequences the product mix in Table 10 may not be acceptable, but this is less important, since some modification in the structure of land use (which *inter alia* may mean imports of food grain, but not necessarily as some cereals undoubtedly are used for feeding purposes, and it would be possible to replace these by fodder crops) should not affect the income forecasts substantially.

On the basis of the predicted pattern of land use and output per acre, the value added of agriculture and livestock when 'fully developed' can be estimated at 11,600 million dinars and net income (i.e. value added less depreciation) at 10,500 million dinars.[1] These figures are consistent with the assumption in the Constantine Plan that net output in agriculture could be increased three to four times. In the late 1950's it fluctuated between 2,500 and 2,700 million dinars, so that the figures suggest that the value added in agriculture could be increased fourfold. A tentative breakdown of the figures between the former non-Moslem and Moslem farms shows that value added on non-Moslem owned land should increase by 50 per cent and on Moslem land more than 7 times (or about 6½ times if depreciation is deducted). This figure is in the opinion of several French experts who have discussed the agricultural potential of Algeria, by no means out of reach.

What would be the implications on employment and income of such an agrarian revolution? The employment aspects can be approached by using the data of labour requirements that are contained in the Constantine Plan.[2] By supplementing these with rough estimates for crops for which no labour requirements data are available, and assuming that value added per man year is the same in animal husbandry as in crop production, it was concluded that at full efficiency the Algerian agriculture would employ 1·5 million men and 0·07 million women: (assumed to be working 250 days a year). This is *less* than the 1·63 million men and 0·07 million women who worked on Algerian farms in 1954 (excluding female family members). Is this employment estimate too low? Globally it may be on the low side, although it implies that in crop production the income per day should be about 30 dinars, which is high at present, but which will not be high in 20 to 30 years time. What is more important is that the daily earnings for people on fruit farms, whether half forests or

[1] Details on these calculations are contained in an unpublished manuscript by the present author.

[2] (2), p. 193.

plantations, should merely be about 12 to 13 dinars a day, and these two cultures are expected to provide more than one-quarter of the employment on crop production.

The problem of income and employment can be approached from another angle, namely by stating an income target in agriculture. The average income per head in Algeria was around 1,000 dinars a year in 1963. If we assume that national income per head will grow by 3½ per cent a year—a fairly modest target for a poor nation—and that income per head in agriculture will catch up with the national income per head, the income per head in agriculture must reach 2,000 dinars if the full production target is reached in 20 years, and 2,800 dinars per head if it takes 30 years to reach this target. These figures would result in very low figures for employment, so low that it would probably not be technically possible to reach the postulated output targets. If we accept that the income per head in agriculture should only be half of the national average, we arrive at more reasonable figures for the population that would be dependent on agriculture: 10½ million 20 years from now and 7 million 30 years from now. The latter figure should correspond to about 2·1 million working persons, and a total agricultural population which would be about 20 per cent higher than it was about ten years ago.

These conclusions are significant for national planning since they imply that even if the agrarian revolution were extremely successful, other economic activities would have to absorb practically the entire growth in the working population. If not, under-employment in agriculture would become very grave, and income per head would in that sector be far below the national average. It should be pointed out that with 2·1 million working in agriculture, not counting women, the average working year would only be 180 days on the basis of the employment estimates referred to earlier in this section.

Changes in agriculture since Independence

At the end of 1964 about 7½ million acres of agricultural land was under 'self-management' (*auto-gestion*). Self-management is a form of nationalization inspired by the Yugoslav experience. The units (former large farms or groups of former smaller farms) are run by committees of workers, with managers appointed by the state. In fact, because of shortage of experienced managers, the management of the nationalized farms has to a great extent been exercised by the workers themselves.

The land under self-management is state property, although the form of organization is close to that of co-operatives. The story of nationalization of land in Algeria can be summarized as follows:

About 750,000 acres of land was at the beginning of 1963 owned by CAPER, an organization set up in 1956 by the French Government, in order to acquire land, improve it and distribute it to landless farmers. Another 2,250,000 acres of land had been abandoned by the former European owners. Furthermore, in March 1963 the Government nationalized about 400 to 500,000 acres of land that belonged to some very rich European settlers and to Algerians who had collaborated with the French against the nationalist movement during the war. At the end of September 1963, 3,430,000 acres were nationalized and put under self-management. In October 1963 the Government decided to nationalize all remaining European properties. One year later, the Government proclaimed nationalization of land belonging to former 'collaborators' (including people who had served as chiefs, on elected assemblies etc.), and in December 1964 it was announced that 500,000 acres of land had been nationalized in this manner. In total at least 7½ million acres have been nationalized and put under self-management.[1]

The bulk of the nationalized land was the 6·75 million acres of land previously owned by 22,000 European farmers (or companies—see Table 2, page 479). This land was organized into 2,300 units ('domaines') with an average size of 3,000 acres. It has been estimated that this land which amounted to about one-quarter of the agricultural area of the country and produced 60 per cent of the value added in agriculture, employed only 150,000 workers or about one-tenth of the labour force in agriculture.[2]

Thus, the value added per worker in the former European owned sector of Algerian agriculture was between 13 and 14 times as high as in the rest of agriculture. The implication is obvious—if the workers on nationalized farms were able to retain the bulk of the output of the farms (and at least almost maintain the level of output), they would be in a very privileged position in relation to the rest of the Algerian peasants. This gap might become even more glaring if the Government proceeds to nationalize the remainder of the Moslem owned farms over 250 acres (there were 8,500 of them, with a total area of 4·25 million acres but some have certainly been expropriated).[3] It is fairly obvious that the Government neither can, nor intends to retain so much of the profit on the nationalized farms that the average income of the workers would be brought down to

[1] Source of information in this and two preceding paragraphs, (14), pp. 21–25.

[2] (14), pp. 23, 24.

[3] It was apparently the intention of the Algerian Government to extend the land reform to all farms with more than 250 acres of land—see (14), page 25. Since the fall of Ben Bella in 1965 the Government has tended to aim at a period of consolidation, rather than of further revolutionary steps.

anywhere in the neighbourhood of the average peasant income. The Algerian Government is thus faced with a dilemma the solution to which cannot yet be seen. In some respects the problem is similar to that in Kenya, but it is far more complex.[1]

It is understandable that the Algerian Government does not want to endanger the agricultural development of the country and the export trade by experiments in breaking up the former European farms in order to settle large numbers of landless workers. But the policy followed implies that a rapid transformation of the peasant farming areas must be pursued very vigorously and at very heavy costs in order to avoid a lasting and deep gap between the economic conditions of privileged self-managing workers on the former European and large Moslem farms and of the great mass of poor peasants.

Has the policy of self-management been successful from the point of view of productivity? It is too early to form a firm opinion about this, but a recent French study draws some conclusions. The main products of the former European agriculture were wine, cereals, fruit, and vegetables (see Table 7, page 495). In 1963 the output of wine fell to 12·6 million hectolitres, of which only 11 million were of a quality that could be sold. This compares with an average output of 15–16 million in earlier years, and weather conditions in 1963 were so good that the output should normally have reached 17 million hectolitres. Only part of the vineyards were nationalized that year, but available acreage figures suggest that output on European managed units fell by 20 per cent, and on units in the nationalized sector by 50 per cent. The failure seems first of all to have been caused by a shortage of people with experience in making wine. As regards cereals the output was very high—2·45 million tons which was the second best harvest after World War II. It is, of course, impossible to pass an objective judgement as to whether the crop would have been higher or not under the old management. The out-

[1] In Kenya, European settlers also owned about 7½ million acres of land. Much of the land, however, was either under labour intensive plantation crops, such as coffee, tea, pyrethrum and sisal (and was to a considerable extent used to grow crops that represented the best possible use of the land), while much of the land under mixed and often less labour intensive farming, in fact has been bought by the Government, broken up into small farms and sold to smallholders. In addition, there is, on the average, no shortage of land in Kenya at present, and the land owned by African smallholders includes about 80% of the high potential land in Kenya. In Algeria, much of the former European land is under mechanized, labour-extensive farming, while much of the land owned by peasants is very poor, and it will take a long time and it will involve heavy investments to raise the productivity on peasant owned land to the extent suggested in the previous part of the present section on agriculture.

put—and exports—of citrus fruits reached a new record level in 1963 (and promised to be even 12 per cent higher in 1965), while the output of fresh vegetables in 1963 was barely above half the output of 1960.

The conclusions drawn on the basis of this material and other evidence are that the agricultural workers have succeeded very well in maintaining the output, and that the bottlenecks have been in processing (notably wine) and in marketing (notably fresh vegetables). It should be noted that a fall in production could not merely be ascribed to a change in management, but also to a shortage of credit. Thus, in 1960 the agricultural credit organizations distributed 39,000 million old francs to European farmers, i.e. about 70 per cent of the recurrent costs of these farms. Such credits were considerably lower in 1963 and 1964, which clearly must have had some influence on the ability of the nationalized farms to buy necessary 'inputs'. In short, the lower Moslem management personnel and workers who took over the management of the former European farms have done astonishingly well.[1]

5. LABOUR AND WAGES

The employment structure in 1954 is summarized in Table 11. The table illustrates the weak representation of Moslems in all categories of jobs which required specialized training and resulted in high incomes. We have already shown how this led to a low average income for Moslems in non-farming activities, compared to non-Moslems. The second and equally serious effect was that with the exodus of the Europeans it became very difficult to fill many specialized jobs. The most striking example was that of female office workers. In 1954 there were barely 2 Moslem women for 100 non-Moslem women in office jobs. After Independence it proved impossible to find typists, shorthand typists, and switch-board operators.

Amongst Moslem men working in agriculture, 35 per cent were wage earners and 65 per cent were self-employed, while the proportion of self-employed was 72 per cent amongst non-Moslem men in agriculture. Superficially, the employment structure in agriculture was therefore rather similar for Moslems and non-Moslems, but while the majority of non-Moslem self-employed in agriculture were rich farmers, the majority of Moslems were poor peasants, and, similarly, while non-Moslems mostly held well paid managerial positions in farming, the Moslems provided the cheap farm labour.

Outside agriculture the employment structure amongst men differed considerably between Moslems and non-Moslems, mainly

[1] *Source:* (14), pp. 51 to 53, and 62 to 71.

Table 11. *Labour force distributed by professional categories*
('000 persons, October 31, 1954)

	Men		Women	
	Moslem	Non-Moslem	Moslem	Non-Moslem
Agriculture				
Owners, tenants, family members, etc.	1,032·3	20·9	970·3	3·2
Wage earners	564·0	8·3	7·0	0·1
Total	1,596·3	29·2	977·3	3·3
Non-agriculture				
Employers, self-employed				
Craftsmen	27·5	16·3	2·6	2·6
Small traders	61·5	18·0	0·8	6·3
Other traders, industrialists	5·7	9·4	0·1	0·6
Liberal professions	2·1	9·2	0·1	1·8
Other	20·3	3·0	0·1	1·4
	117·1	55·9	3·7	12·7
Wage earners				
Top management, profns.	1·3	15·1	—	1·6
Technicians, foremen etc.	7·9	26·6	0·5	13·0
Office workers	9·0	26·3	0·4	21·0
Skilled workers	38·3	44·4	1·2	5·3
Specialized workers	58·9	25·2	2·0	2·9
Unskilled workers	139·4	6·5	1·9	0·7
Char-women	—	—	20·3	6·0
Others	43·8	32·6	5·0	12·1
	298·6	176·7	31·4	62·6
Total employed, non-ag.	415·7	232·6	35·1	75·3
Unemployed	130·5	12·9	2·6	1·2
Total, non-agricultural labour force	546·2	245·5	37·7	76·5
Total labour force	2,142·5	274·7	1,015·0	79·8

Source: (1), pp. 26–27.

because of the much larger proportion of unemployed in the Moslem male labour force (24 per cent against 5 per cent for non-Moslems). 21 per cent of the Moslems and 23 per cent of the non-Moslems were self-employed, so that the proportion of wage earners who actually had jobs was 72 per cent for non-Moslems and 55 per cent for Moslems. Less than 10 per cent of Moslem women in the non-agricultural labour force were self-employed (against 17 per cent of the non-Moslem women), and 7 per cent were unemployed (against 1½ per cent of the non-Moslem).

Moslems provided 89 per cent of the total male labour force overall; 98 per cent of those who worked in agriculture but only 69 per cent of workers in other industries. For women the differences were even more striking; while 93 per cent of the total female labour force were Moslems, the proportion reached 99·7 per cent in farming, but was only 33 per cent elsewhere. 76 per cent of all Moslem men were in agriculture, 19 per cent held non-agricultural jobs and 6 per cent were unemployed (not counting rural unemployment and under-employment). Only 11 per cent of the non-Moslems worked in agriculture, 5 per cent were unemployed and 85 per cent were self-employed or wage earners in non-farming activities. Amongst women the occupational distribution of Moslem and non-Moslem was diametrically opposite: 96 per cent of Moslem women worked in farming, while 94 per cent of non-Moslem women worked in industry, commerce, administration and the professions.

Moslem workers in France were not included in Table 11. There were about 150,000 of them in 1954. If we add these to the male Moslem labour force in Table 11, we find the following distribution: in agriculture 70 per cent, in non-agricultural activities in Algeria 18 per cent, in France 6½ per cent, and unemployed 5½ per cent.

Changes in the employment situation between 1954 and 1960

An enquiry on non-agricultural employment during the summer 1960 suggests that it rose by 350,000 during the 5½ year period from the end of 1954. More than half of the jobs (180,000) were government jobs. 240,000 jobs went to Moslems and almost 110,000 to non-Moslems. Employment of Moslems thus rose by more than 50 per cent, while employment of non-Moslems rose by one-third. Nevertheless, unemployment probably rose amongst Moslems while amongst non-Moslems unemployment must have fallen and many unoccupied persons must have joined the labour force. The natural increase of the Moslem *male* labour force was probably around 330,000 persons, of whom approximately 80,000 found work in France. Thus 240,000 new jobs were not enough to absorb the entire increase in the Moslem male labour force. Moreover, 130,000 jobs in farming apparently disappeared during that period. The natural increase in the non-Moslem labour force can be estimated at 20,000 to which must be added a net immigration of perhaps 25,000, against

110,000 new jobs. 65,000 additional workers were thus drawn from unoccupied persons (and farmers who had to leave their farms due to the war).[1]

Post-independence developments

No statistics are available for the period 1962 to 1966. The only thing that we know with certainty is that about nine-tenths of the non-Moslem population has left Algeria. The decline in non-Moslem employment has not been as noticeable in some sectors as the exodus of Europeans should suggest. Thus the number of Frenchmen in the administration fell only from 10,700 in January 1963 to 6,000 in January 1965 while the number of French teachers only fell from 12,500 to 11,100.[2] In many other fields European management and skilled workers have certainly remained in Algeria or new people have replaced those who left—the petroleum industry is a significant case.

As shown in Table 7, the Gross Domestic Product fell by 28 per cent between 1959 and 1963, and the fall in relation to 1960 or 1961 was even larger. Moreover, Gross Domestic Product less agriculture fell by no less than 35 per cent. A very crude estimate of the impact on employment of this fall in the GDP (assuming on the average a 10 per cent fall in productivity per sector) suggests that employment also fell by more than 35 per cent. This is due to the sharp fall in the output of labour intensive industries such as construction and services. In 1960 non-Moslems accounted for 30 per cent of the total non-agricultural employment. If employment of non-Moslems dropped by 80 per cent, total employment should have dropped by almost 25 per cent, everything else being equal. Thus, total employment is likely to have fallen more than the fall in employment of non-Moslems. It should also be remembered that in many cases there were no trained Moslems who could move into jobs vacated by non-Moslems—in fact, Algeria suffered by increased overall unemployment and at the same time serious shortages of certain types of skilled and semi-skilled workers. All reports from Algeria confirm the picture drawn above—very serious urban unemployment and drastic shortages of some categories of trained workers.

The seriousness of the unemployment situation in Algeria shortly after Independence can be shown by the following illustrative figures:

[1] Figures for employment 1954 and 1960, (3) pp. 73 to 75. Emigration to France, estimate based on (3) pp. 15–16. European immigration (1), p. 20. Loss of jobs in farming, (3), p. 70.

[2] (15), p. 137.

	Changes from 1960 to 1963
Non-Moslem employment	−280,000
Total employment	−400,000
Residuum, Moslem employment	−120,000
Increase, Moslem male labour force	180,000
Estimated increase in unemployment[a]	300,000

Note: [a] These estimates are based on the figures for non-agricultural employment in 1960 (*source:* (3), p. 73); the assumption that non-Moslem employment (350,000) fell by 80 per cent; crude estimate of about 35 per cent fall in total employment—see the text above; and 2½ per cent annual increase in the labour forces.

The above estimates do not take into account the return to Algeria of tens of thousands of men who had been outside the country during the war—some of these remained in the armed forces, but others joined the labour force.

Wages and Salaries

Data on salaries are only available up to the end of 1959. The legal minimum wage for workers outside agriculture was fixed at between 1.03 francs and 1.24 francs per hour in December 1959 (depending on the place of work—the highest scale applied to the larger cities and their suburbs). Between April 1955 and December 1959 the minimum daily wage rates were raised by about 30 per cent. The minimum wage rates for agricultural workers at the end of 1959 were between 5·88 francs and 6·91 francs, again depending on region, but these had been raised by between 61½ per cent for the highest paid and 73 per cent for the lowest paid workers between 1955 and 1959. It should be noted that between 1955 and November 1959 the cost of living rose by about 35 per cent. Thus, the real wages of urban workers on minimum wage rates appear to have fallen somewhat, while those of agricultural workers increased substantially.

Available wage statistics show that the average hourly wage of unskilled workers rose by 29½ per cent between 1955 and November 1959, or at the same rate as the legal minimum wage, while the wages of the highest category of workers rose by 41 per cent. There were significant differences in the increase in wages by industrial groups—within manufacturing the increase during 4½ years varied from 26 per cent for workers in the textile and the wood industries to 39 per cent in the printing and publishing industry.[1]

The wage level in Algeria was not much lower than in France. Thus, in 1959 average wages in manufacturing were 1·86 francs in Algeria

[1] Source of data on wages and cost of living: (1), pp. 38 to 43.

against 1·95 francs in France.[1] The comparison is not fully relevant, since the number of female workers in manufacturing certainly was relatively much higher in France than in Algeria. Nevertheless, earnings in urban occupations in Algeria were not low and were far above those of most African countries.

There are no official statistics on average earnings of Moslems and non-Moslems. The gap between the hourly wages of higher and lower paid workers was not wider than about 2 to 1 for most sectors, and was below 2 for some sectors. So even though the Moslem workers mostly held the lowest jobs in urban occupations, their incomes were not too unfavourable compared to those of the many '*pieds noirs*' who worked as workers in industry and trade. In some sectors the earnings of the Moslems were depressed due to the seasonal and unstable character of the employment. In a study of the economy of Maghreb, Samir Amin made some interesting attempts to estimate the earnings of Moslems and non-Moslems in 1960. He maintains that in manufacturing, construction and transport the average earnings of Moslem workers in large firms were only 1,500 francs a year against 4,000 fiancs for non-Moslem workers.[2] His estimate is based on the assumption that the employment pattern for Moslems is irregular, and this must be so, otherwise the average earnings per hour worked would have been well below the legal minimum wage. In small firms in industry, construction and trade he concluded, earnings of non-Moslem wage earners were of the order of 5,000 francs against 2,000 for Moslems, while the differences in larger commercial firms and in Government services were smaller (5,000 francs to 3,000 francs in the first case; 6,000 francs to 4,000 francs in the latter). His estimates are ingenious, but rather speculative. These are nevertheless supported by the sample enquiry on the consumption pattern of the urban Moslem population which showed that almost half the urban Moslem families earned less than 3,000 francs per year (and many families had several wage earners).[3]

His estimate of rural incomes suggest that about 100,000 permanent agricultural workers had an average income of 1,000 francs per year (which is consistent with the minimum wage pattern) whereas the bulk of Moslem land workers who only worked during certain seasons, probably only earned between 400 and 600 francs per year.[4] The difference in income between urban and rural Moslems were therefore considerably larger than between Moslem and non-Moslem *workers* in urban areas. It should be added, of course, that well-to-do non-Moslems—both land owners, self-employed profes-

[1] (16), table 159.
[2] (17), Vol. 1, p. 151.
[3] *Ibid.*, p. 144.
[4] *Ibid.*, p. 130.

sionals and salary earners in leading positions—represented the rich classes in Algeria, together with a small number of Moslems in similar positions. The general picture which emerges is that the permanent land workers probably were not much better off than land workers in many other African countries, that landless seasonal workers were as poor as small peasants and landless workers in the poorest of the developing countries, but that urban workers—if they were lucky enough to have permanent employment—were comparatively well off, even though they earned less and occupied less skilled jobs than workers of European origin.

6. INDUSTRIALIZATION

Algeria's industrial structure before Independence was determined by the close relationship with France. Local industries had great difficulties in competing with French industries the products of which entered Algeria duty free. Industrial development was therefore based

Table 12. *Structure of manufacturing industries—percentage distribution of output in 1959*

Industry	Per cent of total output	index 1959 (1954 = 100)
Food processing	29·6	203
Tobacco, matches	15·4	126
Textiles	2·5	58
Paper	1·3	142
Printing	5·9	157
Chemical (incl. oils and fats)	10·5	179
Glass	1·8	161
Building materials	12·0	141
Base metals	0·4	156
Metal working, engineering	20·6	137
Total	100·0	150

Notes: This breakdown is based on the industrial production index, and its weighting (*source;* (1), p. 155). Smaller industries, like clothing, wood etc. are excluded.

on some few export industries, and industries that could supply the local market in competition with French industries.

Food processing includes *inter alia* production of wine which was Algeria's largest export product (until surpassed by petroleum in recent years). The metal working and engineering industries were dominated by repair units, the building materials industry was competitive due to the bulkiness of its products, while breweries and cigarette factories catering for the local market (although a large proportion of the output of cigarettes was exported) constituted a large proportion of total industrial output. It is noteworthy that the textile industry was very under-developed. Many important industries suffered heavy setbacks after Independence.

Thus, the output of wine fell from a level of 18 to 19 million hl. in several years during the 1950's to 12·3 m hl. in 1962 and 10·5 m hl. in 1964, while the output of beer fell drastically, from 1·27 m hl. in 1961 to 0·20 m hl. in 1963, and the output of cigarettes fell from 10,558 million in 1961 to 5,294 million in 1964. The fall in output of wine was partly caused by inability to maintain production after the exodus of the European wine growers, but in the case of beer and cigarettes, the immediate cause was a strong fall in demand. Output of non-consumer goods has, on the contrary, not fallen—thus the output of sulphuric acid rose from 30,000 tons in 1961 to 33,000 tons in 1964, of superphosphate from 55,000 tons in 1961 to 89,000 tons in 1964 (but the output had reached 101,000 tons in 1958) and caustic soda from 2,400 tons in 1961 to 2,500 tons in 1964.

With Independence the approach to industrialization was changed in two important respects: state owned enterprises became accepted as a desirable form of industrial enterprise, not as an emergency solution, while it also was decided to foster import substitution industries. With assistance from a number of countries, notably communist countries, the Algerian Government has built a number of new factories. An example is the increase of looms in the cotton industry from 604 ordinary and 96 automatic looms in 1952 to 1,000 ordinary and 4,000 automatic looms in 1964.[1]

This emphasis on certain consumer goods industries, which have been a basis for industrialization in many developing countries, does not mean that other aspects of industrialization have been neglected. Algeria is keen to exploit its large resources of petroleum and natural gas. A large gas liquefaction plant is in operation and plans for new petro-chemical units are under consideration or execution.

Algeria will necessarily have to put much emphasis on more labour intensive industries than the petro-chemical industries whose value mainly lies in their profitability and earning capacity in foreign exchange.

Industrialization in Algeria—and in the other Maghreb countries—would be facilitated considerably if closer economic relationships with Morocco and Tunisia and thus a larger market could be

[1] (18), Table 97.

established. With its very limited possibilities in the agricultural field, and its large unemployment Algeria is in fact condemned to industrialize for the sake of industrialization. But unless export markets can be opened up, there is a danger that the cost of industrialization, both in the form of investment, and through relatively high prices on many products, will become heavy.

The petroleum industry.

In September 1956 the most important oil field was discovered in the Algerian part of Sahara. Already at the end of 1957 commercial production started and in the course of a couple of years Algeria became one of the large oil producing countries. Before 1958 only one oil field, not far south of Algiers, was in operation. It was discovered in 1949 and reached a maximum output of 85,000 tons in 1953.[1] The large Hassi-Messaoud oil field in Sahara is situated about 400 miles south of the port of Bougie, and the transport problem had to be solved before commercial production could be started, first through a 'baby-pipeline' leading to a railhead, and later through a net-work of pipelines to Bougie and to La Skhirra in Tunisia.

Natural gas in large quantities was first discovered in March 1954 in Djebel Berga, but the distance to the coast was about 700 miles and it has so far not been exploited. However, in November 1956 another large deposit of natural gas was discovered in Hassi-R'Mel, only 300 miles South of Algiers.[2] This gas field is now linked with the port of Arzew and the cities of Algiers and Oran by a 552 miles long system of pipelines, of which the main line measures 312 miles.[3]

The French Government took a very active part in the exploration and the development of petroleum and natural gas production in Sahara. Until the end of 1962 about 6,700 million francs (£475 million) had been spent by the Government and private companies on exploration, development and transportation. 42 per cent had gone into exploration, 34 per cent into development and 24 per cent into pipelines etc.[4] These figures do not cover development costs relating to natural gas. Neither do they cover development costs in recent years, such as the construction of a third major pipeline to the coast.

What is the impact of the wealth of oil and natural gas on the economy of Algeria? It is well-known that the direct employment effect of the petroleum industry is very limited. This is an unfortunate fact in a country with very severe employment problems. However, the financial impact, both in terms of government revenue

[1] (19), p. 174. [2] (3), pp. 195–96.
[3] (19), pp. 66 to 68. [4] (19), p. 164.

and foreign exchange earnings, is considerable. Moreover, the discovery of natural gas has provided Algeria with a cheap form of energy, which permits cheap generation of electricity, direct use of gas for many purposes, and perhaps most important, the establishment of chemical industries based on natural gas.

A private estimate puts income from exports of petroleum products in 1963 at 2,130 million dinars which was used as follows: In Algeria 680 million dinars, of which 330 mn was for purchases of local inputs, 20 mn for local salaries, 30 mn was for wages and

Table 13. *Output of petroleum and natural gas*

	Petroleum ('000 metric tons)	Natural gas (m cu. feet)
1958	429	—
1959	1,232	—
1960	8,633	250
1961	15,660	8,150
1962	20,498	12,450
1963	23,641	14,150
1964	26,227	28,550

Source: (18), tables 74 and 75.

construction work and 300 mn for taxes and royalties. Of the remaining 1,450 million dinars, 150 mn was re-invested and 1,300 million dinars 'exported'.[1]

The classification above is not entirely satisfactory, both because 'local purchases' may include imported goods, and because the 'exported' income may include profits which eventually will accrue to the Algerian Government through its investments in oil companies. But it is certain that petroleum exports, which accounted for 59 per cent of all exports in 1963, are not as important to the economy as this very high figure might suggest.

In 1965 new oil and natural gas agreements were concluded between Algeria and France. They apparently 'give Algeria considerable advantages in financial terms and in terms of control, greater than those that have yet been accorded to other oil-producing countries.'[2] In addition, France provides 200 million francs in aid for industrialization during the five year period 1966 to 1970, in order to assist in industrialization based on Algeria's oil and gas resources.

In the long run, the large resources of natural gas may prove to be

[1] (17), p. 275. Note that an official estimate ((13), p. 267) puts petroleum exports at 2,033 million dinars.

[2] (15), p. 134.

far more important for the country's economic development than the petroleum resources. It can be sold to the consumers in Algeria at a very reasonable price. The average price fixed in 1961 was 0·05 francs per cubic metre (or less than 1 sh. per 1000 cu feet), which made it competitive with fuel oil. The price of manufactured gas was at the same time 0·36 francs per cubic metre.[1] The potential output of gas is far larger than the present demand in Algeria. The production of manufactured gas reached about 5,000 m cu feet in 1960, but only about 90 per cent of the output was actually sold, and between 85 and 90 per cent of the sales went to households. Thus the industrial market was virtually untouched, and the estimates of future domestic demand for natural gas take into account the substantial scope for use of natural gas in manufacturing. The Plan de Constantine estimated that initially demand for natural gas in the Algiers and Oran regions would not exceed 18,000 m cu feet, of which almost 11,000 m cu feet would be for production of electric power. Fully developed, the gas pipeline will be able to transport nearly 110,000 m cu feet per year, or 6 times the estimated initial domestic consumption, which nevertheless was estimated to be several times larger than the past consumption of manufactured gas.[2] The future industrial development of the town of Arzew should require another 18,000 m cu feet of natural gas annually, while the Constantine Plan assumed that 36,000 m cu feet of natural gas could be exported annually in the course of some few years.[3]

Another official source[4] contained far more optimistic estimates than the Plan de Constantine. Thus, the domestic consumption was estimated to grow from 18,000 m cu feet already in 1961 to 53,000 m cu feet in 1965, while exports were estimated at 36,000 m cu feet in 1962 and about 70,000 m cu feet in 1964. Total output should thus exceed the capacity of the existing pipeline already in 1965.

These ambitious plans were considerably delayed due to the political changes after 1962. But basically the plans proceed as outlined at the beginning of the 1960's. Arzew is being developed into an important centre for chemical industries based on natural gas (fertilizers, plastics etc.), and exports have started in the form of shipments of liquefied gas to the British Gas Board. Initially 35,000 m cu feet are exported annually, and the contract foresees an expansion up to 100,000 m cu feet in the course of 15 years. The gas is sold in England at a price which is considerably lower than the price of manufactured gas.

Plans have been discussed for further exports of gas, at a much

[1] (19), pp. 130 and 202.
[2] (2), p. 160.
[3] *Ibid.*, p. 270.
[4] Quoted in (19), p. 127.

larger scale, either as liquefied gas or through a pipeline with a capacity of 350,000 m cu feet per annum. However, the pipeline would be very long, and would have to cross the Mediterranean at one place or another, and the Algerian gas would not be able to compete with Dutch natural gas on the European continent. Such a project will probably only be realized if the gas off-take in South Europe (e.g. in Spain) were high enough so that the price to consumers further North could be reduced. Another way of exporting energy would be to convert natural gas to electricity and transmit the electricity to Europe through an underwater cable.[1]

Undoubtedly, the major importance of the natural gas and petroleum resources in Algeria lies in their value as bases of a whole series of manufacturing industries. This is very important for Algeria which has few other raw material resources (mainly in the field of food processing, while other mineral resources are rather poor), and, in addition, few traditional skills of value for further industrialization.

7. FOREIGN TRADE AND BALANCE OF PAYMENTS

To a greater extent than in many other former colonies Algeria was and still is completely dependent on the former colonial power as a trading partner. Even the petroleum industry depends on France, which pays comparatively high prices for Algerian oil that moreover has a composition which makes it somewhat difficult to sell on the European continent. Many Algerian export products were developed for sale to the French market, notably wine which was Algeria's dominant export product until the oil export started.

Algerian exports up to 1960 were heavily dominated by wine, which during the period 1955 to 1962 represented more than half of total exports less petroleum. Wine alone explains the heavy dependence on France as an export market. In 1960 wine exports reached 1,040 million francs and this was the last year in which wine was export product number one.

Algeria can count on a steady growth of petroleum exports during the next few years, but the rate of growth will probably not be as spectacular as in the past. The future of its wine exports to France and possibly also to other countries is uncertain. It is by no means sure that the output of wine will regain its previous level, and there is considerable resistance in France against continued large scale imports of Algerian wine, though Algerian wine is widely used for blending purposes, and it is unlikely that Algerian wine exports to France will

[1] For information on the economics of various plans, see (19), pp. 131 to 135.

Table 14. *Foreign trade*
(m dinars = m new francs = 100 m old francs)

	1954	1957	1959	1960	1961	1963
Imports						
Food, beverages tobacco	484·9	806·2	1,251·9	1,455·5	1,442·5	n.a.
Raw materials, fuels, fats, oils	272·4	537·7	581·7	633·4	578·6	n.a.
Manufactured articles	1,419·9	2,482·4	3,793·8	4,152·5	3,033·4	n.a.
of which:						
textiles, clothing, footwear	166·0	445·5	552·4	604·0	471·0	406·3
metal and metal products	99·0	187·7	365·0	453·3	364·9	190·2
machinery and equipment	n.a.	317·5	592·7	574·8	421·7	288·4
passenger cars	81·0	114·5	233·3	253·6	110·4	94·2
other transport equipment	139·6	340·7	326·0	369·1	217·6	119·2
Total	2,177·1	3,826·4	5,627·5	6,241·1	5,054·5	3,090·1
of which from (%):						
France	73·9	73·3	82·5	79·9	77·5	75·3
USA	3·2	6·1	2·9	1·4	3·6	n.a.
Morocco	2·1	1·8	2·1	2·0	1·9	n.a.
French West Africa	4·8	2·7	1·8	n.a.	n.a.	n.a.

completely disappear.[1] Other markets may be developed, but they will in any case be small compared to the present French market.

In order to make total exports grow at a satisfactory rate Algeria must aim at a rapid expansion of exports of other products than petroleum and wine. Growth prospects for exports of citrus fruit and fresh vegetables are reasonably good, but competition is stiff, and no spectacular growth can be counted upon. Exports of minerals have been static in recent years, and although some expansion should be possible, minerals (other than petrolum) are not expected to contribute strongly to the rise in exports. Probably, manufactured goods may in the future become the driving factor behind the growth

[1] The recent French Government decree prohibiting the mixture of French and foreign wines will clearly have a very serious effect. See comment in *El Moudjahid*, August 31, 1967.

Table 14—*continued*

Exports	1954	1957	1959	1960	1961	1963
Food, beverages, tobacco	986·1	1,336·6	1,353·4	1,513·0	1,373·5	n.a.
of which:						
wine	568·8	835·7	894·7	1,040·7	935·2	465·0
citrus fruits	76·9	154·8	126·2	121·9	135·1	168·4
Raw materials, fats, and oils	281·9	245·2	338·1	1,093·5	1,760·6	n.a.
of which:						
petroleum, crude	—	0·8	83·7	800·0	1,511·4	2,131·5
all others	281·9	244·4	254·4	293·5	249·2	n.a.
Manufactured articles	134·9	135·6	113·1	139·5	191·3	n.a.
of which:						
phosphates	22·1	20·3	23·0	20·9	16·3	34·4
machinery and transport equipment[a]	20·5	15·8	13·9	23·7	50·1	n.a.
all others	92·3	99·5	76·2	94·9	124·9	n.a.
Total	1,403·0	1,717·4	1,804·6	2,746·0	3,325·4	3,476·5
excluding petroleum	1,403·0	1,716·6	1,721·0	1,946·0	1,814·0	1,345·0
Exports to (in % of total)						
France	72·8	79·9	82·3	80·8	78·6	74·5
United Kingdom	8·0	4·6	5·3	4·1	(5·9)[b]	n.a.
Trade balance	−774·1	−2,109·0	−3,822·9	−3,495·4	−1,729·1	+376·4
excluding petroleum exports	−774·1	−2,109·8	−3,906·6	−4,295·4	−3,240·5	−1,745·0

Notes: [a] Mainly re-exports;
[b] Excluding crude petroleum.

Sources: All figures, except crude petroleum exports 1960–61, (20) 1957, 1960 and 1964. Remaining figures (13) pp. 267–68.

of Algeria's exports. There are two reasons why such a development is possible and likely: firstly, the bright prospects for industries based on natural gas as raw material or source of cheap energy; secondly, the scope for industrial growth in general, based on interchange of manufactured goods with Morocco, Tunisia and other African countries. More diversified exports will automatically reduce Algeria's dependence on France as a market, but due to petroleum, France will remain the principal client for the foreseeable future.

France was also the principal supplier of Algeria's imports, and during the war France's share of imports rose to more than 4/5. Imports almost tripled between 1954 and 1960, due to the war, and from 1959 due to the development programme. In 1961 when the French policy towards Algerian independence had changed, imports of capital equipment and durable consumer goods fell sharply. No satisfactory breakdown is available for imports in 1962 and 1963, but much of the further fall in imports resulted from the exodus of the larger part of the non-Moslem community with the resulting further fall of imports of consumer goods, including the great variety of manufactured food products from France. But also imports of investment goods fell sharply, as a result of the fall in investment activity.

Algeria's import pattern was that of a typical colonial economy—with a large proportion of imports being consumer goods (almost 60 per cent in 1961). Consumer goods imports in Algeria were particularly high because of the large number of French and other European inhabitants, with relatively large incomes and a highly developed taste for imported, and in particular, French consumer goods.

During the late 1950's and early 1960's consumer goods imports were further inflated by the presence of half a million French soldiers. Nevertheless, during the period 1954 to 1959 imports of investment goods like machinery and equipment, and metals and metal products rose faster than total imports.

As Algeria was administratively a part of France, it was not surprising that between three-quarters and four-fifths of total imports normally came from France. It is likely that France's share in imports will decline considerably in the future, but French suppliers will retain a relative advantage on the Algerian market since their products are well established there, and Algeria will probably be associated with the European Economic Community in one way or another. Thus French goods will continue to have relatively easy access to the Algerian market. Because of strong French interests in petroleum, in aid and in industrial development, France will undoubtedly remain by far Algeria's main trading partner, not only as a market for Algeria's products but also as supplier of Algeria's imports.

Balance of Payments

Since Algeria before Independence was administratively part of France, no data were published on the balance of payments, and no official estimate has hitherto been published except a table in the Constantine Plan.[1] That table, which covered 1959, showed a trade

[1] (2), pp. 462 and 464.

Table 15. *Balance of payments 1963*
(million dinars)

Current expenditure	
Invisibles:	
Algerian Government	20
Tourism, students abroad etc.	50
Enterprises	50
Foreign personnel	380
Oil companies' transfers[a]	1,300
Total	1,800
Current income	
Trade surplus	240
Foreign governments (including technical assistance)	1,310
Wages earned abroad	500
Foreign aid for current govt. exp.	540
Total	2,590
Current surplus	790
Capital receipts	
Current surplus	790
Foreign capital aid	440
Total	1,230
Capital expenditure	
Non-identified capital expenditure	1,010
Increase in foreign exchange holdings	220
Total	1,230

Note: [a] Part of these may more correctly be treated as capital transfers.
Source: (17), pp. 274–75. Note that this source estimates imports at 3,360 million dinars against 3,090 million dinars and exports at 3,600 million dinars against 3,477 million dinars in table 14. If we use the figure for the trade surplus—375 million dinars—that results from the official figures instead of 240 million dinars, and leave all other figures unchanged, the residual item—non-identified capital expenditure, would be increased from 1,010 million dinars to 1,145 million dinars.

deficit of 4,080 million francs (= dinars), and a current deficit of 1,150 million francs. Four-fifths of the trade deficit were covered by the net expenditure of the French Government in Algeria. Other invisibles were in deficit, both because of high tourist expenditure abroad, and because current income transfers out of Algeria (including transfers of military pay) exceeded the inflow from Algerian workers in France. Capital receipts amounted to close to 3,200 million francs, of which, however, more than 500 million were drawings by banks abroad. The French Government invested more than 400 million francs, and contributed 1,400 million francs to the development programme, while the petroleum industry invested nearly 800 million francs. Almost 1,100 million francs went out of Algeria in the form of 'non-identified capital movements'.

1959 was in many respects an abnormal year. There was clearly a link between the very high French expenditure in Algeria and the large import surplus. The non-identified capital movements include financial transactions by Algerian residents. In 1959 they had not reached such a high level that they could be called large scale flight of capital.

In 1959 the trade deficit represented more than 80 per cent of the current expenditure. It is of interest to study its development over time. As Table 14 shows, it increased rapidly between 1954 and 1960, and—if petroleum is excluded—was still three times as large in 1963 as it was nine years earlier. It would be erroneous to use the figures including petroleum as a basis for a straight comparison, since a large part of the petroleum exports is offset by invisible expenditure. Thus, it is apparent that Algeria after Independence has a fairly substantial current balance of payments deficit that has so far been covered by French aid.

An unofficial estimate of the balance of payments in 1963 is shown in Table 15. This estimate is certainly crude, and as pointed out before, it may underestimate the income from the petroleum industry that accrues to Algeria. An underestimate on this point would raise the figure for unidentified capital transfers abroad. In the years 1960 and 1961 there were very large capital transfers from Algeria to abroad (mainly France). Figures which show total private payments abroad in 1960 and 1961 can be presented as follows:

(million dinars)

	1959	1960	1961
Total private payments	4,763	5,750	6,163
of which:			
Trade deficit, without oil	3,910	4,299	3,237
Trade deficit, with oil	3,701	3,495	1,727
Residuum:			
without oil	853	1,451	2,931
with oil	1,062	2,255	4,441

None of the figures shown as a residuum represent the capital transfers abroad, but they show the approximate order of magnitude of the capital flight that took place before Independence. Similar figures for 1962 were probably even larger.

These transfers represent merely a temporary phenomenon. The crude picture of the balance of payments in 1963 gives some idea of the present balance of payments situation. Algeria's trade deficit is now much smaller, but invisible payments are substantial, and balance is achieved through foreign expenditure in Algeria and direct foreign aid.

8. CONCLUSION

Algeria is in a unique position amongst all the developing countries, not only in Africa, but in the whole world. During the colonial period it was not regarded as a colony by the French government, but as an integral part of France. For this and other reasons parts of Algeria were like parts of France in a great many respects. The Europeans represented more than one-tenth of the total population and had an average income above that in France itself. The regions of Algeria which were dominated by French settlers and city dwellers were amongst the most prosperous and rapidly progressing areas of the French empire, including France.

But the Moslems were on the whole spectators and outsiders in their own country. Most of them lived by traditional farming and became increasingly impoverished due to both population pressure and serious soil erosion. The Moslems in towns and cities on the whole occupied unskilled jobs or earned their living as petty traders and poor artisans who lost out against modern manufactured products.

This dual economy, which can only be compared with that of South Africa, broke down completely in 1962 when Algeria gained its independence after eight years of bitter war. Most of the non-Moslem population emigrated and the bottom fell out of the modern economy which to a large extent was built up to satisfy the needs of the European population. Algeria was left with a good infrastructure, some areas of well-developed, modern agriculture, a rapidly expanding petroleum and natural gas industry, and some manufacturing industries on which future industrial development could be built. But Algeria was also left with its large population of peasants on extremely poor land, with a tremendous unemployment problem and with serious shortages of many types of skilled manpower.

Statistical information on Algeria in 1967 is extremely scanty. We know that the national income fell very considerably from 1960–61 to 1963, mostly due to a very drastic reduction in construction activities, a severe drop in output of services, a substantial fall in industrial output and a sharp fall in the output of the main agricultural product, wine, although agriculture on the whole did well in the first years after Independence.

Unemployment is probably worse than ever before, and only the fact that hundreds of thousands of Algerians work in France makes the situation tolerable in the poorest and most over-populated parts of Algeria. France wisely has continued to give Algeria considerable technical and financial assistance, and Algeria has obtained a very favourable agreement for the exploitation of its petroleum and natural gas resources. However, until recently Algeria has not been able to continue a development programme on the scale which the French started under the Constantine Plan. Due to lack of fertile land, and market limitations for some of its most profitable crops, Algeria must speed up industrialization. It is likely that a Maghreb Common Market would greatly facilitate this task.

SELECTED READING

1. *Tableaux de l'économie Algérienne 1960*, de la Service de Statistique Générale de l'Algérie (Imprimerie Baconnier, Algiers, 1960).
2. *Plan de Constantine 1959–63.* Rapport Général, République Française, Délégation Générale du Gouvernement en Algérie, Direction du Plan et des Études Économiques (Imprimerie Officielle, Algiers, 1960).
3. *L'Algérie de demain.* Étude présentée par François Perroux. Série Tiers-Monde. Institut d'Étude du Développement Économique et Social (Paris, Presses Universitaires de France, 1962).
4. *Rapport sur l'exécution du programme d'équipement de l'Algérie en 1961* (Caisse d'Équipement pour le Développement de l'Algérie, Paris, 1962).
5. *Le développement économique de l'Algérie*, par J. Guillot, Série F.—Développement, croissance, progrès (15). Cahiers de l'Institut de Science Économique Appliqué, Supplt. No. 108, (Paris, Décembre, 1960).
6. *L'Agriculture Algérienne.* Numéro Special. Le Développement Africain (Paris, Octobre 1961).
7. *La Consommation des Familles d'Algérie.* Association pour la Recherche Démographique, Économique et Sociale, INSEE, Statistique Générale de l'Algérie et Caisse d'Equipement pour le Développement de l'Algérie (Presses Universitaires de France, Paris, 1961).
8. *Produits Agricoles—Projections pour 1970.* FAO (Rome, 1962).
9. *Le développement agricole en Algérie*, présenté par Maurice Byé,

Études Tiers-Monde. Institut d'Étude de Développement Économique et Social (Paris, Presses Universitaires de France, 1962).
10. *Plan 62, Les chances industriélles de l'Algérie*. Bulletin de la Caisse d'Equipement pour le Développement de l'Algérie, No. 15 (Juin–Juillet 1962, Paris).
11. *Statistical Bulletin for Africa*, No. 1, Part 1, November 1965 (United Nations, Economic Commission for Africa, Addis Ababa).
12. *Évaluation du revenu national de l'Algérie pour les années 1962–63*. (République Algérienne—Direction Générale du Plan et des Études Économiques, Algiers).
13. *La Zone Franc en 1963*, rapport publié par le Secretariat du Comité Monétaire de la Zone Franc (Paris 1965).
14. Lazarev, G., et Dubois, J., *Institutions et développement agricole du Maghreb*, Études Tiers-Monde, Institut d'Étude du Développement Économique et Social de l'Université de Paris (Presses Universitaires de France, Paris, 1965).
15. Hayter, T., *French Aid*, (Overseas Development Institute, London, 1966).
16. *Statistical Yearbook 1962* (United Nations, New York, 1963).
17. Amin, S., *L'économie du Maghreb* (Les Éditions de Minuit, Paris, 1965).
18. *Statistical Yearbook 1965* (United Nations, New York, 1966).
19. Pawera, J. C., *Algeria's Infrastructure*, Praeger Special Studies in International Economics (Frederick A. Praeger, New York, London, 1964).
20. *Yearbook of International Trade Statistics* (United Nations, New York).

INDEX